Culture and Environment

Researching Environmental Learning

Series Editor

David B. Zandvliet (*Simon Fraser University, Canada*)

VOLUME 4

The titles published in this series are listed at *brill.com/rele*

Culture and Environment

Weaving New Connections

Edited by

David Zandvliet

BRILL
SENSE

LEIDEN | BOSTON

All chapters in this book have undergone peer review.

The Library of Congress Cataloging-in-Publication Data is available online at http://catalog.loc.gov

ISSN 2542-9639
ISBN 978-90-04-39667-8 (paperback)
ISBN 978-90-04-39634-0 (hardback)
ISBN 978-90-04-39668-5 (e-book)

Copyright 2019 by Koninklijke Brill NV, Leiden, The Netherlands.
Koninklijke Brill NV incorporates the imprints Brill, Brill Hes & De Graaf, Brill Nijhoff, Brill Rodopi, Brill Sense, Hotei Publishing, mentis Verlag, Verlag Ferdinand Schöningh and Wilhelm Fink Verlag.
All rights reserved. No part of this publication may be reproduced, translated, stored in a retrieval system, or transmitted in any form or by any means, electronic, mechanical, photocopying, recording or otherwise, without prior written permission from the publisher.
Authorization to photocopy items for internal or personal use is granted by Koninklijke Brill NV provided that the appropriate fees are paid directly to The Copyright Clearance Center, 222 Rosewood Drive, Suite 910, Danvers, MA 01923, USA. Fees are subject to change.

This book is printed on acid-free paper and produced in a sustainable manner.

CONTENTS

	List of Figures and Tables	ix
1.	Culture and Environment: Weaving New Connections *David B. Zandvliet*	1

Part 1: Research

2.	A Methodological Approach to the Study of Environmental Education through Drawings *Antonio Fernández Crispín, Marisela de Niz Robles, Verónica Ruíz Pérez, Norma A. Hernández and Javier Benayas del Álamo*	15
3.	Paradigms in the Relationship between Human Beings and Nature in the Andes *Germán Vargas Callejas*	41
4.	Using a Digital Picture Book to Promote Understanding of Human-Wildlife Conflict *Shiho Miyake*	59
5.	Examining the Role of Indigenous Knowledge in Sustainable Living in the North Rupununi (Guyana) *Paulette Bynoe*	75
6.	How Many Butterflies Will Lose Their Habitats? Communicating Biodiversity Research Using the Example of European Butterflies *Karin Ulbrich, Elisabeth Kühn, Oliver Schweiger and Josef Settele*	93
7.	The Agroecological Movement in Galicia (Spain) *Kylyan M. Bisquert and Pablo Á. Meira*	107
8.	The Sacred Sites of Dan Populations in Côte d'Ivoire: Environmental Conservation Factors *Dien Kouaye Olivier*	127
9.	From the Bubble to the Forest: Nature School Environmental Education *Barry Wood*	139

10. Developing and Motivating Young Leaders for Sustainability:
    A Developmental Framework 163
    Patricia Armstrong and Annette Gough

Part 2: Case Studies

11. Teaching Global Indigenous Content to Young Learners 191
    Sophia Hunter and Carolynn Beaty

12. Climate Change and Agricultural Production: Hands-on Active
    Classroom Learning in Estonia 201
    Margit Säre

13. Outdoor Education in the Slovenian School System Supports
    Cultural and Environmental Education 209
    Darja Skribe Dimec

14. Environmental Power Plant Project: Environmental Education in a
    Conservation Area 231
    *Micheli Kowalczuk Machado, Estevão Brasil Ruas Vernalha and
    João Luiz Hoeffel*

15. A Pilot Program on Avifauna in French Guiana 249
    Judith Priam, Jean-Pierre Avril and Alain Ayong Le Kama

16. Renewable Energies: A Thematic Connection between Subjects 261
    *Nelson Arias Ávila, Verónica Tricio Gómez, Jessica Mayorga Buchelly
    and Jenny Ortega Vásquez*

17. The Environmental Sustainability Game 269
    *Mauricio Guerrero Alarcón, Olivia León Valle and
    Alfonso Rivas Cruces*

18. Drawing Meaning from Nature: Observation, Symbols and Stories 285
    Zuzana Vasko and Robi Smith

19. Youth Engagement for Environmental Education and Sustainable
    Lifestyles 305
    *Brian Olewe Waswala, Otieno Nickson Otieno and
    Jared Buoga*

20. Case Studies for Maintaining and Enhancing Urban Greenery 319
    *Kieu Lan Phuong Nguyen, Ho-Wen Chen, Khanh Ly Le and
    Xuan Hoan Nguyen*

21. Integrating Teaching and Learning around the Seven Sustainable
    Development Goals of the Well-Being of Future Generations
    Act 2015 (Wales)   343
    Carolyn S. Hayles

22. Sustainable Education: Essential Contributions to a 'Quadruple Helix'
    Interaction and Sustainable Paradigm Shift   367
    *Dirk Franco, Alain De Vocht, Tom Kuppens, Hilda Martens,
    Theo Thewys, Bernard Vanheusden, Marleen Schepers and
    Jean Pierre Segers*

23. Communicating about Greater Burlington Regional Centre of
    Expertise on Education for Sustainable Development (GBRCE)
    with Sustainability Stories   395
    Thomas R. Hudspeth

24. Ecomuseums in Saskatchewan: Viewing Networks and Partnerships
    through a Regional and Project-Specific Lens   407
    Adela Tesarek Kincaid, Glenn C. Sutter and Anna M. H. Hall

25. Weaving Traditional Ecological Knowledge into Indigenous
    Youth Education: A Case Study in an Indigenous Rice Paddy
    Cultural Landscape, Taiwan   425
    Kuang-Chung Lee

26. Discovering Nature in the Technological Age   445
    Dylan Leech

FIGURES AND TABLES

FIGURES

1.1.	Theme of the project	1
2.1.	Lowenfeld's stages in the development of drawing in children	22
2.2.	Common elements in the representation of the environment in different drawings	23
2.3.	Representation of the environment in the different drawings	24
2.4.	Representation of space in the different drawn subjects	26
2.5.	Space representation. Differences between type of school and gender. U PU = Urban Public school, U PR = Urban Private school, RI = Rural Indigenous school, B = Boy, G = Girl	27
2.6.	Good and bad animals depicted in the drawings of nature: U PU = Urban Public school, U PR = Urban Private school, RI = Rural Indigenous school	28
2.7.	Diversity Index of animals. Good and bad regarding school and sex in the drawings of nature. U PU = Urban Public school, U PR = Urban Private school, RI = Rural Indigenous school	28
2.8.	Main good and bad animals depicted in the drawings of nature	29
2.9.	Reasons why an animal is good or bad in the drawings of nature	30
2.10.	Reasons to consider an animal as good in the drawings of nature. U PU = Urban Public school, U PR = Urban Private school, RI = Rural Indigenous school	30
2.11.	Reasons to consider an animal as bad in the drawings of nature. U PU = Urban Public school, U PR = Urban Private school, RI = Rural Indigenous school	31
2.12.	Percentage of neutral or evasive answers in the drawings of nature. U PU = Urban Public school, U PR = Urban Private school, RI = Rural Indigenous school	31
2.13.	Environmental attitudes by drawing context	33
2.14.	Feelings in different contexts by drawing context	34
2.15.	Correspondence analysis of attitudes in different contexts	34
3.1.	Perception of nature in the Andean world	43
3.2.	Seminal thought and natural cycle	45
3.3.	Relationship of dialogue between human beings and Nature in the Andes	49
3.4.	Vertical relationship human beings and Nature	51
4.1.	The digital picture book	66
4.2.	Word categories	70

FIGURES AND TABLES

4.3.	Rubric	70
5.1.	Map of Guyana showing communities in the Annai District	79
5.2.	The importance of indigenous knowledge to sustainable development	82
6.1.	Results of survey 2 and 3. School students were asked (a) about their attitudes for out-of-classroom learning, and (b) about their participation in outdoor excursions (natural science subjects). Participants: 90 school students from 20 schools (28 students 7 to 10 years, 41 students 11 to 14 years, 21 students 15 to 18 years)	98
6.2.	Knowledge about butterflies. Sustainability course ($n = 18$; $n = 14$. vs. Control group ($n = 15$; $n = 14$). Differences are significant (t-test)	99
6.3.	The educational software SITAS. Butterfly simulation tool	100
7.1.	Methodological design	115
7.2.	Map of agroecological collective and self-managed projects in Galicia	117
7.3.	Poster of sustainable projects national meetings	118
7.4.	Main features of observed projects and processes	122
8.1.	Example of sacred natural sites of Dan populations in Yorodougou	133
8.2.	Traces of farming activities in the sacred natural sites of Yorodougou	135
10.1.	Overview of the development framework	169
10.2.	Students' levels of leadership for sustainability for each round of interviews	171
12.1.	"Climate change and agricultural production" class	204
12.2.	Student measuring plant's length and searching the presence of nodule bacteria	205
12.3.	Using a refractometer to measure the sugar levels in the plant	206
13.1.	Slovenia's location on the map of Europe	210
13.2.	Endemic olm or proteus (*Proteus anguinus*) living in karst caves in Slovenia	212
13.3.	Number of implemented Outdoor Schools and types of Outdoor Schools in Slovenia	219
13.4.	Locations of CŠOD centres. Note: CŠOD centres (n.d.)	221
13.5.	Model that defines outdoor education (from Higgins & Loynes, 1997, p. 6)	223
13.6.	Activities carried out by students in various CŠOD centres	225
14.1.	EPA Bairro da Usina location	239
14.2.	Hydroelectric power plant	240
14.3.	EPA Represa Bairro da Usina overview	240
15.1.	Saint-Laurent-du-Maroni city along the Maroni River, in French Guiana	250

15.2.	The territory of French Guiana presents a concentration of the population on the coast. The two main cities are Cayenne and Saint-Laurent-du-Maroni, also the name of the two municipalities, among the 22, are delimited on the map	252
15.3.	Mana along the Mana River	253
15.4.	Troglodytes aedon is one of those species nesting in College Arsene Bouyer d'Angoma (pictures taken on the fence). Euphonia violacea uses natural supports to stop	253
15.5.	Different views inside and from College Arsene Bouyer d'Angoma that allow us to identify these diverse environments	254
15.6.	The College Arsene Bouyer D'Angoma (also called College V) is near the Maroni River and some forest patches (image extracted from Google Earth in January 2018)	254
15.7.	Travis H., Marvin A. and Markus G., participating in the Pilot Program on Avifaune and making observations of birds in the Amana Reserve in March 2019	255
15.8.	Students participating in the Pilot Program on Avifauna present great knowledge of their environment and abilities in observing and capturing insects. Here are two grasshoppers captured by Rogely E. and Silciano T. and shown to the others before being released in the gardens of the college January 2018	256
15.9.	A circular interaction of ideas beyond the bottom-up and up-down approaches makes the knowledge of French-Guiana students fundamental in the process of interpreting the environment/milieu	258
15.10.	The Maroni River as seen from the French side. In the background, Suriname	258
16.1.	Front and back cover of the publication of CEER	263
16.2.	Website home page	264
16.3.	Principal sections of the website	265
17.1.	Perinole	277
17.2.	Game board and chips	278
17.3.	The Capital	279
17.4.	Merchandise transport in FTA	280
17.5.	Summit meetings	281
18.1.	Our "table" of natural materials	292
18.2.	Connecting objects, drawings and symbolic meanings	296
18.3.	Starting the mind-mapping	297
18.4.	Adding stories and connections to the map	298
18.5.	Completed group maps	299
18.6.	Reflecting on the map	300
18.7.	Sharing maps, stories and symbols	301
20.1.	Campus 8 of Nguyen Tat Thanh University	325
20.2.	Students' activities during the project period	326

20.3.	Status of greenery	327
20.4.	Species recommendation planted nearby National Highway 1A a) Tectona grandis; b) Chukrasia tabularis; c) Pterocarpus macrocarpus; d) Hopea odorata; e) Dipterocarpus alatus; f) Delonix regia	330
20.5.	Species recommendation planted on campus a) Cassia fistula; b) Terminalia mantel; c) Lagerstroemia indica; d) Lagerstroemia peciosa; e) Mimusops elengi; f) Syzygium oleinum; g) Zoysia japonoca; h) Typha orientalis	330
20.6.	Species recommendation planted on campus a) Dracontomelon duperreanum; b) Peltophorum pterocarpum; c) Lysidice rhodostegia; d) Cinnamomum camphora; e) Michelia champaca; f) Axonopus compressus; g) Chrysopogon zizanioides	331
20.7.	Some reference models for roof garden on the L1 building	331
20.8.	Some indoor greenery ideas	332
20.9.	Species recommendation planted on campus a) Aglaonema Pseudobracteatum; b) Pride of sumatra; c) Cyrtostachys renda; d) Dieffenbachia; e) Aglaoocma; f) Cordyline terminalis; g) Tillandsia imperalis; h) Aglaonema modestum Schott	332
20.10.	Some standing garden ideas	333
20.11.	Species recommendation for standing garden a) Nephrolepis cordifolia; b) Coleus blumei Benth; c) Tradescantia pallida; d) Angelica dahurica; e) Petunia hybrida; f) Spathiphyllum; g) Aglaonema muntifolium; h) Aglaonema hybrid	333
20.12.	Before and after enhancing greenery on campus	334
20.13.	Habitat condition analysis	336
20.14.	NDVI analysis results in the study area in spring and winter seasons	337
20.15.	Study area selected by change level of NDVI value displayed as a grid layout	337
20.16.	Classification of environmental aspects results	338
20.17.	Classification of biological aspects results	338
20.18.	Ecological corridor establishment	339
21.1.	The seven sustainable development or well-being goals	346
21.2.	United Nations sustainable development goals (UN, 2018)	355
21.3.	Certificate introductory session – English and Welsh language provision	356
21.4.	A wales of cohesive communities and a Resilient Wales as illustrated and animated by students from UWTSD's Swansea college of art	357
22.1.	Profile of S curve	369
22.2.	Position of S curves in transition	370
22.3.	Kuhn Paradigm shift	371
22.4.	ESD from the empowerment and the behaviour modification perspective (based on Læssøe, 2009)	376

FIGURES AND TABLES

22.5.	CleanTech categories (Berger, 2012)	377
22.6.	Timeline StudentStartUp PXL-UHasselt	379
22.7.	Different types of interaction in order to obtain good energy performance	389
23.1.	Sustainable Development Goals (2015)	398
24.1.	The Saskatchewan Ecomuseum Partnership (SEP) currently consists of 7 provincial heritage organizations, a group of Indigenous consultants (Raven Consortium), and a representative of the Saskatchewan Ecomuseum Network (SEN). The SEP is currently chaired by the Royal Saskatchewan Museum (RSM), which is also connected to other organizations involved in ecomuseum or heritage-related research and programs. The SEN is overseen by the Museums Association of Saskatchewan (MAS), with input from the RSM	409
24.2.	Theoretical project analysis: to advance and connect theoretical approaches to determine future opportunities for community-based science/research	415
25.1.	Location and boundary of the Cihalaay Cultural Landscape	426
25.2.	The Cihalaay Cultural Landscape covers about 1,040 hectares and comprises mosaic landscapes of an indigenous village, rice terraces and irrigation channels, orchards, secondary forest, natural forests and streams	426
25.3.	Theory of collaborative planning (Healey, 1998, p. 1542)	428
25.4.	Development of basic, middle and advanced levels of the EE courses	430
25.5.	Stakeholder Matrix according to their importance and influence (based on DFID, 2002)	436
25.6.	Interactive framework of stakeholders' roles and functions in the development of Basic, Intermediate, and Advanced Levels of the Pakalongay Interpreters Training Course from September 2012 to December 2014	437
25.6.	Local youngsters learnt to observe and record the agro-biodiversity data of the rice paddies	439

TABLES

2.1.	Drawings obtained by educational modality	17
2.2.	Missing elements, very rare or highlighted	25
4.1.	Results of the word association task	69
4.2.	Example comments by rubric index	71
5.1.	Definitions of indigenous knowledge	81
5.2.	Biodiversity knowledge that is transmitted through generations	84
6.1.	Risk assessment for European butterflies in terms of habitat loss, assuming that there is no dispersal to new habitats, in 2080 (Settele et al., 2008)	95

6.2.	Surveys used to evaluate attitudes and knowledge among students from 14 to 18	96
6.3.	Results of survey 1 (see Table 6.2). Time spent outside a) Students were asked: How many hours per week do you spend outside? Age of students: 15 to 18 years b) Students were asked to select one of the given time periods (0–7; 8–14; or 15–21 hours). Age of students: 14 to 15 years	97
6.4.	Questionnaire used in survey 4 (see Table 6.2). (+) and (–) indicate "right answer" and "wrong answer" respectively	101
6.5.	Questionnaire according to survey 5 (Knowledge about butterflies, part 2). (+) and (–) indicate "right answer" and "wrong answer"	102
6.6.	Questionnaire according to survey 6. (+) and (–) indicate "right answer" and "wrong answer"	103
8.1.	Typology of sacred natural sites of Dan populations in Yorodougou. Investigations in Yorodougou, September to October 2016–January to February 2017	131
8.2.	Modes of management of the sacred natural sites of Dan populations of Yorodougou. Investigations in Yorodougou, September to October 2016 and January to February 2017	134
10.1.	Adolescent leadership for sustainability matrix	175
11.1.	Student inquiry question (Grade three students, 2017, January). (Navigation work booklet, unpublished raw data)	195
13.1.	Days of activities in the Slovenian primary and lower secondary schools	215
13.2.	Days of activities at Vide Pregarc Basic School for 1st grade for year 2017/18	216
13.3.	Outdoor School at the Basic School Dravlje for the year 2017	220
13.4.	Historical review of the opening of CŠOD centres	222
20.1.	Status of greenery species	328
20.2.	Weights of aspects and factors were calculated by questionnaires	338
21.1.	The seven sustainable development or well-being goals (Welsh Government, 2016a)	347
21.2.	The five ways of working of the well-being of future generations (Wales) Act 2015 (Welsh Government, 2016a)	348
21.3.	Example on-line discussion topics from certificate	361
22.1.	Key competencies in ESD (Ploum, 2017)	375
22.2.	Research transition in ESD	376
22.3.	Start-up initiatives in PXL University College	380
22.4.	Different scopes for an EPC contracting	387
22.5.	Base and enhanced case PXL buildings	388

DAVID B. ZANDVLIET

1. CULTURE AND ENVIRONMENT

Weaving New Connections

INTRODUCTION

The original inspiration for this project arose out of a large international conference that I chaired (alongside other colleagues) in September 2017. The conference constituted the ninth in a series of biennial conferences known as the World Environmental Education Congress (or WEEC) and the meeting was held at the Vancouver Convention Centre and various other urban/field locations throughout my home city over five days. Importantly, the ninth World Environmental Education Congress (or WEEC) was organized under the title theme of *Culture/Environment: Weaving New Connections*. The organizing committee for the congress was the Institute for Environmental Learning (British Columbia, Canada) in cooperation with the WEEC Permanent Secretariat (Italy).

The success of the Vancouver congress has been well documented with approximately 1000 attendees and three UN agencies participating. In addition, the conference was given UN patronage as an official *Tblisi +40* event. Attendees hailed from over 60 countries and presented several hundred papers across 14 sub-themes embracing a diversity of approaches in the conceptualization and implementation of EE worldwide. In our evaluations of the meeting, many attendees remarked that the cultural aspects of the congress were especially timely and that the practice of inviting educators (both formal and informal) to dialogue with policy makers and academics was important. This dialogue set the stage for this 'follow on' book project. In this, I wanted to commission a volume of work that spoke to both researchers and practitioners and that would adhere closely to a theme of culture *and* environment.

Figure 1.1. Theme of the project

© KONINKLIJKE BRILL NV, LEIDEN, 2019 | DOI: 10.1163/9789004396685_001

WORLD ENVIRONMENTAL EDUCATION CONGRESSES

Since 2003 the World Environmental Education Congress (WEEC) has been a globally important event in the field of the Environmental Education (EE). The overarching goal of the WEEC network is to enhance worldwide the notion that EE is a 'win-win' in promoting both social and ecological sustainability. In keeping with this philosophy, all major groups and actors from within EE (including public, private, nonprofit and for-profit members) are encouraged to participate in the congresses, having the academic community as a supervisor (or guarantor) of quality, but having participation open to non-academic participants as well. In valuing this openness, different levels of expertise and different approaches are generally accepted for all aspects of the WEEC meetings.

The initiative to have periodic World Environmental Education Congresses was first taken at the WEEC meeting held in Espinho (Portugal), in 2003. Following this initial success, a second WEEC meeting was held in Rio (Brazil) and a Third WEEC meeting was held in Turin (Italy). These early meetings successfully concluded a 'constituent phase' that paved the way for the establishment of an International Network of Environmental Educators. The Fourth WEEC, held in Durban (South Africa) inaugurated the beginning of a second phase of biennial WEECs, adhering to a calendar of regular meetings to be convened every two years.

In terms of the level of participation, and the cultural and scientific quality of its contributions, the World Environmental Education Congress and its network has proven to be an important instrument for the progress of environmental education worldwide. The proposal to establish a Permanent Secretariat, based in Turin (Italy), was advanced at the First Congress with the aim of guaranteeing the continuity of the events and the handover from one congress to another. This has ensured the ongoing exchange of reflections, information and proposals among members of the network and congress attendees.

The WEEC network believes that it is important to facilitate mutual cooperation and exchange among those who are committed to reflecting on the link between the environment and education and also for EE to be considered in all of its formal and informal components (teaching, training, communication and theory) Further, the network maintains that there is a need to establish an international network of researchers and practitioners in environmental education. This is seen as:

- promoting active, informed and responsible citizenship,
- as a condition for a more peaceful, fair and ecological society,
- guaranteeing equitable access to natural resources,
- promoting a harmonious relationship among human beings, other living beings and the planet.

CULTURE/ENVIRONMENT

The theme for this book focuses on a Culture/Environment nexus. All papers selected for inclusion focus on the multi-disciplinarity of Environmental Education with a developing view that Culture and Environment may be inseparable and arise from/within each other. Such a theme underscores the need to abandon notions that everything is measurable or under human control. The real paradigm of environmental thinking is an *uncertainty* in the ways forward vs. the idea that 'progress' is unavoidable. Cultural change is a necessary condition/requirement to rebuild and reinvent our relationship with nature and to live more sustainably.

Importantly, all submissions accepted for this book were previously accepted for presentation at the Vancouver WEEC meeting and subjected to a second round of blinded peer review. All submissions addressed one or more of the interconnected congress sub-themes (see below) and in the spirit of supporting our *praxis*, submissions were directed towards both an educator and/or researcher audience. At a minimum, each submission describes original research or curriculum development work.

ENVIRONMENTAL EDUCATION THEMES

- Early Childhood Education
- Place-based Education and Outdoor Learning
- Architecture and Green Design Principles
- Arts Based Approaches in Education
- Agriculture and Garden-Based Learning
- Global and Cultural Diversity in Education
- Urban Eco-systems Approaches
- Environmental Communication (and Uncertainty)
- Indigenous Knowledge and its Role in Education
- Ethics Lead Learning and Sustainability
- Social Responsibility and Agency/Activism
- Nature as Teacher/Nature as Researcher
- Global Policy and Environmental Education
- Perspectives, Challenges and Innovation in Research

DIVERSITY IN RESEARCH AND PRACTICE

Diversity in environmental education is important when one considers the various cultures, epistemologies, practices and research traditions that can inform our thinking on 'environment.' This complexity accounts for a range of forms for environmental education whether it occurs in formal, informal or non-formal contexts. This book hopes to in a small way mirror the complexity inherent in the broader field. In so doing, it is important to consider two important and linked aspects of diversity: (1) diversity of voice and (2) diversity of method.

Cultural diversity is often talked about in educational circles, and it is assumed that benefits are to be gained through careful attention to a range of perspectives. Accordingly, as culturally informed researchers or practitioners we should insist that since variation exists according to culture within the fields we study, then also, our practice, pedagogies, and research methodologies should reflect this diversity.

A 'diversity of method' is also important for the overall quality of environmental education research. To locate new ideas and approaches in this area, one needs to look outside traditional environmental education, towards general educational research, or to other fields such as environmental justice, indigenous education, science education and health education to name a few examples. Diversity of method speaks also to the question of *"what counts as research?"*

The structure of what follows is this: Part 1 consists of a series of research studies selected from a diverse selection of researchers from all corners of the globe, whereas Part 2 consists of a selection of 'case studies' of practice from an equally diverse selection of global practitioners. In so doing, the intent was to augment and highlight the diversity of both cultural method and cultural voice in our descriptions of environmental education research and practice.

The hope in organizing the book in this way was largely pragmatic in that I assumed that readers may wish to interact specifically with one discourse or another (research or practice) initially. The organization of the parts also does not imply a hierarchy as both research and practice are seen as central to developing a 'praxis' in environmental education as we move forward with the field. The organization of each part however is not entirely random: though the selections and contributors are 'eclectic' in that a range of perspectives and methods are deliberately mixed together in the hopes of 'stirring the pot'.

SYNOPSIS OF PART 1

In Chapter 2, Antonio Fernandez Crispin and co-authors share a research project entitled: *A Methodological Approach to Studying Environmental Education through Drawings*. Crispin et al. relate that the most common assessments of their environmental knowledge and attitudes of young children are tests and questionnaires, but not all preschool children are able to read and write. However, drawings are an ideal methodological option, because they go beyond language barriers and socio-economic contexts. The research focuses on children who are finishing preschool and are aged 5 to 6 years and their study was conducted in rural and urban schools located in Puebla Municipality, Mexico.

In Chapter 3, German Vargas Calleja shares a research study entitled: *Paradigms in the Relationship between Human Beings and Nature in the Andes.* Callejas relates that the global development model-born within and fostered by a Eurocentric culture-profoundly affects the way of life and the cosmo-vision of the indigenous peoples of the planet. In this work, he discusses the contemporary paradigms of understanding Nature among the Bolivian Andes Quechua population. Data underpinning this analysis stem from a research project titled: "Development perception, conception and practices in the Andes. An ethnographic study of the Quechua community of Aramasí in the Tapacarí district of Bolivia".

In Chapter 4, Japanese researcher, Shiho Miyake shares a study entitled: *Using a Digital Picture Book to Promote Understanding of Human-Wildlife Conflict.* Her research aims to develop methodology and create awareness for the Japanese public on biodiversity and sustainability issues. The author endeavoured to increase awareness about biodiversity and sustainability by developing a pilot educational tool (a picture story) focusing on the Asian elephant based on sustained collaboration with a local zoo. One of the project outcomes suggested that story-telling events for zoo visitors had a significant impact on the awareness it promoted among non-zoo visitors. In summary, the developed animation effectively communicated the environmental problem of a discord between humans and wildlife as both 'victim' and 'dilemma.'

In Chapter 5, Paulette Bynoe shares research entitled: *The Role of Indigenous Knowledge in Sustainable Living in the North Rupununi (Guyana).* Her research relates that Indigenous knowledge is often challenged by conventional science in some parts of the world; yet it remains relevant to many local cultures., Indigenous knowledge has been promoted as a means of safegaurding natural and cultural resources and ultimately, promoting a more sustainable way of living. Her study presents a case for the preservation, as well as integration of indigenous knowledge into education for sustainability. To this end, a qualitative case study design, using multiple data sources and methods of collection was employed to examine the role of indigenous knowledge in the *Annai* District of Guyana.

In Chapter 6, German researcher, Karin Ulbrich presents a study entitled: *How Many Butterflies Will Lose Their Habitats? Communicating Biodiversity Research Using the Example of European Butterflies.* Ulbrich describes work developing the SITIS learning environment combining an educational software tool with students' own observations of nature. Research findings on climatic impacts on species habitats are presented using the example of fifteen types of European butterflies in a simulation environment. In this research, the learning environment was tested with students from different schools, aged from 12 to 18. Learning success was evaluated using pre-test and post-test questionnaires and the evaluation results showed that by using the SITIS learning environment students gained a significant increase in their level of knowledge about biodiversity.

In Chapter 7, Kylyan Bisquert and Pablo Meira share a study entitled: *The Agroecological Movement in Galicia (Spain).* The research describes a social movement and their analytical approach explores current and potential socio-educational implications for the agro-ecological movement in Galicia through a description of practice and discourse around food, diet and agri-food systems. The purpose is to look for lines of collaboration and feedback among social actors and the environmental education field, to leverage theoretical-practical contributions and to reinforce socio-educational activity as a component of active citizenship. The goal of their research is to promote social and environmentally sustainable food cultures, which in turn acts to support a new culture of sustainability.

In Chapter 8, Dien Olivier shares research entitled: *The Sacred Sites of the Dan people in Cote d'Ivoire: Environmental Conservation Factors.* Olivier relates that the forest region in the western part of Cote d'Ivoire is home to many sacred natural sites that are dependent on the traditional practices of local communities. In the locality of Yorodougou, some fifty sacred sites were studied. The results show that these sites (composed of forests, rivers and mountains) are still intact and are the object of special care because they are perceived by the Dan populations of Yorodougou as houses and places of encounter with ancestors, divinities and spirits. His study concludes with a series of recommendations aimed at the sustainable management of these important and sacred natural sites.

In Chapter 9, Barry Wood shares an essay entitled *From the Bubble to the Forest: Nature School Environmental Education*. In this work, the 'bubble' metaphor refers to the built environment of urban civilization. Wood relates that for children, the Bubble consists of artificial enclosures: family homes, vehicles, school buses, classrooms, and shopping centers all of which effectively eliminate serious possibilities for environmental education. Wood relates that an important corrective occurs in the concept of the Forest or Nature-based School, a European innovation that is slowly spreading to the US and other countries, Various studies have documented Nature School benefits including physical, and emotional wellbeing.

In Chapter 10, the final chapter in the first part of this book, Australian researchers Patricia Armstrong and Annette Gough share findings from a qualitative study that investigated adolescents' understandings of leadership and the critical factors that helped motivate them as leaders for sustainability. The study involved focus groups and a 3–4 year longitudinal study of students, teachers and principals in five secondary schools in Melbourne, Australia. They describe how students understood leadership and leadership for sustainability and construct a framework for the development of adolescent leaders for sustainability, based around seven key elements (focus, description, examples of actions, practices, understandings, key attributes and key capabilities) for five levels of leadership. This framework includes strategies for motivating and supporting adolescent leaders for each of the five levels around three key areas, plus several instruments and tools. The findings of their study have implications for educators who are working to engage and support adolescent leaders for sustainability, giving these educators matrices, instruments and tools to foster learning that will facilitate and encourage active citizenship and social responsibility.

SYNOPSIS OF PART 2

In Chapter 11, Sophia Hunter and Carolynn Beaty share practices in a case study: *Teaching Global Indigenous Content To Young Learners*. This chapter explores British Columbia's new Social Studies curriculum for grade 3 and its focus on Global Indigenous peoples, particularly the relationship humans have with their environment and the cultural and technological innovations these relationships foster. Students are required to develop an understanding of the interconnected nature of these cultural and technological innovations in both local and global Indigenous communities. The topic is fascinating to students but the authors relate that finding age-appropriate contemporary resources is challenging. Through Simon Fraser University's President's Dream Colloquium on *Returning to the Teachings: Justice, Identity and Belonging*, ideas and resources were borrowed and adapted to allow grade 3 students to discuss concepts such as the Whanganui River gaining legal personhood or the significance of the Hōkūle'a's journey around the world. These contemporary examples of Indigenous technologies and culture allow students to develop relevant and authentic understandings of place-based innovation.

In Chapter 12, Margit Säre shares a case study entitled: *Climate Change and Agricultural Production*. The work describes a program implemented in rural Estonian primary schools in 2017. The author discusses methods used in the classroom to create young peoples' understanding that sustainable agriculture is one of the important players in decreasing the impact of climate change, and everybody has a possible contribution to that process. One important finding was that teachers' competence building was an important component of the project and that educators' practices and attitudes are equally important for improving educational processes.

In Chapter 13, Darja Dimec shares her case study entitled: *Outdoor Education in the Slovenian School System Supports Cultural and Environmental Education.* Slovenia is characterized by extremely diverse and relatively well-preserved natural areas. The author relates that in Slovenia (according to the National School Act) outdoor education is integrated into the national curriculum for lower and upper primary schools, Every student must attend outdoor school at least twice in their 9-year compulsory education. To implement these activities in primary schools, Slovenia has a network of 23 outdoor residential centers which are funded entirely by the state. In these centres, place-based educational programs are implemented, fostering outdoor learning in the natural environment. Most centres are located in abandoned and renovated military buildings, in deep forests or in mountains, mainly along the border with Italy, Austria, Hungary and Croatia. All programs in the centres are strongly connected to the local environment and cultural traditions.

In Chapter 14, Micheli Machado, Estevão Vernalha and João Hoeffel describe the *Environmental Power Plant Project*. Their case study has been carried out at the Paulo Freire Municipal School, located in the Bairro da Usina Environmental Protected Area located near Sao Paulo, Brazil. Their activities were based on a participatory methodology and the actions were divided into three modules: a diagnostic module; "hands in the mass", which consisted of project's execution, through practices carried out in the school environment and in the EPA; and a Participatory Community Module in which the results of the activities developed were presented to the local community. Since its beginning, approximately 400 children have been involved in the process involving outdoor activities, raising data on local flora, construction of a nursery, and organic food production.

In Chapter 15, Judith Priam and Jean-Pierre Avril share their case study : *A Pilot Program On Avifauna In French Guiana*. The authors describe a 'place-relational pedagogy' that takes advantage by integrating local knowledge of the local territory by these students during their bird studies.. The project provides voice to marginalized and underrepresented populations who know and feel displaced when environmental communication highlights only scientific facts. Through the Pilot Program on Avifauna, 11 to 15 years old students validate a level of knowledge in Avifauna by a special exam at the end of the year, developed by the College and contribute in documenting their environment by a Booklet. By spreading this Pilot Program with neighbors and interconnecting their observations with other young students like them, this Pilot Program in Avifauna can contribute to new ways of thinking about environmental education.

In Chapter 16, Columbian authors Nelson Ávila, Verónica Gómez, Jessica Buchelly and Jenny Vásquez share their case study: *Renewable Energies: A Thematic Connection between Subjects*. In their study, the authors relate that education and the teaching of Renewable Energies (RE) at secondary and pre-university levels, has a mainstream role to play within the change towards a more sustainable world. As a contribution to this goal, the University of Burgos (UBU) and the District University Francisco José de Caldas of Bogota (UDFJC) have presented and developed the "Collaborative Project in Renewable Energies" with which teachers and students from these universities and associated schools participated. The project is based on a series of educational materials. A summary of these and the initial results of their implementation in schools in both Bogota and Burgos are presented in this case study.

In Chapter 17, Mauricio Alarcón, Olivia Valle and Alfonso Cruces share their work with: *The Environmental Sustainability Game*. They relate this is a resource to stimulate environmental education by criticizing the behavior of decision-makers in the world, both in economic and environmental policy. It promotes through informal communication, that there is an adverse pattern in the environmental performance indices –such as global warming: conditioned by economic interests. Through the strategy of a casino-style table game, the main agenda of Western civilization is discussed in its development model, confronting it with natural resources, asking if "sustainability", as it is conceived, is just one more panacea. Finally, they conclude that visual arts, design, and play can contribute effectively to critical forms of environmental learning.

In Chapter 18, Zuzana Vasko and Robi Smith share a case study entitled *Drawing Meaning From Nature*. The authors share a description of a hands-on workshop process facilitated by two practicing artists. Their workshop involves talking participants outside, where they work with natural 'found' materials and explore symbolic meanings they might embody. Activities involve close observation through a process-oriented practice of drawing as well as storytelling derived from natural materials. The authors emphasize how dynamics and processes of nature relate to us and teach us about our own lives.

In Chapter 19, Brian Waswala, and co-authors share their work on *Youth Engagement in Environmental Education and Sustainable Lifestyles*. As youth EE specialists, the authors share stories of active involvement in EE policy formulation and the mainstreaming of various institutional, national, regional and international EE initiatives. These include the Eco-School Program in Kenya, Green Universities Networks for Kenya, the African Environmental Education and Training Action Plan (2015–2024) and the Kenya Climate Change Action Plan. The authors urge policy makers to invest in youth participation especially when developing EE policies, as this would be a sustainable 'low hanging fruit' in the achievement of national and regional agenda and the SDGs.

In Chapter 20, Kieu Lan Phuong Nguyen and co-authors share their *Case Studies for Maintaining and Enhancing Urban Greenery*. In the Asian context, environmental education was enacted at the university level through project-based learning (PBL) approaches as solutions for preserving and improving trees in cities. In a case study in Vietnam, students were requested to solve two driving questions: "What are the potential areas to enhance greenery on campus?" and "Which kind of trees are suitable for planting in these areas?" To deal with the problem, the students designed as an investigation, in which 100 teachers and students were randomly sampled combining field survey to collect data on architecture, topography, current land use and so on. The other case study was to maintain greenery in megacities based on system analysis to plan the ecological corridor for a developed urban area in Taiwan. The driving question for students was "How do you establish ecological corridors within urban green spaces?" In summary, both groups of students participating in the PBL activities (Vietnam and Taiwan) achieved knowledge and problem solving skills for current urban green spaces management through this case study approach.

In Chapter 21, Carolyn Hayles, shares a case study of policy and practice entitled: *Integrating Teaching and Learning around the Seven Sustainable Development Goals of the Well-Being of Future Generations Act 2015 (Wales)*. In this Act, Sustainable Development means the process of improving the economic, social, environmental and cultural well-being of Wales by taking actions, aimed at achieving seven well-being goals. As context, University of Wales Trinity Saint David (UWTSD) has a clear National profile, with many of its staff and students speaking the Welsh language. In this chapter the development of a University-wide stand-alone certificate set up by UWTSD is presented. The primary aim of the certificate is to support student engagement with the Act. The online certificate takes students on a journey through the seven Sustainable Development or Well-being Goals, giving them an insight into the aspirations of the goals, supported by research and case studies, which cut across a range of sectors. As part of this certification, students are also expected to take part in University-based activities that reflect the ambitions of the Act.

In Chapter 22, Dirk Franco and co-authors share their efforts and results of Education for Sustainable Development (ESD) in technical and business schools (including research, education, and campus greening efforts). These are reported for two case studies of Higher Education Institutions located in Flanders, Belgium. All of these initiatives deal with the involvement and behaviour of future generations as 'decision-makers' (while *the realization of new start-ups and spin-offs are also reported). They* are an essential contribution of a unique type of partnership known as 'a quadruple helix interaction' towards promoting a sustainable paradigm shift into the *Post Fossil-Carbon Society.*

In Chapter 23, Thomas Hudspeth shares a case study entitled: *Communicating about Unique Aspects of RCE Greater Burlington via Sustainability Stories.* The author shares that the Greater Burlington Regional Center of Expertise (RCE) on Education for Sustainable Development is one of 154 networks recognized by the United Nations University. The network draws from various sectors: individuals, NGOs, higher education, K-12 schools, businesses, government, faith communities and the media. It uses education as a tool to create a sustainable future for the greater Burlington region through promoting the work of sustainability practitioners there and encouraging collaboration to strengthen existing sustainability initiatives. Storytelling is an amazingly effective form of communication that helps us recognize new and better solutions to problems and, ultimately, work toward more sustainable futures. This case study utilizes Sustainability Stories about positive role models (sustainability heroes and heroines) in the RCE region for others to emulate in transitioning/downshifting to more environmentally-sustainable communities.

In Chapter 24, Adela Kincaid, Glenn Sutter and Anna Hall share their research on *Ecomuseums in Saskatchewan: Viewing Networks and Partnerships through a Regional and Project-specific Lens.* In this study, the authors describe that ecomuseums (as an example of living labs) are heavily dependent on networks and systems. Their research describes two scales of networks related to the United Nations 2030 Agenda. First they focus on the process of building the ecomuseum network and the partnerships associated with it, as they help guide and develop democratic community development projects that focus on connections to local cultural and natural heritage. The second focus of their work provides an example of one specific ecomuseum project. This case study concentrates on the White Butte Ecomuseum, situated in a rural part of southern Saskatchewan with increasing urban development.

In Chapter 25, Kuang-Chung Lee shares a curriculum development case study based on intergenerational learning and the transfer of traditional ecological knowledge. The study involved a collaboration with local indigenous people in the Cihalaay rice paddy Cultural Landscape of the Fon-nan village, Hualien, Taiwan. Researchers from the National Dong-Hwa University worked together with local people to launch a series of community-based environmental education courses. The case study analyzes the development processes and outcomes of the program in the first three years. The findings show that the program was planned based on traditional knowledge and involved economic, social, ecological and cultural resources of the whole area rather than specific professional aspects. The collaboration and complementary relationship between local teachers and the research team was the key to the curriculum development and implementation. Most students reported outcomes such as a sense of belonging, cultural identity and increased confidence through their involvement with the courses.

In Chapter 26, the final chapter in this book, Dylan Leech shares an autoethnographic study entitled: *Discovering Nature in the Technological Age*. In this study, Leech explores the relationship, meaning, and qualities of nature and technology using both exploration of relevant literature and his own qualitative experience during two 3-week experiments, one in nature and one in technology. By looking at how digital technology shapes his own life, and by contextualizing this personal experience within a dominant Western culture, Leech relates through his autoethnography many qualities of natural and technological life. Among the discoveries in his thesis are the sense that life 'in technology' involves a high degree of replacement, while life in nature involves coming into a more phenomenal contact with the processes and rhythms of the world.

David B. Zandvliet
Faculty of Education/Institute for Environmental Learning
Simon Fraser University
Vancouver, Canada

PART 1
RESEARCH

ANTONIO FERNÁNDEZ CRISPÍN, MARISELA DE NIZ ROBLES, VERÓNICA RUÍZ PÉREZ, NORMA A. HERNÁNDEZ AND JAVIER BENAYAS DEL ÁLAMO

2. A METHODOLOGICAL APPROACH TO THE STUDY OF ENVIRONMENTAL EDUCATION THROUGH DRAWINGS

INTRODUCTION

All of the great change experienced by humanity has been worsened by problems such as pollution, social inequality and racism, among others. These problems are placed in new demographic, economic, cultural and political contexts. The solutions need to take into account social and cultural factors that are at the root of such problems, and education must adopt a holistic perspective examining the multiple dimension of these environmental issues (UNESCO, 1977).

We believe that Environmental Education should start in the early years of human life. According to the Ministry of Education of Mexico (Secretaría de Educación Pública, SEP), the main objective of preschool education (3 to 6 years old children) is to promote the physical, intellectual, emotional, moral, artistic, social and family development of the child. Among the skills that are expected to be developed by these preschool children is to raise their interest in the observation of natural phenomena and the characteristics of living beings; participate in experimental situations that lead them to describe, question, predict, compare, record, elaborate explanations and exchange points of view about transformation processes of the natural and immediate social world, and *acquire positive attitudes towards environmental care* (SNIE-SEP, 2014).

In Mexico, preschool education is offered in three different categories: General, Indigenous and Community Courses.

- General preschool education is a service offered by the SEP through state governments and individuals in rural and urban areas.
- Indigenous preschool education is delivered by the SEP through its General Management for Indigenous Education, is addressed to the attention of the various indigenous populations in the country and is staffed by teachers with knowledge of the languages of the respective ethnic groups.
- Community courses are a service for the communities with a lack of preschools and elementary schools and having less than 35 children of school age. Classes are given by high school graduates who are trained as instructors; hiring and

payment are managed by the community. This service depends on the National Council for Educational Development (Consejo Nacional de Fomento Educativo, CONAFE), which is a decentralized organization of the SEP (Public Education System, 1994).

Children begin to read and write in preschool, but in many of them these skills are lacking, thus the use of tests and questionnaires is not very useful. However Yilmaz et al. (2012) consider drawings as an ideal methodological option for studying very young children because according to their literature review: (a) drawing is a powerful instrument to gain insight about children's thinking, emotions, experiences and perceptions (Piaget & Inhelder, 1969; Prokop & Fančovičová, 2006); (b) provides a comfortable atmosphere for the children to express their thoughts and emotions freely and drawings also carry many communicative messages (Weber & Mitchell, 1996); (c) drawing is a more convenient way of communicating for those children who are afraid of expressing themselves verbally or who have speaking difficulties (Reiss & Tunnicliffe, 2001) and (d) drawings provide a multidimensional view of children (Borthwick, 2011). Furthermore, childrens' graphical representations are subjected to cultural conventions and local symbolism (Barraza, 1999; Anning & Ring, 2004; Stokas, Strezou, Malandrakis, & Papadopoulou, 2017). We also believe that in addition, it allows comparison between children with different languages and cultures.

The evolution of drawing parallels psychomotor development and has a close relationship with the child's overall development. The period in which the child attends preschool (from 3 to 6 years) can be a period where the child shows considerable progress in doing drawings; at the end of the stage between 5 and 6 years each child can begin to perform drawings in their own way, and we can begin to glimpse a difference between girls and boys. Children are at the stage of intellectual realism hence the explanation of transparency in the drawings and lack of perspective (i.e. the superimposition of planes) in the drawings (Samyn, 2005).

Given this reasoning, we decided to focus this research on children who are finishing preschool, between 5 and 6 years old. The study was conducted in rural schools (CONAFE and indigenous) and urban schools (public and private), situated in Puebla Municipality, Mexico.

To carry out this project the following research question was proposed: How do the third grade preschool rural and urban schools students in Puebla Municipality, Mexico, represent their environment through drawings of different contexts (family, school, neighborhood and nature)? Does this representation correspond to that of an environmentally responsible citizenship?

METHODOLOGY

The study population is composed of students from different preschool modalities identified by the Secretaría de Educación Pública in the Municipality of Puebla for the 2005–2006 school year; there were a total of 843 preschool-level schools of which 821 (97%) belonged to the general modality (both private and public or official), 6 (1%) corresponded to the CONAFE modality and 16 (2%) to the indigenous modality.

The Municipality of Puebla is located in the western-center area of the state of Puebla; it has an area of 544.65 km^2, and an elevation of 2,140 m with a climate that is temperate humid with summer rains. It has a varied topography, from flat areas to major morphological formations such as Malinche volcano, Amozoc and Tenzo ridge. In the distance, one can see the Iztaccihuatl and Popocatepetl volcanoes (the last one is an active volcano) more than 5000 meters high. The Municipality belongs in the Basin of Atoyac River that runs through the west of the town from north to south (INAFED, 2010).

From the existing preschools, a non-random sample was chosen, trying to meet a quota of 50 students per educational modality. Thus, two general schools were chosen in the urban area, one with private financing (U PR) and another with public (U PU). In rural areas, an indigenous school was chosen (RI) and five from the CONAFE since they have very small groups of students. With just 5 CONAFE schools we could barely find 38 children. By contrast the private schools are very numerous. In all cases we worked with all the attending children, so the private school was somewhat overrepresented in our sample. Schools were contacted through their school administrators who were asked permission orally and in writing to allow us to work with their children.

Four visits were made to each school. At every visit, we had the permission and the presence of the teacher to ensure a climate of confidence. At each visit the children were asked to give us a drawing on a different subject (family, school, neighborhood, nature) and at the end of the visit, each child was asked to identify each of the drawing elements.

Children's attendance was not regular so on each visit the number of drawings was different. There were a total of 915 drawings. The distribution of analyzed drawings is shown in Table 2.1.

Table 2.1. Drawings obtained by educational modality

Educational modality	Number of schools	Family drawings	School drawings	Neighbourhood drawings	Nature drawings
General Urban Public U PU	1	43	41	45	48
General Urban Private U PR	1	99	100	101	100
Community Courses CONAFE	5	29	35	37	38
Rural Indigenous RI	1	52	52	48	47
TOTAL	8	223	228	231	233

Examining preschool children's environmental representations produced specific methodological difficulties, as it is an assessment tool rarely used in the environmental sciences. Still, its application has proven to be an important qualitative tool for assessing knowledge, perceptions and environmental attitudes in the population (Barraza, 2006). It is a relatively simple technique to obtain information from and about children (King, 1995) and provides valuable information to the researcher concerning the children's perception of reality, and may indicate the degree to which children perceive that they are part of the natural environment (Schultz, 2002).

Four central subjects were chosen in order to interpret the environmental representations of children. The children were familiar with the subject themes and they could easily be represented by a drawing of (1) family, (2) school, (3) neighborhood and (4) nature.

A content analysis of the drawings was also made. This is a research methodology that goes back to the work of Berelson (1971) and may be used with either qualitative or quantitative data and in an inductive or deductive way. In inductive content analysis, the concepts are derived from the data while deductive content analysis is used when the structure of analysis is operationalized on the basis of previous knowledge. Inductive content analysis is used in cases where there are no previous studies dealing with the phenomenon or when it is fragmented. A deductive approach is useful if the general aim was to test a previous theory in a different situation or to compare categories at different time periods (Elo & Kyngas, 2008).

Elo and Kyngas (2008) based on the work of Dey (1993) and Kyngas and Vanhanen (1999) consider that creating categories is both an empirical and a conceptual challenge, as categories must be conceptually and empirically grounded. Successful content analysis requires that the researcher can analyse and simplify the data and form categories that reflect the subject of study in a reliable manner. Having many categories is usually a sign of being unable to adequately categorize the data. It is important that the observed elements only belong to one category at a time. The challenge is to not establish categories that are too wide-ranging, so that researchers differentiate between categories, and not have them so close so they can identify the distinct groupings (not individuals).

One challenge of content analysis is the fact that it is very flexible and there is no simple 'right' way of doing it. Researchers must judge what variations are most appropriate for their particular problems (Weber, 1990). Each inquiry is distinctive, and the results depend on the skills, insights, analytic abilities and style of the investigator (Hoskins & Marino, 2004).

Once the categories are established the next step is to develop a categorization matrix and to code the data according to the categories. This chapter established four analytical approaches with their respective categories:

- *Representation of the environment:* Biotic and abiotic factors were identified. Biotic factors were subdivided into plants, animals and people. Abiotic factors were subdivided into water, earth, air, fire and sky. To these categories were added the anthropogenic elements; we identified buildings, services and objects. To these preset categories, the presence of food and animated objects were added. The categories constructed basically deductively have different subcategories that are inductively built and allow a more detailed analysis.

- *Space representation:* indoors, outdoors, both interior and open, and undefined spaces (when the child divides his drawings without an order on the sheet and does not intend to place it somewhere in particular).
- *Attitudes towards animals:* In the drawing of nature children were asked to draw bad and good animals and to explain why they were good or bad.
- *Attitudes:* The shape of the mouth in animate beings and other graphic elements like tears are drawn, allowing us to identify if the child draws happy, sad or seemly emotionless characters. The presence of both feelings (happiness and sadness) were added to these categories, the perception of hostile elements in the environment, the presence of people or objects as weapons representing evil, symbols representing love (e.g. Hearts) and the presence of environmentally friendly behavior or, by contrast, environmental perturbations.

For a better understanding of the drawings, these are complemented by an interview in which the child is asked to explain his or her drawing and the researcher writes what the child says. In this way, the child is asked about all relevant elements in the drawing. The analysis of the children's attitudes was conducted through their direct manifestation in the drawings. Regarding animals, a list of the good, bad and those who do not belong to any of these categories, was made.

We applied a three-dimensional analysis of representations showed in the drawings. The three dimensions considered in this approach are: Information Analysis, Field of Representation and Attitudes (Moscovici, 1979).

Information Analysis is the study of the existent and sometimes absent elements in the drawings made by third grade preschool students. In the drawing of nature, the Shannon diversity index (Krebs, 1999) of good and bad animals was obtained.

The Factorial Correspondence Analysis (CA) was used to analyze the representation field. This is a multivariate method to reduce dimensions, valid for qualitative variables at nominal levels that allows summarizing information from a frequency table and also calculates quantitative factors. According to Doise et al. (1992), CA is not limited to finding a link between numerous components of social representations; it also can shed light on the relationships between the relational components and integration of individuals within groups, such as those from dissimilar social conditions.

The analysis allowed us to detect the structure, the evaluative tendency and the specific content on which the child's representation is based. Moreover, our analysis provides a chance to analyze social groups according to their socio-cultural characteristics. It allows an understanding of how far the groups' representations are based on one or another subject, and in what way they are articulated in a certain quantity and quality of information or are oriented in a specific direction (Fernández-Crispín & Lara, 2016).

THEORY

Characteristics of the Third-Grade Preschool Child

To understand how a preschool child thinks, it is necessary to know the cognitive, language, social-emotional, adaptive and physical aspects of a child's development.

The most important in this period is the development of children's intelligence. Piaget described this stage as Preoperative or Pre-operational and is where the symbolic function, which will represent the child places and events in their own world, takes hold; such depictions are based on static configurations (Bejerano, 2009).

The preoperative stage is a period of preparation for specific operations; next comes Intuitive Thinking (4 to 6 or 7 years). There is a tension between assimilation and accommodation, the child learns reality through actions and results, and does not use abstract constructions yet; they tend to focus attention on some aspects of the situation so arises a deformation of judgment. The Preoperative stage lacks mobility and reversibility of mental acts, and highlights Egocentrism, which leads the child to see their own view as unique (Bejerano, 2009). The symbolic function is manifested through language and is limited by self-centeredness and irreversibility without taking into account the needs of the listener.

Piaget raises the child's conception of the world as an analogy, where objects and natural phenomena appear as living beings, endowed with conscience or as a product of intensive activity (Ibarra, 1994) known as Animism.

Children's Drawings

The role and utility of drawing in children's learning has generally been underestimated despite being one of the ways by which children can "talk" about their world. Through the child, drawings may represent action, emotion, ideas and experiences and tell complex stories (Malchiodi, 1998; Matthews, 1994, 1999). Thomas and Silk (1990) and Kelly (2004) considers the drawing as a "window" through which the drawing as an objective representation of reality can be analyzed. It is a relatively simple technique to obtain information about the child (King, 1995); the drawing provides information on the perception of the reality of the infant, and a preschooler discourse also represents its most effective form of communication.

Luquet (1927) considers drawing as one of the objective manifestations that shows cognitive or emotional facets of the child. He is the pioneer in these studies and lays the foundation for the study of realistic drawing later regained by Piaget and Kellogg (1970). Recently, there has been a boom to regain children's drawing as a research tool (Ring, 2001) but in this type of work, it is still important to consider the 'classical' authors.

Drawings provide a record from the point of view of the child, constituting an index of more general phenomena of human life. Drawings can reveal something not only about children, but also about the nature of thought and the way to solve problems in both children and adults (Goodnow, 1979). Children can paint pictures and tell a story, and as they act a role they are creating their own lives (Vygotsky, 1995).

According to Luquet (1927) there are four stages of realistic children's drawing:

- *Fortuitous Realism* (18 months to 2 years old).
- *Failed Realism* (2 to 3 years old).
- *Intellectual Realism* (4 to 10–12 years old)
- *Visual Realism* (10–12 years and older).

Lowenfeld (1947), from the perspective of art education, handles the following six stages in the development of drawing in children:

- *The Scribbling Stage* (2 years) are simply records of enjoyable kinesthetic activity.
- *The Preschematic Stage* (3–4 years) provides a tangible record of the child's thinking process.
- *The Schematic Stage* (5–6 years) the schema represents the child's active knowledge of the subject. Children develop a set of symbols.
- *The Gang Stage* (7–10 years) finds the schematic generalization no longer suffices to express reality and compare their work and become more critical of it.
- *The Pseudo-Naturalistic Stage* (11–13 years) they strive to create adult-like naturalistic drawings.
- *The Period of Decision* (14 years and older). Natural development will cease unless a conscious decision is made to improve drawing skills.

These stages are presented as an example in Figure 2.1, through some of the drawings included in this research.

According to Goodnow (1979), it is convenient in the study of children's drawings to consider each graphic work as a series of parts or units combined to form a whole or a model. Overall we can say that the main features of the drawings of the child are:

a. Children are economical in their use of units, i.e. constantly use a graphics unit.
b. When they make a change they are usually conservative. In younger children some changes are generated in a typical way, varying only in one unit (sometimes only the name of the drawing).
c. The parts relate to each other according to specific principles. Children follow certain rules, which cannot be ours; however, are not mere whims.
d. The parts are linked together to form a sequence. Each step taken in a graphic work has consequences for the next steps. You must discover the consequences and how the child tries to solve them.
e. Children's graphic works illustrate the child's thinking and also our thinking. The features that child graphic work exhibits are characteristics of all troubleshooting, either by children or by adults (Goodnow, 1979).

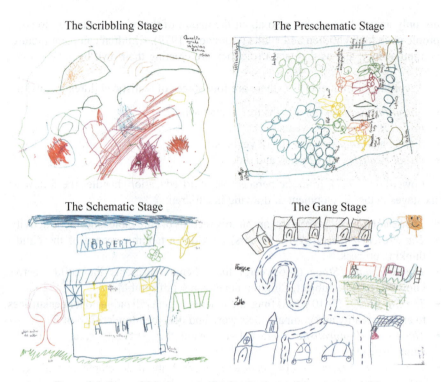

Figure 2.1. Lowenfeld's stages in the development of drawing in children

The study of children's drawings generally focuses on a socio-cognitive knowledge of child development. Although analysis of child's drawing has been little-used as an assessment tool in environmental science, its application has proved to be an important qualitative tool for assessing culture, knowledge, perceptions and environmental attitudes in the population (Barraza, 1999). A more contemporary approach considers the development of drawing not as an intent to copy the exact reality but as the acquisition of a graphic language, sharing affinities with other representational systems, including the verbal language (Picard & Zarhbouch, 2014).

RESULTS AND DISCUSSION

Representation of the Environment

As shown in Figure 2.2, the representation of the environment has many common elements. The most common are the sky and plants. In these representations, the sun usually appears as an animated being (more commonly in drawings of nature), and grass with flowering plants.

Turkish students from kindergarten through 8th Grade (K-8) draw nature pictures in a certain way: mountains range at the background, a sun, a couple of clouds, a river

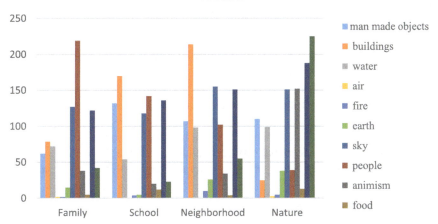

Figure 2.2. Common elements in the representation of the environment in different drawings

emerging from the mountains (Ulker, 2012). In comparison, six-year-old students from the Czech Republic also drew some certain nature elements in their drawings: a couple of linear and curvy clouds and they allocated specific space for sky. Also, the majority of Czech students (76 % of drawings) drew the sun either in the middle of the sky or on the left or right corner of the sky. On the other hand, they did not draw, mountains range at the back and a river emerging from the mountains (Yilmaz et al., 2012).

The possible reasons for why younger children typically draw sun and clouds in their drawings is because students need to draw 3-D objects onto 2-D drawing paper. In addition, some of the nature objects are difficult to draw and include complexity that requires spatial sense. Piaget and Inhelder (1967) consider that younger children started to discover topological relations, but they did not recognize the Euclidean relations such as shape, location, proportion and area. Since sun and clouds could be two of the least complex items in nature to draw for children, young children could prefer to draw a coin size sun and linear curvy clouds, transferring observed 3-D objects onto 2-D paper. Consequently, drawing the sky and clouds allows improvement in children's spatial sense (Yilmaz et al., 2012).

The cultural approach (Wilson, 1997; Baldy, 2005; Picard & Zarhbouch, 2014) considers drawing as a language based on meaningful graphic shapes that take their power from figuration conventions shared by the members of a given culture. They involve a lexicon of graphic forms and syntax to organize, in time and space, the graphic forms. According to Lowenfeld (1947), children develop a set of symbols to create a landscape that eventually becomes a single variation repeated endlessly. A blue line and sun at the top of the page and a green line at the bottom become symbolic representations of the sky and ground. Landscapes are composed carefully, giving the impression that removing any single form would throw off the balance of the whole picture. Lowenfield also noted that in addition to the sky, and the clouds, children also draw grass. Most drawings are in his Schematic Stage, in which it is very important to frame drawing a place by defining the top (sky) and down, generally represented by grass.

Thus, besides the cultural context and the particular child's experience, many of the elements in the drawings are determined by their stage of development.

The correspondence analysis (Figure 2.3) in our data shows that despite the differences, no significant differences were seen in the drawings, except that most children drew people on the family designs and animals on the nature ones. This may also be because they were explicitly asked to represent animals on their nature drawings. It is generally seen that services, buildings and people are more frequent in the drawings of family, school and neighbourhood and less common in nature.

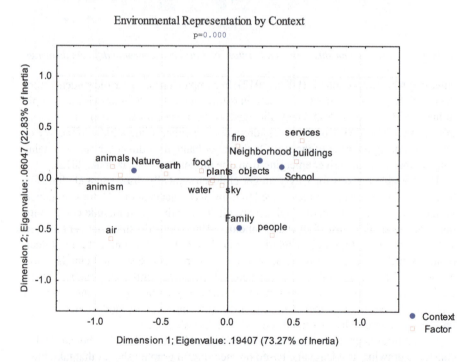

Figure 2.3. Representation of the environment in the different drawings

The data show that there are no significant differences between types of school children regarding the representation of the environment in different contexts, except in nature. In this case, although the difference is significant (p = 0.02) the CA does not show any clear trend.

Barraza (1999) reports that children from United Kingdom and Mexico, with significant structural and cultural differences, manifested more similarities in their drawings than differences. However, Mexican children gave significantly greater importance to their drawing of rural places.

To see differences, we must analyze the categories. Table 2.2 shows missing elements in the different scenarios, which are unusual and highlighted.

Table 2.2. Missing elements, very rare or highlighted

Categories	Missing elements	Rare elements	Highlighted elements
Family	Evil, wildlife, trade, school, pots, signage, government, flag, trades.	Trash	Myself, people, happiness, sadness, undefined spaces
School	Government, air, hostile environment, pro-environment actions, evil.	Religion, media	Flag, teacher, constructed objects, services, recreational items, people without emotion, trash
Neighborhood	Air, technology, flag, gun, exotic animals and aquatic	Trash, bad person	Trade, religion, signage, transportation, roads, buildings, housing, fire, water
Nature	Government, trade, signage, Festivities	Education, Religion, bad person, flag, interiors.	Animals, plants, soil, water, hostile environment, environmental disturbances, evil, both emotions, food, grass, trees, sky phenomena.

Family is represented as a safe place, where people expressing feelings, happiness basically dominate. The space is not necessarily important in drawing the family, although it can also be interpreted that this is a more affective stage and therefore its representation is less intellectual as reflected in more drawings near this level of development are categorized as examples of failed realism.

Moreover, in *school*, which is a more academic space, the children less frequently draw unconfined spaces and instead represent both open and closed spaces. The school is a building in which the flag appears frequently. We assume that the most important school activities occur in an enclosed space, but children usually represent the schoolyard and playground, the place where most children draw unexpressed feelings and also where trash is most often indicated.

The *neighborhood* is represented in open spaces where different types of buildings and roads with vehicles and signaling predominate. Many services, including trade and religion are represented. They draw water and erupting volcanoes more frequently. There are few animals and many plants. Happy people are represented. Neither houses nor vehicles emit smoke, there is no garbage and very rarely are there drawings of violent actions.

Nature is represented with open spaces and the presence of animals and plants. There is the presence of volcanoes, mountains and water. In the sky, besides the sun (usually with eyes and mouth) and clouds, there are also other elements such as rainbows, lightning, rain, etc. There is not much of a presence of people or houses, but the other elements are usually animated and show various feelings, especially happiness. Sometimes nature is drawn as a hostile environment. There are very few disturbances, and pro-environmental actions, such as the care of animals or plants, drawn.

Space Representation

As shown in Figure 2.4, children prefer to draw open/outdoor spaces, especially to represent nature and their neighborhood. The way the space is used is different in different contexts. At school, closed/indoor spaces are represented, although they prefer to combine them with open spaces. Indefinite spaces, which generally indicate that the developmental stage of the drawing is close to Failed Realism, appear more frequently in the drawings of the family and secondly in nature.

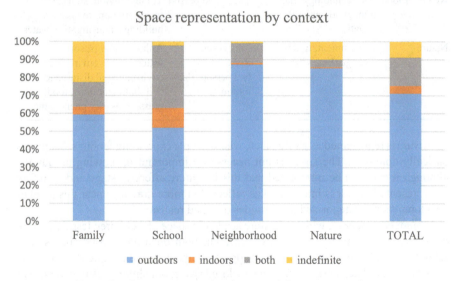

Figure 2.4. Representation of space in the different drawn subjects

No differences between school types or gender in the way the space is represented in different contexts were found, excluding the family drawings, where the CA indicates that there are differences between rural children and urban children (Figure 2.5). Dimension 1 shows that rural children (on the right) and especially indigenous children, tend to draw the family without a defined space, while urban children prefer open spaces (on the left). Dimension 2 shows that children from urban public schools and girls from CONAFE tend more to draw closed spaces or both spaces.

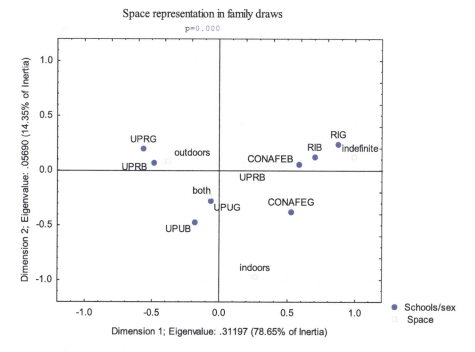

Figure 2.5. Space representation. Differences between type of school and gender.
U PU = Urban Public school, U PR = Urban Private school,
RI = Rural Indigenous school, B = Boy, G = Girl

Animals

Children represented 86 kinds of animals, of which 67 were "bad" and 61 "good". Most animals were represented in both categories, sometimes in the same drawing. In general, boys drew more kinds of animals than girls (Figure 2.6).

While the children of private urban school drew more kinds of animals than rural children, this figure is likely influenced by the size of the sample. The comparison between the diversity indices is less sensitive to sample size (Figure 2.7) and this parameter does not show much difference between types of school.

Figure 2.8 depicts the animals appearing in the drawings, and how often were considered as good or bad. The butterfly is the animal that most frequently appears in the drawings. It is followed by lions and snakes as bad animals. The dog, fish, cats and turtles are common pets, they appear in 4th, 5th, 11th and 12th place respectively.

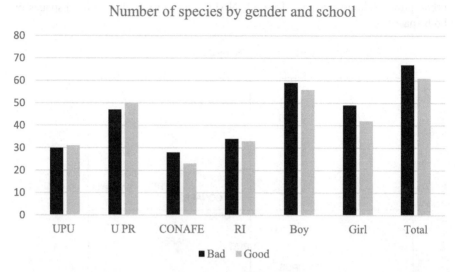

Figure 2.6. Good and bad animals depicted in the drawings of nature: U PU = Urban Public school, U PR = Urban Private school, RI = Rural Indigenous school

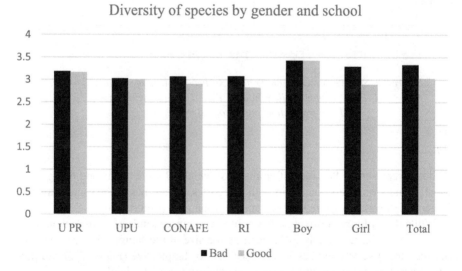

Figure 2.7. Diversity index of animals. Good and bad regarding school and sex in the drawings of nature. U PU = Urban Public school, U PR = Urban Private school, RI = Rural Indigenous school

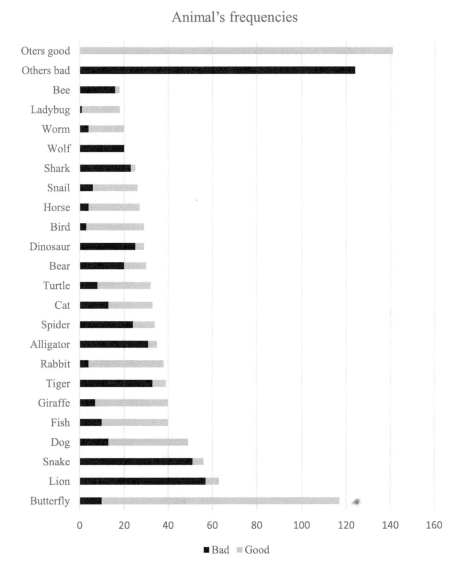

Figure 2.8. Main good and bad animals depicted in the drawings of nature

Figure 2.9 shows the main reason why an animal is considered bad; it is because it is aggressive, a characteristic generally associated with predators, that can even eat people and be dangerous or venomous. In contrast, an animal is good if it is not aggressive or does not eat meat.

Normally, it is hard for children to explain why they perceive that an animal is good, especially the children in urban schools. The benefits to humans or the

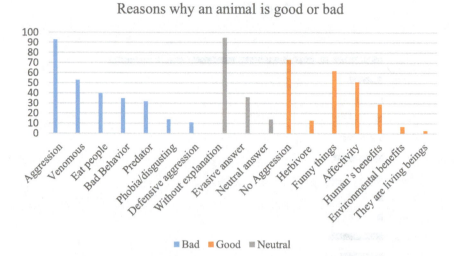

Figure 2.9. Reasons why an animal is good or bad in the drawings of nature

environment are reasons less-often mentioned compared to evasions or those with a strong emotional component, for example: the reasons mentioned are because they do funny things or are pretty. Children of urban public school do not mention the benefits to the environment, while rural schools, especially CONAFE (Figures 2.10 and 2.11) mentioned more benefits to the environment.

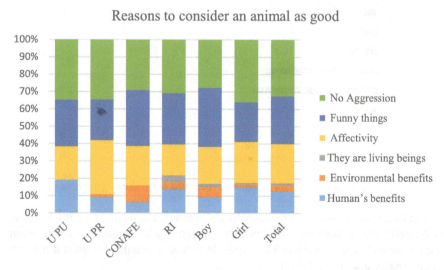

Figure 2.10. Reasons to consider an animal as good in the drawings of nature. U PU = Urban Public school, U PR = Urban Private school, RI = Rural Indigenous school

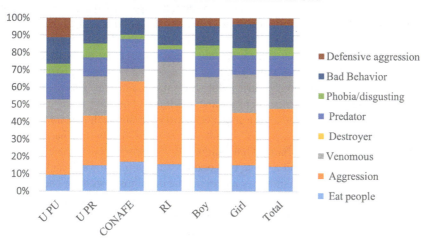

Figure 2.11. Reasons to consider an animal as bad in the drawings of nature.
U PU = Urban Public school, U PR = Urban Private school,
RI = Rural Indigenous school

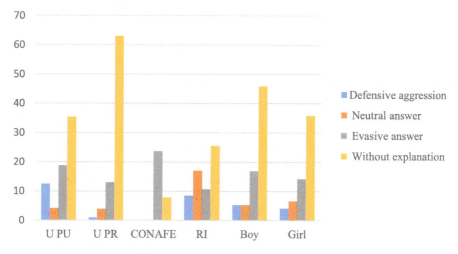

Figure 2.12. Percentage of neutral or evasive answers in the drawings of nature.
U PU = Urban Public school, U PR = Urban Private school,
RI = Rural Indigenous school

Within the type of explanations given by children about why animals are perceived as good or bad, we note that children in urban schools, especially most of the children in private school (76%), cannot explain why an animal is good or bad, giving evasive answers (Figure 2.12). By contrast, children in rural schools gave more specific answers. For example, a child of the indigenous rural school mentions that snakes are bad because one bit his sister and a girl drew a dog as bad because it chases people, and drew another one as good because it does not chase them. They also mention that a donkey is good because it does not kick and a bull is bad because it lunges.

Children may say that animals are good because they do funny things, for example: a rabbit is good "because it jumps", a monkey is good "because it hangs and is happy" or because they are funny. Other animals are good because they are beautiful like snails or butterflies, and a horse is "good because you can ride it and he loves us" (indigenous girl). Few children could argue that there are no good or bad animals or make a more complex judgment about them. For example: a girl mentions that a dog "is good, but it bites when it is disturbed" (defensive aggression), and another indigenous child mentions that a hen "is good because it does not kill and allows itself to be eaten".

This results suggests, not surprisingly, that rural children respond according to their experience of contact with animals, while urban children, despite drawing a greater diversity of animals, have no contact with them and have difficulties making judgments about them (resulting in evasive answers, neutral and without explanation). Similarly, when urban children have contact with pets, they can also make judgments based on their experience, as in the case of a girl of a public urban school: in the same drawing she represented a bad dog that does not like to be in a house and a good one because he likes to stay at home.

According to psychoanalytic theory, a preschool child between 4 and 6 years does not have a clear awareness of his/her own subjectivity; as both egocentrism and preconception merge in the child there is no distinction between internal processes and external reality. Hence, as Piaget says, this state is characterized by working with an "imagined thought" (Chamizo, 1992). Thus, when children say that an animal is bad because it is aggressive or misbehaves, they probably do that based on their own subjectivity and self-centered thought and they still do not understand the trophic relationships of ecosystems as a natural process.

There are also some phobias associated with the presence of many legs and fear of venomous animals, which may have an adaptive function. Fear is an alarm system that helps the child to avoid potentially dangerous situations. Some studies show that between 30% and 50% of children have intense fears. During the first year, fears of intense stimuli or the unknown are more frequent, and up to six years of age, physical fears such as those related to animals, darkness, storms, disasters, fantasy creatures or separation of the parents are the most common (Mendez et al., 1997).

If, as suggested Bejerano (2009), the sources of knowledge of the children in this age group are plants, animals, people, toys and natural phenomena, then it is important to stimulate and develop cognition influenced by contact with the physical, social and individual environment. Preschoolers tend to develop emotional ties to what is familiar and enjoyable for them, so they may be receptive if people around them are concerned about environmental issues and engage in constructive efforts to improve the quality of the environment (Wilson R., 1996).

Attitudes

As shown in Figure 2.13, most children represent feelings of joy in their drawings. More happiness is depicted in the family than elsewhere, whereas the neighborhood and school is where most drawings are emotionless. Nature is where more sadness is represented, but combined with happy characters. The greatest diversity of feelings is represented in the drawings of nature. It is noteworthy that few environmental disturbances and also few pro-environmental actions are represented.

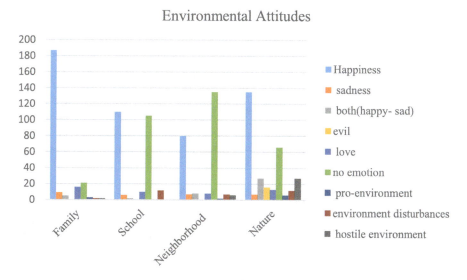

Figure 2.13. Environmental attitudes by drawing context

It is particularly relevant that in school, where the presence of disturbances is perceived, no pro-environmental actions were drawn, where they should be part of the educational program. Finally, in some drawings of nature and neighborhood, the environment is shown as hostile; however this finding is only significant for nature, which also represents 'wickedness'. The representation of a hostile environment contrasts with the representation of pro-environmental actions (though they are rare) as it can be seen at Figures 2.14 and 2.15.

The school is a very different context regarding family. The school is the institution responsible for transmitting knowledge and values of culture and preparing children for their adult role. At school, the language is characterized by a tendency to

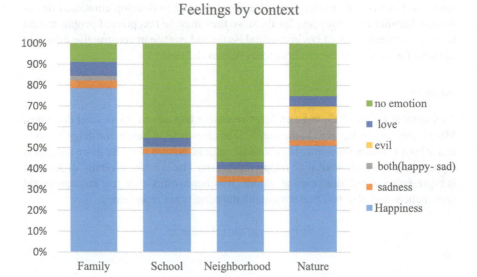

Figure 2.14. Feelings in different contexts by drawing context

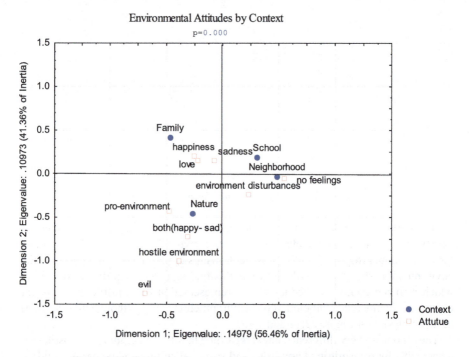

Figure 2.15. Correspondence analysis of attitudes in different contexts

refer to objects and phenomena by placing them out of context. So while school is responsible for transmitting organized knowledge, the family is responsible for transmitting the common knowledge and close relationship with people; at school, with more people present, relationships are less close. Generally, preschool children are more sensitive to the truths about family situations than with those most remote from their experience (Palacios et al., 1994). This may explain why the school is a less happy place than family.

No significant differences in feelings and attitudes represented among the types of schools and gender in the drawings of family, school and neighborhood were found.

Barraza (1999), in a study that compares the perception of nature among Mexican children and English from 7 to 9 years, found there was a sense of well-being, where flowers, trees, water, sun, animals and people share the environment in harmony amongst 45% of Mexican children in their drawings about a place on Earth. Moreover 37% drew at least one problem (pollution, trash, violence, war, deforestation, global warming, etc.). The trend was similar in English children, but they perceive more environmental issues than Mexicans.

Bonnett and Williams (1998) interviewed 5 to 6 years old children in United Kingdom about how they perceived nature, who demonstrated high levels of feeling and general concern towards nature and the environment. These authors highlighted the children's strong empathy towards certain aspects of nature, particularly animals and trees.

Uzzell, Rutland, and Whistance (1995) found that children rate distant global problems as more serious than local ones and they tend not to make connections between local actions and global effects. This may explain why environmental problems are perceived in the distant or academic contexts and not in the family.

Apparently children have more environmental problems when are given instructions like "you have to save the planet" (King, 1995). Barraza (1999) and Stokas et al. (2017) suggest that children perceive more environmental problems when they are asked to compare the present with the future or when children are older.

According to Kollmuss and Agyeman (2002) to be familiar with environmental problems and their causes is an important factor to responsible pro-environmental behaviour. In this sense, Yilmaz, Kubiatko, and Topal (2012) consider it important to help students to understand the changes caused by human activity that can protect and improve the environment as well as to damage and destroy, and build up the awareness of fellow feeling to the world, to the animated and unanimated nature, to humanity, society and to the planet Earth.

CONCLUSIONS

This methodology has proved to be useful for the study of environmental awareness by third grade preschool children that do not yet read or write. Additionally, it is applicable to older children. The methodology transcends language barriers and socio-economic context. It also provides vast and complex data on several topics the researcher may want to address.

Common elements were observed in the four different subjects, for example: it was observed that third grade preschool children have an idealistic "everything looks right" vision of the natural and built environments and most of them have a clear separation between these two contexts. Children prefer to draw open environments and feelings are usually that of happiness. Few environmental disturbances are drawn and consequently few pro-environmental actions; instead they are presented as emotional relationships to animals or plants.

In the drawings about family, most people are in a happy environment. The children drawing elements about school represent it as a building with a flag and a playground, and animals are minimally represented. The childrens' representation of school manifests as impersonal and far from their family life. The drawings about neighborhood show dynamism and constant human activity in constructed and working elements. They also show more distance and indifference in caring for the environment. In the drawings about nature, children observed it as something that exists but is not close to them. Children identify many bad animals that are generally carnivorous or venomous and are bad because they are aggressive. Good animals are usually butterflies and other herbivores that are cute or funny. City children have great difficulty explaining why they perceive an animal is good or bad, while rural children refer to more concrete experiences.

Most drawings are in Schematic Stage. In them, the sky, clouds, sun and grass, as elements that define what is above and below, are present. In everyday environments, closer (the family) or more distant (nature) there may be some regression in the drawings to the Preschematic Stage.

Although the drawings represent aspects of affective and cognitive life of the child with an influence of their culture and environment, many elements are determined by the stage of development of the child in the preoperative stage, which is characterized, among other things, of egocentrism and the attribution of human qualities to non-human beings (animism).

Although it is important that a happy environment is perceived by young children, we feel that it isimportant that they can also perceive human actions that threaten themselves and the environment, so they can be educated as environmentally responsible citizens. In order to do this, it is important that children get involve in environmental issues within the family, school, community and nature.

Given this diversity of contexts found in a country like Mexico, it is a challenge to educate children in environmental issues: to encourage them to become actors and not merely spectators of what happens around them.

ACKNOWLEDGMENTS

Thanks to Armando Noé Rodríguez, Ivette Isabella Otero and María Estela Ruiz Primo for their help.

REFERENCES

Anning, A., & Ring, K. (2004). *Making sense of children's drawings*. London: McGraw-Hill Education.
Baldy, R. (2005). Dessin et développement cognitif. *Enfance, 57*(1), 34–44.
Barraza, L. (1999). Children's drawings about the environment. *Environmental Education Research, 5*, 49–66.
Barraza, L. (2006). Educating to preserve: An example in the socio-environmental research. In A. Barahona, & L. Almeida (Eds.), *Educación para la conservación* (pp. 255–276.). México: Facultad de Ciencias. UNAM.
Bejerano, G. F. (2009). Características generales del niño y la niña de 0 a 6 años. *Cuadernos de Educación y Desarrollo, 1*(5).
Berelson, B. (1971). *Content Analysis in Communication* (First edition from 1952 ed.). Research. Glencoe, Ill: Free Press.
Bonnett, M., & Williams, J. (1998). Environmental education and primary children's attitudes towards nature and the environment. *Cambridge Journal of Education, 28*(2), 159–174.
Borthwick, A. (2011). Children's perceptions of, and attitudes towards, their mathematics lessons. *Proceedings of the British Society for Research into Learning Mathematics, 31*(1), 37–42.
Chamizo, G. O. (1990). Los contenidos ambientales en el nivel preescolar. *Cero en conducta, 5*(17), 41–44.
Dey, I. (1993). *Qualitative data analysis. A user-friendly guide for social scientists*. London: Routledge.
Dey, I. (2003). *Qualitative data analysis: A user friendly guide for social scientists*. London: Routledge.
Doise, W., Clémence, A., & Lorenzi-Cioldi, F. (1992). *Representations sociales et analyses de données*. Grenoble: PUG.
Elo, S., & Kyngäs, H. (2008). The qualitative content analysis process. *Journal of Advanced Nursing, 62*(1), 107–115.
Fernández-Crispín, A., & Lara, D. (2016). Social representation of sustainable development models in students at a Mexican public university. In M. Barth, G. Michelsen, M. Rieckmann, & I. Thomas (Eds.), *Routledge handbook of higher education for sustainable development* (pp. 371–382). New York, NY: Routledge.
Goodnow, J. (1979). *Children's drawing*. London: Open books publishing, Ltd.
Hoskins, N., & Marino, C. (2004). *Research in nursing and health. Understanding and using quantitative and qualitative methods* (2nd ed.). Springer Series on the Teaching of Nursing.
Ibarra, L. (1994). Las dificultades de Jean Piaget para vincular el desarrollo ontogenético y filogenético del conocimiento. *Iztapalapa 35. Extraordinario*, 77–88.
INAFED, Estado de Puebla. (2010). Enciclopedia de los Municipios y Delegaciones de México, Instituto para el Federalismo y el Desarrollo Municipal. Retrieved July 16, 2016, from http://www.inafed.gob.mx/work/enciclopedia/EMM21puebla/
Kellogg, R. (1970). *Analyzing children's art*. Palo Alto, Cal.: Mayfield.
Kelly, D. D. (2004). *Uncovering the history of children's drawing and art*. Westport, CT: Greenwood Publishing Group.
King, L. (1995). *Doing to save the planet. Children and environmental crisis*. New Brunswick, NJ: Rutgers University Press.
Kollmuss, A., & Agyeman, J. (2002). Mind the gap: Why do people act environmentally and what are the barriers to pro-environmental behavior? *Environmental Education Research, 8*(3), 239–260.
Krebs, C. (1999). *Ecological methodology* (2nd ed.). E.E.U.U: Cummings Imp. Addison Wesley Lugman, Inc.
Kyngas, H., & Vanhanen, L. (1999). Content analysis. *Hoitotiede, 11*, 3–12.
Lowenfeld, V. (1947). *Drawing development in children. Adapted from the works of Viktor Lowenfeld and Betty Edwards. Creative and Mental Growth*. New York, NY: Macmillan, Co.
Luquet, G. H. (1927). *De dessin enfantin*. Paris: Press Universitaries de France.
Malchiodi, C. (1998). *Understanding children's drawings*. London: Jessica Kingsley.
Matthews, J. (1994). *Helping children to draw and paint in early childhood*. London: Hodder & Stoughton.

Matthews, J. (1999). *The art of childhood and adolescence: The construction of meaning.* London: Falmer Press.
Méndez, F. X., Inglés, C. J., Hidalgo, M. D., García-Fernández, J. M., & Quiles, M. J. (2003). Los miedos en la infancia y la adolescencia: un estudio descriptivo. *Revista Electrónica de Motivación y Emoción, 6*(13), 150–163.
Moscovici, S. (1979). *Psychoanalysis, its image and public.* Buenos Aires: Editorial Huemul S.A.
Palacios, J., Marchesi, A., y Coll, C. (1994). *Desarrollo psicológico y educación,* Madrid: I. Alianza Psicología.
Piaget, J., & Inhelder, B. (1969). *La Psychologie de l'enfant* (10th ed.). Paris: Presses Universitaries de France.
Picard, D., & Zarhbouch, B. (2014). Le dessin comme langage graphique. *Approches, Revue des Sciences Humaines, 14,* 28–40.
Prokop, P., & Fančovičová, J. (2006). Students' ideas about the human body: Do they really draw what they know? *Journal of Baltic Science Education, 2*(10), 86–95.
Reiss, M. J., & Tunnicliffe, S. D. (2001). Students' understandings of human organs and organ systems. *Research in Science Education, 31*(3), 383–399.
Ring, K. (2001, September 13–15). *Young children drawing: The significance of the context.* College of Ripon and York, British Educational Research Annual Conference, University of Leeds, Leeds.
Samyn, I. (2005). *Le dessin et l'enfant.* Emseigment et Recherche en Psycopathologie.
Schultz, P. (2002). Inclusion with nature: The psychology of human-nature relations. In P. Schmuck & P. Schultz (Eds.), *Psychology of sustainable development* (pp. 61–78). Boston, MA: Springer.
SISTEMA EDUCATIVO Nacional de México. (1994.) Secretaría de Educación Pública y Organización de Estados Iberoamericanos; [informe realizado por Germán Álvarez Mendiola ... (et al.)]. México D. F.
SNIE-SEP. (2014). *Estadística del Sistema Educativo Puebla, Ciclo escolar 2013–2014.* Retrieved June 30, 2010, from http://www.snie.sep.gob.mx/descargas/estadistica_e_indicadores/estadistica_e_indicadores_educativos_21PUE.pdf
Stokas, D., Strezou, E., Malandrakis, G., & Papadopoulou, P. (2017). Greek primary school children's representations of the urban environment as seen through their drawings. *Environmental Education Research, 23*(8), 1088–1114.
Ulker, R. (2012). Turkish children's drawing of nature in a certain way: Range of mountains in the back, the sun, couple of clouds, a river rising from the mountains. *Educational Sciences: Theory and Practice, 12*(4), 3173–3180.
UNESCO. (1977). *Intergovernmental Conference on Environmental Education.* Final Report Tbilisi, 14–26 October. Retrieved August 5, 2016, from http://www.gdrc.org/uem/ee/EE-Tbilisi_1977.pdf
Uzzell, D. L., Rutland, A., & Whistance, D. (1995). Questioning values in environmental education. In Y. Guerrier, N. Alexander, J. Chase, & M. O'Brien (Eds.), *Values and environment: A social science perspective* (pp. 171–182). New York, NY: Wiley.
Weber, R. P. (1990). *1990 basic content analysis.* Newburry Park, CA: Sage Publications.
Weber, S., & Mitchell, C. (1996). Drawing ourselves into teaching: Studying the images that shape and distort teacher education. *Teaching and Teacher Education, 12*(3), 303–313.
Wilson, B. (1997). Types of child art and alternative developmental accounts: Interpreting the interpreters. *Human development, 40*(3), 155–168.
Wilson, R. A. (1996). Starting early: Environmental education during the early childhood years. *ERIC Digest.* Retrieved June, 29, 2016, from http://www.ericdigest.org/1998-1/early.htm
Yilmaz, Z., Kubiatko, M., & Topal, H. (2012). Czech children's drawing of nature. Educational Sciences: Theory & Practice. *Educational Consultancy and Research Center. Special Issue.*(Autumn), 3111–3119.

Antonio Fernández Crispín
Department of Biology
Benemérita Universidad Autónoma de Puebla [Meritorious Autonomous University of Puebla]
Mexico

STUDY OF ENVIRONMENTAL EDUCATION THROUGH DRAWINGS

Marisela de Niz Robles
Institute of University Studies Campus Puebla
Mexico

Verónica Ruíz Pérez
Autonomous University of Madrid
Spain

Norma A. Hernández
Autonomous University of Madrid
Spain

Javier Benayas del Álamo
Department of Ecology
Autonomous University of Madrid
Spain

GERMÁN VARGAS CALLEJAS

3. PARADIGMS IN THE RELATIONSHIP BETWEEN HUMAN BEINGS AND NATURE IN THE ANDES

INTRODUCTION

The global development model: born within and fostered by a Eurocentric Western culture, and the environmental crisis, which reaches its greatest expression in climate change, profoundly affect the way of life and the cosmovision of the indigenous peoples of the planet (Ticehurst, Urgel, & Best, 2009; Marzo, 2010). Most of these are also at risk of cultural extinction. This reality also affects the Quechua populations in the Andes who despite their demographic extension, are on a path of cultural restructuring that among other things, involves the construction of new ways of conceiving nature and relating to it.

Despite Nature being the common denominator for all human beings, it is not conceived nor understood in the same way by all cultures, with many variables that condition the vision and identification of this reality. One's perception of Nature defines the conceptual construction, as well as the forms of use and exploitation of resources (Gudynas, 1999). This is also the case in the Andes where according to the dominant paradigm, Quechua, Aymara and Uru Indians foster a relationship of proximity and respect to Nature or, on the contrary, feel disconnected from this reality (Vargas, 2005).

We are guided by the aim of studying these types of relationships between human beings and Nature and on focusing on the understanding of this reality. In this chapter, we discuss the contemporary paradigms in understanding Nature among the Bolivian Andes Quechua population. The data underpinning this analysis stem from the research titled "Development perception, conception and practices in the Andes. An ethnographic study of the Quechua community of Aramasí in the Tapacarí district of Bolivia" (Vargas, 2002). This information is complemented with a documentary review of bibliographical sources.

UNDERSTANDING THE CONCEPT OF NATURE

Concepts are products of social representations, a body of knowledge developed and shared by a specific society, with the practical objective of understanding, interpreting and controlling its environment. According to this idea, it is claimed that the concept of Nature corresponds to the relationships of human beings with their environment and allows the creation of a type of knowledge that enables the control of space and the use of the opportunities it offers for life. Given the diversity of relationships between human beings and their environment, the types of knowledge developed about the world and its elements are diverse, and, consequently, the concepts 'of' and 'about' Nature are different, insofar as the processes of conceptual construction are a result of unique experiences.

From a global perspective, Nature is conceived as all that is and exists, the totality of things in order, and the arrangement of all that comprises the universe. Thus, in all cultures, Nature implies something that exists, animate or inanimate, and that is endowed with meaning; that it may be a basis for life and social construction, or that may *not* be so. Nature, understood as something that exists, may be structured on two levels; the first, the physical-material, which is an aspect perceptible through sensory experience, but does not comprise the totality of one being, and that, apart from a material nature, consists of an arrangement, a location and an order. Second, a symbolic-spiritual level: a product of human rationality that seeks to assign a meaning to things and beings, beyond mere materiality.

Nature exists as a material and conceptual reality thanks to the human beings' sensory perception and capacity for abstraction. Thus, the idea of Nature is in direct correlation with people's cosmovision and experience. In this sense, it is human beings who bestow it with a specific identity and meaning. Consequently, there is no unique and uniform vision of Nature, as different human groups understand and define Nature according to their cultural traditions and in the way in which it satisfies their needs and circumstances. This results in a plurality of behaviours and actions within and with respect to this reality.

Humanness as a part of Nature influences and conditions us to the vital processes of transformation that take place in ecosystems. However, "there is no natural environment and, consequently, a context that might be independent of human beings, given that nature is continuously suffering their transforming activity that affects and determines a dialectic process of constant actions and interactions" (Caride, 2000, p. 49). This idea relates to the interdependence of human beings and their natural environment, the reciprocity in the transformation, and the interaction in the construction of a sense of reality.

Although all cultures have their own representations of Nature, is it necessary to point out that not all images enjoy the same degree of acceptance, dissemination, and effect on people's lives. What stands out is the modern Western image that, moreover, is closely linked to a specific model of economic, social, and environmental development, seeking to become universal through multiple forms of cultural penetration and imposition (Gudynas, 1999). Peripherally, some indigenous peoples have also developed their own concepts of Nature, thus configuring a collection of conceptual creations that condition the relationships between human beings and their environment.

THE TRADITIONAL PARADIGM OF NATURE IN THE ANDES

Among the so-called "native", "aboriginal", "traditional", or "indigenous" populations, developed outside Western Culture, in many cases there is a noteworthy presence, living and timely, of particular and unique ways of understanding Nature, expressed in the cosmovisions that are rooted in the land, and through forms of use and resource exploitation that are completely different from modern practices. This contrast between the "indigenous-traditional" and the "Western-modern" should not lead to an idealization of peripheral cultures, which, despite a profound knowledge of natural processes and appropriate forms of coexistence, still suffer from the lack of specific services and products generated by Western culture.

From within the framework of the Andean vision of Nature, it is noticeable that one of its distinctive features is the multi-dimensional perception of the natural world, which is conceived as a vital construct structured in three dimensions; the material, the social, and the spiritual. Thus, Nature is presented as a complex existence that integrates it all (Huanacuni, 2013). An ecosystem where human beings, flora, fauna, and supernatural beings constitute a social and spiritual whole, which lends purpose and meaning to daily life things and actions. A global and holistic reality where human beings represent only one more element in the whole (Figure 3.1).

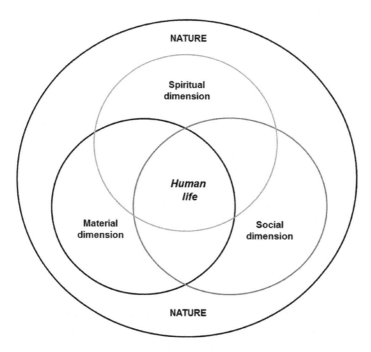

Figure 3.1. Perception of nature in the Andean world

The Andean traditional paradigm on Nature corresponds to a knowledge pattern developed throughout centuries of observation and experimentation, which, in many cases, still serves as a guide that governs the relationships between human beings and their living environment, an interaction which is characterized by analyzing the following factors.

Conceiving Objects as Living Beings

The transformation of reality is conditioned by human beings' perception of the elements that comprise Nature. If all that exists is interpreted as lifeless matter, the tendency would be to exploit it without hesitation. However, if it is conceived that "material objects all have a life of their own" (Kessel, 1993a, p. 18), then Nature and its components are a source of life and a basis for all action and concept of well-being. In the Andean world, according to Kessel (1993b, pp. 9–12), all "phenomena and events always occur because of living things: rocks, plants, animals, tools, farms, houses, human beings, villages, hills, rivers, and even personified phenomena such as rain, frost, hail, disease (…) have life". From this perspective, the interaction with environmental elements is not mediated by feelings of exploitation and domination, but instead by respectful, effective dialogue, an interpersonal relationship of cohabitation and coexistence between indigenous individuals and environments consisting of plants, animals, mountains, rocks, etc.

In the Andes, Nature is conceived and consecrated as *Pachamama,* Mother Earth; source of life and sustenance. According to this idea, in the Andean tradition, *Pachamama* takes female form, which expresses in its fertility the vital quality of the elements of the world. Thus, *Pachamama* (Nature) is a mother that can give, take, suffer, and rejoice (Bettin, 1994). Its existence is neither metaphorical nor symbolic. For the indigenous individual, Nature is an actual mother that one must love and respect.

In this vision of the world, the components of Nature – both animate and inanimate – are perceived as part of a vital reality, where all beings have life and, therefore, a personality that distinguishes, identifies, and transforms them into entities worthy of respect. In this framework of thought, all forms of existence have their place and meaning in the world, where the presence of the human being is no more than one more element of the vital landscape, just another life that deserves the same status as the other beings present in the universe.

Human Being as an Entity Integrated in Nature

If "everything" has life, human beings do not live apart from other existences. Their being is inserted in a context of which they are an integral part and where they seek to adjust as sons, as brothers, as lives that are integrated into the cycle of seasons, phenomena, the ecological environment and events. Within the framework of this vision of Nature, the attitude of human beings in their relationship with the environment is not one of exploitation or submission, but on the contrary, it is mediated by an awareness of their dependence on and interdependence with other existences. In agreement with this idea, Berg (1991) points out that the Andean man does not violate Nature, does not force the earth in order to take its fruit, nor does he mistreat life in order to subdue it, instead he respects her, is fond of her and asks for her permission to consume her resources.

The relationship of the Andean man with Nature is based on the balanced and respectful coexistence with other forms of being, whose presence, in many cases, is interpreted as sacred. In this relational model, the rational being is a part of the natural surroundings, transformed into just another being, integrated and open to coexistence.

Seminal Thought and Cyclical Time

Kessel (1993a) states that the inhabitants of the Andes have a particular way of understanding the transformations in Nature, that is critical thinking. A vision of change that is based on a biological method and rationale, by which:

> events and things occur as in the realm of flora and fauna. They sprout by the vital and driving force of the divine universe – *Pachamama* – grow, bloom, bear fruit and multiply when conditions are favourable and when they are cultivated with affection and understanding. (Kessel, 1993a, p. 11)

To finally die and start the life cycle anew.

Seminal thought, modelled in the life cycle of the seed, is presented as the paradigmatic prototype of life in the Andes, where all the processes of change in phenomena, events, and history respond to the natural sequence of the cycle of life. From this perspective, observes Kessel (1993b), in life, there are no abbreviated, nor accelerated processes. All things are born, grow, reproduce, die, and are reborn. This manner of thinking is represented in Figure 3.2.

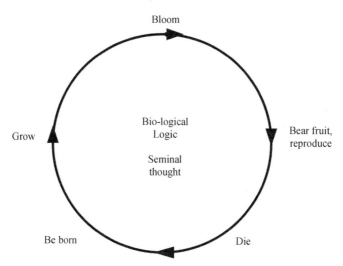

Figure 3.2. Seminal thought and natural cycle

This seminal thought is complemented by a cyclical conception of time. A manner of understanding the world that endows Nature with a dynamic quality, which implies constant change and renewal at fixed and repetitive times, and which, synthetically, represents the cycles of life. A context in which the crucial role of human beings is to seek balance and maintain harmony.

The "Contemplative Midwife"

Within the framework of the cycles of Nature, the action of the Andean indigenous people focuses on the cultivation of the land and the care of animals. In the words of Kessel (1993b, p. 8), "work consists in cultivating the earth, that is, helping Mother Earth to give birth". This vision of the transformation of the world in terms of helping to give birth represents a biological-natural process through which the Andean indigenous people encourage the earth to bear fruit. Assuming the task of "matron" who attends to Nature in the birth of life, helping and encouraging, but without forcing.

Prior, during and after his work, the Andean midwife or cultivator focuses on a contemplative activity. He constantly observes, influences and penetrates the phenomena trying to understand them. Kessel states (1993b, p. 12) that his "understanding is his capacity to feel the life within things, alive and dead, to understand their secret language and to tune in, delicately, with the objects and phenomena with which he is working". Because of his contemplative attitude, he becomes permeable to the mystery of life that he apprehends and memorizes, in order to offer an adequate response to its demands, in such a way that his activity upon Nature does not mean a unilateral dominance, but a reciprocal coexistence (Berg, 1991).

Equilibrium and Harmony

Traditionally, the central concern of the Andean indigenous people has been to preserve the balance "in" and "with" Nature, in order to ensure their existence. The achievement of this objective implies resorting to techniques, religious rites, and social processes that justify and foster the balanced, concrete, and symbolic appropriation of natural resources. As a whole, these interactions compose a complex cultural framework, with economic, social, and spiritual connotations which are at the base of production and consumption in its most material sense.

In the traditional Andean world, the production of goods is destined for the satisfaction of vital needs. Profit and unlimited achievement of economic benefits have no meaning in their context and way of life. What matters are the fulfilment of daily needs and the protection of the harmony with their environment. In this sense, the accumulation of material goods or the concentration of power, which derives from the accumulation of wealth, is irrelevant. The principle that governs indigenous life is "sufficiency", a production logic oriented to the effective and sufficient fulfilling of vital needs, detached from the expectations of generating surpluses for economic profit.

In an environment defined by the search for balance and harmony, production and consumption are based on the management and transformation of elements within the limits of Nature, biodegradable resources whose residues are easily reabsorbed and recycled by the natural metabolism. For example, in traditional communities, garbage is an unknown factor and issue. This harmonious interaction requires limited production and consumption, the use of sustainable techniques for the cultivation and creation of goods, the responsible use of resources, and the application of self-regulatory mechanisms that avoid any destructive and violent pressure on Nature.

The Mythical, Spiritual, and Ethical Dimension of the Relationship between Human Beings and Nature

The relationship between human beings and Nature in the Andes is not reduced to rational interpretations, but it is also conditioned by dimensions that appeal to the mythical-spiritual sense and to an ethical vision that structure the indigenous identity and being.

In the Andean communities, the phenomena that comprise Nature are understood and explained through myths. Myth is a cultural construction that serves to account for the origin, sense, and meaning of elements and events; on the other hand, it is useful for describing ideal realities of the past, when things were what they had to be and, at the same time, it is a conceptual resource that seeks to reveal an ideal future (Jolicoeur, 1994). Through its explanatory and prospective function, myth allows us to understand the transformations in Nature. Insofar as it points out the coordinates of change, maintains an idealized vision of Nature, and facilitates the vision of a hopeful and harmonious future. The mythical reading of Nature in the Andes, despite all the transformations that have taken place, allows dreaming of a life of balance and harmony, in other words, myth fosters the hope in the return to a world that was "perfect".

The validity of myth as an explanatory factor of reality conditions human behaviour in the present and offers clues for future action. In this sense, myth as an expression of the cultural tradition of peoples, especially in societies characterized by orality, marks the boundaries of human action and points out the coordinates within which it is legitimate to act without hurting Nature nor putting in danger the materialization of a utopian reality.

The mythical understanding of reality is complemented by a sacred vision of the elements that comprise Nature. For the Andean being, space is inhabited by deities; nothing can be done without them, who constitute the spirit of the world and life. Thus, the reality is always transformed with respect to the natural and the supernatural. In this regard, Claros (1994, p. 199) expresses that, "when the objective of the indigenous people is to successfully achieve an agricultural production, they use symbolic technology to mobilize the forces of nature present in Mother Earth

(*Pachamama*), the clouds and hills-dwelling spirits who provide rain (*Apus*), the deceased ancestors (*Achachilas*) and other collaborating forces, such as the spirits of the seeds, the protective stones of the farm, the spirits of the irrigation canals, streams or lagoons". Therefore, all human action in Nature is mediated by communication and dialogue with the spiritual dimension of beings and things.

The sacred dimension of Nature is real, insofar as there is no one-dimensional conception of the elements, but rather a global perception that connects the supernatural with concrete things. A duality of realities experience their relationship through rites, which put the subject in contact with the spirits of Nature and with divinity.

The sacred conception of Nature implies a specific ethical practice for the human being, whose behaviour is fundamental for the preservation of harmony and balance in the universe, as well as a condition for good or bad production. Thus, "the earth produces according to man's behaviour towards it. If man's behaviour is good, there is production and protection. If it is bad, there will be no production due to natural catastrophes" Berg (1991, p. 74). This observation highlights the interdependence between human behaviour and the productive and reproductive quality of Nature.

The ethical dimension explains the responsible behaviour of the indigenous people in their natural environment, an idea that also constitutes the most solid frontier that avoids indiscriminate and destructive behaviour towards other beings and resources. This ethical vision, in general, does not correspond to processes of rationalization or social regulation, but rather it is simply practiced as part of the tradition, that is, as a manner of being and acting that is internalized unconsciously by means of educational and cultural processes experienced in everyday life.

The relationship of human beings with Nature in the traditional Andean context is based on these three dimensions; mythical, sacred, and ethical, from which the productive, ecological, cultural, social practices, and everything related to human existence derive. For this reason, in order to obtain the necessary goods for life, the secularized and technified effort of the rational subject is not enough. The spiritual experience and the ethical relationship with all the components of Nature are also relevant.

From a global perspective, it can be asserted that the relationship between human beings and Nature in the Andes corresponds to a "dialogic" model, a process in which the indigenous individual perceives and learns from the other beings and phenomena's messages, and uses this information to transform his environment on the basis of an attitude of respect and care. The relationship of dialogue between the human being and Nature in the Andes is represented in Figure 3.3.

This figure expresses, firstly, the manner in which the Andean man feels that he is a part of Nature and secondly, the relationship with his environment through messages of gratefulness, fear, and supplication of Mother Earth. In addition, the frustration and anger of the indigenous individual when faced with poor production, drafts, or disasters caused by hail or lightning. A collection of messages that receive Nature's response in the form of good crops, plentiful rain, better reproduction of

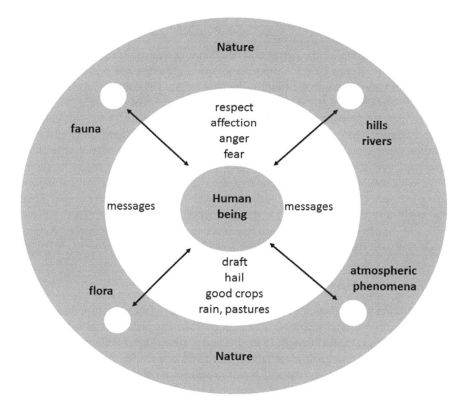

Figure 3.3. Relationship of dialogue between human beings and Nature in the Andes

livestock or, in contrast, Nature's wrath represented by phenomena such as draft, erosion, diseases, etc., which have devastating effects on communal life. This relationship of constant communication and interaction between human beings and Nature in the Andes does not conform to the paradigms of understanding of the Modern-Western rationality, given that it represents a unique manner of interpreting the world and experimenting life.

THE MODERN-WESTERN PARADIGM IN THE ANDES

Due to the phenomenon of economic and cultural globalization, especially in the last three decades, the Western vision has colonized to a significant extent the worldview of the Andean indigenous peoples. To such an extent that, in many traditional settings, the Western model has become institutionalized as the dominant paradigm that conditions and guides the relationship between human beings and their environment. Consequently, despite their resilience and cultural resistance, one of the current traits that single out the situation and perception of Nature in indigenous communities is their proximity to the modern world.

In the Western world, the perception of Nature corresponds, historically, to the Aristotelean difference between matter and spirit, idea that has permeated man's coexistence with Nature to the point of leading to the conception of the human as something significantly disengaged from the other elements of the world, while also on a mission to govern and transform these other elements. Although all cultures have developed the capacity of abstraction as something significantly different from the other components of Nature (Altner, 1994). This possibility has reached alarming levels in the Western world where human beings have come to represent the other elements of Nature as something alien to their existence. Thus running the risk of becoming "denatured" and losing their feeling of belonging to the ecosystem as a whole, an attitude that has led to the destruction of (*their*) Nature. This dualistic rationality has been the basis for the construction of the representation of Nature, which, more specifically, is characterized by the following traits.

The Separation between Human Beings and Nature

The separation between human beings and Nature is one of the more prominent traits of the Modern-Western society, where a man considers himself to be an independent being, superior to the other beings. From this perspective, Nature understood in terms of flora, fauna and inorganic materials, is perceived as a reality that is remote from daily existence, alien to culture and social organization. Nature is not represented as the whole that encompasses and sustains life, but rather as just another element of reality.

Human beings' alienation from Nature has negative consequences, insofar as it reduces the chances of interacting with other beings. Thus, Nature comes to be perceived as a distant reality where the harmful effects of human actions are ignored or, as the case may be, acknowledged as part of a natural process and, sometimes, as an inherent right of rational subjects. This ontological division between man and Nature creates anthropocentric rationality that devalues other beings, whose existence is understood in terms such as "thing"; devoid of their vital dimension and their rights. An existential context in which the rational being lives *against* Nature.

A Hierarchical View of Nature

In the Western world, the relationship between human beings and Nature projects a vertical structure of these elements (Maurice, 1996). In the emergence of Western culture, Nature was regarded as a divine gift for human beings to master and bend to their designs (Huanacuni, 2010). Thus, a vertical relationship was formed, which places divinity at the top of the pyramid, human beings underneath, and Nature on the basis of this relationship. Currently, God has stepped from the top of the hierarchy, that position now being filled by the confidence in Science and Technology that,

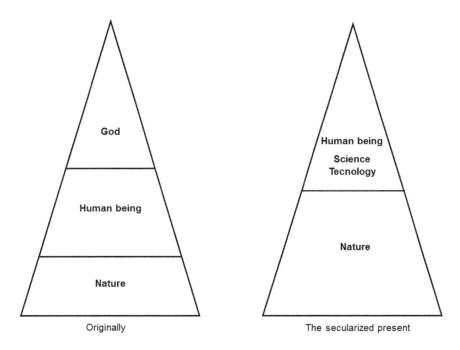

Figure 3.4. Vertical relationship human beings and Nature

apart from the concept of divinity, increase the control that rational beings have over Nature.

In this hierarchical structure, Nature is presented as a residual element, whose existence is meaningful due to its usefulness to human beings. Consequently, it is conceived as a "resource", destined to feed the machinery of industry and the transforming actions of man. This utilitarian conception has led to the destruction, overexploitation, and disregard of other beings, therefore to accelerated destruction of natural equilibria.

Anthropocentrism

In conjunction with the hierarchical structure of Nature, in the Western world, human beings still regard themselves as the center of the Universe, with the mission of dominating the elements of their environment. In this respect, Kessel (1993a, p. 17) states

> with the secularization of Western culture, God was taken out of the picture. The man remained as the sole owner of Earth and its things, absolute and autonomous. Because he feels like the owner, the relation of ownership

has alienated him from his natural environment to such an extent that he represents himself as completely different from the world he lives in, and even transcendent and contrary to it.

Human beings' activity has focused on the unbalanced manipulation and exploitation of the elements of Nature, without in-depth consideration of its negative impact on the balance of the ecosystem. At present, the negative repercussions of the "irrational" activity of man on the environment are known. However, the consensus necessary to reverse these situations has not yet been reached. Human beings remain the conquerors of Nature, even at the expense of their future. The perverse rationality that has led to consider man as a "suicidal" (Meadows, Meadows, & Randers, 1992), a being who is aware of the dangers of his actions but consciously and unconsciously avoids changing course.

Nature as a Resource

Anthropocentrism has had devastating consequences for the rest of beings, which as a whole have been reduced to their quality of "resources" destined to meet human needs, devoid of their vital meaning and with an existence whose reason depends exclusively on their usefulness to human beings. This "objectified" vision of Nature and Utilitarian thought have reached extreme levels, to the point of thinking about human beings themselves in terms of resources.

Therefore, Nature is the totality of resources and raw material available for production. The earth, the flora, the fauna, including the human being, are resources whose energy must be used to achieve higher production (Kessel, 1993a). The desacralized vision and the ideology of profit have reduced the beings in Nature to the status of things, including the rational beings who, for the market, are just another element among the wheels of industry and technological production.

In contrast with the traditional vision of indigenous peoples in the Andes, in the Western World Nature loses its vital meaning and its spiritual connotation, only to become a "thing", a resource, a means for the accumulation of wealth.

Nature as a Source of Profit and Economic Security

In the Western world, well-being is equated with material abundance (Sampedro & Berzosa, 1996) and personal success corresponds exclusively with the ability to accumulate goods of economic value. This perspective has given rise to one of the most outstanding characteristics of Western culture: conceptualizing the transformation of Nature and society in economic terms (Marzo, 2010). A vision that gives rise to processes of deterioration and destruction of ecosystems and cultures.

Focusing security and well-being on the accumulation of economic goods imply producing more, consuming more, creating new needs and, consequently, exhausting and irrationally exploiting natural goods, a set of processes that give rise to social and environmental problems of uncontrollable dimensions, such as climate change.

Disruption of Natural Equilibria

As a vital whole, Nature is the expression of a system of rules and regularities in balance, a reality where nothing is in excess, and everything is regulated through the very act of its elements. In this context, the Western lifestyle, centred on unlimited production and consumption, alters natural processes. An example is the production of non-biodegradable waste or the emission of polluting gases, whose accumulation tends to upset the rules of natural balance. Something similar happens with other productive processes based on the massive use of a specific resource, an abusive use that disrupts rules and natural cycles.

The model of global development associated with the Western lifestyle imposes forced transformations of Nature, insofar as it accelerates the stages of production through the introduction of artificial cycles that do not coincide with natural rhythms, disrupting the balance and harmony. That, among other things, causes catastrophes, waste and, in general terms, discomfort and destruction in the ecosystems.

Destruction of Nature as Part of a "Natural" Process

In the process of industrial and technological production, the considerations on the nature and origin of raw materials are residual, and the ignorance is greater in relation to the specific impacts on the local environment and the global ecosystem. A similar phenomenon occurs with services, everything that is offered and sold seems to be the result of magic, apparently

> services exist by their own nature; they simply must exist. We do not know how they originated, nor how they function, we only know that when we need them, they must meet our expectations. Services are responsible for fulfilling our needs. They are magical. We are not responsible, we disengage. (Pol, 1997, p. 318)

This ignorance distances human beings from Nature, to the extreme of considering that all products are "natural" results of the technical apparatus, detached from biological, social and cultural factors.

The loss and wear of things and beings in the processes of transformation that are forced and destructive are justified as part of a "normal" logic of development, an unavoidable demand of the market and the need for consumption. The disappearance of species and the destruction of aboriginal cultures is accepted as the "natural" price that we must pay to live in a society that has overcome its dependence on Nature. For this rationality, the natural destiny of humanity is the maximum economic development, regardless of the means used to achieve this goal.

This modern vision, based on the separation of man and Nature, has also become institutionalized in the indigenous communities of the Andes, where a new conception of Nature and the processes of interaction with the human being are gradually being developed.

THE HYBRID PARADIGM

The hybrid vision of the relationship between human beings and Nature in the Andes is a recent cultural creation, which is a result of the penetration of the Western lifestyle into indigenous communities: an external vision that is integrated through the education system, including mechanisms of consumption and market logic. Within the framework of this new paradigm converge traditional Andean cultural practices and modern forms of the West, an integration that takes place through processes of imposition and cultural negotiation that, in everyday life, are visible in the interaction of subjects of different origin and in the application of diverse methods, strategies and techniques in the transformation of Nature.

This paradigm is the product of the imposition of a dominant culture, but also of the resistance of the indigenous peoples. Therefore, it is an expression of the encounter and cultural clash and miscegenation of worldviews that shape new ways of explaining and experiencing the relationship of human beings with their environment.

Within the framework of this new vision, indigenous individuals adopt a constant attitude of synthesizing, in one single perspective, two different models of existence (Vargas, 2015). Despite the tension that involves living with two readings of reality, the Andean inhabitant strives to harmonize his own with the alien one, without renouncing his past nor ignoring the present. In this sense, the development of a hybrid paradigm to understand, interact and exploit Nature corresponds to a realistic and resigned vision of life, as the indigenous people know that little or nothing can address cultural globalization and the inevitable advance of the Western model. Consequently, their only alternative is to assimilate the new and redevelop tradition, with the aim of obtaining, in this new context, the greatest advantages in order to ensure their existence and maintain their culture.

An analytical reading of the new relationships between the human being and Nature allows us to understand that, forcefully, in the hybrid paradigm we try to converge both a cyclical and the linear vision of life, the utilitarian and the spiritualized conception of the beings of Nature, as well as an ethical perspective with a more mercantilist approach. Thus, the coexistence with Nature and the appropriation and exploitation of its resources are based on two opposing views that are synthesized into one, to a large extent thanks to the interest of the indigenous peoples to live in harmony with everything and everyone.

Currently, the frequent cultural and economic exchange, the omnipresence of the media and the education system, together with the high degree of institutionalization of the indigenous interpretation of Nature and its recognition in the Political

Constitution of Bolivia and Ecuador, make it impossible to conceive of an Andean vision of Nature that is not contaminated by the Western approach.

The hybrid understanding of Nature places the indigenous people in a constant attitude of assimilation of the new and conservation of the old (Vargas, 2015). Therefore, it is a matter of being productive without losing the spiritual dimension of one's own and without letting oneself be carried away by exclusively instrumental rationality, which results in unbalanced exploitation of Nature. In essence, the hybrid reading of the relationship between human beings and Nature in the Andes allows the mitigation of the conflicts that arise from the conjunction of divergent visions about the world and life.

Despite the effort of indigenous people to synthesize in a single experience the different ways of relating to Nature, the traditional perspective is in decline, due to factors such as the extensive capacity of the Western model to create and meet needs, the high percentages of emigration from rural Andean communities to the cities, the application of educational, social economic policies that privilege the understanding and modern use of Nature and, finally, the gradual transition from a limited, subsistence economy to an economic logic based on profit, consumerism and unlimited growth.

CONCLUSION

Following the logical triad of thesis-antithesis-synthesis, three paradigms of the relationship between human beings and Nature in the Andes have been presented. The intention was to demonstrate the significant difference between the traditional indigenous perspective and the Western-modern, with the objective of making patent the incompatibility between these two perspectives, which only come to a synthesis through the renunciation or subjugation of the indigenous tradition to the globalizing cultural process of the West. A reality is, that in cultural terms, this signifies the rapid destruction of the Andean worldview of Nature.

In order to ensure their survival in a globalized context, indigenous peoples are forced to play by the rules imposed by modern culture, despite the risk that this implies for the continuity of their cultural tradition. To this respect, the universalization of the Western perspective on Nature hampers, and in most cases, nullifies the presence of different logic and rationality systems. The omnipresence of a Western economic model and way of life is gradually giving rise to a univocal perspective on Nature, which is perceived and defined specifically as a "resource" destined to foster economic development.

The presence of the indigenous movement in the Governmental decision-making sphere in Bolivia and Ecuador has fostered, from an institutional point of view, the indigenous cultures' perspective on Nature. Nevertheless, this support of the indigenous discourse and knowledge has clashed with the economic logic of these States. Consequently, the appropriation of the indigenous discourse by the Government has been a mere token, given the low levels of implementation. In this context, for instance, in Bolivia, there have been schizoid situations. On the one hand, both officially and through social movements, the Government highlighted the virtues of the traditional worldview while, on the other hand, at the level of administrative actions and decisions, it promoted economic practices and policies based on the destruction of ecosystems (Cullinan, 2014). This contradiction makes patent the difficult reconciliation between the indigenous vision of Nature and economic interests, which rank higher than any intention of respecting and caring for the things and beings of the world.

Despite the marginal situation and the risk of extinction that threaten the indigenous vision of Nature, it is important to reclaim and update it, given that its insights are necessary in order to address the environmental crisis caused by the Western development model (Armellin, 2011). Given their sustainable essence, the forms of relationship between human beings and Nature in the Andes hold the most appropriate knowledge and practices for the improvement of the interaction between humans and the environment we live in.

At a global level, by not disregarding the importance of the concept of sustainability proposed by the Brundland (1987) Report and the Earth Summits, it is relevant to focus on a new paradigm, the "culture of sustainability" which, in the context of the global cultural and economic development, might integrate concepts and practices from traditional indigenous communities into the contemporary societies manner of transforming the world (Vanhulst & Beling, 2013). The sustainability perspective, innate in Andean peoples, must be recovered, disseminated, and implemented, especially with regard to the limits and cycles of Nature, the preservation of the equilibrium in the ecosystems, the respect of all life forms, and the development of an interdependent and eco-dependent awareness.

REFERENCES

Altner, G. (1994). *Zusammenhangwissen, Lebensverträglichkeit und individuelle Verantwortung. Schirtt zur Versöhnung von Natur und Kultur?*. Kempfenhausener Gespräche. München: Hipo – Bank.

Armellin, M. (2011). Ciencia moderna y conocimientos tradicionales en la adaptación al cambio climático. In *Memoria del taller: Experiencias exitosas de gestión de riesgo en el sector agropecuario para la adaptación al cambio climático* (pp. 183–198). La Paz: FAO Bolivia.

Berg, H. (1991). Conviven con la tierra. In *Cuarto Intermedio, 18* (pp. 64–83), Cochabamba: Compañía de Jesús.

Bettin, I. (1994). Weltbild und denken in den Zentral Anden. In P. Baumann (Coord.), *Kosmos der Anden* (pp. 14–39). München: Diederichs.

Caride, J. A. (2000). *Estudiar ambientes. El análisis de contextos como práctica educativo – ambiental*. A Coruña: Centro de Documentación Domingo Quiroga.

Claros, E. (1994). Hombre y naturaleza en los Andes. In *Yachay, 19–20* (pp. 183–206). Cochabamba: Universidad Católica Boliviana.

Cullinan, C. (2014). The government of the people as members of the Earth community . In T. Prugh & M. Renner (Drs.), *Governing for sustainability*. Washington: The Worldwatch Institute.

Gudynas, E. (1999). Concepciones de la naturaleza y desarrollo en América Latina. In *Persona y Sociedad, 13*(1), 101–125.

Huanacuni, F. (2010). *Buen vivir/vivir bien. Filosofías, políticas, estrategias y experiencias regionales andinas*. Lima: Coordinadora Andina de Organizaciones Indígenas – CAOI.

Huanacuni, F. (2013). Cosmovisión andina y vivir bien. In I. Farah & V. Tejerina (Eds.), *Vivir bien: infancia, género y economía*. La Paz: CIDES-UMSA.

Jolicoeur, L. (1994). *El cristianismo aymara: ¿inculturación o culturización?*. Cochabamba: Universidad Católica Boliviana.

Kessel, J. (1993a). *Tecnología aymara: un enfoque cultural*. Cuadernos de investigación en cultura y tecnología andina, 3. Puno – Perú: CIDSA.

Kessel, J. (1993b). *Ritual de producción y discurso tecnológico andino*. Cuadernos de investigación en cultura y tecnología andina, 5. Puno, Perú: CIDSA.

Marzo, G. (2010). *Buen vivir. Para una democracia de la tierra*. La Paz: Plural.

Maurice, H. (1996). Nature's Nature: Ideas of nature in curricula for environmental education. In *Environmental Education Research*, 2(2), 141–148.

Meadows, D. H., Meadows, D. L. & Randers, J. (1992). *Más allá de los límites del crecimiento*. Madrid: El País – Aguilar.

Pol, E. (1997). Entre el idílico pasado y el cruento ahora. La psicología ambiental frente al cambio. In R. Mira, C. Arce, & J. M. Sabucedo (Eds.), *Responsabilidad ecológica y gestión de los recursos ambientales*. A Coruña: Diputación provincial de A Coruña.

Sampedro, J. L., & Berzosa, C. (1996). *Conciencia del subdesarrollo veinticinco años después*. Madrid: Taurus.

Ticehurst, S., Urgel, S., & Best, S. (2009). *Bolivia, cambio climático, pobreza y adaptación*. Retrieved from http://www.oxfaminternacional

United Nations. (1987). *Our common future: Report of the World Commission on Environment and Development*. Retrieved from http://www.exteriores.gob.es/Portal/es/PoliticaExteriorCooperacion/Desarrollosostenible/Documents/Informe%20Brundtland%20(En%20ingl%C3%A9s).pdf

Vanhulst, J., & Beling, A. (2013). El Buen vivir: una utopía latinoamericana en el campo discursivo global de la sustentabilidad. In *Polis*, nº 36 | 2013. Retrieved from http://polis.revues.org/9638

Vargas, G. (2002). *Prácticas educativas y procesos de desarrollo en los Andes. Estudio etnográfico de la comunidad quechua de Aramasí – provincia Tamaparí, Bolivia* (Doctoral Thesis). Universidad de Santiago de Compostela.

Vargas, G. (2005). *Educación y desarrollo en los Andes*. Frankfurt: Peter Lang, Europäicher Verlag der Wissenschaften.

Vargas, G. (2015). El desarrollo sostenible y local en las comunidades indígenas de los Andes, un enfoque educativo y social. In F. Ilidio, G. Vargas, & O. Freitas (Eds.), *Educação, Desenvolvimento e Ação da Local Comunitaria*. Setúbal: Instituto das comunidades educativas.

Germán Vargas Callejas
Institute of Higher Education
University of Santiago de Compostela
Spain

SHIHO MIYAKE

4. USING A DIGITAL PICTURE BOOK TO PROMOTE UNDERSTANDING OF HUMAN-WILDLIFE CONFLICT

INTRODUCTION: HUMAN-WILDLIFE CONFLICTS

The Global Issue of Human-Wildlife Conflict

Human-wildlife conflict is described as a hostile relationship between wild animals and humans. This relationship is caused as a result of human population expansion and natural habitat shrinkage. People and animals are increasingly coming into conflict over living space and food (WWF, 2017). The World Wildlife Fund for Nature (WWF) as one of the world's largest and historical conservation organizations also reported the gravity of the situation as follows:

> Human-wildlife conflict is a severe and growing problem in today's world. Unlike many environmental issues of our time, it involves not only the impoverishment of human communities but direct human injury and death. On the biodiversity side, it can cause dramatic population declines and potential extinctions, as is currently the concern for the Sumatran elephant in Indonesia. Increasing human population combined with climate change and the alternative movements of both humans and wildlife that it will generate, mean that human-wildlife conflict is likely to increase rapidly in the coming years. (WWF, 2008, p. 11)

> The conflict between people and animals is one of the main threats to the continued survival of many species in different parts of the world and is also a significant threat to local human populations. If solutions to conflicts are not adequate, local support for conservation also decline. The impacts are often tremendous – people lose their crops, livestock, property, and sometimes their lives. The animals, many of which are already threatened or endangered, are often killed in retaliation or to 'prevent' future conflicts. (WWF, 2017)

Why are human-wildlife conflict issues so important? According to the WWF (2008) they are 'one of the important indicators of our ability to keep the world's environment in a healthy state, that enables the majority of people to live a life free from poverty without jeopardizing the future environmental sustainability of our planet' (p. 5). However, no definitive solution has not been found:

> Various socioeconomic and ecological factors that create or aggravate conflicts between humans and wildlife. There are also various technical, institutional and political means to avoid and mitigate them. Potential solutions, of course, are different in different places, depending on a vast variety of factors, such as the species of animals involved and the prevailing attitudes of the local people towards wildlife. (p. 5)

The World Bank (2016) in developing conservation policies from an economic perspective, addressed the difficulty of solving the human-wildlife conflict by examining a case concerning elephants in Botswana, Africa. Woodroffe, Thirgood, and Rabinowitz (2005) described several patterns of the impact of human-wildlife conflict on their work. They noted that:

> Human-wildlife conflict is a significant issue in conservation. As people encroach into natural habitats, and as conservation efforts restore wildlife to areas where they may have been absent for generations, contact between people and wild animals is growing. Some species, even the beautiful and endangered, can have serious impacts on human lives and livelihoods. Tigers kill people, elephants destroy crops and African wild dogs devastate sheep herds left unattended. Historically, people have responded to these threats by killing wildlife wherever possible and has led to the endangerment of many species that are difficult neighbours. The urgent need to conserve such species, however, demands coexistence of people and endangered wildlife. (Inscription page)

In this way, human-wildlife conflicts are currently a serious global environmental problem in terms of biodiversity conservation and sustainable development.

In other several academic research, human-wildlife conflicts have been drawing significant attention. According to a research survey on human-wildlife conflict in India, this problem has been increasing in over 90% of the country over the last 40 years, implying that currently, it occurs almost across the entire country. Moreover, the report contained conflict issues with 88 species (Anand & Radhakrishna, 2017). Quigley and Herrero (2005) categorized conflicts with 15 animal species. It is noteworthy that some of the species are designated as vulnerable, endangered species such as the polar bear (*Ursus maritimus*) and the giant panda (*Ailuropoda melanoleuca*) (IUCN, 2017). Karanth and Gopal (2005) also reported on ecological policies focusing on tigers. Hudenko (2012) and Jacobs, Fehres, and Campbell (2012) examined the emotional aspects of humans, suggesting psychological models and measurement methods and instruments based on literature surveys. In addition, psychological investigations are being conducted on the extent to which people accept wild animals (Whittaker, Vaske, & Manfredo, 2006). Practical approaches are also being attempted to solve indigenous human-wildlife conflicts. For example, Espinosa and Jacobson (2012) studied bear conservation in a Quichua community to evaluate knowledge, attitudes, and behavioural intentions among those living near the animal habitat. Treves, Wallace, Naughton-Treves, and Morales (2006) studied human-wildlife conflict in terms of risk management and human security based on the Bolivia, Uganda, and Wisconsin project studies. These research outcomes indicate that human-wildlife conflicts are examined from various perspectives including ecology, psychology, and sociology.

Conversely, research on the design and implementation of educational tools for the public (including young people) is minimal. It is essential to synthesize research related to the design and development of educational tools that communicate about human-wildlife conflict.

Animals are 'good to think about', since they represent symbolic vehicles for our work representing social relationships and cultural ideas (Lévi-Strauss, 1969). We can also consider and explore how our future society and culture could be if we attend to the situation of animals. In addition, every species that seeks conservation attention also has a cultural meaning that reflects on historical, social, and economic tensions (Richards, 2000).

While considering the environment's future in relation to improving our own lifestyles and livelihoods, we should also study how we can better live with wildlife with cultural meaning. Research outcomes thus far indicate that human-wildlife conflict is an important theme since it communicates about our actual (current) environmental situation and provides an opportunity to coexist with nature and wildlife.

Human-Wildlife Conflict in Japan

The issue of human-wildlife conflict is more evident when we look at daily regional affairs. In Japan, human-wildlife conflicts occur with deer, monkeys, bears, boars and other species. Some incidents occur more frequently such as stolen food and injuries because of our encounters with these animals. For example, Mainichi newspaper reported on 4 December 2017:

> On April 4 at 11:15 am, there was a call to the police concerning 'a boar in school' from Higashiyama junior high school in Kyoto. According to the school principal, two boars invaded the school and were soon captured. Although the glass door of the building entrance had been broken, there were no reported injuries. In Kyoto, wild boars also appeared in November, and road construction workers were injured. (Nakatsugawa & Daito, 2017)

These types of encounters with wild animals in residential areas are no longer rare. However, most people do not know why the problem occurs. If they see a wild animal in town, they might be surprised or scared. In addition, people in urban areas do not have an experience of this problem as much as people in places of Satoyama, a semi-forested area with an urban population. According to the Ministry of Environment of Japan (2004), 'Satoyama is a region with native nature, urban towns, and villages. Secondary forests, farmland, ponds, and grasslands surround Satoyama. It is an important area because there are habitats of many unique organisms, a supply of natural resources for food and wood, and an aestehetic landscape. Also, it is significant in terms of its cultural traditions (p. 2).

On the other hand, an international survey conducted by the Relevance of Science Education (ROSE) reported interesting data. The data on the Japan region, analyzed by Simode (2004), suggested that Japanese secondary school students showed more positive attitudes toward working with animals (mean B3) than students in other countries. However, when they were asked 'how people, animals, plants and the environment depend on each other (mean A16)', their responses were average. This would suggest that young Japanese students prefer to be with animals, however, on the other hand, they are not sure how to relate to wild animals. They could not decide what kind of behavior was most appropriate.

It has been reported that young people in their early 20s are less aware of the management of animals (Cabinet Office Government of Japan, 2010). It has also been reported that people living in urban areas have a lower awareness of human-wildlife conflicts (Matsukane, Eto, & Yokoyama, 2015). However, if we do nothing to improve people's awareness, this problem will become worse. Thus, it is important not only for people to be aware of news articles and occasional events, but also, people should learn about how human-wildlife conflict occurs. This includes an understanding of the culture of coexistence with animals in the history of human society (Berns & Atran, 2012). Now, can people learn more about the processes of human-wildlife conflict? How can people in Japan learn more about human-wildlife conflicts from a global perspective?

PURPOSE OF THE RESEARCH

In this study, I created a digital picture book that illustrates human-wildlife conflict. Using the picture book, I examined young people's understanding of ideas about human-wildlife conflicts. This study aims to suggest methods about how to promote greater student understanding of environmental problems through a multimedia teaching tool. It also seeks to promote consciousness of environmental problems specifically in the younger generation, who will soon be the citizens responsible for protecting our global environments.

This study specifically targeted the human-wildlife conflict of Asian elephants and habitat loss due to the palm oil industry. In the next sections, I will explain why the study focused on students in their late teens, why the elephant was focused on, and why an animated picture book tool was developed.

RATIONALE FOR DEVELOPMENT AND EVALUATION OF THE EDUCATIONAL TOOL

Why Target the Young Generation?

Cultivating students' attitudes and behaviours toward biodiversity and socio-scientific issues have been highlighted as important by previous studies on environmental education and science education (e.g. Nisiforou & Charalambides, 2012; Sadler, Chambers, & Zeidler, 2004). Recently, ecological citizenship, which focuses on the relationship between citizens' environmental actions and their social values, has become a critical framework for fostering sustainable development (Dobson, 2003). However, it is hard to say to what degree the concept of biodiversity conservation has been spreading among the general public. According to a Japanese public-opinion survey on environmental issues, the younger generation, especially people in their twenties, displayed less interest in the natural environment and biodiversity conservation than older generations (Cabinet Office Government of Japan, 2014).

In recent years, the educational setting has significantly changed and educational tools utilizing information and communication technologies (ICT) have also become widespread. Livingstone (2002) states:

> The potential impact of new forms of Information and Communication Technologies (ICT) has been speculatively related to almost every aspect of society; from home to work, from education to leisure, from citizenship to consumerism, from the local to global; perhaps their most radical impact appears to be the blurring of these traditionally important distinctions. (p. 2)

In fact, young people's use of digital tools including smartphones and the Internet is significantly higher than for other generations. A study on the duration of smartphone-based Internet use on an average weekday basis by age group indicated that the overall average use increased by 82 minutes in 2016. The averages are as much as 143 minutes (per day) for teens and 129 minutes (per day) for people in their 20s (Ministry of Internal Affairs and Communications, Japan, 2018). Digital tools are familiar to the young generation. Therefore, when creating teaching materials that will focus attention on complicated problems such as the human-wildlife conflict and biodiversity conservation, it is essential that an engaging digital tool be used to reach this generation.

Why an Elephant for the Theme?

There are three main reasons why an elephant was chosen as the theme of the picture book. The first reason is that elephants have one of the longest histories of being bred in Japanese zoos, with the first elephant arriving at the Ueno (Tokyo) Zoo in 1888 (Tokyo Zoological Park Society, n.d.). Since that time, more than 120 years ago, several zoos in Japan have kept elephants. Nowadays, among the 91 zoos registered in the Japan Zoo Association (JAZA), 51 zoos currently breed elephants (Japan Zoo Association, 2011). Among them, 34 zoos keep Asian elephants, and 17 zoos keep African elephants. Elephants also tend to be the most popular animal among visitors to Japanese zoos.

The second reason that an elephant was selected for the story is that elephants have been designated as an endangered species. Asian elephants (*Elephas maximus*) have been designated at a more critical level of 'endangered' on the IUCN Red

List of Threatened Species than African elephants (*Loxodonta africana*), which have been placed at the 'vulnerable' level (International Union for Conservation Nature and Natural Resources [IUCN], 2017). As the Asian elephant, which is bred in one-third of Japanese zoos is endangered, anything that leads to population decrease is of serious concern. In fact, the loss of the Asian elephant's habitat caused by the palm oil industry is a crucial issue for biodiversity conservation.

The third reason that an elephant was selected for the story is because Japan is deeply involved in the loss of the Asian elephant's habitat, which is caused by palm oil plantations. Palm oil is used to produce food and household products such as chocolates, crisps, ice creams, and kitchen and laundry detergents. In 2014, 543,000 MTs (metric tons) of palm oil were consumed in Japan. This corresponds to 23% of the total amount of vegetable oil consumption (Paulson & Hayashi, 2016). Despite such mass consumption, Japanese people are not aware of the problem, which is at the root of this human-wildlife conflict. Although the Asian elephants' habitat is not in Japan, the human-wildlife conflict that is occurring as a result of habitat destruction directly involves Japanese people. Thus for the above-mentioned reasons, the Asian elephant habitat problem was incorporated into the story material.

Why a Picture Book?

Picture books are fundamental and effective educational tools. In general, they are used with young children. Jalongo (2004) said that all children enjoy reading picture books and take the time to read. Avraamidou and Osborn (2009) asserted that a story has the role of converting readers' experiences into knowledge. More specifically, people's experiences represented in or as a story, lead to the growth of the sense of a community's values (Schank & Berman, 2002). According to Nikolajeva (2010), 'Visual literacy is just an essential component of a child's intellectual growth as the ability to read verbal texts. In addition, if verbal literacy can be and is trained, so should be visual literacy' (p. 27). Other studies from the perspective of psychology and childcare, and children's health (e.g. Reid & Beveridge, 1986; Holzheimer, Mohay, & Masters, 2002) have shown that using picture books promotes an independent attitude in children. In sum, picture books are a simple yet effective educational tool for children.

According to Nikolajeva and Scott (2006), the interpretation of picture books depended on the individual readers:

> For a look at situations where ownership of the book is problematic dramatizes the complexity of the relationship between verbal communication and the iconic communication that picture books embody–that dynamic interrelationship and creative tension between the two modes of communication. Pursuits may declare that the context is all and supports whatever interpretation seem appropriate. While the interpretation of the relationship between image and text also becomes increasingly complex as the number of people involved in its creation and their collaboration diminishes. (p. 29)

In sum, a picture book is a tool that allows the readers to form their thoughts, answers, and interpretations to complicated questions. Thus, the research tool is expected to promote social, global, and complicated values and attitudes for young people, around 20 years old who have passed school age.

RESEARCH QUESTIONS

The author and the students in an environmental sociology and environmental education course have been creating human-wildlife conflict educational tools since 2015. The pilot version of a picture story (the picture and story were separate) was produced and demonstrated for visitors at the zoo in 2015 (Kato, Okuda, Fukumithsu, Kobayashi, & Miyake, 2015). In the present study, the author reproduced the picture book as a digital version using iMovie (version 9.0.8). Using this simple digital tool, the author attempted to convey the environmental problem of human-wildlife conflict to young people and to examine how the digital picture book helped them to understand biodiversity and conservation issues. For the 18-year-old students in the author's environmental sociology course, the following three points were examined:

1. How many students were aware of the issue of human-wildlife conflict prior to the study?
2. What were their impressions after watching the digital picture book?
3. What did they learn and understand about human-wildlife conflict by watching the digital picture book?

RESEARCH PROCEDURE

The Development of a Digital Picture Book to Introduce the Conflict between Humans and Elephants

With the cooperation of the Tennoji Zoo in the city of Osaka, I have been developing an environmental picture book based on the Asian elephant since 2015. I have been conducted several practical investigations to let the visitors read the picture books since then. The story, entitled: *The Story of an Asian Elephant Named Rani-Hiroko* shows how she came to be at the zoo and explains the impact of the oil palm industry on Asian elephants. It also contains the story of Rani-Hiroko's unfortunate childhood, when her mother died due to deforestation. Several pictures from the book and their descriptions are presented in Figure 4.1.

Thirty-seven 18-year-old students participated in the present study. The following two issues were included in the process:

a. A three-minute animation of Rani-Hiroko's story was delivered.
b. The candidates answered a questionnaire to describe their impressions with a word association inquiry of up to ten words.

c. The candidates wrote free comments to describe of their understanding of the human-wildlife conflict. These comments were evaluated according to a four-level rubric.

Rani-Hiroko: I'm Rani-Hiroko in the Osaka zoo. I attack things around me with my trunk.

Zookeeper: Rani-Hiroko is so naughty. She attacks with her nose. Oddly, she steps on the poop, no other elephants do so. Why is she so strange?

Narrator: Hiroko's mother was killed in the forest in India when she was a child. Elephants are believed that they mourn the death and shed tears like humans. They can even make memory. How sad for Rani-Hiroko to lose he mother.

Rani-Hiroko: I'm lost in the forest.

Narration: Rani-Hiroko was taken to an animal shelter when she got lost nearby her dead mother. 3rd May, 1970, only one year old she came to Osaka where the international exhibition was held as a bridge of friendship between India and Japan.

Zookeeper: Why do humans kill elephants?

Narration: Our common food such as chocolate, and 'cup noodles' relate on the reason why elephants are killed. These foods contain vegetable oil. The oil is mainly produced from oil palms. Planting oil palms destroy the natural forests of the elephants habitat.

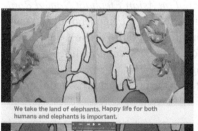

Zoo keeper: We deprive the land of elephants. Happy life for both humans and elephants is important.

Narration: Rani-Hiroko is 46 years old and one of the most longevity among 70 number of elephants in Japan. Keita-a keeper- hopes that elephants live much longer. What can we do for elephants living much happily and longer?

Figure 4.1. The digital picture book

Evaluation Tools for Assessing Student Understanding

Word association. Word association, which is sometimes used with a word 'test' or 'game', is a tool for assessing personality traits and conflicts, in which the subject responds to the given word with the first word that comes to mind or with a predetermined type of word, such as an antonym (The American Heritage Medical Dictionary, 2007). The tool is often used to study on children's and students' understanding. White and Gunston (1992), science education researchers, defined word association as 'a procedure designed to elicit the relations people have formed between concepts. As concepts can be units within topics, word association can be used to measure understanding not only of concepts themselves but also of whole disciplines, of situations, and even of people' (p. 142). This method supports the understanding of students' ideas 'as components of learners' cognitive structure that have "personal meaning" and hence may affect everyday behaviour' (Fensham & Johnson, 1985). The meaning of the word associative method is further explained as follows:

> Word associations arise in the human's mind when reading or saying a word, or just thinking about the word. Association is one of the basic mechanisms of memory. In a sense, they can be called natural classifiers of the conceptual content of the vocabulary of the language. Ideas and concepts, which are available to the memory of a man are related. This relationship is based on the past experience of a man and, in the final analysis, more or less accurately reproduces objectively existing relationships between the phenomena of the real world. Under certain conditions, a revival of one idea or concept is accompanied by a revival of other ideas correlated with it. (Word Association Network, 2018)

Therefore, the word association technique is an appropriate measure to assess students' understanding of the human-wildlife conflict issue.

Rubric

A rubric is an evaluation tool used in education. According to Flinders University (n.d.), a rubric is defined as follows:

> A rubric is a descriptive scoring (or marking) scheme developed by teachers, sometimes in consultation with students, to guide judgments about the products or processes of students' learning through an assessment task. A rubric is often presented as a type of matrix that provides scaled levels of achievement or performance for a set of criteria or dimensions of quality for a particular assessment task. For example, a paper, an oral presentation, use of teamwork skills or a work placement. The descriptions of the possible levels of attainment for each of the criteria or dimensions of performance are described adequately

enough to make them useful for judgment of, or reflection on, progress toward intended learning outcomes.

Analyzes of rubrics and their effectiveness as an evaluation tool have been carried out by Reddy and Andre (2010) and Allen and Tanner (2006). The former comprehensively analyzed case examples of rubric usage. The latter analyzed the use of rubrics in biology education for higher education students. These studies present a way to evaluate the student's description as a result of learning performance. In other words, by using rubrics, it is possible to visualize and evaluate learner understanding, content and degree. For the above reasons, the rubric was adopted as part of the qualitative analysis in this study.

RESULTS

How Many Students Were Aware of the Issue of Human-Wildlife Conflict Prior to the Study?

A questionnaire survey was given to the 37 participants. One question asked, 'Are you aware of the environmental problems concerning elephants?'. Thirty-three students (89.2%) answered 'No' (I do not know) and 4 (10.8%) answered 'Yes' (I know). Thus, most students were not aware of the environmental problems concerning elephants.

What Were Their Impressions after Watching the Digital Picture Book?

A total of 318 words were obtained from the word association task. Table 4.1 shows the candidates' representative impression words extracted in descending order. More than 60% of the students ranked the following three words in first, second, or third place. These three words – 'sad', 'pitiful', and 'cruel'– revealed the strongest impressions made on the viewers. Considering that the word 'painful' came in fourth place, it seems that the story seemed to reflect a pessimistic aspect of the environmental problems facing elephants and its seriousness by illustrating the relationship between Rani-Hiroko's story and the problem of habitat destruction that is affecting elephants.

'Lovely pictures', 'intelligible', and 'dark', which came in fifth to seventh rank describe the students' visual impressions of the digital picture book. Since the background colour was black, this might explain why the students used the word 'dark'.

'Selfish people' in the eighth rank and 'coexistence' in the ninth rank demonstrate the students' reflection on the cause of elephant habitat loss and how cohabitation between humans and wildlife can be difficult in the modern world. In addition, 'affectionate', which was ranked tenth, may have expressed the aspect of the story in which the zookeeper wished Rani-Hiroko would live a longer life, although she had not been happy when she was young.

The words 'environment' and 'value of knowledge', which both ranked tenth (eleventh and twelfth positions in Table 4.1), demonstrated that the awareness of environmental problems and the importance of this knowledge were effectively conveyed to students.

Table 4.1. Results of the word association task

Rank No.	Associated word	Number of responses (%)
1	Sad	27 (75.0)
2	Pitiful	22 (61.1)
2	Cruel	22 (61.1)
4	Painful	17 (47.2)
5	Lovely pictures	12 (33.3)
6	Intelligible	10 (27.8)
7	Dark	9 (25.0)
8	Selfish people	8 (22.2)
9	Coexistence	7 (19.4)
10	Affectionate (care for the elephant called Rani)	6 (16.7)
10	Environment	6 (16.7)
10	Value of knowledge (we need to know)	6 (16.7)
Sub total		152 (47.8)
Total		318 (100)

When categorizing each word, four influential aspects of this digital picture book were found; (1) an ethical/moral aspect, (2) an emotional aspect, (3) an ecological aspect, and (4) the tool's appearance, as shown in Figure 4.2. These were interpreted as the direct responses of the readers to the Rani-Hiroko story of a human-wildlife conflict problem. It is believed that his tool prompted the students' consideration of the ethical, emotional, and ecological aspects of the issue, as well as their appreciation of the tool's visual aspect. Thus, it can be said that a digital picture book is a useful tool in the cultivation of ethical and ecologically aware citizens.

How Did the Students' Understanding of Human-Wildlife Conflict Differ after Watching the Digital Book?

Each student's comment was evaluated using a four-level rubric in terms of keywords, as shown in Figure 4.3. Fourteen students responded at level 2 for 'descriptions of considering humans' impact on wildlife.' Eleven students wrote comments displaying consideration of humans' responsibility at level 3. Some

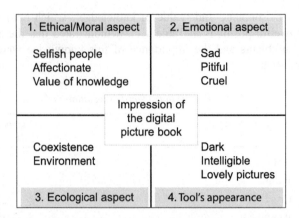

Figure 4.2. Word categories

comments showed understanding that human lifestyle is related to the elephant habitat problem, and this problem is caused not only by those living close to elephants' habitats but also by the people who consume palm oil products, such as Japanese people. Through the story, the students realized that it is necessary to change their minds and attitudes toward the environment. There are several passages in the digital picture book that describe how elephants' habitats are destroyed because of human activities. The students also understood these reasons and factors. Further, one student communicated that everyone, including each of us, should take action to protect the future environment. Through the story of the elephant called Rani-Hiroko, the students' awareness of the issue of human-wildlife conflict improved.

	1	2	3	4
	Description of story contents and understanding of the facts	Descriptions of considering humans' impact on wildlife	Description of consideration on humans' responsibility	Description of how we should behave for future environment
Key words in the phrases	elephant, forest destruction	human and wildlife, sacrifice,	protection, conservation, coexistence,	future, global view, ecosystem, extinction
Number of responses	8	14	11	4

Figure 4.3. Rubric

Table 4.2. Example comments by rubric index

---

1. *Description of story contents and understanding of the facts*
   a. I learned that mothers are necessary for baby elephants, just like for human children. I also learned that animals have emotions and personalities.
   b. I learned that elephants have strong connections between parents and children. During the scene when Rani-Hiroko shed tears, I felt sorrow.
2. *Descriptions of considering humans' impact on wildlife*
   a. Palm fields are increasing to produce food and items for humans. This reduces the space where elephants can live. To make matters worse, this leads to elephants going into villages and being killed by people. We must consider animals' environment as well as humans' environment.
   b. I found that the impact of humans on other animals is also huge.
3. *Description of consideration on humans' responsibility*
   a. Coexisting, knowing the current situation that human beings cut down trees, which robs elephants as well as other plants and animals of their habitat. That is why I realised that the existence of zoos is great because they play a wonderful role in protecting animals.
   b. We destroy animals' lives for selfish reasons, ruin their homes, and kill them because elephants are dangerous. I now understand how selfish human beings are. However, I also understand that it is not only a local problem, but a global one because all of us who buy and use palm oil products are partly responsible.
4. *Description of how we should behave for future environment*
   a. Although it has nothing to do with the Japanese environment, I was able to learn about deforestation in other countries through the elephant story. I thought that people should think seriously about what we should do for elephants to live happily without being killed.
   b. I think that elephants and human beings should live together in cooperation and harmony. For this purpose, I think it is important for humans to actively protect the global environment.

CONCLUSION

The survey results showed that nearly 90% of participants did not previously know about the environmental problem about elephants' habitat loss. Some reasons why the students were not aware of this human-wildlife conflict may be because the elephants' habitat is far from Japan, and there is little information available on this topic. In Japan, approximately 60% of zoos have elephants, and the history of animal breeding in Japan is a long one. Elephants are well-known and familiar animals so we have the responsibility to understand what is happening to their habitat and to adopt personal behaviours that will help ensure their future survival.

In this study, I created a digital picture book about an Asian elephant named Rani-Hiroko who lives at the Osaka zoo. The participants showed interest in watching and reading the story. The students commented on the appearance of the digital picture book, but many also expressed interest in the human-wildlife conflict of the elephants' habitat loss and humanity's responsibility for the problem. They also recognized that knowing and obtaining information itself was significant.

People sometimes resort to the use of violence to solve environmental problems. However, it is more effective to raise people's consciousness and awareness of such problems than to fight for solutions. Raising awareness and knowledge of real environmental problems, mainly through education, is a more effective way of resolving human-wildlife conflicts. Dobson (2003) stated that 'value' is more important than 'literacy' in current environmental education for citizenship:

> This is to say that just as environmental education has moved on from the acquisition of knowledge to the negotiation of values, so citizenship education is no longer only about learning how parliament functions, but also has to do with the moral and ethical dimension of social life. We might say, in other words, that just as environmental education now includes but goes beyond 'environmental literacy,' so citizenship education now includes but goes beyond 'political literacy'. (p. 178)

Based on the results of the present study, I would like to continue producing teaching materials that effectively convey the values of knowledge and awareness of environmental problems related to the loss of wildlife habitats, especially those linked to the lives of Japanese people. Unfortunately, the Asian elephant at Osaka Tennoji Zoo, Rani-Hiroko died on January 25, 2017, at the age of 48. I hope that her picture story contributes to the conservation of the global environment.

ACKNOWLEDGEMENTS

This study was supported by the JSPS KEKNHI [Japan Society for the Promotion of Science Grants-in-Aid for Scientific Research] 16H01814 for Tomoyuki Nogami (Kobe University) and 15K00998 for Shiho Miyake (Kobe College) from the Ministry of Education, Culture, Sports, and Technology.

This chapter was revised and reconstructed for publication in this volume. The original manuscript was titled 'A study on developing a pilot biodiversity educational tool to communicate the discord between wildlife and humans' and presented at the 9th World Congress of Environmental Education held in Vancouver, Canada, 9–15 September, 2017.

REFERENCES

Allen, D., & Tanner, K. (2006). Rubrics: Tools for making learning goals and evaluation criteria explicit for both teachers and learners. *CBE-Life Sciences Education, 5*, 197–203.

Anand, S., & Radhakrishna, S. (2017). Investigating trends in human-wildlife conflicts: Is conflict escalation real or imaginaed? *Journal of Asia-Pacific Biodiversity, 10*(2), 154–161.

Avraamidou, L., & Osborn, J. (2009). The role of narrative in communicating science. *International Journal of Science Education, 31*(12), 1683–1707.

Berns, G. S., & Atran, S. (2012). The biology of cultural conflict. *Philosophical Transactions of the Royal Society B, 367*(1589), 633–639.

Cabinet Office Government of Japan. (2010). *Doubutsu-aigo ni kakawaru yoron chosa* [Public opinion survey of animal welfare and management]. Retrieved from https://survey.gov-online.go.jp/h22/h22-doubutu/index.html (in Japanese)

Cabinet Office Government of Japan. (2014). *Kankyo-mondai ni kansuru yoron chosa* [Public opinion survey on environmental issues]. Retrieved from http://survey.gov-online.go.jp/h26/h26-kankyou/gairyaku.pdf (in Japanese)

Dobson, A. (2003). *Citizenship and the environment* (pp. 174–207). New York, NY: Oxford University Press.

Espinosa, S., & Jacobson, S. K. (2012). Human-wildlife conflict and environmental education: Evaluating a community program to protect the Andean Bear in Ecuador. *The Journal of Environmental Education, 43*(1), 55–65.

Fensham, P., & Johnson, B. (1985). Learner's response to the idea of environment. *Research in Science Education, 15*, 131–139.

Flinders University. (n.d.). *What is a rubric?*. Retrieved from http://www.flinders.edu.au/teaching/teaching-strategies/assessment/grading/rubric.cfm

Holzheimer, L., Mohay, H., & Masters, I. B. (2002). Educating young children about asthma: Comparing the effectiveness of a developmentally appropriate asthma education video tape and picture book. *Child: Care, Health and Development, 24*(1), 85–99.

Hudenko, H. W. (2012). Exploring the influence of emotion on human decision making in human-wildlife conflict. *Human Dimensions of Wildlife, 17*(1), 16–28.

International Union for Conservation of Nature and Natural Resources [IUCN]. (2017, January 28). *The IUCN red list of threatened species, 2017-3*. Retrieved from http://www.iucnredlist.org/search

Jacobs, M. H. (2012). Human emotions toward wildlife. *Human Dimensions of Wildlife, 17*(1), 1–3.

Jacobs, M. H., Fehres, P., & Campbell, M. (2012). Measuring emotions towards wildlife: A review of generic methods and instruments. *Human Dimensions of Wildlife, 17*(4), 233–247.

Jalongo, M. R. (2004). *Introduction–engagement of picture books, Young children and picture books* (pp. 1–5), Washington, DC: National Association for the Education of Young Children.

Japan Zoo Association. (2011.) *Shiiku doubutsu kensaku* [Search for breeding animals]. Retrieved from http://www.jaza.jp/animals/zukan.php

Karanth, K. U., & Gopal, R. (2005). An ecology-based policy framework for human-tiger coexistence in India. In R. Woodroffe, S. Thirgood, & A. Rabinowitz (Eds.), *People and wildlife: Conflict or coexistence?* (pp. 373–387). Cambridge: Cambridge University Press.

Kato, R., Okuda, R., Fukumitsu, M., Kobayashi, M., & Miyake, S. (2015). Doubutsuen no zou wo mochifu ni shita yomigatariyou kankyo ehon no kaihatsu [How we developed an environmental awareness picturebook of an Elephant at a Zoo]. *JSSE Research Report, 30*(3), 95–100. (in Japanese)

Lévi-Strauss, C. (2004). *The savage mind*. New York, NY: Oxford University Press. (Reprinted from *The savage mind*, C. Lévi-Strauss, 1962, Paris: Librairie Plon.)

Livingstone, S. (2002). *Young people and new media: Childhood and the changing media environment*. London: Sage Publications.

Matsukane, C., Eto, K., & Yokoyama, M. (2015). Toshibu jyumin no inoshishi ni taisuru isikityousa [Survey of urban residents' consciousness of wild boar and conservation efforts]. *Hyogo wildlife monograph, 8*, 66–89. Wildlife management research centre, Hyogo. (in Japanese)

Ministry of Environment of Japan. (2004). *The Satoyama initiative*. Retrieved from http://www.env.go.jp/nature/satoyama/pamph/pamph2/full.pdf

Ministry of Internal Affairs and Communications, Japan. (2017). Present and future of smartphone economy. *2017 white paper on information and communications in Japan* (pp. 2–11). Retrieved from http://www.soumu.go.jp/johotsusintokei/whitepaper/eng/WP2017/chapter-1.pdf#page=1

Nakatsugawa, H., & Daito, Y. (2017, 12 4). Inoshishi syutubotsu gakkoude hokaku keganinn nashi Kyoto [A boar appears and is caught in a school]. *The Mainichi* (morning). Retrieved from https://mainichi.jp/articles/20171204/k00/00e/040/200000c (in Japanese)

Nikolajeva, M. (2010). Interpretative codes and implied readers of children's picture books. In T. Colomer, B. Kümmerling-Meibauer, & C. Silva-Díaz (Eds.), *New directions in picture book research* (pp. 27–40). New York, NY: Routledge.

Nikolajeva, M., & Scott, C. (2006). *Whose book is it? How picture books work* (pp. 29–60). New York, NY: Routledge.

Nisiforou, O., & Charalambides, A. G. (2012). Assessing undergraduate university students' level of knowledge, attitudes and behaviour towards biodiversity: A case study in Cyprus. *International Journal of Science Education, 34*(7), 1027–1052.

Paulson, J. K., & Hayashi, Y. (2016). *Japan oilseeds and products. Annual 2016 Japan oilseeds and products situation and outlook.* Tokyo, Japan: United States Department of Agriculture [USDA] Foreign Agricultural Service. Retrieved from https://gain.fas.usda.gov/Recent%20GAIN%20 Publications/Oilseeds%20and%20Products%20Annual_Tokyo_Japan_4-7-2016.pdf

Quigley, H., & Herrero, S. (2005). Characterization and prevention of attacks on humans. In R. Woodroffe, S. Thirgood, & A. Rabinowitz (Eds.), *People and wildlife conflict or coexistence?* (pp. 27–48). Cambridge: Cambridge University Press.

Reddy, Y. M., & Andre, H. (2010). A review of rubric use in higher education. *Assessment & Evaluation in Higher Education, 35*(4), 435–448.

Reid, D. J., & Beveridge, M. (1986). Effects of text illustration on children's learning of a school science topic. *British Journal of Educational Psychology, 56*(3), 294–303.

Richards, P. (2000). Chimpanzees as political animals in Sierra Leone. In J. Knight (Ed.), *Natural enemies: People-wildlife conflicts in anthropological perspective* (pp. 78–103). New York, NY: Routledge.

Sadler, T. D., Chambers, F. W., & Zeidler, D. L. (2004). Student conceptualizations of the nature of science in response to a socioscientific issue. *International Journal of Science Education, 26*(4), 387–409.

Schank, R. C., & Berman, T. R. (2002). Narrative impact: Social and cognitive foundations. In M. C. Green, J. J. Strange, & T. C. Brock (Eds.), *The pervasive role of stories in knowledge and action* (pp. 287–314). Mahwah, NJ: Lawrence Erlbaum Associates.

Simodo, S. (2004). *A comparative study on interests in, attitudes toward and experiences in science among Japanese 'science-lover' and 'science-hater' students: Through the analysis of an international comparative survey, ROSE* (Unpublished bachelor's thesis). Kobe University, Kobe, Hyogo, Japan.

The American Heritage Medical Dictionary. (2007). Boston, MA: Houghton Mifflin Harcourt.

The World Bank. (2016). *5 things you may not know about human-wildlife conflict in Botswana.* Retrieved from http://www.worldbank.org/en/news/feature/2016/03/03/5-things-you-may-not-have-known-about-human-wildlife-conflict-in-botswana

Tokyo Zoological Park Society. (n.d.). *Ueno doubutsuen no rekishi* [History of Ueno Zoo]. Retrieved from http://www.tokyo-zoo.net/zoo/ueno/history.html (in Japanese)

Treves, A., Wallace, R. B., Naughton-Treves, L., & Morales, A. (2006). Co-managing human-wildlife conflicts: A review. *Human Dimensions of Wildlife, 11*(6), 383–396.

White, R., & Gunston, W. (1992). *Word association. Probing understanding* (pp. 142–157). New York, NY: Routledge.

Whittaker, D., Vaske, J. J., & Manfredo, M. J. (2006). Specificity and the cognitive hierarchy: Value orientations and the acceptability of urban wildlife management actions. *Society & Natural Resources, 19*(6), 515–530.

Woodroffe, R., Thirgood, S., & Rabinowits, A. (2005). People and wildlife conflict or coexistence? *People and wildlife* (Inscription page). Cambridge: Cambridge University Press.

Word Association Network. (2018). *The definition of word association.* Retrieved from https://wordassociations.net/en

World Wide Fund for Nature [WWF]. (2008). Summary analysis. *Common ground – Solutions for reducing, the human, economic and conservation costs of human wildlife conflict* (pp. 5–12). Retrieved from http://wwf.panda.org/about_our_earth/all_publications/?133121/Common-Ground-Reducing-human-wildlife-conflict

World Wide Fund for Nature [WWF]. (2017). *Human-wildlife conflict.* Retrieved from http://wwf.panda.org/about_our_earth/species/problems/human_animal_conflict/

Shiho Miyake
School of Human Sciences
Kobe College, Japan

PAULETTE BYNOE

5. EXAMINING THE ROLE OF INDIGENOUS KNOWLEDGE IN SUSTAINABLE LIVING IN THE NORTH RUPUNUNI (GUYANA)

INTRODUCTION: DEMYSTIFYING SUSTAINABILITY
AND INDIGENOUS KNOWLEDGE

The concepts of sustainability and sustainability education have diverse interpretations. The former encompasses environment, economy and society is based on three principal pillars; namely a flourishing environment, a vibrant community, and an equitable economy (Hopkins & McKeown, 2002; McFarlane & Ogazon, 2011). These principles help to prevent the depletion of natural resources and increase the chances of future generations in respect of their access, while the latter recognizes the importance of awareness building and the sharing and acquisition of knowledge and skills that motivate people to inculcate a caring attitude for the environment. This caring attitude can then influence our individual and collective decisions and actions that impact our environment. Summarily, one can argue that education is indispensable to and a critical tool for achieving sustainability (Hopkins & McKeown, 2002). Notably, Chapter 36 of Agenda 21 titled "Promoting Education, Awareness, and Training" (UNESCO, 1992), argues that there is need to reorient education towards sustainable development and that:

> Education, including formal education, public awareness and training should be recognized as a process by which human beings and societies can reach their fullest potential. Education is critical for promoting sustainable development and improving the capacity of the people to address environment and development issues. …Both formal and non-formal education are indispensable to changing people's attitudes so that they have the capacity to assess and address their sustainable development concerns. It is also critical for achieving environmental and ethical awareness, values and attitudes, skills and behaviour consistent with sustainable development and for effective public participation in decision-making. (UNESCO, 1992, p. 320)

UNESCO, the lead agency to promote, implement and monitor progress throughout the Decade of Education for Sustainable Development (DESD), 2005–2014 declared that the DESD was launched "to promote education as a basis for sustainable human society and to strengthen international cooperation toward the development of innovative policies, programmes and practices of education for sustainable development" (Pigozzi, 2003, p. 1). Innovation necessitates a global recognition of the importance of flexibility and diversity and consequently an acknowledgement and appreciation of the critical role of Indigenous Knowledge in promoting sustainability (Ministry of Education, Guyana, 2008). In fact, Battiste (2002) reminds us that Indigenous Knowledge is an evolving field of inquiry, both nationally and internationally, particularly for those interested in educational innovation.

Indigenous knowledge is also referred to as "local knowledge or wisdom", "nonformal knowledge", "culture", "indigenous technical knowledge", "traditional ecological knowledge", and "traditional knowledge" (Battiste, 2005). According to Owuor (2007, p. 23), the term 'Indigenous Knowledge' is typical, and belongs to peoples from specific places with common cultural and social ties. The author contends that Indigenous Knowledge "is a process of learning and sharing social life, histories, identities, economic, and political practices unique to each cultural group" and that this is indicative of the unique ways specific societies construct their realities and use such forms of knowledge to resolve local problems. Indigenous Knowledge, though challenged by conventional science in some parts of the world, remains relevant to many local cultures, particularly in geographically marginal areas where formal education has not been widely available or accessible to local residents. The conduit of transmission of this knowledge is through symbols, art, proverbs, songs, storytelling, and dances, among others (Dei, 2002; Turray, 2002). Owuor's notion of Indigenous Knowledge is a timely reminder of the purpose of indigenous education, that is, to place knowledge within the context of the user (Dei, Hall, & Rosenberg, 2002; Wane, 2002).

Indigenous Knowledge has been promoted by proponents of the preservation of indigenous customs, habits of traditional customs, habits, and a general way of life, as a means of safeguarding natural and cultural resources and ultimately, promoting a more sustainable way of living. In fact, Clarkson, Morrisette, and Regallet (1992, p. 81) draw attention to the fact that the United Nations Convention on Biological Diversity (UNCBD) recognizes the significance of Indigenous Knowledge, innovations, and practices to scientific knowledge, conservation studies, and sustainable development. The authors argue that Indigenous Knowledge is invaluable to the development of sustainable societies given that local communities have struggled to maintain a harmonious relationship with the land as such, traditional peoples "can become a contributing force in the community, a force of change".

An essential characteristic of Indigenous Knowledge is its changing nature. Dei, Hall, and Rosenberg (2002) argued that knowledge cannot be perceived as fixed categories, experiences, and social practices. Moreover, Wane (2002) underscores a similar point in his statement that indigenous forms of knowledge have accrued over time, which is a critical aspect of culture.

Arguably, the incorporation of Indigenous Knowledge in education for sustainability represents a paradigm shift from the more conventional approach to development and strict enforcement of a national school curriculum to "the adoption of an endogenous approach to education that involves the contextualization of the school curriculum by integrating Indigenous Knowledge" (Owuor, 2007, p. 6).

Proponents of the integration of Indigenous Knowledge in a formal education that promotes sustainability have encountered two principal challenges; the first relates to the complex nature of Indigenous Knowledge and practices which are incorporated into their ways of life, and as such, are difficult to identify as innovations. For example, Owuor (2008, p. 30) notes that:

> Among the Luo of Western Kenya, emphasis in indigenous education is placed on learning by doing through repeated practice over time rather than observation and replication. Thus, the knowledge is passed on in the context of personal relationships between the learners and mentors actively involved in the everyday interaction with the natural environment and activities necessary for survival.

Second, the formal acceptance of incorporating culture into the design of formal curricula on sustainability requires flexibility that is rarely seen in the education system. Teachers would cite barriers such as time constraint, lack of approval for their subordinates, and the absence of culture as a salient issue in the examination orientated syllabus that addresses sustainability.

AIM OF CHAPTER

This chapter presents a case for the integration and preservation of Indigenous Knowledge into education for sustainability that targets indigenous peoples in Guyana, using the experiencing of communities in the North Rupununi in Region 9 in Guyana.

METHODOLOGICAL APPROACH

Case Study Design

A case study design was employed as the distinctive form of empirical inquiry of the role of Indigenous Knowledge in promoting sustainable living among five communities in Annai, an Amerindian District in the north Rupununi in Guyana. This research strategy allowed for the use of multiple data sources and methods of data collection, which in turn, fostered data triangulation, as well as the observation and analysis of a phenomenon (and in this context sustainability education) that may not be possible through a more scientific investigation (Yin, 1994). As Zainal contends, a case study research design enables a researcher to examine the data within a specific context closely and can be considered a robust research method particularly when a holistic, in-depth investigation is required" (Zainal, 2007, p. 1). To this end, qualitative data were collected, using survey and interview methods to provide a complete understanding of a research problem, rather than for either method alone (Creswell, 2014).

THE LOCAL CONTEXT

The North Rupununi is located in south-western Guyana, in Region 9 and is part of the savannah lowlands of Amazonia. It extends from the Siparuni River to the Kanuku Mountains and from the Essequibo River to the Brazilian Border (https://rupununi.org/). Within these lowlands are some distinct mountain ranges, including the Iwokrama Mountain. The tropical rainforest that includes the Iwokrama forest reserve accounting for more than 50% of Guyana's estimated birds, reptiles and amphibians.

Annai is a District in the North Rupununi, Region 9, in Guyana. It comprises five Amerindians communities (referred also as villages) that are titled under the Amerindian Act (2006). These villages are Annai Central, Rupertee, Wowetta, Kwatamang, and Surama (see Figure 5.1) with populations of 550, 343, 313, 415, and 287 respectively (North Rupununi District Development Board, 2017), comprised of mainly the Makushi tribe with approximately 81 percent (Funnel & Bynoe, 2007). It is noteworthy that the nine Amerindian tribes were historically differentiated linguistically in Guyana. Amerindians are referred to as the indigenous peoples of Guyana.

The Bina Hill Institute, located in the Annai District, was established in 2001, to cater to the educational and training needs of Amerindian youths who do not have access to secondary and post-secondary educational opportunities. This is because of the distance from the coast, and due to transportation and living costs, among other factors. The institution also caters to those youths that have no formal schooling but are interested in acquiring technical skills to enhance their chances of employment in a region where the dominant economic activities are agriculture, forestry, mining and tourism. Students are expected to spend two years at the institute.

The Institute, therefore, works with several partners such as the Iwokrama International Centre for Rainforest Conservation, Development, and with Conservation International, to develop training, research and other resources in the North Rupununi. It supports adult and distance education and literacy programmes that target all communities. Importantly, the Bina Hill Institute also established Radio Paiwomak and The Youth Learning Centre and has expanded (over the years) its training efforts to include natural resource management, traditional knowledge systems, among other themes (http://nrddb.org/bhi%20 and personal communication). To this end, the Institute offers nine subjects including forestry, natural resources management, agriculture, business, sewing, language and culture, home economics and tourism.

DATA COLLECTION METHODS

A semi-structured interview was designed and administered to 7 of the 10 teachers of the Bina Hill Institute, using an interview plan. Questions posed to teachers related to the meanings of sustainable development and Indigenous Knowledge, the role of Indigenous Knowledge in sustainable development, challenges posed to Indigenous Knowledge, and recommendations for preserving indigenous language.

SUSTAINABLE LIVING IN THE NORTH RUPUNUNI (GUYANA)

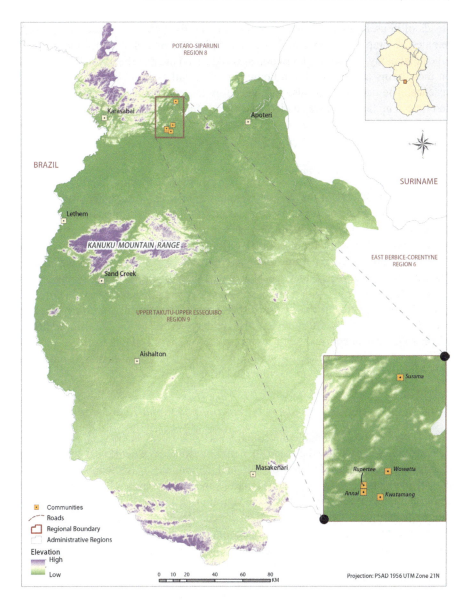

Figure 5.1. Map of Guyana showing communities in the Annai District

In an effort to complement the semi-structured interviews of teachers a cross-sectional survey was designed, using a piloted questionnaire which comprised sections with the following themes; personal and demographic data, knowledge of key concepts and views of Indigenous Knowledge for promoting sustainable living, challenges posed to indigenous and recommendations. The survey targeted 109

Heads of households of whom approximately 47.7% were males, and 52.3% were females. A simple random sample was applied to the household selection process, given that many indigenous households would spend most of the day or several days on their farms and would return home late in the afternoons or after several days absence. The decision was also influenced by the constraints of accessibility, cost and time. The fieldwork was undertaken during June and August 2017.

ANALYSIS OF RESULTS

Demographic Profile of Households

Approximately 47.7% of the sample were males and 52.3% were females with an average age of 42.5 and a standard deviation of 13.8 years. Approximately three-quarters of the respondents were 53 years of age or less. Of the 109 respondents of the survey, 28.4% lived in the Annai Village, 20.2% were from Wowetta, 20.2% were from Surama, 16.5% were from Rupertee and 14.7% were from Kwatamang. The survey data revealed that the average number of years living in the Annai District was 34.9 years, with a mode value of 33 years and a median value of 35.5 years. Further, about 70.1% of the respondents had attained a primary level of education while 15.9% had attained a secondary level of education. In addition, 7.5% of the respondents had graduated from the Teachers Training College, 3.7% of the respondents had graduated from the Georgetown Technical Institute, and 1.9% of the respondents had graduated from the University of Guyana.

Sustainable Development and the Importance of Indigenous Knowledge

When asked about sustainable development, 19.6% of respondents considered the term to mean avoiding exhaustion of natural resources, whereas 16.3% referred to ongoing development/plans for self and community. Additionally, 12.0% of the respondents equally cited conservation and preservation of resources while using them for development, but in recognition of the need to ensure access by future generations. Other responses included: development without significant environmental destruction; long-term benefits for a village; sustainable community projects; leaders' vision of development; maintaining culture, tradition, practices and ways of life; development that meets the needs of present generations without compromising the needs of future generations; and ongoing process of decision making to develop management arrangement for future development of village.

Responses provided by teachers were somewhat similar and included: development that utilizes indigenous resources to sustain itself not destroying environment; a plan or programme of activities that will last forever when you do things in a sustainable way as well as maintain your language; not to over-use resources, but know how to manage them in the environment and the way resources are used; not to over-use and managing your human and natural resources.

Table 5.1. Definitions of Indigenous knowledge

		Frequency	Percent
Valid	Knowledge passed down from forefathers or ancestors to younger generations	38	34.9
	Other	8	7.3
	Knowledge unique to Amerindians/ Indigenous peoples	24	22.0
	Traditions, history, myths, language, beliefs, culture, songs and dance	8	7.3
	Capacity and ability of using knowledge to maintain a living and survive in our communities	16	14.7
	True and real in life and nature	3	2.8
	Total	97	89.0
Missing	System	12	11.0
Total		109	100.0

Of the 109 respondents, 97 provided a definition for Indigenous Knowledge. Approximately 39.3% of the respondents considered the term to mean knowledge passed down from forefathers or ancestors to younger generations while 24.7% referred to it as knowledge unique to Amerindians/Indigenous peoples. Additionally, 16.5% of respondents cited capacity and ability to use knowledge to maintain a living and survive in our communities. Other responses included traditions, history, myths, language, beliefs, culture, songs and dance, and knowledge that are true and real in life and nature. Details are presented in Table 5.1.

Teachers defined the term as follows; knowledge passed down by elders to children and the youth from one generation to another, practical knowledge of traditional culture and language that could also be written to pass on to future generations and keeping your knowledge 'alive' by doing and sharing with your children.

When asked about the importance of passing on knowledge to children and grandchildren, 72.4% of respondents believed that it was very important to pass on knowledge to children and grandchildren while 22.9% believed that it was extremely important to do so. Moreover, 2.9% of respondents believed that it was not very important to pass on knowledge to children and grandchildren and 1.9% believed that it was not important to do so. Respondents who felt that the transmission of knowledge had some degree of importance cited the main reasons as: preservation of knowledge and culture for future generations; raising awareness of traditions, knowledge and culture passed down from forefathers which are part of their identity and the role of knowledge in supporting sustainable livelihoods for survival.

A closely related question about the role of Indigenous Knowledge in promoting sustainable development and sustainable living. can be gleaned from Figure 5.2, where 68.3% of the respondents believed that Indigenous Knowledge is very important to sustainable development, while 22.1% believed that it was extremely important to sustainable development, and 1.9% of the respondents believed that indigenous knowledge is not very important to sustainable development. On the contrary, 7.7% believed that it is not important to sustainable development.

Notably, teachers at the Bina Hill Institute expressed the view that Indigenous Knowledge is critical for sustainable development, citing the following several reasons for such a position:

- Youth are losing their culture and language
- Sustainable development is an essential part of Indigenous Knowledge
- Indigenous children and youth must know their identity.
- For future generation to enjoy as well
- Help young people to do things.
- It is the base for transformation for modern society
- Indigenous Knowledge has sustained our natural resources and helped maintained our way of life.
- Using traditional farming, fishing and hunting, as well as maintain your language will enable us to survive.

Notably, respondents from the households surveyed cited the main reason for their views on the importance of Indigenous Knowledge to sustainable development

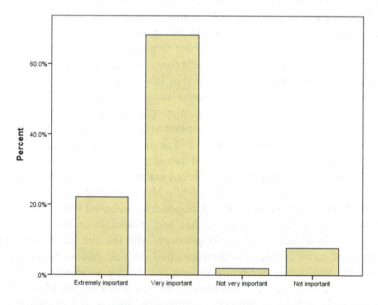

Figure 5.2. The importance of indigenous knowledge to sustainable development

as the *preservation of knowledge and culture for use by future generations*. Other responses included the *sustainable use or management of resources; and maintaining livelihood, health, development and environment*. Parents, therefore, pass on the knowledge to their children and grandchildren about respect for nature, subsistence living, the value of trees and wildlife, and the risk of eating certain species of fish, birds and animals during their reproductive years and when they are still very 'young'.

THEMES OF INDIGENOUS KNOWLEDGE TRANSMITTED THROUGH GENERATIONS

The views held by the teachers on the importance of indigenous knowledge is validated by the curriculum on biodiversity conservation in which several issues regarding sustainable development in the local context are incorporated using non-traditional teaching methods such as song, drama and story-telling. Issues include; how to care for the forest and its resources: for example, to stop burning the savannah, stop excessive logging, stop poisoning the creeks to access fish, and the importance of forests for human existence. Others focused on the importance of conserving natural resources to ensure we will always have access to those resources, not to over-harvest animals and birds, but keep some for future generations, the intrinsic value of resources and the role of the forest as a home for biodiversity, especially, birds, fishes and mammals.

Similarly, parents considered biodiversity issues central to the sustenance of local communities. Table 5.2 indicates that approximately, 39.6% of respondents cited that Indigenous Knowledge with respect to biodiversity conservation centred on the conservation of natural resources. Some examples of responses included conserving nature as a whole within the community. The importance of conserving resources as part of the culture and conserving biodiversity is to ensure the continuation of different species of fish, birds, animals and trees for generations to come.

Additionally, 37.6% of respondents cited that indigenous knowledge of biodiversity conservation focused on the value of trees and wildlife. Some examples of responses included teaching the importance of wildlife in the forest and how it connects and supports others, teaching the values of the trees and medicinal plants and knowing the names of the birds and habitats. Additionally, 22.8% of respondents cited that indigenous knowledge on biodiversity conservation is based on its links to livelihood. Some examples of responses included telling of stories of when to fish and types of trees for building, what type of animals to kill and eat, teaching song, dance, handicraft, and not trapping birds and other animals.

Moreover, 5.0% of respondents equally cited that Indigenous Knowledge on biodiversity conservation focused on arespect for nature and subsistence living respectively. Some examples of responses included rules to respect and protect our nature, connecting to the environment and nature, not disturbing sacred places like ponds creeks and trees of values, and farming and hunting for home use and to maintain

Table 5.2. Biodiversity knowledge that is transmitted through generations

Main themes	Percentage of respondents	Examples of responses
Respect for nature	5.0%	There are rules to respect and protect our nature Our knowledge is the one connecting to the environment and in respect to nature We were taught not to disturb sacred places like ponds creeks and trees of values
Subsistence living	5.0%	We don't harvest lumber on a large scale and fish and hunt for commercial purposes. We use them just for food and housing Farming and hunting for home use but not for commercial business Farming on a small scale to maintain family
Conservation of national resources	39.6%	Conserve our nature as a whole within our community Conserve our resources which is very important to our culture If biodiversity is conserved the continuation of different species of fish, birds, animals and trees will be preserved for generation to come.
Value of trees and wildlife	37.6%	Teaching the importance of wildlife in the forest, how it connects and supports the others Teaching the values of the trees by naming them and knowing the names of the birds and habitats To know that the things we have in our forest and savannah Importance of medicinal plants
Links to Livelihood	22.8%	Telling of stories – when to fish, cut trees for building Knowledge is shared through song and dance, by making craft, by not trapping the birds. We also tell them what type of fish and animals to eat. We do not trap animals Instructions from elders as to what to cut, what to eat, what to kill
Diet	2.97%	We were told to not eat certain trees because of its value and use. The same for birds, fish and animals – we cannot eat certain species of fish, birds and animals at certain time like during pregnancy and after birth What type of animal, fish and bird we should consume when parents are expecting (having a baby)

family but not for commercial business. Only 2.97% of respondents referred to diet, and some examples of responses included not eating certain trees, birds, fish and animals because of its value and use and type of animals to eat during and after pregnancy.

Since agriculture is the dominant livelihood activity in the North Rupununi, teachers have also integrated aspects that are best described as sustainable agricultural practices in the curriculum. These include cultivating the land for sustenance and reducing households' dependence on retail grocery shops. Other examples included: when to 'cut' our farms, when to plant; the types of crops to be planted on a small scale and use of varieties of cassava strains to mitigate the effects of climate variability particularly droughts and floods; avoidance of clearing large amounts of forests or traditionally degrading the land and planting. This knowledge is complemented by the more elderly persons in the five communities and relates to the following:

- Plant certain species or varieties of cassava at a specific time of the year and there are different crop seasons in the year
- Varieties of cassava which are drought resistant and some that are not drought resistant
- Farming is done twice yearly: May–July and August–September
- There is a short season and a long season and the month of August is a short season for planting watermelon, pumpkin etc.
- Knowledge about how to treat the pests
- Plant staples (cassava, bananas, potatoes)
- Fallowing and changing farming grounds every 3–4 years
- When to clear land for farming
- Engage in small scale farming on small plots of land for subsistence and income
- How to select farming ground
- Farming must be done seasonally at the beginning of the rainy season and plant cassava during March to May before the start of the rainy season.
- Plant several crops on one farm
- Organic farming
- Being guided by nature (biological indicators) to know when and what to farm to avoid pests and insects
- Amerindians are the first people to convert poisonous cassava into food
- Farming methods for planting cassava and other species of crops

With regard to climate change, teachers explained that attention is given in their lessons to changing weather patterns (floods and droughts) using videos. Topics include: the difficulty in predicting weather due to human pollution and negligence; how weather patterns have changed; and the relationship between changing weather patterns and the deforestation. Importantly, the curriculum facilitates discussion on the role of humans in changing climatic variables such as rainfall and temperature and how a Western model of development has contributed to pollution amongst other environmental problems. This specific topic is only discussed by a few parents who are confident in their knowledge of the subject with respect to the causes and effects of climate change, even though over 90% of those surveyed said that they had experienced unpredictable weather, warmer weather, changes in the rainy and dry seasons, and an increase in the frequency of floods and droughts in the past 15–30 years. Undoubtedly, knowledge of climate change, its impacts and local adaptations are critical to indigenous people's survival in Guyana's hinterland, given their experiences with frequent droughts and the concomitant risk of water and food insecurity.

Given the relative geographic isolation, economic poverty and limited access to healthcare facilities prevalent in the indigenous communities of the study area. The issue of health and medicine was also considered central to sustainability. To this end, the relational question was posed to respondents. The survey results revealed that the in general the use of local, traditional 'bush' medicines extracted from parts of trees, including their barks, roots, leaves, vines, fruit and seeds to treat either snake bites, skin rashes, wounds, cuts, 'ringworm' infection, hypertension, diarrhoea, malaria, common cold, among others demonstrated this knowledge. Household use of this type of medicine is commonly used to treat minor illnesses, especially when modern medicine is inaccessible, unaffordable or scarce. It was therefore important for parents to share their knowledge of local medicines with their children and grandchildren. Some of the specific responses are captured below:

- Boil and drink guava leaves and jamoon leaves to treat diarrhea.
- Boil Savannah cedar bark to treat tapeworm infections
- Lemon grass leaves are good for high pressure
- Use barks, seeds, leaves, and fruit from the forest to treat snake bites and diarrhea
- Prepare local medicine from plants from the forest e.g. seeds from greenheart, crabwood tree, barks and leaves

The final theme explored in the study related to sustainable livelihoods. As Allison and Horemans (2006, p. 759) noted "A livelihood is sustainable if people are able to maintain or improve their standard of living related to well-being and income or other human development goals, reduce their vulnerability to external shocks and trends, and ensure their activities are compatible with maintaining the natural resource base…".

Teachers explained that their curricula enforce five principal points: (i) Be self-sufficient using resources in communities; their farms and livestock; the way you earn your livelihood financially you are stable and independent, (ii) How knowledge of fore-parents have been significant to our sustainable way of life, (iii) Living the same way as fore-parents: fishing, hunting, farming and being connected to our forest and nature, (iv) The importance of continuing to use and manage the forest in a sustainable way by not over-harvesting what we have and (v) maintaining their traditional way of life.

Responses from surveyed respondents varied as shown in the examples of statements below. Notably, respondents explained that this information is shared mainly through 'face to face' dialogues, storytelling, songs and dances. The messages of parents are ostensibly an echo of what Dei (2002) refers to as locally defined models of sustainability.

- Farming is a steady and important source of income for households
- Use the environment wisely and have a job that maintains their home
- Avoid too many purchases from shops
- Living with nature and valuing tradition and indigenous way of life is important.
- Acquire food from hunting and farming and ensure we do not eliminate all aspects of plants and animals from forest
- Avoid excessive hunting, fishing and farming
- Families help each other on farms, building homes, and having feasts
- Do not overuse resources while making handicrafts
- Do not overharvest fish and other animals and keep forest intact.
- Using the forest in a sustainable way preserves a traditional way of life

A sustainable livelihood is essential to the indigenous way of life, given their high dependence on surrounding natural resources such as land, landscape, water, climate, vegetation, and fauna. Their socio-economic profiles suggest that in each household there is a diverse livelihood portfolio and that most persons are involved in income generating activities such as farming, fishing and ecotourism. Therefore, conservation of the natural resource base will help guarantee their sustainable development. Arguably, local, indigenous communities best demonstrate the interrelatedness and interdependence of environment and development.

Challenges to the Preservation of Indigenous Knowledge

This study sought to highlight challenges to the preservation of indigenous knowledge. Firstly, from the teachers' perspective there are four major challenges, namely:

i. Some elders' unwillingness to share knowledge with the youth.
ii. Modern science challenges traditional knowledge and as a consequence the latter is less respected: Indigenous knowledge must first be recognized as being vital to sustainability and as such, be accepted as a critical topic for inclusion in the formal curriculum.
iii. There is an absence of any systematic documentation of indigenous knowledge.
iv. Some youth are not interested as they are continually influenced by the 'modern' way of life of people who live on the costs in Guyana, as well as 'foreign' cultures from across the borders (mainly Brazil that is south of Guyana).

The cross-sectional survey revealed the following eight challenges, as articulated by respondents.

i. Youth are not interested in preserving our culture, tradition and knowledge due to the introduction of modern technology and lifestyles
ii. Youth are engaged with non-Amerindians i.e. foreigners and foreign teachers
iii. No proper documentation and storage of indigenous knowledge
iv. Culture is not practiced daily and language is being neglected
v. English is encouraged in schools and culture and tradition is not taught.
vi. Migration of youth out of the village in search of jobs
vii. It is not taught to children by families in the communities, and parents rarely speak to their children in the native language.
viii. Indigenous knowledge is not part of the school curriculum and there are no examinations in indigenous languages

Importantly, the challenges identified by teachers and parents (survey respondents) also draw attention to other issues that must be addressed by policymakers at the national level. These include, but are not limited to: the creation of employment opportunities (particularly for youth) in the indigenous area to address current migration trends; incorporation of indigenous knowledge as a critical element of education for sustainability in the formal curricula; and documentation and dissemination of indigenous knowledge systems particularly in respect to sustainability.

RECOMMENDATIONS

Several recommendations on addressing indigenous knowledge and sustainable living were made by teachers and survey respondents. Direct quotes are indicated below.

Documenting Culture and Language

- Seek assistance from partners and NGOs to document local culture and language: There are few nongovernmental organizations that support indigenous initiatives in Guyana. Chief among these are the Iwokrama International Centre for Rainforest Conservation and Development, Conservation International and the World Wildlife Fund who have provided financial support and have facilitated countless training seminars and workshops for local communities on issues related to ecotourism, sustainable livelihood, forest conservation, monitoring, reporting and verification, among others.
- Use technology to document, store, analyze and research indigenous knowledge: In the digital age, it is important to capture, store and retrieve indigenous knowledge that is transmitted during socialization processes (from one generation to another), and can be made readily accessible to young people. It should be noted that there is a notable effort on the part of the government to improve ICT access to remote communities in Guyana; hence the possibility of a digital

database that can be developed and maintained by the Ministry of Indigenous Peoples Affairs, in collaboration with the North Rupununi District Development Board (NRDDB).
- Hold teaching sessions on language in the villages and seek funding from NGOs to document knowledge. This recommendation can be tied to the digitization process since 'lessons' should be recorded for use by future generations.

Incorporation in the School's Curriculum

- Teach language and culture to youth at home,, schools, Bina Hill Institute and the university: there must be a concerted effort at all levels of formal education to ensure the preservation of indigenous language and culture. Any such initiatives must be fully supported by policy on education and especially, education for sustainable development.
- Establish a training centre for interested youth to receive training on indigenous culture such as hunting, fishing, building construction, planting and plaiting or weaving. Since the Bina Training Institute has already been established; therefore, teachers can enhance their delivery of the written curricula with demonstration projects that provide students opportunities to be involved in more hand on/practical learning activities that will definitely support critical thinking and decision making; thereby empowering them to apply local sustainability measures to their unique situations.
- Respect traditional knowledge and incorporate it into school curriculum. As mentioned earlier, policymakers must first acknowledge and respect indigenous knowledge for its vital contribution to sustainable living as a prerequisite to legitimizing the same in the formal educational process.
- Establish a separate Makushi Institute for research and preservation of indigenous knowledge and culture; also, Makushi researchers should be teaching the language in schools. There is already the formal establishment of the Makushi Researchers; therefore, their involvement in the training workshops and the digitization process of the language and culture is vital. It is noteworthy that the Makushi researchers had already begun a process of documenting indigenous knowledge under the supervision of Janet Forte (now referred to as Janet Bulkan).
- Set up Makushi programmes in schools and on radio. Currently, there is Radio Paiwomak – the first radio indigenous community radio station in Guyana that caters to the hinterland communities of the North Rupununi District of Region #9. According to the stations's 97.1 FM is one of the more popular programmes associated with the hinterland communities and has kept the tradition alive by broadcasting daily in the Amerindian dialect.

Other recommendations provided by respondents include: (i) formation of a group of elders to teach our language and craft to interested youth in the village, (ii) encourage elders to share traditional knowledge and skills, (iii) having classes in schools and workshops aimed to teach the language; as well as appreciate the importance of their culture, and (iv) develop/enhance Makushi programmes for schools and broadcast on "Radio Paiwomak".

CONCLUSIONS

This study conducted in the Annai District of Guyana provides evidence to support the view that Indigenous knowledge is vital to sustainability knowledge and that it places emphasis on the specific local economic, environmental, social, and cultural conditions. The efforts of teachers at the Bina Hill Training Institute are commendable, given the absence of any formal or explicit educational policy that seeks to promote education as a pillar for sustainable living in Guyana. Additionally, the complementary initiatives of parents in educating young people-through informal, sociological processes must not be discounted. This informal approach often reinforces what is taught in formal curricula, thereby providing opportunities for empowerment in local communities to take individual and collection actions to resolve problems of sustainability within their local settings.

Further, these findings enhance the academic discourse on the relevance of indigenous knowledge to local solutions to developing a sustainable society. The human-environment interaction within the context of indigenous communities provides compelling evidence of the need for conservation of our natural capital to foster and sustain human well-being.

The study also highlights several challenges that are not unique to Guyana and should be debated at high levels to gain support for resources devoted to finding practical solutions to transmitting indigenous knowledge to future generations. This discourse is not merely a local issue but one that has substantial and global significance. Given the multiplicity and severity of current global environmental problems, including climate change and biodiversity loss. Much can be learned from indigenous peoples in respect to living in harmony with our natural environment.

REFERENCES

Allison, E. H., & Horemans, B. (2006). Putting the principles of the sustainable livelihoods approach into fisheries development policy and practice. *Marine Policy, 30,* 757–766.
Battiste, M. (2005). *Indigenous knowledge: Foundations for first nations.* Retrieved from https://www2.viu.ca/integratedplanning/documents/IndegenousKnowledgePaperbyMarieBattistecopy.pdf
Clarkson, L., Morrisette, V., & Regallet, G. (1992). *Our responsibility to the seventh generation: Indigenous Peoples and sustainable development.* Winnipeg: International Institute for Sustainable Development.
Creswell, J. W. (2014). *Research design: Quantitative, qualitative and mixed methods approaches.* London: Sage Publications.
Dei, S. G. J., Hall, B. L., & Rosenberg, D. G. (2002). *Indigenous knowledge in global contexts: Multiple readings of our world.* Toronto: University of Toronto Press.
Dei, S. G. J. (2002). African development: The relevance and implications of indigenousness. In G. J. S. Dei, B. L. Hall, & D. G. Rosenberg (Ed.), *Indigenous knowledge in global contexts: Multiple readings of our world* (pp. vii–x). Toronto: University of Toronto Press.

Funnel, D., & Bynoe, P. (2007). Ecotourism and institutional structures: The case of North Rupununi, Guyana. *Journal of Ecotourism, 6*(3), 163–183.

Government of Guyana. (2006) *Amerindian act. No. 6 of 2006*. Retrieved from http://parliament.gov.gy/documents/acts/4680-act_no_6_of_2006.pdf

Hopkins, C., & McKeown, R. (2002). Education for sustainable development: An international perspective. In D. Tilbury, R. B. Stevenson, J. Fien, & D. Schreuder (Eds.), *Education and sustainability: Responding to the global challenge* (pp. 13–24). Switzerland & Cambridge: Commission on Education and Communication, IUCN, Gland.

McFarlane, A., & Ogazon, A. G. (2011). The challenges of sustainability education. *Journal of Multidisciplinary Research, 3*(3), 81–107.

Ministry of Education Guyana. (2008). *Strategic plan 2008–2013: Meeting the quality imperative*. Georgetown: Ministry of Education.

Pigozzi, M. J. (2003). UNESCO and the international decade of education for sustainable development (2005–2015). *Connect: UNESCO International Science, Technology and Environmental Education Newsletter, 28*(1–2), 1–7.

Turay, T. M. (2002). Peace research and African development: An indigenous African perspective. In G. J. S. Dei, B. L. Hall, & D. G. Rosenberg (Ed.), *Indigenous knowledges in global contexts: Multiple readings of our world* (pp. 248–263). Toronto: University of Toronto Press.

United Nations Educational, Scientific and Cultural Organization. (1992). *Education and sustainable development: UNESCO's contribution to agenda 21*. Retrieved from http://portal.unesco.org/en/ev.php-URL_ID=5434&URL_DO=DO_TOPIC&URL_SECTION=201.html

Wane, N. N. (2002). African women and spirituality: Connection between thought and education. In E. O'Sullivan, A. Morrell, & M. O'Connor (Eds.), *Expanding the boundaries of transformative learning: Essays on theory and praxis* (pp. 135–150). New York, NY: Palgrave, St. Martin's Press.

Wilson, W., Bulkan, J., Piperata, B., Hicks, K., & Ehlers, P. (2011). Nutritional status of Makushi Amerindian children and adolescents of Guyana. *Annals of Human Biology, 38*(5), 615–629.

Yin, R. K. (1994). *Case study research: Design and methods* (2nd ed.). Newbury Park, CA: Sage Publications.

Zainal, J. K. (2007). *Case study as a research method Zaidah Zainal m-zaidah@utm.my Faculty of Management and Human Resource Development*. Malaysia: Universiti Teknologi.

Paulette Bynoe
Faculty of Earth and Environmental Sciences
University of Guyana
Guyana

KARIN ULBRICH, ELISABETH KÜHN, OLIVER SCHWEIGER
AND JOSEF SETTELE

6. HOW MANY BUTTERFLIES WILL LOSE THEIR HABITATS?

Communicating Biodiversity Research Using the Example of European Butterflies

INTRODUCTION

In times where biodiversity is highly endangered, only little of recent biodiversity research is implemented in school curricula of German gymnasiums and secondary schools. In this chapter we discuss how closer collaboration among scientists and educators can fill this gap. Most of Europe's ecosystems are now assessed to be degraded: Nearly 30% of the EU-27 territory is considered to be highly to moderately fragmented. Europeans currently consume more than twice what the EU's land and sea can provide in terms of natural resources (European Union, 2011; COP, 2013). Studies also suggest that global terrestrial biodiversity will decline by at least another 10% by 2050 (EEA, 2015; OECD, 2012), and that intensive global use of food, water, energy and materials will lead to global ecosystem depletion and biodiversity loss to continue or accelerate. Moreover, European terrestrial ecosystems are expected to increasingly be affected by drought, wildfires, floods, and glacier melt in the next decades (EEA, 2015).

Meeting the challenge of these global megatrends requires credible information on other possible developments and choices in the face of global risk and uncertainty. Foresight methods, such as horizon scanning, scenario development and visioning bring together different perspectives and disciplines, and develop systemic understanding (Carpenter et al., 2006; Sutherland et al., 2013; Neus et al., 2017). In this way, these methods could strengthen long-term decision-making and improve our understanding of future trends and uncertainties (EEA, 2015). Consequently, it is essential to enable the young generation – the decision-makers of tomorrow – to acquire knowledge about risk assessment and uncertainty. As early as 1992 the Rio Summit stated that scientists have the responsibility to inform the public about their research and to contribute to raising the awareness for biodiversity preservation (United Nations, 1992; UNESCO, 2005).

A previous paper (Ulbrich et al., 2015) described our educational software PRONAS that presented results of the integrated project ALARM (Settele et al., 2005).

PRONAS aimed at passing research results from the sphere of science "down to earth" – to the classrooms.

The ALARM project focused on the assessment and forecast of changes particularly in biodiversity but also in structure, function, and dynamics of ecosystems. Socio-economic scenarios have been applied to simulate future environmental threats and to quantify risks subsequent on these (Spangenberg et al., 2012). Those scenarios do not represent predictions but instead possible development paths: SEDG (Sustainable European Development Goal) aims at integrated ecological, social, institutional, and economic sustainability; BAMBU (business as might be usual) includes measures for mitigation or adaptation to climate change, but not for explicit protection of biodiversity; and GRAS (growth applied strategy) is a scenario of unlimited economic growth considering adaptation to climate change but no measures for its reduction (Settele et al., 2008; Spangenberg et al., 2012).

The educational software PRONAS deals with key results of the ALARM scenarios demonstrating that completely different species – such as plants, reptiles and amphibians, birds, butterflies – will suffer significantly from climate change, as climatic conditions in their habitats become hostile and they cannot reach new areas in a conceivable timeframe. Moreover, disturbed biotic interactions could increase these impacts (Schweiger et al., 2012).

In our educational project, we focus on butterflies as indicators for biological diversity. As they are typical insects, butterflies' responses may reflect changes amongst other insect groups. It is crucial to assess the fate of insects in order to monitor the overall state of biodiversity as they make up the largest proportion of terrestrial wildlife (Costello et al., 2013; Stork, 2018). Insect diversity and abundance is described to be heavily declining in Germany (Hallmann et al., 2017). Impact factors include: the ubiquitous use of pesticides; the spread of monoculture crops such as corn and soybeans; urbanization; and habitat destruction (IPBES 2016). It is also important to know that pollinating insects improve or stabilize the yield of three-quarters of all crop types globally – one-third of global crop production by volume (IPBES, 2016). The decline is dramatic and depressing and it affects all kinds of insects, including butterflies, wild bees, and hoverflies.

Butterflies are increasingly being recognized as valuable environmental indicators (Settele et al., 2008). Due to their short life cycles, butterflies react quickly to environmental changes. Unlike most other insects, they are easy to recognize and their ecology, life-histories, and taxonomy are well-documented.

Europe's butterflies are facing enormous changes in their environment (Van Swaay et al., 2010):

- Changes in farming practice result in semi-natural grasslands being either abandoned or intensified.
- Growing human population and increasing urbanization are leading to an enhanced pressure on the remaining semi-natural habitats.
- Climate change may affect the abiotic environment, the vegetation structure, species composition and interactions as well as butterflies' physiology.

DeVictor et al. (2012) found that bird and butterfly populations are not keeping up with changing temperatures and, on average, European bird and butterfly species lag around 212km and 135km, respectively, behind climate changes.

As birds and butterflies are more dispersive than many other species groups, terrestrial species that cannot disperse as easily may be slower to adapt to climate change. Environmental changes have a direct impact on the reproductive success of individual butterflies and, therefore, on local population sizes. At a larger scale species will shift their range, distributing to new areas that have become suitable and leaving areas that have become less suitable (Settele et al., 2008). However, the risk varies considerably under the three scenarios considered (Table 6.1).

Table 6.1. Risk assessment for European butterflies in terms of habitat loss, assuming that there is no dispersal to new habitats, in 2080 (Settele et al., 2008)

Scenario	Percentage of butterflies losing more than 95% of habitats (%)	Percentage of butterflies losing more than 50% of habitats (%)
SEDG	3	48
BAMBU	9	66
GRAS	24	78

Many butterfly species are sensitive to small-scale changes because of their limited dispersal ability, larval food plant specialization and dependence on weather and climate. Examples are the "Large Blues" – the *Maculinea* butterflies. *M.nausithous* and *M.teleius*. Their life cycle is strongly related to the herbaceous plant *Sanguisorba officinalis* (great burnet) and to ants of the genus *Myrmica*. The butterflies are usually found on or near their foodplant. Having lived on the flowerheads of this plant for a few weeks, the small caterpillars go down to the ground, in order to be carried away usually by workers of the ant *Myrmica rubra* (for *M. nausithous*) or *Myrmica scabrinodis* (for *M. teleius*) into their nests. There, they remain feeding on ant grubs, hibernating and pupating in the early summer. The newly-emerged butterflies leave the nest in a consecutive year or even one year later (Thomas & Settele, 2004).

Living in times of uncertainty and complexity, but also in times of digitalization and information overload, also has consequences for education and the role of research in society. It is not helpful to maintain the narratives of stable and unchanging societies, with relationships, needs, and demands that have remained the same for decades. The new challenge of uncertainty requires the development of new forms of learning and research-school collaboration. Future active citizens require knowledge as well as a set of skills in order to manage these change processes and make decisions in the conditions of uncertainty and resilience.

To meet this challenge we developed the educational software SITAS (Simulation of buTterflies and scenArios for Schools) that will represent the basis of a new learning environment. We hoped to

- raise the awareness for biodiversity protection,
- develop skills that help to understand and manage uncertainty and risk assessment,
- combine learning at the computer with learning in living nature,
- motivate school students to undertake their own research.

The aim of the present study is to better understand our target group: secondary school students aged from 12 to 19.
We addressed the following questions:

- How strong is the engagement of students in exploring nature in terms of (i) time spent outside and (ii) attitudes towards out-of-classroom learning?
- What about students' knowledge on biodiversity and butterflies? Does the participation in a special "sustainability course" increase students' learning success?
- Can we identify knowledge gaps related to resilience studies in terms of uncertainty and modeling?
- How could a concept of educational software look like that presents our biodiversity research to our target groups?

METHODS

Evaluation of Attitudes and Knowledge

We conducted surveys to evaluate the attitudes of being and learning outside, to address the knowledge about butterflies and their habitats and of risk assessment and modelling as well (Table 6.2).

Table 6.2. Surveys used to evaluate attitudes and knowledge among students from 14 to 18

Survey pos.	Objectives of the questionnaire	Number and age of students
1	Time per week spent outside	99; 14 to 18 years
2	Attitudes for out-of-classroom learning	28; 7 to 10 years
3	Participation in excursions	41; 11 to 14 years
		21; 15 to 18 years
4	Knowledge about butterflies	33; 17 to 18 years
5		28; 17 to 18 years
6	Knowledge about butterflies, climate, and risk assessment	55; 15 to 18 years

Developing the Educational Software SITAS

The software designed responds to the requirements of the target groups. It include sites dedicated to scientific knowledge about butterflies, biodiversity, and risk assessment. Special emphasis will be put on adequate didactic approaches such as story-telling, user-friendly design, and test questions.

RESULTS

Spending Time Outside

Ninety-nine students aged 14 to 18 years were asked in November 2016 "How many hours per week do you spend outside". In this context, "outside" means any location outside school, home and other buildings.

Table 6.3. Results of survey 1 (see Table 6.2). Time spent outside.
a) Students were asked: How many hours per week do you spend outside?
Age of students: 15 to 18 years

Students' place of domicile	h	Number of students
I'm living in the city	15,08	42
I'm living in the countryside	18,52	43

b) Students were asked to select one of the given time periods (0–7; 8–14; or 15–21 hours).
Age of students: 14 to 15 years

Students' place of domicile	Selected time span (h)	Number of students
I'm living in the city	0–7	5
	8–14	1
	15–21	2
I'm living in the countryside	0–7	3
	8–14	2
	15–21	1

Twenty-one students aged 14 to 15 years and 78 students aged 16 to 18 years participated in the survey. 38% of 14 to 15 year old students said that they are less than 7 hours per week outside, while only 10% of older students are spending so little time outside. There is also a difference between students living in the city and those from countryside: land dwellers spend nearly four hours per week more outside than towners.

Out-of-classroom Learning

We found that attitudes for out-of-classroom learning change with students' age (Survey 2 and 3, Figure 6.1a). Where 90% of children aged 7 to 10 said "Yes, it

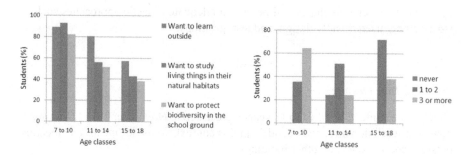

Figure 6.1. Results of survey 2 and 3. School students were asked (a) about their attitudes for out-of-classroom learning, and (b) about their participation in outdoor excursions (natural science subjects). Participants: 90 school students from 20 schools (28 students 7 to 10 years, 41 students 11 to 14 years, 21 students 15 to 18 years)

would be great if we would go out of the school to study plants and animals. It is more interesting than looking them on pictures, because I can see how they move", only 57% of 15 to 18 year olds confirmed this statement. Even more contrasting, the statement "I would like to learn how I can study living things in their natural habitats" confirmed 93% of 7 to 10 year olds, but just 56% and 43% of 11 to 14 year olds and 15 to 18 year old students, respectively. The question "Are you interested in protecting biodiversity in your school ground?" was positively answered by 82% of 7 to 10 olds, but only by 51% of 11 to 14 year olds and by 38% of 15 to 18 year olds.

The number of outdoor excursions is also lower in higher grades (Figure 6.1b). 64% of children from elementary schools go out for excursion three or more times a year, while only 24% and 38% of the older students do so.

Evaluating the Knowledge Base of Students

Two evaluation tests (survey 4 and 5) were conducted among students of a special class termed the "Sustainability course" compared to a control group (see Table 6.4 and Figure 6.2). The students were 17 and 18 years old. Where the first test was performed in the beginning of the 11 grade (autumn 2015), the second test was conducted after finishing the year-long course (January 2017). Results show that students in the "Sustainability course" performed significantly better.

Evaluating the Knowledge about Butterfly Ecology, Uncertainty, and Modeling

Survey 6 addressed questions related to climatic impacts on butterflies as well as of climatic modeling aspects (Table 6.6). Analyzing the answers of 55 students (aged 15 to 18) we found that questions related to butterfly ecology were partly understood (Questions 1, 2), but modelling and uncertainty aspects are widely unclear (Questions 3, 4, 9, 10).

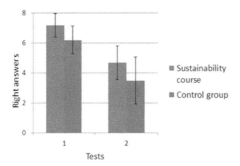

Figure 6.2. Knowledge about butterflies. Sustainability course (n = 18; n = 14) vs. Control group (n = 15; n = 14). Differences are significant (t-test)

Educational Software

A concept for the educational software SITAS has been developed. The target groups of SITAS are students from 12 to 19 and their teachers and the learning targets of SITAS include

- Raising the awareness for biodiversity protection in general,
- Understanding the role of butterflies as indicators for biodiversity,
- Understanding the impact of climate change on habitats of plants and animals,
- Understanding the potential but also the limitations of modeling,
- Understanding that uncertainty is evident and should not be ignored when we tackle the actual local and global issues and events.

More than thirty interactive pages and videos have been arranged around a simulation tool (Figure 6.3). After the user has selected one of fifteen butterflies he can simulate the butterfly's future climatically suitable habitats for the three scenarios GREEN, YELLOW and RED. Those scenarios correspond to the scenarios SEDG, BAMBU, and GRAS used in the ALARM project. The time step for the simulation is one year – from 2000 to 2100.

Simulation results are based on the method of climate niche modeling. This method and its four underlying key parameters are explained in SITAS. The software will be freely available in autumn 2018 on www.ufz.de/sitas.

CONCLUSIONS

Close collaboration between scientists and educators is essential for effective knowledge transfer and to ensure the development of the next generation of scientists (Ledley et al., 2011). Our networks of environmental researchers, pedagogical researchers, and teachers have provided the basis for our study and for future collaboration.

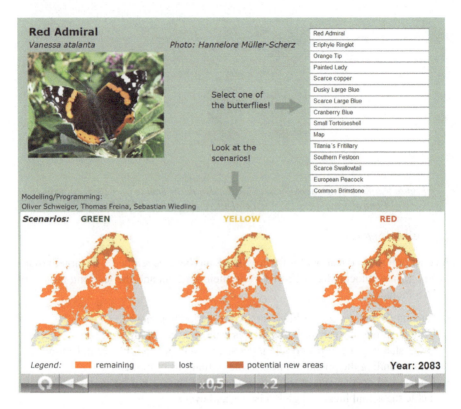

Figure 6.3. The educational software SITAS. Butterfly simulation tool

The survey data allowed for a better understanding of our target group (students from 12 to 19) and helpful indications of how to develop the educational software SITAS.

According to our evaluation results, students living in the city spend significantly less time outside compared to students from the countryside (Table 6.3). Our study confirmed that there are young people who spend just one hour per day outside. Also, the engagement in learning outside the classroom seems to decrease with age (Figure 6.1). Feierabend et al. (2017) surveyed 12 to 18 year olds in Germany. They found that 89% of young people in Germany are using the internet daily. Time of internet use has doubled in the last decade – from 106 minutes per day in 2007 to 221 minutes per day in 2017. Also, the study indicated that 47% of girls and 34% of boys are interested in environmental topics.

Therefore, we faced a challenge to make the software SITAS appealing for those users who are not yet engaged in nature studies in a way that gets them outside, preferably combining software with fieldwork. On the other hand, students who enjoy spending time in nature may learn to deepen their knowledge about butterflies

Table 6.4. Questionnaire used in survey 4 (see Table 6.2). (+) and (–) indicate "right answer" and "wrong answer" respectively

Pos.	Questions
1	What do you know about the relationship between caterpillar and butterfly? a. Caterpillars attract butterflies b. Each butterfly was a caterpillar (+) c. There is no relationship
2	Which name is used for butterflies? a. Large Blue (+) b. Large Yellow c. Large Orange
3	How many diurnal butterflies occur in Germany? a. 15 b. 150 (+) c. 50
4	The Brimstone is feeding on a. Sure liquids b. Bacteria c. Nectar (+)
5	How do butterflies take their food? By a. Proboscis (+) b. Teeth c. Antenna
6	The Peacock butterfly lives about a. 1 year (+) b. 5 years c. 4 weeks
7	This is the life cycle of butterflies: a. Egg → butterfly b. Egg→ larva→pupa→butterfly (+) c. Larva→pupa→butterfly
8	Why has the number of butterfly species decreased for the last hundred years? a. They have been galled by birds b. No, they have not gone. c. They could not find the right habitats. (+)

and biodiversity risk assessment with the SITAS software. Compelling narratives are helpful to successfully transfer scientific knowledge to non-scientific scholars (Vervoort et al., 2014). In SITAS, a video is included that tells the "story" about the "Large blues" – the *Maculinea* butterflies.

The evaluation survey indicated that students have deficits in the understanding of uncertainty and modeling (Table 6.6). Therefore, the method of climatic modeling

Table 6.5. Questionnaire according to survey 5 (Knowledge about butterflies, part 2). (+) and (–) indicate "right answer" and "wrong answer"

Pos.	Questions
1	Who appears later in the year? a. Brimstone b. Small heath (+) c. Small tortoiseshell
2	Who has two generations per year? a. Orange tip b. Peacock (+) c. Purple emperor
3	Who is the smallest one? a. Dusky meadow brown b. Small heath (+) c. Small tortoiseshell
4	Who does not belong to the family of the "Whites"? a. Brimstone b. Green-veined white c. Marbled white (+)
5	Which butterflies cannot be seen together? a. Peacock and Red admiral b. Small tortoiseshell and Orange tip c. Marbled white and Orange tip (+)
6	Who occurs only in summertime? a. Ringlet (+) b. Peacock c. Red admiral
7	Whose caterpillars feed on stinging nettles? a. Silver-washed fritillary b. Small tortoiseshell (+) c. Small heath
8	Where do most butterflies live? a. In the forest b. In the park c. On meadows (+)

is explained in a user-friendly way using science-based content alternating with test questions and also completed by short videos. Building the model, the researchers aimed at including "as little as possible but as much as necessary" parameters. Settele et al. (2008) applied four climatic parameters to assess the climatic risks for butterflies:

- Annual temperature range,
- Annual precipitation range,

Table 6.6. Questionnaire according to survey 6. (+) and (−) indicate "right answer" and "wrong answer"

N	Question	Students' right answers (%)
1	From butterfly abundance we cannot conclude on the presence of other species. (−)	56
2	Whether an area is suitable for butterflies, is determined by precipitation. (+)	82
3	Climatic niches are small-scale retreats for endangered species. (−)	16
4	Scientist can predict species' occurrence in 2050 based on current distributions. (−)	31
5	Differences between the temperatures of the hottest and the coldest months have a stronger climatic impact than mean annual temperature. (+)	55
6	Differences in monthly precipitation will decrease in Germany in the next years. (−)	18
7	Climatic niche is an abstract term dealing with climatic parameters. (+)	47
8	Researchers present at least three different answers if they are asked about the presence of the Brimstone butterfly in 2050. (+)	51
9	Modelling of future species distribution means including as many parameters as possible. (−)	4
10	Methods applied to butterfly modelling can be applied also to amphibians. (+)	29

- Soil water content,
- Growth degree days.

In the software, two difficulty levels are provided for the explanation of the parameters and the modeling approach itself: a basic and a more detailed one. To deal with uncertainty, the three future scenarios GREEN, YELLOW, and RED are applied. In the butterfly simulation tool, habitat losses and gains for each time step are presented for each of those scenarios (Figure 6.3). In this way, we highlight that researchers cannot predict future species' distributions, but instead project possible futures (see Table 6.6).

Comparing the knowledge of the two student groups it became obvious that students attending the "Sustainability course" knew significantly more about nature than other students (Figure 6.2). This is probably due to the fact that students who join the one-year facultative "Sustainability course" are generally more engaged in nature studies and also participated in the German butterfly monitoring scheme (www.tagfalter-monitoring.de, Kühn et al., 2008). Taking part in Citizen Science projects enhances consciousness for science-society collaboration and responsible citizenship (Bonn et al., 2016). Supervising students' research and participation in citizen science projects also requires additional resources from researchers. As the most evident result of this kind of collaboration is "only" the learning success of students (Jordan et al., 2012; Zoellick et al., 2012), those efforts are rarely rewarded by scientific research institutions.

The software SITAS provides an educational tool that is based on a multidisciplinary approach. Through biodiversity risk assessment, and using the popular characteristics of butterflies as an example, students deal with scientific methods and develop skills of future decision-makers such as critical and dynamic thinking.

REFERENCES

Bonn, A., Richter, A., Vohland, K. et al. (2016). Grünbuch Citizen Science Strategie 2020 für Deutschland, UFZ, iDiv, MfN, BBIB, Berlin, 2016.

Carpenter, S. R., Bennett, E. M., & Peterson, G. D. (2006). Scenarios for ecosystem services: An overview. *Ecology and Society, 11*(1), 29. (Online) Retrieved from http://www.ecologyandsociety.org/vol11/iss1/art29/

COP 13. (2016). Summary of the UN biodiversity conference: 2–17 DECEMBER 2016. *Earth Negotiations Bulletin, 9,* 678. Retrieved January 26, 2018, from http://www.iisd.ca/biodiv/cop13/enb/

Costello, M. J., Wilson, S., & Houlding, B. (2011). Predicting total global species richness using rates of species description and estimates of taxonomic effort. *Systematic Biology, 61*(5), 871–883. doi:10.1093/sysbio/syr080

Devictor, V., Van Swaay, C., Brereton, T., Brotons, L., & Chamberlain, D. (2012). Differences in the climatic debts of birds and butterflies at a continental scale. *Nature Climate Change, 2,* 121–124.

EEA. (2015). European environment – State and outlook. (2015). *Assessment of global megatrends, European Environment Agency, Copenhagen.* Retrieved January 26, 2018, from https://www.eea.europa.eu/soer-2015/global/action-download-pdf

European Union. (2011). *The EU biodiversity strategy to 2020.* Luxembourg: Publications Office of the European Union. Retrieved January 23, 2018, from http://ec.europa.eu/environment/nature/info/pubs/docs/brochures/2020%20Biod%20brochure%20final%20lowres.pdf

Feierabend, S., Plankenhorn, T., & Rathgeb, T. (2017). *JIM-Studie. Medienpädagogischer Forschungsverbund Südwest.* Stuttgart.

Hallmann, C. A., Sorg, M., Jongejans, E., Siepel, H., Hofland, N., Schwan, H., ... de Kroon, H. (2017). More than 75 percent decline over 27 years in total flying insect biomass in protected areas. *PLoS ONE, 12*(10), e0185809. Retrieved from https://doi.org/10.1371/journal.pone.0185809

IPBES. (2016). Summary for policymakers of the assessment report of the Intergovernmental Science-Policy Platform on Biodiversity and Ecosystem Services on pollinators, pollination and food production. In S. G. Potts, V. L. Imperatriz-Fonseca, H. T. Ngo, J. C. Biesmeijer, T. D. Breeze, L. V. Dicks, ... B. F. Viana (Eds.), *Secretariat of the Intergovernmental Science-Policy Platform on Biodiversity and Ecosystem Services.* Bonn, Germany.

Jordan, R. C., Ballard, H., & Phillips, T. B. (2012). Key issues and new approaches for evaluating citizen-science learning outcomes. *Frontiers in Ecology and the Environment, 10*(6), 307–309.

Kühn, E., Feldmann, R., Harpke, A., Hirneisen, N., Musche, M., Leopold, P., & Settele, J. (2008). Getting the public involved into butterfly conservation – Lessons learned from a new monitoring scheme in Germany. *Israel Journal of Ecology and Evolution, 54,* 89–104.

Ledley, T. S., Dahlman, L., McAuliffe, C., Haddad, N., Taber, M. R., Domenico, B., Lynds, S., & Grogan, M. (2011). Making earth science data accessible and usable in education. *Science, 333,* 1838–1839.

Neus, E., Stevenson, R. B., Lasen, M., Ferreira, J. A., & Davis, J. (2017). Approaches to embedding sustainability in teacher education: A synthesis oft he literature. *Teaching and Teacher Education, 63*, 405–417.

OECD. (2012). *OECD environmental outlook to 2050*. Paris: Organisation for Economic Co-operation and Development. Retrieved January 26, 2018, from http://www.keepeek.com/Digital-Asset-Management/oecd/environment/oecd-environmental-outlook-to-2050_9789264122246-en#.WmsS62dG1YM

Settele, J., Hammen, V., Hulme, P., Karlson, U., Klotz, S., Kotarac, M., ... Kuhn, I. (2005). ALARM – Assessing LArge-scale environmental Risks for biodiversity with tested Methods. *Gaia-Ecological Perspectives for Science and Society, 14*(1), 69–72.

Settele, J., Kudrna, O., Harpke, A., Kühn, I., Swaay, C. van, Verovnik, R., ... Schweiger, O. (2008). Climatic risk atlas of European butterflies. *Biorisk, 1*, 1–710.

Spangenberg, J. H., Carter, T. R., Fronzek, S., Jaeger, J. A. G., Jylhä, K., Kühn, I., Omann, I., Paul, A., Reginster, I., Rounsevell, M., Stocker, A., Sykes, M. T., & Settele, J. (2012). Scenarios for investigating risks to biodiversity. *Global Ecol. Biogeography, 21*, 5–18.

Stork, N. E. (2017). How many species of insects and other terrestrial arthropods are there on Earth? *Annual Review of Entomology, 63*, 31–45. doi:10.1146/annurev-ento-020117-043348

Sutherland, W. J., Bardsley, S., Clout, M., Depledge, M. H., Dicks, L. V., Fellman, L., Fleishman, E., Gibbons, D. W., Keim, B., Lickorish, F., Margerison, C., Monk, K. A., Norris, K., Peck, L. S., Prior, S. V., Scharlemann, P. W., Spalding, M. D., & Watkinson, A. R. (2013). A horizon scan of global conservation issues for 2013. *Trends in Ecology & Evolution, 28*, 16–22.

Thomas, J. A., & Settele, J. (2004). Evolutionary biology: Butterfly mimics of ants. *Nature, 432*, 283–284.

Ulbrich, K., Schweiger, O., Klotz, S., & Settele, J. (2015). Biodiversity impacts of climate change – The PRONAS software as educational tool. *Web Ecology, 15*, 49–58.

UNESCO. (2005). *United Nations Decade of Education for Sustainable Development (2004–2015): International implementation scheme*. Paris: UNESCO.

United Nations. (1992). Multilateral Convention on biological diversity (with annexes), Concluded at Rio de Janeiro on 5 June 1992. *United Nations Treaty Series, 1760*, 146. (Article 2. Use of Terms)

Van Swaay, C. A. M., Harpke, A., Van Strien, A., Fontaine, B., Stefanescu, C., Roy, D., ... Devictor, V. (2010). *The impact of climate change on butterfly communities 1990–2009*. Report VS2010.025, Butterfly Conservation Europe & De Vlinderstichting, Wageningen.

Vervoort, J. M., Keuskamp, D. H., Kok, K., van Lammeren, R., Stolk, T., Veldkamp, T. A., ... Rowlands, H. (2014). A sense of change: Media designers and artists communicating about complexity in social-ecological systems. *Ecology and Society, 19*, 10, doi:10.5751/ES-06613-190310

Zoellick, B., Nelson, S. J., & Schauffler, M. (2012). Participatory science and education: Bringing both views into focus. *Frontiers in Ecology and the Environment, 10*(6), 310–313. Retrieved June 5, 2018, from http://www.edupolicy.net/wp-content/uploads/2016/04/Summer-School-concept-VF.pdf

Karin Ulbrich
Department Community Ecology
Helmholtz Centre for Environmental Research – UFZ
Leipzig, Germany

Elisabeth Kühn
Department Community Ecology
Helmholtz Centre for Environmental Research – UFZ
Leipzig, Germany

Oliver Schweiger
Department Community Ecology
Helmholtz Centre for Environmental Research – UFZ
Leipzig, Germany

Josef Settele
Department Community Ecology
Helmholtz Centre for Environmental Research – UFZ
Leipzig, Germany

KYLYAN M. BISQUERT AND PABLO Á. MEIRA

7. THE AGROECOLOGICAL MOVEMENT IN GALICIA (SPAIN)

INTRODUCTION

This chapter aims to show an analytic approach to the current situation of the agroecological movement in Galicia (Spain) similar to that of Andalusia (Sevilla, 2012). The movement is composed by a significant heterogeneity of initiatives characterized by a social nature, a critical position toward the socioeconomic and agri-food paradigm, and a goal of transforming vocation which transcends and transgresses the institutional frame of certified organic farming. It is a social movement relatively new to the territory although it has consolidated precedents in other regions of Spain. Furthermore, it is immersed in a process of articulation and search for identity of its own, recognizable in different platforms and tools that it has been endowed with over the last few years: forums for reflection and debate, participatory guarantee systems and other local organizational structures, such as coordination networks, media, etc.

Some of the notable features of these initiatives are: their horizontal and assembly organization, their community orientation; their engagement with the revitalization of rural contexts and economic relocation; their organization based on principles of self-management and autonomy; as well as the promotion of relationships based on mutual support and trust.

The analytical approach used in this research explores the current and potential socio-educational implications offered by the agroecological movement in Galicia through its practices and discourses around food and its model of construction of diet and agri-food systems. The purpose is to look for possible lines of collaboration and feedback between these social actors and the Environmental Education field, both to leverage their theoretical-practical contributions and to reinforce their socio-educational activity as a mobilized sector of citizenship. Consequently, the ultimate goal is to promote social and environmentally sustainable food cultures, which in turn act as an axis to reach more profound and more complicated transformations in society in our search for a new Culture of Sustainability.

ENVIRONMENTAL EDUCATION AND AGRI-FOOD SYSTEMS

A Hegemonic, Global and Unsustainable Agri-food System

Food is a fundamental satisfier for the human need of subsistence (Max-Neef, 1994). It also constitutes a central element in the configuration of our societies. To supply the growing demand for food, we have endowed ourselves with many agri-food systems throughout history and planetary geography. At a local level, these systems are being adapted to the particularities of the regions and ecosystems, in which they developed, allowing, together with other socioeconomic, political and cultural conditions, the emergence of a vast diversity of agrarian practices (Sevilla, 2006).

This diversity is evident in the multitude of different models of diet construction, as a cultural manifestation of adaptation to the environment in the way of feeding for different human groups. However, after a process of the agrarian sector modernization occurred through the named green revolutions happened during the second half of the last century, the hegemony of a global food system based on the industrialization of agricultural production, liberalization and globalization of food markets and the concentration of power in an increasingly smaller number of transnational corporations it was consolidated. This paradigm shift in agrarian practices in the management and organization of food has undoubtedly converted the globalized agri-food system as an element of high relevance in the generation of severe social and environmental imbalances (Sevilla, 2006; Cuéllar & Sevilla, 2013).

According to the fifth report of the United Nations Intergovernmental Panel on Climate Change, (when disaggregated by economic sectors) about a quarter of anthropogenic origin greenhouse gases (GHGs) correspond to agriculture, forestry and other land uses (Intergovernmental Panel on Climate Change, 2015). Nevertheless, if this analysis is applied to the overall agri-food system, including all the links in the chain, from the production and supply of agricultural inputs to final consumption, through changes in land uses and deforestation undertaken to expand the agricultural frontier, the global transport of food commodities, their processing and packaging, their refrigeration, storage and distribution, and the waste generated in all parts of the process, the sum to the total computation of emissions would be much higher (Garnett, 2011). New estimates range between 44% and 57% according to the international peasant organization GRAIN (GRAIN, 2014). It is in this way that the patterns of consumption that make up the diet are directly linked to GHGs emissions and, consequently, to Climate Change (Faber et al., 2012), especially if we observe them in relation to agri-food systems.

In addition, the globalized agro-industrial model is behind multiple environmental impacts of very diverse nature, due to, among other causes, "it has incorporated highly polluting technologies (pesticides, chemical fertilizers, etc.), it has developed practices of equal destructive capability (burning of crop residues, deep and repetitive tillage, etc.) and it has standardized its basic raw material (seeds and animal breeds) […], [with which] it exerts a devastating effect […] on the air, water, land and biodiversity" (Cuéllar & Sevilla, 2013, p. 15). To all this we must add the impacts caused by the transport of food over long distances and the construction of large infrastructures to facilitate it, the deforestation caused by the agrarian frontier enlargement, the use of genetically modified organisms (GMOs), the occupation of vast territories with enormous extensions of monocultures, the breakdown of biochemical cycles, the exhaustion and contamination of freshwater reserves, the erosion of soils or waste generated by agro-industry and large distribution chains (packaging, packages, plastic bags, etc.), among others.

This globalized and industrialized agri-food system has led to a great loss of cultural and biological diversity in the set of local cultivated species and varieties because of this uniform character (Shiva, 2008). However, it has led to the marginalization or disappearance of local agrarian cultures through the imposition of agro-industrial management on traditional peasant and indigenous practices (Van der Ploeg, 2010). Through technological packages linked to subsidies or commercial treaties, the growing hoarding of lands and resources by companies and governments in foreign territories, the bio-piracy denounced by Shiva (2001), or the homogenization of the different cultural constructions of diet in favour of a global diet that offers the consumer a false perception to have a vast diversity of options to choose from. But in reality, it is composed of an ever decreasing diversity and quality of raw materials (Patel, 2008).

From a socioeconomic perspective, the interaction of a hegemonic agri-food system with an industrial production system, global trade and the logic of the dominant economic system has led to serious imbalances at the global level in the distribution of wealth, access to natural resources and services, or the ability to take decisions relating to the production, distribution and consumption of food. For decades we have witnessed the effects of a growing concentration of power in gigantic transnational corporations related to agribusiness (supply of seeds and other inputs, transformation and marketing, large distribution, etc.). This is further compounded by the important role played by supranational institutions such as the World Bank, the International Monetary Fund or the World Trade Organization in shaping national agricultural policies in many countries, especially those considered as developing, through reform sets associated with funding, or by the policies of agricultural subsidies developed by, among others, the US or the European Union through the Common Agricultural Policy.

Some of these effects lead to the plundering of natural resources and services in impoverished countries, the extreme indebtedness to which peasants and small producers from around the world are subjected by the adaptation of small farms to the needs of the agro-industry and the purchase of the inputs, and the waves of suicides among the rural population in countries such as Mexico or India due to this indebtedness (Ziegler, 2006; Shiva, 2007; Patel, 2008). Conflicts generated by the shortage and the rise in the price of the food or the increase of migratory flows contribute to what we could call agri-food refugees (Bisquert, 2016).

To all this we must add the increasing nutritional imbalances and the resulting serious health problems, either by the undernutrition and malnutrition. As many as 800 million humans suffer because of persistent food insecurity in vast regions of the planet, aggravated by the effects of Climate Change, or by the spread of diets of high caloric value and based on processed foods which are also behind the over-nutrition of upwards of 1 billion people who suffer obesity or are overweight in the world (Patel, 2008; FAO, 2016).

Therefore, the hegemonic agri-food system proves to be an element of obvious importance in our current socio-environmental crisis and shows clear signs of incompatibility with the requirements of social and environmental sustainability. Consequently, it is essential that from an Environmental Education perspective we begin to propose strategies to counteract the impacts these causes, whether acting through the social construction of diet or recognizing and promoting alternative agri-food systems that are more consistent with the aims and principles of our field.

Agroecology: Transdisciplinary Field and Social Movement

Agroecology as a research field, is complementary to Environmental Education in this work, is based on the recovery of peasant and indigenous knowledge and the exploration of new approaches and techniques to identify the best configurations to build socially and environmentally sustainable local agri-food systems. It is a field with an eminently transdisciplinary and multi-epistemological character that sinks its roots in the intellectual tradition of Peasant Studies, and therefore it arises mainly from Sociology, although it integrates the concurrence of a great number of disciplines of Natural, Social and Human Sciences (Morales, 2011). Likewise, contributions from other extra-academic knowledge based on cultural traditions of peasant and indigenous peoples and communities are also important for this field (Sevilla & Soler, 2010). In fact, from this approach, it is understood that traditional knowledge is the most relevant reference to establish local agri-food systems in terms of sustainability in each region. This perspective is based on historical and contextualized cultural adaptations of these traditions with the ecosystems where they developed, in terms of farming techniques, but also in other forms of socioeconomic organization, decision-making processes, distribution channels or diet configurations. Therefore, agroecology tries to revalue and recover an environmentally adapted cultural heritage to build on, including technical and social innovations, socially and environmentally sustainable agri-food models, based on local culture, but also in accordance with current challenges.

Agroecology proposes three dimensions of analysis; technical-productive, socioeconomic, and cultural-political. The first refers specifically to agricultural production and its degree of adaptation to ecological principles. The second one focuses on social and economic elements present in the processes of production, distribution and consumption of agricultural products, as well as in the different ways of the relation between the different actors who compose agri-food systems. The last is referred to the degree of empowerment or respect for the cultural features of each region in the development of the agri-food system, as well as the level of democracy and autonomy present in these processes and among the different actors involved (Cuéllar & Sevilla, 2013).

On the other hand, Agroecology is a field that exceeds the academic framework and moves in the social contexts through its political dimension (Calle, Gallar, & Candón, 2013). We refer here to the agroecological 'social movement,' current heir to the peasant movements (Van der Ploeg, 2010). Its discourses and practices are structured precisely around the three dimensions, from a systemic and transformative perspective that transcends the limited framework of organic farming, towards a food democracy (Calle, Soler, & Rivera, 2011). Through "collective social action proposals that reveal the predatory logic of the hegemonic agro-industrial productive model, to replace it with another that points towards agriculture socially fairer, economically viable and environmentally appropriate" (Sevilla, 2006, p. 14). The contributions of this movement are also important to the field of Agroecology, given its multi-epistemological character, and these are appreciated as social innovations that work to implement its proposals from an emerging practice in real-world spaces.

Agroecology is a very heterogeneous social movement, but with a common political objective that aims at achieving food sovereignty through an social transition that concerns the whole of society, integrating personal, microsocial, eco-structural and meso/macro-social dimensions (Calle et al., 2013). At the international level, the organization named La Vía Campesina[1] stands out as a unifying reference for all these struggles. This organization maintains a close relationship with partners that operate at a national and regional level. In Spain, there are also trade unions and peasant organizations that represent this organization as part of their collaboration network.

Apart from these organizational structures, according to the principles and practices of Agroecology, there are also many small initiatives that operate from the principles of autonomy and self-management. This trend, inspired by both historical and current peasant and indigenous struggles (agrarianism, landless workers, zapatism, mapuche people, etc.), as well as in anarchist tradition and libertarian socialism currents, these reject classic forms of organization based on structures that, despite these are not truly democratic. These initiatives are organized in networks and other channels of participation, practicing what Calle (2011) understands as radical democracy, a form of direct and emancipatory democratic practice. In other words, this kind of initiatives works "betting on horizontality in decision making (assemblies, decision-making by consensus), through working in small groups (commissions, consumer groups, production groups) and by daily communication and cyclic *groups-assembly-groups* feedback, with multiplier and participative effect" (Calle, Soler, Vara, & Gallar, 2012).

The analytical approach to the agroecological movement that is presented here takes place in the framework of a doctoral thesis, of which the authors of this chapter are, respectively, Ph.D. student and thesis director. This project aims, on the one hand, to limit and characterize this social movement in Galicia based on the collective initiatives that compose it, and on the other, to identify and evaluate the most relevant theoretical and practical contributions of this movement for the Environmental Education field in the sense of promoting sustainable diet models among people in general. In addition, it hopes to support and strengthen the development of their socio-educative actions and strategies, as social actors committed with agro-ecological social transition throughout the local agri-food systems transformation. We are particularly interested in the remarkable consistency in the cultural-political dimension of Agroecology and the principles of social and environmental sustainability in that these initiatives and collective processes each operate in an autonomous and self-managed way.

Currently, there are previous studies that point to a notable presence of agroecological initiatives in Galicia (Simón, Copena, & Rodríguez, 2010; Ríos, 2014). However, until now there has not been a systematic analysis of this social reality as a whole and in this region, much less about its socio-educational dimension.

An Environmental Education Approach

In order to address the sustainability problems linked to food, we identified two main areas of action from Environmental Education closely related to the social construction of diet and the agri-food systems, especially on the local scale.

The term diet comes etymologically from classical Greek, in which δίαιτα meant life regime. That is to say, beyond the reductionism associated with the follow-up of nutritional guidelines. It is understood as closer to what we understand as lifestyle. Thus, we understand 'diet' as the set of behaviours, habits and patterns of consumption, mediated by criteria, decisions and socioeconomic and cultural factors, as well as external conditions (advertising, fashion, supply, accessibility). This configures the way in which individuals and human groups satisfy their food needs. Developing educational actions on the construction of diet may have some relevance because its social construction is closely linked to the configuration of the agri-food systems that supply it. However, both are overlapping realities (in fact, consumption is one more link in the agri-food chain), acting only over established conventions of diet that ignore the configuration of agri-food systems.

Thus, beyond the focus of consumer education, we consider that within a socio-critical perspective of Environmental Education we should also consider the analysis of agri-food systems and the relationship we establish with them through diet, as well as which ones should be considered more timely and consistent with the principles of sustainability. We propose to overcome, according to the terminology of Calle et al. (2012), the mere promotion of certain individual and collective consumption strategies to also incorporate into the equation the stimulus of *agri-food resistances* such as:

- networks of *food criticism* and social ecology: platforms for protest and visibility of alternatives to the imbalances of the hegemonic agri-food system;
- new *social crops*: experiences of self-management and autonomy around food through collective action;
- new *agri-food styles*: articulation of different sectors of the agri-food system (production, transformation, distribution and consumption) as interrelated agents and partners in an alternative food praxis in coherence with common values.

The aim is to stimulate the adoption of what Gómez-Benito and Lozano (2014) call food citizenship. But from a perspective closer to the conception of ecological citizenship of Dobson (2003) or the eco-citizenship of Sauvé (2014), for promoting this in the society a collective engagement and agency in the construction of *sustainable diet models* taking part also straightly in the configuration of the agri-food systems, at least to local scale (Johnston, Fanzo, & Cogill, 2014).

Therefore, it is necessary to put the focus of attention on Environmental Education in a proposal of alternative agri-food systems in which the requirements of social and environmental sustainability are at the centre of priorities. Hence the special interest of the agroecological movement for an Environmental Education that seeks a critical social practice genuinely transformative (Caride & Meira, 2001). In this sense, the role of Environmental Education should also be recognized to make visible and to collaborate in the development of the initiatives and processes aimed at promoting and facilitating greater access to sustainable diets. Deepening the reconfiguration of the local agri-food systems towards more sustainable social and environmental models, as well as in democratizing the decision-making related to these.

Environmental Education cannot ignore proposals from mobilized citizens that direct their efforts to the configuration of social and environmentally sustainable agri-food systems. Adapted as they are to the natural cycles and ecosystems where they develop, they are based on networks and horizontal models of socioeconomic relation that go deep into the democratization of the food and agriculture sector, giving major relevancy in the decision making to producers and consumers. In addition, according to Orellana, Sauvé, Marleau, and Labraña (2008), the most honest way to do this will be from a participatory, critical, committed and responsible investigation that is based on wisdom and dialogue, that values and recognizes the contributions of people and collectives participating in the research, their visions, perspectives, questions and interests, with an ever-transformative and constructive purpose.

This research is ultimately designed to reveal ways to contribute to the promotion of a Culture of Sustainability through transformations of the food model. This strong notion of sustainability aspires to overcome the paradigm of sustainable development to situate the issue of social and environmental sustainability at the center of the configuration of human societies and policies (Vargas, Barba, & Diaz, 2015). According to Herrero, Cembranos, and Pascual (2011) this approach proposes, among other things, to adjust growth to the limits of the biosphere, to minimize the use of resources for the satisfaction of human needs, to appreciate austerity and sufficiency, to promote social relations, to adapt our societies to the functioning of the biosphere (closing cycles, minimizing transport, slow paces, cooperation, etc.), to respect the precautionary principle, to promote diversity in all its forms (ecological, social, cultural, epistemological, etc.) and to deploy forms of organization and decision making based on participatory processes and relationships in environments nearby. It would be necessary as an educational approach that transcends the school framework. It is also about making sustainability an inalienable ethical principle. In other words, the ultimate goal of all spheres of human activity. It should also be an education that puts into value all the knowledge about sustainability, close to the land and the means of production, which values and promotes knowledge for articulating the community and collective solutions critical with the socioeconomic model and stimulating alternatives. Thus, if we consider the relevance of didactic models that transfer agroecological ideas to school environments we should also explore the desirability of developing a similar line of work for the development of Environmental education in open contexts, involving the general population (Llerena, 2015).

METHOD

The methodological design of this research is mixed method, but it has a predominant orientation of Participatory Action Research (PAR). Consequently, according to Ganuza, Olivari, Paño, Buitrago, and Lorenzana (2010), we use strategies that "seek to approach a problem from a participatory perspective in order to propose, jointly, proposals oriented to improve the initial situation from which we started" (p. 31). We agree with Malo (2004) that it is a methodological commitment that aims to "be collective and contribute to the transformation of reality, generating a new and fairer reality", which is why we seek to break the duality of "the relation subject (researcher) – object (investigated)" and this is based on "the recognition of the power of action of all social subjects, [and] seeks to produce a process of co-research, in which different subjects, with knowledge-making diverse, are related according to ethical criteria" (pp. 32–33). As in the research line about eco-alimentation developed in the *Université du Québec à Montréal*, we understand that "learning is a transversal dimension of innovative collective action projects […] [and thus] it is about learning together in the movement of the projects that are being developed" (Sauvé, Naoufal, & Anzou, 2013).

Subject to this perspective, we will make use of a set of more classical data collection techniques and instruments, both quantitative (questionnaire) and qualitative (in-depth interviews and discussion groups), organized around different phases of project development. The approach of these techniques and instruments respond to the objectives of this study. However, it also aspires to answer to the needs and concerns expressed by the people and initiatives participating in it. For this, members of these initiatives will be involved partially in the design of instruments and techniques, through workshops and meetings in which we will collect what they need or want to know about themselves as a collective. These contributions will be included, for instance, in the questionnaire, which will be subjected to the corresponding tests of reliability and validity. Depending on each case, the subject participant of study is made up of the initiatives that are part of the universe investigated (the agroecological movement in Galicia) or by some members that compose them.

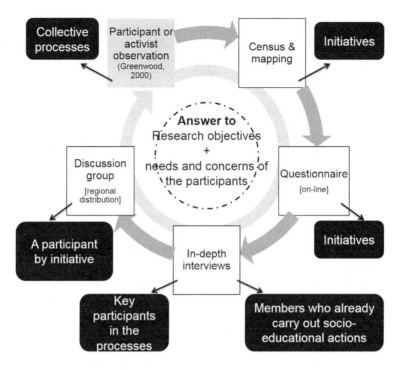

Figure 7.1. Methodological design

However, for this first approximation presented in this chapter, we used the technique of participant or militant observation, closer to a PAR design which will be a process constant during all the phases that make up the methodological design (Greenwood, 2000). The subject of study is the collective processes and dynamics developed by the agro-ecological initiatives. So far, an ethnographic approach has been carried out by this technique, with the personal involvement and direct observation of the researcher. These involve different articulation processes and meeting and dialogue spaces developed between some of the most active initiatives that are part of the studied movement. These observations are contrasted with other primary data sources emanating from these initiatives and processes (records of meetings, web or social network pages, media, etc.).

CURRENT SITUATION OF THE AGROECOLOGICAL MOVEMENT IN GALICIA

As a result of this approach to the current state of the agroecological movement in Galicia through some of the initiatives that compose it and of the different processes and articulation spaces that they develop, it has been possible to confirm the existence of a very heterogeneous set of small production, distribution and consumption initiatives that operate under different organizational formats. These initiatives are disseminated throughout the region and are currently in a moment of emergence and articulation around new networks, tools and common spaces for dialogue and collaboration.

Collective and Self-managed Projects

Among the agroecological initiatives observed, one highlight is the self-managed organization of meetings and markets of local producers on a weekly or biweekly basis by some of these initiatives. These are collective projects in which the decision-making takes place in an assembly-like manner and where all the initiatives concur in a horizontal manner. Among a large number of markets, fairs and other events linked to the commercialization of food products from environmentally sustainable management in Galicia, only some respond to the principles of Agroecology, especially as far as the organization model is concerned. Ethical consumption meetings like the *Entre Lusco e Fusco*'s agroecological market in Santiago de Compostela[2] and *4Ponlas* in Pontevedra,[3] the *Foros Ecolóxicos da Barbanza* (Barbanza's ecologic forums), in the municipalities that make up the homonymous coastal region, specially Ribeira, the *Mercado da Terra* (land's market) in Lugo[4] and the *Encontros Labregos* (peasant meetings) organized by *Labrega Natura* association in A Coruña. It is common practice to offer leisure activities during the celebration of these markets, including the celebration of traditional Galician festivals, music and dance performances, poetry workshops, etc. The markets also include educative activities and skills related to the local agricultural culture (cheese making and preserving, identification of mushrooms, tasting of local varieties of vegetables, exchange of seeds, etc.), with sustainable agricultural techniques (soil regeneration, alternative treatments to diseases of the plants) or with current constructions of diet (elaboration of vegetable alternatives to dairy products -milk, cheese and yoghurts-, healthy nutrition), as well as on topics related to environmentalism and other related social movements (degrowth, social economy and alternative currencies, time banks, fair trade). Although there are many similar events in Galicia, these represent other models in relation to their composition regarding the type of producers and products on offer (handicrafts, second-hand items, etc.), their organization (promoted by public administrations or other organizations), its management (vertically, by an external organizer) or its periodicity (annual or specific events).[5]

Another collective project format with similar characteristics is represented by *A Gavela* (the sheaf) project, a Participatory Guarantee System promoted by a set of production, distribution and consumption initiatives, as well as by people who participate individually as consumers, residents in the regions of southwest Galicia, who work together in an assembly and self-managed way. It is a collective tool alternative to third-party certification -the one used in the official certification of organic farming products, according to current European regulation (Council

Regulation (EC) Nº 834/2007, 2007), which involves the active participation of the entire community in the supervision and support of the productive projects. This approach is a way to guarantee compliance with collectively established precepts, such as the prohibition of the use of agro-toxins and genetically modified organisms, the benefit based on the exploitation of people or the parallel practice of conventional management. The maintenance of soil fertility and biodiversity, active participation in the farm audits, transparency, shortening of marketing circuits, mutual aid and non-competition are also required.

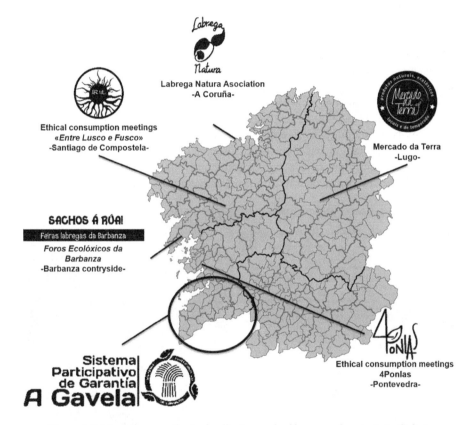

Figure 7.2. Map of agroecological collective and self-managed projects in Galicia

Network Articulation Processes

In turn, these collective projects, integrated by small agroecological initiatives of production and consumption, have been trying to promote a greater articulation of the movement within the Galician region since 2016, through a biannual celebration of sustainable projects. These meetings take place during the celebration of one of the aforementioned self-managed markets, in which a series of recreational and lifestyle activities are developed, as well as an open, horizontal and deliberative decision making process, as a space for communication and coordination among initiatives.

In the different meetings, differences have been expressed with the official certification model, regulated at European level (Council Regulation (EC) N° 834/2007, 2007). In fact, this certification model, its practices and its shortcomings in terms of transparency and democratic functioning, are rejected and perceived by many agroecological initiatives as a distortion of the original philosophy of organic farming, which has been instrumentalized by companies to the detriment of small socially-based initiatives. Moreover, they are seen as reproducing capitalist schemes in their marketing strategies and their organizational model. This conflict has generated one of the first lines of collaboration among participating projects around the disclosure of their position and the nature of their initiatives, which then deepens the dialogue on environmental sustainability. Beyond the idea of productive management, being respectful of the environment, incorporating criteria of proximity, temporality, closure of cycles, recovery of local varieties, etc., place they place a special emphasis on social sustainability (relations of trust between producers and consumers, recovery of community links, etc.) and the radically democratic functioning in their spaces of collective organization.

Figure 7.3. Poster of sustainable projects national meetings

Emerging from these meetings, a coordination group was created, made up of representatives of the different participating projects with the purpose of developing proposals, objectives and common lines of work between the celebrations of each meeting. Particular emphasis is placed on the purely communicative and collaborative nature of this coordination process, as a space to share useful information to solve common problems, practice mutual aid and solidarity between projects and to gain greater visibility and social impact as a collective. However, with there is no power of decision-making as that power resides in the assemblies of each project or market. Similarly, the purpose of the biannual meetings is mainly to create spaces for coexistence and strengthen the market that hosts it in each edition.

The practice of mutual aid and the principle of solidarity is specified in the design of many strategies that respond to the needs or problems that arise in the initiatives or projects that compose the network. In the same way, they coordinate dates and schedules of the different markets to avoid,overlapping with each other. Together with the inclusive nature of this process, a wide variety of initiatives based on common minimum principles, are foreseen in coordinating these efforts. Nonetheless, certain restrictions are placed on this inclusiveness in order to safeguard the autonomous, self-managed and horizontal nature of the projects that make up the network. Leaving out the possibility of integrating other events that do not share this philosophy. Although leaving the possibility of their incorporation if they are endowed with collective structures and assemblies. However, the interference of public administrations, private companies, political parties or trade unions is totally rejected by the network, since they are considered a threat to their collective sovereignty and autonomy.

Other Spaces and Tools

On the other hand, with a biannual character, the *O Rural Quere Xente*[6] (countryside wants people) meetings are organized, as a space for gathering, exchange of experiences, collective education and debate. The eighth edition of this event was held in July 2017 in the municipality of A Lama (Pontevedra). Within its programming, the methodological design proposed for this research was presented, inviting those present to participate. In addition, educational and recreational activities related to sustainable and fair skills and lifestyles in rural settings, social initiatives and alternative economies or traditional popular culture were programmed including: preparation of groceries based on cereals and nuts,; the collection of wild and medicinal plants; flour production; sharpening of tools; bioconstruction; self-care workshops; an exhibition of experiences and projects, colloquia on civil rights in rural areas, traditional and popular games and chants, etc.

In the previous edition of these meetings (March 2017, in Bergondo, A Coruña) the first issue of *A Fenda*[7] was presented. This is a new periodical magazine linked to the movement and the defence and development of common-managed and self-managed projects, de-growth, etc., with special attention to rural Galician contexts.

In this issue it is possible to find a panoramic presentation of this type of initiatives together with other related initiatives that affect areas such as: environmental platforms; urban social centers; feminisms; alternative and community education initiatives in rural areas; self-care and health; social economy, decentralized and free technologies and communication. Moreover, the visions and discourses of the oldest, rural population are put in value, as well as recipes of vegan cuisine, sustainable local food, on-farm work techniques or documents of interest on environmental issues and struggles in Galicia.

Common Characteristics

Overall, among all the collective projects and processes observed they all include the following common features:

Mutual aid, cooperation and defence of the commons. In all these initiatives and processes it has been possible to observe an active interest in collaboration and solidarity, such as the disposition of aid strategies and the exchange of information to face common problems, the celebration of the events in the context of a project or initiative to give it visibility and support, or to help new related initiatives or collective projects that could find difficulties in their creation and consolidation.

Autonomy, self-management and network organization. The projects and processes integrated by agroecological initiatives observed have also as their hallmark a collective will to function autonomously, without inference from an external agent, public or private, or any other organizational structure that is not their own articulation between independent initiatives: neither political parties, nor trade unions, nor non-governmental organizations. Self-management is also perceived in the way that the initiatives themselves and the people who integrate them manage projects and collective processes directly, without delegating to representatives beyond specific functions without decision-making power. This orientation toward self-management is one of the points that makes them reject the official model of accreditation in organic farming, based on agencies with exclusive competencies controlled by the largest companies in the sector, with undemocratic, opaque structures, that exercise production control through audits by a third party. It also emphasizes its way of articulating itself around networks, either those created between their own agroecological initiatives and collective projects that make up, or through the participation in other related ones: of seeds, of social economy, of degrowth, of alternative education, etc.

Horizontality and inclusiveness. The movements organizational functioning is based on assemblies in many cases that opened for the participation of the one who wishes it, and the possibility of taking part as producer, distributor, consumer or exercising other roles in the food and agriculture chain, always in a position of equality. ,This makes the projects and processes observed good examples of the practice of radical democracy. Similarly, all decisions are taken by consensus and not by voting, avoiding imposing majorities on minorities and by trying to include all proposals and perspectives in a common discourse. In this way they define themselves as collective.

Conservation of the biocultural diversity of the region. Although these initiatives raise important technical and social innovations, in the farm management and in its ways of organizing itself, one of its fundamental bases is the recovery and conservation of traditional peasant knowledge and practices, which they try to reproduce whenever they are consistent with the principles of environmental and social sustainability. In the same way, the recovery and conservation of autochthonous or traditionally cultivated species and varieties in Galicia is another one of its greatest priorities. This is partly due to the existence of seed banks and networks that they have helped to consolidate. This is another difference with the model of organic farming certification, which obliges producers to acquire certified seeds, whose purchase must justify each year, instead of allowing to be the peasants who guard the local genetic heredity.

Attention to their impacts than the requirements of official certification. Another element of differentiation and critique by agro-ecological initiatives towards the hegemonic model of organic farming is its careful attention to the impacts that farm management puts on the ecosystems in which they take place, beyond the prohibition of the use of certain pesticides and fertilizers, or the cultivation of GMOs. Generally, these initiatives tend to go more in depth in their requirements for environmental sustainability for their farms, developing techniques, permaculture or other trends and traditions that allow having a greater care of the organic and inorganic systems and cycles present in the lands they occupy. In addition, unlike conventional organic farming, they are also concerned about social sustainability. That is to say that the initiatives are viable and allow for decent working conditions for peasants, but also they must be used for the recovery of community linkages, the socioeconomic network and the repopulation in rural areas. Moreover, they make a special effort to popularize the accessibility of all type of consumers to this model of feeding, trying to counteract the elitism towards which has tended the consumption of ecological products in Spain through high prices. They attempt to do this by shortening distribution channels, involving consumers in their projects or by celebrating events in streets and squares to bring their production closer to the general public.

Political orientation to social transformation. Finally, the movement's positions infer motivations of an ideological nature, beyond the economic character inherent in these initiatives. This is another characteristic that differentiates it from typical organic farming companies. This is observable, for instance, in its rejection of the use of the conventional channels of marketing of agri-food products, such as supermarkets or other formats of the large distribution chains. They also reject the official certification agencies in this sense, because they understand that the role is not so much of assuring the fulfillment of standards in the farm management, but to the position in the market a differentiated type of product, coming from an exclusively business perspective. For agroecological initiatives, the main objective is not to make money, but to promote social changes while developing a life project based on ethical values. The search for food sovereignty or the recovery of living rural zones as a collective purpose is appreciated both in the discourse and in the nature of the articulation processes it undertakes.

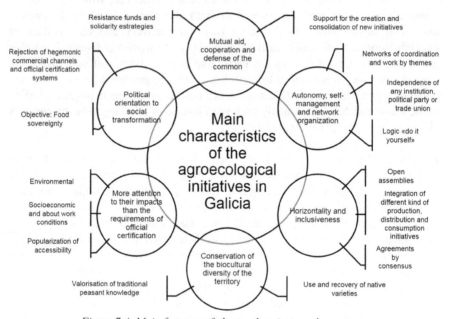

Figure 7.4. *Main features of observed projects and processes*

CONCLUSIONS

After this initial approach, we have been able to appreciate that initiatives that make up the agroecological movement in Galicia observed, as well their projects and collective processes undertaken, are a clear example of promotion of social and environmental sustainability in the agri-food sector. It is also clear the connection between culture and environment that is set within this movement and in the spaces and processes that are promoted, especially:

Peasant culture. These initiatives aim to revitalize rural contexts, increasingly depopulated and industrialized, recovering traditional knowledge and practices of the Galician peasantry, like the collective management of the common good, mutual help in farm works and in response to common problems of any nature, the movment promotes recovery and conservation of a great diversity of species and varieties indigenous or adapted to the local ecosystems, or the establishment of forms of direct and nearby commercialization.

Environmental culture. In addition, these initiatives disseminate and promote the values and practices of environmentalism, especially around issues related to food. Indeed, they also support and disseminate other related struggles, against polluting industries and predatory natural resource exploitations (minning, timber and paper industry, energy production, etc.). Moreover, they go beyond the standards of the official organic agriculture, integrating criteria of proximity, temporality, an adaptation of crops, the closing of natural cycles or protection and conservation of wild vegetal and animal species that interact with their farms.

Community culture. One of the outstanding features of these initiatives is their concern in recovering and promoting the consolidation of community links that have traditionally marked social life in rural contexts in Galicia and which are currently seen as deteriorating. Understanding the community as the best context of relation and action makes them organize in collective projects and processes between related initiatives, but also to work for promoting a community lifestyle in places where they develop their daily activities.

Democratic culture. As has been observed, deepening the democratization of relationships is another of the characteristic values of these initiatives, both in developing socioeconomic relationships that support the alternative agri-food systems that try to build, as in the internal functioning of the collective projects and articulation processes that they drive.

Culture of sustainability. Consistently, we understand that the agroecological movement in Galicia coincides perfectly with our conception of Culture of Sustainability, and that is also why we consider it a strategic element for promoting the movement between citizens across diet and their participation in the rebuilding of local agri-food systems.

Because of all this, and still in further expanding and developing this research project, we foresee that the agroecological movement can be a collective of great interest for the development of Environmental Education in Galicia. Particularly as it transcends a consumer education framework to draw on other educational strategies that are able to promote and support the configuration of socially and environmentally sustainable agri-food systems. In this way, we are advancing the establishment of a Culture of Sustainability in Galician society. Specifically, we consider especially interesting the discourses and practices raised by these initiatives, as well as meetings, markets and other events organized as spaces where further Environmental Education activities can be developed.

Finally, it is necessary to emphasize the engagement that Environmental Education must undertake to support and to promote the consolidation and joint development of this movement, while also completely respecting its autonomy and self-management, as well as to offer encourage as it it assumes a socio-educative role : so that we may share with them our resources, tools and strategies as field.

NOTES

[1] https://viacampesina.org/en/
[2] https://www.facebook.com/mercadoentreluscoefusco
[3] https://www.facebook.com/4ponlas/
[4] https://www.facebook.com/Mercado-da-Terra-160291954066359/
[5] There is a list made by *MaOs Innovación Social* that includes other types of events related to organic farming in the following link: http://maos.gal/recursos/mercados-ecoloxicos-de-galiza/
[6] https://www.oruralquerexente.net
[7] https://afenda.org/

REFERENCES

Bisquert, K. M. (2016). Migración y conflictos armados. Expresiones de violencia del sistema agroalimentario. *Soberanía Alimentaria. Biodiversidad y Culturas, 26*, 5–9.
Calle, Á. (2011). *Democracia radical: entre vínculos y utopías*. Barcelona: Icaria.
Calle, Á., Gallar, D., & Candón, J. (2013). Agroecología política: la transición social hacia sistemas agroalimentarios sustentables. *Revista de Economía Crítica, 16*, 244–277.
Calle, Á., Soler, M., & Rivera, M. (2011). Soberanía alimentaria y Agroecología Emergente: la democracia alimentaria. In A. Calle (Ed.), *Democracia radical. Entre vínculos y utopías* (pp. 213–238). Barcelona: Icaria.
Calle, A., Soler, M., Vara, I., & Gallar, D. (2012). La desafección al sistema agroalimentario: ciudadanía y redes sociales. *Interface: a journal for and about social movements, 4*(2), 459–489.
Caride, J. A., & Meira, P. Á. (2001). *Educación Ambiental y Desarrollo Humano*. Barcelona: Ariel.
Council Regulation (EC) N° 834/2007 of 28 June 2007 on organic production and labelling of organic products and repealing Regulation (EEC) n° 2092/91. Retrieved from http://eur-lex.europa.eu/legal-content/EN/TXT/?uri=uriserv:OJ.L_.2007.189.01.0001.01.ENG
Cuéllar, M., & Sevilla, E. (2013). La soberanía alimentaria: la dimensión política de la Agroecología. En, M., Cuéllar, Á., Calle, & D. Gallar (Eds.), *Procesos hacia la soberanía alimentaria* (pp. 15–32). Barcelona: Icaria.
Dobson, A. (2003). *Citizenship and the environment*. Oxford: OUP.
Faber, J., Schroten, A., Bles, M., Sevenster, M., Markowska, A., Smit, M., ... van't Riet, J. (2012). *Behavioural climate change mitigation options and their appropriate inclusion in quantitative longer term policy scenarios*. Delft: CE Delft.
FAO. (2016). *El estado mundial de la agricultura. Cambio Climático, agricultura y seguridad alimentaria*. Roma: FAO. Retrieved from http://www.fao.org/3/a-i6030s.pdf
Ganuza, E., Olivari, L., Paño, P., Buitrago, L., & Lorenzana, C. (2010). *La democracia en acción. Una visión desde las metodologías participativas*. Madrid: Antígona Procesos Participativos.
Garnett, T. (2011). Where are the best opportunities for reducing greenhouse gas emissions in the food system (including the food chain)? *Food Policy, 36*, S23–S32.
Gómez-Benito, C., & Lozano, C. (2014). Constructing food citizenship: Theoretical premises and social practices. *Italian Sociological Review, 4*(2), 135–156.
GRAIN. (2014). *La soberanía alimentaria: 5 pasos para enfriar el planeta y alimentar a su gente*. Retrieved from https://www.grain.org/article/entries/5100-la-soberania-alimentaria-5-pasos-para-enfriar-el-planeta-y-alimentar-a-su-gente

Greenwood, D. (2000). De la observación a la investigación-acción participativa: una visión crítica de las prácticas antropológicas. *Revista de Antropologia Social, 9*, 27–49.
Herrero, Y., Cembranos, F., & Pascual, M. (2011). *Cambiar las gafas para mirar el mundo*. Madrid: Libros en Acción.
Intergovernmental Panel on Climate Change. (2015). Technical summary. In O. Edenhofer, R. Pichs-Madruga, Y. Sokona, E. Farahani, S. Kadner, K. Seyboth, A. Adler, I. Baum, S. Brunner, P. Eickemeier, B. Kriemann, J. Savolainen, S. Schlömer, C. von Stechow, T. Zwickel, & J. C. Minx (Eds.), *Climate change 2014: Mitigation of climate change. Contribution of working group III to the fifth assessment report of the intergovernmental panel on climate change*. Cambridge: Cambridge University Press. Retrieved from http://www.ipcc.ch/pdf/assessment-report/ar5/wg3/ipcc_wg3_ar5_technical-summary.pdf
Johnston, J. L., Fanzo, J. C., & Cogill, B. (2014). Understanding sustainable diets: A descriptive analysis of the determinants and processes that influences diets and their impacts on health, food security, and environmental sustainability. *Advances in Nutrition: An International Review Journal, 5*, 418–429.
Llerena, G. (2015). *Agroecología escolar. Fundamentación teórica y estudio de casos sobre el desarrollo de huertos escolares con el referente de la agroecología* (PhD thesis). Universitat Autònoma de Barcelona, Bellaterra.
Malo, M. (Ed.). (2004). *Nociones comunes. Experiencias y ensayos entre investigación y militancia*. Madrid: Traficantes de Sueños.
Max-Neef, M. (1994). *Desarrollo a escala humana: conceptos, aplicaciones y algunas reflexiones*. Barcelona: Icaria.
Morales, J. (Coord.). (2011). *La Agroecología en la construcción de alternativas hacia la sustentabilidad rural*. Jalisco: ITESO.
Orellana, I., Sauvé, L., Marleau, M. E., & Labraña, R. (2008). La recherche critique en education relative à l'environnement au sien du mouvement de résistance sociale face au projet minier Pascua Lama. *Éducation relative à l'environnement, 7*, 23–47.
Patel, R. (2008). *Obesos y famélicos. El impacto de la globalización en el sistema alimentario mundial*. Barcelona: Los Libros del Lince.
Ríos, R. (2014). Os circuitos curtos de comércio de alimentos na Galiza atual: na procura de alternativas ao oligopólio da distribuiçom. *Icede Working Paper Series, 10*.
Sauvé, L. (2014). Educación ambiental y ecociudadanía. Dimensiones claves de un proyecto político-pedagógico. *Revista Científica, 18*, 12–23.
Sauvé, L., Naoufal, N., & Auzou, E. (2013). *Pour une écoalimentation: dix belles histoires*. Québec: Presses de l'Université du Québec.
Sevilla, E. (2006). *Desde el pensamiento social agrario*. Córdoba: UCOPress.
Sevilla, E. (2012). *Canales cortos de comercialización alimentaria en Andalucía*. Sevilla: Fundación Pública Andaluza Centro de Estudios Andaluces.
Sevilla, E., & Soler, M. (2010). Agroecología y soberanía alimentaria: alternativas a la globalización agroalimentaria. In M. Soler & C. Guerrero (Coords.), *Patrimonio Cultural en la nueva ruralidad andaluza* (pp. 190–217). Sevilla: Junta de Andalucía.
Shiva, V. (2001). *Biopiratería. El saqueo de la naturaleza y del conocimiento*. Barcelona: Icaria.
Shiva, V. (2007). *Las nuevas Guerras de la Globalización: Semillas, agua y formas de vida*. Madrid: Popular.
Shiva, V. (2008). *Los monocultivos de la mente*. México: Fineo.
Simón, X., Copena, D., & Rodríguez, L. (2010). Construyendo alternativas agroecológicas al sistema agroalimentario global: acción y reacción en el Estado español. *Revista de Economía Crítica, 10*, 138–175.
Van der Ploeg, J. D. (2010). *Nuevos campesinos. Campesinos e imperios alimentarios*. Barcelona: Itaca.
Vargas, G., Barba, M., & Díaz, A. (2015). Cultura da sostibilidade e cooperación ao desenvolvemento en centros educativos de Galicia e República Dominicana. *AmbientalMENTEsustentable, 2*(20), 715–731.
Ziegler, J. (2006). *El imperio de la vergüenza*. Madrid: Taurus.

Kylyan M. Bisquert
SEPA-interea (Social Pedagogy and Environmental Education Research Group)
Pedagoy and Didactics Department
Universidade de Santiago de Compostela, Spain

Pablo Á. Meira
SEPA-interea (Social Pedagogy and Environmental Education Research Group)
Pedagoy and Didactics Department
Universidade de Santiago de Compostela, Spain

DIEN KOUAYE OLIVIER

8. THE SACRED SITES OF DAN POPULATIONS IN CÔTE D'IVOIRE

Environmental Conservation Factors

INTRODUCTION

Recent studies reveal that Côte d'Ivoire is faced with diverse environmental issues which include the disappearance of the forest cover, the impoverishment of the soils, water eutrophication and air pollution, urban area degradation, but also with the harmful effects of climate change (DSRP, 2009; Boko, 2010). In this context of ongoing natural resources degradation, special attention is being paid to traditional practices in the management of the environment which are now seen as alternatives to be explored for the conservation of ecosystems and biodiversity (Ibo, 2005). Indeed, these practices have, for millennia, permitted the conservation of spaces deemed "sacred" and shelter many plant and animal species (Yéo, 2016). However, few studies directly highlight the connections between these practices and the conservation of the environment performed to date.

This work has been motivated by the insufficiency of scientific data on the matter. Thus, this study of the Dan populations in Yorodougou sub-prefecture will bring about answers on the functions and the social, cultural and religious values of the sacred natural sites on the one hand, and on traditional upholding and perpetuation systems and the associated ancestral cultural values of those sites, on the other hand. This could lead to the suggestion of adequate mechanisms for the management of the sacred natural sites.

METHODOLOGY

Field of Study

The study field is made up of the villages of Gangbapleu, Gbangompleu, Samapleu, Yèpleu, Yorodougou and Zokoma. They are all located in the new Yorodougou sub-prefecture in the department of Sipilou.[1] All of these villages were created before colonial time and their native populations are the Dan who belong to the Mandé ethnocultural group. The Dan in Yorodougou sub-prefecture are organized in patrilineal lineages or clans. All of them identify themselves with a common ancestor and are characterized by the respect of many prohibitions and the possession of one or several masks which help to tell them apart.

The founding ancestor of Yorodougou's villages was named *Plé*, a native of one component of the Dan group called Tompimins and based in the mountains around the city of Touba. *Plé* settled in the region long before colonial time. To protect himself against enemies, he set up a camp on the mountain *Klo*, in the vicinity of the present village of Samapleu. Then, he married a woman who gave birth to seven (7) sons. As they grew up, *Plé's* sons scattered in the region creating different villages according to soothsayers' recommendations. These villages have been chosen because they are located in the forest region in the west of Côte d'Ivoire which is considered as one of the last representations of what the Ivorian natural forest once was (Arnaud & Sournia, 1979). The native populations of these villages still practice cultural rites involving a variety of sacred places.

Surveyed Population

To reach this study's main objective, which is comprehending, through sacred natural sites, traditional practices and behaviors which testify to the management and conservation of the environment by the Dan populations in Côte d'Ivoire, a survey was carried out among three main groups of people according to criteria of knowledge and responsibility in the management of those sites:

- The guardians or trustees, that is initiated persons who have been assigned special responsibilities towards those sacred natural sites by tradition. Twenty-five (25) people were surveyed in this category (one guardian per site).
- Traditional chiefs, especially village and land chiefs who, according to the Dan tradition, are from the village founder's close lineage. Eighteen (18) people were surveyed in this category.
- Nephew (or *bèhè* in local language) who are in direct contact with the sacred forests guardians and who are sometimes their confidents and loudhailers. They are in charge of the maintenance of the sacred sites and of the successful organization of ceremonies. Eleven (11) people were surveyed here.

In total, 54 people have been surveyed in this study.

Data Collection Technique

Data collection for this study has been made through the research techniques, of literature review, interviews and participant observation.

For the literature review, we focused on available publications, namely from Senegal, Guinea, Cameroon and Côte d'Ivoire. Those documents were accessed on the internet.

Interview guides were used to carry out semi-structured interviews and focus-group interviews that, favored the construction of discourse rather than short answers. The interviews permitted the respondents to talk quite freely about the subject matter.

The observation regime included visiting sacred natural sites and participating in traditional ceremonies. This permitted researchers to grasp the events in their natural context of occurrence namely the practices governing the access to those sites.

The data collection was conducted in two stages. The first took place from September to October 2016. At this time, we examined written sources and interviewed traditional chiefs and sacred site's guardians. This stage permitted us to better be immersed in the local realities and to select the sacred sites on the ground for their importance to the villages and their relevance for highlighting practices, behaviors and representations testifying to the management and conservation of the environment. It also permitted the preparation of the second stage which was carried out from January to February 2017. On this occasion, we went deeper into our investigations through the visit of the shortlisted sites, the participation in traditional ceremonies and by conducting the focus-groups.

Data Analysis Methods

The data collected during our investigation were analyzed with a qualitative analysis method. On this account, the interviews conducted with the help of a portable recorder were first fully transcribed using the Word software. Then, the data were classified and the corpus obtained was the subject of a thematic content analysis. At this stage, we preferred phenomenological and ethnological approaches. The phenomenological one seems most appropriate, as Kragbe and Tahoux (2010) posit, for restoring the meaning of social phenomena in the exploitation of natural habitats and for how local communities perceive biodiversity and natural resources. As for the ethnological approach, it permitted us to focus on the culture that shapes the conduct of our subjects. What is predominant here, is their words chosen and the respondents' discourse.

FINDINGS

Characteristics of Sacred Natural Sites of Dan Populations in Yorodougou

The study listed forty-two (42) sacred natural sites of Dan populations in the Yorodougou sub-prefecture. These special places drew attention due to a certain homogeneity. They are present in all villages, and in each one of them, these sites occupy an important place in tradition and are linked to a more or less remote past. Beside this uniqueness, the large variety of sites leads to specific appellations and usages linked to their assigned functions and to their respective social, cultural and religious values. Among those sacred sites, there are five (5) watercourses in the village of Gangbapleu (Ouédieu, Tiapleuyigbêba, Gueukpalé, Téguieu and Dêngbê) which belong to Gouépleu, Tiapleu, Toueu, Gboampleu and Guê families respectively. There is also a forest (Danta) hosting the graves of the dignitaries of the village. In Gbangompleu, there exists two (2) mountains (Lohô and Blagbeu) and two (2) watercourses revered by the whole population. We can also mention two (2) water sources, respectively belonging to the Koné (village founder's family) and Touré families. In Samapleu, in the Plé or Gbapleu family which is the founding ancestor's family, the researchers noticed two (2) watercourses (Doueuhiba and Mouhounba), one (1) cave (Gangbihileu, one (1) forest (Danta) and one (1) mountain Gangbo). In addition to these sites, two (2) water sources have been mentioned and they respectively belong to the Golé and Monlé families. In the locality of Yèpleu, one (1) forest belonging to three (3) families (Bêdeu, Gbeu Kessé and Peudeu) from the village founder's lineage. Along with these sites, we counted one (1) water source (Nonbôhibâ) belonging to the Soumahoro Plétomba family, two (2) forests (Guépleu and Oulakpanlé), one (1) watercourse (Yétrouba) and one (1) cave (Goueugondrileu) which are properties of the Oulaleu family, and two (2) water sources (Zonyoglouleu and Zooyiba) worshiped, respectively, by the Zonneu and Zôôleu families. In Yorodougou, a women-owned forest (Kohounpleu) has been mentioned. Besides, the existence of some sacred sites owned by each one of the biggest two families of the village has been reported. Thus, the Lôhbanous own three (3) watercourses (Souêba, Jahaba and Munzeuhiba), one (1) mountain (Yékayan) and one (1) forest (Danta). As for the Toueu family, they own one (1) sacred mountain (Minhatôba). Finally, in the village of Zocoma, there are two (2) sacred forests (Goueupeulougogui and Kpoklobâ) which shelter the grave of the dignitaries of the village. Moreover, there are sacred sites belonging to each large family. In the Soumahoro family, the family of the village founder's ancestor, one (1) forest (Gbêguilé) and one (1) watercourses (Zouzeuguinbâ) are recorded. Then, in the Diomandé family, three (3) sacred forests are mentioned (Gôgôguinon, Zokonbli and Fagoualé).

Every one of these sacred natural sites possesses several places where ceremonies and rituals in honor of the deities and the spirits of the ancestors are organized according to special situations or on dignitaries' initiative. If we consider the sacredness given to them, three (3) types of sacred natural sites can be identified, to wit the sites hosting the graves of the ancestors and used as burial places for the dignitaries of the village, the sites where the masks live and the places for special practices.

Functions and Value of the Sacred Natural Sites among Dan Populations of Yorodougou

In the traditional society of the Dan of Yorodougou, sacred natural sites are deemed as meeting places with deities and the spirits of the ancestors who have the power to intervene any time in the livings' lives. Members of a given family feel connected to these immaterial forces through the trustee of the sites, who is usually an adult, wise and reserved person and who has scrupulous respect for traditional values.

Generally speaking, in Dan populations of Yorodougou, the natural sites sacredness lies not only in the connections they permit to establish with the deities and the

Table 8.1. Typology of sacred natural sites of Dan populations in Yorodougou. Investigations in Yorodougou, September to October 2016–January to February 2017

	Forests	Mountains	Water sources	Watercourses	Caves
Burial places	Danta (3)* Goueupeulougogui Kpoklobâ Kohounpleu				
Masks' residence	Gué Bli Guépleu				
Places for special practices	Sandeukoueuleu Oulakpanlé Gbêguilé Gôgôguinon Zokonbli Fagoualé	Lohô Blagbeu Gangbo Yékayan Minhatôba	Doubonleu Doungoualé Nonbôhibâ Zonyoglouleu Zooyiba	Ouédieu Tiapleuyigbêba Gueukpalé Téguieu Dêngbê Zranmiy Goyi Doueuhiba Mouhounba Dogbahi Tomaha Yétrouba Souêba Jahaba Munzeuhiba Zouzeuguinbâ	Gangbihileu Goueugondrileu

* *Three sacred forests have the same name in different villages*

spirits of the ancestors but also in the functions they fulfill for the community. There are four (04) main functions as described by the study populations. The first one is religious and is concerned with the sacred natural sites worshiping at important events such as initiation, the search for answers to everyday problems (search for equilibrium, warding off misfortunes, appeasing the wrath of the spirits or asking for blessings). The second, the political function, is focused on legislation and ruling the community's life: sacred natural sites meeting places for the dignitaries and places where important decisions for the village are made; whatever decision made in these sacred places is binding on every villager. The third one, of a cultural nature, proceeds from the fact that sacred natural sites are conservation places of ancient objects and venues of knowledge transmission. Finally, the fourth function which is a social one, lies in the fact that the different lineages or large families of the villages identify themselves and develop membership links in reference to the sacred natural sites they are associated with.

D. K. OLIVIER

Traditional Systems of Conservation and Management of Sacred Natural Sites among Dan Populations of Yorodougou

The sacred natural sites as a whole are called *dègbalè*, which is the translation for a different quality the sacred and implies a spatial distinction. Thus, *dègbalè* (sacred space) is opposed to *dèwèlè* which designates the ordinary space where all kinds of activities are allowed (farming, logging, hunting, etc.). Beyond this common denomination, every sacred natural site has a name related to the story of the village or to particular circumstances justifying the attachment of the populations to it. Thus, places of the first encounter between the village founder's ancestor and protective deities, places for confession, propitiatory places, thanksgiving places and fulfilment places. Before starting any ceremony on these sites, the populations conform to an invocation ritual in the honor of the deities and the spirits of the ancestors who inhabit them. That ritual is called *dôhôn* and is important to ensure the protection and the safety of the guests and the success of the ceremony. It is carried out by the manager of the site who is the driving belt between the people and the spiritual forces. On this account, he is given a special treatment. For instance, when he dies, the news of his death is not broken directly. It is done so by means of a metaphor. It must not be said that he is dead, but it must be said under such circumstances that he has gone to "*danta*". The interment strictly takes place in private with the initiated people and it is impossible for the public to see or recognize his grave.

In addition to the existence of a specific vocabulary, the conservation and the management of the sacred natural sites of the Dan population of Yorodougou are guaranteed by a social organization which gives prominence to family or lineage initiates hierarchy. Indeed, in all villages of Yorodougou, the assignment and the advantage of the power as the responsible for or the manager of the sacred sites, rest on the restricted circle of the oldest insiders. This power is granted after consultation of the deities and of the spirits of the ancestors who are the only ones to have the ability to reveal the name of the most qualified person to manage a sacred site. Therefore, the sacred site responsible or manager is a person who, though living a common life, is surrounded by mystery and inspires fear in populations. He is responsible for carrying out ritual functions on the sacred natural sites and perpetuating the tradition.

During his term, responsibility for the sacred site is assisted by his nephews from the lineage or from the family in charge of the maintenance of the sites and of the organization of ceremonies and rituals taking place there. Moreover, he is supported by notables consisting of people coming from the village's large families. The latter are chosen on the ground of their age and their ability to express their different families' concerns to the deities and spirits of the ancestors.

Dan populations of Yorodougou have also set up rules and interdicts ensuring the protection of their sacred natural sites. Thus, they use still closed terminal bud palm leaves to tell apart these sites from those common to all. These leaves, horizontally attached to two pieces of wood, constitute a curtain to deny access to the site. Their presence not only indicates the inviolability of the site, but also the presence of deities and spirits of the ancestors.

The ability to communicate with the deities and the spirits of the ancestors is gained through initiation rites which start in boys by circumcision between 7 and 15 years of age. This practice which takes place on the sacred natural sites (generally in the forest) is surrounded by quite a lot of secrets which the recipients are to keep preciously. During the subsequent retreat period, the youngsters are led by elders and the masks' dignitaries. They are taught how to be a man and also the restrictions contributing to protect the environment. This comes to down mainly to the prohibition to exploit the sacred natural sites, to kill totem animals or to kill a pregnant animal.

Figure 8.1. Example of sacred natural sites of Dan populations in Yorodougou

In the villages of Yorodougou, resource exploitation is completely denied on some sacred natural sites, except for specific moments when they become the focus of ritual practices and samplings are allowed on other sites under precise rules. Not abiding by these rules and interdicts brings about consequences for the guilty ones. To avoid being exposed to the wrath of the deities and of the spirits of the ancestors, the latter can be forgiven by the community by making sacrifices and by giving donations in kind, worthy of the offence. In the event of a minor act, the inflicted punishment is made up of a donation of 7 white kola nuts, some rice powder and a white rooster. The financial value of such a donation is estimated at 15,000 CFA francs. If it is a serious offence such as the violation the site secrecy, namely by a woman, the purification rite requires the payment of 1,000 CFA francs representing prosternation (tôbli), a request for the acceptance of the offering with

5,000 CFA francs (tôbliguipeu), the payment of a 25,000 CFA francs fine (tôhoun) and the donation of a child of age. Besides, in the course of the expiation ceremony, the guilty one remains in prosternation posture, his arms crossed in the back, until being granted pardon by the dignitaries of the violated site. If the profanation occurs on sites where the masks are sheltered, the offender is likely to be cast a spell. To prevent this, he shall stand on one foot and beg for the mercy of the notables through the donation of a dog, a white chicken and 4 white kola nuts.

Many anecdotes related to the mysterious consequences of the sacred natural sites profanation and the non-performance of sacrifices and of required donations permeate the populations' everyday tales. These anecdotes are passed on orally and contribute to strengthen the attention given to the sacred natural sites. For example, a story goes that the managers of a mining exploration company accessed the sacred site of *Gangbihileu* without previously informing the village, and that, once they got onto the site, all their devices got damaged by the genies. There is also the story of a man who persisted in killing and eating monkeys found on a tree adjoining the river *Jahaba* and who died the following day in that watercourse.

Table 8.2. Modes of management of the sacred natural sites of Dan populations of Yorodougou. Investigations in Yorodougou, September to October 2016 and January to February 2017

Types of sites	Interdicts	Types of protection
Burial places	No exploitation No women No hat No red garments No griots	complete
Masks' residence	No exploitation No women No hat	complete
Places for special practices	No red garments No exploitation No shoes No griots	partial

Pressures and Threats to the Sustainable Management of the Sacred Natural Sites of the Dan Populations of Yorodougou

The pressures and threats pertaining to the sustainable management of the sacred natural sites of the Dan populations of Yorodougou are mainly of demographics and land settlement. Indeed, long remaining stable, this sub-prefecture experienced an fluctuation in its population during the military-political crisis in Côte d'Ivoire from 2002 to 2011. That crisis caused the arrival of massive non-native and immigrant populations who settled mostly in rural areas in search of farming lands. The anarchic occupation of farming lands and the development of perennial crops (namely cocoa) which followed as a main impact was the total or partial annexation of many sacred sites relatively well preserved prior to these migrations. Tensions between native and immigrant populations concerning the destruction of those sacred natural sites were tangible in most villages at the time of our survey. Thus, it may be said that the traditional system of conservation and management of sacred natural sites of Dan populations of Yorodougou is somehow called into question at present, mostly since the land of which they could only have the right to use so far, has now been turned into a commodity there.

Figure 8.2. Traces of farming activities in the sacred natural sites of Yorodougou

DISCUSSION

As demonstrated by the findings of our work, the villages of Yorodougou abound in multiple sacred natural sites to which Dan populations assign religious, political, cultural and social functions. The abundance of this kind of sites could mainly be explained by the fact African cultures derive their vitality, their spiritual and immaterial treasures from the relationship they have with nature and in particular with those sacred places (Sow et al., 2011). Thus, those sites not only testify to the cultural dynamism of those populations, but they also express a certain worldview from which populations gain their equilibrium at the psycho-sociological level.

Each one of the sacred natural sites is the focus a specific denomination beside its common appellation. This could imply that the populations of Yorodougou are aware of the existence of the constituents of the environment; as naming indicates that the subject has an idea of what is named. This idea has particularly been highlighted by Sawadogo (2012) in his work on traditional practices of environment management by population in Burkina-Faso.

At the level of the regulation of the interactions between individuals and the sacred natural sites, the traditional management system set up by the populations of Yorodougou involves initiation rites, cults, prohibitory norms, and reparation requirements in the event of infraction and anecdotes. This system is similar to the one described by Claudette et al. (2017) concerning marine and coastal resources conservation in traditional environments by Diola populations in Lower Casamance (in the south of Senegal) and it suggests, as noticed in these authors, that it first aims at preserving those important cultural places, the harmony with the ancestors, the genies and deities. However, the findings of our study show that through this same traditional management by Dan populations of Yorodougou, natural resources (animals and plants) located on those sacred natural sites are relatively well preserved. They confirm work giving a prominent role to sacred sites in the conservation of ecosystems and of biodiversity (Kokouet Sokpon, 2006; Tchouamo, 1998; Wangari, 1996 cited in Malan, 2009). In the same context, Yéo (2016) notices in his investigations that the interdicts enunciated by the guardian of the custom contribute to preserve the forest, the fauna and the flora. Every man, woman or child knows, from very young age, that, in those forests, it is not permissible to cut or pick up fruits, deadwood, even more so to cut down green wood, to hunt, to fish or kill a pregnant animal, to set fire (even accidentally), to have a farm or sell medicinal plants. Thus, though their first objective is the protection of the environment, those sacred natural sites indirectly contribute to the conservation of animal and plant natural resources, for their very functions have a positive impact on the environment (Diatta et al., 2017).

CONCLUSION

In the dynamics of enhancing ancestral practices deemed worthy of interest today, the study of the sacred natural sites of Dan populations of Yorodougou aimed at highlighting the connections between those practices and the conservation of the environment. In the light of our findings, it can be stated that in the Dan populations, there is a real potential for the conservation of biodiversity through the knowledge they have developed to preserve those sites from anthropogenic pressures. This knowledge is characterized by the denomination of sites with reference to their social, cultural and religious functions and values, the regulation of the interactions between individuals and the sacred sites and to the existing multiple anecdotes which strengthen the fear about those sites.

In view of the agricultural threat which is hanging over these sites at present, protecting them cannot be considered without a proactive attitude. In this perspective, the steps which seem necessary to be taken are the development of a participatory management policy by including into the national system of protected areas, the inventory of their fauna and flora potential and a clear definition of their ecological limits.

NOTE

[1] The department of Sipilou belongs to the Tonkpi Region, in the Mountain District in the far west of Côte d'Ivoire. It was created from a subdivision of Biankouma's department.

REFERENCES

Adou Yao, C. Y., Kpangui, K. B., Kouao, K. J., Adou, L. M. D., Vroh, B. T. A., & N'Gussan, K. E. (2013). Floristic diversity and the value of the Bokasso sacred forest (Eastern Côte d'Ivoire) for conservation. *VertigO – The Environment Sciences Electronic Journal* [Online], *13*(1).

Arnaud, J., & Sournia, G. (1979, July–September). Forest of Côte-d'Ivoire: An endangered natural resource. In *Overseas Notebooks, No. 127 – 32nd year*, 281–301.

Boko, N. K. (2010, September 20–23). *Biodiversity conservation and unequal access to "sacred woods" in the north of Côte d'Ivoire, under climate change circumstances.* Paper presented at 15th International Environmental Assessment Conference, Paris, France.

Claudette, S. D., Malick, D., Charlotte, K., & Amadou, A. S. (2017, September 11). Natural sacred sites and conservation of marine and coastal resources in Diola traditional milieu (Senegal). *Ethnoecology Journal* [Online], *11*.

Claudine, F. (1999). "Natural" sacred sites, cultural diversity and biological diversity. *Symposium Report NSS*, *7*(1), 78–81.

François, M. D. (2009, September). Traditional religion and sustainable management of floristic resources in Côte d'Ivoire : The Ehotilé case, residents living near the National Park of Ehotilé Island. *VertigO – The Environment Sciences Electronic Journal* [Online], *9*(2) (accessed 30 May 2014).

IBO, J. (2005, June). Ecologist non-governmental organisations' contribution to the management of sacred sites in Côte d'Ivoire: The Green Cross experience. *VertigO – The Environment Sciences Journal*, *6*(1).

Juhé-Beaulaton, D. (2009). An unknown urban heritage, memories trees, sacred forests and plant gardens of Porto Novo (Benin) Sciences Presses Po (P.F.N.S.P.). *"Autrepart"*, *3*(51), 75–98.

Kragbe, A. G., & Tahoux, T. (2010). The sacralization of nature in the management of the environment, the case of Dida populations in Côte d'Ivoire. *Social Sciences Journal* (Humour and derision), *43*.

Republic of Côte d'Ivoire. (2009). *Strategy for the revival of the development and for poverty reduction.*

Sawadogo, R. C. (2012). *Knowledge of traditional practices of management of the environment: Prerequisite and sociological basis of the effectiveness of present conservation strategies.* IRD Éditions.

Sow, M., Camara, L., & Camara, O. A. (2011). *Identification and characterization of coastal and marine natural sacred sites in West Africa.* Guinea report.

Yeo, A. D. (2016). *Custom to the rescue of the environment: The example of sacred forests in Senoufo populations in Côte d'Ivoire.* Research notes.

Dien Kouaye Olivier
Centre de Recherche en Ecologie
Université Nangui Abrogoua d'Abidjan
Côte d'Ivoire

BARRY WOOD

9. FROM THE BUBBLE TO THE FOREST

Nature School Environmental Education

INTRODUCTION

Awareness of the human impact on nature began in the nineteenth century, but recognition of the severity of environmental problems traces to well-documented studies in the decades after WW II. In the 1970s, under the impetus of the United Nations Education, Scientific, and Cultural Organization (UNESCO), Environmental Education (EE) emerged as a worldwide priority, though the various declarations and charters tended to address educational administrators and assume EE as a subject to be taught within the traditional education system. This amounts to an implicit endorsement of the classroom as a sufficient site for environmental education. But the indoor classroom, the traditional school system, and the dominant educational establishment is a certification body. As a state-funded system, brick-and-mortar schools certify children, adolescents, and college graduates for employment in the industrial-age technosphere – the source and ongoing instrument of overconsumption, energy waste, atmospheric and ocean pollution, biodiversity loss, and general environmental degradation.

Alongside these developments, a less known tradition of outdoor education has emerged. In the 1920s, outdoor schooling developed against a romanticized background of nature and rural living. People living in villages and small towns with childhood memories of countryside and farmsteads chose outdoor schooling for their children. Trekking and camping gained popularity with the establishment of national parks, recreational camp grounds, and the Appalachian Trail in 1937. As outdoor schools and forest kindergartens emerged, the benefits for children – physical, social, mental and emotional – were recognized and acknowledged and documented. But research has uncovered other benefits. A childhood of deep immersion in nature is common to the classical environmentalists from John Muir to Al Gore, and contemporary research with ecologists shows "significant life experiences" of nature regularly cited as instrumental in their choice of profession. This chapter suggests that Outdoor Education and Forest Kindergartens provide the best foundation for politically neutral environmental education, and thus ideal as platforms for developing committed environmentalists capable of addressing the wicked problems of environmental degradation.

EARLY NATURALISTS

Recognition of environmental problems began, though sporadically, in the nineteenth century. John Muir, founder of the Sierra Club, may be the symbolic reference point: his *Mountains of California* (1894) brought attention to Yosemite Canyon, the Tuolumne Meadows, and what he called the Big Trees (giant sequoias) scattered through the rugged wilderness of the Sierra Nevada mountains which even then were in danger from logging. But the need for preservation of nature was implicit in Henry David Thoreau's *Walden, or Life in the Woods* (1854), and his excursion books, *A Week on the Concord and Merrimack Rivers* (1849), *The Maine Woods* (1864), *Cape Cod* (1865), and his voluminous journals. Thoreau's most famous quotation, "In wildness is the preservation of the world" from his essay "Walking" (1863) has achieved enduring recognition with Eliot Porter's flagship volume for the Sierra Club, *In Wildness is the Preservation of the World* (1962). John Burroughs' *Signs and Seasons* (1886) and a dozen other books set forth the beauty of nature in language reminiscent of the transcendentalist writer, Ralph Waldo Emerson, with whom his writing is often compared. Theodore Roosevelt's *Wilderness Hunter* (1893), despite the numerous animals he hunted, championed wilderness:

> In hunting, the finding and killing of the game is after all but a part of the whole. The free, self-reliant, adventurous life, with its rugged and stalwart democracy; the wild surroundings, the grand beauty of the scenery, the chance to study the ways and habits of the woodland creatures – all these unite to give to the career of the wilderness hunter its peculiar charm. (1996, p. 329)

Together Thoreau, Burroughs, and Roosevelt forged a tradition of environmental stewardship that continued far into the twentieth century in Rachel Carson's trilogy, *Under the Sea Wind* (1941), *The Sea Around Us* (1951), and *The Edge of the Sea* (1955); Edward Abbey's *Desert Solitaire* (1968); David Rains Wallace's *The Klamath Knot* (1983); and Thomas Berry's *Dream of the Earth* (1988). But alongside these landmarks of environmental writing, a counter tradition was developing, dating perhaps to the pointed indictment of George Perkins Marsh in *Man and Nature* (1864): "Man has too long forgotten that the earth was given to him for usufruct alone, not for consumption, still less for profligate waste .... The ravages committed by man subvert the relations and destroy the balance which nature had established between her organized and her inorganic creations" (2008, pp. 71, 78). The emblem for profligate destruction is surely an American bird, the most populous on the continent – five billion strong when Europeans arrived. Aldo Leopold identifies 1871 as the year that "pigeon hunters by the scores plied their trade with net and gun, club and salt lick, and", and virtually wiped out an estimated 136 million passenger pigeons in Wisconsin. "It was the last big nesting in Wisconsin, and nearly the last in any state" (1949, pp. 14–15). They were driven to extinction; the last one in captivity, Martha, fell off her roost in a Cincinnati zoo on September 1, 1914. The tragic story is retold by Gene Stratton-Porter, famous for her writings on Limberlost Swamp, in her personal essay, "The Last Passenger Pigeon" (1925).

Full-throated voices detailing environmental stress and degradation broke like a tidal wave following World War II. Three best sellers alerted a whole generation. Fairfield Osborn's *Our Plundered Planet* surveyed humanity's misuse of the environment through forest clearance and over-cultivation of farmlands, pinpointing human blindness to the impact of civilizational development on the planet. It is "amazing", Osborne wrote, "how far one has to travel to find a person, even among those most widely informed, who is aware of the processes of mounting destruction that we are inflicting upon our life's sources" (1948, p. 194). In *The Road to Survival*, William Vogt identified continuing population growth – world population had reached 2.5 billion – with concomitant demand of Earth's resources as a growing crisis that would eventually lead to civilizational disaster. "By excessive breeding and abuse of the land mankind has backed itself into an ecological trap. By a lopsided use of applied science it has been living on promissory notes. Now, all over the world, the notes are falling due. Payment cannot be postponed much longer" (1948, p. 284). A year later, Aldo Leopold published *A Sand County Almanac*, a book that transcends its twelve-month account of a year in the Wisconsin wilds to set forth a "conservation esthetic", a peroration on the value of wilderness, and the first and justly famous "land ethic". Even the use of nature for recreation comes under his scrutiny, for post-War affluence was already leading to a huge increase in travel and overuse of the American wilderness, with trails and access roads progressively pushing farther into wildlife ecosystems. Writing of "our dependency on the soil-plant-animal-man food chain", Leopold remarked that "civilization has so cluttered this elemental man-earth relation with gadgets and middlemen that awareness of it is growing dim. We fancy that industry supports us, forgetting what supports industry" (1949, p. 178).

ENVIRONMENTALISM EMERGES

Environmental awareness resurfaced in the 1960s. A collage of mothers, children, and babies crowded the cover of the January 11, 1960, *Time* magazine with the title "The Population Explosion", visually defining a major theme of the decade. Rachel Carson's *Silent Spring* (1963) introduced another, detailing the impact of pesticides on wildlife that eventually led to a ban on DDT in the United States. Upon election, the environmentally astute President Kennedy appointed Stewart Udall as Secretary of State (1961–1969), then wrote the introduction to his book, *The Quiet Crisis*: "The modern American record in conservation ... came just in time in our own land .... As Mr. Udall's vivid narrative makes clear, the race between education and erosion, wisdom and waste, has not run its course ... we must expand the concept of conservation to meet the imperious problems of the new age" (1963, xii-xiii). President Lyndon Johnson added government authority to environmental concern. Three weeks after his 1965 inauguration, with the shocking mushroom clouds of WW II atomic bombs haunting the background – along with their acquisition by the USSR and China – Johnson delivered his "Special Message to Congress on Conservation and Restoration of Natural Beauty": "Air pollution is no longer confined to isolated places. This generation has altered the composition of the atmosphere on a global scale through radioactive materials and a steady increase in carbon dioxide from the burning of fossil fuels". Through the abbreviated Johnson presidency (1963–1968), Udall inspired six acts signed into law to protect wilderness, endangered species, wild and scenic rivers and ocean coasts, along with the creation of eight national seashores, fifty-six wildlife refuges, and three national parks, culminating in the creation of the Environmental Protection Agency (EPA), officially established during the Nixon administration in 1970.

Meanwhile, under the influence of the alarmist language of Osborn and Vogt, Stanford biologist Paul Ehrlich published *The Population Bomb* (1968), a Malthusian warning which projected crisis and disaster from a world population now approaching 3.5 billion, with no indications of slowdown in the foreseeable future. Perhaps the most striking work of the decade was Robert and Leona Train Rienow's *Moment in the Sun* (1969) which catalogued a plethora of American environmental issues: city blight, excessive river damming, farmland exhaustion, topsoil loss, and wildlife poisoning. The way was paved for the most data-driven, evidence-based compilation, the seventeen-member Club of Rome's *Limits of Growth* (1972), which has been updated twice (1993, 2004). Full of dire scenarios, this work has had a huge influence with 30 million copies sold in 30 languages. Alarming graphs which indicated immanent chaos on every front came under deep criticism, and in fact did not materialize. They might have, except for an effective Green Revolution that dramatically increased food availability worldwide. With food production increased, the Club of Rome's expected hunger and nutrition crisis was delayed, effectively allowing world population to more than double to its present 7.5 billion. But the underlying stresses of the Green Revolution – reliance on single-crop foodstuffs at the expense of genetic diversity, massive amounts of fertilizers applied to counteract soil exhaustion – would eventually catch up.

A decade after *Limits of Growth*, William R. Catton, Jr., published *Overshoot: The Ecological Basis of Revolutionary Change* (1982), where he described what humans have done to the environment: they have exceeded the "carrying capacity" of the planet by an excessive ecological load – the result of overwhelming population numbers combined with an equally overwhelming per capita extraction of earth resources. To this, Mathis Wackernagel and William Rees added a clarifying metaphor in *Our Ecological Footprint* (1996), a volume rich in line drawings which duplicate and crystalize the overshoot theme. Following perspectives drawn from an extended perspective on human history, Catton summarized the "tragic story of human success …. We are already living on an overloaded world. Our future will be a product of that fact … overshoot has already happened" (1982, pp. 17, 213). A third of a century later, we are living in that future.

Even before *Limits to Growth* and *Overshoot*, warnings in the 1960s had laid the foundation for a popular movement in the 1970s. An outrageously romantic response that drew on environmental imagery was a runaway best seller by Yale law professor, Charles Reich – *The Greening of American* – which held out salvation by consciousness change while naively remarking that "the world is ample for all" (1970, p. 166). Publicized by an excerpt in *The New Yorker* (September 26), the book enjoyed momentary countercultural fame, then disappeared, as counterculture perorations of the period tended to do. Meanwhile, a serious, scientifically-based movement was brewing. Building on the activism growing out of the Draft Lottery and Vietnam War protest, Senator Gaylord Nelson proposed the creation of Earth Day on April 22.

This initiative effectively defined 1970 as the year of the environment. *Newsweek* (January 26) heralded the idea with a cover story titled "The Ravaged Environment". *Saturday Review* (March 7) entered the discussion with a cover story titled "Cleaning Humanities Nest" and a cover photo of the earth from space, and a month later (April 4) an essay by Paul and Anne Ehrlich on "The Food-from-the-Sea Myth". *Saturday Review* came back to the environment three times in 1970: The August 1 cover story focused on "The Threat to Life in the Sea"; the September 5 cover pictured a planet with rocket parts circling overhead with the cover story, "The Orbiting Junkyard"; and the December 5 issue provided a note of hope with "Clean Power from Inside the Earth". Attention to the environment spread beyond the American border: a Canadian edition of *Time* (June 29) focused on "Canada's Threatened Environment". Meanwhile, radical publications provided their own predictable spin, blaming industry, corporations, and lending banks for environmental degradation. *Ramparts* (May 1970) published an "Ecology Special" that featured "The Making of a Pollution-Industrial Complex" and "Science and the Gross National Pollution". But the *Ramparts* cover provided the most dramatic blame assessment: a brilliant fire-red photo of a conflagration – the February 25th student burning of the Bank of America in Isla Vista near Santa Barbara, accompanied by a quotation: "The students who burned the Bank of America in Santa Barbara may have done more towards saving the environment than all the Teach-ins put together".

Earth Day itself was prefaced by a compilation of essays in *The Environmental Handbook* (1970) and set the event in an educational context as a "national teach-in on the environment". The general population came to understand that population growth, air and water pollution, aquifer depletion, pesticide poisoning, and the growing crush of automobiles amounted to a new era in history: "the quiet crisis" had become "the perpetual crisis" (Wood 1970), that has been memorialized on April 22 for 48 years. Pogo Possum's line, "We have found the enemy and he is us", may be the most repeated summation – one of the barely humorous perspectives available. Four decades later, the impact of humans as the major geological force on the planet would lead to a name for the contemporary geological period: the Anthropocene.

ENVIRONMENTAL EDUCATION

With environmental issues now framed in educational terms, the United Nations (UN) Secretary-General commissioned a report on "the care and maintenance of a small planet". Authored by René Dubos and Barbara Ward, *Only One Earth* (1972) was published simultaneously in nine languages, in time for the first UN Conference on the Human Environment, held in Stockholm (June 5–12, 1972). The General Assembly set broad parameters, suggesting an emphasis on "stimulating and providing guidelines for action by national and international organizations". The mandate was sweeping; in retrospect, so broad that it lacked focus – a difficulty issuing from the complexity of every task undertaken by the UN: the history, needs, resources, politics, and cultures of nations are so varied that formulation of unified strategies is almost impossible. The conference summary report, praised by President Nixon (June 20), set forth seven proclamations and twenty-six principles that struck a tenuous balance between conservation, elimination of pollution, and attention to social and economic environments in developed and undeveloped regions, with resolutions for a moratorium on whale killing and ocean dumping of waste. In keeping with the sovereignty of member nations, recommendations were couched in general terms: Principle 19 emphasized the importance of "education in environmental matters, for the younger generation as well as adults" as a key component "essential in order to broaden the basis for an enlightened opinion and responsible conduct by individuals, enterprises and communities in protecting an improving the environment in its full human dimension" (UN, 1972, p. 6) This kind of vague idealism set forth without concrete parameters virtually guaranteed that it would rarely be translated into education programs and thus would remain largely unrealized. But the ground was at least cleared for some approach to environmental education – a UN theme that has been reiterated for the last forty years.

Three years after the Stockholm conference, a ten-day workshop was held in Belgrade (October 13–22, 1975). Based on the recent UN formulation of a "new economic order", *The Belgrade Charter* (1975) – subtitled *A Global Framework for Environmental Education* – called for goals and objectives that would "take into account the satisfaction of the needs and wants of every citizen of the earth … [through] the eradication of the basic causes of poverty, hunger, illiteracy, pollution, exploitation and domination". An implicit ideal of sustaining existing lifestyles and extending them to people of the developing world was evident in the emphasis on "measures that will support the kind of economic growth which will not have harmful repercussions on people, that will not in any way diminish their environment and their living conditions". Sustainability here meant protection and extension of the "new economic order" – a necessary prerequisite for a Cold War initiative suspended between Western capitalism and the state-run economies of the USSR and China. Avoiding any definition of this new economic order, the *Charter* called for a "new global ethic" based on "the reform of educational processes … a new environmental education … related to the basic principles outlined in the *United Nations Declaration on the New International Economic Order* [1974]" (Belgrade, 1–2). The vagueness of these "principles" and concomitant difficulty in activating them is evident in their abstract components – Awareness, Knowledge, Attitude, Skills, and Participation – which navigated carefully between competing economic and political interests.

The environment, of course, lies outside all political, economic, or ideological frameworks, but the various sacred cows of sovereign nations continued to exert an influence on educational proposals. Two years after the Belgrade workshop, the United Nations Education, Scientific, and Cultural Organization (UNESCO) organized the world's "first intergovernmental conference on environmental education" which was held in the USSR at Tbilisi, Georgia – a location chosen to establish environmental education as beyond ideological differences. The resulting *Tbilisi Declaration* (1977) has been to some extent forgotten, though it received much mention leading up to its forty-year anniversary (2017) – more mention, one suspects, than careful rereading. Its language retains the difficult-to-apply generalities of its forerunners. It advocates understanding the "economic dimensions ... whereby people may understand and make better use of natural resources in satisfying their needs", wording that again implies sustaining present lifestyles as the benchmark of environmental education. It will be necessary, the report argues, for people to understand the "complex nature of the natural and built environments ... the economic, political, and ecological interdependence of the modern world". Its grandest suggestions included "the development of conduct compatible with the preservation and improvement of the environment ... a closer kink between educational processes and real life ... an interdisciplinary, comprehensive approach which will permit a proper understanding of environmental problems ... [by] all ages and socio-professional groups in the population ... linked with legislation, policies, measures of control, and the decisions that governments may adopt in relation to the human environment" (UNESCO, 1977, pp. 1–2). But these recommendations are defined so nebulously that it is virtually impossible to translate them into a grass-roots educational program or curriculum. Additionally, they address ideas, attitudes, and principles at the level of higher and adult education. How environmental education might occur for children is left untouched.

Undoubtedly, we need to commend UNESCO for its early and continuing focus on environmental education. At the same time, we must recognize that these early declarations and charters have had little impact nationally or internationally, having fallen short of developing an effective educational methodology adaptable on a local or global scale. The later United Nations Conference on Environment & Development, held in Rio de Janerio (June 3–14, 1992), resulted in a 31-chapter report on Sustainable Development, with goals aligned for the year 2000. Chapter 25, "Children and Youth in Sustainable Development", addressed "involvement of today's youth in environment and development decision-making". Its "objectives" focused on increasing enrollment in secondary education and vocational training programs, equal educational opportunity for girls, and avenues for youth involvement in relevant decisions and participation in UN processes. "Children", the report noted in its first acknowledgment that their education might be an important consideration, "will inherit the responsibility of looking after the Earth" and are "highly vulnerable to the effects of environmental degradation" (UN, 1992), but the report lacks any outline of procedures for educating children or how they are to gain cognitive leverage sufficient for exercising their responsibility.

The recent release of the United Nations *Sustainable Development Goals* (2017), with a target date now projected to 2030, was available at the WEEC 2017 in Vancouver. With the anticipation created by earlier charters and declarations, one would expect incisive, precisely defined policies related to environmental education. But Goal 4, "Quality Education", veers away from the actual environment, favoring individual and national goals: to "ensure that all learners acquire the knowledge and skills needed to promote sustainable development, including, among others, through education for sustainable development and sustainable lifestyles". This is placed in a context of politically correct nods to "human rights, gender equality, promotion of a culture of peace and non-violence, global citizenship and appreciation of cultural diversity and of culture's contribution to sustainable development". Forty years after the *Tbilisi Declaration*, it appears that the development of environmental education has stalled at sustainable development goals, which is easily mistranslated in the popular mind as "sustaining" the status quo, though we know that status-quo reliance on fossil fuels, wasteful consumerism, and un-recycled waste disposal must necessarily change.

It is revealing that forty years of UN conference reports, declarations, and charters from 1977 to 2017 made no mention of outdoor education. The idea seems to have not occurred to many. Hundreds of participants – educators, leaders, and politicians from every corner of the globe – have assumed a status-quo educational context: a traditional brick-and-mortar classroom setting. Curricular *content* remained the focus, with environmental education reduced to one more "subject" in competition with basic skills of language and mathematics, social studies and physical education. If the *Declaration* is attended to, it is soon clear that neither the actual environment nor the learner to be educated enters the equation.

Despite this overly generalized language of United Nations charters and declarations, and the confinement of environmental education to one chapter of *Sustainability Development Goals* (SDG), there are slight – very slight – signs that the science establishment may be developing a broader vision. The US based National Science Foundation *Next Generation Science Standards* (2013) include elementary units on the environment for children as early as Kindergarten, though these are so few that any transformation of a child's mind is minimal to nil. But twenty-five years after the Union of Concerned Scientists (UCS) issued a Warning to Humanity (1992), the Alliance of World Scientists (AWS) issued a second warning signed (by the time of press release, October 23, 2017) by 15,364 scientists from 184 counties, with 1,000 signatures being added per month. Among its suggestions, the document includes a quiet, unobtrusive call for "increasing outdoor nature education for children". Someone in the committee that drafted the warning had discovered a new idea: education for children in the outdoors.

THE TECHNOSPHERIC BUBBLE

As a youth growing up in Scarborough, Ontario, I enjoyed exploring on my bicycle. I once followed Warden Avenue to St. Clair and Eglinton Avenue – traffic-free graveled roads running between farmlands stretching across grain fields and pasture to distant barns and farm homes. Two decades later, these had become heavily-trafficked four-lane paved roads lined with factories and stores lit up at night, fronted by huge parking lots. A much-publicized shopping area called "The Golden Mile" marked the consumer supply center for dozens of new subdivisions. Decades later, now in Texas, I have listened to accounts of how Houston's numerous suburbs and malls were once open cropland and forest – about the same time I was exploring open country in Canada. Versions of this rural/urban contrast between Then and Now are familiar to people in nearly every city, especially those whose age provides perspective on the changes. But young people – in fact, anyone under the age of forty – lack this perspective.

Driving my kindergarten grandson to school one morning along Houston's Beltway 8, I am aware of the chasm between my youth and his. He looks out the window at a multi-lane car-congested highway, a concrete center barrier, and sweeping interchanges three or four levels high spreading over hundreds of acres – gazing with calm acceptance at the only world he has ever known: endless housing tracts, high rises, parking lots, and traffic noise, with forest lands, lakes, and running streams a car ride miles away. This is the world he was born into – dominated by crowded malls, urban development, computers, Internet, and smart phones; it is the world hundreds of millions of millennials have been born into. It is their normal world; they are virtually unable to conceive of anything else. "Environment" is a word found in phrases like "home environment", "school environment", and "urban environment"; for many, its larger context of water, air, life, and the earth lie below the level of conscious attention. Angela Hanscom (2016) has assembled research to show that experience in Nature is calming; that it relieves anxiety; that it is therapeutic in smoothing out the fragmented world of the technosphere which is inherently stressful. Happily, my grandson is dealing with the urbanized, industrialized, paved world he was born into; a nurturing family provides an antidote to the jumble of urban life. A forest school, were one available, would be even better.

For his generation, awareness of our real environmental problems is eliminated by what I call "the tyranny of the normal": how can youth, soon to be adults in the workforce, learn to see and understand that their normal world just beyond the car window is disastrously abnormal? Without even knowing it, they are victims of what Richard Louv (2006) so aptly called "nature-deficit disorder". At night in the city, polluted air hides all but the brightest stars; throughout the day, birds perch in long lines on power lines; sounds of nature are blotted out by the roar of eighteen wheelers and engines drilling foundations for still more highway access ramps. This scene, which occupies my grandson's attention, is part of an enormous problem that will affect his world, his future, his children, and coming generations. The dilemma is the recognition that much of it cannot be undone. Schools and workplaces are no longer within walking distance. The movement of people is so voluminous that a radiating wheel of four-lane highways is needed for any venture from home. My grandson now sees this is usual, normal, and quite okay. And for the few who will somehow came to an environmental awareness, will they know how to address the seemingly irresistible fact of mushrooming population, roads congested day and night, more and more pavement, continuous construction, urban expanse – and now the looming fact of global warming?

The environmental foundations of our existence include four interlocking spheres: aquasphere, atmosphere, biosphere, and geosphere – water, air, life, and earth. Working together, they constitute an ecosphere. Moisture-laden clouds formed over oceans are blown ashore where they drop their burden on hills and mountains; streams and rivers carry water through lowlands, replenishing lakes and wetlands, eventually finding a way to the sea where clouds will be replenished. Wind-blown air distributes the Sun's warmth over the land, regulating climate, and delivering energy to every living thing. The biosphere, the sum total of vegetable and animal life, extends to every part of the aquasphere and atmosphere, adding up to as many as 100 million species, providing a food chain from plankton to plant life, trilobites to turtles, and eventually humans. The geosphere underlies the other three, providing mineral nutrients for plant life and habitat for microbial life, with enrichment through volcanic eruptions and erosion of rock providing a foundation for biotic material reconstituted as topsoil. The interaction of these four spheres provides a complex "household" (*ekos*), an *eco-logical* system upon which we depend.

Over the past century, awareness of human dependence on the environment has all but disappeared, and with it knowledge of the environment itself. The reason: increasing human dependence on a fifth sphere – the industrial-age *technosphere*. The term has been adopted in the new millennium for the sum total of the man-made world: houses, vehicles, stores, factories, ports and airports, and the necessary power installations to keep everything going. Life, experience, and employment are dominated by our technospheric surroundings: city workplaces (offices, factories), urban transportation (cars, subways, airplanes), and human structures (roads, subdivisions, shopping malls). Hundreds of cities from America to Africa and Asia with populations in the millions spread across the land for miles in all directions, limiting contact with the natural spheres to landscape available only beyond the most distant suburbs. We are separated from the earth by cushioned car seats, well-resistant chassis, rubber tires, and millions of acres of pavement. This urban technosphere surrounds, immerses, envelops, contains, and isolates us, confining us to an enclosing industrial-age "bubble", an image suggested by Peter Senge's "Life Beyond the Bubble" (2010). Richard Louv expands its connotations based on the smart phone revolution with its network connections to the Internet, social websites, the Cloud, and GPS satellites; together they enclose us in an "electronic bubble" (2012, p. 17). We are containerized.

The Tbilisi Report recognized that "environmental problems lie outside the direct experience of young people. In certain countries ... schools are in urban surroundings and the pupils are cut off from any contact with nature" (UNESCO, pp. 20–21), but it provided no solution to this dilemma. As rural is replaced with urban living, the technosphere exerts an ever greater influence on our children who grow up in the same industrial-age bubble. They are unknowingly containerized, moving from crib to playpen, bedroom, kitchen, family vehicle, to the inside of Walgreen's or Walmart. Once they reach school age they are containerized by the school bus, the classroom, the lunchroom, and the gymnasium. Education – which literally means to escape from traditional containers, to be led-out (*e-ducere*), has beome a process of induction, being led-into (*in-ducere*), enclosed in the technospheric system, where they are "graded" like so much bulldozed terrain until they can be certified for another container – office space, the employee lunch room, or factory workshop in the city.

Meanwhile, the earth has been strip mined, logged, land filled, drilled and fracked to the point of eliminating wildlife habitat, destabilizing hillsides, and causing earthquake tremors from Oklahoma to Italy. Our urbanized, consumer society is engaged in a massive conversion of earth materials for the construction of the technosphere, with exorbitant waste and mountainous landfills, which have become an "intractable environmental issue" (Wood, 2017). The biosphere is shrink wrapped for purchase at the grocery store, sold in decorated planter pots, or fenced in at the city zoo. Nature is outsourced to gardeners who cultivate park plots watered by sprinkler systems. Wildlife is endangered and reduced to programs to "conserve" it by setting aside tracts of "protected" land, with littered roadsides and beaches "adopted" by schoolchildren and volunteers organized to clean up the highways, wash oil off seabirds, and run rescue programs for owls, tigers, bonobos, and whooping cranes. The natural world, too, has been containerized and reduced to footnotes of the technosphere.

FROM THE BUBBLE TO THE FOREST

The forerunner of this chapter was delivered on September 11, 2017, at Lynn Canyon near, Vancouver, located in a 250-hectare (617-acre) temperate rainforest spreading along several miles of rushing water flowing through a deep canyon from mountains to the north. After conversing on outdoor education and forest kindergartens in an open meadow a few yards from the river, we discovered this was the opening day of the *Fresh Air Forest School* which meets on the park upland under towering hemlocks, Douglas-firs, and western red cedars. Children of four and five were busy exploring: a boy balancing on the exposed root of a giant tree trunk; a girl watching something crawling among the leaves – perhaps a banana slug; another trying to spot a chattering squirrel somewhere overhead. Dark-stained picnic benches provided a workspace for projects and handcrafts; canopied spaces assured shelter from rain showers, a regular occurrence in Vancouver where westward running clouds run into the mountains. Of course, it is easy to romanticize pre-Kindergarten children in nature – by a stream, in a meadow, under a canopy of trees – and it may well be this idealism that makes it easy for skeptics to dismiss the Forest School to a "nice idea! … But how will our children learn reading, math, and social studies if they are just playing in the woods?" The question reveals how far we have come from our natural world – how the standard containerized classroom has become so deeply embedded as the educational norm that alternatives are now almost inconceivable.

But the fact is that the school classroom mirrors the larger technospheric context that defines educational goals aligned with occupational tasks – the planning, building, maintenance, repairing, and renovation of an industrial-age technosphere. From a traditional perspective, some observers are apt to doubt that children of the Lynn Canyon *Fresh Air Forest School* will be prepared to work in and maintain the technosphere. That perspective is too small, too conditioned, too lacking in imagination, and too demeaning of an evolving environment that originated and has nurtured life for four billion years, building our bodies, brains and imaginations, evolving our species to cast our vision beyond the stars. While these children are playing in the woods, they are experiencing an original ecological context where humans began; something of profound importance is going on that will enrich not only their later lives, but prepare them for an endangered technospheric world desperately in need of a new vision.

Forest-school education has a logic and value that has been applied too seldom, though it has been understood for more than half a century. Nearly seventy years ago, L. B. Sharp remarked, "Most of the things children learn about are brought to school .... Outdoor education, in its simplest aspect, merely says: Don't try to bring the whole world into the school. Rather take the children to where the world is .... Those things which can best be taught outdoors should there be taught" (1952, pp. 2, 7). Long-time Head of the Outdoor Teacher Education Department at Illinois University, Donald Hammerman, pointed out that "the outdoor school setting provides the natural environment where pupils have the opportunity to come to grips with reality – where close, first-hand observation, independent investigation, analysis of data, and problem solving are the order of the day" (1963, p. 46). James Ward provides a philosophic perspective: "The outdoors has a strong *being quality*, a quality of being real, alive, and in the process of happening. Things can be seen in actual contexts, relationships and processes. One is actually involved in and learning about what *is*. The tangible quality appeals. It pulls the senses .... An infinite number of principles wait to be inferred from the world of natural events" (1968, pp. 118, 121).

Vancouver is the site of another outdoor school, the *Maple Ridge Environmental School* founded in 2011 with the help of grants and support of Simon Fraser University. While many such schools are forest kindergartens, *Maple Ridge* enrolls students up to the seventh grade. It turns out that the idea has a long history: forest schools were first created in Cradon, Laona, and Wabeno, Wisconsin, in the 1920s. The idea was introduced in Sweden and Denmark in the 1950s, and in the 1990s in the United Kingdom, with 140 founded in the UK by 2006 and 180 in Sweden by 2008. New Zealand's *Play and Learn Early Education Programmes* was established in 1995. The American west coast has been aggressive in adopting the idea: *Fiddleheads Forest School* in Seattle was founded in 2012; *Tiny Trees* was operating six outdoor preschools in Seattle parks during the 2016–2017 year, aiming at twenty by 2020. Around the world, forest schools are found in Germany, Scotland,

Japan, and the Indonesian island of Bali. In Puerto Rico, *Bosque Escuela* (Forest School) for youth up to high-school age operates on 150 acres. Forest schools may be located in expansive environments beyond the clutter of the city; the *Juniper Hill Nature Preschool and Forest Kindergarten* operates at Alna, Maine, on 42 acres, but fewer acres of undeveloped urban land may provide a convenient site. In the unlikely environment of New York City, *Brooklyn Forest School* operates three schools in Prospect Park and two in Central Park. Arguably, locating a forest school for children on a patch of wild forest land in an urban setting may be the most environmentally sound use of undeveloped land.

The various locations of existing Forest Schools lead us to further considerations of how and where. Inner city institutions like, for instance, University of London or Columbia University in New York City, may be hemmed in by urban development, eliminating available wild acreage, while branches of Foothill College in California have easy access to wild forest land. Communities adjacent to the Appalachians, Rockies, the Sierra Nevadas, or the Cascades of the Pacific Northwest have vast tracts of wild parkland nearby. Canadian and Russian cities have enormous tracts of adjacent undeveloped land; so do Malaysia, Indonesia, and Australia. A forest school has minimal effect on the land; such low-impact usage may often be permitted at little or no cost. Existing forest schools are found in parks, arboretums, and on donated private land.

And why not exercise imagination? Why not propose establishing a Forest School on the wild acreage of Jefferson's *Monticello* in Charlottesville, or his ultimate retreat, *Popular Forest* in Lynchburg, Virginia? Locating outdoor schools on available wild lands adjacent to historical sites, colleges, or universities adds a dimension of meaning and symbolism to the education itself that children will eventually come to appreciate. My own explorations of spectacular botanical gardens in London, Victoria in British Columbia, and Singapore suggest that promising forest-school educational sites abound. A concerted search of locally available property in Africa, Asia, Australia, Europe, North and South America, could well turn up tens of thousands of sites, the establishment of which *on a global scale* would revolutionize childhood education. Virtually any forest, meadow, hillside, or stream-side site will be, by definition, immune to political, ideological, or religions restrictions. And finally, as David Sobel advises in his inspiring *Nature Preschools and Forest Kindergartens*, if the perfect Garden-of-Eden location cannot be found, successful forest schools have been established in what he terms "ratty little thickets" – inner-city oases of "meadows, marshes, gardens, and small patches of forest" (2016, pp. 192–195).

Existing school grounds, even though many have adjacent empty land that could be used for a forest kindergarten, present problems difficult to resolve. Red tape, school district politics, and an educational concept that may be new to a conservative school board is likely to assure long delays, endless discussions about philosophy, questions about curriculum, safety, insurance, and certification of teachers – even though an entire network of support groups and training programs for outdoor-education teachers is now well established and worked out solutions for these concerns. Accustomed to the brick-and-mortar school, school administrators may be the most difficult to persuade. Here I take counsel from my co-presenters at the Lynn Canyon Ecology Center – Debra Harwood and Fran Hughes – and other attendees who are active in the forest-school trenches. The impetus for establishing an Outdoor School may work best if it comes from parents, from members of the community who, if they have young children and want a Forest School, are most likely to find the ways and means. With numerous Internet sites featuring Forest Schools worldwide, a growing list of helpful books, and a visually beautiful film like *School's Out: Lessons from a Forest Kindergarten* (2013) to introduce the idea, community members are a logical place to begin.

THE NATURE PRESCHOOL AND FOREST KINDERGARTEN

Forest kindergartens and outdoor schools provide a potpourri of benefits not realized because we are attuned to the props of classrooms, conventional subject divisions, testing sequences, grade completion, and the technospheric employment doors that open once a graduation diploma has been issued. These are the primary concerns of both teachers and administrators who may be fixated on classrooms and curricula completion rather than the child learner. Carolyn Webster-Stratton (1992) refers to ages 3 to 8 as "the wonder years"; Maria Montessori singled out the child's most important asset in *The Absorbent Mind* (1949). The outdoors provides a better platform for developing the minds of children during these crucial years. The forest environment answers the curiosity and exploratory needs of the child by providing imaginative space and thus a new educational template. In the indoor classroom everything – paper, crayons, scissors, and factory-made construction pieces – is within reach and accessible. The forest includes a dimension of the inaccessible: squirrels disappear in burrows; birds in the treetops live in realm apart; the treetops themselves tower virtually out of sight, emblems of the unreachable. Nature stimulates and symbolizes what Abraham Maslow (1971) called "the farther reaches of human nature". By the end of the first year, a pre-kindergarten child will have laid claim to the forest: she will know and can name every kind of rock, tree, flower, and creature in the surrounding space – with the sole exception of below-ground and behind-bark insects.

The foundation of a child's knowledge is immediate observation of what is real, enhanced by the collection of treasures like various shaped leaves, nuts, flowers, and seeds, with stories to add meaning. Children are not and should not be removed from stories in the outdoor school; they can gather for regular story time on wooden benches, or around a picnic table – or even seated in a circle on the ground – with stories that make sense of their experience. Interpretive nature books for Pre-K children that both teach and entertain range from Eric Carle's half-century-old classic *The Very Hungry Caterpillar* (1969) to Joseph Anthony's cleverly conceived *The Dandelion Seed* (1997) and a recent eco-friendly story by Lola and Adam Schaefer,

Because of an Acorn (2016), with dozens of other books published in the interval. There is much for the child to learn about the value of trees in the forest as habitat for wild birds; Jennifer Ward's illustrated book for Pre-K and Kindergarten children, *The Busy Tree* (2009), and Holling Clancy Holling's *Tree in the Trail* (1942) for older elementary children, provide the ecological contexts for real trees overhead. In the forest setting, children learn where lumber comes from: the forest rather than Home Depot. In home and classroom, heating and air conditioning provide climate control; outdoors it is palpable in sunshine, breezes and rustling leaves.

Whatever is observed in the forest is seen with observable changes through the seasonal cycle, intensely realized because a forest school will meet through sun, rain, and snow, retreating to open-walled shelter only when necessary. The visual documentary by Lisa Molomot and Rona Richter, *School's Out: Lessons from a Forest Kindergarten* (2013), filmed in Switzerland, illustrates how children thrive in any outdoor environment; Anne Stires (2016) description of a winter day at the *Juniper Hill* outdoor schools illustrates how children play with abandon even in a subzero snowy landscape. Dressed appropriately, children of five or six become oblivious to the vagaries of weather, equally happy in a sunny meadow or on a snowy slope, unconcerned if their hands get dirty digging in the mud. After all, what's more important? – clean hands, or digging in the earth?

Edward Wilson once remarked that most children go through a bug period. They also go through a digging-to-China period, a leaf-collecting period, a flower-gathering period, and a damming-up-a-stream period. For me it was climbing trees and building forts. The indoor classroom eliminates this kind of adventure and with it spontaneous activity so natural to children; the forest school provides a terrain for exploring, scrambling, balancing on logs, jumping from rock to rock, wading in whatever water is available – the results being mastery of balance, climbing, and large-muscle motor skills. Group building projects with rocks or branches build communication, social skills, and teamwork. Jane Worrell and Peter Houghton's *Play the Forest Way* (2016) provides teachers with a collection of: "Woodland Games and Crafts for Adventurous Kids". The Council for Environmental Education manual, *Project WILD* (2005) – sponsored by more than fifty environment groups from the U.S. to India, Iceland to Japan – provides a K-12 Curriculum & Activity Guide touching every aspect of the environment. With multiple editions dating since 1983, *Project Wild* was honored by the Reagan White House in 1991, receiving the Gold Medal for Education and Communication in the President's Environment and Conservation Challenge program.

Children instinctively humanize the landscape. Anyone who has read L. M. Montgomery's *Anne of Green Gables* (1908) will recall Anne's naming of places in the natural world: a road becomes the White Way of Delight; a pond is called Lake of Shining Waters; a geranium becomes Bonny; a cherry tree is called Snow Queen; a mundane village becomes Avonlea; a spring is named Dryad's Bubble. At the *Juniper Hill* Forest schools in Maine, where 4-to-6-year-olds are Seeds and 6-to-8-year-olds are Roots and Sprouts, children head to Welcome Woods in the morning; other parts of the forest are named Porcupine Woods and Salamander Woods. Cold weather from the north is called King Winter; hot water for tea is poured from Kelly Kettle; play locations through the woods are Troll Rock, Rhythm Log, Hemlock Home, Bad Cinnamon Tree, and Potion Stump. A spot where children shape cakes and pies of mud is called the Chocolate Factory. Such naming pulls the natural world into a humanized world of imagination – the very foundation of spirituality – as the populating of springs, rivers, groves, and hills with nymphs and spirits by the ancient Greeks makes clear.

By the first and second grade, children can learn to handle a knife correctly and whittle, and bind branches together to form the frame of a shelter or drying rack for wet clothing. Learning to build a fire safely brings pride to any young child, as does roasting potatoes or corn in the outdoors or cooking a meal in a Dutch oven. Meanwhile, daily reading sessions go forward with stories spanning more than a century and a half that interpret the natural world: Louisa May Alcott's *Flower Fables* (1854), Sibylle von Offer's *The Story of the Snow Children* (1905) and *When the Root Children Wake Up* (1906), Elsa Beskow's *Children of the Forest* (1910), Felix Salten's *Bambi* (1928), Holling Clancy Holling's Caldecott Honor book, *Paddle-to-the-Sea* (1941), along with *Minn of the Mississippi* (1951). Stories featuring animals range from Beatrix Potter's *Tale of Peter Rabbit* (1902) and half a dozen others to scores of animal adventure stories by the conservationist, Thornton W. Burgess, now honored in a drop-in museum where children can learn to make jam and his home on Cape Cod on the National Register of Historic Places.

For slightly older children ready for the broader story of the universe, earth, life and human origins, several stand out: Virginia Lee Burton's *Life Story* (1962); Jennifer Morgan's magnificent trilogy – *Born with a Bang* (2002), *From Lava to Life* (2003), and *Animals that Morph* (2006); and Stacy McAnulty's *Earth! My First 4.54 Billion Years* (2017). A full list of children's books relevant to the Forest School is astonishing; the collaborative volume, *1001 Children's Books You Must Read before You Grow Up* (2009), lists enough to nourish a child's mind from Pre-Kindergarten to adolescence. But there is no reason to limit reading to nature books. Children love to sing and dance. The "cultural literacy" program created by E. D. Hirsch, Jr., exists as a series of seven "core knowledge" texts: *What Your Kindergartner Needs to Know*, *What Your First Grader Needs to know*, all the way to *What Your Sixth Grader Needs to Know* (1991–2005). Each one includes compilations of songs, poems, fables, stories, basics of geography and history, mathematical concepts, and elementary science, including ecological projects – a full curriculum, in fact.

There is no reason to regard these guides as limited to an indoor classroom; every lesson can be conducted around work tables in an outdoor setting where culture is seen as a gift of civilization and the environment is a gift of Planet Earth. This gift may be interpreted in the traditional tales of the Grimm Brothers and Hans Christian Andersen, poems such as Emily Dickinson's "A Narrow Fellow in the Grass" and Robert Frost's "Road Not Taken". But children need interludes, captivatingly provided in humorous poems by Edward Lear, Lewis Carroll, and Shel Silverstein, and the linguistic extravaganza of falling water in Robert Southey's "Cataract of Lodore". The outdoor teacher armed with *The Oxford Book of Poetry for Children* (1963) can guarantee that literary education will not be neglected.

Children also love to dramatize, invent plays, and stage them: the remarkable imaginative stories and dramas of the Bronte children of England and Alcott sisters of New England are well documented. Children spontaneously invent dramatic situations and plays, but famous dramas are available for children. A striking two-volume anthology compiled by Coleman Jennings and Aurand Harris, *Plays Children Love* (1981, 1988) offers "a treasury of contemporary and classic plays for children", with each volume divided into "Plays for Adult Performers" and "Plays for Children to Perform". Introduced regularly, stories, poems, and plays assure that the best cultural artifacts of civilization, normally found in the school classroom, easily find their place within the much larger stage of nature.

FOUNDATIONS FOR COSMIC EDUCATION

Early in the twentieth century, the Italian educator, Maria Montessori, began developing an educational system for children housed in a setting called *Casa de Bambini* (Children's House). Her method was to create spaces congenial to children, with project storage shelves low to the floor and work projects that allow for building, drawing, and inventing while sitting on the floor – a habit common to children worldwide. Her innovations, first presented in *The Montessori Method* (1912), attracted attention from India to England and California where she delivered numerous lecture series of. The Montessori Method is typically offered in expensive private schools where an array of concrete materials is assembled to create a "prepared environment" extensive enough that each child can pursue an individual project, learn to care for materials, and reshelve them upon completion of the task. In *Education for a New World* (1946) – an appropriate goal in the aftermath of World War II – she speaks to the education of very young children.

Through the 1930s and the War years, Montessori had developed the concept of "cosmic education", a communication of knowledge about the entire universe. Her book, *To Educate the Human Potential* (1948), summarized what was then known about the ocean, earth, early humans, and civilization, visualized in a series of Big Stories. Her towering optimism about the potential of educating the next generation of youth appears in *Education and Peace* (1949), her response to a century thus far ravished by war. The breadth of her vision was clarified by her son, Mario Montessori, in "Cosmic Education", the final chapter in *Education for Human Development* (1976). More recently, Michael and D'Neil Duffy have expanded treatment in *Children of the Universe: Cosmic Education in The Montessori Elementary Classroom* (2014) where each of Montessori's six Big Stories is given a chapter.

Redefining the method of the "prepared environment" for the Forest School retools it as a "natural environment" sufficiently diverse to present a variety of individual challenges. The cosmic-education structure is more easily transferred and in fact is captured in children's books on wildlife, nature, earth, and the universe listed above. Cosmic Education amounts to the story of the entire cosmos, the long history of the earth, and the rise of life in all its vast diversity, and humans and their civilization. For this imaginative vision, the expansive environment of the forest and the open sky leading to the Sun, Moon, and stars provides superbly appropriate metaphors. Integrated into forest-school education, the Montessori Method – freed up from costly private schools – could well reach its ideal educational potential.

As a coda, it is worth emphasizing that the primary medium for childhood learning is the story. The remarkable fact is that children are born with the ability to understand stories, a fortunate fact since *no teacher knows how to teach a child to understand stories*. A child who cannot understand a story is conceptually impossible; devising a method for correcting this is beyond every educational method ever devised. The efficacy of stories comes wrapped in language, the basics of which are mastered by three-year-old children who are also able to retell simple stories and sometimes devise their own. In addition, they can relate characters in stories across various media, recognizing a TV talking animal, a stuffed animal, and a real animal as the same – a cat or dog or horse. And despite the TV version, she will be quite clear that "animals don't talk". By age four, she understands how the story of Mother Rabbit's love in Margaret Wise Brown's classic, *The Runaway Bunny* (1942), mirrors the story of her own mother' love.

It is relevant here to note that the power of story – a narrative account of events – is now recognized as the most powerful teaching tool from grade school to grad school, with applications all the way up to Brian Swimme and Thomas Berry's presentation of cosmic evolution, *The Universe Story* (1988). Therapists analyze mental, emotional, or social problems from their patients' narratives. Sociologists, evolutionists, and anthropologists now recognize the power of narrative to explain stellar evolution, the rise of life, the demise of the dinosaurs, and the emergence of humans. The six stories that make up Maria Montessori's "cosmic education", updated with children's books informed by the sciences of astronomy, geology, biology, and anthropology are "big story narratives" that have the power to develop in the child and later adolescent a cosmology encompassing all of reality – far surpassing the limited perspectives of technospheric schooling (Wood, 2015). Thomas Berry (1988) referred to this cosmological version "the new story", which we are slowly beginning to learn from the remarkable discoveries of science. But the use of story learning begins with children.

A NEW COMMUNITY OF SCIENTISTS

The study of the environment fits logically within the educational spectrum summarized as STEM, a widely accepted acronym for Science, Technology, Engineering, and Mathematics. Ecology, however, is reduced to one subject within "science" (S) and this makes up one-quarter of the whole, conceptually outweighed by two others, "technology" (T) and "engineering" (E), the prominent fields that design, build, maintain, and renovate the technosphere. Within the field of science (S), ecology is overshadowed by biology, chemistry, genetics, geology, and physics. Each of these includes components and themes relevant to ecology, but typically the sciences are imagined and taught as distinct "disciplines" in academic "departments" – separate knowledge silos with little attention to links or relationship with other fields. The interdisciplinary scope of ecology – spanning the aquasphere, atmosphere, biosphere, and geosphere – is thus relegated to a subfield overseen by few academic specialists, enrolling minimal numbers of students. None of this is surprising given the curtailed focus of the STEM educational template – even in the curricular overhaul, *Next Generation Science Standards* (NGSS), where lesson templates devoted to the environment are overshadowed by units conceived as laying the groundwork for practical applications in technology and engineering and indoor classrooms the assumed site of education. This emphasis is well illustrated in comments by Michigan's Oakland Community College Chancellor Peter Provenzano: "Employment is the legitimate outcome of education …. We're trying to create a pipeline that runs from the middle schools and high schools, through a community college or university, right to employment" (Anon, 2018, p. 77). Provenzano's pipeline metaphor frames the NGSS curricula where we read, "The United States has a leaky K-12 science, technology, engineering, and mathematics (STEM) talent pipeline …. We need new science standards that stimulate and build interest in STEM" (2013, p. xv). Elementary science education is now referred to as a "K-12 pipeline" that requires testable standards and a precise sequence of lessons leading to competence in STEM. But the "standards" offered have been designed by professors and deans of science departments and colleges of education far from the minds and imaginations of children (Wood, 2015).

While the educational authorities in virtually every nation are concerned with developing specialists in STEM, ecology is overlooked, despite a need – a desperate need – for specialists. Richard Louv asks the question, "Where Will Future Stewards of Nature Come From?" – a highly relevant question given what he calls "the endangered environmentalist" (2005, p. 145). The dominance of career-driven STEM education overshadows the less dramatic and less "practical" field of ecology. Given the range of ecological problems we are now facing, bringing ecology and environmental specialties into prominence is an absolute necessity, and how it can be done is clear. This chapter contends that outdoor education that moves children "from the bubble to the forest" provides the best foundation for ecological thinking. The evidence is extensive. In his last book, *The Story of My Boyhood and Youth* (1913), the Scotsman John Muir tells us that he was "fond of everything that was wild". He wandered in fields and along the seashore, watching fierce waves rolling up on the beach, recalling walks in the outdoors with his grandfather. At the age eleven, his family migrated to Wisconsin where he and his brother David discovered a land of inspiring landscape. "This sudden plash into wildness – baptism in Nature's warm heart – how utterly happy it made us!" (1992, p. 45) *A Thousand-Mile Walk to the Gulf* (1913) recounts his journey by foot from Kentucky to Florida, but his reputation is indelibly linked to the West where he explored mountain ranges from California to Alaska, his favorite range providing the name for the most prominent environmental group 125 years later, The Sierra Club, founded by Muir in 1892.

PERSPECTIVES

Within the limits of the modern world which has degraded much of the natural world Muir and many others traversed, the Forest School provides a contemporary firsthand childhood experience of the natural world. Indeed, with Neil Postman's and Charles Weingartner's *Teaching as a Subversive Activity* (1969) as background, it is clear that education in the forest-school context is subversive in the best sense of creating another perspective on the technosphere. While this perspective is absorbed by osmosis, the child will not judge; she will not realize her own developing discrimination, but awareness of the contrast between the cycles of nature and the take-make-waste cycle of consumerism-to-garbage living will dawn eventually, probably by the high-school years, and especially at college and university levels of education that necessarily move her from the forest back to the lecture room and laboratory.

Without the childhood experience of the outdoors, an adult is likely to retain a conservative, institution-based view of education, never realizing their constrained idea of classroom learning assures a constricted education. The problem for most of the adult population, in the innovative terminology of Richard Louv (2012), is a deficit of Nature, a pressing need for "Vitamin N". For the child who spends several years learning in the open air, breathing in Vitamin N, the artificial makeshift world of the technosphere will eventually swim into view. In early childhood, in the Forest School, before the cognitive faculties have fully matured, Nature will nurture the physical, emotional, imaginative, and spiritual child. This is the indisputable foundation for environmental education.

The evidence goes far beyond John Muir's childhood on the Scottish moors and the wilds of Wisconsin. Investigating the biographies of Henry David Thoreau, Theodore Roosevelt, Edward Abbey, Aldo Leopold, Loren Eiseley, and Al Gore we find that each had immersive and transforming experiences in the natural world during childhood. John Burroughs (1837–1921) is a case in point. Born in the Catskills, his childhood experiences included life on a farm and hiking on Old Clump Mountain and Slide Mountain. His observation of migrating birds lay behind his first book, *Wake-Robin* (1871), the first of more than thirty nature-based books. The transformative energy of childhood experience in nature touches American literary artists, too, a case in point being Sarah Orne Jewett's childhood on the wild Maine coast, beautifully recreated in "A White Heron", one of the finest American short stories every penned. A similar experience of nature affected Gene Stratton Porter (1863–1924), born in Wabash County in north-central Indiana near the vast Limberlost swamp. Her love of nature and the mystic beauty of the region exudes from every page of her best-selling novel, *A Girl of the Limberlost* (1909), one of Indiana's finest literary works.

The happiness and delight John Muir experienced, the "indescribable enthusiasm" he felt in the presence of towering Sugar Pines, his sense of the Romantic "sublime" in contemplating the giant sequoias, touches on the spiritual (1992, pp. 574, 578). Exploring the Sierra Nevada, his delighted encounter with nature provided a continuous lifelong education earned at what he once called The University of the Wilderness (1992, p. 111). Half a century ago, in a book of revealing title, *Education and Ecstasy*, George Leonard spoke of direct experience of the world and education itself as an "ecstatic moment. At its best, its most effective, its most unfettered, the moment of learning is a moment of delight", a transformative experience coloring the rest of life (1968, p. 20).

This point has been emphasized in the research of Thomas Tanner (1977) who interviewed dozens of environmentalists: a significant childhood experience in the natural world was named repeatedly as the impetus for their choice of the environment and ecology as their profession and calling. Citing Tanner, Louise Chawla (1999) set out to "explore people's accounts of their environmental interest, concern, and action", casting a broad net to discover the formative experiences of environmental professionals. Common features emerged: significant childhood experiences in nature, admired ecologist role models, organized treks into the natural world, distress over environmental degradation, and environmental literature. The case for experience in nature as a foundation for a career in ecology has subsequently been made by David W. Orr (2004). Richard Louv's question – Where shall we find tomorrow's stewards of nature? – has a decisive answer.

Outdoor education in some version of the Forest School should begin at the pre-Kindergarten level, age 4, and continue at least until age 10, longer if possible, to develop a transformative experience of the world of nature beyond the technosphere – an experience that will lay the groundwork for appreciation of the natural world, create perspective on the fragile civilization we have built, and provide motivation for seeking ways to ameliorate current environmental problems. We have massive numbers of technology specialists, highway designers, petroleum engineers, high-rise architects, and business executives, but we need more active environmentalists. We now face wicked ecological tangles that single-silo-one-subject specialists are not prepared to handle. The result is that environmental work is left for volunteer groups – the World Wildlife Fund (WWF), Rainforest Action Network (RAN), National Audubon Society, The Wilderness Society, the Center for Biological Diversity – with minimal assistance from government. Environmental planning and action by educated and trained ecologists is a pressing need. A deep immersion of youth in the forest-school environment is the surest foundation for the development of an informed public and a new generation of environmental scientists, conservation activists, and engaged and knowledgeable leaders capable of effecting meaningful change.

This provides a new perspective on the long-term but so-far incomplete and ineffective United Nations promotion of environmental education. While an environmental curriculum acceptable to every nation, culture, and religious perseuasion is virtually impossible to imagine, an environmental experience in the natural world for young children is easy to imagine and easy to create. The next UNESCO education conference should be devoted to the promotion of this single idea, with educators and leaders of every nation invited to attend. The Nature Preschool and Forest Kindergarten, tried and tested around the world, is an idea whose time has come. It is easy to visualize it remaking early childhood education everywhere, just as the German concept of *Kindergarten* ("garden for the children") introduced by Friedrich Fröbel (1782–1852) in 1837 has now spread worldwide. Its benefits for children themselves are now well recognized; its benefits for future generations are many and urgently needed. Without a reconnection of future generations of children with their environmental support system, we may continue to see the same patterns of industrial-age technospheric overconsumption and waste continue – taking us down a road of environmental degradation and loss from which there is no return.

REFERENCES

Abbey, E. (1968). *Desert solitaire: A season in the wilderness.* New York, NY: Touchstone.
Alcott, L. M. (1854). *Flower fables.* Bedford, MA: Applewood Books.
Anon. (2018, March). Dossier: Michigan. *Hemispheres.* Coral Gables, FL: Ink.
Anthony, J. (1997). *The dandelion seed.* Nevada City, CA: Dawn Publications.
Berry, T. (1988). *The dream of the earth.* San Francisco, CA: Sierra Club Books.
Beskow, E. (1910). *Children of the forest.* Edinburgh: Floris Books.
Blishen, E., & Wildsmith, B. (Eds.). (1963). *Oxford book of poetry for children.* New York, NY: Franklin Watts.
Burroughs, J. (1904). *The writings of John Burroughs* (Vol. 14). Boston, MA: Houghton Mifflin.
Carle, E. (1969). *The very Hungry Caterpillar.* New York, NY: Philomel Books.
Carson, R. (1941). *Under the sea wind.* New York, NY: Truman Tally Books.
Carson, R. (1951). *The sea around us.* New York, NY: Oxford University Press.
Carson, R. (1955). *The edge of the sea.* Boston, MA: Houghton Mifflin.
Carson, R. (1962). *Silent spring.* Boston, MA: Houghton Mifflin.
Catton Jr., W. R. (1982). *Overshoot: The ecological basis of revolutionary change.* Urbana, IL: University of Illinois Press).
Chawla, L. (1998, Fall). Significant life experiences revisited: A review of research on sources of environmental sensitivity. *Environmental Education Research, 4*(4), 369–382.
Council for Environment Education. (2005). *Project WILD: K-12 curriculum & activity guide.* Houston, TX: Council for Environmental Education.
De Bell, G. (Ed.). (1970). *The environmental handbook: Prepared for the first National environmental teach-in.* New York, NY: Bantam Books.
Duffy, M., & Duffy, D. (2014). *Children of the universe: Cosmic education in the Montessori elementary classroom.* n.p.: Montessori Services.
Eccleshare, J. (Ed.). (2009). *1001 children's books you must read before you grow up.* New York, NY: Universe Publishing.
Hammerman, D. R. (1963). The case for outdoor education. *In Hammerman and Hammerman, 1973,* 45–48.
Hammerman, D. R., & Hammerman, W. M. (Eds.). (1973). *Outdoor education: A book of readings* (2nd ed.). Minneapolis, MN: Burgess Publishing.

Hanscom, A. J. (2016). *Balanced and barefoot: How unrestricted outdoor play makes for strong, confident, and capable children*. Oakland, CA: New Harbinger Publications.
Hirsch Jr., E. D. (1990–205). *The core knowledge series: Resource books for Kindergarten through grade six* (Vol. 7). New York, NY: Bantam Books.
Holling, H. C. (1941). *Paddle-to-the-sea*. Boston, MA: Houghton Mifflin.
Holling, H. C. (1942). *Tree in the trail*. Boston, MA: Houghton Mifflin.
Holling, H. C. (1951). *Minn of the Mississippi*. Boston, MA: Houghton Mifflin.
Jennings, C. A., & Harris, A. (Eds.). (1981, 1988). *Plays children love* (Vol. 2). New York, NY: Doubleday and St. Martins.
Leonard, G. B. (1968). *Education and ecstasy*. New York, NY: Delacorte Press.
Leopold, A. (1949). *A sand county almanac*. New York, NY: Oxford University Press.
Louv, R. (2006). Nature-deficit disorder and the restorative environment. In *Last child in the woods: Saving our children from nature-deficit disorder* (pp. 98–111). Chapel Hill, NC: Algonquin Books.
Louv, R. (2012). Vitamin N. *The nature principle: Reconnecting with life in a virtual age* (pp. 41–88). Chapel Hill, NC: Algonquin Books.
Marsh, G. P. (1864). From man and nature. *In McKibben*, 71–80.
Maslow, A. (1971). *The farther reaches of human nature*. New York, NY: Viking.
McAnulty, S. (2017). *Earth! My first 4.54 billion years*. New York, NY: Henry Hold and Company.
McKibben, B. (Ed.). (2008). *American earth: Environmental writing since Thoreau*. New York, NY: Library of America.
Montgomery, L. M. (1908). *Anne of green gables*. Farrar, Straus & Giroux.
Montessori, M. (1912). *The Montessori method*. Lexington, KY: Renaissance Classics.
Montessori, M. (1946). *Education for a new world*. Madras: Kalakshetra Publications.
Montessori, M. (1948). *To educate the human potential*. Madras: Kalakshetra Publications.
Montessori, M. (1949). *Education and peace* (H. R. Lane, Trans.). New York, NY: Henry Regnery.
Montessori, M. (1967). *The absorbent mind* (C. A. Claremont, Trans.). New York, NY: Holt, Rinehart and Winston.
Montessori, M. M. (1976). Cosmic Education. *Education for human development: Understanding Montessori* (pp. 97–106). New York, NY: Schoecken Books.
Morgan, J. (2002). *Born with a bang: The universe tells our cosmic story*. Nevada City, CA: Dawn Publications.
Morgan, J. (2003). *From lava to life: The universe tells our earth story*. Nevada City, CA: Dawn Publications.
Morgan, J. (2006). *Mammals who Morph: The universe tells our evolution story*. Nevada City, CA: Dawn Publications.
Muir, J. (1992). *The eight wilderness discovery books*. Seattle: Mountaineers.
National Academy of Science, et al. (2013). *Next generation science standards*. Washington, DC: National Academies Press.
Orr, D. W. (2004). *Earth in mind: On education, environment and the human prospect*. Washington, DC: Island Press.
Osborn, F. (1948). *Our plundered planet*. Toronto: Little, Brown and Company.
Porter, E. (Ed.). (1962). *In wildness is the preservation of the world*. New York, NY: Arrowood Press.
Postman, N., & Weingartner, C. (1969). *Teaching as a subversive activity*. New York, NY: Delacorte Press.
Rienow, R., & Rienow, L. T. (1967). *Moment in the sun: A dial report on the deteriorating quality of the american environment*. New York, NY: The Dial Press.
Ripple, W. J., et al. (2017, October 23). World scientists' warning to humanity: A second notice. *Bioscience, 20*(10).
Roosevelt, T. (1976). *Hunting trips of a rancher & The wilderness Hunter*. New York, NY: The Modern Library.
Schaefer, L. M., & Schaefer, A. (2016). *Because of an Acorn*. San Francisco, CA: Chronicle Books.
Senge, P. et al. (2008). Life beyond the bubble. *The necessary revolution: Working together to create a sustainable world* (pp. 33–41). New York, NY: Broadway Books.

Sharp, L. B. (1952). What is outdoor education? *The School Executive, 71*, 19–22.
Sobel, D. (2016). *Nature preschools and forest kindergartens: The handbook for outdoor learning* St. Paul, MN: Redleaf Press.
Stires, A. (2016). A winter day in the life: An east coast nature preschool and forest kindergarten. *In Sobel*, 4–26.
Stratton-Porter, G. (1908). *A girl of the Limberlost*. New York, NY: L. C. Page.
Stratton-Porter, G. (1925). The last passenger pigeon. In *McKibben*, 192–204.
Tanner, T. (1977, Winter). Significant life experiences: A research area in environmental education. *The Journal of Environmental Education, 11*(4), 20–24.
Thoreau, H. D. (1985). *A week on the Concord and Merrimack rivers; Walden; or, life in the woods; The maine woods; Cape cod*. New York, NY: Library of America.
Udall, S. L. (1963). *The quiet crisis*. New York, NY: Holt, Rinehart and Winston.
UNESCO/UNEP. (1975). *The Belgrade charter and recommendations of the Belgrade workshop on environmental education*. Belgrade: International Bureau of Environmental Education.
United Nations. (1972). *Declaration and report of the United Nations conference on the human environment*. Stockholm: United Nations Publication.
United Nations. (1992). *United Nations conference on environment and development*. Rio de Janeiro, Brazil.
United Nations. (2017). *Sustainable Development Goals (SDG) report*. New York, NY: United Nations.
Vogt, W. (1948). *Road to survival*. New York, NY: William Sloane Associates.
Von Olfers, S. (1905). *The story of the snow children*. Edinburgh: Floris Books.
Von Olfers, S. (1906). *The story of the root children*. Edinburgh: Floris Books.
Wackernagel, M., & Rees, W. (1996). *Our ecological footprint: Reducing human impact on the earth*. Gabriola: New Society Publishers.
Wallace, D. R. (1983). *The Klamath Knot: Explorations of myth and evolution*. San Francisco, CA: Sierra Club Books.
Ward, B., & Dubos, R. (1972). *Only one earth: The care and maintenance of a small planet*. New York, NY: W. W. Norton.
Ward, J. (1968). Cognitive learning and outdoor education. *In Hammerman and Hammerman*, 118–122.
Webster-Stratton, C. (1992). *The wonder years*. Toronto: Umbrella Press.
Whipple, W. J. (2017, November 13). World scientists' warning to humanity: Second notice. *Bioscience, 67*(12), 1026–1028.
Wood, B. (1970, October 13). The perpetual crisis. *The Stanford Daily*, p. 3.
Wood, B. (2015, January). *Big story narratives: Reframing K-12 science education*. Proceedings of the 13th Annual Hawaii International Conference on Education, HICE, Honolulu.
Wood, B. (2017, December). Conversion of the earth/ construction of the technosphere: An intractable environmental issue. *International Journal of Arts and Sciences (IJAS), 10*(7), 325–336.
Worroll, J., & Houghton, P. (2016). *Play the forest way: Woodland games and crafts for adventurous kids*. London: Watkins Publishing.
Worldwatch Institute. (2017). *EarthEd: Rethinking education on a changing planet*. Washington, DC: Island Press.

Barry Wood
College of Liberal Arts and Social Science
University of Houston
USA

PATRICIA ARMSTRONG AND ANNETTE GOUGH

10. DEVELOPING AND MOTIVATING YOUNG LEADERS FOR SUSTAINABILITY

A Developmental Framework

INTRODUCTION[1]

Over the past two decades, many Australian schools have been actively involved in sustainability education programs and initiatives, such as the Australian Waste Wise Schools (Armstrong, Sharpley, & Malcolm, 2004; Cutter-Mackenzie, 2010), the Australian Sustainable Schools Initiative (Larri, 2010) and ResourceSmart Schools in Victoria (Guevara, King, & Smith, 2010; Liefman, 2011; Remenyi, 2011). Many schools have also actively encouraged child and adolescent leadership for sustainability (Larri, 2010; McLeod, 2013) and education providers have been developing and delivering leadership training programs and resources (Field, 2013; Reddington, 2015; Stewart & Armstrong, 2009; Stoney, 2013). However, there are few research-based studies (e.g. Corriero, (2006); Sacks, (2009) to underpin these programs, resources and initiatives and no developmental framework for child and adolescent leaders, unlike that available for teachers (Department of Education Victoria, 2007).

BACKGROUND

There is an ever-increasing understanding of adult leadership and the attributes and capabilities of leaders and how this applies to leaders working in the areas of sustainability (Taylor, 2008, 2010a, 2010b). This knowledge has been used to develop numerous leadership development programs for adult leaders, both in the workplace and community groups. However, modified adult leadership and leadership for sustainability development programs may not be suitable for adolescent leaders. There are at least three reasons for this. First, research has shown that humans undergo considerable neurological, cognitive, social and developmental changes during adolescence (Siegel, 2013; Steinberg, 2011); what works for adults may not necessarily work for adolescents. Second, there is insufficient knowledge about where and how adolescents lead. Adult leadership development programs may not be relevant for adolescent leaders in schools and their community groups. Third, there is little research about what adolescents themselves understand by leadership and what motivates them to lead. Roach et al. (1999, p. 13) found that "emerging youth leadership differs from established measures and leadership theories drawn from adults" and we wondered if this could also be the case for adolescent leaders for sustainability.

Understandings and Definitions of Leadership

There is little consensus about what leadership means in the literature on adult leadership. For example, Bass and Bass (2008) concluded that "the search for the one and only proper and true definition of leadership seems to be fruitless" (p. 23). However, they cited a cross-cultural leadership study that developed a more "universal" definition of leadership: "the ability to influence, motivate and enable others to contribute to the effectiveness and success of the organisations of which they are members" (House, Hanges, Javidan, Dorfman, & Gupta, 2004, p. 23).

Northouse (2012) concluded that leadership could be viewed in several ways: as a *trait* ("a distinguishing quality of an individual, which is often inherited"); as an *ability* (having "the capacity to lead"); a *skill* or competency ("to accomplish the task efficiently"); as a *behaviour* ("what leaders do"); as a *relationship* ("a process of collaboration that occurs between leaders and followers"); and as an *influence process* (pp. 4, 5). However, his definition of leadership emphasised the *influence process*: "Leadership is a process whereby an individual influences a group of individuals to achieve a common goal" (p. 6), as it is not the trait or ability of the leader that is important, but the interaction between the leader and followers to achieve an agreed outcome.

Taylor (2008) incorporated emphases on influence and relationships in a definition of adult leadership as it relates to sustainability: "a process of influence that occurs within the context of relationships between leaders and their collaborators, and involves establishing direction, aligning resources, generating motivation and providing inspiration to achieve mutual interests" (2008, p. 2). He added that this definition also applies when leaders and collaborators swap roles, for individual leadership and when leadership is distributed across a team.

Several authors have proposed definitions of youth leadership. For van Linden and Fertman (1998), the definition of leaders is the same for adults and adolescents: "those ... who think for themselves, communicate their thoughts and feelings to others, and help others understand and act on their own beliefs; they influence others in an ethical and socially responsible way" (p. 30).

Participants in a 2006 global study of young leaders defined leadership as "the process of leading, facilitating, mobilizing, influencing, energizing, organizing and guiding people towards a common vision/goal" (Corriero, p. 36). An earlier study of community leaders (aged 8–28 years) suggested that adolescents are more interested in developing leadership in groups, rather than as an individual and that leadership is more about "group participation and distribution of knowledge and skills in collaborative efforts towards team defined goals" (Roach et al., 1999, p. 21). To the young people in this study, leadership was more about "doing leadership" than in "being a leader", a distinction also raised by van Linden and Fertman (1998). It was also about negotiation and consensus, rather than influence or position, as is often the case in adult leadership (Bass & Bass, 2008; Northouse, 2012).

Attributes and Capabilities

The literature on the qualities of leaders uses confusing terminology. Some of the terms used were characteristics, traits, attributes, skills, competencies or capabilities. For the purposes of this chapter and for consistency, we use the term "attributes" for those qualities that adolescents may bring to leadership and which possibly could be enhanced and "capabilities" as those they could learn and develop over time.[2]

Northouse (2015) concluded that while there is no "definitive list" of leadership traits, there is some evidence that certain traits contribute to leadership: "intelligence, self-confidence, determination, integrity, and sociability"; and emotional intelligence. Northouse also looked at research about the skills approach of adult leaders, identifying the three skills approach (technical, human, and conceptual), with different levels of each skill appropriate for different levels of management (p. 68).

Taylor (2008) reviewed a number of studies that highlighted the traits of effective adult environmental leaders. These traits showed a strong emphasis on values, consistent with van Linden and Fertman's (1998) work on the role of emerging values on adolescent leadership.

Regarding the characteristics/traits of adolescent leaders, Rogers' (2009) research with a small group of "gifted" adolescent leaders identified several innate characteristics (intelligence, wisdom and creativity) and several that seemed to have been learnt (self-confidence, planning and perseverance).

Although there were few studies about the attributes of adolescent leaders, one study gave some insights as the research participants listed the attributes of leaders as: "selfless, responsible, enables others, sets an example, has integrity and is a problem solver. They create environments for both action and personal learning and development" (Corriero, 2006, p. 36).

Numerous publications described adolescent leadership capabilities or skills (e.g. Karnes & Chauvin, 2000). However, we failed to find equivalent studies that identified the capabilities or skills required of adolescent leadership for sustainability.

Motivational Factors

Researchers have been investigating what motivates people for almost a century, led at first by psychiatrists and psychologists such as Maslow (1943) who proposed the idea of the hierarchy of needs (basic, safety, love, esteem and self actualisation). According to Maslow, a person is only able to attend to their "higher order" needs when their "lower needs" are partially or fully met. Psychologist, David McClelland, another major contributor to theories of human motivation, proposed that there are four human motives: Achievement; Power; Affiliation; and Avoidance (1987).

More recently, researchers from other disciplines have been investigating human motivation and, in particular, how it relates to leadership (Adair, 2009; Rabas, 2013) and taking environmental actions (Arnold, Cohen, & Warner, 2009; Chawla, 1998, 1999, 2001). Arnold, Cohen and Warner (2009) investigated motivational factors with a small group (12) of young leaders, aged 16–19 years. They found the key factors that influenced them to take action were a combination of "influential people" (parents, teachers, friends and role models) and "influential experiences" ("time spent outdoors and in youth groups, conferences and gatherings") (p. 30). These factors are similar to those described by Chawla (1999) for adults, except that adolescents were also influenced by friends, role models, groups, conferences and gatherings, but less by negative environmental experiences, books and the media. Cox (1988) found in a retrospective study of established leaders in the United States that among the seven key factors recommended by these leaders for the development of adolescent leadership were "having mentors and other nurturers" and "significant life experiences". Another study found that families and schools that encouraged learning for its own sake (academic intrinsic motivation) would help adolescents to be more motivated to lead when adults (Gottfried et al., 2011, p. 517). As indicated by Annette Gough, more research is needed to address this blank spot in our understanding of adolescents' motivation to take environmental actions and leadership roles for sustainability (1999).

Developmental Learning Frameworks

Van Linden and Fertman (1998) argued that adolescent leadership development progresses through three stages (awareness, interaction, and mastery), with five dimensions within each stage: Leadership information; Leadership attitude; Communication skills; Decision-making skills; and Stress management skills (p. 41), but did not develop this concept further into a framework.

Levels of leadership are commonly used in the literature of adult management. Charan, Drotter, and Noel (2011), for example, described six levels of adult management and the skills and values required to move from one level to another. The levels of their pipeline start with Level 1 "from managing self to managing others" progressing to Level 6 "from group manager to enterprise manager".

Many businesses and government departments use levels of leadership and matrices as developmental frameworks for their staff, such as *The developmental learning framework for school leaders* (Department of Education Victoria, 2007) and the *VPS HR capability framework* (Victorian Public Service Commission, 2015). These two matrices used a similar format, e.g. the *VPS HR capability framework* used a grid with five leadership levels across the columns, five categories down the rows (Roles, Membership levels, HR activity, HR Knowledge Acumen and HR Capabilities) and relevant descriptors in each cell (p. 4). Development Dimensions International Inc. (DDI) have developed success profiles, using matrices built from four elements: Knowledge; Experience; Competencies; and Personal Attributes (Cosentino & Tefft, 2015).

RESEARCH DESIGN

This study was part of a larger three to four-year longitudinal study of adolescent leadership for sustainability using social constructivist grounded theory methodology (Charmaz, 2008, 2014). The purpose of this study was to investigate how adolescents' understandings of sustainability, leadership, leadership for sustainability, capabilities, attributes, leadership styles and motivational factors help shape their identity, emergence and development as leaders. This chapter reports some of the findings of this study, in particular:

- Adolescents' understandings of leadership and leadership for sustainability and how these changed over time
- Adolescents' understandings of the key attributes and capabilities of adolescent leaders and how these changed over time
- The key factors that motivated adolescents as leaders in sustainability
- A developmental framework for adolescent leadership for sustainability

Preliminary data was collected in Melbourne, Australia from two focus groups of students, aged from 15 to 18 years, in a secondary school (a total of 23 students). Data for the longitudinal study was obtained from 93 semi-structured interviews over a three to four year period with 20 secondary school students (with a starting age of 15 to 16 years), 13 principals and teachers from five secondary schools (three government schools and two private schools), plus seven others. The schools were selected on the basis of their prior active participation and leadership in sustainability programs (ResourceSmart Schools and Tomorrow's Leaders for Sustainability). The students for both the focus groups and the interviews were nominated by teachers in their respective school as leaders in sustainability.

FINDINGS

Understandings of Leadership

Students' understandings of adolescent leadership in this study were as follows.

There are several ways of categorising understandings of adolescent leadership. These are: leading *for* the group (working as either an individual or in a small team on a project that would benefit a larger group such as club or a school, e.g. Lachlan worked, at first in a small team, then on his own on a school solar energy project that will benefit his school); leading *a* group (to take charge of the group/team, e.g. "taking charge when no one is in charge", Patrick, Round 1); and leading *in* a group (and speak on behalf of the group/team, e.g. "Not taking over something, but guiding the group or a couple of people to help themselves", Jodie, Round 1).

Students commonly described leadership in terms of four dimensions as capabilities, attributes, purposes and relationships.

When younger, students more commonly described leadership as *taking initiative, influencing others* and *taking charge* (e.g. "takes charge of a group in a project", Ange, Round 1), but when older, more commonly described leadership as about *taking initiative, leading a group to complete a task* and *inspiring others* (e.g. "leading a group in the best way you see fit to address some challenge or agenda or objective", Lachlan, Round 3).

When students were older, they more commonly combined two or more of these dimensions into more complete, coherent statements ("It's the initiative giving some people the determination to help others and to take charge and to try and make everything the slight bit better", Emma, Round 3).

Adolescent leadership was considered by a few students as both *leadership of self* and *leadership of or within a group* (e.g. leadership means having "the initiative to work with a group of people or individually to make something happen or to use team work to make an event happen", Kylie, Round 3).

Finally, adolescent leadership can be described by *relationships between members of the group and by the nature or situation of the project* (e.g. Beth spoke about being a leader at home, in friendship groups and in projects).

Understandings of Leadership for Sustainability

Students' had a range of understandings of adolescent leadership for sustainability.

They described leadership for sustainability in four ways; as capabilities, aptitudes, purposes and relationships.

When younger, students more commonly described their understanding as *teaching others, raising awareness* and *promoting change ideas*, but when older, more commonly described it as *a group effort, leading for a sustainable future, convincing/showing others to get involved in sustainability issues* and *doing things for the environment*, with group effort the most commonly mentioned. A possible explanation for this change was that, when in Year 9, students' understandings reflected their observations of other student leaders. However, by Years 11 and 12, they may have learnt that just telling people and raising awareness is not enough and that a team approach that engages others is needed. Jason (Round 3) highlighted this in the following statement: "encourage people and work with them, getting them to work with you and with people who are passionate for ... the greater good of the environment".

When students were older, as Jason's quote demonstrates, they also often combined two or more of these understanding into more complex, coherent statements.

A DEVELOPMENTAL FRAMEWORK FOR ADOLESCENT LEADERSHIP FOR SUSTAINABILITY

Overview

Using the above understandings of leadership, plus other key findings from this study, we developed an *Adolescent leadership for sustainability developmental framework*.

The Framework provides several instruments across five key levels of adolescent leadership for sustainability (Citizen, Initiator, Apprentice, Change agent and Connector). These instruments include: *a development matrix* for seven elements (Focus, Description, Examples of actions, Practices, Understandings, Key capabilities and Key attributes) for each of the five levels; *a Capabilities map* (of the capabilities in the Framework to those in the Australian Curriculum); and *Expanded descriptors* (for each of the capabilities and attributes). The Framework also provides additional tools: Leadership principles (principles of adolescent leadership for sustainability); Leadership definitions; Strategies for motivating adolescent leaders for sustainability (Mentoring and supporting, Personal development and Curriculum and co-curriculum); and Assessment tools (for teachers and students).

The study showed that the development of adolescent leaders for sustainability does not occur in isolation, but within the influences of their home, school and other activities in their personal life and the community. This emergence and context of adolescent leadership is the focus of another paper.

Figure 10.1 provides an overview of the Framework.

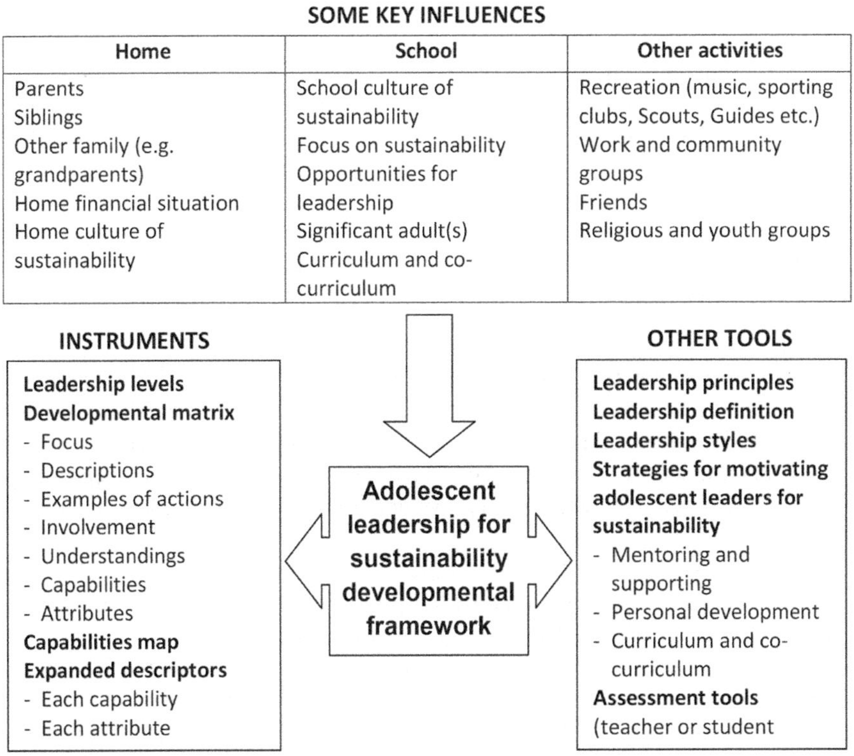

SOME KEY INFLUENCES

Home	School	Other activities
Parents	School culture of sustainability	Recreation (music, sporting clubs, Scouts, Guides etc.)
Siblings	Focus on sustainability	Work and community groups
Other family (e.g. grandparents)	Opportunities for leadership	Friends
Home financial situation	Significant adult(s)	Religious and youth groups
Home culture of sustainability	Curriculum and co-curriculum	

INSTRUMENTS		OTHER TOOLS
Leadership levels **Developmental matrix** - Focus - Descriptions - Examples of actions - Involvement - Understandings - Capabilities - Attributes **Capabilities map** **Expanded descriptors** - Each capability - Each attribute	Adolescent leadership for sustainability developmental framework	**Leadership principles** **Leadership definition** **Leadership styles** **Strategies for motivating adolescent leaders for sustainability** - Mentoring and supporting - Personal development - Curriculum and co-curriculum **Assessment tools** (teacher or student)

Figure 10.1. Overview of the development framework

Leadership Levels and the Developmental Matrix

In his first interview, Mr Black described adolescent leadership as being on a spectrum ("Leadership is on a spectrum which depends on the situation"). As three students had also raised this concept when asked about leadership styles, we looked more closely at the data.

In the interviews, students had been questioned about their involvement in sustainability activities and projects. Analysis of these answers identified a number of key concepts about how these leaders were involved, suggesting that there may be several levels of leadership for sustainability among students, based on increasing responsibility. At first, this appeared similar to the six levels of adult management advocated by Charan et al. (2011). However, our data suggests that in schools, the levels were based on increasing responsibility. To the students, it was also important, as Jodie suggested, to give them "opportunities to lead things" and to have faith in them.

After the first two interviews, we devised a draft scale to develop case histories of student participants, giving criteria for a five-level rating system for students, based on increasing responsibility. However, we found that the scale was incomplete with some students' scores changing markedly from Round 2 to Round 3, i.e. it was fluid. In many cases, a student's personal circumstances and his or her school had changed so dramatically, that the student was either no longer able or wanted to be involved in leadership initiatives. Our scale needed to reflect this. We then used a recursive process, similar to that described by other authors, e.g. Birks and Mills (2011, p. 185), in which we went back and forth from our early leadership level scores of the students, their answers to the questions of *how* they were leading sustainability projects and our evolving descriptions of the levels. This process led us to propose that there are five levels of adolescent leadership for sustainability, as summarised below:

1. *Eco-citizen:* Moderately committed to sustainability, will take actions to model sustainability at home, youth groups and at school, but may have limited understanding of sustainability and practical opportunities for leadership.
   Or Takes actions, has a very good understanding of sustainability and leadership, but for either personal reasons or lack of opportunity is unable to lead at a higher level
2. *Initiator:* Highly committed to a particular sustainability issue and shows great tenacity in conducting a particular project about that issue. Is developing capabilities, attributes, understandings and practice through the project.
3. *Apprentice:* Interested in sustainability and belonging to a sustainability group, club or committee. Motivated to develop understandings and learn from others.
4. *Change Agent:* Growing passion for sustainability and ability to hold leadership positions within a sustainability group, club or committee. Works collaboratively with others. Takes on increasing responsibilities and initiatives.

Or Unable to join or form a sustainability group (for personal reasons or through lack of opportunity), but leads by coaching others.
5. *Connector:* Exceptional leader, passionate about sustainability, has had extensive practice in leading sustainability and has a deep understanding about leadership and sustainability. Demonstrates high levels of capabilities and attributes to lead significant sustainability initiatives.

Our data showed that the path of students on this spectrum was different for each student and fluid. For example, a student could start and stay at the same level (e.g. Lachlan) or start at a middle level, advance and then shift back to an earlier level, depending on opportunities and their personal circumstances (e.g. David).

Figure 10.2 shows the number of students for each level of leadership for each round of interviews. The shifting nature of the number of students categorised for each level between rounds reflects changes in the social and cognitive maturity of the students, changes occurring in their schools and changes in their personal circumstances.

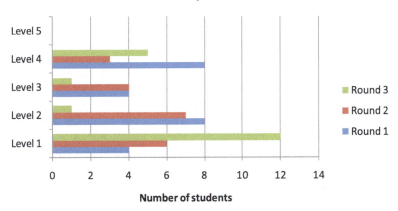

Figure 10.2. Students' levels of leadership for sustainability for each round of interviews

As we worked through our data, we began to see that the leadership scale could be further organised into a matrix for each of the levels of leadership that we had already identified.

Using abductive reasoning (Charmaz, 2014, p. 201), we hypothesised that seven elements were of importance and could be used as headings for rows of the matrix, with descriptors for each element for each leadership level. We returned to the empirical data to check, re-examining and recoding the data where required, using NVivo software. Based on this process, we selected seven elements to construct the matrix as described below:

- Focus
- Description
- Examples of actions
- Practices (How they contribute/what they do)
- Understandings (of sustainability and leadership)
- Key capabilities (Shows the earliest level where relevant)
- Key attributes (Shows the earliest level where relevant)

The final matrix is shown in Table 10.1.

In the section below, we give further explanation of the descriptors for the seven elements in the matrix for each of the five levels.

Focus

Our scale for levels of leadership for sustainability is based on increasing responsibility. We initially used these scales for each of the levels of Focus in the Framework. The first three foci were clear-cut, but after a while we realised the fourth which we had called, *Organising school sustainability projects and activities*, was more than just "organising"; it was also about inspiring and motivating others. The concept that seemed to fit best was the term *Leadership through school or community influence*. This described what students such as David, Declan, Olivia and Patrick in Round 1 were really doing – influencing others in the school through their environment group. David and Patrick were also influencing others in the surrounding community through their many activities.

At the fifth level, however, the focus appeared to be on making a difference through a group of schools and community groups. Three examples from the study demonstrate student leaders operating at this level. First, when in Year 9, the four students at Red Gum College (David, Olivia, Michelle and Patrick) all spoke about the impact of the School Captain/Environment Captain, both in their school and in bringing schools together. Second, Zac (a 19 year old past student) had attended a school where there was no environment team, but this didn't deter him from leading and, when in Year 12, he became a valued leader in a community environment group. Third, three high school students from the United States were part of a District committee which organised themes for their Interact (school-aged Rotary clubs) projects in both the International and Community areas. These themes were taken up by dozens of school clubs in their District (with about 7,000 members). The focus of these Interact leaders was making an impact within a school, between schools and international and local communities.

Again through a recursive process, we concluded that the focus of each level of leadership is best described as:

- *Self* leadership: Participates in positive environmental behaviours and projects (in school, outside school or at home).

- Leadership through *projects*: Initiates and participates in team sustainability projects.
- Leadership *within a group*: Learns and helps organise school sustainability projects and activities.
- Leadership through *school or community influence*: Inspires and motivates others, initiates and organises sustainability projects and activities at school or in a community group.
- Leadership *through a group of schools or community groups*: Inspires and motivates others, initiates and organises sustainability projects and activities across schools or community groups.

Description

From the five foci we built up descriptions of student leadership for each of the five levels. By re-analysing the students' interviews, we developed descriptions for each level, constantly testing them against what we had documented about each student in their respective case history. However, as noted earlier, students' ratings often changed between rounds, making this task very complicated. At one point, we arrived at a description for each level which seemed to fit all the student participants for the three rounds of the study, with the exception of two students, Emma and Michelle from Red Gum College.

We had developed the description, consistent with the summaries of each level discussed earlier, for Level 4 as:

> Growing passion for sustainability and ability to hold leadership positions within a sustainability group, club or committee. Works collaboratively with others. Takes on increasing responsibilities and initiatives.

We had included the expression "growing passion for sustainability", as this was a quality possessed by the five students who demonstrated this level of leadership in Round 3 (Declan, Emma, Jake, Luke and Olivia).

Emma had been operating at Level 3 for the first two rounds of interviews, then in her senior school years circumstances changed significantly for her. She experienced a number of major health issues and a teacher, who had been coordinating the school environment team, left the school. Because she was unable to join the environment group (lack of opportunity) in Year 11 and had experienced health problems (personal reasons), Emma did not seem to fit into either Level 3 or 4. During the final interview, we learnt that during Year 12, she had coached a number of students in sustainability projects, modelling the coaching style used by the environment coordinator at the school. She was displaying the focus of "influence" and hence belonged in Level 4.

One solution to this dilemma was to create an alternative description to Level 4:

> Unable to join or form a sustainability group (for personal reasons or through lack of opportunity), but leads by coaching others.

Michelle, who was a close friend of Emma, had been rated at a high leadership level for the first two interviews and, like Emma, had experienced several health issues and the loss of the key teacher in Year 12. However, while still very passionate about sustainability, unlike Emma, she did not coach other students, and, as she was so time-poor, she could really only take environmental actions, i.e. she was operating at Level I. So at Level 1, it seems that there may be two types of students; those who are moderately committed to sustainability and take sustainability actions, and those that are passionate about sustainability, take personal actions, but, for some reason, are unable to contribute further. As with Level 4, a solution was to create an alternative description for Level I:

> Passionate about sustainability, has a deep understanding of sustainability and has demonstrated leadership through team or environment group projects, but for either personal reasons or lack of opportunity is unable to contribute further

The final descriptions for the five levels are shown in Table 10.1.

Examples of Actions

Examples of actions for each of the five levels (shown in Table 10.1) were derived from the answers to several student questions.

Practices (How They Contribute/What They Do)

Similarly, the descriptors for the practices for each of the five levels were also derived from the answers to the appropriate students' questions and from additional NVivo coding for the three rounds of interviews. These practices are shown in Table 10.1.

Understandings (for Leading Sustainability Actions, Projects and Events)

In order to provide descriptors for this section, we looked carefully at the descriptors for the previous sections – the descriptions, examples and practices – and reviewed the case histories for each of the students, looking for common themes for understandings that would apply across all five levels. We hypothesised, then checked our hypotheses by returning to the data, that four themes of understandings were important in distinguishing the different levels of leadership: the minimum requirement for understanding of sustainability; necessary rules, procedures and relationships; sets of capabilities; and where to seek further advice and information. Note that we first thought that we could distinguish student leadership levels by their growing understanding of sustainability, but this was not the case. We found instead that by Round 3, the majority of students had a good or very good understanding of sustainability and there seemed to be no relationship between students' level of leadership and their understanding of sustainability.

Table 10.1. Adolescent leadership for sustainability matrix

Level	Eco-citizen	Initiator	Apprentice	Change agent	Connector
In essence	"Doing the right thing most of the time!"	"If I don't do it, who will?"	"People feeding off each other, makes it easier"	"Fighting the big issues and are less concerned about themselves"	"Serving the environment"
Focus	*Self* leadership	Leadership through *projects*	Leadership *within a group*	Leadership *through school or community influence*	Leadership *through a group of schools or community groups*
Description	Committed to sustainability, will take actions to model sustainability at home, in youth groups and at school. Shows personal responsibility and self leadership. Or Passionate about sustainability, takes personal sustainability actions, has a deep understanding of sustainability and has demonstrated leadership through team or environment group projects, but for either personal reasons or lack of opportunity is unable to contribute further	Highly committed to and knowledgeable about a particular sustainability issue and shows great tenacity in conducting a particular project about that issue. Is developing capabilities, attributes, understandings and confidence through the project.	Very interested in sustainability and belonging to an environment/ sustainability group, club or committee. Motivated to learn from others.	Growing passion for sustainability and ability to hold leadership positions within a sustainability group, club or committee. Works collaboratively with others. Takes on increasing responsibilities and initiatives. Or	Exceptional leader, passionate about sustainability and has had extensive experience in working with others and leading sustainability projects. Displays advanced capabilities in many areas, especially in communicating, planning, interpersonal and networking

(*cont.*)

Table 10.1. Adolescent leadership for sustainability matrix (cont.)

Level	Eco-citizen	Initiator	Apprentice	Change agent	Connector
Examples of actions	Uses refillable lunch boxes and drink bottles Rides a bike or walks to school Puts litter in bin Turns off lights when leaving a room Participates in school energy awareness day	Sets up a project to collect unwanted mobile phones for charity Works with a team to build a vegetable garden at the local primary school	Joins the school environment team Assists in the organisation of a project to clean up the local creek	Unable to join or form a sustainability group (for personal reasons or through lack of opportunity), but leads by coaching others. Leads an activity at a sustainability conference Organises activities for the whole school on World Environment Day	Organises an interschool conference for students in sustainability Participates on a regional student sustainability committee
Practices (How they contribute/what they do)	Takes sustainability actions at home, school and possibly the community Participates in school sustainability projects and events Communicates about sustainability to friends and family	Initiates and completes projects either alone or with a small team Communicates to classes or groups about their projects Builds relationships within the project group	Participates in a environment/ sustainability club or committee outside of the curriculum May co-facilitate activities/events in school or out of school	Leads teams and committees Initiates new school sustainability projects and events Gives presentations to a year level or the whole school	Organises inter-school sustainability events Gives presentations at inter-school sustainability events Builds partnerships and networks with people and groups within and outside the school

(cont.)

Table 10.1. Adolescent leadership for sustainability matrix (cont.)

Level	Eco-citizen	Initiator	Apprentice	Change agent	Connector
			Helps to organise school sustainability events Gives presentations to classes or groups about projects of the club or committee Communicates with people outside the school about school sustainability projects Builds relationships in environment groups	Builds partnerships with school council committees (e.g. finance or grounds) May work with people outside the school on sustainability projects (e.g. clean up the local creek Coaches other students with their sustainability projects Mentors other student leaders Supports the sustainability activities of others	
Understandings (for leading sustainability actions, projects and events)	At least, a basic understanding about sustainability issues and personal sustainability actions The rules of their class/year level/school	An in-depth understanding of at least one sustainability issue How to work in teams How to manage projects Who to ask for support with a project	At least, a good understanding of several sustainability issues How school co-curriculum committees operate	At least, a good understanding of a wide range of sustainability issues	A deep understanding of a wide range of sustainability issues How to lead groups drawn from several schools

(cont.)

Table 10.1. Adolescent leadership for sustainability matrix (cont.)

Level	Eco-citizen	Initiator	Apprentice	Change agent	Connector
	How to lead when situations arise (to step up) Who to ask for the additional information about sustainability		How to lead and manage activities Who to ask for advice for group activities	How to lead school clubs/ committees How school decisions are made Who to ask for advice for leading groups and setting up projects and events	Sustainability/ environment organisations outside the school and the relationships between them Who to ask for advice for leading major events
Key capabilities (Shows the earliest level where relevant)	Communicating effectively Modelling sustainability behaviours	Analytical Inter-personal Resilience Project and time management Social	Planning Research and self-education	Managing teams and groups Networking and collaborating	
Key attributes (Shows the earliest level where relevant)	Passionate about sustainability	Determined Innovative (and entrepreneurial) Persistent Positive	Confident Trustworthy Open-minded	Caring	

The groups of understandings for each level are listed in Table 10.1. Below, we give an explanation, together with examples of how this combination of understandings helped students in the study to lead at that level.

Level 1

Students operating at this level needed a basic understanding of the sorts of sustainability actions they can take and the reasons for this, but they also needed to understand which ones they could take at school. It was also helpful if students appreciated that leadership is sometimes about modelling appropriate behaviours and when to do this within the context of school rules. They also needed to know where they could access additional information. As an example, Chloe in Rounds 1 and 2 was rated at Level 1 for leadership, although she moved up to Level 3 in Round 3. Chloe set an example to her friends by riding her bike to school and collecting aluminium cans to raise money for an overseas school trip.

Level 2

Students operating at this level of leadership commonly lead through a sustainability project, requiring them to understand the issue around that particular project. Most of the students at this level in this study have worked in teams on other projects and described how they collaboratively planned and undertook their projects. In order to complete a project, students needed to know where they could gain information, both inside and outside the school. As an example, four girls from Melaleuca College worked as a team on a community project in the local community. They told how they sought advice from teachers and people from different organisations outside the school.

Level 3

Students operating at this level had joined an environment team or club, either bringing with them a good understanding of sustainability issues or developing them through the work of the team. Patrick, for example, described one of the benefits of being part of the team was that he could learn new things about sustainability and spoke of how Ms Blue was always available to assist him.

Level 4

Students at this level were expected to have a good understanding of sustainability either through their own research or through the projects and events of their team or committee. They needed to know about leading a club or committee and how decisions were made in the school and how to fix things, as, for example, when Luke needed to find out how to fix the leaking water taps in the school.

Level 5

Students operating at this level needed a strong understanding of sustainability and highly developed leadership capabilities to have the credibility and capacity to lead either students from several schools or members of the community. When in Year 9, all four students from Red Gum College and their teacher, Ms Blue, spoke about the advanced capabilities of the school Environment Captain who we believed would have been operating at Level 5.

Capabilities

The key capabilities of adolescent leaders for sustainability identified in the study were: *analytical* (logical thinking and problem solving); *communicating effectively* (writing and speaking persuasively, giving presentations, public speaking); *interpersonal* (active listening, empathy); *managing teams and groups* (delegating, teaching others, fairness, involving others, inspiring others, negotiating); *modelling sustainability behaviours*; *planning* (for the short and long term); *project and time management* (organisational); *research and self-education* (about sustainability and leadership); *resilience*; and *social* (people skills). The most commonly reported capabilities for the three rounds were communicating effectively, project and time management and social. Students mentioned all the above capabilities in all three rounds of interviews with three exceptions; no student mentioned the skill of problem-solving in the first round and no student mentioned logical thinking or research in the third round.

We did not have sufficient data to precisely place each of the capabilities in each box of the matrix, as the students were only asked about what they believed were the key capabilities of adolescent leaders in general. We had to return to the data to predict which of these capabilities would have been helpful for a student when he or she was operating at a particular level. These capabilities are listed in Table 10.1, with each listed in the earliest level where we reasoned it would have been most relevant to a student leader operating at that level. We further reasoned that as a student progressed from Level 1 to Level 5, his or her capabilities would have developed. A student operating at Level 5 would have been expected to use all 11 capabilities to a high level. This is an area requiring further research.

Key Attributes

The key attributes identified from this study were: *caring* (about people and the group); *confident*; *determined*; *innovative* (and entrepreneurial); *open-minded*; *passionate about sustainability*; *persistent*; *positive*; and *trustworthy*, with the most commonly reported attribute being confident. Students mentioned all the above attributes in all three rounds of interviews with one exception; no student mentioned the attribute of caring in the first round.

These attributes are listed in Table 10.1. As for the 11 capabilities above, each attribute is listed in the earliest level where it would have been most relevant to a student leader.

Leadership for Sustainability Definition

Based on the findings discussed earlier about how adolescents understand leadership for sustainability, we propose the following definition:

> Adolescent leadership for sustainability is the ability to work either individually or within a group to create ideas, take initiatives, influence, educate and motivate others and to undertake actions that will bring about change for a more sustainable future.

David's quote illustrates this definition: "Working with people to help achieve sustainability" (Round 3).

Strategies for Motivating Adolescent Leaders for Sustainability

The data from this study showed that adolescent leaders are motivated by four key factors: *influence of people* (influential teacher at school or at home or in the community – the significant others or people of influence in an adolescent's life); *personal motivation and capitalising on opportunities*; *school/community influences*; and *self learning/experiences.* The first two were the most commonly reported.

Many strategies were recommended by teachers and students for motivating adolescent leaders for the sustainability. These were coded into three key categories, through:

- co-curriculum activities
- the school curriculum in education for sustainability
- school student mentoring, leadership structures and training

Through their personal stories, we learnt that there were further ways in which students seem to have been motivated to lead. For example, Declan had learned how to lead teams from observing his father manage his business. Chloe had observed leadership practices from a community group who campaigned to protect established trees at a local train station and Jake had done voluntary work in an African orphanage. These students were motivated from both their school programs and from people and initiatives outside school. We then created an additional category of personal development outside school; experiences, observations, training and activities outside of formal and informal school learning. Schools can play an important role in encouraging their students to participate in these types of initiatives.

We developed a second matrix, with levels of leadership for sustainability and three categories of strategies, combining the first two categories above *curriculum* and *co-curriculum* and adding *personal development outside school*. The final three categories (in order of importance) were:

- *Mentoring, leadership structures and training* (Teachers initiate at school)
- *Curriculum and co-curriculum* (Teachers or principals initiate)
- *Personal development* outside school (Teachers encourage students)

The strategies for motivating adolescent leaders for sustainability matrix, developed from the suggestions from participants in the study, is the focus of further writing (contact authors for details).

Assessment Tools

We developed a number of (at this stage) paper-based, self-assessment measures that corresponded to the various elements in the Framework. (Contact the authors for details.)

DISCUSSION

Through this research we have developed deep insights into how adolescents understand leadership during mid-adolescence and how these understandings changes with age. One of the key findings was that the participants viewed leadership in several ways as: leading *for* a group; leading *a* group; and leading *in* a group. A few even recognised that there is "self" or individual leadership as well as working within a team, a concept different from adult models of self leadership (Neck & Houghton, 2006). Their explanations could also be categorised as either capabilities, aptitudes, purposes or relationships, showing some parallels with the work of Northouse (2012, 2015) for adult leadership.

Another key finding was that participants, when older, frequently referred to leadership as working with and in groups, consistent with previous adolescent studies (Roach et al., 1999), although, when younger, commonly described leadership as "influencing others", similar to some definitions of adult leadership (Bass & Bass, 2008; Northouse, 2012). The adolescents in this study also showed that their understandings changed with age from "taking charge" to "working with a group towards an outcome", i.e. being more collaborative. There are several possible reasons for this: cognitive and social maturation; greater opportunities for leadership experiences; observations of the behaviours of other leaders; and through formal leadership training programs.

There were some similarities of the key attributes identified in this study to those in other studies e.g. the traits of adult leaders (self-confidence, determination and sociability) identified by Northouse (2012) and attributes of adolescent leaders (selfless, responsible, enables others, sets an example and problem solving) Corriero (2006).

For many students in the study, leadership for sustainability was understood as being the same as for leadership, but with a focus on sustainability. When younger, they spoke more commonly about educating people about sustainability issues (raising awareness, promoting change ideas, teaching others), when older, their understandings emphasised working together for a purpose (engaging others for the environment/a sustainable future).

As with understandings of leadership, we found that the students' understanding of leadership for sustainability changed throughout the study from "changing others" to "working as a group for a sustainable future". Jason highlighted this in the following comment:

> encourage people and work with them, getting them to work with you and with people who are passionate for ... the greater good of the environment. (Round 3)

The Developmental Framework is a significant contribution to our knowledge of the development of adolescent leadership for sustainability. It is also a practical tool that will be useful for secondary students to map their leadership development, and for teachers and educators to develop leadership programs and motivate students to become more effective leaders. It could also be used by students to self-assess their leadership levels, capabilities and attributes and to work with a teacher, parent or community leader to develop a personal leadership development profile and plan. The matrix of motivational strategies is a practical resource for teachers to help them to further develop their adolescent leaders.

These nine measures of the self-assessment tools would give students (and teachers or educators) a snapshot of where they are at a point in time and an indication of areas where they might improve. Students could then work out a course of leadership development activities, perhaps with support from either their teacher or other environmental leader. Further assessments could judge whether these leadership development activities had been effective. The matrix strategies would provide a basis for these activities.

The matrix of motivational strategies is similar to the 70:20:10 model used by many organisations to structure the development of their staff, based on three categories and percentages of development: informal/on the job (70%); coaching and mentoring (20%); and formal learning (10%) (Kajewski & Madsen, 2013). The results of this study, however, suggest that for adolescent leaders, the categories of motivational strategies, in order, are: mentoring/training; curriculum/co-curriculum and personal development outside of school. The results of a community study reported earlier suggested that educators can best help young leaders through "group engagement through sustained work on projects and products", and encouraging "group outcomes held high as possible standards of excellence" (Roach et al., 1999, p. 22). Many of the recommended strategies involve engaging and involving students in learning about sustainability, i.e. encouraging "academic intrinsic motivation", or enjoying learning for its own sake. There is evidence that when schools and families provide opportunities for this kind of learning for a child, the person is more motivated to lead as an adult (Gottfried et al., 2011).

Our findings on motivational factors, in part, support the work of Arnold, Cohen, and Warner (2009) who found (from a small study of 12 participants) that the key factors that influenced young environmental leaders to take action were a combination of "influential people" (parents, teachers, friends and role models) and "influential experiences" ("time spent outdoors and in youth groups, conferences and gatherings") (p. 30). This present study proposes additional factors of personal motivation, school and community influences and self learning/experiences.

A significant finding was the importance of persons of influence on the motivation of the students to become engaged in sustainability projects. These persons of influence can be a parent, grandparent, sibling, supportive teacher, another parent or someone outside the school, such as a Girl Guide leader. The following story exemplifies this finding. At a school where an influential teacher had retired, the two students in the study approached another teacher to help them set up an informal Enviro Warriors group, even though both students had heavy school workloads. The teacher agreed, the group was great success and the students went on to become school environment captains. The results of this study are consistent with the retrospective study of established leaders in the United States Cox (1988), which found in that included in the seven key factors for the development of adolescent leadership were "having mentors and other nurturers" and "significant life experiences".

There were some limitations to this study: it was limited to a relatively small number of participants (93); the emphasis was on leadership of adolescents in a narrow age range (mid-adolescence); it was conducted in a small number of schools (five) in just one city (Melbourne); and all schools had similar educational structures (the Victorian Curriculum). Two of the schools were private schools and three were government schools. Despite these limitations, the study has generated rich data and findings made more reliable by the repeat interviews of many participants and with theoretical sampling of additional participants. The longitudinal sampling allowed for a deeper understanding of how adolescent leadership changes with age, opportunities and personal circumstances.

Further research studies could investigate how the understandings of leadership, motivational strategies and the developmental framework outlined in this study compare with those of children and older adolescents. They could also consider differences with gender, education systems and culture. It would also be revealing to follow up the students from this study as they enter young adulthood.

In summary, adolescents view leadership for sustainability predominantly as working with others to deliver an outcome for sustainability, but they also see it as a process of influencing and educating others. There are many strategies educators can use to help motivate adolescent leaders, but, at the very heart, it is about creating opportunities for adolescents to learn about sustainability, themselves and leadership and encouraging them to learn through practical and challenging projects, within a supportive and nurturing environment. The findings in this study can provide a framework to achieve this.

CONCLUSIONS

This longitudinal study of a small group of students in mid adolescence, teachers and principals has contributed to our knowledge of how adolescents understand leadership and leadership for sustainability, the key attributes and capabilities of adolescent leaders and the strategies that can help motivate them to become leaders for sustainability. The study also identified that adolescent leadership for sustainability occurred across a spectrum of five levels and that these levels can be used in a developmental framework for adolescent leaders, based on two matrices. One matrix was constructed using seven elements for each of the five levels of leadership. A second focused on strategies to motivate adolescents to become leaders at each level of development for three key areas: mentoring, leadership structures and training; curriculum and co-curriculum; and personal development outside school.

NOTES

[1] Pseudonyms were used for the participants and their schools in this chapter.
[2] An "attribute" is "A quality or feature regarded as a characteristic or inherent part of someone or something" (2016). We chose the term "capability", as it is a commonly used term in education and would be familiar to educators. The Australian Curriculum defines a "capability" for students as encompassing "knowledge, skills, behaviours and dispositions" (ACARA, 2013, p. 5). These capabilities are used by students in school, home and the community.

REFERENCES

ACARA. (2013). *General capabilities in the Australian curriculum.* Retrieved June 1, 2013, from http://www.australiancurriculum.edu.au/generalcapabilities/pdf/overview

Adair, J. E. (2009). *Leadership and motivation: The fifty-fifty rule and the eight key principles of motivating others.* London: Kogan Page, Ltd.

Armstrong, P., Sharpley, B., & Malcolm, S. (2004). The Waste Wise Schools program: Evidence of educational, environmental, social and economic outcomes at the school and community level. *Australian Journal of Environmental Education, 20*(2), 1–12.

Arnold, E. A., Cohen, F. G., & Warner, A. (2009). Perspectives of young environmental leaders on their formative influences. *Journal of Environmental Education, 40*(3), 27–36.

Bass, B. M., & Bass, R. (2008). *The bass handbook of leadership: Theory, research & managerial applications* (4th ed.). New York, NY: Free Press.

Birks, M., & Mills, J. (2011). *Grounded theory: A practical guide.* London: Sage Publications.

Charan, R., Drotter, S., & Noel, J. (2011). *The leadership pipeline: How to build the leadership powered company* (2nd ed.). San Francisco, CA: Josey-Bass.

Charmaz, K. (2008). Constructionism and the grounded theory. In J. A. Holstein & J. F. Gubrium (Eds.), *Handbook of constructionist research* (pp. 397–412). New York, NY: The Guilford Press.

Charmaz, K. (2014). *Constructing grounded theory* (2nd ed.). Thousand Oaks, CA: Sage Publications.

Chawla, L. (1998). Significant life experiences revisited: A review of research on sources of environmental sensitivity. *The Journal of Environmental Education, 29*(3), 11–21. doi:10.1080/00958969809599114

Chawla, L. (1999). Life paths into effective environmental action. *The Journal of Environmental Education, 31*(1), 15–26.

Chawla, L. (2001). Significant life experiences revisited once again: Response to Vol. 5(4) 'Five critical commentaries on significant life experience research in environmental education'. *Environmental Education Research in the Schools, 7*(4), 451–461.

Corriero, J. (2006). *Youth-led action in an international context: Major project report* (Master in Environmental Studies Masters). York University, Ontario, Canada.

Cosentino, C., & Tefft, M. (2015). *Competency management at its most competent.* Retrieved from http://www.ddiworld.com/DDI/media/white-papers/competencymanagementatitsmostcompetent_wp_ddi.pdf

Cox, K. J. (1988). *Significant adolescent leadership development experiences identified by established leaders in the United States* (Doctor of Philosophy). Ohio State University, Ohio.

Cutter-Mackenzie, A. (2010). Australian Waste Wise Schools program: Its past, present, and future. *The Journal of Environmental Education, 41*(3), 165–178.

Department of Education Victoria. (2007). *The developmental learning framework for school leaders.* Melbourne: Department of Education Victoria. Retrieved from http://www.education.vic.gov.au/Documents/school/principals/profdev/developmentallearn.pdf

Field, C. (2013). Leadership: What do you think of? *Eingana, 36*(2), 10–13.

Gottfried, A. E., Gottfried, A. W., Reichard, R. J., Guerin, D. W., Oliver, P. H., & Riggio, R. E. (2011). Motivational roots of leadership: A longitudinal study from childhood through adulthood. *The Leadership Quartlery, 22*, 510–519.

Gough, A. (1999). Kids don't like wearing the same jeans as their mums and dads: So whose 'life' should be in life experience research? *Environmental Education Research, 5*(4), 383–394.

Guevara, R., King, J., & Smith, J. M. (2010). *Most significant change stories: Lessons learned from the implementation of ResourceSmart AuSSI Vic 2009.* Retrieved from http://www.resourcesmart.vic.gov.au/documents/ResourceSmart_AuSSI_Vic_most_significant_change_stories_2009.pdf

House, R. J., Hanges, P. J., Javidan, M., Dorfman, P. W., & Gupta, V. (Eds.). (2004). *Culture, leadership and organisations: The globe study of 62 societies.* Thousand Oaks, CA: Sage Publications.

Kajewski, K., & Madsen, V. (2013). *Demystifying 70:20:10 white paper.* Retrieved from http://deakinprime.com/media/47821/002978_dpw_70-20-10wp_v01_fa.pdf

Karnes, F. A., & Chauvin, J. C. (2000). *The leadership skills inventory.* Scottsdale, AZ: Great Potential Press, Inc.

Larri, L. (2010). *Evaluation of the Australian sustainable schools initiative ACT.* Canberra: Climate Change and Natural Environment, Program Implementation. Retrieved from http://www.sustainableschools.act.gov.au/__data/assets/pdf_file/0006/261348/Evaluation_of_the_AuSSI_ACT_2010FINAL1111.pdf

Liefman, J. (2011). A national and local reflection on education for sustainability (EfS). *Eingana, 34*(2), 6–7.

Maslow, A. H. (1943). A theory of motivation. *Psychological Review, 50*(4), 370–396.

McClelland, D. C. (1987). *Human motivation.* Cambridge: Cambridge University Press.

McLeod, S. (2013). Student leadership at Bentleigh West Primary School. *Eingana, 36*(2), 4.

Neck, C. P., & Houghton, J. D. (2006). Two decades of sel-leadership theory and research. *Journal of Managerial Psychology, 21*(4), 270–295.

Northouse, P. G. (2012). *Introduction to leadership concepts and practice* (2nd ed.). Thousand Oaks, CA: Sage Publications.

Northouse, P. G. (2015). *Leadership: Theory and practice* [Kindle version] (pp. 496). Retrieved from https://www.amazon.com.au/Leadership-Practice-Peter-G-Northouse-ebook/dp/B00TKEOIVE

Oxford Dictionaries, Oxford University Press. (2016). *Oxford dictionaries.* Retrieved December 31, 2016, from https://en.oxforddictionaries.com/definition/attribute

Rabas, A. (2013). *The barriers, fears and motivations encountered by women leaders in higher education leadership roles.* Chicago, IL: The Chicago School of Professional Psychology.

Reddington, T. (2015). An environment for change: AYCCs Switched on Schools program. *Eingana, 38*(2), 11–14.

Remenyi, C. (2011). The resourceSmart AuSSI Vic story: A short history of how sustainability in schools in Victoria has developed. *Eingana, 34*(2), 12–15.

Roach, A. A., Wyman, L. T., Brookes, H., Chavez, C., Brice, H. S., & Valdes, G. (1999). Leadership giftedness: Models revisited. *Gifted Children Quarterly, 43*(3), 13–24.

Sacks, R. E. (2009). *Natural born leaders: An exploration of leadership development in children and adolescents* (A thesis submitted in conformity with the requirements for the Degree of Doctor of Philosophy). Ontario Institute for Studies in Education at the University of Toronto, Ontario, Canada.

Siegel, D. J. (2013). *Brainstorm: The power and purpose of the teenage brain.* New York, NY: Penguin Group.

Steinberg, L. (2011). *Adolescence* (9th ed.). New York, NY: McGraw-Hill Companies Inc.

Stewart, J., & Armstrong, P. (2009). Tomorrow's leaders for sustainability. *Eingana, 12*(2), 18–22.

Stoney, K. (2013). Youth leadership: Let's ride. *Eingana, 36*(2), 15.

Taylor, A. C. (2008). *Promoting sustainable practices: The importance of building leadership capacity.* Paper presented at the Enviro 08, Melbourne, Australia.

Taylor, A. C. (2010a). *Sustainable urban water management: The champion phenomenon* (Unpublished PhD). Monash University, Melbourne, Australia.

Taylor, A. C. (2010b). *Using the lever of leadership to drive environmental change: Ten tips for practitioners.* Paper presented at the Enviro 2010, Melbourne.

van Linden, J. A., & Fertman, C. I. (1998). *Youth leadership: A guide to understanding leadership development in adolescents.* San Francisco, CA: Jossey-Boss.

Victorian Public Service Commission. (2015). *VPS HR capability framework.* Retrieved January 15, 2016, from http://vpsc.vic.gov.au/wp-content/pdf-download.php?postID=27641

Patricia Armstrong
RMIT University
Australia

Annette Gough
RMIT University
Australia

PART 2
CASE STUDIES

SOPHIA HUNTER AND CAROLYNN BEATY

11. TEACHING GLOBAL INDIGENOUS CONTENT TO YOUNG LEARNERS

TACKLING A NEW CURRICULUM

This chapter sets out to explore British Columbia's new Social Studies curriculum for grade 3 and its focus on global indigenous peoples (BC's new curriculum, 2016). As part of the new curriculum, students develop an understanding of the interconnected nature of cultural and technological innovations in both local and global indigenous communities. We will focus on the relationship humans have with their environment and the cultural and technological innovations these relationships foster. This topic is fascinating to students, but we found it challenging to locate age-appropriate contemporary resources for our school library to support this requirement. Through Simon Fraser University's President's Dream Colloquium on Returning to the Teachings: Justice, Identity and Belonging, ideas and resources were used and adapted to allow grade 3 students to discuss concepts such as New Zealand's Whanganui River gaining legal personhood or understand the significance of the Hōkūle'a's journey around the world (Colloquium Course, 2016). We hope these contemporary examples of indigenous technologies and culture allow students to develop relevant and authentic understandings of place-based innovation.

The expansion of indigenous content throughout the new curriculum for K-12 is a response to the Calls to Action that emerged from the Truth and Reconciliation Commission's work to address the legacies of the racist and colonial Residential School system (*Truth and Reconciliation Commission of Canada: Calls to action*, (2015). This curriculum was developed and implemented in the last five years with most school-age children now being taught through these lenses and expectations.

In our opinion, effective exploration of any indigenous culture begins with a connection to the student's own natural environment. Developing a sense of place is the foundational piece before understanding how indigenous peoples build culture and technology. This dual approach allows unique opportunities to shift assumptions that young learners, particularly in urban environments, might have about dominant ways of being and interacting with nature. As Gregory Cajete noted, "American Indian people's inherent identification with their Place presents one of the most viable alternative paradigms for practicing the art of relationship to the natural world" (Cajete, 1994, p. 81).

This research focuses on how this approach was developed, examples of student learning and our own teacher-librarian reflection on the process. This, in turn, shows how teachers in British Columbia can work successfully with the new curriculum while helping students to think critically about their environment and all the possible ways to live in it. Teachers outside of British Columbia will find it a useful look at contemporary studies of global indigenous peoples in the elementary school classroom.

ABOUT THE AUTHORS

We are both teacher-librarians. We worked with two grade three (8–9-year-olds) classes of 20 students each. All forty were girls of high socio-economic status. The classroom teachers co-guided the inquiry with us. They shared our concern about the dearth of resources on global indigenous peoples and were keen to try the Hōkūle'a and Whanganui River as areas of inquiry to be used to scaffold the unit. Both classroom teachers had been working with a local elder during the previous term as part of their inquiry into local indigenous ways of being.

BRITISH COLUMBIA'S NEW CURRICULUM

As discussed, British Columbia has a new curriculum (Social Studies 3, 2016). Indigenous content is embedded throughout this new curriculum (*First Peoples Principles of Learning*, n.d.).

As part of the grade three Social Studies curriculum, the following *content* is part of the new direction:

- cultural characteristics and ways of life of local First Peoples and global indigenous peoples
- aspects of life shared by and common to peoples and cultures
- interconnections of cultural and technological innovations of global and local indigenous peoples
- governance and social organization in local and global indigenous societies
- oral history, traditional stories, and artifacts as evidence about past First Peoples cultures
- relationship between humans and their environment (Social Studies 3, 2016).

This content is part of these *big ideas:*

- Learning about indigenous peoples nurtures multicultural awareness and respect for diversity.
- People from diverse cultures and societies share some common experiences and aspects of life.
- Indigenous knowledge is passed down through oral history, traditions, and collective memory.
- Indigenous societies throughout the world value the well-being of the self, the land, spirits, and ancestors (Social Studies 3, 2016).

Core competencies are central to the new curriculum. They are sets of "proficiencies" that students need to develop over time to engage in in-depth lifelong learning. There are three main competencies: Communication, Thinking, and Personal and Social Responsibility. Students express their progress in 'I' statements. One facet of the Personal and Social proficiencies is well-being (Core Competencies, 2016).

Challenges

Many of the available resources on global indigenous peoples were not age appropriate in reading level or content. In addition, some resources perpetuated the notion that indigenous peoples and societies are unchanging. We were concerned that this would limit young learners by depriving them of examples of contemporary applications of indigenous ways of being that are based on traditions but not dictated by them. Such a limitation could thwart discussions with young learners about the possible benefits of indigenous ways of being in non-indigenous communities.

Navigating Resources – Inspiring a New Approach

Speaker Wade Davis' book *The Wayfinders: Why Ancient Wisdom Matters in the Modern World* (2009), based on his CBC Massey Lecture, explores the origins and history of the Hōkūle'a, which provides students with a rich look at a global indigenous peoples tackling a modern problem with traditional knowledge passed down through oral culture: sustainable travel. As Davis (2009) notes, "Navigation fundamentally defined the Polynesian identity" (p. 10).

The Hōkūle'a is a double-hulled canoe that has sailed around the world and on numerous long open-water journeys using traditional Polynesian navigation techniques. These techniques are based on "the fundamental elements of the Polynesian world: wind, waves, clouds, stars, sun, moon, birds, fish and the water itself" (Davis, 2009, p. 52). The Polynesian Voyaging Society, which launched the Hōkūle'a, works to preserve this unique cultural knowledge and bring a message of environmental awareness to its ports of call. We believe that this endeavor matched the objectives of our curriculum, especially "interconnections of cultural and technological innovations" and the "relationship between humans and the environment", in an age-appropriate and age-appealing manner (Social Studies 3, 2016). It became an integral resource in our unit and was a successful and inspiring tool for teaching nature-connectedness to our young learners.

Indigenous legal scholar John Borrows spoke to the Dream Colloquium at Simon Fraser University about the Whanganui River in New Zealand being granted legal status as a person due to its importance to the Maori people (Borrows, 2016). The decision to make this designation was based on the Maori belief that the well-being of the river and the well-being of the people are inextricable. This provides students with a contemporary look at the link between well-being and place.

IMPLEMENTATION

We began our work with our students by reviewing our background knowledge of local indigenous peoples and their technologies and culture, and the link between these and their natural environment. The significance of the salmon and its habitat was a considerable focus from the previous year's teaching in science and local indigenous cultures. To build on previous learning, related technologies like salmon weirs and drying racks were reviewed. These connections help set the stage to make our thinking international.

The Hōkūle'a website contains a wealth of information, including videos, photographs and blog entries, that can be adapted for use in the elementary school classroom, in addition to some ready-made lesson plans (Polynesian Voyaging Society, n.d.). These resources are excellent quality and allow an intimate view of life on the Hōkūle'a. Students can follow the voyages in real time, adding to the relevance of the lessons. To encourage engaged learning and critical thinking about the material, we relied on questioning techniques to encourage students to interact deeply with the resources. For example, the introductory video to the world voyage contains several phrases and images that are worth exploring in depth with young learners. When the narrator says, "They were the astronauts of our ancestors. They were the greatest explorers on the face of the earth", we showed students Polynesia on a globe and asked them to discuss why the double-hulled canoe sailors might be called "the astronauts of our ancestors" (Hōkūle'a Worldwide Voyage, 2016). Grade three students had no trouble understanding the distances they were sailing in the past were similar in adventure and exploration to space travel now. This was also a great hook. The students were mesmerized, and we were able to easily connect technologies past and present.

One scene in the same video has a bird flying over the ocean while the narrator says, "Relying solely on a complex understanding of the stars, the winds, the waves and other cues from nature …" (Hōkūle'a Worldwide Voyage, 2016). We asked students what the bird might mean to navigators? We were surprised when all of the students were able to figure out in their partner groupings that birds meant land was nearby. We would periodically supplement their understanding with information from *The Wayfinders* (Davis, 2009). In this instance, we added that different birds could fly different distances from land, so specific birds represented specific distances from land.

After asking these questions, we had children come up with their own questions, which would drive our focus for the rest of the inquiry. Their questions are compiled in Table 11.1. We used numerous resources from the Hōkūle'a website to help the children find answers to their questions, especially photographs and blog entries (it turns out "How do they go to the bathroom?" is a very popular question). The former allowed the children to infer from visual sources and they were able to answer many of their questions this way. We were pleased to see the connections forged by using authentic indigenous resources and primary documents.

Table 11.1. Student inquiry question (Grade three students, 2017, January). (Navigation work booklet, Unpublished raw data)

Life on the boat	Time sailing	Learning to sail
How much food do they eat?	How long were they out sailing the most?	How do they learn to sail and tell direction?
Do they eat fish?	When will they stop travelling?	Did they always follow birds and stars?
How do they catch fish?	Did they stay at the destinations?	Types of birds used for navigation?
Do they eat plants?	What was the farthest they sailed?	How did they learn how far birds can fly?
What type of water did they drink?	Did they go to the Arctic?	Types of birds used for navigation?
How many hours do they sleep?		How do the wind and stars help them?
Did they know what day it was?		How do they never get lost?
What do they make sails out of?		How do they know where they are going?
How did they make things?		How does the boat move?
Do they read any books?		How does the boat work?
How do children get educated?		What is the boat made of?
Do they have candy?		How does the sail stay up?
Do they have instruments?		How do they make the boat?
Do they celebrate any holidays?		How do they get so far with no motor?
Did they use oil?		How do they stay up all night to steer?
How do they bathe?		What happens if a big wave comes?
How do they change?		Could their boat break?
What happens if they get hurt?		What if there is thunder and lightning?
Where do they go to the washroom?		Is *Moana* based on this?
If they are sick, where do they put it?		
Are they all boys?		

As we worked through the online resources, many of the students' questions were answered. We invited a guest speaker, Candace K. Galla, PhD, an indigenous Hawaiian scholar from the University of British Columbia to speak to the children about why the Hōkūle'a was meaningful to her and to talk more about the islands, culture, and language. Dr. Galla is also a hula master, so she shared some dances and songs with us, one of which we were given permission to perform for other people.

Throughout the inquiry, we highlighted that the crew of the Hōkūle'a always met with local indigenous peoples in their ports of call, as shown in the videos on the website. This helped students to understand the connections between indigenous communities, and to grasp that there are different indigenous communities around the world, with many commonalities and differences.

We regularly highlighted the environmental message of the voyage, Mālama Honua, which means "to care for our Island Earth" (How do you malama honua?, n.d.). Students noted on their own from photographs and videos that the Hōkūle'a has solar panels on its back. Elements like this of the voyage helped to keep students engaged and enabled them to see different technologies integrated with traditional knowledge. In the videos and photographs, styles of dress were mixed to reflect both ways of being. One man on the Hōkūle'a wore traditional Hawaiian clothing, whilemany others wore surf shorts, tank tops and baseball caps, but with a lei or other traditional piece. Indigenous groups at the ports of call often wore regalia to host their special guests.

Since our students are from a high socio-economic group, many of them have been to Hawaii on vacation. Studying the Hōkūle'a presented them with knowledge of the islands that was not part of their past trips for various reasons which are beyond the scope of this chapter. It is our hope that students who visit the islands now will have a very different understanding of them than previous visits fostered.

John Borrows introduced us to the legal personhood of the Whanganui River. There are not a lot of resources on this for grade three and elucidating the legal concept is obviously ambitious for the age group. What is challenging, but manageable, is unraveling the reasoning behind the river's status. The river is viewed as central to the well-being of the Maori people. As noted by Labour's Te Tai Hauauru MP Adrian Rurawhe, the well-being of the river is directly connected to the well-being of the people (Davison, 2017). He says that there is a well-known Maori saying: I am the river, and the river is me (ibid.).

After watching a simple news clip that clearly explained that there is a connection between the Whanganui River and the well-being of the people, we asked students to talk with their partner about what the video meant to them (Lui, 2017). It quickly came to our attention that grade 3 students do not know what well-being means. We ascertained that this would need to be rectified before we could continue. We knew the concept was not only fundamental to understanding current global indigenous cultures but also would be relevant to each students' understanding of nature and self.

Well-being is a profile in the previously mentioned Core Competencies. According to the teacher guides, well-being is defined as:

> Students who are personally aware and responsible recognize how their decisions and actions affect their mental, physical, emotional, social, cognitive, and spiritual wellness, and take increasing responsibility for caring for themselves. They keep themselves healthy and physically active, manage stress, and express a sense of personal well-being. They make choices that contribute to their safety in their communities, including online interactions. They recognize the importance of happiness, and have strategies that help them find peace in challenging situations". (Personal awareness and responsibility: Competency profiles, n.d.)

A sample 'I' statement for this competency is "I can use strategies to find peace in stressful times" (ibid.).

With this example in mind, we helped students to break down the word and started by just talking about the meaning of 'well'. Compared to their remarkable insights about what birds might mean to navigators on the Hōkūleʻa, they struggled to define the word. They knew little more than it was the opposite of sick. They could not easily outline what makes them the opposite of sick. With some prompting, they were able to connect a safe home, food on the table to being well. Finally, a student yelled out "love" (Student, personal interview by the author, 2017, March 5). Once this happened, students were able to expand on their definition to include things that make them happy, calm and safe.

On our school grounds, there is an old tree with a curve at the base. It is a favourite hangout for students of all ages as it is the perfect place to sit. It is called the horse tree because you can easily swing your legs over the trunk like a horse. Returning adult students often ask if the tree is still there. Next, we asked the students how the horse tree might be connected to their well-being. This was also difficult for them, which is not too surprising considering this way of thinking about the word 'well' was new to them. We prompted them to think about why they like to hang out at the tree. Why do students of all ages gather there? Why do former students remember it?

Once again, the responses began at a literal level. There were mentions of it being shady or fun. Students needed help to acknowledge that they feel better in a cozy nook of nature, leaning against a beautiful old tree. They know it is more "fun" being outside under a big tree, but it had never occurred to them that it might be good for them or their well-being. Once these connections were apparent to students and they had a working definition of well-being, we returned to the river, and so we returned to global indigenous cultures and other environments.

Students each had a dry-erase marker and had written their definition of well-being on a section of the library windows. We asked them to discuss and jot down how a river might be important to the Maori people. They were quickly able to determine that the river was most likely a food source and somewhere to get drinking water. It was easy for them to make the next connection between well-being and the river. As a food and water source, the river needed to be free of pollution. It could not be overfished. Interestingly, they were very concerned about it being drained of water. We could clearly connect environmental needs to personal needs of people far away.

It was hard for students to connect to the spiritual aspect of well-being. The closest they came was when they referred to love. The ineffable quality of connection and happiness that we sometimes feel being outside or under a lush green canopy eluded them. Many of our students live quite structured lives and outside time often means an organized activity, such a soccer practice or ski lessons. This can fragment their connection to nature and reduce their ability to recognize the restorative qualities of time outside. It also thwarts the deeper connection required to begin to understand the what Gregory Cajete means when he writes, "indigenous means being so completely identified with a place that you reflect its very entrails, its soul"

(Cajete, 1994, p. 87). We recognize that we need to continue to work with all of our students to help them build a meaningful connection to their natural environment. Nurturing this connection will help them to explore the curriculum more deeply and understand its intentions.

CURRICULAR OBJECTIVES

When we reflect back on the content and big ideas central to the new grade three Social Studies curriculum, we believe that our study of the Hōkūle'a and Whanganui River have been aligned with both the spirit and goals of the curriculum. The students explored the "cultural characteristics and ways of life" of global indigenous peoples when they investigated the history of Polynesian navigation and its resurgence through the Hōkūle'a (Social Studies 3, 2016). The technologies that the crew of the Hōkūle'a used to stay in touch with supporters, such as video blogs and photographs, helped the students understand "aspects of life shared by and common to peoples and cultures" (ibid.). The link between well-being and the Whanganui River allowed our student to find common understanding with their own cherished natural spaces. The Hōkūle'a is a perfect and accessible manifestation of the "interconnections of cultural and technological innovations" and the "relationship between humans and their environment" (ibid.).

The big ideas driving the grade three Social Studies curriculum were also prominent throughout our inquiry. The way our students embraced the exploration of the Hōkūle'a, and the Whanganui River showed that "[l]earning about indigenous peoples nurtures multicultural awareness and respect for diversity" (ibid.). Finally, it allowed the students to understand that indigenous groups "value the well-being of the self, the land, spirits, and ancestors" (ibid.).

We believe that the discussion around well-being fostered by the importance of the Whanganui River to the Maori people was aligned with some of the Core Competency profiles.

CONCLUSIONS

A key objective of the new curriculum is to help Canadians live in a society that includes indigenous perspectives, traditions, and beliefs. British Columbia's new curriculum strives to prepare students for living in a reconciled Canada where Indigenous philosophies are part of our lives and our legal framework. Helping young learners understand indigenous technologies and worldviews from a young age enables them to thrive and engage in such a society. There is always new intriguing information to get students thinking: traveling without modern navigational devices, traveling with no pollution, understanding your natural environment so we that you can travel far beyond your point of origin, viewing the well-being of your surrounding place as central to your well-being. Finding age-appropriate and engaging resources that connect to the lives of young learners is essential to this process.

This was a wonderful inquiry to teach and was a highlight for us and our students. They were often deeply engaged in thinking activities and challenging assumptions about how to be in the world. We look forward to starting this work with another group of girls next year. We hope that more teachers who work with grade three in British Columbia will take up the Hōkūleʻa and the Whanganui River as windows into the curriculum.

One of our closing reflection questions for our students after their Hōkūleʻa inquiry was "Why is the Hōkūleʻa important and why are we learning about it?" One student responded that it proves "that we can live in the old ways" (personal interview, 9 May 2017). Place-based innovation, environmental connectedness, and an understanding of cultures other than ours, both rooted in the past and deeply entrenched in the present, were introduced and explored with quality and age-appropriate resources with encouraging success. We believe that seeing global indigenous cultures and technologies in contemporary life is the best way for young learners to explore the curriculum.

REFERENCES

BC's new curriculum. (2016). Retrieved January 15, 2018, from https://curriculum.gov.bc.ca/

Borrows, J. (Presenter). (2016, November 17). *Justice, identity and belonging*. Speech presented at President's Dream Colloquium on Returning to the Teachings, Simon Fraser University, Burnaby, BC.

Bryce, O. (2017, April 20). *Nelson socials 3 classroom set* [PDF]. Retrieved from http://www.nelson.com/bc/wp-content/uploads/2016/10/SC-SAM-Nelson-Socials-3-2017-New-Brand-LR.pdf

Cajete, G. (1994). *Look to the mountain: An ecology of indigenous education*. Durango, CO: Kivaki Press.

Colloquium Course. (2016). In V. Kelly & B. Morrison (Chair.), *President's dream colloquium on returning to the teachings: Justice, identity and belonging*. Symposium conducted at Simon Fraser University, Burnaby, BC. Retrieved from http://www.sfu.ca/dean-gradstudies/events/dreamcolloquium/DreamColloquium-Reconciliation.html

Core Competencies. (2016). Retrieved September 6, 2017, from https://curriculum.gov.bc.ca/competencies

Davis, W. (2009). *The wayfinders: Why ancient wisdom matters in the modern world*. Toronto: House of Anansi.

Davison, I. (2017, March 15). *Whanganui river given legal status of a person*. Retrieved January 4, 2018, from https://www.earthlawcenter.org/newsfeed/2017/3/whanganui-river-given-legal-status-of-a-person

First Peoples Principles of Learning. (n.d.). Retrieved January 15, 2018, from https://www2.gov.bc.ca/assets/gov/education/kindergarten-to-grade-12/teach/teaching-tools/aboriginal-education/principles_of_learning.pdf

Grade three students. (2017, January). [Navigation work booklet]. Unpublished raw data. How do you malama honua? (n.d.). Retrieved January 15, 2018, from http://www.hokulea.com/malamahonua/

Hōkūleʻa Worldwide Voyage. (2016, November 15). *Worldwide voyage overview* [Video file]. Retrieved from https://www.youtube.com/watch?v=9yjNUbJquKI

Lui, K. (2017, March 16). New Zealand's Whanganui river has been granted the same legal rights as a person. *Time*. Retrieved January 4, 2018, from http://time.com/4703251/new-zealand-whanganui-river-wanganui-rights/

Personal awareness and responsibility: Competency profiles. (n.d.). Retrieved January 4, 2018, from https://curriculum.gov.bc.ca/sites/curriculum.gov.bc.ca/files/pdf/PersonalAwarenessResponsibilityCompetencyProfiles.pdf

Polynesian Voyaging Society. (n.d.). Retrieved September 7, 2017, from http://www.hokulea.com
Social Studies 3. (2016). Retrieved September 6, 2017, from https://curriculum.gov.bc.ca/curriculum/social-studies/3
Truth and Reconciliation Commission of Canada: Calls to action. (2015). Retrieved January 7, 2018, from http://www.trc.ca/websites/trcinstitution/File/2015/Findings/Calls_to_Action_English2.pdf

Sophia Hunter
Crofton House School
Canada

Carolynn Beaty
Crofton House School
Canada

MARGIT SÄRE

12. CLIMATE CHANGE AND AGRICULTURAL PRODUCTION

Hands-on Active Classroom Learning in Estonia

INTRODUCTION

Education is an essential element of the global response to climate change as it helps young people understand the impact of global warming and encourages changes in their attitudes and behaviour. European project S.A.M.E. WORLD (www.sameworld.eu) worked out different online materials, developed and tested new programs for schools focusing climate change, environmental justice and climate migration topics. The activities took place in nine European Union countries.

The chapter introduces the Climate Change and Agricultural Production Program implemented in rural Estonian primary schools in 2017. The author discusses methods used in the classroom to create young people understanding that sustainable agriculture is one of the important players in decreasing the impact of climate change, and everybody has a possible contribution to that process.

This experimental learning helped students to evaluate the effectiveness, pros, and cons of the traditional and sustainable agricultural production; giving an opportunity to understand the interconnections of today's world (nature, economy, society) and make them aware of the fact that individual (food) consumption choices have an impact not only on the present but also on the future. Teachers' competence building was also an important component of the project as educators' practices and attitudes are equally important for improving educational processes.

ENVIRONMENTAL AND GLOBAL EDUCATION POLICIES AND PROGRAMS

With a world population over 7 billion people and limited natural resources, individuals and societies need urgently to learn to live together sustainably and to take actions based on the understanding that today's actions have implications on the lives of people and the planet in future. The United Nations has through its programs aimed to improve quality education on sustainable development at all levels and social contexts, to transform society by reorienting. Very importantly, UNESCO Education for Sustainable Development (ESD) empowers participatory teaching and learning methods that motivate learners to change their behaviours and take action for sustainable development (https://en.unesco.org/themes/education-sustainable-development).

In line with the United Nations 2030 Sustainable Development Goals, Europe 2020 Strategy and other important policy documents European Commission has through its various programmes financed development education and awareness raising on global issues. For example, the DEAR (Development Education and Awareness raising) programme is taken forward to inform European Union (EU) citizens about development issues and foster awareness and understanding of global development and recognition of interdependences; also change attitude sand provide the public with tools to engage critically with global developments.

In 2015 the EU celebrated a special year for development, aiming to increase the awareness of citizens about how EU development aid works and foster direct involvement and critical thinking of citizens and stakeholders in development co-operation. With European Commission support, numerous non-state actors started their multinational DEAR projects. One of those – S.A.M.E. WORLD project (www.sameworld.eu) – was elaborated and implemented during 2015–2018 by thirteen European partners in response to the need to develop interdisciplinary teaching methods, materials, and training on local languages on climate change, environmental justice, and environmental migrations. The main purpose of the project was to promote global environmental citizenship, climate friendly practices and cultural/change of attitude toward immigrants.

Project partners from formal and non-formal educational institutions created multilingual online tools and educational materials; interdisciplinary programs were tested in schools and outdoor programs were carried out, which represent climate change not only as an environmental issue but a moral one (human rights based approach). Importantly, besides students also their families and teachers were involved in learning. It is also worth mentioning that teaching and training materials were developed by a multinational team of experts, taking into account different historical, political, cultural, educational and other contexts.

Estonian partner – NGO Peipsi Center for Transboundary Cooperation – focused their activities on rural East Estonian schools. Although Estonia has strong environmental education policies, targeting especially young people, in more underdeveloped /rural regions schools are not so much involved in innovative projects or retraining programs for educators. That is why our SAME World project was of big importance to that region.

KEY COMPETENCIES TO BE DEVELOPED

As stated in the UNESCO Education for Sustainable Development Goals, global issues, such as climate change, require a transformation of the way we think and act. Parents, teachers, and educators have an important task to develop new skills, values, and attitudes to the new generation. Thus, Education for Sustainable Development

(ESD) was a holistic and transformational concept followed while developing new methods and programs in the S.A.M.E. WORLD project.

Education for Sustainable Development addresses mostly learning content and outcomes, pedagogy and the learning environment. ESD does not only integrate contents such as climate change, sustainable production, and consumption into the curriculum but interactive, learner-centered teaching and learning settings are required. ESD foresees a shift from teaching to learning and supports self-directed learning, participation and collaboration and the linking of formal and informal learning. However, the conflict between a fast-changing society and a largely traditional school system has become a serious obstacle for many countries, especially in schools of more disadvantaged regions. Thus, we should not forget about teachers and educators while trying to develop new programs / new educational paradigm.

While developing S.A.M.E. WORLD project educational programs, ESD concepts were taken as the core of our teaching-learning activities. Our team believes in the importance of learner-centered, problem-orientation teaching, where the bigger role is given to learners than traditionally in Estonian schools.

Thus, before testing new climate change focused programs in schools, special teacher training sessions and consultations were carried out. During our project, we discovered that not all schools were eager to introduce new programs and teaching methods in their schools, still, we established very good collaboration with four schools, where pilot programs were eventually carried out. Short evaluations were also conducted in classrooms before the programs started, in order to understand learners starting point and awareness on global and sustainable development issues.

Methodology

"Climate change and agricultural production" program, aiming to introduce the interconnections of climate change and agricultural production, was developed and tested by Peipsi Center for Transboundary Cooperation in four schools in 2017.

The program was run by non-formal educators from Peipsi Center for Transboundary Cooperation and assisted by the class teacher.

The program is suitable for 6th graders and older (13+ years). The themes of the program correspond to the Geography, Biology, and Society subject syllabuses.

The full program takes 2–3 months to complete and is a unique mix of theoretical knowledge and practical experiments; both formal and non-formal educational settings are used. The program supports self-directed learning and requires active participation from each child and collaboration in the classroom.

The workshop follows four main steps, where very different skills are used and developed:

1. The workshop starts with warming up "barometer"-game, that helps students share their opinions by asking them to line up along a continuum based on their position on an issue. It is especially useful when you want to discuss an issue about

Figure 12.1. "Climate change and agricultural production" class

which students have a wide range of opinion. In our program, we had "barometer" on main causes of climate change and your personal contribution to it. After that theoretical introduction to the topic of climate change and agricultural practices, interconnections are made. Short video clips of the film "Vanishing the bees" are also watched and importance of insects in ecosystems for biological welfare is analyzed.

2. For practical work: each child receives pots to plant different seeds – peas, beans, buckwheat, wheat, rye, barley. During the two-month period they have a task to water each pot either with the natural nutrient mixture, chemical fertilizer solutions or tap water. They work in pairs (or alone) and need to observe and photograph weekly the plant's growth.
Students will record the process, as a result, a digital diary (PowerPoint format) is compiled.
3. Short study and interviews with local farmers about their agricultural practices, pesticides used, their remark on climate change etc. is also encouraged.
4. At the end of the 2-month program, a concluding session was held with educators. The plant's growth was measured and the presence (or absence) of nodule bacteria was confirmed. Refractometer analysis was also done to measure plant sugars and differences depending on watering mixture used were discovered. Research work conclusions were then prepared in a written format.

Figure 12.2. Student measuring plant's length and searching the presence of nodule bacteria

Evaluation and Results of the Workshop

The workshops oral and written evaluations were conducted with teachers and students. The results showed that program was especially highly evaluated by teachers who appreciated its interdisciplinarity and novelty. However, the main concern from the teacher's side was that it is quite a time and money consuming activity (need to purchase fertilizers, soil, seeds, refractometer etc.) and also that the topics are from different syllabuses and much coordination, cooperation between teachers and management is needed.

Students appreciated the highly non-formal, non-regular class setting, and the interaction and joint work that was promoted with their classmates (which is not so common in rural schools). Still, some of them were not happy with dirty planting work. Short questionnaires also showed that most of the students were aware of climate change concepts, but that the interconnection with our own consumption habits (organic/non-organic products, energy use etc.) and climate change were not as clear.

As a result, we can say that the workshop helped students to create understanding of the systemic and interconnected nature of today's world and made them aware of the fact that individual (food) consumption choices have an impact not only on the present but also the future. The personal commitment to the experiment of growing cereals, analyzing results and interpreting these in the context of climate change, enhanced the development of critical thinking and had an effect on values

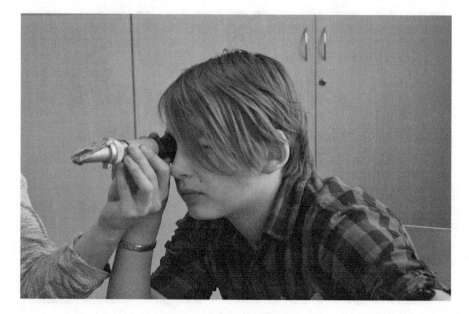

Figure 12.3. Using a refractometer to measure the sugar levels in the plant

concerning a sustainable lifestyle. As our test schools were from an agricultural region, students also learned about agricultural practices used by local farmers. In addition, the program strengthened the competencies needed for carrying out practical experiments, making conclusions and presenting your research work.

FURTHER DEVELOPMENT AND DISCUSSION

The positive reception of this particular Climate Change and Agricultural production Program and other interdisciplinary workshops (such as Climate Breakfast or Green Drama) developed within the S.A.M.E. WORLD project made our team develop programs further and expand them to other schools in Estonia. Still, there are various challenges that we noticed while working with a global education topic in our regional schools.

First, for now global topics are scattered in the syllabus through various lessons of Geography, Biology, Society etc. As education plays a vital role in helping young people recognize their contribution as global citizens, it is necessary to equip them with the information and skills to make informed decisions. We believe it is crucial to develop a global dimension to the Estonian school curriculum in a more systematic manner, bringing more discussions and links between local and global topics to the lessons. Both students and teachers are eager to be engaged in hands-on, more practical educational activities, but these require more time and more money as these resources are often not available.

Another challenge lies in training of educators both from the formal system (schools) and non-formal systems such as NGOs or environmental centres. Global learning facilitators, teachers or educators need constantly to enhance their knowledge and improve practices, in order to develop inclusive, learner-centered teaching. The S.A.M.E. WORLD project and online multilingual Educational Kit, along with several other training and information materials are available for educators but as our global world is changing fast and new challenges arise, then the need for new training materials, and teacher training will be constant.

We have also noticed that sometimes the qualifications of non-formal system educators is doubted, and we believe that the evaluation and accreditation of non-formal educational programs is needed. Another important aspect of teacher training is the need for a transformation to the Education for Sustainable Development (ESD) concept: meaning enhanced learner-centered and problem-orientation teaching, higher participation and collaboration in the classroom and a linking of formal and informal learning. This new type of pedagogy requires a big change in schools and teachers. But as we know, change is often a painful process.

Lastly, we can say that our experiences with interdisciplinary climate change programs in rural schools were successful; they proved the need that the younger generation can be given an opportunity to understand the interconnections of today's world and make them aware of the fact that our own (consumption) choices can change the world. It is undeniable that behavioral choices have a substantial impact upon emissions, energy and water use, and on waste produced. Citizens' education and participation is a key tool to promote changes in sustainable behaviours and to develop a sense of environmental identity and global citizenship.

ACKNOWLEDGEMENTS

This chapter is based on the results obtained in the processes of implementing Europe Aid project: S.A.M.E. WORLD.SUSTAINABILITY. AWARENESS. MOBILIZATION. ENVIRONMENT in the Global Education for EYD 2015 – http://www.sameworld.eu/

To read more about the Estonian partner, Peipsi Center for Transboundary Cooperation activities, visit www.ctc.ee.

REFERENCES

European Commission. (2015, December). *European year for development 2015*. Retrieved from https://ec.europa.eu/europeaid/tags/european-year-development-2015-eyd2015_en

European Commission. (2017, April 8). *DEAR programme*. Retrieved from https://ec.europa.eu/europeaid/sectors/human-rights-and-governance/development-education-and-awareness-raising_en

Facing History and Ourselves. (n.d.). *Barometer: Taking a stand on controversial issues*. Retrieved from https://www.facinghistory.org/resource-library/teaching-strategies/barometer-taking-stand-controversial-issues

Europe 2020 Strategy. (n.d.). Retrieved from https://ec.europa.eu/info/business-economy-euro/economic-and-fiscal-policy-coordination/eu-economic-governance-monitoring-prevention-correction/european-semester/framework/europe-2020-strategy_en

UNESCO. (2017). *Education for sustainable development learning objectives*. Retrieved from http://unesdoc.unesco.org/images/0024/002474/247444e.pdf
UNESCO. (2018). *Education for sustainable development*. Retrieved from https://en.unesco.org/themes/education-sustainable-development
United Nations. (n.d.). *UN 2030 sustainable development goals*. Retrieved from https://www.un.org/sustainabledevelopment/sustainable-development-goals/
Peipsi Center for Transboundary Cooperation. (2017, January 18). *SAME world project*. Retrieved from http://www.ctc.ee/running/same-world
Sameworld. (2018). *S.A.M.E. WORLD Edu Kit*. Retrieved from http://edu-kit.sameworld.eu

Margit Säre
NGO – Peipsi Center for Transboundary Cooperation
Estonia

DARJA SKRIBE DIMEC

13. OUTDOOR EDUCATION IN THE SLOVENIAN SCHOOL SYSTEM SUPPORTS CULTURAL AND ENVIRONMENTAL EDUCATION

INTRODUCTION

The unique school system in Slovenia, which includes obligatory forms of outdoor and environmental education during a compulsory nine-year basic education, highly supports a close connection with culture and environment. The Basic School Act defining the curriculum for basic education was adopted in 1996. According to this document, outdoor education is integrated into the national curriculum for primary and lower secondary education, materialized by the "Days of Activities" and "Outdoor School". The curriculum defines 15 days of cultural, sports, science and technical activities per year while an Outdoor School is an activity that takes place for three or more days in a row outside the school area. Every basic school student must attend Outdoor School at least twice in their 9-year compulsory education. To implement these activities in primary and lower secondary schools, Slovenia has a network of 24 outdoor residential centres (CŠOD centres), which are funded entirely by the state (Ministry of Education, Science and Sport). In CŠOD centres place-based educational programs are implemented, fostering outdoor learning in the natural environment. Most centres are in abandoned and renovated military buildings, in deep forests or in the mountains, along the borders with Italy, Austria, Hungary and Croatia. Slovenia is characterized by extremely diverse and relatively well-preserved nature. Significant diversity in land, climate, plant and animal species, and culture enables the students to stay connected with variety of local traditions and their natural and cultural heritage. All programs in the CŠOD centres are strongly connected to the local environment and cultural traditions. As globalization increasingly creates a risk of neglecting historical tradition and the loss of cultural identity, it is essential that outdoor education emphasize locality, which allows us to stay connected with tradition, and heritage and by that, successfully weaving together culture and environment.

ABOUT SLOVENIA

Slovenia is a small country located in the heart of Europe (Figure 13.1). It shares borders with Austria on the north, Hungary on the east, Croatia on the south and Italy on the west. Slovenia occupies an area of little more than 20,000 km². and so

Slovenia is about 493 times smaller than Canada and about two times smaller than the Netherlands. In total it has 1,382 km of borders (Country size comparison, 2017). In less than 2.5 hours you can easily across the country by car from east to west or from south to north. In Slovenia, there is a population of about 2 million people. Slovenia's capital city, Ljubljana, is located near the centre of the country. Slovenia has been an independent state since 1991 (as it was formerly part of Yugoslavia) and a member of the European Union since May 1st, 2004, a member of NATO since April 7th, 2004. It is also a member of many other international organizations.

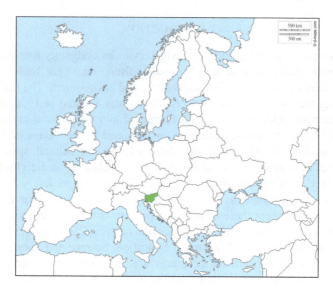

Figure 13.1. Slovenia's location on the map of Europe
Note: Slovenia location on the Europe map (n.d.). Retrieved from https://d-maps.com/carte.php?num_car=2232&lang=en

Slovenia lies in the place where the Alps meet the Mediterranean Sea, and the Pannonian Plain meets the Karst. The topography of Slovenia features a small coastal strip on the Adriatic with 46 km of coastline (approximately two fingers for every citizen), the Julian Alps adjacent to Italy, the Karavanke Mountains of the northern border with Austria, and a mixture of mountains and valleys with numerous rivers in the central and eastern regions. According to a newer natural geographic regionalization, the country consists of four macro-regions. These are the Alpine, the Mediterranean, the Dinaric, and the Pannonian landscapes with three prevailing climate types – mountain, submediterranean, and temperate continental. The highest point of Slovenia Mt. Triglav (three heads) lies in the Julian Alps with an elevation of 2,864 m. The longest river is the Sava, which flows through the centre of the country for 221 km. A unique feature of Slovenia is the presence of over 10,000 underground caves formed in karst, the most well-known being the Škocjan caves in the southwest, which have been designated a natural UNESCO World Heritage Site since 1986.

Slovenia is also distinguished by a vast variety of habitats (Hlad & Skoberne, 2001), due to the contact of various geological units and biogeographical regions, and due to human influences. Over half of the country (11,823 km^2) is covered by forests (Statistical Office of the Republic of Slovenia, 2017). This makes Slovenia the third most forested country in Europe, after Finland and Sweden (Forests, forestry and logging, 2017). Slovenia is (in terms of the quality of water) one of the most water-rich counties in the world, with a dense river network, a rich aquifer system, and significant karst underground watercourses (Žitnik, Čuček, & Pograjc, 2014). The term "Karst topography" refers to that of southwestern Slovenia's Karst Plateau, a limestone region of underground rivers, gorges, and caves, located between the capital city Ljubljana and the Mediterranean. The term "karst" originated from this region. Around 12.5% of the territory is protected, 35.5% of the protected territory being in the "Natura 2000" ecological network, which is the largest percentage among European Union states (Bibič, 2007). The protected areas of Slovenia include national parks, regional parks, and nature parks, the largest of which is Triglav National Park. There are 286 Natura 2000 designated protected areas. Slovenia also signed the Rio Convention on Biological Diversity on June 13th, 1992 and became a party to the convention on July 9th, 1996. It subsequently produced a National Biodiversity Strategy and Action Plan, which was received by the convention on May 30th, 2002. According to Yale University's Environmental Performance Index, Slovenia is considered a "strong performer" in environmental protection efforts (Environmental Performance Index [EPI], 2012).

Diverse geological units, relief and biogeographical regions enable great diversity in plant and animal species. Slovenia is marked by a significant biological diversity (Blažič, Arih, Nartnik, & Turk, 2008; Hlad & Skoberne, 2001). From this point of view, Slovenia is a 'hot spot' in Europe (Mršić, 1997). Slovenia is one of the few European countries in which the three larger European predators permanently live: brown bear, wolf and lynx. Within the framework of the "Life Dinalp Bear" project, a genetic analysis estimated that at the end of 2015 there were about 564 bears in Slovenia (A new estimate of brown bear numbers in Slovenia, 2017). There are also many animal and plant endemic species, where the fauna from karst caves standing out with the world-famous 'olm' or 'proteus' (*Proteus anguinus*). Olm is a cave vertebrate, aquatic salamander, blind, 20 – 30 cm long and the only exclusively cave-dwelling chordate species found in Europe (Figure 13.2). In Slovenian language, it is called "človeška ribica (human fish)" because of its skin colour. It is also a symbol of Slovenian natural heritage.

Slovenia's geographical and biological diversity determines the cultural diversity of the country's various regions. Because Slovenia lies at the crossroads of the Alps, the Mediterranean, the Pannonian Plain, and the Dinaric Mountain Range, through the centuries the individual Slovenian regions have developed various forms of economic activities, ways of life and cultural creativity. Among the greatest

Figure 13.2. Endemic olm or proteus (Proteus anguinus) living in karst caves in Slovenia. Note: The Dragon is celebrating his first birthday (2017). Retrieved from https://siol.net/novice/slovenija/zmajcek-praznuje-prvi-rojstni-dan-442294

treasures of these regions are the diversity of dialects of the Slovenian language, different lifestyles, gastronomic traditions, and other aspects of the everyday life of the local people. Ljubljana was proclaimed the European Green Capital 2016 (European Green Capital, n.d.).

From the above-mentioned data, compiled from Pavlič Možina and Prešeren (2011) and different websites: Slovenian Environment Agency (n.d.), Worldmark Encyclopedia of Nations (n.d.), Slovenia (2018), Diversity (n.d.) and European State of the Environment (2010), it is clear that Slovenia is an outstanding mosaic of biological, landscape and cultural traits, which are the basis for its outdoor education programs.

THE SLOVENIAN SCHOOL SYSTEM

Many important changes in the Slovenian school system have been made after 1992, soon after the independence of Slovenia. These changes have been introduced gradually. The new educational laws approved in 1996 on the basis of the White Paper on Education in Slovenia are based on the principles of democracy, freedom of choice, autonomy and professionalism, quality and excellence, and equal opportunity (Krek, 1996).

Education in Slovenia starts with pre-school (children aged 1–6), followed by a basic education (children aged 6–15) that encompasses primary and lower secondary education, then follows with upper secondary education (students aged 15–19) and higher education from 19 years onwards. The whole education system from pre-school to higher education is under the responsibility of the Ministry of Education, Science and Sport. The education system in Slovenia is fully financed from the state budget.

In Slovenia, pre-school education is not compulsory. In 2013 and 2014 there were 75.6% of children of pre-school age who attended kindergartens and early childhood education and care families. In the same school year, over 90% of all five-year olds attended pre-school education (Taštanoska, 2015, p. 21). Public kindergartens are founded by local communities. The Kindergarten Curriculum is an essential program document adopted in 1999 that specifies pre-school education as part of the education system.

In accordance with the Constitution of the Republic of Slovenia, basic school education is compulsory, and it is state-financed. Education is organized in a single-structure nine-year basic school (integrated primary and lower secondary education). Basic education is divided into three cycles, with each covering three grades. During the first cycle, generalist teachers provide for all of a child's education. The second cycle includes some subject specialist teachers, and the third cycle uses subject specialist teachers almost exclusively. External, national exams are compulsory for all pupils at the end of the second and at the end of the third cycle. Further, exams are compulsory for three subjects: the native language, mathematics and a third compulsory subject that is annually determined by the ministry.

In Slovenia, post-compulsory education begins with upper secondary education. Students can choose among general upper secondary education, technical upper secondary education and vocational upper secondary education. General upper secondary education prepares pupils for further studies. The duration of this educational level is 4 years, and at the end of the studies, an external exam is conducted. The upper secondary vocational and technical education provides the skills and knowledge required for employment or for higher education. Upper secondary schooling is free.

There are several types of higher education institutions in Slovenia, namely universities, faculties, art academies and independent higher education institutions. Slovenia joined the Bologna Reform in 1999, and as a result, a three-cycle study structure was introduced in 2004. Higher education attainment and student performance are measured in ECTS (the European Credit Transfer and Accumulation System) credits. The government also funds full-time studies at the first and second levels of the Bologna structure.

Because basic schooling is mandatory and financed by the state, we will look at this organization in more detail. The Organization and Financing of Education Act regulates the terms and conditions of the basic school, through its management and funding methods. The Basic School Act was adopted in 1996. It defines general basic education objectives; gives parents the right to choose the educational method for their child; prescribes components and the scope of compulsory and elective basic school programs; regulates enrolments, rights and responsibilities of pupils, basic assessment and testing rules, conditions for pupils' progression to next years and the reporting of end-of-year results. The act also regulates basic school education for children with special needs, the rights of migrant children, home education and basic school education for adults.

The basic school program is specified by a timetable and curricula of compulsory and elective subjects, as well as by guidelines and educational concepts that define other methods of working with children (morning care, afterschool classes, extra-curricular activities, outdoor school), cross-curricular contents (days of activities, how to use libraries and information technologies) and other documents to guide the work of the education staff. Along with compulsory and compulsory optional subjects, class discussion periods and days of activities (Cultural, Sports, Technical and Science Days), all basic schools undertake the activities of the extended program. These include extracurricular activities, non-compulsory optional subjects and morning care for pupils in grade 1, as well as after-school classes for pupils of grades 1 to 5. Among the 15 main basic education objectives we can find, some are strongly connected with a cultural and environmental education for example; "to develop awareness of belonging to the nation, national identity and cultural heritage, and to nurture general cultural values to develop respect for human rights, tolerance and acceptance of diversity; to facilitate sustainable development and to take responsibility for one's actions, one's health, for other people and the environment" (2nd article of The Basic School Act, 1996).

The presentation of the school system in Slovenia is mainly based on the following internet sources: Education system Slovenia (2015), Single structure education (2016), Education policy outlook, Slovenia (2016), Slovenia education (n.d.) and Higher education system in Slovenia (n.d.).

OUTDOOR EDUCATION IN SLOVENIA

According to the Basic School Act (1996), outdoor education in Slovenia is integrated into the national curriculum for primary and lower secondary education. At the organizational level, outdoor education is organized primarily by (a) Days of Activities and (b) Outdoor School. Both types of activities are part of the regular schooling organized during the school year in order to achieve the educational goal of outdoor learning. Being a part of the national curriculum, these are financed by the state. This structure seems to be unique.

In many countries, educators and policymakers want to find closer links between formal education and out-of-school learning to create an inclusive education system and to bring together school science and life outside of schools (Rennie, 2010). According to Cooper (2016), outdoor education in the United Kingdom is part of both the formal and non-formal sectors. Schools organize field work as part of the geography and science curriculum, and outdoor education centres may offer programs that relate to physical education, environmental education, and personal and social development. However, there are few other solutions concerning outdoor education in basic education. "In countries, such as Slovenia, outdoor learning is predominantly linked to the school curriculum, while in others, such as Iceland, it is mainly provided by the non-formal sector" (Cooper, 2016, p. 399).

Activity Days

In 1998, the Expert Council of the Republic of Slovenia adopted the concept of 'Activity Days' for basic education. They established four types of days: Cultural,

Science, Technical, and Sports Days. Activity Days are part of the compulsory basic school program (The Concept of Days of Activities, 1998; Act Amending and Supplementing the Basic School Act, article 19.a, 2011). The purpose of Activity Days is to enable students to consolidate their knowledge of individual subjects and integrate its various components and practical skills into problem-solving activities. This is crucial in the context of cooperation and the ability to participate in any given social context. In the different years of schooling, the distribution of different types of Days of Activities varies, and at the end of each year, each student receives a total of 15 Days of Activities. Fifteen Days of Activities are envisaged for each and every school year, which translates to three weeks out of a total of 38 weeks per school year. Each Day lasts for five teaching hours. Table 13.1 shows the structure of Activity Days according to subjects and school year, but despite the explicit subject definitions, the implementation is often interdisciplinary.

Table 13.1. Days of activities in the Slovenian primary and lower secondary schools

Days of activities	School year									Hours
	1	2	3	4	5	6	7	8	9	
Cultural	4	4	4	3	3	3	3	3	3	150
Science	3	3	3	3	3	3	3	3	3	135
Technical	3	3	3	4	4	4	4	4	4	165
Sports	5	5	5	5	5	5	5	5	5	225
Total	15	15	15	15	15	15	15	15	15	675

Source: Basic school curriculum (2014), retrieved from http://www.mizs.gov.si/fileadmin/ mizs.gov.si/pageuploads/podrocje/os/devetletka/predmetniki/Pred_14_OS_4_12.pdf

According to the definition and objectives of the "Concept of Days (of activities)" (1998), Activity Days should inspire students to be creative, inquisitive and to show initiative. In addition, Activity Days enable students to observe precisely and to gain experiences, skills and knowledge that can increase their problem-solving abilities. Clear educational goals are set for each of the four types of activities.

Schools also have to include the content and organizational structure of Days of activities in their Annual Work Plan. The schools themselves deploy the organization of the Activity Days, and they mostly decide to organize these outside the school buildings. For Cultural Days, cultural institutions such as theatre, opera or cinema are most often used. All Sports Days are taking place outside. Students are sometimes offered alternative options. For example, in winter, pupils can go skiing, snowboarding, sledding, skating or walking/hiking near the school. For Science Days, students often go on excursions, to the House of experiments, museums, zoos, arboretums, etc. For Technical Days, students visit a technical museum, railway museum, coal mining museum, artificial handicrafts, etc. Teachers often organize the projects so the objectives of different subject areas are intertwined. Parents must pay only for transport and entrance fees. Some schools offer alternative activities without any costs, or parents can apply for financial support as every school typically keeps a special budget for such cases. A random selection among the school websites is an example of an organization of Activity Days for one year for 1st grade in Vide Pregarc Basic School, which is situated in the capital city (Table 13.2).

Table 13.2. Days of activities at Vide Pregarc Basic School for 1st grade for year 2017/18

Activity	Content	Time
Science Days (3)	1. Meadow/Forest	Term ŠVN
	2. Water – Stream	Term ŠVN
	3. Healthy way of growing up	October 2017
Cultural Days (4)	1. National gallery	December 2017
	2. Viewing the theatre performance	Jan.–March 2018
	3. Prešeren Day (cultural holiday)	February 2018
	4. Day of the school (The 60 years anniversary)	June 2018
Sports Days (5)	1. Autumn trip	September 2017
	2. Orientation hike	Term ŠVN
	3. Winter games	Jan.–Feb. 2018
	4. "March along barbed wire"	May 2018
	5. Sports games	June 2018
Technical Days (3)	1. New Year's products	November 2017
	2. Travel to the past	November 2017
	3. Earth Day	April 2018

Note: ŠVN = Outdoor School for 3 or more days.
Source: Vide Pregarc Basic school (n.d.). Retrieved from https://www.osvp.si/solski-koledar/solsko-leto/

From Table 13.2, it is clear that wide variety of activities is offered to students in the first year of schooling. For Science Days two out of three days are planned to be taken outdoors (Meadow/Forest and Water – Stream) and at least two Cultural Days will be conducted out of the school (gallery and theatre). All five Sports Days will be held outdoors. The "March along barbed wire" is an almost 35 km long route around Ljubljana, where during World War II the wire fence of Italian and German occupiers was constructed. School students join this traditional walking route just for a small part of it. From the title of these activities, it is difficult to figure out how many Technical Days are planned to be out of school. However, we can guess that at least "Earth Day" will be held outside and probably "Travel to the past" for example. From Table 13.2, we can also see that dates of events are distributed in a way that each month at least one day of activity will happen. The phrase "term ŠVN" means that the Activity Days will be carried out within the framework of one-week activities in Outdoor School. For all other grades Activity Days are planned similarly.

Outdoor School

Outdoor School is another government-prescribed way of reaching educational goals outdoors. It is defined as "an organized form of educational work, which takes place three or more days in a row out of the school" (Outdoor School, n.d.). As mentioned before Outdoor School is integrated into the national curriculum for primary and lower secondary education (Basic School Act, 1996). It is obligatory for each school to organize at least two Outdoor Schools in 9-year schooling and it is recommended to organize them at least three times – at the end of each 3-year cycle, but many schools tend to offer their students one Outdoor School each year (Gros et al., 2001). This can be done because schools often combine Activity Days with Outdoor School (Table 13.2).

Because of the diverse landscape with mountains, the sea, a Mediterranean and continental climate, Slovenia has very good natural conditions for outdoor sport activities. Therefore, in Slovenia there is long tradition that basic school students learn to ski and to swim. According to Kristan (1998), the concept of Outdoor School dates back to 1962.

> An Outdoor School is defined as a special educational form, the essence of which is that a whole class or more of the parallels go for some time to a natural environment, as little urban as possible, outside the place of permanent residence (to the sea, the river, the lake, in forests, mountains, snow-covered nature, etc.), where in special circumstances and after a special education program, the practical pedagogical work continues. (Kristan, 1998, p. 8)

If the Outdoor School in the past was intended only for sports activities, the new concept differs considerably. In 2001, Gros and many other experts prepared "The Concept of Outdoor School", which is the foundation for nowadays implementation of Outdoor School. The following is a conceptual definition of Outdoor School.

> The specific organization of the work of the Outdoor School primarily implements a program whose goals, activities and contents from several different subject curricula are linked to a different implementation (for example, fieldwork, projects, sports activities), and for which it is particularly important to have a cross-curricular connecting and intertwining (of) the knowledge of different subject areas and integrating (these) into the natural and social space, that is, the connection with the environment in which the Outdoor School takes place in nature. The program of the Outdoor School is generally carried out

in the natural environment. It is precisely this specific organizational form that provides a greater possibility of implementing all elements of the social-integration role of the educational program (Gros et al., 2001, p. 4).

The design of the implementation program of Outdoor School is based on three foundations:

- The Concept of Outdoor School (goals, principles, specific forms of work);
- the curriculum in a specific educational environment (curricula for each subject in a particular class and educational period);
- the specific options offered by the environment and the space in which program of Outdoor School is conducted (Gros et al., 2001, pp. 7–8).

Because Outdoor School is part of the curriculum, the Slovenian Ministry of Education, Science and Sport covers all costs for one Outdoor School (Act of Financing Outdoor School, 2004) and provides funding for teachers for additional Outdoor Schools, while parents must also contribute to the material costs (accommodation and transport). The Law on the Organization and Financing of Education (2007) in Article 83 stipulates that for parents who (due to socio-economic status) cannot pay the full contribution for their children, these funds are provided by the state in accordance with the norms and standards determined by the minister.

Since 2003 the Ministry of Education, Science and Sport has systematically monitored the implementation of the Outdoor School. Schools report to the ministry once a year on the number of implemented Outdoor Schools, the number of students who attended the Outdoor School, their program and type of accommodation. The Ministry of Education, Science and Sport has published two analyses of Outdoor Schools program for the year 2005 (Kresal Sterniša, n.d.) and the year 2014 (Analysis of Outdoor School, 2014). The two analyses are very similar indicating the stability of Outdoor School program in Slovenia. The number of implemented Outdoor Schools was 1591 in the year 2005 and 1590 in the year 2014 (Figure 13.3). Outdoor Schools were attended by 65.400 students in the year 2005 and 63.230 students in the year 2014. This decrease in the number of participants is seen as a consequence of a decrease in birth rate.

Most Outdoor Schools included topics from natural sciences (41.9% in 2005 and 46.1% in 2014), followed by swimming courses (24.7% in 2005 and 25.4% in 2014), and skiing courses (21.8% in 2005 and 19.8% in 2014). In smaller proportions, the schools also provided topics from the social sciences as well as mountain camps and some other activities.

As stated, schools have the autonomy to decide when, where and how often they will organize Outdoor Schools. Table 13.3 shows the organization of an Outdoor School in the Dravlje basic school for the year 2017. Dravlje basic school is placed in the capital city of Slovenia, and it was randomly selected from the list of basic school websites.

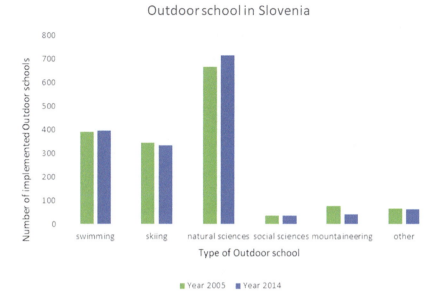

Figure 13.3. Number of implemented Outdoor Schools and types of Outdoor Schools in Slovenia

Dravlje Basic School organizes Outdoor School for every grade except for the last grade. As we can see from Table 13.3 students from that school receive outdoor experiences from different school subjects in different parts of Slovenia.

The Ministry of Education, Science and Sport analyzed venues of Outdoor Schools in 2014 (Analysis of Outdoor School, 2014). According to the report, more than half of the Outdoor Schools were conducted in CŠOD centres (54.8%). In almost the same proportion schools choose other holiday facilities (17.9%) or hotels (16.5%). Tourist farms or mountain lodges were used in 10.1% of cases, and student dormitories in less than one percent (0.7%) of cases.

CŠOD: CENTRE FOR SCHOOL AND OUTDOOR EDUCATION

As reported, many basic schools implement Activity Days and Outdoor Schools in CŠOD. The Centre for School and Outdoor Education (CŠOD) is a network of 24 outdoor residential centres widely spread across the country (Figure 13.4). They were established in 1992 by the Government of the Republic of Slovenia in order to integrate outdoor learning systematically into the program of basic schools. They were established by the Ministry of Education, Science and Sport, and are part of the ministry and that is why the state completely funds them. In the CŠOD centres place-based educational programs are implemented, fostering outdoor learning in the natural environment. Most centres are located in abandoned and renovated

Table 13.3. Outdoor School at the Basic School Dravlje for the year 2017

School year	Type of outdoor school	Place	Time
1.	Natural science camp	CŠOD Jurček (Kočevje)	29. 11. – 01. 12. 2017 (3 days)
2.	Natural science camp	CŠOD Jurček (Kočevje)	27. 11. – 29. 11. 2017 (3 days)
3.	Natural science camp	CŠOD Čebelica (Litija)	02. 10. – 04. 10. 2017 (3 days)
4.	Swimming school in nature	Dom ZPM LJ – Moste (Zambratija)	04. 06. – 08. 06. 2017 (5 days)
5.	Mountain camp	CŠOD Planica (Rateče)	04. 06. – 08. 06. 2017 (5 days)
6.	Winter school in nature	Dom Videc (Mariborsko Pohorje)	February (5 days)
7. + 8.	Natural sciences & mathematical camp	CŠOD Brežanka (Fiesa)	16. 04. – 20. 04. 2017 (5 days)

Note. CŠOD = Centre for school and Outdoor Education, Dom = lodge.
Source: Basic school Dravlje (n.d.). Retrieved from http://www.osdravlje.si/ola-v-naravi/

buildings, in deep forests or in the mountains, mainly along the border with Italy, Austria, Hungary and Croatia.

The beginnings of CŠOD date back to 1992 when the "Decree of Establishing CŠOD" was issued by the Government. In 1996, the "Basic School Act" was issued. This defined the program 'Life in nature' and indicated that Outdoor School was part of an expanded program. In 2001, a document called "Concept of Outdoor School" was published, which defined the purpose and goals of the Outdoor School more precisely. In 2011, the Basic School Act was amended, and the Outdoor School became part of the mandatory program. At the end of 2017 CŠOD also celebrated its 25th anniversary. On this occasion, they prepared a presentation which gives a complete insight into the development and operation of the CŠOD network (25th anniversary of CŠOD Centres, 2017). A historical review of the opening of the centres is shown in Table 13.4.

From 1993 to 2003, at least one new centre was opened every year, with four of them opened in 1996 and one, Kurent in the centre of a small town Ptuj, closed recently. In Figure 13.4, we can see that the first two centres were established in the north of the country, just next to the border with Austria. The reason for this is that after the independence of Slovenia, empty military barracks formerly belonging to the Yugoslav Army were abandoned at the borders. Some of these were not used by the Slovenian army, and so they were restored and put into the use of CŠOD. Later,

OUTDOOR EDUCATION IN THE SLOVENIAN SCHOOL SYSTEM

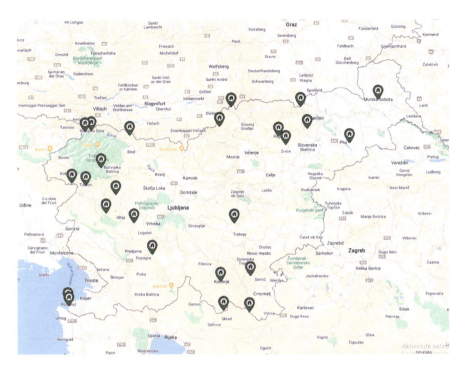

Figure 13.4. Locations of CŠOD centres (CŠOD centres, n.d.)

several other facilities and installations were put under the CŠOD's management, including abandoned village schools, mountain lodges, forest cabins and closed hotel resorts. Today, CŠOD centres are located well away from the major urban centres (Figure 13.4).

In parallel with the program for residential centres, CŠOD network also developed Day centres that carry out Activity Days. These programs started in 1995 with a Science Day in the Arboretum. Today we have a network of 19 Day centres that also supplement the educational activities of CŠOD centres throughout Slovenia. About 95,000 students per year visit the CŠOD system, with a total of 1,988,543 participants in 25 years.

CŠOD centres follow the definition of outdoor education presented by the model (Figure 13.5), which was made by Higgins & Loynes (1997). In this model, outdoor education comprises outdoor activities, environmental education, personal and social education.

In 2002, a three-year international project was completed within the framework of Comenius Education, aimed at integrating theoretical and practical knowledge related to teaching in nature. Experts from Austria, Czech Republic, Germany, Sweden and the United Kingdom have linked different perspectives and practices into a common starting point. As a result of the project, a brochure titled Outdoor

Table 13.4. Historical review of the opening of CŠOD centres

Year	CŠOD
1993	1. Škorpijon (April), 2. Trilobit (June)
1994	3. Ajda (September), 4. Rak (October), 5. Medved (November)
1995	6. Čebelica (September)
1996	7. Kranjska gora (January), 8. Bohinj (May), 9. Štrk (May), 10. Breženka (June)
1997	11. Lipa (October)
1998	12. Kavka (September), 13. Fara (September)
1999	14. Burja (May), 15. Vojsko (September)
2000	16. Planinka (January)
2001	17. Gorenje (January)
2002	18. Jurček (March), 19. Soča (March), 20. Radenci (June)
2003	21. Peca (April), 22. Kurent* (June)
2005	23. Planica (March)
2015	24. Cerkno (January)
2017	25. Murska Sobota (June)

* This centre is not operating any more.
Source: 25th anniversary of CŠOD centres (2017). [Video file]. Retrieved from https://www.youtube.com/watch?v=Az__-QOUIBU&feature=youtu.be

Education: Authentic Learning in the Context of Landscapes was created, which is the theoretical basis for new training courses for teachers from EU countries and teachers from countries that seek to join the EU (Higgins & Nicol, 2002). Teachers, who were preparing programs for CŠOD, took this and some other similar publications as extremely valuable resources. According to Gregorčič (2005), Slovenia is very strong in the field of Outdoor School compared to other European countries, mainly due to the favourable natural conditions and excellent organization and positioning in the educational system. The results are the product of the long-standing practice and experience of the CŠOD institution in this field.

Gros (2004) explains that the program for Outdoor School, implemented by CŠOD, is mostly carried out in a natural environment, thus enriching the learning. Socialization, socializing with classmates and teachers, mentors and other associates is also important. It enables a deep and broader cooperation and more effective achievement of the educational goals set. Outdoor School takes into account, in the context of didactics, the possibility of greater consonance with direct observation, learning in the natural environment (in snowy nature, in unspoiled nature, etc.) and in artificial places (ski resort, swimming pool, museum, laboratory). It is a multi-day process based on the interconnection of content and experiential components. It is

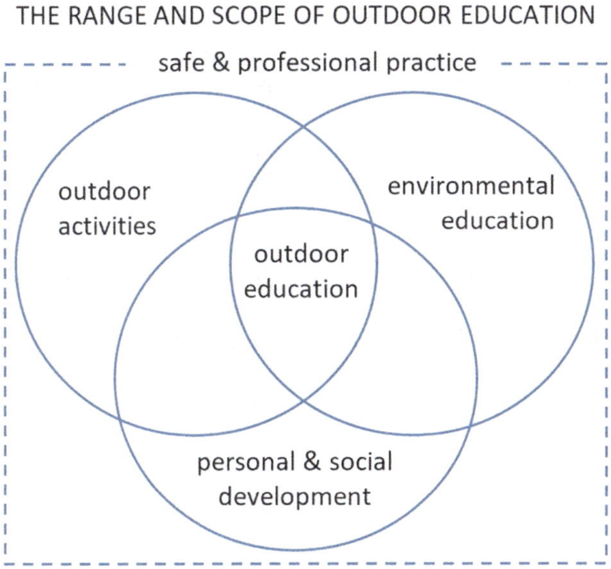

THE RANGE AND SCOPE OF OUTDOOR EDUCATION

Figure 13.5. Model that defines outdoor education (from Higgins & Loynes, 1997, p. 6)

important to emphasize that the activities conducted by CŠOD are in accordance with the national curriculum for basic education.

As mentioned earlier, most centres are situated in nature, far from tourist centres, which is very suitable for outdoor education. Out of 24 centres, five are located in the Alps, two are on the coast, one in the heart of the Karst region, a few in villages, and the rest in forests. Some centres are located by rivers and lakes and so have opportunities to offer various sports activities. In these centres, students engage in canoeing, kayaking or rafting. Ten centres are located near ski resorts, and students can ski during the winter. The surroundings for all the centres support active exploration of the local environment: weather, climate, land, flora and fauna as well as diverse cultural heritages.

The activities carried out in CŠOD connect the goals of the national basic school curricula for sports, natural sciences, and social sciences, all in an interdisciplinary way. Besides having cognitive and psychomotor objectives, students also achieve affective objectives. Students develop creativity with activities such as land art, created with natural materials, handicrafts, learning how to build a fire, baking bread, making Easter eggs and homemade soap, etc. These activities are based on experience-based learning and experiential pedagogy: learning by doing, hands-on approach, inquiry-based learning, etc. (Cornell, 1994; Dewey, 1938; Kolb, 1984; Krajnčan, 2007; Skribe Dimec, 1998). The purpose of these activities is to facilitate the educational process, promote environmental education and sustainable development, demonstrate the value of spending free time constructively, teaching the importance of respecting and protecting nature, as well as the importance of taking responsibility for one's actions. The importance of organized outdoor learning is also confirmed by the following thought: "If young people are not experiencing the natural world independently or in the company of family or friends, the role of guided outdoor experiences becomes increasingly significant" (Beams, Higgins, & Nicol, 2012, p. 34).

CŠOD offers a variety of programs from which schools can choose: five- and three-day programs, theme weeks, project weeks, single-day programs (Activity Days), programs for gifted students, kindergarten programs and programs for children with disabilities. There are also various activities that schools can choose.

Figure 13.6 displays some of the activities carried out in different CŠOD centres including: rowing, camping, learning how to give first aid in nature and too many activities to list here.

CONCLUSION

All programs in CŠOD are running place-based educational programs, which are strongly connected to the local environment and cultural traditions. Because Slovenia is very diverse in terms of both its environment and cultural traditions, and because the CŠOD network is all over Slovenia, Slovenian basic school students have plenty of opportunities for diverse environmental learning. With the systematic promotion of environmental and outdoor education, we are already implementing the desire expressed by Zandvliet (2009, 2016) in the introduction to the Researching Environmental Learning series:

> ... to make change and develop a new ethic – a responsible attitude toward caring for the earth. Working to integrate environmental learning within all subject areas promotes this change in attitude by providing students with opportunities to experience and investigate the relationships linking individuals, societies, and natural surroundings. (p. 1)

Slovenia's success in environmental education is proven by the fact that we were invited among 15 countries from all over the world to present our practice in the book entitled Environmental Education in the 21st Century (Palmer, 1998).

Today globalization increases the risk of us neglecting our historical traditions with a corresponding loss of cultural identity. Therefore, it is extremely important that outdoor education emphasize place and locality, which allows us to stay connected with the traditions, and our natural and cultural heritage, thereby successfully weaving culture and environment. Perhaps globalization was the reason that the year 2018 was proclaimed as the European Year of Cultural Heritage (2018). The slogan for the year 2018 is: "Our heritage where the past meets the future". It is planned that in 2018 Europeans will celebrate its diverse cultural heritage across Europe – at the EU, national, regional and local levels.

OUTDOOR EDUCATION IN THE SLOVENIAN SCHOOL SYSTEM

Figure 13.6. Activities carried out by students in various CŠOD centres.
Source: CŠOD archives

The aim of the European Year of Cultural Heritage is to enable people to become closer to and more involved with their cultural heritage. Cultural heritage shapes our identities and everyday lives. It surrounds us in Europe's towns and cities, natural landscapes and archaeological sites. It is found in literature, art and objects but also in the crafts we learn from our ancestors, the stories we tell to our children, the food we enjoy in the company of others, and the films we watch and recognize ourselves in. Cultural heritage has a universal value for us as individuals, communities and societies. This is important to preserve and pass on to future generations. Similarly, the United Nations General Assembly has declared 2019 as the "International Year of Indigenous Languages" (UN International Year 2019, n.d.). Its aim is to raise awareness about languages of indigenous peoples all over the world.

This key finding, which I came to at the 9th World Environmental Education Congress, in Vancouver, Canada was about how important it is to respect indigenous peoples and their ways, which are based on a deep connection with nature. This was also the message of many of the plenary session speakers. At the congress, somebody asked me what kind of attitude Slovenes have towards nature. I said that I think we have quite a good one, and that is probably because almost all of us still have some kind of contact with nature, gardens or countryside (weekend cottages, houses of parents or grandparents, etc.). I received additional confirmation of this statement on the very last day of the congress in a story told by plenary speaker David Suzuki (2017). In his speech, he related the case of his friend, a businessman living in an air-conditioned apartment. In the morning, this friend moves to the basement with an elevator sits in his air-conditioned car and drives to his workplace. There, in the garage, he leaves his car and takes the elevator to his office, which is also air-conditioned. After work, he goes back to the air-conditioned car and drives to the shopping centre, which is also air-conditioned. Then he drives with his air-conditioned car back home, and returns with an elevator to his air-conditioned apartment. And just like that – day after day. In the end, he boasts that he did not have to step outdoors for 14 days.

Moreover, this is not a story about an exception. It should be noted that more and more people live in cities and are losing contact with nature. We are witnessing the remarkable technological development of computers, tablets and smartphones, which quickly take today's youth into a virtual world. Ten years ago, Louv (2008) drew attention to the phenomenon, which he called nature-deficit disorder, exposing our alienation from nature, demonstrated by our diminished use of our senses, attention difficulties, and higher rates of physical and emotional illness. In fact, we do not know where humanity will go in the future with our increasing use of the virtual world. I think that we must become aware as soon as possible, that humanity cannot survive if we do not keep in touch with nature. I hope that the Slovenian school system, which, by integrating Activity Days and Outdoor School into the regular program of schools, can slow down this process of alienation from nature among Slovenian students and be an outstanding example for other countries.

REFERENCES

25th anniversary of CŠOD Centres. (2017). [Video file]. Retrieved from https://www.youtube.com/watch?v=Az__-QOUIBU&feature=youtu.be

9th World Environmental Education Congress (WEEC). Vancouver, Canada (September 9–15, 2017).

A new estimate of brown bear numbers in Slovenia. (2017). Retrieved from http://dinalpbear.eu/a-new-estimate-of-brown-bear-numbers-in-slovenia-the-population-has-increased/

Act amending and supplementing the basic school act. (2011). Retrieved from http://www.pisrs.si/Pis.web/pregledPredpisa?id=ZAKO6129

Act of Financing Outdoor School. (2004). *Pravilnik o financiranju šole v naravi. Uradni list 61/2004, 7874.* Retrieved from https://www.uradni-list.si/glasilo-uradni-list-rs/vsebina?urlid=200461&stevilka=2810

Analysis of Outdoor School. (2014). *Analiza ŠVN za koledarsko leto 2014.* Retrieved from http://www.mizs.gov.si/fileadmin/mizs.gov.si/pageuploads/podrocje/os/pdf/Analiza_SVN_2014.pdf

Basic School Act. (1996). Retrieved from http://pisrs.si/Pis.web/pregledPredpisa?id=ZAKO448

Basic school curriculum. (2014). *Predmetnik osnovne šole.* Retrieved from http://www.mizs.gov.si/fileadmin/mizs.gov.si/pageuploads/podrocje/os/devetletka/predmetniki/Pred_14_OS_4_12.pdf

Basic school Dravlje. (n.d.). Retrieved from http://www.osdravlje.si/ola-v-naravi/

Beams, S., Higgins, P., & Nicol, R. (2012). *Learning outside the classroom. Theory and guidelines for practice.* New York, NY: Routledge.

Bibič, A. (2007). *Natura 2000 site management programm: 2007–2013: Operational programme.* Ljubljana: Ministry of the Environment and Spatial Planning.

Blažič, M., Arih, A., Nartnik, I., & Turk, I. (2008). *Endangered species.* Ljubljana: Environmental Agency of the Republic of Slovenia, Ministry of the Environment and Spatial Planning.

Cooper, G. (2016). Outdoor education, environment and sustainability: Youth, society and environment. In B. Humberstone, H. Prince, & K. A. Henderson (Eds.), *Routledge international handbook of outdoor studies* (pp. 398–408). London: Routledge.

Cornell, J. (1984). *Sharing nature with children. The classic parents' and teachers' nature awareness guidebook.* Nevada City, CA: DAWN Publications.

Country size comparison. (2017). Retrieved from http://www.mylifeelsewhere.com/country-size-comparison.

CŠOD centres. (n.d.). Retrieved from http://www.csod.si/dom

Dewey, J. (1938). *Experience and education.* New York, NY: Collier Books.

Diversity. (n.d.). Retrieved from http://www.slovenia.si/si/visit/diversity/

Education policy outlook. Slovenia. (2016). *OECD.* Retrieved from http://www.oecd.org/slovenia/Education-Policy-Outlook-Country-Profile-Slovenia.pdf

Education system Slovenia. (2015). Retrieved from https://www.nuffic.nl/en/publications/find-a-publication/education-system-slovenia.pdf

Environmental Performance Index. (2012). Retrieved from https://epi.envirocenter.yale.edu/

European Green Capital. (n.d.). Retrieved from http://ec.europa.eu/environment/europeangreencapital/winning-cities/

European state of the environment. Contributions from Slovenia. (2010). *Environmental Agency of the Republic of Slovenia, Ministry of the Environment and Spatial Planning.* Retrieved from http://www.arso.gov.si/en/soer/

European Year of Cultural Heritage. (2018). Retrieved from https://europa.eu/cultural-heritage/european-year-cultural-heritage_en

Forests, forestry and logging. (2017). Retrieved from http://ec.europa.eu/eurostat/statistics-explained/index.php/Forests,_forestry_and_logging

Gregorčič, B. (2005). *Šola v naravi v evropskem prostoru in položaj Slovenije v njem* [Outdoor School in Europe and Slovenia's position in it]. Retrieved from http://www.csod.si/uploads/file/SVN_CLANKI/SVN_v_evropskem_prostoru_in_brigita_gregorcic.pdf

Gros, G. (2004). *Interdisciplinarnost in šola v naravi* [Interdisciplinarity and outdoor school]. Retrieved from http://www.csod.si/uploads/file/SVN_CLANKI/Interdisciplinarnost_in_SVN_gabrijel_gros.pdf

Gros, J., Marinčič, M., Komljanc, N., Brcar, P. Rusjan, N. Rudman, I., … Ajtnik, M. (2001). *The Concept of Outdoor School* [Šola v naravi za devetletno osnovno šolo. Koncept]. Retrieved from http://www.mizs.gov.si/fileadmin/mizs.gov.si/pageuploads/podrocje/os/devetletka/program_drugo/Sola__v__naravi.pdf

Higgins, P., & Loynes, C. (1997). On the nature of outdoor education. In P. Higgins, C. Loynes & N. Crowther (Eds.), *A Guide for outdoor educators in Scotland* (pp. 6–8). Penrith: Adventure Education.

Higgins, P., & Nicol, R. (2002). *Outdoor education: Authentic learning in the context of landscapes* (Vol. 2). Kisa: Kinda Education Centre.
Higher education system in Slovenia. (n.d.). Retrieved from http://www.mizs.gov.si/en/areas_of_work/ directorate_of_higher_education/higher_education_system_in_slovenia/
Hlad, B., & Skoberne, P. (Eds.). (2001). *Characteristics of biological and landscape diversity in Slovenia. Biological and landscape diversity in Slovenia: An overview*. Ljubljana: Environmental Agency of the Republic of Slovenia, Ministry of the Environment and Spatial Planning.
Kolb, D. A. (1984). *Experiential learning: Experience as the source of learning and development*. Englewood Cliffs, NJ: Prentice Hall.
Krajnčan, M. (2007). *Osnove doživljajske pedagogike* [The basics of experiential pedagogy]. Ljubljana: Pedagoška fakulteta.
Krek, J. (1996). *White paper on education in the Republic of Slovenia*. Ljubljana: Ministry of Education and Sport.
Kresal Sterniša, B. (n.d.). *Analiza šole v naravi v letu 2005* [Analysis of the outdoor school in 2005]. Retrieved from www.mizs.gov.si/fileadmin/.../sola_v_naravi_analiza_4_9_06.doc
Kristan, S. (1998). *Šola v naravi* [Outdoor School]. Radovljica: Didakta.
Louv, R. (2008). *Last child in the woods: Saving our children from nature-deficit disorder*. Chapel Hill, NC: Algonquin Books.
Mršić, N. (1997). *Biotska raznovrstnost v Sloveniji: Slovenija – »vroča točka« Evrope* [Biodiversity in Slovenia: Slovenia – the "hot spot" of Europe]. Ljubljana: Ministrstvo za okolje in prostor, Uprava RS za varstvo narave.
Outdoor School. (n.d.). *Šola v naravi*. Retrieved from http://www.mizs.gov.si/si/delovna_podrocja/ direktorat_za_predsolsko_vzgojo_in_osnovno_solstvo/osnovno_solstvo/sola_v_naravi/
Palmer, J. A. (1998). *Environmental education in the 21st century: Theory, practice, progress, and promise*. New York, NY: Routledge.
Pavlič Možina, S., & Prešeren, P. (Eds.). (2011). *Facts about Slovenia*. Ljubljana: Government Communication Office.
Rennie, L. J. (2010). Learning science outside of school. In S. K. Abell & N. G. Lederman (Eds.), *Handbook of research on science education* (pp. 125–167). New York, NY: Routledge.
Single structure education. (2016). Retrieved from https://webgate.ec.europa.eu/fpfis/mwikis/eurydice/ index.php/Slovenia:Single_Structure_Education_(Integrated_Primary_and_Lower_Secondary_ Education)
Skribe Dimec, D. (1998). *Raziskovalne škatle* [Inquiry boxes]. Ljubljana: Modrijan.
Slovenia. (2018). Retrieved from https://sl.wikipedia.org/wiki/Slovenija
Slovenia education. (n.d.). Retrieved from http://www.sloveniaeducation.info/Education-System/ Slovenia-Education-Overview.html
Slovenia location on the Europe map. (n.d.). Retrieved from http://ontheworldmap.com/slovenia/ slovenia-location-on-the-europe-map.html
Slovenian Environment Agency. (n.d.). Retrieved from http://www.arso.gov.si/en/
Statistical Office of the Republic of Slovenia. (2017). Retrieved from http://www.stat.si/StatWebPDF/ PrikaziPDF.aspx?id=6963&lang=en
Structure of the education system in the republic of Slovenia. (2016/17). Retrieved from http://www.mizs.gov.si/fileadmin/mizs.gov.si/pageuploads/ministrstvo/Shema_ izobrazevanja_2016_17_AN.pdf
Suzuki, D. (2017, September 9–15). Keynote speaker at 9th World Environmental Education Congress, Vancouver, Canada.
Taštanoska, T. (Ed.). (2015). *The education system in the Republic of Slovenia 2016/2017*. Ljubljana: Ministry of Education, Science and Sport of the Republic of Slovenia.
The concept of Days of Activities. (1998). *Dnevi dejavnosti*. Retrieved from http://www.mizs.gov.si/ fileadmin/mizs.gov.si/pageuploads/podrocje/os/devetletka/program_drugo/Dnevi_dejavnosti.pdf
The Dragon is celebrating his first birthday. (2017). Retrieved from https://siol.net/novice/slovenija/ zmajcek-praznuje-prvi-rojstni-dan-442294

The Law on the Organization and Financing of Education. (2007). *Zakon o organizaciji in financiranju vzgoje in izobraževanja.* Retrieved from https://zakonodaja.com/zakon/zofvi

UN International Year 2019. (n.d.). Retrieved from https://www.timeanddate.com/year/2019/

Vide Pregarc Basic School. (n.d.). Retrieved from https://www.osvp.si/solski-koledar/solsko-leto/

Worldmark Encyclopedia of Nations. (n.d.). Retrieved from http://www.encyclopedia.com/places/spain-portugal-italy-greece-and-balkans/former-yugoslavian-political-geography/slovenia

Zandvliet, D. B. (Ed.). (2009). *Diversity in environmental education research.* Rotterdam, The Netherlands: Sense Publishers.

Zandvliet, D. B. (Ed.). (2016). *The ecology of home.* Rotterdam, The Netherlands: Sense Publishers.

Žitnik, M., Čuček, S., & Pograjc, M. (2014). *Water – From the source to the outflow.* Ljubljana: Statistical Office of the Republic of Slovenia.

Darja Skribe Dimec
Faculty of Education
University of Ljubljana
Slovenia

MICHELI KOWALCZUK MACHADO,
ESTEVÃO BRASIL RUAS VERNALHA AND
JOÃO LUIZ HOEFFEL

14. ENVIRONMENTAL POWER PLANT PROJECT

Environmental Education in a Conservation Area

INTRODUCTION

Debates about socio-environmental problems and the possible risks that their aggravation may have for our survival and the diversity of the world's ecosystems has been intensified in the last decades. However, today's society still faces several sustainability challenges, which are closely associated, with the current development model that has contributed to generations of socio-environmental impacts.

The unsustainability of the dominant economic model is evidenced by the depletion of renewable and non-renewable resources, exploitation and loss of biodiversity, diverse socio-environmental problems, an ethical values crisis and increasing global poverty. This reality reinforces the need to redefine existing development models and policies (Philippi, 2002).

In this sense, it is important to mention the role of ecological movements in the elaboration of a critical analysis related to modernity and our current development models. These are proposing self-management, disarmament, pacifism, environmental conservation, social equity, among other objectives (Reigota, 2002). An important step in awakening the international community to these criticisms came at the First International Conference on Human Environment, held in Stockholm, in 1972, by United Nations.

In this conference, the key role of education was identified to assist the world community to solve problems arising from conflicts over natural resource use and pollution. Thus, defending and improving the environment for present and future generations became a primary goal. Since then, discussions on environmental issues began to extrapolate to wider economic and political problems, as these challenged the relation between nature and societies. Such an education, which focuses on a recognition that human beings are an integral part of the ecosystem and not a species apart.

In response to the recommendations of this conference, UNESCO promoted an international meeting in Environmental Education, in Belgrade, Yugoslavia (Dias, 2003). During this meeting, in 1975, Environmental Education was defined as the fundamental instrument for the world population to become aware of threats related to the environment and the importance of both individual and collective actions taken to avoid and minimize such threats.

Despite the importance of these events to the environmental movement, social problems were still dissociated from so-called environmental ones. However, while at Stockholm Conference, in 1972, environmental issues were viewed with distrust by developing countries, at UN Conference on Environment and Development, in Rio de Janeiro, in 1992, environmental and development issues were closely linked (Stahel, 1995). Environmental Education then began to incorporate discussions of Sustainable Development and Inclusion, recognizing lack of focus given to the education of marginalized groups in society such as Indigenous peoples, women, and children (Serrão, 1999).

Thus, the discussion of environmental problems, initially involved with essentially biological issues, expanded to encompass several areas of knowledge and is now present in all sectors of human life. In this way, it is possible to see that the causes of our environmental problems go beyond the current economic system, which presents a development strategy based on profit making at all costs and that disregards ethical values. This question goes beyond our economic system and considers cultural values, especially with regard to the western way of life that is being established throughout the world (Hoeffel et al., 2004).

More recently, considering the urgency and importance of this issue, in September 2015, 193 member states of United Nations formally adopted a new global agenda on sustainability. Termed Agenda 2030 for Sustainable Development, it presents 17 goals, successors to the eight-millennium development goals, and 169 goals (United Nations, 2015). Among the issues, the document recognizes that education is fundamental to guarantee quality of life of human beings and conservation of environment on the planet.

Among the 17 objectives, Goal 4 seeks to "ensure inclusive and equitable quality education, and promote lifelong learning opportunities for all Regarding the proposals related to this objective and that must be fulfilled by 2030, it includes: "ensuring that all students acquire knowledge and skills necessary to promote sustainable development, including, among others, through education for sustainable development and sustainable lifestyles, human rights, gender equality, promotion of a culture of peace and non-violence, global citizenship, and enhancement of cultural diversity and contribution of culture to sustainable development" (United Nations, 2015).

Given the above, it is possible to observe that educational processes have been consolidated as an essential tool in the formation of citizens able to understand the complexity of environmental problems and to then propose and execute equally complex solutions to these questions. Environmental problems are understood to mean not only the conflicts generated between person(s) and nature but also those generated between person(s) and person(s), from a perspective that it is not the nature that is in crisis, but the basis and livelihood by which most of today's societies are maintained (Leff, 2003).

Thus, to transform a functioning structure, as suggested by Gadotti (2000), it is necessary to build a new model of education that is capable of describing and solving social inequalities, the natural resources crisis, cultural homogenization and many others problems. Luzzi (2005, p. 399) reinforces this approach by mentioning that environmental education "is not only a dimension, nor a transversal axis, but is responsible for the transformation of education as a whole, in search of a sustainable society".

In this sense, the Environmental Power Plant Project proposes a reflection on the importance of environmental education in schools with the effective participation of students, teachers and the local community. The project has been carried out at Paulo Freire Municipal School, which is located in the surroundings of Bairro da Usina Environmental Protected Area (Bairro da Usina EPA), located in Atibaia, São Paulo, Brazil. The activities are based on a participatory methodology and the actions were divided into three modules: a Diagnostic Module, that sought to understand local reality and environmental perception of actors involved; a "Hands On" Module, which consisted of the project's execution, through practices carried out in the school environment and in Bairro da Usina EPA; and a Participatory Community Module, in which the results of activities developed within the project were presented to the local community. The development of this project also reveals and reiterates the need to carry out environmental education programs in a conception that includes human beings and their complex interactions as part of the environment.

ENVIRONMENTAL EDUCATION IN BRAZIL

Until the 1970s, environmental education was based mainly on a naturalistic perspective, which created a dichotomy between nature and society. According to Saito (2002), experiences in environmental education during this period prioritized the awareness and importance of defending nature. Since then, one of the major challenges of environmental education has been to overcome this vision and to instead understand the inherent complexity of social and environmental issues. Carvalho (2012) emphasizes that a socio-environmental view constitutes a field of dynamic interaction between culture, society and the physical and biological basis of vital life processes., This conception is oriented by a complex and interdisciplinary rationality that does not consider the environment as synonymous with nature.

In this way, human beings are part of the environment and this interaction acts as a transforming agent. Although this process does not always bring good results with regard to conservation and environmental quality, on the other hand, it can contribute to sustainability. According to Carvalho (2012) a reductionist view of the environment, considering only one of its dimensions and neglecting the richness of the interaction between nature and human culture, prevents a glimpse of the ultimate solution to environmental problems.

Loureiro (2004) points out that every conception of environmental education that has as its principle that social dynamics are disconnected from natural ones:, disregards sustainability as a permanent construction resulting from the social and ecological mediations that constitute human beings and denies an education-citizenship-participation interaction.

Changes in our current socio-environmental reality will only be possible if this reality is understood objectively. Therefore, the development of environmental education processes implies, among other factors, there is a cause and effect relationship between processes of degradation and the dynamics of social systems. In order to do so, it is necessary that "knowledge and skills be incorporated, and that attitudes are first formed from ethical values and social justice, because it is these attitudes that predispose action" (Pelicioni & Phillipi, 2014, p. 6).

From this perspective, it should also be mentioned that a critical environmental education is linked to formation of a person capable of reading his/her environment and interpreting relationships, conflicts and problems present there. For the exercise of environmental citizenship, it is also necessary to critically diagnose environmental issues and the self-understanding of the place occupied by subject in these relations (Carvalho, 2012).

Today there remains a naive vision of environmental education understood as a generic term for something next to "everything that could be accepted as the umbrella of 'good environmental practices' or 'good environmental behavior'" (Carvalho, 2012, p. 153). In addition to this view, critical environmental education aims to understand that educational practice is related to a process that aims to form the subject as a social and historically situated being. Thus, it is necessary to contribute to a change of values and attitudes, in a process in which the learner can identify and problematize socio-environmental issues and act upon them (Carvalho, 2012; Pelicioni & Philippi, 2014).

Understanding environmental education as a form of intervention in the world, in all its social, economic, political, cultural, ethical and aesthetic aspects, is fundamental to the formation of a conscious, critical, competent and proactive citizen (Philippi & Pelicioni, 2002). Therefore, environmental education is a life-long learning process, based on respect for all life forms, affirming values and actions that contribute to human and social transformation and environmental conservation. This process stimulates the formation of "socially more equitable and ecologically balanced societies that maintain a relationship of interdependence and diversity" (Sato, 2002, p. 17).

Given the above, it can be stated that, at present, our theoretical conception of environmental education goes beyond a reductionist perspective based on environment understanding of nature where the human being is a separate element.

In Brazil, in 1981, an important step towards environmental education was instituted in the National Environmental Policy, sanctioned by Federal Law n. 6,938. This document aims to guarantee preservation, improvement, and recovery of the environmental quality conducive to life, aiming at ensuring, in the country, conditions for socioeconomic development, interests of national security and the dignity of human life . To that end, it includes in its principles that environmental education must be present at all education levels, including community education, to enable it to actively participate in environment protection. In 1988, the Federal Constitution, in its article 255, reinforced this need to "promote environmental education at all education levels and public awareness for environment preservation".

According to Saito (2002), the 1980s brought changes to the socio-political scenario of the country, due to the redemocratization process, new terms such as political openness and redemocratization became more common in the Brazilian vocabulary. This process had its critical moment with the promulgation of a new Federal Constitution in 1988, leading to the advancement of debate on environmental issues and explicitly mentioning the importance of the environment for Brazil. The author further emphasizes that even before the constitution: this importance was already observed in the National Environmental Policy of 1981.

In 1999, Law 9,795 instituted the National Environmental Education Policy.[1] This policy defined environmental education as the processes through which individual and community can construct social values, knowledge, skills, attitudes, and competencies aimed at conservation of the environment, and is essential to the healthy quality of life and its sustainability. According to this law, environmental education must be present and articulated at all levels and modalities of the educational process, both formal and non-formal, and should be considered an essential and permanent component. This document outlines *the basic* principles of environmental education: the conception of the environment in an integrated way, considering its multiple and complex interactions; democratic and participatory approach; pluralism of ideas and pedagogical conceptions, under the perspective of inter, multi and trans-disciplinarity; recognition and respect for individual and cultural diversity; among others.

The approach proposed by the National Environmental Education Policy refers to an understanding that due to interrelationships complexity that occurs in the environment, creating an environmental education discipline would be insufficient and ineffective, since phenomena that interact and constitute certain environmental realities belong to different disciplines of knowledge (Philippi, Pelicioni, & Coimbra, 2002). Sato (2002) reinforces this view by showing that the quality of life on the planet has deteriorated, in a process where not only physical or biological aspects are being compromised, but also social, economic and political factors. In this way, the environment must be approached with a dimension that involves such factors and not as an objective of each discipline.

In the 1990s, the National Curriculum Parameters (1997), which guide the practice of education in Brazilian schools, consolidated the approach to environmental issues not as a discipline, but as a cross-cutting theme. According to curricular parameters, addressing environmental issues encompasses all of human actions in their complexity. Thus, environmental contents must be integrated into the curriculum through transversality, since they need to be addressed in different areas of knowledge, and allowed to permeate the entire educational practice. This, at the same time would enable a global and comprehensive view of environmental issues (Ministério da Educação e do Desporto, 1997). This view is in agreement with the one proposed by National Environmental Education Policy (1999), which, in its article 10, also mentions that "environmental education should not be implanted as a specific discipline in teaching curriculum".

Interdisciplinarity, while obviously fundamental to environmental education, can also be considered a challenge, since it is about going beyond integrating contents or subjects into different disciplines. For Cascino (1999, p. 68), interdisciplinary action is not about "simple intersection of similar things; Rather, it is a question of constructing dialogues founded on the difference, concretely embracing the wealth derived from diversity".

Regarding democratic and participatory practices proposed in the National Environmental Education Policy, Pelicioni and Philipi (2014) mention that educating for responsible citizenship requires new strategies to strengthen critical awareness that should generate praxis. Thus, environmental education, when educating for citizenship, social participation and representativeness can contribute to public policies and a democratic culture. Saito (2002) also points out that within the foundations of this document, it is possible to identify four major challenges for environmental education in Brazil: the search for a socially just and democratic society; an unveiling of social oppression conditions; the practice of an intentional transformational action; and the need for a continuous search for knowledge. According to the author, the four challenges "articulate among themselves and focus on strengthening exercise of citizenship as an expression of a more just and egalitarian society construction" (Saito, 2002, p. 50).

In this sense, critical environmental education plays a fundamental role in the formation of the individual and social being and our need to be historically situated. Therefore, educational process cannot be reduced to an intervention focused exclusively on individuals, but instead its form should focus on individual-society relations (Carvalho, 2004). Unlike critical environmental education, conservation education is grounded on a worldview that fragments reality by simplifying and reducing it. Thus, it does not include the perspective that education occurs in a human transformation movement within a process of collective transformation of socio-environmental reality, in a dialectical and complex view. In contrast to this approach, critical environmental education aims to promote educational environments to mobilize these intervention processes on the reality of environmental problems and provides educational processes in which educators and learners are formed by the exercise of citizenship to transform the socio-environmental crisis that society lives in the present time (Guimarães, 2004).

Critical perspectives of environmental education can be present in several environments with educational potential: formal or non-formal, rural or urban, built or natural. In this sense, it is important to highlight the National Program of Environmental Education (Ministério do Meio Ambiente, 2005) and the National Strategy for Communication and Environmental Education in Conservation

Units (Ministério do Meio Ambiente Instituto Chico Mendes de Conservação da Biodiversidade, 2011).

The National Program of Environmental Education presents as its guidelines: transversality and interdisciplinarity; spatial and institutional decentralization; social and environmental sustainability; democracy and social participation and improvement of education, environment and other systems that interface with environmental education. Among the objectives, it is worth mentioning: "to foment processes of continuous environmental education formation, formal and non-formal, giving conditions for performance of various sectors of society" (Ministério do Meio Ambiente, 2005).

The National Environmental Communication and Education Strategy aims to stimulate and strengthen the implementation of communication and environmental education actions in Environmental Protection Areas. These could be Conservation Units, Ecological Corridors, Mosaics of Conservation Units and Biosphere Reserves, in their surroundings and cushioning zones; promoting participation and social control in the processes of creation, implementation and management of these territories and ensuring dialogue between different subjects and institutions affected and/or involved with the issue in the country Units (Ministério do Meio Ambiente Instituto Chico Mendes de Conservação da Biodiversidade, 2011).

According to Toledo and Pelicioni (2014), environmental education, due to its integrating characteristics, can be conducted in varied contexts, as in Conservation Units, for instance. However, activities carried out at these sites should not only be characterized by their ecological aspects, nor occur in a restricted manner. Such actions need to open spaces for a generation of new values regarding human beings and respect for life. Therefore, they must be permanent, emphasizing, the ecological aspects, but also economic, social, political, cultural and ethical perspectives.

In 2012, Resolution No. 2, from June 15, approved by the National Education Council, established the National Curricular Guidelines for Environmental Education, to be observed by education systems and their institutions of Basic Education and Higher Education (Resolução no. 2, 2012). According to the guidelines, among other issues, Environmental Education must contemplate the "deepening of critical-reflexive thinking through scientific, socioeconomic, political and historical studies, from the socio-environmental dimension, valuing participation, cooperation, sense of justice and responsibility of the educational community as opposed to relations of domination and exploitation present in current reality". Guerra and Orsi (2017) emphasize that this document also strengthens Brazilian environmental education.

Environmental education as seen as interdisciplinary, participatory, promoting citizenship, critical, transforming socio-environmental reality – does not occur only in informal teaching environments. Through an analysis of the documents guiding environmental education in Brazil, it is possible to verify that they mention the inclusion of community in educational processes related to socio-environmental issues. Even the National Curriculum Parameters (1997), designed to guide educational practices in elementary education, emphasize this school-community relationship in the educational process.

Given the above, it is worth emphasizing, as proposed by Jacobi (2005), that in environmental education practices, participation must be a structuring axis and represent an essential instrument for the transformation of relations between society and the environment. For the author, this relationship between environment and education for citizenship has an increasingly challenging role, which requires the emergence of new knowledge to understand the complexity of social processes and the intensity of environmental risks.

Considering this proposed basis for environmental education, it is also important to mention several different approaches for actions that include socio-environmental themes in educational processes. Sauvé (2005) shows in her research that in the environmental education field, there is a common concern with the environment and human relations and there are several ways of conceiving and practicing educational action in this context. The author has identified, in North American and European cultural contexts, fifteen different environmental education streams including: naturalistic, conservationist/recursive, resolutive, systemic, scientific, humanistic, moral/ethical, holistic, bioregional, practical, critical, feminist, ethnographic, of eco-education and sustainability.

Regarding the diversity of these propositions, Coimbra (2004, p. 528), states that environmental issue have many faces, and are not a closed issue onto itself. On the contrary, it must be considered open because, from many sides and at all times, human beings must point the way out, a rescue to the victory of environmentally correct solutions and a continuity of life that favours the environment. Sauvé (2002), when considering the relationship between humans and nature, brings a range of different and additional points of view, such as the environment as a problem to prevent and solve; as a system to understand in order to make better decisions; as a place where people live; as a biosphere and as a community project. For Hoeffel and Fadini (2007), the different perceptions on the environment offer several social actors that act in the environmental area, orient practices of environmental education, and are reflected in decision-making, actions, and formulation of public policies.

The plurality of environmental education proposals, resulting from the many different forms of perception and interaction between human beings and the environment, are fundamental for the amplification and maturation of critical, reflexive and participative pedagogical propositions inherent to this transformative educational process. According to Loureiro (2004, p. 10), "environmental educators, in their most diverse understandings, have generated, in Brazil, experiences, theories, and methodologies of great value and meaning for world environmental education".

Given the above, the Environmental Power Plant Project, based on the proposals developed in a Brazilian context for environmental education, are presented as a case study, which seeks to consider local reality, interdisciplinarity, participation and critical and citizenship formation.

ENVIRONMENTAL POWER PLANT PROJECT

The environmental power plant project has been developed by Faculdades Atibaia – FAAT, a college located in the city of Atibaia, State of São Paulo, Brazil. This college has a Research Center with four main lines of research, one of them focused on sustainability and cultural issues to which this project is linked. The project involved 400 children aged 6 to 10 years old and has been in effect since 2016 at Paulo Freire Municipal Elementary School, located in the surroundings of the Environmental Protected Area (EPA) called Bairro da Usina, in Atibaia (Figure 14.1).

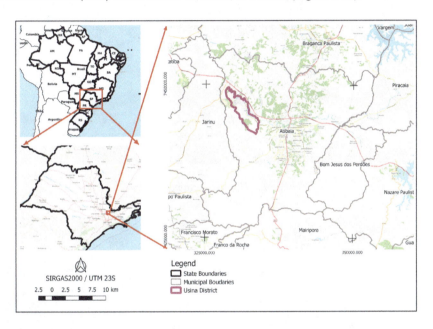

Figure 14.1. EPA Bairro da Usina location

The neighborhood was named in 1928, after a Hydroelectric Power Plant had been built (Figure 14.2) and remained operational until January 1970. It supplied energy to Atibaia, and the cities of Jarinu, Bragança Paulista and Bom Jesus dos Perdões.

Due to its environmental importance, considering that the region is inserted in an area rich in water springs, on September 4, 1986, Represa Bairro da Usina EPA (Figure 14.3) was created, established by State Law 5,280. An EPA is characterized as a strip around the reservoir, and the purpose is the protection of the springs area that contributes to the city's water supply, as well as that of the landscape.

Although protected by law, the EPA region and its surroundings have been undergoing a range of environmental impacts, such as uncontrolled land use and occupation, garbage left in inappropriate areas (including in the reservoir itself), tourism conducted in a damaging manner and even cases of the hunting of wild animals.

Figure 14.2. Hydroelectric power plant

Figure 14.3. EPA Represa Bairro da Usina overview

Given these issues, it is essential that the community in this context has the opportunity to reflect on their actions, aiming to minimize these problems. This proposal, therefore, is focused on environmental education as a teaching-learning process in the exercise of citizenship and social and political responsibility. It seeks also to build new values and social relations between human beings and nature, to form attitudes within a new perspective, and to improve the quality of life for all (Philippi & Pelicioni, 2002). This project proposes an escape from the reductionist view of environmental education as a practice centered solely on natural resources conservation. To preserve the environment, human beings must be included as agents belonging to and transforming their reality.

The activities were based on a participatory methodology, and actions were divided into three modules: "Diagnostic"; "Hands-on" and "Participatory Community". This modular proposal stressed the collective construction of the educational process. For Coimbra (2002, p. 156) "environmental education must be a collective construction process since it proposes to contribute to man and world construction […]".

Within the Diagnostic Module, concerns over the environmental education projects were investigated with school teachers. The results were used as a base to elaborate an action plan for environmental education, considering local aspects. At the same time, an environmental perception survey was done with those involved – teachers and students – so that the necessary actions could be taken.

This module showed, for instance, the existence of a great amount of knowledge about the ecological characteristics of the EPA, such as varied species of fauna and flora. On the other hand, it was also possible to verify little existing knowledge regarding the creation and importance of the protected area. In other words, this phase of the project not only collaborated with understandings of the local reality but gave rise to an educational process based on the premise that education happens as part of the human action to transform nature in culture and that in this process different senses are attributed, as per Carvalho (2012). To consider this characteristic is fundamental for an environmental educational project, as the teacher is always involved in the reflection task to enhance new understandings and versions about the world people live and their actions towards this world.

The "Hands-on" module consisted in the project execution, through practices carried out within the school environment and Bairro da Usina EPA. This module followed four basic guidelines: (1) Direct intervention of environmental educators with teachers and students; (2) Conducting interdisciplinary activities by school teachers involving topics addressed to practical activities; (3) Carrying out students integrating activities to share experiences collected from different practices; (4) constant project evaluation.

The activities carried out with teachers and students involved interpretative walks around the school and Bairro da Usina EPA so that they could understand the socio-environmental reality, as well as to share knowledge about the place they live in; a survey on local flora and construction of a pedagogical seedling nursery, through collection and planting of 26 current native species seeds, to be used as an instrument of environmental education; elaboration of a terrarium from which students and teachers could reflect on how life on earth unfolds and what the role of human beings are in this process, both for its protection and generation of impacts. The objective was to promote a process of teaching-learning in which children could reflect on causes and consequences of various environmental problems, and understand their role in this scenario.

The terrarium was built using a 5-liter PET bottle simulating life on planet Earth; production of organic food and elaboration of a worm farm provided a discussion on ways to produce and consume food in a healthier and less environmentally harmful way. This approach allowed work on topics such as: organic food production (pesticide free); Importance of forests, soil, air and water conservation, for food production; understanding that human beings play a fundamental role in the quest for sustainability and, in this process, contribute to health and quality of life of individuals; understand how food is produced and propose a reflection on unbridled consumption; encourage improvement in eating habits and environment conservation.

In addition to planting, children tasted healthier foods and visited organic production sites. On the day of the visit, they had a healthy snack, replacing the usual industrialized options. Still during the visit students ate organic carrots and strawberries that they had picked straight from the plant. In addition to these activities, a Workshop of the Future (Matthäus, 2001) was held with children, so that it was possible to exercise citizenship through proposals made by students themselves within the school environment.

The workshop included the elaboration of a grieving wall (Critical phase), a tree of dreams (Utopia Phase), a field class at Bairro da Usina EPA and a proposal for community environmental awareness developed by children (Phase of achievement). At the end of the workshop activities, the students elaborated two environmental awareness actions – a short film and educational posters – used in the Module "Participatory Community".

During the development of the "Hands-on" module, teachers used themes developed on environmental education in other school disciplines: Science, Mathematics, Portuguese Language, History, Geography, and the Arts. Thus, it was possible to bring an interdisciplinary approach to the project, enriching the proposal and bringing environmental themes to students and teachers daily life.

The experiment showed that integral view of socio-environmental issues, environmental education requires knowledge of several disciplines so that an interdisciplinary understanding is necessary (Philippi & Pelocioni, 2002).

Philippi et al. (2002) show evidence of society's insistence in an inter-disciplinary process for environmental education, so that both stimuli and recommendations are present. However, the students represented only occasional shallow interventions. Besides, there are also limitations and real difficulties for the implementation of content and methodology. For the authors, "those who want to work with interdisciplinary need to confront a real change in their own way to viewing and acting"

(Philippi et al., 2002, p. 184). Therefore, this project tried to stimulate teachers' reflection, regarding environmental education, triggering the beginning of a transformation in the educational practice in the school setting.

In the "Participatory Community" Module, the results of activities were presented through actions developed by the students themselves, aiming to raise awareness in the community. We highlighted actions such as a short film, photo exhibition, and workshops with environmental themes. The results were presented in a school fair, divided among four rooms – in the first, guests watched a short film containing the results of projects carried out at school and the short film "The Tree of Dreams" (idealized by children themselves). This way, it was possible to present the actions carried out in the school environment and to encourage a reflection on the themes presented.

In the second room, the community learned about the students' trees of dreams and grieving wall and built their own tree of dreams and grieving wall as well. This activity, in addition to being reflective and participative, made it possible to understand more about the participants perception of the socio-environmental reality of the place they live. In this room, visitors also had contact with a panel containing native trees identified by students around the school. They were also able to observe posters prepared by the students to sensitize the community about environmental conservation issues (the result of the workshop of the future).

In the third room the terrariums constructed by students were presented. In addition, guests could pick up cherry tomatoes and chamomile seedlings planted by the students – as a way of publicizing the project and also mobilizing community about the importance of medicinal plants, local culture, and healthy food.

The development of these three modules and their activities lead to dialogue, reflection and participation from the wider community. These are fundamental factors for environmental education, once they deal with human beings with substantially different perceptions and ways of living. In addition to developing modules with this participatory process, we sought to address themes that involve environmental issues through a perspective of joy and creativity. Thus, the larger objective was to develop activities that enable new ways of interacting with art, culture, and nature. The development of this project reveals and reiterates the need to carry out environmental education programs in a conception that includes human beings and their complex interactions as an integral part of the environment.

FINAL CONSIDERATIONS

Through this project, it became clear that, at present, human beings face a great challenge concerning socio-environmental issues. It is a task which goes beyond a question of survival. It demands us to construct a new form of interaction and relationship with all elements that make up the environment: physical, biological, ecological, cultural, social, political or economic. In this context, Philippi and Pelicioni (2003) cite that humanity needs a new scientific conception, a new civilizational project, in which it is necessary to establish an ethics of life promotion. In order to do so, it is necessary to reflect and take actions "on inequalities, poverty, and the exclusion of a majority from access to goods and services, and on consumer practices and relations. This requires a reconstruction of paradigms and relations with nature, as well as imposing a continuous reflection on the consequences of our actions taken (Philippi & Pelicioni, 2002, p. 3).

Often environmental education is considered as a solution to all of our environmental problems, without taking into account other factors involved in this reality, such as our current development model. Certainly, as it has been affirmed in the last few decades, the educational process plays a fundamental role in the search for a more sustainable society. However, if this is based only on the promotion of individual attitudes and behaviors, the construction of a solution to environmental problems becomes distant. Philippi et al. (2002) endorse this view by citing that this solution also depends on collective responsibility, public policies, financing, socioeconomic status and current policies.

In this context, the Environmental Power Plant Project sought, with students and teachers, to think collectively about local environmental problems and to encourage actions to involve the local community in this process. The project mobilized and encouraged those evolved to rethink their interactions with the environment, in each phase, continuously building knowledge and intervention actions. Given this, it is worth mentioning that for Ingold (2003), knowledge is inseparable from the practices and relationships of individuals with the environment, where humans and nonhumans make up a single landscape, and in this process connect and mingle. For the author, learning does not involve the acquisition of a mental schema to construct a meaning of the environment, but instead involves the acquisition of skills for a direct perceptive engagement with the elements of the world that human inhabits. "This means that in dwelling in the world, we do not act upon it, or do things to it; rather we move along with it. Our actions do not transform the world; they are part and parcel of the world's transforming itself" (Ingold, 2003, p. 200).

The development of this case study research demonstrates that environmental education is facing the challenge of including human beings in the place where they live, not as agents that interact and transform the environment but also that may promote changes in this process. Understanding this view is fundamental so that educators and learners can develop a process of teaching and learning that goes beyond the simple transmission of information related to environmental topics, but which creates possibilities for the collective production and construction of knowledge. Education needs to create challenges, in which those involved "are developing the power of capturing and understanding the world that appears to them in their relations with it, no longer as a static reality, but as a transforming reality in process" (Freire, 2011, p. 100).

The conceptual basis for the project made it possible to use in a more, analytical and critical way, the recurrent methods and educational processes that are often used only superficially. As an example, it is possible to mention activities conducted like planting, terrarium building, and hiking trails, methods that, if practiced in isolation, would have little chance of achieving their stated environmental education goals.

Finally, educators need to have a critical view of the reality in which they are situated, so that they may better perceive the interrelationships of socioeconomic, political and cultural factors. They must, therefore, be prepared to recognize causes and consequences of environmental problems that interfere with the quality of life without worrying about geopolitical borders (Philippi & Pelicioni, 2002).

Considering these issues, interdisciplinarity deserves special attention, because a new holistic and systemic approach is essential to building new relationships with the environment. In the Environmental Power Plant Project, this issue presents itself with great potential, given teachers interest in participating in the interdisciplinary project, but also as a challenge, due to the difficulty of inserting this perspective into their day-to-day practice. Coimbra (2002, p. 182) points out that the model sought to be built "must deal with man in the environment, and not only with man and environment". According to the author, it is necessary to deepen the foundations that drive the interaction of these two terms: man (human being, society) and natural world (ecosystems, natural resources), since these fundamentals explain the meaning of actions and reactions found in the relationship (Coimbra, 2002).

The Environmental Power Plant Project can be considered an initial step towards this deepening, as it can be reviewed and improved. In perspective of this praxis, it is a natural process for environmental education. It is necessary to construct and reconstruct our practices, concepts, and approaches, so as to, in a participatory, critical and transforming perspective, inform citizens that are committed to building a more sustainable society.

NOTE

[1] The National Environmental Education Policy was regulated in 2002 by Decree no. 4.281.

REFERENCES

Carvalho, I. C. M. (2012). *Educação ambiental: a formação do sujeito ecológico* (6th ed.). São Paulo, SP, Cortez.

Carvalho, I. C. M. (2004). Educação ambiental crítica: nomes e endereçamentos da educação. In Ministério do Meio Ambiente. *Identidades da educação brasileira.* Brasília.

Cascino, F. (1999). *Educação ambiental: princípios, história, formação de educadores.* São Paulo, SP: SENAC.

Coimbra, J. A. A. (2002). Considerações resultantes da construção coletiva. In A. Phillipi Jr. & M. C. F. Pelicioni (Eds.), *Educação ambiental: desenvolvimento de cursos e projetos.* Barueri, SP: Manole.

Coimbra, J. A. A. (2002). Linguagem e percepção ambiental. In A. Philippi Jr., M. A. Romerio, & G. G. Bruna (Eds.), *Curso de gestão ambiental.* Barueri, SP: Manole.

Constituição da República Federativa do Brasil de 1988. (1998). Brasília.

Decreto n. 4.281, de 25 de junho de 2002. (2002). *Regulamenta a Lei no 9.795, de 27 de abril de 1999, que institui a Política Nacional de Educação Ambiental, e dá outras providências.* Brasília, DF. Retrieved January 24, 2018, from http://www.planalto.gov.br/ccivil_03/decreto/2002/d4281.htm

Dias, G. (2003). *Educação ambiental: princípios e práticas* (8th ed). São Paulo, SP: Gaia.

Freire, P. (2011). *Pedagogia do Oprimido* (50th ed.). Rio de Janeiro, RJ: Paz e Terra.
Hoeffel, J. L., Fadini, & A. A. B. (2007). Percepção ambiental. In L. A. Ferraro Jr. (Coord.), *Encontros e caminhos: formação de educadoras (es) ambientais e coletivos educadores* (Vol. 2). Brasília, DF. Ministério do Meio Ambiente.
Hoeffel, J. L., Sorrentino, M., & Machado, M. (2004). Concepções sobre a natureza e sustentabilidade: Um estudo sobre percepção ambiental na Bacia do Rio Atibainha. *Anais do Encontro da Associação Nacional de Pós-Graduação e Pesquisa em Ambiente e Sociedade.* Indaiatuba, SP: Brasil, 2.
Gadotti, M. (2000). *Pedagogia da terra.* São Paulo, SP: Fundação Peirópolis.
Guerra, A. F. S., & Orsi, R. F. M. (2017). O PRONEA como política pública: a educação ambiental e a arte do (re)encontro. *Revista Eletrônica do Mestrado em Educação Ambiental,* Ed. Esp., 25–39. Retrieved January 24, 2018, from https://www.seer.furg.br/remea/article/view/7140
Guimarães, M. (2004). Educação ambiental crítica. In Ministério do Meio Ambiente. *Identidades da educação brasileira.* Brasília, DF.
Ingold, T. (2003). *The perception of the environment.* London: Routledge.
Jacobi, P. (2005). Participação. In L. A. Ferraro Jr. (Coord.), *Encontros e caminhos: formação de educadoras (es) ambientais e coletivos educadores* (Vol. 1). Brasília, DF. Ministério do Meio Ambiente.
Leff, H. (2003). *Complexidade ambiental.* São Paulo, SP: Cortez.
Lei n. 5.280, de 04 de setembro de 1986. (1986). *Declara área de proteção ambiental a região que circunda a represa hidrelétrica do Bairro da Usina no Município de Atibaia.* São Paulo. Retrieved January 24, 2018, from http://www.al.sp.gov.br/repositorio/legislacao/lei/1986/lei-5280-04.09.1986.html
Lei n. 6.938, de 31 de agosto de 1981. (1981). *Dispõe sobre a Política Nacional do Meio Ambiente, seus fins e mecanismos de formulação e aplicação, e dá outras providências.* Dispõe sobre a Política Nacional do Meio Ambiente, seus fins e mecanismos de formulação e aplicação, e dá outras providências. Brasília, DF. Retrieved January 24, 2018, from http://www.planalto.gov.br/Ccivil_03/leis/L6938.html
Lei n. 9.795, de 27 de abril de 1999. (1999). *Dispõe sobre a educação ambiental, institui a Política Nacional de Educação Ambiental e dá outras providências.* Brasília, DF. Retrieved 24 January 2018 from http://www.planalto.gov.br/ccivil_03/Leis/L9795.htm
Loureiro, C. F. B. (2004). Educar, participar e transformar em educação ambiental. *Revista Brasileira de Educação Ambiental,* 13–20.
Luzzi, D. (2014). Educação ambiental: pedagogia, política e sociedade. In A. Phillip Jr. & M. C. F. Pelicioni (Eds.), *Educação ambiental e sustentabilidade* (2nd ed.). Barueri, SP: Manole.
Matthäus, H. (2001). Oficina do futuro como metodologia de planejamento e avaliação de projetos de desenvolvimento local. In M. Brose (Ed.), *Metotodologia participativa: uma introdução a 29 instrumentos.* Porto Alegre, RS: Tomo Editorial.
Ministério da Educação e do Desporto. (1997). *Parâmetros Curriculares Nacionais: meio ambiente.* Brasília, DF: Secretaria de Educação Fundamental.
Ministério do Meio Ambiente. Instituto Chico Mendes de Conservação da Biodiversidade. (2011). *Estratégia Nacional de Comunicação e Educação Ambiental em Unidades de Conservação (ENCEA).* Brasília, DF. Recuperado em 24 de janeiro de 2018 de http://www.mma.gov.br/images/arquivo/80219/publicacao_encea.pdf
Ministério do Meio Ambiente. (2005). *Programa Nacional de Educação Ambiental* (3rd ed.). Brasília, DF: Ministério do Meio Ambiente.
Pelicioni, M. C. F., & Philippi Jr., A. (2014). Bases políticas, conceituais, filosóficas e ideológicas da educação ambiental. In A. Phillip Jr. & M. C. F. Pelicioni (Eds.), *Educação ambiental e Sustentabilidade* (2nd ed.). Barueri, SP: Manole.
Philippi Jr., A., & Pelicioni, M. C. F. (2002). Alguns pressupostos da educação ambiental. In A. Phillip Jr. & M. C. F. Pelicioni (Eds.), *Educação ambiental: desenvolvimento de cursos e projetos.* Barueri, SP: Manole.
Philippi Jr., A., Pelicioni, M. C. F., & Coimbra, J. A. A. (2002). Visão de Interdisciplinaridade na educação ambiental. In A. Phillip Jr. & M. C. F. Pelicioni (Eds.), *Educação ambiental: desenvolvimento de cursos e projetos.* Barueri, SP: Manole.

Philippi, L. S. (2002). Desafios da aplicação de princípios básicos na implementação de projetos e educação ambiental. In A. Phillip Jr. & M. C. F. Pelicioni (Eds.), *Educação Ambiental: desenvolvimento de cursos e projetos*. Barueri, SP: Manole.

Reigota, M. (2002). *Meio Ambiente e representação social* (5th ed). São Paulo, SP, Cortez.

Resolução n. 2, de 15 de junho de 2012. (2012). *Estabelece as Diretrizes Curriculares Nacionais para a Educação Ambiental*. Brasília, DF. Retrieved January 24, 2018, from http://portal.mec.gov.br/index.php?option=com_docman&view=download&alias=10988-rcp002-12-pdf&category_slug=maio-2012-pdf&Itemid=30192

Saito, C. H. (2002). Política Nacional de Educação ambiental e construção da cidadania: desafios contemporâneos. In A. Ruscheinsky (Ed.), *Educação ambiental abordagens mútliplas*. Porto Alegre, RS: Artmed.

Sauvé, L. (2002). Environmental education: Possibilities and constraints. *Connect, XXVII*(1–2), 1–4.

Sauvé, L. (2005). Currents in environmental education: Mapping a complex and evolving pedagogical field. *Canadian Journal of Environmental Education, 10*(1), 11–37.

Sato, M. (2002). *Educação ambiental*. São Carlos, SP: Rima.

Serrão, S. M. (1999). Conferências, Tendências e Concepções de Educação Ambiental. *Gestão e Desenvovimento, 4*(1), 19–32.

Stahel, A. W. (1995). De Estocolmo ao Rio: a mutação da problemática do movimento ecológico. *Ciências Ambientais*, Ed. Esp., 07–95.

Toledo, R. F., & Pelicioni, M. C. F. (2014). Educação Ambiental em Unidades de Conservação. In A. Phillip Jr. & M. C. F. Pelicioni (Eds.), *Educação ambiental e sustentabilidade* (2nd ed.). Barueri, SP: Manole.

United Nations. (2015). *The 2030 agenda for sustainable development*. Retrieved January 24, 2018, from https://sustainabledevelopment.un.org/content/documents/21252030%20Agenda%20for%20Sustainable%20Development%20web.pdf

Micheli Kowalczuk Machado
Núcleo de Estudos em Sustentabilidade e Cultura
Centro de Estudos, Pesquisas e Extensão
Centro Universitário UNIFAAT
Brazil

Estevão Brasil Ruas Vernalha
Núcleo de Estudos em Sustentabilidade e Cultura
Centro de Estudos, Pesquisas e Extensão
Centro Universitário UNIFAAT
Brazil

João Luiz Hoeffel
Núcleo de Estudos em Sustentabilidade e Cultura
Centro de Estudos, Pesquisas e Extensão
Centro Universitário UNIFAAT
Brazil

JUDITH PRIAM, JEAN-PIERRE AVRIL AND
ALAIN AYONG LE KAMA

15. A PILOT PROGRAM ON AVIFAUNA IN FRENCH GUIANA

INTRODUCTION

To our knowledge, the *Pilot Program on Avifauna* (Priam, 2016, *Projet Pilote en Avifaune*, internal document, Academy of French Guiana, Arsène Bouyer d'Angoma Middle School, 2 pp.) validated by J-P. Avril, co-author of this chapter and director of Collège Arsene Bouyer d'Angoma, is the first of its kind in France or worldwide. It makes sense in that in this peculiar part of France, Saint-Laurent-du-Maroni in French Guiana (see Figure 15.1), students are living in an *environment* or even *milieu*, that they are part of. They integrate many aspects of it as the birds and their interrelations within this *milieu*. French Guiana belongs to the Neotropics, where we find the highest number of bird species: 32% of the total i.e. 86 families with French Guiana having at least 707 species according to Birdife International (2018). A local association even identified as many as 729 species.

The *Pilot Program on Avifauna* was developed on what we call a *circular bottom-up approach*. It goes beyond the traditional *Bottom-up* and *Up-down* approaches. We foresee that it will be part of the future of ongoing and future climate change evaluations. Youth are part of our future comprehension and solutions. In fact, "few have studied whether and how youth-focused community and citizen science [CCS] contributes to conservation" (Ballard al., 2017, p. 66). This appears to us as evidence. As Ballard et al. (2017, p. 66) mentioned, "we define youth-focused CCS as activities by youth that produce data or results disseminated to and usable by professional scientists, agencies and/or managers".

In this case study, we provide brief elements of context about Saint-Laurent-du-Maroni and education in French Guiana. Then we present a methodology to empower youth that looks partly traducing endeavour of our *Pilot Project on Avifauna*: the Environmental Science Agency. Finally, we explain how our *circular bottom-up approach* goes beyond traditional methodologies of integrating youth, that we connect with a deep culture environment nexus.

Figure 15.1. Saint-Laurent-du-Maroni city along the Maroni River, in French Guiana

SAINT-LAURENT-DU-MARONI: ELEMENTS OF CONTEXT

Milieu and Environment

The distinction between Milieu and Environment makes sense in French Guiana. *Environment* appears when human beings have such modified Nature, that the limits are well identified because of huge anthropogenic changes. The *Environment* surrounds. The *Milieu*, on the opposite, is a core area where humans are part of. We can identify some concentrations of population along the coast from the main transect Saint-Georges-de-l'Oyapock on the East to Apatou in the West. However, some more isolated communities (villages or hamlets) exist, without roads to access from the two main cities of Cayenne and Saint-Laurent-du-Maroni.[1] In these cases, the river becomes the main way for transportation even if in some cases small planes reach a few of those remote places. They are by example the villages of Grand-Santi, Papaïchton, Maripasoula, Saül, along the Maroni River and Camopi along the Oyapock River. Mana is along the Mana River, to the West. Nature is part of the daily life in those remote places, or is part of it for the others, as in Saint-Laurent-du-Maroni (see Figure 15.2). The case of Mana is illustrated in Figure 15.3, that we classify as an intermediary remote case, as Apatou and Awala-Yalimapo: are far from the main cities, but are connected by roads.

Nature is very close to the city of Saint-Laurent-du-Maroni even if the changes are coming fast. The existing environment near the Collège Arsène Bouyer D'angoma allows for the identification of punctual and permanent species of birds during the day due to their displacement for feeding (see Figure 15.6). Some of these even nest in the College (see Figure 15.4). The College area covers above 17,000 square meters (see Figure 15.5).

Let's consider the context of education that brings together students living nearby or visiting us from remote places.

The Students

The students seen here (see Figure 15.7) are 11 to 15 years old. It is obligatory to be in school in the French educational system between the ages of 6 and 16 years old Some families from remote communities have to send their children far away, to cities, or the nearest place to study. In the Municipality of Saint-Laurent-du-Maroni (see Figure 15.2) this is the case as there are five *Collèges* concentrated in the city with the same name, near the Maroni River. That Municipality covers 4,830 km² (CCOG online, http://ouestguyane.fr/la-ccog/le-territoire/saint-laurent-maroni/) with 43,600 inhabitants in 2015 (https://www.insee.fr/fr/statistiques/3291260).

Those students involved in the *Pilot Program* demonstrate strong abilities in knowing and observing their environment (see Figure 15.6). They even are also very good at capturing insects such as grasshoppers (see Figure 15.8). That's why we consider that Methodologies regarding Nature must leave liberty in observing and analysing without constraining the scientific imagination of those students.

SOME WAYS TO CONSIDER YOUTH' EMPOWERMENT

Some methodologies address youth's sense of place, such as the ESA, Environmental Science Agency where "ESA[2] combines not only an understanding of environmental

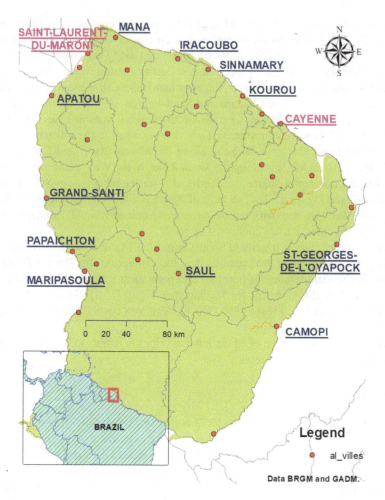

Figure 15.2. The territory of French Guiana presents a concentration of the population on the coast. The two main cities are Cayenne and Saint-Laurent-du-Maroni, also the name of the two municipalities, among the 22, are delimited on the map

science and inquiry practices, but also youths' identification with those practices and their developing belief that the ecosystem is something on which they act" (Ballard et al., 2017, p. 65). One element underlined through case studies presented and carried out by youth in San Francisco Bay, California, with the *Long-term Monitoring Program and Experiential Training for Students* (LiMPETS) program or the *East Bay Academy for Young Scientists* (EBAYS) program (Yin, 2013 in Ballard) is that "Most participation by youth in CCS occurs during the field data collection process" (Sadler et al., 2010 cited in Ballard et al., 2017, p. 67).

Figure 15.3. Mana along the Mana River

Troglodytes aedon   *Euphonia violacea*

Figure 15.4. Troglodytes aedon is one of those species nesting in College Arsene Bouyer d'Angoma (pictures taken on the fence). Euphonia violacea uses natural supports to stop

For example regarding LiMPETS it is stated that "All focal youth used or described new ecological knowledge specific to their research question, which varied across sites: for the in- and out-of-school LiMPETS participants, most often this meant youth explained the relationships between … populations and … environmental factors, ecological relationships … and food sources or predators, and improved understanding of and skills in field data collection focused on accurately collecting and measuring …" (Ballard, 2017, p. 69).

Our hypothesis, stated at the onset of our *Pilot Program on Avifauna,* was that youth may observe and capture some components of the environment that adults do not. That means that a free approach for students is the best way to develop key ideas for answering questions:

Figure 15.5. Different views inside and from College Arsene Bouyer d'Angoma that allow us to identify these diverse environments

Figure 15.6. The College Arsene Bouyer D'Angoma (also called College V) is near the Maroni River and some forest patches (image extracted from Google Earth in January 2018)

Figure 15.7. Travis H., Marvin A. and Markus G., participating in the Pilot Program on Avifaune and making observations of birds in the Amana Reserve in March 2019

We recall an experience a few years ago, with a heterogeneous group of children, that didn't know each other but then began to interact. It was in the context of waiting for of a small boat that was delayed, off an archipelago of the Caribbean. They (the children) were gathered behind a barrier and looking at birds moving behind cars that were bringing passengers to the boat terminal. No adult paid attention to this.

We consider that the ESA demonstrates limits regarding ongoing issues and norms. We think that in the context of complexities and uncertainties related to ecosystems and climate change, we don't have the exact answers to act: humans are trying to solve by experimenting.

We think that another manner to consider the contribution of youth, is through what we call a *circular bottom-up approach* that can constitute an innovative manner to deal with climate change issues and loss of biodiversity, among others. We take advantage of Mannion and Lynch (2016) about the *Place-relational pedagogies*, and *Planning with place*.

Figure 15.8. Students participating in the Pilot Program on Avifauna present great knowledge of their environment and abilities in observing and capturing insects. Here are two grasshoppers captured by Rogely E. and Silciano T. and shown to the others before being released in the gardens of the College January 2018

A CIRCULAR APPROACH GOING BEYOND A BOTTOM-UP AND UP-DOWN APPROACHES

This approach is based on the recognition of the knowledge of some students studying in French Guiana. *Place-relational pedagogies* (Mannion & Lynch, 2016) can take advantage of integrating local knowledge of the territory by these students. Our *Pilot Program* demonstrates a from of *Place-based Education and Local Outdoor Learning* through which the key ideas for interpretation can arise. This also provides a voice to marginalized and underrepresented populations who know and feel differently when an Environmental communication tries to simply highlight some facts (out of the local context).

Our approach can be interpreted as a new category difeerentiated from the three identified by Mannion et al. (2011) regarding *Planning with place*: "place-ambivalent", "place-sensitive" or "place-essential". Furthermore, as Mannion et al. (2013) have found, "taking a place-essential approach will mean educators are likely to benefit from knowing well the places where the teaching and learning experiences are to be enacted or knowing in some depth the kinds of things that are likely to happen in the place visited" (Mannion & Lynch, 2016, pp. 85–94). Ours is more unpredictable. In fact in our "Place", we are capturing moments of ecological equilibrium in process, and that's why we term it *place-in-process*.

In our work, we can't predict with any certainty what will be the components regarding avifauna by example, because climate change is driving slow changes. During the lessons, we don't speak of educator and learners, as there are continuous interactions between both levels: students and professor. This approach generates a hypothesis-deduction game based on knowledge: the indigenous and the academic. We consider that the students are fundamental in the interpretation of the Environment/Milieu's complexities through a circular interaction of ideas going beyond the bottom-up and up-down approaches as presented in Figure 15.9.

This hypothesis depends on an intrinsic cultural knowledge regarding birds that we present in the next section of this case study.

CULTURAL KNOWLEDGE REGARDING BIRDS

The study of birds is dependant on the capabilities and abilities developed by observers. In French Guiana, these great capabilities are due to long-term integration of knowledge and a particular way of living in (or not far from) the forest and the rivers (see Figure 15.10). We believe that we can't discredit this type of local knowledge, as Cox stated in 2000, "local knowledge systems are disappearing at a rate that may not allow us even to know what value if any, such systems had" (as cited in Pandey, 2003, p. 633). We argue that in the Caribbean, as in French Guiana, an up-down approach is the rule that can prevent access to this long-term form of acquired knowledge. For example, "Through the Caribbean BirdSleuth program we train teachers in the Caribbean to involve young people in the natural world and to build their science skills" (see for example http://www.birdscaribbean.org/outreach-and-education/).

Parents also know about birds and young people hear and confront themselves with these past souvenirs of the environment/milieu owned by 'the ancients'. Birds even paint memories with images. Nowadays in parts of the countryside where I lived in the Caribbean, some birds have disappeared and so has the magic of their songs ... like the *Vireo sp*. However, in some parts of the Caribbean, new species are generating visual images based on bird song, for example, Mimus sp. That kind of knowledge of sites is fundamental ....

With this brief case study, we argue that resilience of Nature and humans integrated into Nature is based on a close interaction and ongoing understanding of these changes. When "outdoor education and outdoor learning" depend on local

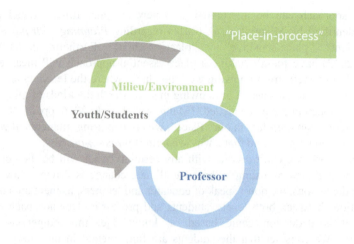

Figure 15.9. A circular interaction of ideas beyond the bottom-up and up-down approaches makes the knowledge of French-Guiana students fundamental in the process of interpreting the environment/milieu

Figure 15.10. The Maroni River as seen from the French side. In the background, Suriname

knowledge, a big challenge is to unlock key ideas for the understanding and gathering of knowledge. Climate Change is seen as one of the largest issues in this regard. It will need to be addressed through the integration of knowledge from scientists and the local community.

NOTES

[1] 57,614 inhabitants in Cayenne and 43,600 inhabitants in Saint-Laurent-du-Maroni in 2015 (INSEE online, published in 2017, https://www.insee.fr/fr/statistiques/3291260).
[2] "Some programs oriented toward development of ESA support young people in becoming agents of change" (Freire, 2000), and ask educators and researchers to look for small, incremental changes young people make in their lives and local communities, alongside larger changes made through participation in collective actions and activities" in Ballard et al. (2017, p. 66).

REFERENCES

Ballard, H. I., Dixon, G. H., & Harris, E. M. (2017). Youth-focused citizen science: Examining the role of environmental science learning and agency for conservation. *Biological Conservation, 208*, 65–75.

BirdLife International. (2018). *Country profile: French Guiana*. Retrieved from http://www.birdlife.org/datazone/country/french-guiana

Birds Caribbean online. (2018, February), *Outreach and education*. http://www.birdscaribbean.org/outreach-and-education/

CCOG online. *Saint-Laurent-du-Maroni*. Retrieved from http://ouestguyane.fr/la-ccog/le-territoire/saint-laurent-maroni/

Encyclopaedia Britannica. (2011). Vol. Dinosaurios, reptiles y aves, 68–69.

INSEE online. (2017). Retrieved from https://www.insee.fr/fr/statistiques/3291260

Mannion, G., & Lynch, J. (2016). The primacy of place in education in outdoor settings. In B. Humberstone, H. Prince, & K. A. Henderson (Eds.), *International handbook of outdoor studies* (pp. 85–94). New York, NY: Routledge.

Ministry of National Education, online. *Controle de l'obligation scolaire*. Retrieved form http://eduscol.education.fr/cid46688/controle-de-l-obligation-scolaire.html?rub=253

Pandey, D. N. (2003). Cultural resources for conservation science. *Conservation Biology, 17*(2), 633–635.

Priam, J. (2016). *Projet pilote en avifaune*. Unpublished paper. Academy of French Guiana, 2 pp.

Priam, J. (2017). *La maison créole et son avifaune*. Proposal College Arsene Bouyer d'Angoma, submitted to the Patrimoine Project Maison de Kaw, Acdemy of French Guiana, 2 pp.

Judith Priam
Academy of French Guiana and
Servicios Científicos y Técnicos San Juan, Puerto Rico
French Guiana

Jean-Pierre Avril
Academy of French Guiana
Collège Arsène Bouyer d'Angoma
French Guiana

Alain Ayong Le Kama
Academy of French Guiana and
Servicios Científicos y Técnicos San Juan, Puerto Rico
French Guiana

NELSON ARIAS ÁVILA, VERÓNICA TRICIO GÓMEZ,
JESSICA MAYORGA BUCHELLY AND
JENNY ORTEGA VÁSQUEZ

16. RENEWABLE ENERGIES

A Thematic Connection between Subjects

INTRODUCTION

In the current interconnected world, with a massive advance of technological development, a scientific culture should be a part of the general culture that the citizens of all countries have.

In relation to three aspects, energy, environment and education, we can say that for years, the evidence has been abundant and unquestionable that present-day energy production schemes based on fossil-fuel sources are fundamentally unsustainable, highly vulnerable, and dependent on dwindling supplies of fossil-fuel resources. It has also been confirmed that excessive and irrational energy consumption and indiscriminate use of fossil fuels have had toxic environmental side effects.

Today, there is a clear need to modify the current energy model as soon as possible: substituting the use of those fuels for others and, likewise, generating a radical change in energy savings and the rational use of energy at all levels (García, 2013; Gutiérrez & Gutiérrez, 2009; Heras, 2008; Jaén & Calventus, 2006; Tricio, Vilches, & Gil, 2014). As the importance of energy for sustainable development is urgent, education has an essential and irreplaceable role in the required changes in attitudes of our society towards it. In the framework of an education system that favours the transition to sustainability, it is very necessary to teach renewable energies (RE) and to weave new connections between culture and the environment. In doing so, particularly at secondary and pre-university levels of education, RE can become a thematic connection between subjects (Arias & Tricio, 2014; Vilches, Macías, & Gil, 2014; Merino, 2010; Tricio & Arias, 2011).

In presenting a proposal to the requirements of this teaching, content was prepared on standard topics of renewable energies and its related themes (sustainability, non-renewable sources, and environmental impacts among others), thereby integrating a large part of these materials into the teaching programs.

A compilation of these materials has been published by the University of Burgos, with the title "Booklet for the teaching of Renewable Energies" (Cartilla para la Enseñanza de las Energías Renovables [CEER]) (Arias & Tricio, 2013). The resource contains a presentation of global problems relating to RE, an outline of scientific concepts relating to the thematic content, practical activities, exercises, and guidance on situating those items in conventional courses. Based on this work and on the experiences of the University of Burgos (UBU) and the District University Francisco José de Caldas of Bogotá (UDFJC), the "Renewable Energies Collaborative Project" (Proyecto Colaborativo en Energías Renovables) (PROCOLER) has been developed, in which teachers and students from the university and associated schools participate in a multidisciplinary approach that allows students to comprehend RE in their world, relating these energies with different subject modules in their education and daily life.

The PROCOLER has a double objective; first, to promote the increase of a scientific culture and in second, to educate young people in an energy culture based on renewable energy sources, the saving of energy and on energy efficiency.

Multidisciplinary Project on Renewable Energies

The methods, forms, and proposals that have been followed for the teaching and the dissemination of RE at different levels of education vary (Barrio & Andrés, 2008; Comisión Europea, 2006; Organización de Estados Iberoamericanos para la Educación, la Ciencia y la Cultura (OEI), 2010; Rau, 2011; Renewable Energy [Teacher Resource Guide], 2008). However, the majority of these proposals can clash with different types of problems teachers face as they (typically) have not the knowledge background to teach these topics. Inappropriate preparation for these themes for many teachers stems from a single subject approach that is generally taken when addressing these themes. The lack of appropriate resources for teaching the above-mentioned themes (especially in Spanish and for secondary and pre-university education) is a further problem. In addition, some of the proposals that have been advanced have yet to be implemented.

As a contribution to the RE teaching-learning process, PROCOLER as an educational resource has been developed between the UBU and the UDFJC (with some associated schools). It seeks to provide a tool to secondary and pre-university school teachers to help them in the process of teaching RE related themes (Tricio & Arias, 2016).

The project is based on the CEER (Figure 16.1), where a direction that is presented distinguishes it from other earlier implementations.

The objective of the Booklet is to approach the teaching of RE and related themes with a different and innovative approach, applying collaborative, multidisciplinary and horizontal working methodologies, at all educational levels that form part of secondary and pre-university teaching.

The Teaching Booklet is not intended to fit in with the needs of a specific or particular plan, but it can be useful for any particular school or educational institute. The primary idea of the resource is the importance and need for a multidisciplinary perspective which permits students to comprehend RE in context and to relate energy use with their daily life, although teachers can also use it on an individual basis.

Figure 16.1. Front and back cover of the publication of CEER

One focus throughout the resource is Science, Technology, Society and Environment (Ciencia, Tecnología, Sociedad y Ambiente) (CTSA). It is expected that pre-university students will not only gain a specific basic knowledge of those themes, but that they will adopt personal positions that will permit and make possible exchanges in both of the ideas and experiences with their family members and social circle in general. In this way the resource may influence behavior throughout their life supporting sustainable development for their region and country.

The active participation of the school teachers involved in the project is vital, and our approach is framed within an action-research methodology (Uttech, 2006). For this reason, many of the concrete goals and objectives of the project are generated as part of this process, both within and outside the classroom.

As a general objective, PROCOLER intends to arrive at an evaluation of the themes, structure, and methodologies proposed in the Booklet (CEER) through this implementation. To date the schools associated with the project include:; San Pedro y San Felices, and Jesús María, both in Burgos and Marco Antonio Carreño Silva, of Bogotá. In addition, students completing their end-of-degree project have joined with the project as active co-researchers.

Multiple activities have been developed within the framework of the resource and the implementation of its activities such as surveys, questionnaires for students and teachers, mental maps, and conceptual maps among others. One of the activities that is emphasized in the Booklet is the construction of low-cost devices, such as solar ovens, biodigesters, and simple home-made solar cells. Some of these involve student activities in the laboratory, in which the formulation of hypotheses and the analysis of the data obtained from the assembly of the devices mentioned above were all encouraged. The students also prepared informative leaflets, using software programs such as Publisher to show the construction process of their different home-made devices.

In those educational centres where the so-called *World Environment Day* or similar events were celebrated, the students have also shown the results obtained in the different product activities of the implementation of the CEER. To do this, exhibitions were organized in various public spaces, where posters, models, and tasks completed with recyclable material among others, were presented.

Design and Previews of a Website

As part of the implementation of PROCOLER, work also began on the design of a website centred on the dissemination and the teaching of RE, which is still under development; the Joomla! Platform, version 3.1, was used (https://www.joomla.org/).

Its basic structure is presented as follows. Starting at the home page (Figure 16.2), a general introduction may be accessed with a brief description of the most widely used energetic sources at present (fossil fuels), the reason for their use has led to various environmental problems and how RE can be incorporated, from different perspectives, as one of the possible solutions to those problems.

The website comprises four principal sections (Figure 16.3). The first section is called *The Sources of Renewable Energies*; it includes historical and general information on each of the energy sources, emphasizing the different devices that

Figure 16.2. Website home page

Figure 16.3. Principal sections of the website

they power. A series of informational links (various materials) is also presented that supplements the main content of the web.

The second section, called *The Teachers' Room*, contains a series of teaching tools designed intending to provide a guide to the teacher, so that topics focused on RE may be integrated with the essential topics in the study plan of an ordinary school. With a view to mainstreaming the teaching of renewable energies in the teaching units of a secondary education institute, emphasis is placed on the *Teaching Activity Sheets*, which cover activities, from the perspective of each subject (Biology, Spanish Language and Literature, Physics, English, Mathematics, Social Studies – Geography and History – Technology and Computing, etc.) on one or more thematic aspects of RE.

The activities that are proposed in the sheets vary from simple laboratory work to the construction of home-made devices in the classroom. At the end of each sheet, complementary material (lectures, articles, videos, etc.) of a scientific nature are suggested for dissemination, with which the teacher can propose various projects to the students, whether in the classroom or as homework. Among the general themes of the information sheets thermal solar energy and photovoltaic solar energy are also considered.

Another tool that is proposed are the *Laboratories*, which are separated between: direct laboratory work on RE, a space in which practices may be found that are principally related to the home-made devices that are constructed, and corresponds to the indirect laboratories, a space in which practices are presented and suggested that involve fundamental concepts in the study of different disciplines such as Physics, Chemistry, and Biology among others, but oriented towards RE-related phenomena. For example, the theme of a direct laboratory is the home-made solar kitchen, and an indirect one is thermal conductivity. Open "exercises" are also proposed and suggested, based on a problematic aspect.

Different didactic proposals on the teaching of RE are also presented as the culmination of this section, among which the one outlined in the Booklet.

A list of documents (articles, videos, etc.) on the teaching of RE in secondary education and university education as well as the informative articles on renewable energies are presented in the third section, referred to as the *Press Office*; whenever possible, the respective hyperlinks are provided. As a complement, hyperlinks to book and journal downloads were found that centre their themes on both the teaching and the dissemination of RE.

Also, in this section, current affairs news is provided that focuses on technological advances for RE and similar topics as well as a list of commemorative days. For example, The Day of the Earth, Day of the Sun, and World Environment Day among others. Likewise, a calendar of academic events on the teaching of RE at a national/ and international scope, as well as some events related to the dissemination of renewable energies.

In the fourth section, called the *Debating Room*, a range of tools will soon be available in which the user will have the opportunity to interact with others who are interested in a particular topic among those shown on the website. The main tools are an environmental forum and an interactive student blog, in which the user can propose some topic or article of interest or share an experience with other users of the site. In addition to this, the space includes a "forum for teachers" where teachers from different knowledge areas can contribute their experiences in the classroom in the form of a field diary. In doing so, their colleagues can be made more aware of the new learning methodologies focused on RE and how these are developed at present in Colombia and elsewhere in the world.

CONCLUSIONS

In this section, we summarize some of the results that have been reached to date and the most significant conclusions for our project.

- A didactic methodology has been proposed in this work centred on collaborative and transversal working practice, with a multidisciplinary approach, that allows students to understand RE, relating these forms of energy to both the different subjects on their educational courses and in their daily life.
- PROCOLER, based on the Booklet (CEER), presents an interdisciplinary approach as a guide for the teacher in the RE teaching/learning process and in related topics, in secondary education. In both, the proposed methodology is centred on collaborative work with a multidisciplinary approach that encourages students to understand RE, linking these sources of energy to different subjects and their daily lives.
- It can be used in any educational institution, with no limitation to a specific curricular plan. The Booklet can be approached in any order depending on the characteristics and needs of each institution, and there is no need for it to be implemented as a whole.

- Its development implies no increase in hours of the different subjects. Although it suggests the creation of interest groups to complement the thematic topics, it incentivizes the construction of low-cost devices, encouraging students to develop their manual skills within a context of project planning and development.
- The world of the student is involved, by analyzing daily situations and by developing practices that differ from those in which the student is limited to following a set of guidelines established as a "type" of template.
- The results of the implementation to date offer a better vision from the perspective of both student and teacher towards the learning and the teaching of RE in their educational circles.
- A website has been designed and partially developed (still under construction), that will soon be on-line and available to the public.

REFERENCES

Arias Ávila, N., & Tricio Gómez, V. (2013). *Cartilla para la enseñanza de las Energías Renovables* (p. 150). Burgos, Spain: Servicio de Publicaciones Universidad de Burgos. Información disponible en. https://e-libro.net/libros/libro.aspx?idlibro=12741

Arias Ávila, N., & Tricio Gómez, V. (2014). Energías renovables: una propuesta para su enseñanza, *Lat. Am. J. Phys. Educ.*, 8(3), 487–493.

Barrio, J., & Andrés, D. (2008). *Ciencias para el mundo contemporáneo*. Madrid, Spain: Ediciones Editex.

Comisión Europea (Luxemburgo). (2006). *Educación energética: Enseñar a los futuros consumidores de energía*. Retrieved from https://es.scribd.com/document/87999311/educacion-energetica

García, P. (2013). Nuevas energías. *Revista Española de Física*, 27(1), 34–40. Retrieved from http://revistadefisica.es/index.php/ref/article/view/1834

Gutiérrez, C., & Gutiérrez, C. (2009). *La actuación frente al cambio climático: guía para un consumo sostenible*. Murcia, Spain: Universidad de Murcia.

Heras, M. (2008). *Fuentes de energía para el futuro*. Madrid, Spain: Ministerio de Educación de Madrid.

Jaén, A., & Calventus, Y. (2006). *Tecnología energética y medio ambiente I*. Cataluña, Spain: Universidad Politécnica de Cataluña.

Merino, L. (2010). *Las Energías Renovables*. Madrid, Spain: Fundación de la Energía de la Comunidad de Madrid.

Organización de Estados Iberoamericanos para la Educación, la Ciencia y la Cultura (OEI) (España). (2010). *Metas Educativas 2021*. Retrieved from www.oei.es/metas2021/libro.htm

Rau, M. (2011). *Moja Island: una forma amena de acercarse al mundo de las energías renovables*. Retrieved from www.scienceinschool.org/2011/issue19/moja/spanish

Renewable Energy. (2008). *Adding energy to the classroom. High school. Teacher resource guide*. Austin, TX: State Energy Conservation Office.

Tricio, V., Vilches, A., & Gil Pérez, D. (2014). Ciencia de la Sostenibilidad: un nuevo enfoque científico. Spain: *Revista Española de Física (Temas de Física)*, 28(4), 8–9. Retrieved from http://revistadefisica.es/index.php/ref/article/view/1997

Tricio Gómez, V., & Arias Ávila, N. (2011). Propuesta para la enseñanza de las energías renovables en la educación secundaria. *Memorias XXXIII Reunión Bienal de la Real Sociedad Española de Física, 2*, 163–164.

Tricio Gómez, V., & Arias Ávila, N. (2016). Proyecto Colaborativo en Energías Renovables – PROCOLER. Presentación y resultados iniciales de esta propuesta en educación científica. La Habana, Cuba: *Materiales IX Congreso Internacional de Didácticas de las Ciencias y XIV Taller Internacional sobre la Enseñanza de la Física, 3*, 28–31.

Uttech, M. (2006). ¿Qué es la investigación-acción y qué es un maestro investigador? *Revista de Educación, XXI*(8), 139–150.

Vilches, A., Macías, O., & Gil, D. (2014). *La transición a la sostenibilidad: Un desafío urgente para la ciencia, la educación y la acción ciudadana. Temas clave de reflexión y acción*. Retrieved from http://www.oei.es/divulgacioncientifica/?La-transicion-a-la-sostenibilidad

Nelson Arias Ávila
District University Francisco José de Caldas of Bogotá
Colombia

Verónica Tricio Gómez
University of Burgos
Burgos, Spain

Jessica Mayorga Buchelly
District University Francisco José de Caldas of Bogotá
Colombia

Jenny Ortega Vásquez
District University Francisco José de Caldas of Bogotá
Colombia

MAURICIO GUERRERO ALARCÓN, OLIVIA LEÓN VALLE
AND ALFONSO RIVAS CRUCES

17. THE ENVIRONMENTAL SUSTAINABILITY GAME

INTRODUCTION

Visual arts, design, and play, can effectively contribute to a critical and ethical Environmental Education (EE) by demonstrating that economic interests prevail over environmental ones.

The relationship between the visual arts and Environmental Education (EE) allows us to reflect on the fragility of ecosystems. In this regard, we consider that there is a hostile relationship between Western civilization and the natural environment.

The Environmental Sustainability Game (ESG) is a resource to stimulate environmental education by criticizing the behavior of decision-makers in the world, both in economic and environmental policy.

It promotes among the players, through informal communication, that there is an adverse pattern in the environmental performance indices – such as global warming – strongly conditioned by economic interests.

In this work we have proposed to problematize the interests of ecological order with those of the economic one, to transmit to the people interested in this issue the uncertainty that hangs over humanity and the planet when observing the delay of the objectives set out in the summits.

Through the strategy of a casino-style table game, the main agenda of Western civilization is discussed in its development model, confronting it with natural resources, asking if "sustainability", as it is conceived, is just one panacea more than a goal to fulfill with high priority.

Finally, we will conclude that the visual arts, design, and play can contribute effectively to critical environmental learning, giving the message that the unsustainability of the planet will always be present, as long as social awareness does not change, and this will only be possible with the participation of society.

ART-DESIGN, SOCIETY AND ENVIRONMENT

The attention of the arts towards the things of nature in general, particularly in the western world, is recognized for example in remarkable musical compositions, literature, theatre, dance, film, and so on. Traditional painting has reflected themes such as "La primavera" by Boticelli, "The Sunflowers" by Van Gogh, "Landscape of the Valley of Mexico" by José María Velasco, "Landscape of Eragny" by Camile Pizarro. In Baroque and Churrigueresque religious architecture, art recreates nature with fruits and vegetables; just as in Art Nouveau it manifests itself in stairs, windows, and balconies. All these are some few examples throughout the history of this Art-Nature relationship that has undergone a metamorphosis, to move from works that represented the elements, to works where nature itself is part of these (Morgan, 2003, p. 12).

The design, in particular, the graphic, for its ability to communicate with a defined purpose and, despite its still young existence, promotes awareness through awareness campaigns and warning calls to the most urgent environmental problems.

The attitude of some artists and designers to question the functions conventionally assigned to their disciplines – because of their relationship with the market – has derived in the realization of pieces that recover the social function, and not only aesthetics, that art and design should have, and that we also recognize as the ethical function.

Ethics along with aesthetics and morphology are axiological categories that establish value judgments regarding our perception of reality. Those of aesthetic order attend sensorial stimuli, comfort, pleasure and, those of ethical order, the moral judgment, the sense of truth, the social responsibility, the community and, of course, the care of the environment.

The progressive deterioration of the environment implies that the expectations of recovering a habitable space that means a better level of subsistence leads us to the promotion of a culture of preservation of the natural environment.

It is a task for all fields of knowledge, including for the visual arts and design that must assume and insist, with the means at their disposal, on the indissoluble nexus of man and nature, the subject of the highest priority.

WHAT ARE THE CRITICISM AND ETHICS IN ENVIRONMENTAL EDUCATION?

It is necessary to focus on opportunities rather than obstacles. The opportunity is to move from ignorant consumerism to responsible production, based on a culture of self-sufficiency in sustainable consumption. That is, to a progressive reduction in the consumption of resources and energy, that is more inclusive of what and who constitute the planetary whole.

It is needed a critical ethical position that guarantees cultural and biological survival, in the long term. An ethic that helps replace the idea of 'development and progress' with another of stability; which seeks the preservation, recovery, and strengthening of the natural environment, traditions, and ways of life. Before welfare is further reduced, environmental education must take a critical stance on the values and principles that lead to sustainable development.

It is not just about assuming that a sustainable development is one that will consume resources and energy without detriment to future generations to meet present needs within ecological limits. It is more about promoting a sustainable development nurtured by ethical principles that are synonymous with stability, responsible for all forms of life and natural resources.

For 25 years permaculture has raised three principles, which by their approach, assume a critical stance to the present way of life-based on consumption and mercantilism. These are, caring for the earth – soil, forests, water, ecosystems; caring for people – respect and preservation of values, traditions, worldviews, taking care of the individual to the familiar, and then the local, and the global; and sharing resources, where corporate and investment returns are not the centre of human existence, much less the reason for their existence.

To conceive a structure of the social and economic organization that seeks a just distribution is, in fact, a transcendent motive for human existence. Environmental education must contribute to the construction of ethical principles and values that define a new paradigm of harmonious development. An environmental education in which the natural and obvious ways of living are based on the self-sufficiency of sustainable consumption, based on responsible production. An environmental education that provides for the care of the land, the care of people and a way of thinking and acting where sharing resources means stability. Promoting "good living" or Sumac Kawsay (Kichwa concept about the good living actually developed in Andean countries) with a responsible relationship with the environment (Biodiversidadla, 2018).

ART AND EDUCATION

The arts, in addition to fulfilling the aesthetic function by which they are historically recognized, also plays an ethical function relative to the social content. It was a compromise that was distorted privileging beauty for economic interests. However, we see clear examples of how the visual arts were committed to their time and the society they lived. Such is the case of The Mexican Painting School, better known as Mexican Muralist Movement. Booming in the early twentieth century, and encouraged by José Vasconcelos, who in front of the critical situation that lived the country of the Post Revolution (90% was illiterate) commissioned the painter Gerardo Murillo to gather other artists to educate these masses through murals in public buildings that explain the history of Mexico (Rodriguez, 1970, p. 151). The contribution that mural painting made to education has been widely recognized.

Another example is the work of artisans and artists dedicated to the dissemination of the Sacred Scriptures from antiquity and after the Renaissance. The first Christian temples that were built for the celebration of the cult of the new religion date from the Roman emperor Constantine in 313 AD, already almost two thousand years ago. Once again, it is clear the power of both space and image and its treatment in the visual transmission of – this time – a spiritual belief. This power was soon recognized by the Catholic hierarchy and prompted her to do artistic commissions that still today they produce juicy profits.

What seems to be a history of the past – linked to the link art-religious education – acquires relevance in contemporary art, by ceasing to be nature ornamentation, or reason for representation, to become another form of ecological reflection.

In 1968 several artists in different parts of the western world (Lailach, 2007, p. 6) were interested in working with the earth (Earth Art) in a real sense and not figuratively (some moved by a kind of annoyance for the commodification of art, others by a philosophical drive with their experiments in nature under the name of Land Art, art of the earth, ecological art, nature art, earth works). They make a tacit acknowledgment of a problem that is already perceived as urgent; and, they are pioneers in exhibiting, not only the beauty of their works but other things so far not considered in art. This happens even before international environmental law measures were agreed upon in Stockholm (Klein, 2015, pp. 252–253) in view of the progressive deterioration of the environment.

These works of unconventional art were drawn upon scientific data or were the product of empirical intuitions based on criticizing the consumer society or social inequity.

Throughout the world, there are artists and groups that unintentionally carry out works or actions with a pro-environmental content, or propose something in relation to the biological issue. There we recognize that indeed there is a tendency to want to raise awareness and environmentally educate the population in a non-formal way.

The issue of environmental education is a latent demand since the first summits of the United Nations and it is considered a long-term strategic objective. Its total fulfillment will be recognized with the passage of some generations, but today we can anticipate that in the achievement of the short and medium term objectives some progress is observed; such is the case of the inclusion of topics and subjects in the plans and study programs at all levels of school education (SEMARNAT, 2006, p. 64). However, this occurs from the perspective of 'sustainable development', which is why some specialists have emphasized the advisability of presenting a critical vision of this orientation. Since, in order to arrive at a sustainable culture, the construction of other values is necessary and its achievement will be accomplished through a didactic for the change of mentality (Barbosa, 2015, p. 32).

Next, are described three examples of what we consider a hostile relationship between Western culture and the environment.

The Foundation of Mexico City in Texcoco Lake and the Consequent Desiccation of this Ecosystem

Since Colonial times, Mexico City is the best evidence of a hostile and irrational attitude towards nature in the West, since at that time the desiccation of the Texcoco Lake began, where the great Tenochtitlan, now Mexico City, was originally settled. The gradual drying process put at risk the very existence of this city, militarily and politically justified because on the water resource this city based its existence.

THE ENVIRONMENTAL SUSTAINABILITY GAME

If we consider that a large percentage of cities in the world have settled, and developed, and grown on the banks of some river, or at its mouth on the shores of the oceans, the common denominator is always the water resource in all of them, and Mexico had it too.

Until 1538, the basin of the Valley of Mexico drained freely and naturally its waters towards Cuernavaca by the south (Department of the Federal District, 1969, pp. 12, 13). The lake had been 'domesticated' since the fresh waters of the salt flats were separated; the levees were built to prevent overflow and the mixture of fresh and salt water.

As hydraulic systems were altered by the colony, floods increased, giving rise to the 1604–1607 construction of the Nochistongo tunnel to the Northeast of the city.

From then on the works continued until the basin was emptied with the consequent desertification of the valley, the proliferation of respiratory diseases and worsening of the general health of the population of the city.

The Constant or Persistent Extinction of Species Is Another Example of the Hostile Relationship with Other Living Beings

For example, during 2017 "… the marine vaquitas were about to disappear. In 1995 there was a record of approximately 600 specimens, there are currently about 30, in little more than 20 years, the population of this species has decreased 72%" (Animal Político, 2017).

Fracking

Actually, fracking is a procedure that is done to extract gas from the bottom of the earth with an impact on the pollution of the oceans. This requires a large consumption of water that involves contaminated wastewater, noise and visual impacts, chemical substances with harmful effects on health, contamination of groundwater, as well as contamination of land and surface water, unleashes small earthquakes, and pollution from the air (Fractura hidráulica NO, 2018).

Under the pretext of avoiding damage to health and discomfort due to floods, favoring development and economic growth, nature is subject to any environmental risk.

THE RELATIONSHIP OF ANCESTRAL CULTURES WITH THE ENVIRONMENT

The societies of the East consider the environment and animals a divine creation through their religions, so its value is greater than the respect that exists in the West. Chinese thought has a special appreciation for natural forces, sun and rain; in India, Indra is the god of thunder and moisture, and Shiva is the goddess associated with drought, destruction, and the transformation; in Egypt, the Nile River is the entity around which all life revolves. There was a strong association to stellar constellations and their gods were represented with characteristics of totemic animals, such as the bull, the cat, the ram, but also the sun, the desert, and the land were part of the cult.

Persia had a naturalistic religion whose central cult was fire, in addition to worshiping the sun, the moon, the stars, water, and plants.

In the pre-American cultures, mainly in Mesoamerica and the Inca region, the cosmos and the forces of nature governed all through life. From the Mayans and among the Mexicas the observation of the Tlamatinime (the wise people, the ones who know, philosophers in the Nahuatl culture) was always placed in the constant and the natural so that the Nahuatl thought was true and scientific (León Portilla, 1974). The close relationship of nature with Mesoamerican civilization was a consequence of a worldview that harmonized things, time and space in their daily lives.

WESTERN CRITICISM REGARDING THE HIGH ESTIMATE OF NATURE

In the old Nahuatl language, the sign Calli (house) refers to the Earth, which in turn, in the words of Fray Diego Durán, is associated with the meaning of the woman-mother, Tonantzin. Beyer refers this: "The earth denying its fruits, witnessing the death of beings and enclosing their spoils in its bosom, naked its greenness during the winter, presents an anguished and harsh face, while its fertility abounds (sic). [She grants] the constant birth of new individuals, the reappearance of plants in the spring, the offer as tender and loving: from here as mother and stepmother at the same time" (Beyer, 1910, p. 240).

This metaphor summarizes how nature was conceived among our ancestors. Historically, however, this idea was not well assimilated by the Western culture, and perceiving it as different it was interpreted as insane. From the sixteenth century the friars judged all behaviour of the ancient settlers of America as a product of evil, and to them as minors, or even came to doubt that they were humans.

In this case, to consider that nature can be known in a different way from the usual one in Western society suggests that it is an anachronistic vision, that it is surpassed, and that it belongs to archaic societies. The strategy to disqualify any thought other than the prevailing official understanding is based on the development and implementation of its own evaluation instruments, applying established measurement parameters developed since the sixteenth century in the Positivism.

Psychoanalysis is the tool that allows us to see how the West structures dominant thought, since, on the one hand, to the ancestral link with nature it attributes ill fixations, complexes in the behaviour of individuals and the societies that share them (Guerrero Alarcón, 1998, p. 27); and on the other, it overestimates industrialization "by the domination of nature, as manifested in industrial production, man gets rid of his fixation on the bonds of blood and soil, humanizes nature and naturalizes himself" (Fromm, 1990, p. 45).

Erich Fromm explains it this way:

Although it has come out of nature [man], the natural world is still its homeland; its roots are still there. Try to find security by returning to the world of plants and animals and identifying with it. This attempt to open up to nature is clearly seen in many myths and primitive religious rites. When man worships as idols trees and animals, he adores particularizations of nature: they are the powerful protective forces whose cult is the cult of nature itself.

The sustainability game makes evident when putting on the table the interests that predominate today, where the emphasis is placed on the development of economic policies shared by the countries. When applied these apparently do not realize the consequences they have on the environment and habitat of all species. Environmental indicators always show red numbers and economic indicators in black numbers.

The constant protection that is made of the capital so that it is inverted and generates gains is evident when always presenting growth and the elements of nature a scarce development seen in proportions of 2 to 1.

THE COMMITMENTS MADE IN THE MEETINGS

The proposal by the Chairman of the COP21 Summit Conference, for the draft decision issued on 12 December 2015 in Paris, states in its ninth subparagraph (unfccc.int, United Nations, 2015):

> Emphasizing *with grave concern* the urgent need to resolve *the significant gap between the aggregate effect* of the Parts mitigation promises, expressed in terms of the annual global greenhouse gas emissions in the Year 2020, and the trajectories that should follow the aggregate emissions to be able to maintain the global average temperature rise well below 2°C with respect to the pre-industrial levels, and to continue striving to limit the increase of the temperature to 1.5°C.

A promise is different from commitment, to the promise only a moral obligation can make it fulfilled, unlike the commitment that is more concrete, detailed and subject to sanction.

And in section II "Contributions previews determined at the national level", of the aforementioned agreement in number 17th:

> Observes with concern that the estimated levels of aggregate greenhouse gas emissions in 2025 and 2030 resulting from the expected contributions (…) at the national level *are not compatible* with the 2°C scenarios (…) but lead to a level (…) of 55 Gigatons in 2030, and also notes that, to maintain the global average temperature rise below 2°C (should be reduced) emissions to 40 Gigatons, or below 1.5°C with respect to preindustrial levels, (…) level to be defined in the special report referred to in paragraph 21 below, a larger emission-reduction effort is required than the provided by nationally-determined contributions; (…)

Paragraph 21 invites the Intergovernmental Panel on Climate Change to submit, in 2018, a special report on the effects of global warming of 1.5°C on pre-industrial levels and trajectories that should be followed by global greenhouse gas emissions.

The commitments of developed nations, in particular of the European Union, are the environmental type and attends the climate change. There are probably advances in them but in the above quotation we talk about the concern that exists when declaring that there is a gap and not lag in the goals, we mean, there is an added effect, a cumulative and non-fulfillment of the agreements. Because of this, a new summit is convened for experts to prospect for a possible scenario if we reach 1.5°C sooner than expected; in other words, we are facing a climate crisis (Gore, 2017) On the opposite side are trade agreements and the economic bonanza always surplus. Any progress in the commitments outlined above are at least in three areas: the first is economic development or economic growth; the second is the paradigm of culture-civilization, the idea of wellbeing in the west; and the third is the politics and the idea of global power or hegemony, that is, those who define what to do and when.

Among the economic indicators that are contrary to "sustainability policies", we find the globally multicited: manufacturing index and services, gross domestic product, trade balance, inflation, interest rates. All of them are susceptible to manipulation and because of their behaviour they have, according to analysts, a very unclear origin (Grandgerard, 2015).

Taking as an example the trade surplus of cars in Mexico, if the sale of private vehicles matches the statistics of the previous year it is said to have been a bad year; to be considered successful would have to surpass that percentage. For example, the following text: "At the end of 2016, the sale of a 1,603,672 cars was recorded, the highest figure in the history for the Mexican market and an increase of 18.6% compared to the one year before" (Sanchez, 2017).

In its Marrakesh Declaration (Climate Change Conference, COP22), Mexico plans to reduce its dependence on fossil fuels – oil and thus GHG emissions by half in the year 2050 (El Financiero, 2016). But in recent days the fifth largest oilfield in the world was discovered in the Gulf of Mexico, the Zama-1. The finding surpassed the expected estimates. "According to Mexican company Sierra Oil information, the finding found total estimated reserves of between 1.400 and 2 million of crude barrels in the primary objective, (…) generated a higher result than expected" (García, 2017). This makes it possible to assume that with the extraction until its depletion of that richness it will be able to subsist for many years.

Through its agency Secretariat of Environment and Natural Resources (SEMARNAT), the Mexican government declares that "… the oil activity involves large dimensions actions that affect drastically the environment. This is particularly true in relation to refining and petrochemical activities which, although they become an important stimulus to the formation of industrial poles, generally show high levels of pollution, as well as deterioration of their natural environment" (SEMARNAT, 2007).

In terms of commitments, the above-mentioned highlights the palpable lack of interest of the Mexican government to invest in applied research in the field of clean energies.

(…) Mexico currently earmarks 0.57 percent of GDP for science and technology, while developed countries allocate between 1.5 and 3.8 percent of their GDP to spending on scientific research and Experimental Development (GIDE). (Villaseñor, 2016)

Compared to the global paradigm of sustainability implemented by Denmark, only its investment in education is about 7.8% of gross domestic product: it is the country that most invests in this area within the European Union and is only responsible for 0.1% of the GHG emissions (Altares, 2015, pp. 48–57).

THE GAME SYSTEM BETWEEN ECONOMY, ENVIRONMENT AND SUSTAINABILITY

The ESG is originally created as an artistic piece of participation with the aim of educating in a non-formal mode and proposing unusual parameters such as the economy, capital, and seemingly disconnected policies. The purpose of the game is to put in evidence how the rules that we follow, always condition an unfavourable result to the environment.

Figure 17.1. Perinole

Using a six-player game board, a seven-sided perinole showing the rounds, described below, that recall policies, the game is structured into three main aspects: Economic interests (politics), environmental interests (resources), and the multimodal

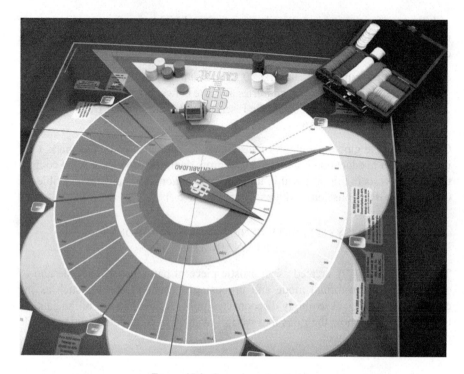

Figure 17.2. Game board and chips

factor of omnipresent Capital. The three slopes meet by chance and coexist based on exogenous rules given in advance.

Capital

This resource only plays in business, just invest where you see a profit, just risk where you can win. The profit must be seen in the short term and the income or utility that it receives must be greater than the investment.

Natural Resources as a Counterpart

Called in the game *Elements*, it acquire importance only when the Capital crosses them, gives them a value and enter in the market, otherwise, their value in the capitalist and/or socialist economy would not have meaning. Its value transcends the economy because its usefulness in ecosystems is vital.

The valuation of the elements conditioned by the *objectification* makes us realize a parody or representation of what happens in reality within a consumer society governed by the law of supply-demand.

Figure 17.3. The Capital

In the ESG system, the assigned scores are arbitrary, it reflects the inequity of commercial and social relations. All the elements gathered together and summed up barely exceed the value of Capital.

The Rounds

These phases are dedicated to certain policies adopted by the governments of developed and emerging countries.

Free Trade Agreements (FTA)

Free Trade Agreements are trade relations between countries that seem to promote the growth of the economy and encourage investment and employment. These treaties like the one that Canada has signed with USA and Mexico oblige to import goods of consumption and raw material of distant countries without considering the risks for health or the environment, the expenditure of energy in its transport, the pollution it entails and the extraordinary sanitary measures.

The Idea of More Consumption = More Development

In capitalist societies, it is considered that, as greater is the consumption of food, household goods, pleasure trips, luxury articles, there will be further development. This model is promoted because it stimulates production; it has been permeated even a communist country like China.

> Indeed, to tackle the challenge of restructuring the Chinese economy has to stimulate consumption. While the rest of the world struggles to increase

Figure 17.4. Merchandise transport in FTA

savings, China, with a saving rate of more than 40%, struggles to get its population to consume more. (Stiglitz, 2007)

The Polluter Must Pay

The phrase refers to the idea that the goods, not the services, of the ecosystems, are quantifiable in monetary terms. In Mexico, an ecologist political party promotes the vision that it is enough that the response of the degradation of the environment takes a penalty and "pay" the damage as if nature were rebuilt with money. The idea that law is a path to a civilized life in democracies can help as long as it is not in the service of those who only seek to benefit from what nature has.

These first three rounds have a decisive economic implication aided by the euro-centrist ideology that maintains order in favor of a determined economic and political power.

Environmental Education Round

Focus on the one that does not propose an analysis and critique of certain policies and actions that make it functional. It is accepted that EE at a general level, is a strategic objective to change the vision of society, but it should not be functional almost informative but critical to the complexity and advantages that some actors have.

Summit Meeting Agreements

For 45 years the environmental problem emergency has demanded agreements between scientists, activists, officials, and politicians who meet at summits or international conferences. Which they have proliferated worldwide counting with first level media coverage to undertake actions favourable to the environment and, as it is said today, human sustainable development against climate change. It is worth to mention that these onerous meetings, spend large budgets with meager results.

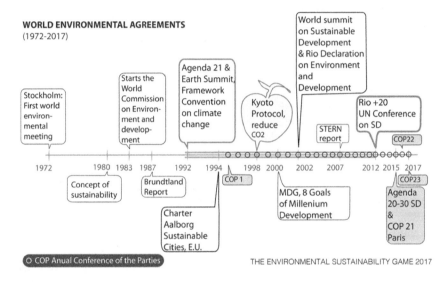

Figure 17.5. Summit meetings

Environmental Actions

The sixth round of the game dedicated to environmental actions against climate change and in favor of sustainability. The actions must, truly, be understood as changing our consumption habits, consider other living species above our environmental comfort, be responsible to the degradation of the biosphere, reduce the emission of greenhouse gases, undertake the reforestation of forests, social and political organization to the anthropogenic causes of climate change and against intensive exploitation of nature's goods, including mitigating the impacts to the environment or reciprocity in the benefit obtained. In short, it is the promotion of an environmental ethic (Noguera de Echeverri, 2007, p. 6).

The board and the perinole are subjected to random rules that pose crisis situations for the elements, but not for Capital. Using casino-style chips this ubiquitous resource grows despite the taxes applied in each move.

The ESG is a ludic educational project that proposes an experience of learning about the inequitable logic of the interests of Capital over environmental ones.

CONCLUSIONS

It is concluded that the vision and conception of nature or environment must change. We have a history of a sacred bond that has survived for centuries and has been distorted by Positivism coupled with the rule of reason over any effective valuation of nature. In this case, contemporary psychoanalysis is the ideological apparatus that imposes for us our values and behaviours.

The ideal space for creating a game that combines different types of knowledge is the art and freedom inherent in it. Subjectivity in the approach of the environment-economy tension helps to simplify concepts in a manageable way.

The critique that permeates all ESG is a principle that must prevail in any educational process. Through the game we show environmental elements such as flora and fauna, water, sun and land that, to a greater or lesser extent, are implicated in the dilemma of economic development and the deterioration of the planet. Climate change, deforestation, the disappearance of species, pollution and degradation of the environment are all the result of this dilemma.

The commitments that are signed summit after summit are assumed as mere promises. They reveal that, despite the importance of these meetings, a certain form of sustainable development is conceived that will take much longer than the one available for a real climate change.

Sustainability is a concept that coupled with "development", shows its obvious contradiction when an urgent aspect is the change in the habits of life and development model.

Instrumenting mechanisms and norms that measure the impact of the presence of the human species in the cities of the West can regulate and raise awareness of something that has been present in our society since we were born: a lifestyle incompatible with nature and its resources.

Playing environmental sustainability is a parody that through its randomness lets us see how by accepting the rules of the game in the economy – that they overlap with the needs of environmental care, allowing players a critical reflection on the limited protection of the ecosystem and the accelerated progress of capital.

REFERENCES

Altares, G. (2015, June 7). La Revolución Verde de Copenhague (M. Rico, Ed.). *El País Semanal, 2019*, 48–57.
Animal Político. (2017). *La vaquita marina, a punto de desaparecer por negligencia del gobierno, acusan organizaciones*. Animal Político. Retrieved from http://www.animalpolitico.com/2017/08/vaquita-marina-extincion-negligencia-gobierno/
Barbosa, A. (2015). *Educación y arte para la sustentabilidad* (J. Pablos, Ed.). Cuernavaca, Morelos, México: Juan Pablos Editor/ Autonomous University of the State of Morelos.

Beyer, H. (1910). *La astronomía de los antiguos mexicanos* (3rd season, volume II). Mexico City, Mexico: Annals of the National Museum of Mexico.
Biodiversidadla. (2018). *El Sumak Kawsay en Ecuador y Bolivia: Vivir bien, identidad, alternativa.* Biodiversity in Latin America and the Caribbean. Retrieved from http://www.biodiversidadla.org/Portada_Principal/Documentos/El_Sumak_Kawsay_en_Ecuador_y_Bolivia_Vivir_bien_identidad_alternativa (accessed 26 January 2018).
Departamento Distrito Federal. (1969). *Interceptores profundos y el emisor central, un nuevo sistema de drenaje para el Distrito Federal.* Mexico City, Mexico: General Direction of Works of the Federal District Department.
El Financiero. (2016, November 17). México espera reducir emisiones de gases efecto invernadero en 2050. *El Financiero.* Retrieved from http://www.elfinanciero.com.mx/nacional/mexico-espera-reducir-a-la-mitad-emisiones-de-gases-efecto-invernadero-en-2050.html
Fractura hidráulica NO. (2018). *Fractura hidráulica NO.* Retrieved from http://www.fracturahidraulicano.info/impactos.html
Fromm, E. (1990). *Psicoanálisis de la sociedad contemporánea.* Mexico, México: Fondo de Cultura Económica.
García, G. and E. T. (2017, July 12). 5 claves del hallazgo petrolero en México (G. E. CV, Ed.). *Expansión de CNN.* Retrieved from https://expansion.mx/empresas/2017/07/12/los-5-puntos-que-debes-conocer-sobre-el-hallazgo-en-el-pozo-petrolero
Gore, Al. (2017). *Now this exclusive.* Retrieved August 14, 2017, from https://www.facebook.com/climatereality/videos/1533820006708118/
Grandgerard, J. H. (2015). *Indicadores económicos: Números ficticios.* Tendencias FX. Retrieved August 14, 2017, from https://tendenciasfx.com/indicadores-economicos/
Guerrero Alarcón, M. (1998). *El fenómeno de las aves migratorias en la Ciudad de México, una obra de arte urbano no-objetual* (National School of Plástic Arts, Ed.). Mexico: National Autonomous University of Mexico.
Klein, N. (2015). *Esto lo cambia todo. El capitalismo contra el clima* (1st ed.). (Paidos, Ed.; M. A. Santos, Trans.). Buenos Aires: Paidos.
Lailach, M. (2007). *Land Art* (S. Biebman, Ed.; P. A. Ellacuría, Trans.). Cologne: Taschen.
León Portilla, M. (1974). *La Filosofía Nahuatl* (Historical Research Institute, Ed.). Mexico City, Mexico: National Autonomous University of Mexico.
Morgan, R. C. (2003). *Del arte a la idea, ensayos sobre arte conceptual* (1st ed., 1996 ed.). (M. L. Olivares, Trans.) Madrid, Spain: Akal.
Noguera de Echeverri, A. P. (2007, May 17). Complejidad ambiental: propuestas éticas emergentes del pensamiento ambiental latino-americano. *Reflexión, 10*(4). Retrieved from http://www.bdigital.unal.edu.co/13602/1/1156-6659-1-PB.pdf.P.6
Rodriguez, A. (1970). *Historia de la pintura mural en México, El Hombre en Llamas* (Trans. from German). Mexico City, Mexico/London: Thames and Hudson.
Sánchez, A. (2017, January 4). *Section Empresas* (El Financiero, Ed.). Ventas de autos rompe record en México en 2016.
SEMARNAT. (2006). *Estrategia de educación ambiental para la sustentabilidad en México.* Mexico City, Mexico: Center for Education and Training for Sustainable Development.
SEMARNAT. (2007). 13. *Industria Petrolera, Instituto Nacional de Ecología y Cambio Climático.* http://www2.inecc.gob.mx/publicaciones2/libros/16/parte3_13.html
Stiglitz, J. E. (2007, April 19). *El nuevo modelo economico de China* (M. L. Tapia, Trans.). Obtained from El Pais, Opinion. Retrieved from https://elpais.com/diario/2007/04/19/opinion/1176933612_850215.html
Unfccc.int, United Nations. (2015). *Convención Marco sobre Cambio Climático.* Paris: United Nations. Retrieved from http://unfccc.int/resource/docs/2015/cop21/spa/l09r01s.pdf
Villaseñor, N. (2016, February 5). *Estrategias para impulsar el desarrollo científico de México.* National Council of Science and Technology, Scientific Policy. http://www.conacytprensa.mx/index.php/sociedad/politica-cientifica/4649-ciencia-sexi-para-combatir-rezago-en-mexico

Mauricio Guerrero Alarcón
Environmental Department for Design
Autonomous Metropolitan University, Mexico

Olivia León Valle
Environmental Department for Design
Autonomous Metropolitan University, Mexico

Alfonso Rivas Cruces
Environmental Department for Design
Autonomous Metropolitan University, Mexico

ZUZANA VASKO AND ROBI SMITH

18. DRAWING MEANING FROM NATURE

Observation, Symbols and Stories

INTRODUCTION

For those of us fortunate enough to live close to accessible natural areas, it is not unusual to feel a pull toward them in response to a need to reflect, be with oneself, connect spiritually, or gain needed perspective. Areas of relatively unspoiled nature may be touted in market spheres for the benefits of 'location' or their ability to offer an escape from the humdrum of ordinary life, yet those of us who connect with it regularly know that far more importantly, nature offers refuge. While in urban contexts we are inundated with reminders of all kinds telling us how and who to be, in the silence of the woods we are better able to hear the voice within.

When it is felt, the impulse to connect with the something of the natural world – even in contexts of busy contemporary and urban life – is often deeply inherent. Eco-psychologist Theodore Roszak (2010) speaks of an ecological unconscious – a deep connection between the human psyche and the natural environment out of which we evolved. Edward O. Wilson (1984) similarly addresses our evolution within a vast diversity of species, and finds that when we are immersed in exploring nature – particularly when the exploration is deeply immersive – we engage something "close to the human heart and spirit" (p. 22). He speaks of a "biophilic instinct shared by all", stating, "Humanity is exalted not because we are so far above other living creatures, but because knowing them well elevates our very concept of life" (p. 22).

While Wilson may imply a biologist's scope of knowledge, his own writing reveals a distinctly poetic sensibility; indeed, his call is to a wide population. Peter London (2003) observes this call to connect with the natural world through the eyes of an artist, saying that "Nature appears beautiful to us because we too are Nature, and what we take to be beauty is only like meeting like and celebrating the congruence" (p. 31). In recent years, however, it has become clear that a personal relationship with the natural world, instinctive as it may seem to many, is not something to be taken for granted.

In 2005, Richard Louv incited much concern over our alienation from the natural world. Compared to previous generations, many young people are relatively detached from their natural surroundings – a phenomenon that has far-reaching effects on our emotional and physical well-being. The future health of the planet itself is also much affected, Louv states, for without a genuine personal bond with nature, we are less inclined to protect it. Since the publication of Louv's important work, much literature has been generated on the need to bring children (and all of us) out into nature. The central question becomes how to do this in a way that inspires people to feel more connected to nature – and that invites a desire to do so of our own volition rather than out of a sense of responsibility. Is bringing people out into nature enough, or do we need to find ways to connect more deeply on a spiritual and personal level with the natural world?

Creative and spiritual work, as manifested through arts-based approaches, can provide very fertile soil in which our bond with nature can grow. More specifically, immersive encounters with the natural world – particularly when experienced through the arts – can be a valuable meaning-making practice that enhances, as Wilson suggests, our sense of life itself. In what ways might nature be a source of wisdom, offering a valuable perspective on our own lives and the things that matter to us?

In her plenary address at the 2017 WEEC conference, indigenous scholar Jeanette Armstrong discussed the importance of rituals and practices that connect a people – especially the younger generation – to the land that is their home. The valuable and far-reaching effects of these practices, she said, are that the place then becomes part of our lives, part of who we are. More precisely, her words were that the land is "in" us. Even though Armstrong spoke here specifically of her own people, the Syilx of the Okanagan region of British Columbia in western Canada, we wish to assume here that the "us" she speaks of implies everyone, or even all residents of that general area. For, she said, if the land is in us, it will always be protected.

While not all of us have this kind of heritage bond with the land where we dwell, a deep connection with place – with the ground beneath our feet and all the life it is home to – seems intensely valuable at a time when whole ecologies are being lost, arguably due in part to our not being in right relationship with them. This is particularly so with areas close to home.

Our workshop at WEEC, titled *Drawing meaning from nature: observation, symbols and stories*, was informed by our work as educators and artists whose own practices explore the shifting dynamics between people and nature. We designed the 90-minute workshop to be an active, embodied experience for participants. In a supportive and intimate context, we explored ways of connecting with land and nature on a deeply personal level that sought to intertwine our own human stories and senses of meaning with those of the natural world. The first part of our workshop included contour drawing – a process-oriented activity suitable for all levels. The observation and close noticing that was engendered then led to an exploration of how natural materials connect with symbols that are both personal as well as shared by all within the life sphere. We aimed to share discoveries and stories in the community as a way of embedding learning with the more-than-human realm. Our emphasis is on how the dynamics and processes of nature relate to – and teach us about – our own lives, and how connecting with other lifeforms generates a meaning-making practice.

In this regard, human culture – by which we mean the individual and collective acts of creating meaning and authenticating our connection with the world – has many opportunities to be enriched and deepened through personal and intimate connection with our natural ecologies. Connecting with nature close to home in a way where it becomes part of us, in turn, engenders greater inclination to take on the responsibility to be stewards of the land in the way Jeanette Armstrong suggests.

FINDING MEANING AND WISDOM IN NATURE

Zuzana

For me, seeds for the practice of listening for wisdom from the natural world were sown when, in 2009, I heard of a presentation at Simon Fraser University (SFU) by Narcisse Blood and Cynthia Chambers. The presentation focused around a film which was subtitled, "If the Land Could Speak and We Would Listen …". The film explores learning that is grounded in place – specifically the traditional territory of the Blackfoot First Nation in Alberta – and is informed by the ethic of *kitaowahsinnoon*, which in Blackfoot means, "that which nurtures us". The question posed by the title haunted me for some time and led me to wonder … what might we, if we were to open ourselves enough, hear the land say?

On my walks into wooded and wilderness areas around my home in Maple Ridge outside Vancouver, I began to ask myself this question. I began to listen, to imagine, how the land might respond. While I do not have the ancestral connection to the land where I live as the Blackfoot do, it still felt eminently important and valuable to engage in a practice of listening to the land, the area of my home, in this way. I sensed that if I were to hear a response, it would occur only after I had listened carefully for some time, on repeated visits to a place, once that place and I had come to know each other – once I had seen it through several seasons, witnessed its moods and come to understand something of the dynamics of the life within it. There were several areas I knew this way. Yet it did not depend only on that. I would need to listen with a very open heart, and to "let the ear grow large", as poet Tim Lilburn says (2002), so that "what is in the world comes near" (p. 10).

Over time, I began to take students and fellow researchers into the wooded hillside area on SFU's Burnaby campus. I would ask them to find a quiet place of their own and sit for a while. Often, I would task them to observe something of the place through drawing, taking photographs, or writing. The purpose here was to become present in the space: to connect with it through the senses and embodied perception. My experience of arts-based teaching and learning had shown me that we need to slip away from the 'rational' part of the mind and into a more intuitive mode to connect in a deeper, more genuine way. Then, my participants would write in response to a simpler version of the question I had been working with: "What does this place say to you?" The intent was simply to observe, and to listen, consciously. I had added the "to you" part to convey that there was no 'correct' response: while this did call upon sincere observation of what was in front of them and unique to this area of woods, it relied as much on individual modes of listening, subjectivity and imagination.

When we returned to class and shared these responses, it struck me how what people heard in the woods often said as much about them as individual human beings, as it did about the wooded place and the life they had observed there. At first, I wondered if this work was taking on a self-serving focus. Then I realised that if the natural world shows us something of our own lives, our own perspectives, this is a valuable form of wisdom and worthwhile contemplative practice.

Robi

My art practice for the past 20 years has been rooted in exploring the often complex and changing relationships we humans have with nature. For many years, my paintings focused on highlighting the ways we exploit nature, pollute and poison it, or disregard it completely. I tried to juxtapose the beautiful and mysterious qualities of non-human species with the human-made problems. Over time, I found the darkness in the work alienated those I wanted to engage.

I shifted my focus and began a process of trying to understand social and environmental change. What inspires people to care about the natural world, to work to conserve particular ecosystems and species? The answer kept coming back as a connection. People need to feel connected to the natural world to care enough to work to preserve it.

In my experience, art-making provides a meaningful way for connecting directly with the natural, non-human world, especially for people who are neither inclined to participate in outdoor, nature-based recreation (such as kayaking, hiking, bird watching) nor rely on foraging, fishing or hunting for food. Nature-based art-making can provide a framework for being outside, slowing down, breathing, and closely observing the elements and other species. It can be an entry point to critically questioning our place in the world and our relationships with the Earth and non-human species. Who are we? Why are we here? How do our actions and inactions affect the natural world? How am I contributing to the world, for better or worse?

In my own artwork, I began to create mixed media paintings and site-specific art installations that explore the interconnections between species, and, between humans and the natural world. How are we interrelated, and what are the dynamics at play in those relationships?

I also began to understand the importance of not only creating my own work but inviting and engaging others to join me in creating work together. This impulse coincided with my being awarded a multi-year artist residency with the City of Maple Ridge, a region endowed with noteworthy wilderness areas. This residency, located in a municipal park bordering a salmon-bearing river, has given me a platform to engage community members in art-making connected to nature.

One of the most powerful tools has been to invite people to join me in outdoor nature sketching. I welcome anyone interested in coming along, regardless of their skill or experience drawing. As a group, we spend some time discussing and trying out different drawing materials, as well as strategies for observation and how to approach a blank page. Before long, we head out to the park, and each chooses a spot to sit and draw. I check in with each person periodically, especially if they haven't had much drawing experience and are feeling lost or overwhelmed. With some simple guidance about how to make decisions about what to focus on and reassurance that the process, not the result, is critical, people inevitably settle in and enjoy the quiet, contemplative and communal experience of being in nature and connecting with the subject they are recording. We then close by coming together as a group to share our drawings, observations, and experiences.

HOW ARTS-BASED APPROACHES BUILD PERSONAL RELATIONSHIPS WITH THE NATURAL WORLD

It is not necessary to have any remarkable skill or talent in the arts to do the kind of work we are proposing. All that is required is openness, a sense of exploration and play, and a willingness to be with the creative spirit we believe dwells in all of us.

As with our relationship with nature, involvement with the arts has always been part of the human experience: throughout eras and cultures, we have engaged with some form of creative meaning-making as a way of connecting with each other and with the world around us (Dissanayake, 1992). Indeed, the experience of creative work and aesthetic engagement has much in common with the experience of immersing oneself in nature (Vasko, 2016): both absorb the senses in a very direct way and engage personal and subjective modes of perception. Both call upon embodied experience and emotional involvement, thereby engaging the whole being. Nature and creative engagement both address something ineffable of the human spirit while offering a sense of connection to things beyond ourselves. These experiences are deeply aesthetic in character, offering a sense of beauty and pleasure even with the potential to address the heavier, darker and more challenging aspects of life. Gregory Bateson encapsulates this notion beautifully with his observation that "When we find meaning in art, our thinking is most in sync with nature" (Van Boeckel, 2011, p. 1).

EXPLORING SYMBOLIC MEANINGS

Zuzana

I related to Robi an activity I had been inspired by some years before. On an outing into nature, young students were given the task of finding three objects: one symbolising birth, another life, and a third, death (Van Boeckel, 2009). After sharing their findings with each other, students created a painting or a poem. What struck me as particularly evocative about this activity was how the task of looking for certain natural materials in the outdoors brings participants to look carefully at other life forms, while also deciphering their own individual meanings and images of how birth, life, and death might be represented. These symbols are universal, yet are often interpreted in deeply personal ways. In essence, students were looking closely in the natural world, finding things that echoed their own sense of meaning – their own life experience. Furthermore, they were working with themes that as humans, we share with all of nature.

Robi

Zuzana's enthusiasm for this particular exercise reminded me of a workshop I had led at the 2013 Canadian Network for Environmental Education and Communication (EECOM) conference in Victoria. In the workshop, I used symbols as the starting point for co-creating a series of mind maps with participants. (Mind maps are also known as concept maps – ideas are positioned in an all-over type diagram, where lines show the connections between them.) We rolled out large sheets of white paper on long tables, which I seeded with hand-drawn symbols of animals, such as a crow, and human-made items, such as a plastic water bottle. Participants were invited to write words or phrases that they associated with each symbol, and then travel around the papers adding to what others had written, creating further associations and connections. Finally, I invited participants to notice where they could make connections between different symbols based on the associations described. As the minutes passed, the maps filled in with lines, connecting words and stories. During our closing, we unpacked the ideas represented in the maps, noticing the multiple layers of connection between seemingly disparate items. I now wondered, could a mind mapping exercise like this be adapted to develop a stronger sense of connection between people and an embodied sense of connection with the natural world?

***

Working with symbols invites, and calls upon, imagery and metaphor; it is an inherently intuitive process. On a walk Robi and Zuzana took through the woods in preparation for the WEEC workshop, we considered symbolic themes that were integral to human life, but which were also widely experienced and felt within the natural world. Knowing that our participants would be educators, mature adults with a substantial life already lived, we looked for motifs that would encompass what we know to be necessities of thriving, as well as those that make room for the darker aspects of life, including the attendant hope necessary to take us through its various cycles. We considered many concepts, eventually whittling down to four general groupings. We anticipated participants would be able to connect meaning to these concepts in relation to the objects they might find or use in the workshop exercise:

- Nourishment
- Transformation/Transition
- Birth/Return/Regeneration
- Communication/Voice

If this workshop were to be conducted with a younger audience, the themes could be adapted accordingly.

WORKING WITH NATURAL MATERIALS: CONSIDERATIONS

The experience of handling natural materials first-hand – taking them in with our senses and knowing that this thing was once alive or part of a living ecosystem that developed over time – returns us to a tactile connection with the larger life sphere. In our workshop at WEEC, we wanted to invite participants to work directly with materials from nature.

We spent quite a bit of time considering whether to take participants outside to find natural materials themselves, or to bring such materials into the room where the workshop was held. Our first preference was to be outside in direct contact with the land and with nature. While the workshop would be held in a conference center in downtown Vancouver, we found a grassy area with trees nearby, the ground littered with maple leaves. The waterfront was also right there, teaming seagulls and crows scavenging for a meal. But the outdoors brings its own uncertainties: Would it be too cold? What if it rained? Would people be comfortable sitting on the damp and sloped ground? What about the noise of passing seaplanes or enquiring glances from non-participants out walking? We were also aware of the limitations to the variety of natural materials available on-site in the manicured landscape.

We knew from experience that in a context where an instructor leads a group over a period of time, such as in a school setting, rich opportunities are created when students to grow accustomed to being outdoors in all types of weather. For example, Zuzana once led a series of ecological art projects with a Grade 2 class in Maple Ridge who went to explore a nearby forested park every Tuesday, rain or shine. She recalls well how the children took a downpour completely in stride, even enjoyed going through the puddles on the way back to the school.

Yet most important is to create an enjoyable and meaningful experience for the particular group at hand. After considering the constraints of time we would be working with, the noise factors of passersby, nearby traffic, and seaplanes, we opted to bring a collection of natural materials inside. We also wanted to create an intimate and supportive space for individuals who were coming to know each other, away from public eyes, where participants could have the room necessary to delve deeply into their thoughts, emotions and personal meanings. While an undisturbed natural area and greater freedom with time would generally be ideal, this alternative had advantages too.

Not knowing how many participants would be joining us for the workshop, or whether they would be locals or educators from other countries, we decided to bring a mix of materials to the workshop. Zuzana collected many materials locally the day before: large maple leaves – newly dropped by the autumn season, bits of cedar fallen from decomposing stumps, fir and huckleberry twigs, hemlock cones, salal. It seemed important to emphasise local fauna, both to mirror to locals their home ecologies and also to introduce these species to visitors from other geographies. Robi dug through her own collection of natural materials that she has gathered over the years to add more variety to the mix: a large moon snail and scallop shells, dried bull kelp, a dried dragonfly, paper wasp nest, salmon bones, crow and eagle feathers, and rocks weathered by the ocean tides. We felt the emphasis on ordinary local materials was important, but it was interesting how the less common ones were a large draw to many participants. The two collections complimented each other well.

Figure 18.1. Our "table" of natural materials

EXPERIENTIAL WORKSHOP PROCESS

Setting the Stage

The way in which a room is arranged – and the feeling one gains upon entering – significantly affects how learning occurs. It was important for us to create an intimate and grounded setting, even though our workshop took place in a rectangular conference room with no windows or natural light. Before participants arrived, we moved the tables and chairs to the perimeter of the room and laid a light, cream coloured cloth in the centre of the floor. We then arranged our found, natural materials on the cloth in an aesthetically-pleasing arrangement, assuring that each object was visible yet fit within a larger pattern. It was important to us that this "table" was arranged in a careful, welcoming and inviting way, setting the stage for the experience to come.

As participants arrived, we invited them to sit on the floor in a circle around our "table". We were unsure how many people would show up for our workshop. This seating arrangement gave flexibility; it would work for a small group of a dozen or the large group of more than 30 who did arrive.

We started our welcome with an acknowledgment that we were meeting on the traditional unceded territorial lands of the Squamish, Musqueam and Tseil-Waututh Nations. This acknowledgement is a critical beginning to any work that locates itself in a particular place. It reminds us that people have lived on this land, and have had a deep relationship with the land and all species on it, since time immemorial. We are here as the most recent arrivals and have much to learn.

After welcoming everyone, introducing ourselves, encouraging participants to introduce themselves to others sitting close by, and sharing our aims for the workshop, we expressed that our motive was to create a safe space where individuals were invited to share aspects of their lives, to allow themselves to be vulnerable. We asked that whatever personal thoughts were shared by fellow participants were treated with respect and remain in the space.

We also acknowledged the presence of the natural materials in the centre of the circle as we could feel a palpable desire on the parts of the participants to engage directly with them. We explained that we would be using these materials a little later in the workshop but first wanted to do a drawing exercise as a warm-up.

We passed around sheets of heavy drawing paper and set out sets of colourful felt markers and pens. We chose paper than was smaller than usual 8.5" x 11" to signal that what we were embarking on together was slightly out of the ordinary. The smaller paper size was also intended to be more intimate and less threatening than being faced with a large blank page. We started the workshop with a blind contour drawing exercise where participants drew one of their hands without looking at their paper.

Blind Contour Drawing

Engaging in blind contour drawing is a deeply embodied process. Kimon Nicolaides' very basic exercise for learning to draw is a powerful process of learning to see and to observe very closely (Nicolaides, 1941). This way of drawing emphasizes the process of seeing, rather than the product – the finished drawing itself. Thus, rather than get caught up in concerns about how their drawing is going to look, participants focus instead on what it is that they are drawing. Most of the process of drawing, after all, is about seeing well rather than about the marks that end up on paper.

Participants are reassured, first of all, that how their drawing looks at the end does not matter, that what we are after is sincere observation: a focus on the thing we are looking at. It is helpful, before beginning, to do a few centering, grounding breaths so that we feel the presence of the body and its connection to the earth; this also helps bring about the relaxation and stillness of mind that is helpful to the process.

The instructions for the blind contour drawing go something like this. We will be drawing by looking only at the object you are drawing, not at the paper. Position yourself so you can look at your object comfortably for a sustained time; it may be helpful to sit so the object you are holding is within your field of vision, but your paper is not. In other words, your two hands are quite far apart from each other. Notice the contours on your object: these are the outlines, as well as the lines that are on the inside of your object; for example, the veins in a leaf or the spikes on a fir cone. Begin by focussing on a particular part of your object where you want to begin your contour drawing. Then, position your pen on the paper where you will begin your drawing. Return your eyes to your object, and keep them there.

Now comes the important part: in your mind's eye, picture that the place where you are looking on your object (the part of the contour you are focusing on) and the tip of your pen are one and the same; that the tip of your pen is exactly where your eye is – on your object. Wait until you are convinced in your imagination that the position of your pen and the location where your eyes are focussing are one and the same. This may take a few breaths. Wait until you are ready. Then, begin moving your pen and your gaze together – they move in complete synchronicity; they are one and the same. Your gaze and your pen move very, very slowly, together. When you come to a place where your line ends, and you need to lift and reposition your pen, do so without looking at your paper. Keep going, very slowly, until you have traced your whole object. If, at any moment, you lose the focus of your eye and pen working together, stop and refocus before continuing. It takes some patience; go slowly.

This process is very meditative and grounding. It is important that everyone is silent during this work so that vision – seeing – can work uninterrupted by any activity from the verbal sides of the mind and brain. The drawing may take about 5–8 minutes or so, depending on how long the group can focus. They will need to be reminded once or twice to resist the temptation to look at the paper and to allow themselves the time to refocus if they need to. It also helps to ensure they keep a solid line going, rather than a feathery type of line with stops and starts. When drawings are done, and everyone looks at their paper, it helps to remind them that it is okay to find it funny or wonky, that is part of the beauty of it. Certainly, it is fine to laugh at themselves. It is helpful to give a moment for everyone to share and debrief their experience ("How did this feel for you?"), in small groups of two or three.

It is usually evident when the observation, the looking, has been focused and sincere. The proportions of the drawing may be completely off, but there will be something genuine and beautiful in the contours; something of the character of the thing that is drawn will show through.

In this workshop, we started with a blind contour drawing of one of our hands, then invited participants to come to the centre of the room to choose an object from our tablecloth of natural materials that resonated with them. Because we had so many participants from other places in Canada and around the world, we also took time to introduce a variety of the more unique species, naming them and sharing collective knowledge about their biological qualities and place in the local ecosystem.

Once everyone had chosen an object, we invited them to do a second contour drawing, this time of their object, on a fresh piece of paper. This second time, participants relaxed more easily into the drawing, even though some of the forms were much more complex than a hand – lichen with tiny, curly fronds; pieces of cedar bark with moss hanging off the edges; a large piece of sandstone with holes bored through it by saltwater waves.

These myriad details force an even closer observation of the object. Since the purpose of the blind contour drawing is to concentrate and observe every detail as you draw, a more complex shape becomes both more challenging and more interesting. Conversely, a more conventional approach to drawing, where one is looking at both the object and paper as one draws, can be more difficult as one is engaged in a constant comparison between what is seen and how it is represented. People who are less confident in their drawing skills can easily become frustrated if their work in progress doesn't match their idea of what a realistic drawing should look like. Blind contour drawing, where the page and the marks made are not looked at during drawing, short circuits this inner critic, allowing the artist to focus on observation. One doesn't look at the finished piece until the drawing is complete. At this point, participants are invited to step back and appreciate the whole, relating to the drawing as an expression of self in a process of discovery. What do you see? How do you see it? What feelings does the drawing bring up? What connection do you feel with the object you drew? How does it relate to your life?

Symbols and Stories

The calming and embodying experience of the blind contour drawing provides a good lead-in to the kind of intuitive thought that is helpful for the next activity, which is about symbols and the storied meanings that come from personal interpretations of these symbols.

As a reflection on the object they had chosen and drawn, we invited participants to turn over their paper and write for a few minutes in response to the question, "What does this say to you – about your own life or life in general?" The ideas that came out of their writing were shared with a partner. This sharing provided an opportunity to begin an expansion outward: how we forge meanings that are deeply personal, yet often relatable to others, all in connection with another life form or element of nature.

After this sharing, we handed out small pieces of paper, listing the four groups of symbols:

Figure 18.2. Connecting objects, drawings and symbolic meanings

- Nourishment
- Transformation/Transition
- Birth/Return/Regeneration
- Communication/Voice

In small groups of two or three, participants discussed how these themes connected to the objects or meanings that each group member had drawn and written about on their own. For instance, participants shared that a drawing of a leaf brings up thoughts of regeneration, of reconnecting with one's core values as part of a process of changing careers. The spiral pattern of the moon snail shell brings up ideas of transition, transformation, representing progress from tiny to infinite, while also depicting that life goes in cycles. Looking at the spiral from the other direction, it becomes a symbol of return and rebirth. A piece of branch covered in moss is a reminder of the rainforest and a feeling of deep connection. It also reminds us of a sense of nourishment: for the moss, an environment that provides minerals and moisture, for humans, one that offers softness and comfort. Barnacles on a rock become a symbol for coming together with the community. A small branch of western cedar can be understood as a symbol of nourishment, reminding us that cedar can be made into a sacred tea. Likewise, salmon bones are symbols of nourishment (physical self, as well as ecosystem health) and return, as the salmon return to their birth streams at the end of their lives to spawn. They are also a symbol of regeneration. A crab shell becomes a symbol for transformation; as the crab grows too large for its current home, it sheds and grows a new shell. This process is a reminder of the need to shed old ways of being to transform into a new self, such as happens at different stages of formal education. For one participant, the crab offered a further symbol of nourishment, bringing up memories of eating Dungeness crab with family on a boat as a child.

The participants generated many personal symbolic connections in their small groups: the room buzzed with conversation. After 5 or 10 minutes discussing their objects and the associations and memories they inspired, we divided the entire group into four groups of 6 or so participants each. Each group was given one large paper to work with, either on the floor or the wall. Each piece of blank paper was approximately 3' x 5', giving enough space for all group members to sit around it, or stand in front of it comfortably.

We instructed each participant to place their drawing on the large paper, spaced at a distance from each of the other individual drawings. We then asked them to write a few words next to their drawing about what their chosen object symbolized to them, either reflecting on the themes that we had earlier discussed, or something different. We made sure each group had a variety of coloured felt markers and pens to encourage creativity.

Figure 18.3. Starting the mind-mapping

Connecting Individual Storied Symbols to the Whole

After a few minutes of writing, we asked everyone to shift one place to the left in their group, look at the new drawing in front of them and read what the first participant had written, and then add their own thoughts and connections to it, using a line or arrow or another connecting device. We then kept shifting until each person in the group had an opportunity to add to each person's reflection. Connecting words included: *synthesis, growth, resilience, fragility, seasons, cycles, taking flight, higher consciousness, strength, freedom, interconnectedness, structure, organization, intelligence, beauty, mysteries, time, witnessing, symmetry, opening, interweaving, shape-shifting, endurance, layers, stories, wonder, sunlight, hope, ephemeral, delicate, direction, wonder, shield, home, vulnerable, self-preservation, complexity, community.*

Figure 18.4. Adding stories and connections to the map

There was a thoughtful silence about the room now: everyone immersed in their own interpretations of how all these things connect and linking them to the ideas of others. Soon, the papers were filling up. We invited the groups to take a step back to reflect on the results of their work so far, discussing what emerged for each of them in relation to other's ideas connected to their own drawings, and what they noticed when adding to others. We then invited them to add further lines and colours to show any other connections between the objects and symbolic meanings that became apparent when the papers were viewed as a whole. We gave participants 20 to 30 minutes for this portion of the session, allowing for deeper and more engaged discussion. By this time, the room was buzzing with conversation again, and it was clear by the body language of the participants that they were deeply engaged. The maps became more complex as each group found its own visual language for communicating the ideas members were processing.

Some of the themes that arose in discussion shared with the group as a whole now included: it is not possible for things to always be good, we need to have the dark

DRAWING MEANING FROM NATURE

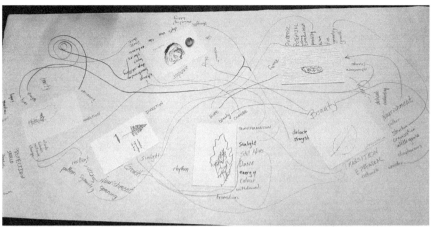

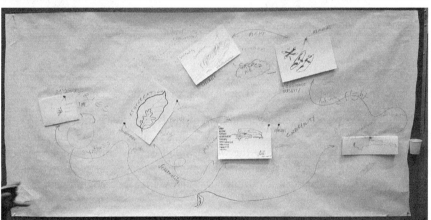

Figure 18.5. Completed group maps

with the light for things go in cycles; no matter how individual we may feel, we are actually all connected; and, it is easy to forget how much we have in common with the natural world.

Before closing the session, we encouraged everyone to walk around and look more closely at the maps of other groups. A reporter from each group stayed with their own map and offered explanations of their group's process, pointing out what was most notable. Back together in a circle as a whole group for the closing of our workshop, we invited each person to share one word about how they were feeling and to offer thoughts about how they might use this kind of work in their own practice. Words shared included *inspired, grounded, grateful, relaxed* and *playful*. After our session closed, conversations continued about the applications of this type of process in the respective educational contexts of the various participants.

Figure 18.6. Reflecting on the map

EXPANDING TO OTHER CONTEXTS: APPLICATIONS

Having physical materials to touch and hold grounds an activity such as this one in the embodied natural world. With the other components of the workshop tending more toward the abstract, centring the work around tactile forms, with their visual qualities, weight, textures, and smells add much-needed balance. It also adds a particular quality otherwise absent from our digital, virtual and cognitively-oriented everyday lives.

The practice of close observation through a creative activity such as drawing connects us on a visceral and intuitive level to the natural world. Yet drawing need not be the only option. Depending on the context, some other modes of expression are possible. If a group can go outside, for example, photography can work well if the photographers are encouraged to look very closely, to see things that would ordinarily escape their notice if they just looked at a place in passing. Zuzana has worked with elementary students who responded to trees and rocks through creative movement. Poetry and narrative writing – again, with a requirement to look closely and observe sincerely – also lend themselves well to coming to personally know, and connect with, elements in the natural world.

It is also possible to think about expanding this activity into a longer workshop. If one had a full or half day and access to the outdoors, the workshop could begin with a nature exploration designed to open the senses. For instance, the workshop leader could invite participants to look for the smallest organism they can see with the naked eye, something sprouting, something that spends time airborne, something that never leaves the ground, something that changes colour, something cold or

DRAWING MEANING FROM NATURE

Figure 18.7. Sharing maps, stories and symbols

warm, something that feels furry or soft, something hard or rough, something that smells delicious, something edible. After sharing their discoveries, the leader could then provide the group with parameters for collecting natural materials to use in the drawings, such as only taking materials that have fallen on the ground, that aren't alive or providing a home for other living species, or, if harvesting from a living tree or plant, only taking a small sample of whatever you are interested in and leaving

301

the rest for nature and others to enjoy. An alternative is to do the drawing exercise directly in nature, so nothing need be disturbed or removed.

After the mind-mapping exercise is complete, the workshop could lead to further individual writing exploring the symbols and personal connection to nature, or into more art-making, such as printmaking using the materials gathered.

In a classroom setting, this activity holds the possibility of expanding into deeper learning about a wide variety of subject areas, from ecology (learning about plants and other life forms and how they work together in the ecosystem, invasive and native species), to biology (biological properties, understanding life cycles and reproduction, using microscopes to learn about cell structures), geography (distribution of plants and animals, understanding climate, mapping, urban planning), and social studies (how have these plants and other natural materials been used by local people over time).

CONCLUSION

Several main ideas are being put forth through this work. One is that culture and meaning are not unique to the human realm. Tim Lilburn (2002) insists that "the culture of humans is not man-made; it is just the human part of the culture of the whole" (p. 161). Like Lilburn, Robert Bringhurst (2008), another British Columbia philosopher-poet, observes that human language and meaning-making is inextricably linked with the land and life-sphere where a human culture develops. A particularly helpful paradigm shift, or at least an invitation to such a paradigm shift, is that as humans, we do not own culture and meaning; the life symbols we examined in this workshop are shared by all of life on the planet.

A second idea concerns itself with how we, for our human part, create culture: for the culture we practice, and in which we participate, has inevitable effects on the natural world. If we see ourselves as disconnected from other-than-human life, these effects are bound to be enormously different from those that are brought about if we see ourselves as part of nature itself, and connected to it in inextricable and life-giving ways.

Taking both of these notions a step further, if wilderness areas and natural spaces are valued as places of refuge, not to escape from ordinary life but to return us to it by offering quiet and healthy, helpful perspective, we begin to see that our own education, well-being and sense of groundedness benefit significantly from time in connection with nature.

Through participation in arts-based activities, such as those described in this chapter, these ideas are introduced in ways that are inviting and accessible to people of a wide range of ages, skills and life experiences. The processes of observation and reflection then become a conduit for deepening participants' sense of connection with the natural world and understanding our human place in it.

REFERENCES

Blood, N., & Chambers, C. (2009). *Event publicity for lecture and film presented at Simon Fraser University.*
Bringhurst, R. (2008). *The tree of meaning: Language, mind and ecology.* Berkeley, CA: Counterpoint.
Dissanayake, E. (1992). *Homo aestheticus: Where art comes from and why.* Seattle, WA: University of Washington Press.
Grimm, E., & Lilburn, T. (2002). *Imaging the sacred: The fruitful alliance between gospel and art* (Vol. 24). Regina, SK: Campion College, University of Regina.
Lilburn, T. (2002) Going home. In T. Lilburn (Ed.), *Thinking and singing: Poetry and the practice of philosophy.* Toronto: Cormorant Books.
London, P. (2003). *Drawing closer to nature: Making art in dialogue with the natural world.* Boston, MA: Shambala Publications.
Louv, R. (2005). *Last child in the woods: Saving our children from nature-deficit disorder.* Chapel Hill, NC: Algonquin Books.
Nicolaides, K. (1941). *The natural way to draw: A working plan for art study.* Boston, MA: Houghton Mifflin Company.
Roszak, T. (2010). Towards an eco-psychology. In *Thinking allowed* [DVD]. Retrieved from http://www.thinkingallowed.com/2troszak.html
Van Boeckel, J. (2009). Arts-based environmental education and the ecological crisis: Between opening the senses and coping with psychic numbing. In B. Drillsma-Milgrom & L. Kirstina (Eds.), *Metamorphoses in children's literature and culture.* Turku: Enostone.
Van Boeckel, J. (2011). When we find meaning in art, our thinking is most in sync with nature: A review of an ecology of mind. *naturearteducation.org.* Retrieved from http://naturearteducation.org/Articles/An%20Ecology%20of%20Mind_Review%20by%20Jan%20van%20Boeckel.pdf
Vasko, Z. (2015). Connections between artistic practice and experiences in nature: Considerations for how art education can engender ecological awareness. *Canadian Review of Art Education, 42*(2), 69–79.
Wilson, E. O. (1984). *Biophilia.* Cambridge, MA: Harvard University Press.

Zuzana Vasko
Faculty of Education
Simon Fraser University
Canada

Robi Smith
Artist-in-Residence
City of Maple Ridge
Canada

BRIAN OLEWE WASWALA, OTIENO NICKSON OTIENO
AND JARED BUOGA

19. YOUTH ENGAGEMENT FOR ENVIRONMENTAL EDUCATION AND SUSTAINABLE LIFESTYLES

INTRODUCTION

Increased environmental degradation in Kenya, Africa, the global south and the world over, has resulted in intensified incidents of food insecurity (FAO, 2009); water quality loss and scarcity; natural resource depletion and conflicts (FAOSTAT, 2009; FAO, 2010); emergence of infectious diseases and spread; increased pollution (Clinton Foundation, 2010); and unsustainable livelihoods, among other anthropogenic challenges including industrialization (UN Habitat, 2009). Natural environmental assets continue to be exploited for economic gain; affecting their ability to provide critical ecological, social, cultural, and economic functions, also known as 'planetary boundaries' (UN, 2012). These negative trends push the planet towards a tipping point that would make the planet less habitable (Frantzeskaki & de Haan 2009; Rockström et al., 2009; UNEP, 2012a, 2012b, 2012c; Pradhan & Waswala, 2014), but also hampers the achievement of the national and global agenda including the Kenya's Vision 2030 (Government of the Republic of Kenya, 2007); the African Union Vision 2063 (African Union Commission, 2013); and a wide range of the Sustainable Development Goals.

Most of these socio-economic and ecological ills are a result of people lacking an appreciation for the environment, as it is viewed as public property open to exploitation, a phenomenon referred to as the *tragedy of the commons* (Ostrom, 2008). This negative mindset is accompanied by poor enforcement; coupled with an economic and ecological disconnect for our decision making and a limited consideration of environmental issues. This economic and ecological disconnect is primarily because environmental sustainability is yet to be mainstreamed into a number of academic disciplines/courses in learning institutions.

Higher Education Institutions (HEIs) have a vital role to play in influencing future societies in a sustainable future by producing new knowledge; development of skills and competencies; and elevating sustainability consciousness. Despite humanity sharing common learning environments and planet, most academic courses taught in HEIs are taught independently, as opposed to interrelated by "systems thinking". This is essential because each dimension of development can either have a positive or negative impact on other dimensions. It is therefore important that interdisciplinary cross-cutting environmental education is promoted in HEIs, as this is a conduit to preserving and improving the world's environment, as envisaged in world's inaugural Intergovernmental Conference on Environmental Education (UNESCO, 1978) and many subsequent conferences. The Tbilisi meeting culminated with a need to promote environmental education at all levels and all age groups both inside and outside the formal school system. This is critical in addressing the emerging environmental challenges that the world grapples with. It is also of great urgency for youth, academia, and future leaders, in collaboration with governments and private entities, to develop and embrace interdisciplinary curriculum, capacity and practical hands-on solutions in environmental ethics and sustainability for our future prosperity as proposed by Karri Holley (2017). This kind of curriculum offers students a platform to work with knowledge drawn from multiple disciplines and to solve cross-cutting problems. It also stimulates intergenerational learning and transformative leadership.

WORLD STUDENT COMMUNITY FOR SUSTAINABLE DEVELOPMENT

The World Student Community for Sustainable Development (WSCSD), a youth-led caucus in Kenya, is using this interdisciplinary model of learning to pro-actively engage youth in environmental education. By instilling essential environmental education and life-long skill development among our young, change agents, WSCSD is catalysing environmental sustainability within universities and at the community level. It is also increasing its capacity development for communities in promoting environmental resilience; while promoting community advocacy in environmental conservation through indigenous knowledge. The organisation also influences youth voices on interdisciplinary institutional and national policy design, development, and implementation.

WSCSD Environmental Education Initiatives

1. Adopt-an-Ecosystem Initiative

This initiative aims at using hands-on environmental education and skill development to conserve and restore degraded water and forest ecosystems, within universities and communities. Students identified a gap in both the Kenyan Constitution and the Vision 2030 Economic Development Blueprint to actively contribute to ecosystem management. Both documents require that Kenya work toward achieving a forest cover of at least 10% of its land area to ensure sustainable resource use, growth, and job creation. In so doing, WSCSD has worked to rehabilitate degraded river and forest ecosystems and increase tree cover in universities and open spaces. It has also promoted citizen science in river quality monitoring, assisting the government to enforce ecosystem health and compliance as further described in the following section.

a. Adopt-a-Forest Initiative

Students engage their universities in planting trees on under-utilised or barren on-campus land resources. As public institutions, Kenyan HEIs are also obligated to plant trees on-site. Our students have also overseen the establishment and maintenance of tree nurseries through affiliate student associations. These tree nurseries supply seedlings/saplings for periodic tree planting exercises on campus and in the adopted forests. Using innovative approaches, students also task universities' top management to take on this initiative as a means of offsetting their travel related carbon emissions. Excess seedlings are also offset into the market during rainy seasons, allowing the initiative to be self-reliant while also offering training in life-long skills and an alternative income. Improved biodiversity on the campus also provides for living labs for experiential learning.

The initiative has so far been adopted by seventeen universities and inspired the formation of four student associations and active projects in six universities.

b. *Adopt-a-River Initiative*

Kenya's State of the Environment and Outlook Report (2010) indicates that wetlands are the most undervalued ecosystems in Kenya, a result of their direct conversion into built-up areas. These fragile ecosystems face irreversible damage ranging from loss of aquatic biodiversity, alterations in ecosystems' productivity, and an inability to discharge ecosystem services.

In response to this, the WSCSD in partnership with the National Environment Management Authority and various stakeholders partnered to implement the 'Adopt-a-River Initiative'. This is a 'people-driven' wetlands monitoring and restoration project that entails "adoption" of a nearby river by secondary school/university student groups, community youth groups, and other interested institutions. The groups are trained and expected to monitor the health of their respective adopted rivers over time using the Mini Stream Assessment Scoring System (Water Research Commission, 2018), a simple, user-friendly community river health bio-monitoring tool. The group then identifies possible sources of pollution and takes local action towards restoration and conservation of the river.

The 'Adopt-a-River Initiative' exemplifies how key curricula components can be used to solve real world sustainability challenges. It is also a perfect model of how the public (especially youth) can be mobilized to manage rivers and other wetlands around them. Through identification of polluted river ecosystems within the Nairobi River Basin, the project is expected to result in enhanced enforcement of environmental and other related regulations to ensure our healthy wetlands.

The Training of Trainers exhibits another excellent case of intergenerational and multidisciplinary learning with most of the young facilitators from WSCSD training university Professors who are then to further train other students of river health monitoring and restoration. The project also promotes Citizen Science and the use of ICT in conservation of natural resources through application of an online community river health and bio-monitoring tool.

c. *Kenya UNEP-DHI Eco Challenge.*

WSCSD is also the local partner responsible for implementing the UNEP DHI Eco-Challenge in Kenya. This challenge is a fun and innovative way of engaging high school students and teachers with sustainable water management issues. This is with the aims of sharing knowledge, creating awareness and providing an avenue for students to offer suggestions on how to tackle existing water challenges. In the challenge, students compete in a game called Aqua Replica. Aqua Replica is a tool for raising awareness on integrated water resource management issues, and how these can be resolved. It is a virtual world that mimics the complexity of the real world, in terms of water environments and it is a tool for education and stakeholder participation.

2. *Nyakongo Water and Sanitation Project*
Located in a remote village in Nyando, Kenya, this project provides household Biosand Water Filters and awareness education on basic hygiene among an HIV/AIDS support groups adversely affected by perennial flooding. So far 124 households have been provided with water filters by the project. WSCSD hopes to eventually provide filters to over 800 households. The project was launched in 2009 in partnership with the spin-off SWALLOW Inc. It also led to the conceptualization of the Nyakongo Sustainable Village Initiative for cross-border and multi-disciplinary collaboration among campus students in co-creating a model sustainable village (WSCSD, 2018a).

3. *Nyakongo Sustainable Village Initiative*
The WSCSD's Sustainable Village Initiative embodies a holistic approach for household and community empowerment through student collaboration and campus outreach programs. The proposed 'Nyakongo Sustainable Village Program' aims at mobilizing university/college students, higher education stakeholders and impoverished communities to collaborate in transforming the poor rural community of Nyakongo, Kenya, into a model sustainable village through evidence-based and 'co-created' development. The master plan for the development of Nyakongo GREEN Center (WSCSD, 2018b) has been developed in discussion with partners and resource mobilization (WSCSD, 2018c) and a plot of land has been donated by the community for the development of this project.

Kenya Green University Network

The demand for higher education is high in Kenya and tertiary education institutions should therefore have an underlying role in promoting development and having an impact within their spheres of influence. However, due to the disjointed 'silo effect' of most curricula, students often do not gain the essential skills needed for sustainable development. This has largely contributed to the growing disconnect between economic growth, social development and environmental conservation.

Following an environmental course audit of 67 universities and tertiary academic institutions in Kenya, it was reported that close to 80% of all public universities offer an environment related course, with approximately 30% of public constituent university colleges and about 12% of the private-chartered universities offering such courses, all of which are taken at different levels (i.e. bachelor BSc, MSc and PhD levels). The study established that these university courses were not interdisciplinary, though they has at least one environmental component. This confirms a lack of environmental knowledge and appreciation at HEIs, despite the environment being the single most important cross-cutting resource providing us with regulatory, revisionary, aesthetic/cultural and supportive services.

Having noted this disconnect, the WSCSD and UN Environment in collaboration with various government agencies (Ministry of Environment and Natural Resources, the National Environment and Management Authority, and Commission of Education) created the Kenya Green University Network (KGUN). This is a growing network of higher education institutions that incorporate environment and sustainability aspects in their education, training, campus operations/management and student engagement. The network seeks to develop the capacity to assist public universities in their performance reporting requirements on environmental targets. The network also plays a significant role in the implementation of the African Environmental Education and Training Action Plan (2015–2024); and Mainstreaming Environment Sustainability in Africa. The network is guided by four pillars namely: Green Campus Development; Green Curricula; Student Engagement; and Community Engagement.

The World Student Community for Sustainable Development is responsible for coordinating the implementation of KGUN's student engagement activities. WSCSD's spin-off social enterprise, NIKO GREEN also offers advisory services to support university management in developing their Institution's Sustainability policies and strategies as well as the development of green campus buildings.

Pillar 1: Green Campus Development

Universities are a strong driver for societal change, not only through education and research, but also by the example they set in its own operations. As universities are often the largest infrastructure developers within many local communities, they can also act as hubs for learning and change towards sustainable construction in their communities. The KGUN is supporting HEIs in Kenya with the necessary tools to develop green campuses and become centres of excellence in environmental sustainability.

A "green campus" can be defined as an environmentally friendly campus. This form of campus ascribes to energy efficiency (production and use); wise use of water; offers safe, eco-friendly transport; conserves biodiversity; reduces and manages its waste, and is built using eco-friendly designs and material. As more tertiary education institutions develop, there is an urgent need that they promote sustainable practices that can later be replicated by students, faculty members, and communities.

Green Campus Case Studies in Kenya

a) *Use of solar energy*

Strathmore University has installed one of the largest rooftop photovoltaic (PV) solar power plants in the region producing over 600 kilowatts consisting of 2,400 solar panels and 30 inverters (Strathmore University, 2011). The system was installed through a public-private partnership and has a daily power production of 2.2 to 2.8-megawatt hours. The university also sells surplus energy to Kenya Power. It is estimated that this form of renewable energy generates enough power, equivalent to light 6,665–8,484 light bulbs per day; plant an equivalent of 90–120 trees monthly; save approximately 862–1097 kg of carbon dioxide daily; with resultant economic savings of 15,000–20,000 US dollars in electricity per month.

The Kenya Energy (Solar Water Heating) Regulations require all establishments with hot water needs of a capacity exceeding one hundred litres per day to install and use solar heating systems (ERC, 2012). It is envisaged that this would significantly reduce water heating costs. Through KGUN, students are also learning about these environmental education initiatives. Acting as agents of change, the students are advocating for their universities' compliance with these energy requirements. These ventures are in line with SDG 7: Access to affordable, reliable, sustainable and modern energy for all.

b) *Rain and surface water harvesting*
It is estimated that close to one billion people lack access to clean drinking water. Kenya Vision 2030 recognizes that Kenya is a water scarce country and emphasizes water conservation and prudent use of the limited available potable water. Access to clean water and sanitation services in Kenya ranges from 41–52 percent and 52–69 percent respectively (Marshall, 2011; Water.org, 2018). It is therefore imperative that citizens, communities, institutions, and governments, invest in good water management practices. This form of investment calls for improved institutional arrangements, payment for ecosystem services, ecosystem conservation. Investment in water infrastructure can accelerate the concept of the green economy and reduce water deficiencies and the time wasted in other unsustainable developments generally.

Oshwal University College has invested in a surface water harvesting system that can collect and store close to 20,000 litres of water in its underground catchment tanks. The water is "cleaned" by an existing wetland and later used to clean lavatories. This reduces not only costs also but overall water demand, in line with SDG 3 and 6. Over time, students have been able to share the merits of rainwater harvesting and advocate for the sustainable use of this scarce but essential resource.

c) *Sustainable Food Production and Use*
Food insecurity is an observable fact in Kenya, a trend contributed to by an over-dependence on subsistence cultivation, a disregard for orphan crops, and increased subdivision of land, climate change among others factors. Masinde Muliro University of Science and Technology, located in western Kenya, promotes mushroom farming as a form of sound environmental education. The Jaramogi Oginga Odinga University of Science and Technology is collaborating with the World Bank to promote the consumption of edible insects as an alternative source of protein in both animal and human diets (Ayieko, 2015; Nyakeri et al., 2015). These harvested mushrooms and

edible insects are now finding their way into diets, promoting alternative nutritious food sources and income to families in line with SDG 1 and SDG 8. Many universities are also sourcing locally available foods (reduction of 'food miles') thus promoting the incomes of local producers; emphasizing food quality over quantity; advocating for reduced food waste in their cafeterias; and collecting waste for composting or alternative livestock feeds. This contributes to SDG 2.

d) *Waste reduction*
Despite efforts to encourage reuse, recycling and recovery, the amount of solid waste generated remains high and appears to be on the increase (National Environment Policy, 2013). Currently, only 8% of recyclable waste and 5% of compostable waste is recovered. The Green Economy Strategy sets a long-term target of 50% waste recovery (17% recycling and 32% composting) by 2030 and a short-term target to achieve 30% waste recovery (15% recycling and 15% composting).

Vocational training institutions in Kenya are major sources of waste due to their multiple status of being training, commercial and domestic entities. For example, in 2010, the 42 technical training institutions in Kenya had a population of about 100,000 students and a staff of 1,602. It was found that 29 out of these institutions (73%) generated about 23 tons of waste per week in 2010, which represents a considerable amount of waste in their respective geographical contexts (Gakungu & Gitau, 2012).

Some of this waste finds its ways into landfills. The management of the waste is also dependent on infrastructure. Currently, many universities have installed marked waste bins in offices, classrooms kitchens, and common areas; promoting waste segregation before disposal, and promote holistic waste management as advocated by a circular economy. University students in collaboration with faculty are also conducting waste audits, especially for plastic waste and e-waste. These would then help guide policy development for the development of the environmental educational material such as the Africa Regional Waste Management Outlook (UNEP, n.d.) and the Africa Waste Management University Curriculum. Promotion of zero waste in the Kenyan HEIs contributes to the achievement of SDG 11 and 12.

e) *Land Management*
Learning institutions also ought to be aware of the cognitive, affective and psychomotor domains of learning, as these greatly impact on teachers' effectiveness and students' academic performance. Students should have enough space, adequate ventilation, be insulated from heat and noise, have sufficient lighting, and be free from pollution while they are learning. Universities can go a step further by promoting open spaces in the landscape, which complement the built environment of classrooms and labs. Through landscaping and tree plantings, universities can create breeze corridors that make the external environment more pleasant for community use, while also having the practical effect of sequestering carbon emissions generated by campus activities. These initiatives compliment Kenya Green Economy Strategy and Implementation Plan (2015, 2017); Kenya's vision of having a minimum 10% tree cover as per UN standards; SDG 12 and 13.

f) *Green Building Designs*

It is estimated that humans spend approximately 70% of our lives inside buildings. The construction of these units have a great impact on the environment, accounting for close to 40% of total energy use; resource consumption and waste generation. Campus buildings offer a great opportunity for improvements, especially when guided by sustainability, during the development of architectural plans and in building.

In Kenya, the Catholic University of Eastern Africa has a green building, also referred to the Learning Resource Centre that stands out (Construction Review Online, 2016). The Centre was designed to allow natural ambient lighting (thus reducing energy costs); is optimally oriented for the climate with the major window facades in the North and South facing walls (preventing excess glare to users); has high thermal mass walls and allows for natural ventilation; built using local material; is naturally cooled using a rock bed cooling system; allows for rainwater harvesting; and has oxidation ponds for sewage. The Learning Resource Centre won a National Green Building Award for its exemplary green features. Architectural students often visit the centre to learn and network with peers, on best practices, which in the future can be replicated in other buildings.

g) *Green Purchasing*

Universities have rigorous procurement procedures. It is increasingly vital that these integrate sustainable procurement standards into campus projects and policies, especially for long-term environmental 'gains' as opposed to short-term budget savings. "Green purchasing" should consider supply chain and disposal. KGUN is advocating for the development of a strategy on sustainable procurement within member institutions' purchasing departments; demystifying the notion that green products are more expensive than conventional alternatives; development of sustainable purchasing guidelines; installation of energy consuming products (cost savings and reduced CO_2 emissions; and procurement of products that have been awarded a environemental certification labels.

Pillar 2: Green Curriculum

Education for Sustainable Education (ESD) underscores a need for balance between human and economic well-being within cultural traditions, and a respect for the earth's natural resources. The role of academia, especially HEIs on contributing to this vision cannot be overlooked. It is believed that close to 20,000 global HEIs institutions graduate over 150 million students annually (UNESCO, 2014). These granduants end up contributing to decision-making in all sectors of the global economy, especially since sustainability is now recognized by governments and international agencies as an essential skill set.

In Africa, UN Environment in collaboration with various HEIs developed Mainstreaming Environment and Sustainability in African Universities (MESA), aimed at *promoting the integration of environment and sustainability concerns into teaching, research and community engagement and management of African universities, as well as to enhance student engagement and participation in sustainability activities both within and beyond universities* (UNEP, 2008). However, these objectives fall within each independent environmental faculty.

In a bid to reverse the environmental challenges in Kenya, WSCSD through the KGUN, challenged the Commission of University Education (a state institution that mandates and offers quality assurance in universities) to develop and implement of a compulsory environmental education course. The examinable course is to be taken by all students, and it is hoped that this would increase environmental literacy and give students the skills and ability to make thoughtful consumption choices. It is hoped that this proposal would meet the burgeoning discourse around 'students being partners' in higher education's transformation.

The course would be guided by the UNESCO Global Action Programme on ESD; the African Environment Education and Training Action Plan; and the UN Environmental Assembly Resolution 2/3 "Investing in human capacity for sustainable development through environmental education and training" (UNEP, 2016); and the UN SDG 4.7 "ensure all learners acquire the knowledge and skills needed to promote sustainable development".

It is worthy to note that in order to achieve the objectives of this green curriculum, priority actions on policy support; whole-institution approaches to education and training; enhancing capacities of educators and trainers to effectively deliver ESD; empowering and mobilizing youth, and accelerating sustainable solutions at the local level all will need to be developed.

Pillar 3: Student Engagement

There is now a shared consensus on the role of students in the university's transformation agenda, yet student engagement in Africa remains largely uncoordinated. Similarly it has not been recognized, measured, reported or rewarded accordingly. Students are not empowered to influence the institutional decisions that will lead to the transformation of the academy.

It has been noted that practical applications of knowledge gained in the classroom remains an issue for student engagement. Students have raised concerns that academic curriculum and education do not promote critical thinking, problem-solving and innovation. Students yearn for real-life work experiences and a practical application of their knowledge , soft skills and values as this would greatly improve their employability and impact on society.

Most HEIs in Kenya also lack student governance policies on how to engage students, a testament of the uncoordinated and thus *ad hoc* nature of this governance – devoid of measurable impacts. The World Student Community on Sustainable Development sought to bridge this gap through policy design and implementation.

The organization applies a 'head-heart-hands' and 'whole-institution' approach to inform, inspire and empower students with values, skills and conditions to enable them to influence the practices of the higher education academy. It advocates for the prioritization of student engagement in policies, strategies, plans and management structures at Kenyan Universities as well as in the coordination of students' sustainability initiatives.

WSCSD is facilitating peer mentoring and training on sustainability principles and practices by conducting sustainability literacy tests and training during its first year student orientation programs, mainstreaming environmental sustainability into student unions and student professional clubs, as well as providing structured and coordinated 'green internships'. These initiatives have had a great impact in stimulating green thinking, advocacy and the adoption of sustainable production and consumption practices on campus as well as in motivating and empowering the youth with skills to create new green jobs. All these contribute to the different tenets of the SDGs.

Due to the success of the Kenya Green University Network, this model has now received global recognition. It has been replicated in Morocco, with other global south nations following suit. The model complements the eco-school models, which have been widely promoted at the primary and secondary school levels.

TEMBEA YOUTH CENTRE FOR SUSTAINABLE DEVELOPMENT

The Tembea Youth Centre for Sustainable Development (Tembea) is a grass root civil society organization based in Ugunja, Siaya County, Kenya. The organization was founded in 2003 and legally exists as a Community Based Organization (CBO). Under its current strategic plan 2017–2022, Tembea envisions *"A Sustainable Community"*, with a mission of "enhanced sustainable development at grass root level through awareness creation, capacity building, advocacy on socio-economic rights, environmental conservation and climate change". This is realized through three program areas namely *Climate Change Education and Innovation*, *Environment and Natural Resource Management* and *Economic and Social Rights* in order to address the most pressing problems facing our target audience.

Climate Change Education and Innovation

Through this program, Tembea enhances the capacity of communities living in Siaya County to develop innovative approaches for mitigating the effects of climate change and to enhance their awareness of climate-smart farming practices. In doing so, it contributes to the long-term outcome of reduced community dependence on non-renewable energy and industrial products.

Tembea has promoted the use of clean energy through the construction of over 45,000 energy efficient cookstoves in households in rural communities in Siaya County. This energy efficient cook stove is a biomass rocket stove designed for burning wood and consists of two cooking units that can be fired separately. The stove is fixed and installed in households and brings multiple benefits to the users. It reduces firewood consumption by approximately 40–50%, thus reduces the burden of firewood collection on women and children and reducing the household fuel budget. Moreover, through cleaner and efficient combustion, harmful smoke emissions are reduced and the quality of indoor air is considerably improved. A reduction in firewood consumption also helps conserve forest vegetation and reduces the carbon emissions responsible for climate change. Further, we have promoted the use of solar energy among local communities and distributed more than 1,500 solar lamps in Siaya County. The organization has also provided over 4,300 pupils with solar light lamps to enable children to study in their homes after school.

Further, Tembea has played a critical role in advancing a low carbon development policy at the County Government levels. The organization has made deliberate efforts as a think tank working with the County legislative assembly in strengthening capacity in climate responsive budgeting, policy, and legislation.

Environment and Natural Resources Management

This program amplifies Tembea's work in environmental conservation as well as its contributions to SDG 11 (sustainable cities and communities). Our goal is to ensure proper management of solid waste, the sustainable use of natural resources and proper land use planning in Siaya County. It contributes to a long-term outcome of having proper systems for land use, solid waste and natural resource management in the County. So far, our environmental conservation efforts have realized the mobilization of local community members to plant over 500,000 trees and establish over 200 tree nurseries across the County. As a strategy for promoting environmental stewardship among local communities, over 100 environmental clubs have been established in schools and villages. Tembea also conduct education and awareness workshops on environmental conservation for youth, women, charcoal burners, quarry, sand harvesters and village elders living around wetlands, tributaries, streams. Our natural resource management efforts have sought to address devastating environmental degradation resulting from human activities along the Nzoia river and other natural resources in Ugenya sub-county and neighboring areas.

REFERENCES

African Union Commission. (2013, June 10). *Agenda 2063: The Africa we want*. Retrieved from https://au.int/en/agenda2063

Atieno, P. (2014, June 19). *The learning resource centre in Catholic University of Eastern Africa*. Retrieved from http://constructionreviewonline.com/2014/06/cuea-library-building-wins-award-best-green-building-kenya/

Ayieko, M. (2015, June 24). *Rearing and processing crickets (Achita domestica) at household level for food security*. Retrieved from http://62.24.102.115:8080/xmlui/handle/123456789/165

Energy Regulatory Commission. (2018, July 30). *Renewable energy and energy efficiency regulations (Public Notice)*. Retrieved from http://www.renewableenergy.go.ke/index.php/news/3

Gakungu, N. K., & Gitau, A. N. (2012). Solid waste management in Kenya: A case study of public technical training institutions. *ICASTOR Journal of Engineering, 5*(3), 127–138.

Government of Republic of Kenya. (2007). *Kenya vision 2030*. Retrieved from http://vision2030.go.ke/about-vision-2030/

Holley, K. (2017). Interdisciplinary curriculum and learning in higher education. *Oxford Research Encyclopedia of Education*. doi:10.1093/acrefore/9780190264093.013.138

Jaramogi Oginga Odinga University for Science and Technology. (2018). *Africa center of excellence in sustainable use of insects as food and feeds (INSEFOODS)*. Retrieved from http://jooust.ac.ke/index.php/insefoods

Kenya State of the Environment Outlook Report. (2010). Retrieved from https://europa.eu/capacity4dev/file/12612/download?token=CfK2v642

Marshall, S. (2011). The water crisis in Kenya: Causes, effects and solutions. *Global Majority E-Journal, 2*, 31–45. Retrieved from https://studylib.net/doc/13016650/the-water-crisis-in-kenya--causes--effects-and-solutions-

National Environment Policy, (2013). Retrieved from, http://www.environment.go.ke/wp-content/uploads/2014/01/NATIONAL-ENVIRONMENT-POLICY-20131.pdf

Nyakeri, E. M., Ogola, H., Ayieko, M. A., & Amimo, F. A. (2015, June 24). *Black soldier fly larvae (Hermetia illucens) organic waste bioremediation potential*. Retrieved from http://62.24.102.115:8080/xmlui/handle/123456789/162

Ostrom, E. (2008). *Tragedy of the commons*. Palgrave Macmillan. Retrieved from http://hdl.handle.net/10535/5887

Pradhan, M., & Waswala, B. M. (2014). *The global universities partnership on environment and sustainability: Promoting intergenerational learning*. Wageningen Academic Publishers. Retrieved from https://doi.org/10.3920/978-90-8686-802-5_26

Strathmore University. (2014, July 11). *Strathmore University 600 KW Roof Top PV solar power plant*. http://sbs.strathmore.edu/blog/2014/07/11/strathmore-university-600-kw-roof-top-pv-solar-power-plant/

UN. (2002, September 4). *Report on the world summit on sustainable development*. Retrieved from www.un-documents.net/aconf199-20.pdf

UNEP. (2008). *Mainstreaming environment sustainability in Africa*. Retrieved from http://www.unenvironment.org/fr/node/10690

UNEP. (2016a). *UNEA resolution 2/3*. Retrieved from http://web.unep.org/about/cpr/resolutions-adopted-un-environment-assembly-its-second-session

UNEP. (2016b). *African environmental education and training action plan 2015–2024*. Retrieved from http://web.unep.org/ourplanet/march-2017/unep-publications/africa-environmental-education-and-training-action-plan-2015-2024

UNEP. (2016). *Kenya green university network*. Retrieved from https://www.unenvironment.org/news-and-stories/story/kenya-green-universities-network-launched-promote-sustainability-practices

UNEP. (2017, July 28). *Africa regional waste management outlook*. Retrieved from http://web.unep.org/ietc/africa-regional-waste-management-outlook-consultations

UNEP. (2012a). *21 issues for the 21st Century*. Retrieved from http://www.unep.org/pdf/Foresight_Report-21_Issues_for_the_21st_Century.pdf

UNEP. (2012b). *Global environment outlook (GEO-5)*. Retrieved from http://www.unep.org/geo/geo5.asp

UNEP. (2012c). *UNEP year book 2014: Emerging issues in our global environment*. Retrieved from www.unep.org/yearbook/2012/

UNESCO. (1978). *Final report: Intergovernmental conference on environmental education*. Retrieved from www.unesdoc.unesco.org/images/0003/000327/032763eo.pdf

UNESCO. (1978). *Intergovernmental conference on environmental education*. Retrieved from http://unesdoc.unesco.org/images/0003/000327/032763eo.pdf

UNESCO. (1992). *Agenda 21 – Chapter 36: Promoting education, public awareness and training.* Retrieved from www.un-documents.net/a21-36.htm

UNESCO. (2014). *Shaping the future we want; UN decade of education for sustainable development.* Retrieved from www.unesdoc.unesco.org/images/0023/002301/230171e.pdf

Water.org. (2018). Retrieved from https://water.org/our-impact/kenya/

Water Research Commission. (2018). *Mini stream assessment scoring system.* Retrieved from http://www.minisass.org/en/

World Student Community for Sustainable Development. (2018a). *Nyakongo Biosand Filters.* Retrieved from http://nyakongo2030.wscsd.org/nyakongo-biosand-filters/

World Student Community for Sustainable Development. (2018b). *Nyakongo GREEN Center.* Retrieved from http://nyakongo2030.wscsd.org/initiatives/nyakongo-green-center/

World Student Community for Sustainable Development. (2018c). *Nyakongo Sustainable Village Initiative.* Retrieved from http://nyakongo2030.wscsd.org/

Brian Olewe Waswala
Regional Centre for Expertise Greater Nairobi and
World Student Community for Sustainable Development – Kenya
Kenya

Otieno Nickson Otieno
World Student Community for Sustainable Development – Kenya
Kenya

Jared Buoga
Tembea Youth Centre for Sustainable Development
Kenya

KIEU LAN PHUONG NGUYEN, HO-WEN CHEN, KHANH LY LE AND XUAN HOAN NGUYEN

20. CASE STUDIES FOR MAINTAINING AND ENHANCING URBAN GREENERY

INTRODUCTION

In this chapter, environmental education (referred as EE) was carried out for university students through a project-based learning (PBL) approach. The projects involved green space management in urban areas in two different metropolises, one located in Vietnam and the other is in Taiwan. Exploring the value of urban green spaces has been increasingly gradually for decades. According to Project Evergreen, green spaces in urban areas play a crucial role in helping regulate air quality and climate, reducing energy consumption, recharging groundwater supplies, increasing aesthetic pleasure and other contributions. Lee, Jordan, and Horsley (2015) explored the value of urban green spaces for health and well-being claiming that urban green spaces provide great environmental benefits in negating urban heat, offsetting greenhouse gas emissions, attenuating stormwater, providing urban residents spaces for physical activity and social interaction, and allowing for psychological restoration to take place. Unfortunately, such green spaces have been shrinking due to a greater demand for space in an increasingly urbanized and industrial era (i.e. more housing, schools, hospitals, better infrastructure). Moreover, Threlfall et al. (2017) that urban green spaces are the most suitable habitat for protecting urban biodiversity, which is also decreasing due to this urbanization. Therefore, a general aim for EE in this study is to create an opportunity for students to be more aware of the challenges to urban green space management and to achieve some skills in service to that problem. One group of students in the Vietnamese case study was requested to propose plans to enhance greenery in a campus area, whereas a group of students at a Taiwanese university was instructed to establish an ecological corridor aimed at the reduction of habitat fragmentation.

This chapter will first briefly review EE literature, especially EE at the university level, and the teaching methods of PBL which was applied in the studies. Next, two individual cases will be presented as case studies of EE activities in urban green spaces management. Finally, the authors close by discussing student's achievement related to the objectives of these EE projects.

BACKGROUND

Environmental Education

Turning to history, the concept of EE was aimed at "producing a citizenry that is knowledgeable concerning the biophysical environment and its associated problems, aware of how to help solve these problems, and motivated to work toward their solution". In the world's first Intergovernmental Conference on Environmental Education held in Tbilisi in 1977, the Tbilisi Declaration defined EE is "a learning process that increases people's knowledge and awareness about the environment and associated challenges, develops the necessary skills and expertise to address the challenges, and fosters attitudes, motivations, and commitments to make informed decisions and take responsible action" (Stapp, 1969). The goals of EE were: (1) to foster clear awareness of, and concern about, economic, social, political, and ecological interdependence in urban and rural areas; (2) to provide every person with opportunities to acquire the knowledge, values, attitudes, commitment, and skills needed to protect and improve the environment; (3) to create new patterns of behavior of individuals, groups, and society as a whole towards the environment. The objectives of EE were to focus on social groups and individuals' (1) *awareness* – to acquire an awareness and sensitivity to the total environment and its allied problems; (2) *knowledge* – to gain a variety of experience in, and acquire a basic understanding of, the environment and its associated problems; (3) *attitudes* – to acquire a set of values and feelings of concern for the environment and the motivation for actively participating in environmental improvement and protection; (4) *skills* – to acquire the skills for identifying and solving environmental problems; (5) *participation* – to have an opportunity to be actively involved at all levels in working toward resolution of environmental problems (UNESCO & UNEP, 1977).

In Vietnam, EE has received attention since the late 1990s which is expressed through the promulgation of legal documents. Typically, this process has been the initial resolution for environmental protection which was regulated in Directive no. 36-CT/TW of the Politburo dated June 25, 1998, on strengthening environmental protection in the period of industrialization and modernization of the country, and then followed by Resolution no. 41-NQ/TW of the Politburo dated November 15, 2004, on environmental protection during periods of promotion of industrializsation and modernization of the country. Afterwards, environmental protection contents have been mainstreamed in an education program approved by Decision no. 1363/2001/QD-TTg of the Prime Minister dated October 17, 2001.

As a result, education for environmental has been conducted through formal and non-formal programs at all levels, kindergarten, high school, vocational school, colleges, and universities. Yet, there is no general EE program which has been unified in the education and training systems in schools. Such programs focused on awareness but did not consider local conditions and circumstances. Hence, in the next phase, it is necessary to have solutions that transfer EE programs from awareness into action for environmental protection.

In Taiwan, the first Environmental Education Act draft was developed in 1993 referencing the U.S. Environmental Education Act of 1990. The Act was approved in 2010 and went into effect one year later. Chang (2016) described the key functions of the Act as follows: (1) Establishment of a National Environmental Education Framework and Environmental Education Action Plan; (2) Budget allocation for environmental education funds; (3) Assignment and certification of personnel to conduct EE through one of six approaches, including education, experiences, expertise, recommendation, examination, and training; (4) EE consultation and EE Facility & Place certification to improve the quality of Non-Formal EE; (5) Certification of Environmental Education Institutes to provide training; and (6) Implementation and monitoring of no less than four hours of EE. Since 2001, EE has been integrated into nationwide school system from grade 1 through grade 9 and will also be implemented in the national curriculum framework, extending through to grade 12 in 2018. Even though the framework has described several goals and EE themes, teaching pedagogy and implementation should also be considered thoroughly as well as school-based approaches. The framework's five EE themes include environmental ethics, sustainable development, climate change, disaster preparedness, and sustainable use of resources and energy (Chang, 2018).

In this chapter, the authors describe EE activities for undergraduate students at the university level. Emmelin (1975) attempted the classification of EE programs by selecting representative examples of various universities throughout Europe. This could be categorized into ten types:

- Integration into all subjects: EE could be integrated into multidisciplines such as engineering, planning, and the education of economists
- Overview courses: cross-sector overview courses conducted in several types and different content and size at most universities.
- Education of specialists: For instance, interdisciplinary seminars and courses at the doctoral level.
- Complementing other education: The purpose of these programs is to broaden the student's understanding of environmental problems.
- Recurrent education: In many British programs, some courses are run as Diploma courses.
- Environmental health sciences: As in other environmental areas, there is a need for teamwork and participation of specialists to strengthen this aspect of EE.
- Environmental conservation and management: Programs in this category exist of variable length at different levels of education.
- Combinations of categories: For instance, in environmental health, planning and management programs, they have recognized both long-term needs for natural resource management and planning and short-term needs for immediate action against pollution which must be consistent with the long-term planning and management principles.

- Training for the educational system: In some British schools EE exists as a new branch of teaching. Several teacher training colleges have set up programs both for the education of new teachers and the retraining of old.
- Education of decision makers: For example, the Pro Deo training course on environmental policy (Italy) is aimed directly at decision makers.

Project-Based Learning

The EE approach taken in this research is project-based learning (PBL) which is defined as an instructional model that is based in the constructivist approach to learning, which entails the construction of knowledge with multiple perspectives, within a social activity, and allows for self-awareness of learning and knowing while being context dependent (Duffy & Cunningham, 1996). Similarly, Krajcik and Blumenfeld (2006) stated PBL is one type of situated learning based on the constructivist finding that students gain a deeper understanding of material when they actively construct they're understandings by working with and using ideas. In PBL, students engage in real, meaningful problems that are important to them (Duffy & Cunningham, 1996), and in rich and authentic learning experiences (State of New South Wales (Department of Education), 2018).

According to Thomas (2000)'s report, projects are comprehensive tasks, based upon given questions or problems, that students are requested to design, problem-solving, decision marking, or investigative activities; are given the opportunity to work relatively autonomously during the project period until realistic products or presentations are completed (Jones, Rasmussen, & Moffitt, 1997; Thomas, Mergendoller, & Michaelson, 1999). To assess the 'real project' among diversity features, Thomas suggested five criteria regarding centrality, driving questions, constructive investigations, autonomy, and realism. This means that PBL projects should be central to the curriculum; be concentrated on question or problems that 'drive' students to encounter the essential concepts and principles of a discipline; involve students in a constructive investigation; are student-driven outcomes that are not predetermined; and are realistic with students about their responsibility in the task, the context that the project is carried out, and collaborators who work with students in real-world social interaction (Thomas, 2000). Kokotsaki, Menzies, and Wiggins (2016) demonstrated the effectiveness of PBL in pre-school and primary school, secondary school and higher education in their research.

With respect to the design of learning environments in the PBL approach, Krajcik and Blumenfeld (2006) suggested five principal features of the learning environment as follows: (1) They start with a driving question, a problem to be solved; (2) Students explore the driving question by participating in authentic, situated inquiry. As students explore the driving question, they learn and apply important ideas in the discipline; (3) Students, teachers, and community members engage in collaborative activities to find solutions to the driving question; (4) students are scaffolded with learning technologies that help them participate in activities normally beyond their ability;

and (5) Students create a set of tangible products that address the driving question (Blumenfeld et al., 1991; Krajcik, Blumenfeld, Marx, & Soloway, 1994; Krajcik, Czerniak, Czerniak, & Berger, 2002). Krajcik and Blumenfeld also proposed criteria to be good driving questions. Such criteria are feasible in that students can design and perform investigations independently to answer the questions; worthwhile in that they consist of any scientific content that adjusts to regulations at different scales; contextualized in that they are real-life and crucial; meaningful in that they are appealing to students; ethical in that they do not injure any human being, organisms or the environment.

In the next section, the authors present two distinct case studies associated with the problems leading to the driving question, expected learning outcomes, and the research methodology which was taught by teachers for the student-lead research.

CASE STUDY 1

Challenges for Urban Green Space Management in Vietnam

The policies of urban greenery in our historical development have had impacts on urban green space management both Hanoi and Ho Chi Minh City which are the largest cities in Vietnam. Hanoi is the oldest capital city among Southeast Asian countries since 1010. During its long history, Hanoi City has experienced many different cultures including Chinese, French, Soviet and other contemporary influences. In each period, greening growth was conducted with different objectives such as in the French Colonial Period (1873–1954) which opened and built new roads, and grew shade trees along the roadsides, while in the Post-Independence Period (1955–1985) and early years of the Renovation (1986–1990s), the idea of 'a hundred flowers blooming' resulted in the planting of decorating trees as quickly as possible with medium sizes which were suitable for smaller sidewalks, but without selecting appropriate trees for its long-term urban development plans. This greening policy lead to challenges in the current state of urban greenery. For instance, in 2015, People's Committee of Hanoi proposed a project replacing 6700 decades-old iconic trees simultaneously without examining the trees that were in a healthy condition. This project sparked a public outcry leading to a protest involving hundreds of Hanoi citizens. Consequently, the chairman of the city People's Committee postponed the project until this could be reviewed. The investor then planned to replace these chopped-down trees with a the tree species *Manglietia Phuthoensis dandyi Dandy*. Some Vietnamese scientists, however, identified that another kind of tree, named *Manglietia Phuthoensis Dandy*, was used instead. Since the soil condition is not appropriate for the growth and development of these replaced trees, the trees could then easily die. These issues demonstrate the poor management of local authorities in managing urban trees in particular, and urban green space in general.

The impact of urban sprawl on green space also occurs in Ho Chi Minh City (HCMC) the commercial hub of Vietnam. According to Tran (2012), the city is a young one, just over 300 years-old, derived from servicing rice agriculture. Since the French colonization of HCMC (1863–1865), opinions on growing trees to cope with a harsh tropical heat were considered. The idea of a master plan for urban development was brought to Vietnam by the French, leading to the development of urban trees. Additionally, the French started to organize sidewalks, broaden the roads and grow more trees. In 1886, many streets were reconstructed and almost all of them were covered with small trees including tamarind trees and mango trees. Planting and watering works were also assigned to the villages by the government. However, not for a long time, there were some unexpected results such as a thin canopy and fallen fruits and leaves. Hence, the city government decided to renovate the streets in the early 1900s.

Ton Duc Thang Street is one of the oldest one in HCMC, with the length of 2361 meters and the width of 25 to 34 meters. Having learned from its failures, the French planted more appropriate trees such as nacre trees along this street before 1873 with a high aesthetic as well as logically allocated algon the length of the street. According to Ho Chi Minh City Greenery Parks Company, these trees are the *Khaya senegalensis* species, belonging to the *Meliaceae* family. This species is a medium-sized, hardwood tree with an extensive root system with origins from Africa. The seeds will germinate and grow rapidly, while the heartwood is light red with a brown-red pigment and is made of coarse interlocking grains. The grains are easy to split and crack which might defect the standing of the tree.

Recently Ho Chi Minh City Department of Transport, starting in October 2017, chopped down and uprooted the trees on Ton Duc Thang Street to prepare for the construction of the Thu Thiem bridge, connecting District 2 to District 1, where is the heart of the city. Out of 258 trees, 115 trees were uprooted and removed, while 143 were chopped down. Despite understanding the purpose of this action, many citizens still regret losing those century-old trees as they were considered as part of the municipal history.

As has been described, the challenges for urban green space management in Vietnam are not just from urban development planning in the past but also from the poor management capacity of some individuals and/or organizations. In this case, the general aim was to increase awareness of the role of green space in a specific landscape on campus where we may be able to extend the greenery. The driving questions were "What are the potential areas to enhance greenery on campus?" and "Which kind of trees are suitable for planting in these areas?"

Expected Learning Outcomes

- Students will be able to compose a questionnaire to do a sociological survey on respondents' opinion on status and demand for green space at the school;
- Students will be able to communicate effectively with collaborators who will work with students on the project;
- Students will be able to recognize the role of green space on campus;

- Students will be able to list potential areas which could be enhanced by greenery;
- Students will be able to analyze and select the appropriate trees to be planted on campus.

Methodology

Study area. The study was carried out on campus 8 of Nguyen Tat Thanh University (referred to as NTTU) which is located in District 12 of Ho Chi Minh City, Vietnam. It fronts just off the National Route 1A linking Ho Chi Minh City with other provinces in the south-eastern region. Moreover, the range of business activities is very wide within 200m of NTTU including mechanical manufacturing and transportation companies, traditional markets, motorcycle repair shops and others activities. Therefore, the environmental quality of the workplace and the learning of the lecturers, staff, and students have undoubtedly been affected.

This campus was put into use in 2015 serves a population of approximately 12,000 employees and students. The total land area is about 8,657 square meters, of which the land area for construction is about 3,673 square meters with two main function buildings:

- L1 building: with an area of 2,096 m², a height of 45 m, and total floor area of 26,092 m² comprising offices, lecture halls, classrooms, cafeteria, basement parking. The architectural design of this building highlights the possible benefit of natural ventilation systems with "I" shape providing natural wind for classrooms and workrooms.
- Building complex: with an area of 1,431 m² comprising library and gymnasium.

The remaining area is mainly for internal traffic on campus and an area of 4,982 square meters of the courtyard for community activities. However, it seems that there is little green space at the university leading to the only shade in internal spaces being provided by high-rise buildings inside and outside of the campus.

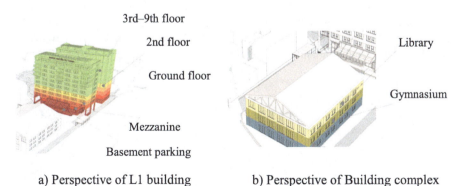

Figure 20.1. Campus 8 of Nguyen Tat Thanh University

Research methods. In the spirit of PBL, the students were taught research methods before conducting their project independently. The students who took part in this course, namely "Environmental conservation", were from faculties of Environmental Science at Nguyen Tat Thanh University and Landscape Architecture at Vietnam National Forestry University. The students all had a fundamental knowledge of the process of scientific research, of plants, conditions affecting the growth and development of plants, environmental impacts on plants, related software, and other factors.

Regarding the sociological survey, the study was designed as a cross-disciplinary investigation, in which 100 questionnaires were delivered randomly to staff, lecturers, and students. A group of students proposed the main contents in the questionnaire including respondents' opinion on the current greenery status, their opinions on each of the green spaces detailed, and the demand and solutions for enhancing green spaces on campus. After doing the survey, the students discussed with their instructors how to analyze the responses.

Next, an observational survey of the current greenery status was conducted, the students were trained in mapping methods in order to mark the location and information of current trees on the campus map. Student groups were also instructed to use tree measurements to determine tree height, canopy diameter, and stem diameter. For instance, in term of shrubs and grass, long rulers were used in determining the area and location. The students then used a camera to record the green space status and to provide data in modeling and post-survey data analysis. In addition, in identifying species in the study area, some could be easily identified, whereas some species required taking a sample or photo to discuss with teachers and experts later.

After analyzing the data, students and teachers held a workshop on solutions for enhancing green space on the campus within a small area. Other students who were interested in the research were welcomed to participate and share their own ideas.

At the end of this study, there was much software used such as Word, Excel, SPSS software for data processing and analysis; AutoCAD, ArcGIS, Photoshop, 3D Max software for developing maps, drawing landscape elements; especially AutoCAD, Photoshop, Sketchup and Lumion software for landscape planning used by students who have background in landscape architecture.

Figure 20.2. Students' activities during the project period

Research Results

- Status of greenery at NTTU

According to field measurements, total greenery on campus occupies just 1.79% compared to the total land area (8,657 m^2). Those are five flower basins situated in front of the L1 building, on the way to the basement parking, and along the entrance as shown in Figure 20.2. The vegetation on the campus is mainly herbaceous and low shrubs, but no shade trees have been planted.

Figure 20.3. Status of greenery

- Sociological survey results

Although 100 questionnaires were distributed to lecturers, staff, and students of NTTU, 94% of the responses were obtained. The proportion of respondents categorized by participants were 88.3%, 9.6%, and 2.1% of students, lectures, and staff respectively. Their perceptions about the campus' landscape was that it was not really appealing. Indeed, responses showed that over half of their perceptions claimed campus' landscape as being "Ordinary", nearly 30%] "Ugly" answers, and the remaining percentages for "Beautiful" and "Very beautiful" as a rating of NTTU's landscape. In addition, the result of the question "Has greenery at NTTU been used at full capacity as recreation, study yet?" Analysis of the questionnaire indicates that over 50% of answers stated "Have not", nearly 14% of answers stated "A part of capacity", and exactly one-third of answers stated "Yes". Regarding "Comment on greenery area at NTTU campus" question, a majority of answers were "Small" and "Very small" accounting for 46.7%, and 28.7% respectively, whereas "Large" and "Moderate" accounted for only 2.1% and 22.5% respectively. The latter question has concerned the question "Have classrooms, offices, library, cafeteria, restrooms of the campus been decorated by plants?" because just under two thirds of response revealed "Have not", over approximately a quarter of response revealed "Have a little", and mere 8.7% of response revealed "Have". Based on field trip observations, indoor greenery has only been flower pots for office decoration which has carried out spontaneously. As far as plant species were concerned, answering for the issue

Table 20.1. Status of greenery species

AA basin

Species	Amount	Image of trees			
Syzygium oleinum	11 trees				
Normanbya normanbyi	11 trees				
Barringtonia asiatica	1 trees	Syzygium oleinum	Normanbya normanbyi	Barringtonia asiatica	Zoysia tenuifolia
Zoysia tenuifolia	52 m^2				

CC basin (doubled)

Species	Amount	Image of trees			
Aglaia duperreana	2 trees				
Acanthus integrifolius	10.8 m^2				
Justicia gendarussa	6.5 m^2	Aglaia duperreana	Acanthus integrifolius	Justicia gendarussa	Pseuderanthemum carruthersii
Pseuderanthemum carruthersii	10.7 m^2				

BB basin (doubled)

Species	Amount	Image of trees			
Wrightia religiosa	2 trees				
Ixora coccinea	1.2 m^2				
Cyathula prostrata	9.7 m2				
Codiaeum variegatum	1.3 m^2	Wrightia religiosa	Ixora coccinea	Cyathula prostrata	Codiaeum variegatum
Acanthus integrifolius	12.4 m^2				
Cordia latifolia	22.1 m2				
Leucophyllum frutescens	3.8 m^2	Acanthus integrifolius	Cordia latifolia	Leucophyllum frutescens	Justicia gendarussa
Justicia gendarussa	13.8 m^2				

"Plant species on campus are rich and diverse", over one in three of response was "Little", nearly a half of response was "Ordinary", and about 15% of responses were "Diverse" and "Very diverse". Regarding the question about what kind of tree should be planted in the campus, 58.7% of the answers suggested shade trees and 25.8% for decorating trees, whereas 2.5% of respondents suggested planting a tree with falling leaves. However, this seems not suitable for a tropical climate in Ho Chi Minh City. Similarly, some answers indicated that the university has shade trees and a roof garden while the field trip observation proved such thoughts were untrue. The writers are of the opinion that green space issue has not received much attention from students or they are not able to recognize exactly different types of trees.

- Greenery enhancement proposals at NTTU

The outcome of the workshop held was a comprehensive solution to enhance green spaces on the campus of NTTU. In this discussion, students proposed the types of modern green spaces suitable for the small space of the school including: (1) National Highway 1A; (2) campus; (3) basement parking; (4) roof garden on L1 building; (5) indoor greenery; and (6) standing garden (Vertical garden). Furthermore, the proposed species selection for the solutions was based on theoretical lectures and several criteria such as locality, aesthetics, environmental improvement and fitness for each space function. The cost factor was also taken into account when selecting species to ensure the feasibility of the study.

1. *National Highway 1A:*
    + Regional characteristics: Located on a road that is always exposed to noise and dust caused by traffic vehicles regularly.
    + Solutions: Growing trees that have the ability to prevent dust and noise, creating shade and improving the landscape of the study area and especially avoiding noise pollution for the university. Growing large trees with a straight body, beautiful to enhance the majesty and stability for the road was recommended.
    + Characteristics selection:
        - Shade, evergreen, thick, wide
        - Aesthetics
        - Roots elongate in the soil, small trees.
        - Having good growth rate
        - Having high tolerance to the harsh environment, less pest and easy to care
        - No odor, no toxic substances
        - Priority to leafy species (good dust retention)
    + Species recommendation:

2. *University campus*
    + Regional characteristics: served as a place for recreation and mutual activities for students.
    + Solutions: Growing highly aesthetic trees for shading and high lighting the campus.
    + Characteristics selection:
        - Large and flowered trees characterized by seasons, combining with other flowers or lower trees to create highlights
        - Comfortable fragrant
        - Less pest and easy to care
    + Species recommendation:

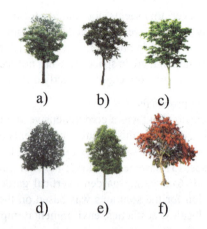

*Figure 20.4. Species recommendation planted nearby National Highway 1A.
a) Tectona grandis; b) Chukrasia tabularis; c) Pterocarpus macrocarpus;
d) Hopea odorata; e) Dipterocarpus alatus; f) Delonix regia*

*Figure 20.5. Species recommendation planted on campus.
a) Cassia fistula; b) Terminalia mantel; c) Lagerstroemia indica; d) Lagerstroemia peciosa;
e) Mimusops elengi; f) Syzygium oleinum; g) Zoysia japonoca; h) Typha orientalis*

3. *Basement parking*
   + Regional characteristics: A bustling place during school-finish hours; the average temperature is always higher than the surrounding area due to the heat generated by the vehicles, so is the emission level.
   + Solutions: Growing strong species that can create shade for the parking lot, paying attention to plants able to absorb air pollutant and improve the atmosphere.

+ Characteristics selection:
  - Highly aesthetic
  - Large-shade and evergreen
  - Having good growth rate
  - Fewer insects and easy to care
  - Capable of filtering and absorbing waste
  - Species recommendation:

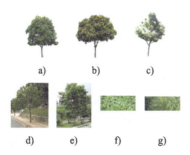

Figure 20.6. Species recommendation planted on campus.
a) Dracontomelon duperreanum; b) Peltophorum pterocarpum;
c) Lysidice rhodostegia; d) Cinnamomum camphora; e) Michelia champaca;
f) Axonopus compressus; g) Chrysopogon zizanioides

4. *Roof garden on the L1 building*
   + Regional characteristics: The roof of the building L1 with the height of 54m, with direct contact and higher influence by environmental factors, especially the sun and wind.
   + Solutions: creating an ecological system on the roof by designing and building gardens.
   + Characteristics selection:
     - Shrubs, no large timber trees
     - Wind resistant (small leaf area)
     - Highly aesthetic
     - Easy to adapt to the surrounding environment
     - Roots that are not too deep in the soil
   + Some reference models:

Figure 20.7. Some reference models for roof garden on the L1 building

5. *Indoor greenery*
   + Regional characteristics: in the library, lobby, meeting rooms, classrooms, offices, and restrooms.
   + Solutions: adding trees indoor to relieve stress, improve the air and create the best environment for studying and working.
   + Characteristics selection:
     • Highly aesthetic
     • Shade-tolerant, easy to care
     • Less pest, no spine or toxic latex
     • Capable of absorbing air pollutant
   + Some indoor greenery ideas:

Figure 20.8. Some indoor greenery ideas

   + Species recommendation:

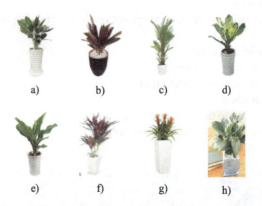

Figure 20.9. Species recommendation planted on campus.
a) Aglaonema Pseudobracteatum; b) Pride of sumatra; c) Cyrtostachys renda;
d) Dieffenbachia; e) Aglaoocma; f) Cordyline terminalis;
g) Tillandsia imperalis; h) Aglaonema modestum Schott

6. Standing Garden

Because the area of the campus is not large so the solution is to design trees in the vertical to maximize the green area. Standing garden is one of the solutions contributing to reducing the temperature caused by solar radiation makes the indoor working environment cooler and pleasant.

+ Regional characteristics: Green spaces at L1 building and Building complex are too few, hence increasing trees at these areas is recommended.
+ Solutions: The use of herbaceous plants combine green walls at the buildings
+ Characteristics selection:
  - Prefer herbaceous plants and groundcover plants
  - Highly aesthetic
  - Easy to adapt to the surrounding environment
  - Cluster roots that able to keep the soil
  - Capable of absorbing air pollutants
+ Some standing garden ideas:

Figure 20.10. Some standing garden ideas

+ Species recommendation:

Figure 20.11. Species recommendation for standing garden.
a) Nephrolepis cordifolia; b) Coleus blumei Benth; c) Tradescantia pallida;
d) Angelica dahurica; e) Petunia hybrida; f) Spathiphyllum;
g) Aglaonema muntifolium; h) Aglaonema hybrid

In summary, the area of green space for NTTU is a very modest number of 155.21 m^2, accounting for 1.79% of the total area. While according to the Vietnam Building Code (QCXDVN 01: 2008/BXD), green space must reach at least 40% of the school's area, so the green area must reach 3,462.6 m^2 (3,307.39 m^2 lacking). By proposing a plan to increase green space, it is clear that green areas are increasing: from 1.79% to 41.52% reached 3,594.3 m^2 (exceeding the minimum standard by 1.52%) not including the area of standing gardens and indoor greenery improvement.

a) Before enhancing b) After enhancing

Figure 20.12. Before and after enhancing greenery on campus

CASE STUDY 2

Challenges for Urban Green Space Management in Taiwan

In a different context is Taichung City, Taiwan's second most populous metropolis located in central-western Taiwan. The population of Taichung City in 2017 was about 2.79 million living in 2215 km^2. Taichung's economy has developed enormously for decades to become a major manufacturing hub for small and medium-sized enterprises: one of the largest service-industry markets in Taiwan. Recently, the development of high-tech industries has increased rapidly. Even though green spaces are given much attention in urban development planning, only a small land area has been allocated for a variety of functions, such as schools, airports, industrial parks, and science parks. This excessive use can cause a habitat fragmentation process which is also decreasing biodiversity in this area. Hence, the general aim of this case study was training the students in methods to establish an ecological corridor aimed at the reduction of habitat fragmentation by using ArcGIS software combined with an Analytic Hierarchy Process (AHP) method. The driving questions were "How do you establish an ecological corridor within urban green spaces?"

Expected Learning Outcome

- Students will be able to gather relevant data from government resources.
- Students will be able to compose a questionnaire to do a survey on experts' opinion on the importance of the data;

- Students will be able to communicate effectively with the collaborators who will work with students on the project;
- Students will be able to calculate the weighting of factors by the AHP method;
- Students will be able to recognize the impact of habitat fragmentation on urban biodiversity;
- Students will be able to establish an ecological corridor through the use of ArcGIS software.

Methodology

Study area. The study was conducted on the Dadu Plateau located on the west of Taichung City. This area acts as a main gate to the heart of the city with express highways on both sides, railway lines of about 85 km and an arterial road to suburban area. As an expected plan, by the end of 2018, the first line of Taichung Metro will also be ready. Moreover, there are a variety of functional constructions on the Dadu Plateau such as Taichung International Airport to the north, the Taichung thermal power plant to the west (the second largest coal-fired worldwide). In order to promote economic development, the government has set up the Taichung Industrial Park, Central Science Park, and the Taichung Metropolitan Park. In 2013, Sea-Air Development Project and Multifunctional Shopping Center tender were also opened. The aim is for a further expansion of Taichung Airport, Sea-Air development, and other external transportation links. Additionally, with the approval of the Executive Yuan for a free economic demonstration zone, Taichung Economic Development Bureau organized a working plan and reviewed a project entitled "Overall development of the surrounding area in Taichung Airport" and proposed planning a Multi-functional Shopping Center with an area of 5 hectares (Taichung City Government, 2013). It is obvious that the level of development within city limits has been significant. As a result, human activities in this area include buildings, roads, farming and irrigation., As a result, growth and surface vegetation height and plant coverage have been affected. Also, the shape and structure of the low-altitude pristine forests on the southwest side of the city are of great importance for land security and ecological preservation. Since the Dadu Plateau covers different patterns and surface features considered a microcosm of the ecology in Taichung City, this study selected this as a study area.

Research methods. As stated previously, students participating in this study were trained in the research methods needed to establish an ecological corridor. The students who took the "Sustainable urban development" course had a background in Environmental Science at Tunghai University. They, therefore, had been taught the fundamental knowledge of the processes of scientific research, biodiversity conservation, ArcGIS software and other related knowledge.

First, the students were asked to collect essential data from government reports on the environmental and biological aspects of the study area. In environmental aspects, there were three factors, namely landscape diversity, carbon fluxes and slope, while the biological aspects, there was land ecology (rodents), plants and birds. After this activity, the students were trained to design a questionnaire and further how to calculate the weight of different factors (by AHP method).

Next, the learners were introduced to a procedure on how to establish an ecological corridor; that is an analysis of the difference between the Normalized Difference Vegetation Index (NDVI) values of two seasons in order to observe the area with less seasonal variation of vegetation in the study area. The selected area will then be gridded into 500 m x 500 m dimensional squares to ensure selection of the "excellent" rank square.

Finally, the ecological corridor was established by integrating all the "excellent" squares with the weightings of the different environmental and biological factors estimated in the preceding section. Despite the procedure being taught to students, there were several issues that the students must think about it such as how to the analysis of the difference of NDVI values in two seasons, and further, how to classify the rank of gridded squares.

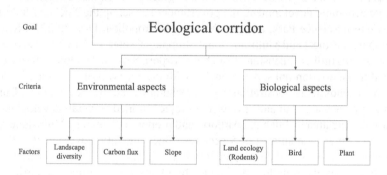

Figure 20.13. Habitat condition analysis

Research Results

- NDVI analysis results

In the analysis of habitat conditions, the vegetation coverage in spring and winter was analyzed by the NDVI index function for ERDAS images. The students proposed a method to differentiate two seasons that: Through NDVI analysis, surface vegetation coverage could be divided into three categories: non-vegetation, sparse vegetation, and dense vegetation. After a two-season vegetation coverage analysis was completed, the two sets of results were overlaid to find the area with the most stable vegetation coverage (see Figure 20.15a). In other words, the area where the vegetation did not decrease significantly with seasonal variation showed the greater degree of change, whereas the lighter color indicates a smaller degree of change. The next step was to select an area with the greater change in order to form a grid network. The dimension of each grid was 350 m x 350 m which is displayed in Figure 20.15b.

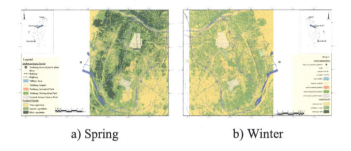

a) Spring b) Winter

Figure 20.14. NDVI analysis results in the study area in spring and winter seasons

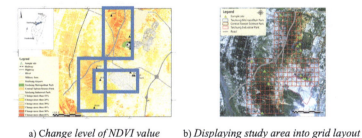

a) *Change level of NDVI value* b) *Displaying study area into grid layout*

Figure 20.15. Study area selected by change level of NDVI value displayed as a grid layout

- Survey results

The questionnaire respondents consisted of ten experts who were from industry (one), public sector (three), and research areas across the economic, environmental and ecological, social and other areas. The response rate was 92.9%. After answers were collected, the students calculated the weight of each factor and each aspect by the AHP method.

As a result, in the first-level assessment structure, the weight of environmental factors was 0.386, the weight of biological abundance surface factors was 0.614, and the analysis weight ratio showed that experts believed the biological abundance factors were more important than the environmental factors.

The second level was subdivided by the aspects of environment and biological abundance. Among all the environmental factors, the most important was the difference in the landscape (0.362), followed by the carbon flux (0.345) and the slope (0.293) respectively. Among the biological abundance factors, the most important was the terrestrial ecosystem (0.390), followed by the plants (0.323) and birds (0.286).

Table 20.2. Weights of aspects and factors were calculated by questionnaires

Level 1		Level 2		
Evaluation aspects	Relative weight	Factors	Relative weight	Overall weight
Environmental aspects	0.386	Landscape diversity	0.362	0.140
		Carbon flux	0.345	0.133
		Slope	0.293	0.113
Biological aspects	0.614	Land ecology	0.390	0.239
		Bird	0.286	0.176
		Plant	0.323	0.198

- Establishing ecological corridor results

After discussing their results with the teachers, the students classified different levels of landscape diversity, carbon flux, slope, land ecology, bird, and plant were into four categories; that is excellent, good, average, and poor. The "excellent" level of habitat condition results was highly recommended for designing an ecological corridor to maintain green spaces in urban areas.

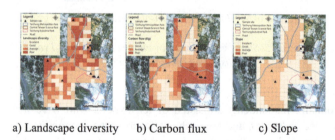

a) Landscape diversity   b) Carbon flux   c) Slope

Figure 20.16. Classification of environmental aspects results

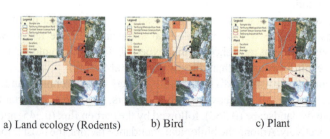

a) Land ecology (Rodents)   b) Bird   c) Plant

Figure 20.17. Classification of biological aspects results

All "excellent" grids in six factors associated with measured overall weights above were integrated into a comprehensive map that indicated the ecological corridor.

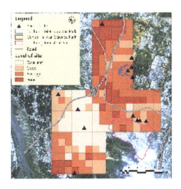

Figure 20.18. Ecological corridor establishment

To summarize, the students established through their PBL activities a complete ecological corridor including Tunghai University area and the Taichung Metropolitan Park area.

CONCLUSION

This chapter described two case studies as typical solutions for maintaining and enhancing urban green spaces in the Taichung City of Taiwan and in a university in HCMC of Vietnam, respectively. The teaching methods used for students at the university level in both studies was a PBL approach which is a product-aimed form of learning where students gain a deeper understanding through the resolution of specific driving question(s).

In the first case study in Vietnam, the students were made aware of the challenge in century-old trees replacement for current urban development planning and gained a knowledge of the characteristics of some trees which are highly recommended to be planted in specific landscapes such as a campus, highway, parking, roof garden, indoor, and standing garden.

In Taiwan, other students gained skills in the use of AHP and ArcGIS software in order to establish an ecological corridor to help prevent the habit fragmentation phenomena occurring in many fast growing urban areas.

ACKNOWLEDGEMENTS

The authors gratefully acknowledgement the support of Tunghai University, and funding from NTTU Foundation for Science and Technology Development of Nguyen Tat Thanh University. We also thank colleagues and students in Nguyen

Tat Thanh University, Tunghai University and the Vietnam National University of Forestry for their participation and contributions to this study.

REFERENCES

Blumenfeld, P. C., Soloway, E., Marx, R. W., Krajcik, J. S., Guzdial, M., & Palincsar, A. (1991). Motivating project-based learning: Sustaining the doing, supporting the learning. *Educational psychologist, 26*(3–4), 369–398.
Chang, T.-C. (2016). *Implementing the Taiwan Environmental Education Act (TEEA)*. Retrieved from https://cdn.naaee.org/sites/default/files/case-study/file/case_study_eea_1.pdf
Chang, T.-C. (2018). *Infusing environmental education into national curriculum framework in Taiwan.*
Duffy, T., & Cunningham, D. (1996). Constructivism: Implications for the design and delivery of instruction. *Handbook of research for educational communications and technology, 51,* 170–198.
Emmelin, L. (1975). *Environmental education at university level.*
Jones, B. F., Rasmussen, C. M., & Moffitt, M. C. (1997). *Real-life problem solving: A collaborative approach to interdisciplinary learning*. Washington, DC: American Psychological Association.
Kokotsaki, D., Menzies, V., & Wiggins, A. (2016). Project-based learning: A review of the literature. *Improving schools, 19*(3), 267–277.
Krajcik, J. S., & Blumenfeld, P. C. (2006). *Project-based learning.*
Krajcik, J. S., Blumenfeld, P. C., Marx, R. W., & Soloway, E. (1994). A collaborative model for helping middle grade science teachers learn project-based instruction. *The Elementary School Journal, 94*(5), 483–497.
Krajcik, J. S., Czerniak, C. M., Czerniak, C. L., & Berger, C. F. (2002). *Teaching science in elementary and middle school classrooms: A project-based approach* (2nd ed.). New York, NY: McGraw-Hill.
Lee, A. C. K., Jordan, H. C., & Horsley, J. (2015). Value of urban green spaces in promoting healthy living and wellbeing: Prospects for planning. *Risk Management and Healthcare Policy, 8,* 131.
Project Evergreen. (2018). *Environmental benefits of green space*. Retrieved from http://projectevergreen.org/resources/environmental-benefits-of-green-space/
Stapp, W. B. (1969). The concept of environmental education. *Environmental Education, 1*(1), 30–31.
State of New South Wales (Department of Education). (2018). *Introducing project-based learning.* Retrieved from https://education.nsw.gov.au/teaching-and-learning/curriculum/learning-for-the-future/future-focused-learning-and-teaching/project-based-learning-resource-guide/introducing-project-based-learning
Taichung City Government. (2013). *Sea-air development project and multifunctional shopping center tender*. Retrieved from http://eng.taichung.gov.tw/fp.aspx?fpage=cp&xItem=14415&ctNode=4715&mp=19
Thomas, J. W. (2000). *A review of research on project-based learning*. San Rafael, CA: The Autodesk Foundation.
Thomas, J. W., Mergendoller, J. R., & Michaelson, A. (1999). *Project based learning: A handbook for middle and high school teachers*. Novato, CA: The Buck Institute for Education.
Threlfall, C. G., Mata, L., Mackie, J. A., Hahs, A. K., Stork, N. E., Williams, N. S., & Livesley, S. J. (2017). Increasing biodiversity in urban green spaces through simple vegetation interventions. *Journal of Applied Ecology, 54*(6), 1874–1883.
Tran, H. Q. (2012). *The early urban infrastructure of Saigon*. Ho Chi Minh City: The Ho Chi Minh City General Publishing House.
UNESCO, & UNEP. (1977). *Final Report*. Paper presented at the Intergovernmental Conference on Environmental Education, Tbilisi.

Kieu Lan Phuong Nguyen
Food, Chemical & Environmental Sciences
Nguyen Tat Thanh University, Vietnam

CASE STUDIES FOR MAINTAINING AND ENHANCING URBAN GREENERY

Ho-Wen Chen
Department of Environmental Science and Engineering
Tunghai University, Vietnam

Khanh Ly Le
College of Landscape Architecture and Interior Design
Vietnam National University of Forestry, Vietnam

Xuan Hoan Nguyen
Ho Chi Minh City University of Food Industry, Vietnam

CAROLYN S. HAYLES

21. INTEGRATING TEACHING AND LEARNING AROUND THE SEVEN SUSTAINABLE DEVELOPMENT GOALS OF THE WELL-BEING OF FUTURE GENERATIONS ACT 2015 (WALES)

INTRODUCTION

The Well-being of Future Generations (Wales) Act of 2015 is the first of its kind where the well-being of future generations is right at the heart of Welsh Government decision making. In the Act, Sustainable Development means the process of improving the economic, social, environmental and cultural well-being of Wales by taking actions aimed at achieving seven 'Sustainable Development' or 'Well-being' goals (Welsh Government, 2015). The goals are a Prosperous Wales, a Resilient Wales, a Healthier Wales, an Equal Wales, a Wales of Cohesive Communities, a Wales of vibrant Culture, thriving Welsh Language and a Globally Responsible Wales. It is still early days for the Act; however, it is important that Welsh universities respond to this Sustainable Development Act and put in place activities that support staff and student engagement through learning, teaching and research activities. In this chapter, the author describes a journey that has led to the development of a stand-alone certificate designed to support learning and teaching around the seven Sustainable Development or Well-being Goals of the Well-being of Future Generations Act (2015.) Using a descriptive case study as the approach allowed for a systematic identification of the process and explores both primary and secondary data collection. The case study looks at who, what, where and when. The aim is not to test a theory or hypothesis, but to record and share in-depth knowledge and insight into the process (Fellows & Lui, 2003; Naoum, 2013). By recording and sharing the University of Wales, Trinity Saint David's whole-institution approach, and in particular: the work of its sustainability institute INSPIRE in developing the certificate, it is hoped that others will be encouraged to explore and deliver similar courses on Sustainable Development or indeed the 17 Sustainable Development Goals (SDGs) of the United Nations (UN, 2018).

DESCRIPTIVE CASE STUDY

Wales

Wales is a small country and a part of Britain and the United Kingdom. It is located to the west of England and is about 170 miles (256 km) long and 60 miles (96 km) wde. It covers just over 8,000 square miles (20,722 km²). Much of Wales is a nature-lovers' playground, with internationally recognized beaches and expansive mountain ranges. Wales' capital, Cardiff, is a thriving city just two hours by train from London. Wales is a modern country, but with a documented heritage of two thousand years which includes its own language (Welsh Government, 2018).

Although people living in Wales speak English, the Welsh language continues to thrive with half a million people in Wales who can speak Welsh. A Celtic language, Welsh is one of Europe's oldest living languages and as a living language, used in conversation by thousands throughout Wales. The Welsh Language Act 1993, Government of Wales Act 1998, and Welsh Language (Wales) measure 2011 stipulate that the Welsh and English languages are to be treated equally. In 2017, the Welsh Government prepared a new strategy, 'Cymraeg 2050', to increase the number of Welsh speakers in Wales to 1 million by 2050 and to build a platform in society for Welsh to be spoken more often (Welsh Government, 2018).

Wales takes the idea of Sustainable Development and Global Citizenship seriously, and it is looking out for future generations as well as the planet's resources. Wales has taken a leading role in coming up with innovative ideas to ensure sustainability is achievable at all levels. For Wales, sustainable development is much broader than perhaps the environmental definition that many of us are familiar with. Sustainable development is about improving the way Wales can achieve economic, social, environmental and cultural well-being. Making sure that the Welsh Government and its citizens are using the most appropriate methods in the long term to achieve short and medium-term goals. Wales was the first Fair Trade Nation and the first nation in the World to legislate for the UN's Sustainable Development Goals (Welsh Government, 2018).

The Well-Being of Future Generations (Wales) Act 2015

Indeed, there is a Sustainable Development Law for Wales called the Well-being of Future Generations (Wales) Act 2015. This law commenced on April 1, 2016. The Act is one of a minimal number of laws in the world that legislates for Sustainable Development, and it is the first of the 'well-being of future generations' that must now be considered at the heart of the (Welsh) Government decision making.

Prior to becoming Law, the Welsh Government ran a national consultation. 'The Wales We Want' as a national conversation, was also the first of its kind and helped inform the groundbreaking Well-being of Future Generations (Wales) Act 2015. The conversation consisted of 20 linked events, 3 launch events and the recruitment of 150 'Futures Champions'. These helped to bring together some 6474 individuals who took part in over 100 conversations across Wales resulting in almost 1000 responses in the form of reports, videos, postcards, drawings and surveys. The following recommendations are based on 'The Wales We Want' National Conversation. They are taken from conversations with nearly 6500 participants, and reflect views on the foundations required for the Well-being of Future Generations (Wales) Act 2015:

1. An Integrated approach to Well-being Plans, including support from pre-birth through early years of life. Positive impacts of early interventions (from pregnancy to the first 1,000 days of a child's life), through environmental and nutritional factors, have significant long-term effects on life (expectancy);
2. People felt disconnected from decision-makers, fatigued and frustrated by limited engagement. The success of Wellbeing Plans will depend on the level of external engagement. Public Service Boards need to ensure a broad ownership of objectives and prioritize engagement, including children and young people.
3. Well-being Plans designed from the bottom up and based on local place plans. Greater empowerment will create resilience and a greater sense of responsibility. It is critical that there is a strong locality-based approach to wellbeing planning.
4. Climate change is considered the most significant factor affecting the long-term well-being of communities. Well-being Plans need to be climate-proof, transitioning to a low carbon economy with adaptations needed for a changing climate.
5. Social and economic benefits and environmental improvements, including access to green space, is fully integrated into well-being plans. Many of the negative impacts of the local environment on the quality of life were in areas with the greatest deprivation with adverse effects on mental and physical health.
6. The need for a stronger, more localized economy to achieve a 'prosperous' and 'more resilient' Wales. Well-being plans need to ensure an integrated approach to growing local economies by leveraging public procurement, enabling distributed low carbon energy schemes and improving the local food supply.
7. A focus on inequality issues is needed for well-being assessments. All aspects of inequality are highlighted, including health inequalities, gender, ethnicity, and age. As older people become the largest and fastest growing demographic in Wales, it becomes urgent to enable older people to maintain their independence and to engage and participate fully in society.
8. Use the assets of culture, language and heritage positively as a legacy for future generations while continuing to be inclusive of all cultures. These assets need to be at the center of well-being plans (Davis, 2015a, 2015b).

Subsequently, 'The Wales We Want' reports became a forerunner to the statutory reports, which have become a requirement of the 'Future Generations Commissioner for Wales' under the Wellbeing of Future Generations (Wales) Act 2015 (Davis, 2015a, 2015b) (see below).

The Wellbeing of Future Generations (Wales) Act 2015 as Wales' Sustainable Development Law, intends to make Wales a better place to live both now and in the future and this national conversation shaped the way forward. Other successful engagement includes a bi-lingual video of 'Megan's story', an animation which explains the positive impact of the Well-being of Future Generations Act will have throughout one girl's life. It explains what the Welsh Government is doing and why it is important for Wales and its citizens to get behind the idea of Sustainable Development (Welsh Government, 2015). The Well-being of Future Generations (Wales) Act 2015 also ensures Wales will make a positive contribution to the achievement of the UN's Sustainable Development Goals (SDGs). This aims to end extreme poverty, fight inequality and tackle Climate Change by 2030, through the introduction of 7 Sustainable Development or Well-being Goals (UN, 2018).

The Well-being of Future Generations (Wales) Act 2015 defines Sustainable Development in Wales as 'the process of improving the economic, social, environmental and cultural well-being of Wales by taking action, following the Sustainable Development principles, aimed at achieving the Well-being Goals' (Welsh Government, 2015). In other words, Sustainable Development means using the things we need to live our lives while making sure that there are still enough resources left for future generations. The Seven Sustainable Development or Well-being Goals are described in Figure 21.1 and Table 21.1.

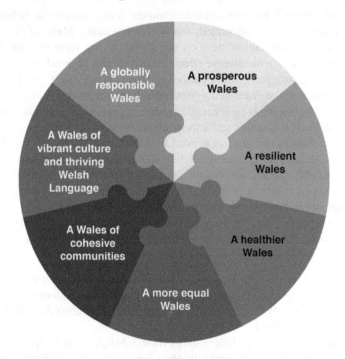

Figure 21.1. The seven sustainable development or well-being goals

Table 21.1. The seven sustainable development or well-being goals
(Welsh Government, 2016a)

Sustainable development/ well-being goal	Example discussion topics
A Globally Responsible Wales	A nation which, when doing anything to improve the economic, social, environmental and cultural well-being of Wales, takes account of whether doing such a thing may make a positive contribution to global well-being.
A Prosperous Wales	An innovative, productive and low carbon society which recognizes the limits of the global environment and therefore uses resources efficiently and proportionately (including acting on climate change), and which develops a skilled and well-educated population in an economy which generates wealth and provides employment opportunities, allowing people to take advantage of the wealth generated through securing decent work.
A Resilient Wales	A nation, which maintains and enhances a biodiverse natural environment with healthy functioning ecosystems that support social, economic and ecological resilience and the capacity to adapt to change (for example climate change).
A Healthier Wales	A society in which people's physical and mental well-being is maximized, and in which choices and behaviors that benefit future health are understood.
A more Equal Wales	A society that enables people to fulfil their potential no matter what their background or circumstances (including their socio-economic circumstances).
A Wales of Cohesive Communities	Attractive, viable, safe and well-connected communities.
A Wales of vibrant Culture and thriving Welsh Language	A society that promotes and protects culture, heritage and the Welsh language, and which encourages people to participate in the arts, sports and recreation.

The Act also sets out 'Five Ways of Working' that are needed to achieve these seven Sustainable Development or Well-being Goals. These support sustainable decision-making. The Five Ways of Working are given in Table 21.2.

Wales' Sustainable Development Law: The Well-being of Future Generations (Wales) Act 2015, states that public bodies in Wales must think about people now and in the future when they make their decisions. The 'Five Ways of Working' approach provides an opportunity for innovative thinking, reflection on the way we live our lives and what we expect of our public services.

Wales has many challenges, including a countrywide response to climate change, poverty, health inequalities, and the future employment prospects of its citizens. In

Table 21.2. *The five ways of working of the well-being of future generations (Wales) Act 2015 (Welsh Government, 2016a)*

Ways of working	Implementation
Long-term	Helping public bodies to plan and build insight as to what the future might look like if we achieve the Goals, or fail to tackle the biggest problems facing future generations.
Integration	Public bodies must work together to understand their collective contribution to all seven of the Well-being Goals.
Involvement	Between communities, individuals and their public services is crucial if we are to meet the needs of current and future generations.
Collaboration	To have a better understanding of how working together can benefit us all.
Prevention	Of problems or early intervention in the first place are key to improving the lives of the people of Wales.

order to make improvements, public bodies must work together to determine what people need now, but also how the decisions are made to improve lives now – impact on people's lives in the future.

Forty-four public bodies must work together to deliver on the Act. These include: Welsh ministers, Local authorities, Local health boards (including Public health Wales NHS trust and the Velindre NHS trust), National park authorities, Fire and rescue authorities, Natural Resources Wales, Higher education funding council for Wales, Arts council of Wales, Sports council of Wales, National library of Wales and National Museum of Wales.

The Well-being of Future Generations (Wales) Act 2015 established statutory Public Service Boards (PSBs), which replaced voluntary Local Service Boards in each local authority area. The purpose of PSBs is to improve the economic, social, environmental and cultural well-being in its area by strengthening joint working across all public services in Wales. Each board must:

- Assess the state for economic, social, environmental and cultural well-being in its area; and
- Set objectives that maximize the PSBs contribution to the Sustainable Development or Well-being Goals.

From 2017, each PSB must prepare and publish a plan setting out its objectives and steps it will take to meet them. This is a 'Local Well-being Plan'. It must say:

- Why the PSB feels their objectives will contribute within their local area to achieving the Well-being Goals; and
- How it has had regard to the assessment of 'Local Well-being' in setting its objectives and steps to take.

Each PSB will carry out an annual review of their plan showing their progress going forward. When producing their assessments of local well-being and Local Well-being Plan, PSBs must consult widely.

PSBs were asked to take account of 'The Wales We Want' report in the production of their Wellbeing Plans, in order to maximize their contribution to the achievement of the national Sustainable Development or Well-being Goals (David, 2015a, 2015b).

Forty-Six National Indicators are in place to measure Wales' progress and a Future Generations Commissioner appointed to oversee the Act (Welsh Government, 2016b). The commissioner's role is to ensure public bodies are working towards the Well-being Goals and to suggest improvements in the services provided. In 2017, the commissioner published the first annual report to demonstrate how public bodies are progressing, and achievements made towards reaching Wales' Sustainable Development or Well-being Goals (Future Generations Commissioner for Wales, 2018).

Although Higher Education Institutions (HEIs) in Wales are not required to deliver the Well-being of Future Generations (Wales) Act 2015, the higher education funding council for Wales (HEFCW) is one of the 44 public bodies that must work with others to deliver on the Act. Several of Wales' Higher Education Institutes (HEIs) have voluntarily adopted the Well-being of Future Generations (Wales) Act 2015 Goals (principles and duty) from 2015 onwards, including the University of Wales, Trinity Saint David.

The University of Wales, Trinity Saint David – A New University for Wales

The University of Wales, Trinity Saint David (UWTSD) is a new university with a historical past. UWTSD formed on November 18th, 2010 through the merger of the University of Wales Lampeter and Trinity University College Carmarthen, under Lampeter's Royal Charter of 1828. On August 1st, 2013, Swansea Metropolitan University became part of UWTSD. The University's Royal Charter is the oldest in Wales and England after the universities of Oxford and Cambridge. In 2011, His Royal Highness (HRH) the Prince of Wales became its Royal Patron (Hayles, 2015; UWTSD, 2015).

The UWTSD Group includes the Further Education colleges of Coleg Sir Gâr and Coleg Ceredigion as part of a dual sector – Higher Education (HE) and Further Education (FE) – group structure. The UWTSD Group has over 25,000 learners across 17 campuses in rural and city locations. UWTSD aims to deliver clear, tangible benefits for learners, employers, industry and communities by offering a vocational approach from entry level to post-doctoral research (UWTSD, 2015). The Group further strengthened through the completion of merger of University of Wales into UWTSD (University of Wales, 2011).

The University has its principal campuses in Carmarthen, Lampeter and Swansea in Wales, as well as an English-based campus in London. It also has a presence in Cardiff with the Wales International Academy of Voice and through its dual sector partners, in Aberystwyth, Ammanford, Cardigan and Llanelli in west Wales. There is no single 'main' or 'home' campus. The geographical spread of the University has seen the development of strategies for multi-campus working, including adequate video-conferencing facilities and shared electronic resources. All staff have a 'home' campus in the sense of an office base, but the majority work across campuses. UWTSD has a clear national profile, with many of its staff and students speaking the Welsh language and there are opportunities for students to undertake their studies through the medium of Welsh. Indeed, the University's strong presence in South West Wales alongside its dual sector delivery makes it an essential voice in the region. Many students are locals, living and working in the region. They also intend to live and work in the region on completion of their studies. In addition, their contribution to the local region, its economy, environment and culture are readily identifiable (Hayles, 2015; UWTSD, 2015).

As a newly formed institution that has placed itself at the heart of a region, the University has an integral role to play in building capacity and importantly in building resilience for a sustainable future for South West Wales. This is timely with the recent introduction of the Well-being of Future Generations (Wales) Act 2015. Going forward there will be a requirement for public bodies to make sure that when they are making decisions, they consider the impact they could have on people living their lives in Wales in the future. It will expect them to work better together, to involve people reflecting the diversity of our communities, to look to the long-term as well as focusing on now and to take action to stop problems getting worse and even stop them happening in the first place (Welsh Government, 2015). The University is well placed to not only meet the requirements of the Well-being of Future Generations (Wales) Act 2015 but also to support others to do so through its learning, teaching and research activities.

Embedding Education for Sustainable Development and Global Citizenship (ESDGC) at a Strategic Level

Transformation, adaptability and flexibility are familiar words to organizations working in times of a merger. Indeed, as a newly formed institution experiencing widespread organizational change, the University has had to make some critical decisions in shaping the new UWTSD group (Hayles, 2015). This has brought about many opportunities, one of which has been to place sustainability at the core of its strategic planning, embedding sustainability within its core operations and culture. The core values of the University as outlined in its Strategic Plan are as follows:

1. *Collaboration*: Through the establishment of a range of strategic relationships at regional, national and international levels. Such networks will have the potential to inspire learners, staff and partners to create exciting new learning futures;
2. *Inclusivity*: Through putting learners first and championing lifelong learning without barriers; and supporting students from all backgrounds and at all stages

of their education;
3. *Employability and creativity*: By harnessing the entrepreneurial, research, creative and enterprising skills of its learners, the university will offer educational programs that allow students to have the best opportunities to gain employment and develop their transferable skills;
4. *Sustainable development*: Through a system-based approach to delivering meaningful and relevant educational pathways, promote learning and social responsibility that supports 'development that meets the needs of the present without compromising the ability of future generations to meet their needs' (World Commission on Environment and Development, 1987);
5. *Wales and its distinctiveness*: Through celebrating the distinctive linguistic and cultural assets and heritage of Wales;
6. *The concept of global citizenship*: Through the development of further multi-national activities and opportunities for learners, staff and partners; and
7. *Research and its impact on policy*: By ensuring, that its research activity and outcomes influence the evidence base of policies developed in Wales and beyond (UWTSD, 2013).

Therefore the University's strategic plan makes the commitment of UWTSD clear, namely to embed sustainability as a core principle across all aspects of the University.

The Institute of Sustainable Practice, Innovation and Resource Effectiveness (INSPIRE)

The Institute of Sustainable Practice, Innovation and Resource Effectiveness (INSPIRE) is a virtual institute that provides a focus for Sustainable Development activities across the University and the broader UWTSD group. INSPIRE was established by Jane Davidson, a former Minister for Environment and Sustainability in Wales, in January 2012. In 2013, INSPIRE became a strategic Sustainability Directorate and formed a Sustainability Committee, which serves the whole UWTSD group. INSPIRE's role is to work across academic and support structures to deliver on the University's strategic priorities and embed Sustainable Development through its learning, teaching, curricula, campus, community and culture. Through INSPIRE the university aims to:

- Develop curriculum-related delivery to ensure that students are provided with the knowledge, skills and attitudes that will equip them for their future contribution to the economy, community and environment;
- Develop a research and innovation capacity focused on the core strengths of the University;
- Develop its campuses to the highest standards of environmental performance; and
- Contribute to local communities by giving particular regard to issues of sustainable rural and urban communities and the development of South West Wales as a low carbon region (Davidson, 2014).

Embedding Education for Sustainable Development and Global Citizenship (ESDGC) at a Faculty Level

The University recognizes 'Education for Sustainable Development and Global Citizenship' (ESDGC) holistically, while deliberately and consciously acknowledging the need for a balance between society, economy and environment to contribute towards individual and community well-being and a reduction in environmental impacts and consequently a more resilient future. The University intends to ensure that it embeds a framework for ESDGC in a way that delivers, where the emphasis is not merely on the content of the modules and programs of study offered, but on the entire learning and teaching experience. Indeed, the University has agreed that Learning, Teaching and Enhancement Strategy includes 'sustainability conscious learning' to enable students to have a clear understanding of the impacts of their future actions on the physical, social and economic environments (Hayles, 2015, 2017; INSPIRE, 2018).

This strategic commitment to introduce ESDGC through its teaching and learning offerings is recorded in Faculty Sustainability Plans which were introduced in 2013 and provided a mechanism for annual reporting on faculty level ESDGC through the University's Sustainability Committee. Each University faculty is required to produce a plan to a standard template, outlining how they are working to embed ESDGC within subject disciplines as well as identifying cross-curricular opportunities. The plans also reflect environmental commitments.

Each faculty plan is required to provide a summary of the key ethos and pedagogical approach of the faculty, and how the faculty intends to take the sustainability commitment forward, including arrangements for plan delivery and reporting structure. For example, area/activity, sustainability element, faculty wide and interdisciplinary approaches and concepts. Specifically, the faculty makes sustainability commitments to:

- Work within environmental limits;
- Explore *how* the faculty teaches;
- Explore *what* the faculty teaches;
- Progress the faculty research and development activity;
- Progress faculty engagement the wider community; and
- Seek competitive advantage.

Faculty Plans demonstrate the link between faculties and the University's strategic agenda on sustainability. The documents are available on the INSPIRE web page and can be used publicly to demonstrate the University's practical application of its commitment to sustainability (Davidson, 2014; INSPIRE, 2018).

Framework Approach

Academics are encouraged to work within existing frameworks when developing new programs and updating existing programs. As part of the validation and revalidation of teaching programs, course directors are required to provide a sustainability statement, demonstrating their pedagogical approach and how sustainability is embedded in their programs, modules, learning outcomes and assessments. Since 2016, they must also demonstrate which of the seven Sustainable Development or Well-being Goals of the Well-being of Future Generations (Wales) Act 2015 are built-in to the curriculum and where are they located. As part of the validation process, all program validation documentation is reviewed by the academic lead for INSPIRE to ensure consistency with the University's sustainability commitments. This is a precious process and is proving to be a useful intervention point with which to shape curriculum in relation to ESDGC.

Academics have been encouraged to use UNESCO's five pedagogic principles to support the development of ESDGC curriculum:

1. Futures thinking;
2. Critical and creative thinking;
3. Participation and participatory learning;
4. Thinking systemically; and
5. Partnerships (UNESCO, 2002).

In addition, the university recognizes the Higher Education Academy (HEA)'s Future Fit Framework and the Quality Assurance Agency for Higher Education (QAA) guidance developed in collaboration with the HEA, 'Education for Sustainable Development Guidance' (Stirling, 2012, 2014). Indeed, the University formally adopted the HEA QAA guidance in March 2015 as the framework for ESDGC curriculum design, delivery and review within the University. Educators are encouraged to use it as a framework within their disciplinary context, rather than as a prescription of a curriculum or pedagogic approach.

This approach to embedding ESDGC is one where academics are asked to conform to a centrally mandated, systematic, whole-of institution policy at a strategic and faculty level. Previous research has demonstrated that cultural change in organizations is most effectively achieved as a process of learning through dialogue and praxis, grounded in systems thinking (Senge, 1990). Therefore, it is necessary to recognize that educational change occurs through cultural changes in the way academics work within their disciplinary expertise. Interacting across interdisciplinary boundaries, negotiating the forms, purposes and pedagogies through which knowledge and learning experiences are prepared for, and experienced by students (Fullan, 1999). The project outlined below is an example of cross-faculty, interdisciplinary and collaborative working. The Well-being of Future Generations (Wales) Act 2015 provided the catalyst to develop new ways of working, which in addition to providing learning and teaching around Sustainable Development and the Well-being of Future Generations, also resulted in the advancement of knowledge, skills and attributes in ESDGC pedagogy amongst a self-selecting group of academics.

Sustainable Development: The Well-being of Future Generations Certificate

The specific project described below is the product of a desire to give students an opportunity to access learning and teaching on Sustainable Development during their time at UWTSD. What has resulted is an extra-curricular certificate that anyone associated with the institution can take part in it and widen participation from just students to staff, including both academic and non-academic employees. The online, institution-wide, stand-alone, non-credit bearing certificate on 'Sustainable Development and the Well-being of Future Generations', delivered bilingually (through the mediums of the Welsh and English languages), was developed by the Academic Lead for INSPIRE with voluntary support from colleagues from across the University's faculties between June 2016–August 2017. The certificate was consequently designed for anyone associated with the broader institution. Giving them an opportunity to access learning and teaching on Sustainable Development and recognize what the Welsh Government are doing to promote Sustainable Development in Wales.

During the certificate, participants predominantly learn about Wales' Sustainable Development Law and the 'Well-being of Future Generations (Wales) Act 2015'. As previously stated, the Well-being of Future Generations (Wales) Act 2015 defines Sustainable Development in Wales as 'the process of improving the economic, social, environmental and cultural well-being of Wales by taking action, in accordance with the Sustainable Development principles, aimed at achieving the Well-being Goals' (Welsh Government, 2015). The certificate takes participants through each of the Sustainable Development or Well-being Goals and looks at why they were established (with a focus on the spirit of the Act, not legislation). It explores and proposes approaches that may move Wales forward towards achieving these goals. It also looks at how the Welsh Goals relate to the UN SDGs (UN, 2018). Participants have an opportunity to consider what the Sustainable Development or Well-being Goals mean for them, their studies/employment, and their future as Welsh citizens. For participants, not physically in Wales or not intending to stay in Wales on completion of their studies, the certificate also provides an insight into the UN SDGs (see Figure 21.2).

The intention was to create an inclusive learning environment. This is particularly pertinent when considering the subject matter. Tisdell (1995) suggests that a learning environment needs to attend inclusivity at three levels. A genuinely inclusive learning environment will therefore be:

1. Reflect the diversity of those present in the learning activity through the curriculum and pedagogical style;
2. Attend to the wider and immediate institutional contexts in which the participants work and live; and
3. Try to reflect the changing needs of an increasingly diverse society.

Figure 21.2. United Nations sustainable development goals (UN, 2018)

Learners do not live in a vacuum. Addressing institutional and societal levels are important, but the most significant level is the selection of appropriate materials and methods that address the characteristics of learning group members (Tisdell, 1995). Addressing the diversity of participants by selecting appropriate curriculum and course content was critical in ensuring all aspects of inclusivity were addressed (Shore, Black, Simpson, & Coombe, 1993). This includes:

1. Developing an understanding of the groups and sub-groups likely to participate;
2. Representing and respecting the knowledge base of all these groups in the learning and teaching content; and
3. Choosing resources and learning activities that met the needs of all the groups and sub-groups identified.

It was also important to develop a collaborative learning environment, where participants from different parts of the same institution come together and attempt to learn something new through shared experience and equal non-threatening and non-hierarchical learning environment (Chiu, 2000).

Seven academics, all volunteers with a passion for sustainability, took part in the development and delivery of the certificate, each taking the lead on one of the seven Sustainable Development or Well-being Goals. As a result, the academics working together were self-selecting, brought together by shared interests and desire for ESDGC.

The academics pre-recorded each online session as two discrete sets of content, one in the Welsh language and the other in English (Figure 21.3). The University's internal translation service provided support to those academics who do not speak Welsh, and one of the volunteers provided all the Welsh-language voice-overs in these circumstances.

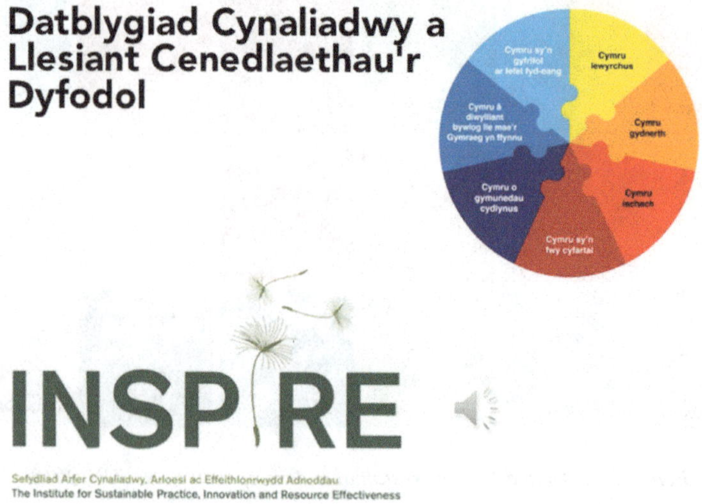

Figure 21.3. Certificate introductory session – English and Welsh language provision

Students access to sessions via Moodle (a learning platform designed to provide educators, administrators and learners with a single robust), a secure and integrated system to create personalized learning environments (Moodle, 2017), choosing their preferred language. Each of the eight sessions includes a 10–15 minute pre-recorded video on each of the Sustainable Development or Well-being Goals:

1. Introduction;
2. A Globally Responsible Wales;
3. A Prosperous Wales;
4. A Resilient Wales;
5. A Healthier Wales;
6. A more Equal Wales;
7. A Wales of Cohesive Communities; and
8. A Wales of vibrant Culture and thriving Welsh Language.

Presentation of the Goals was enhanced by illustration and animation students from UWTSD's Swansea college of Art (see Figure 21.4), who designed the ten minutes' video as part of INSPIRE's student internship program (INSPIRE, 2018).

In addition, included short quizzes, activities and additional resources in each session. If possible, all additional resources are available in both Welsh and English and translated into Welsh for participants. Most Welsh Government websites provide Welsh and English content to support this dual-language approach for learning and teaching.

Each 'session academic' poses a series of questions for certificate participants to discuss with others, who are taking part in the course, over the internet and each

INTEGRATING TEACHING AND LEARNING

Figure 21.4. A wales of cohesive communities and a Resilient Wales as illustrated and animated by students from UWTSD's Swansea college of art

discussion moderated by that session academic. These discussions are undertaken bilingually. When considering Wales' journey towards each of the Sustainable Development or Well-being Goals, the Act's 'Five Ways of Working' (long-term, integration, involvement, collaboration, prevention), designed to support sustainable decision-making, are at the forefront of these discussions. This approach provides an opportunity for innovative thinking, reflecting on the way we live our lives and what we expect of our public services. Expected 'Netiquette' is referring to rules of etiquette that apply to online communication, are shared with participants to make sure they appear respectful, polite and knowledgeable when posting to the certificate's online discussion forums.

In Session 1, participants are encouraged to take part in the Sulitest. Sulitest.org (2016) is an international initiative assessing core sustainability literacy with a standardized test. Academic institutions and non-academic organizations in more than 50 countries use this tool which serves as a reference to raise awareness on Sustainable Development and improve sustainability literacy worldwide. The Sulitest requires participants to answer both international and national questions on sustainability and Sustainable Development. It is an opportunity for the participant to see how much they know and understand about sustainability and Sustainable Development. They can do this through the mediums of Welsh or English with UWTSD providing the Welsh translation for Sulitest and encourages participants to revisit the test at the end of the certificate to see whether their awareness and knowledge of sustainability and Sustainable Development has changed.

In order to obtain a certificate of participation for the course, participants attempt the quizzes embedded in the eight online sessions and contribute to online discussions that are moderated by the academic leading the session. They are also encouraged to take part in the practical action on campus or in their local community. For some people, this might mean joining INSPIRE as an intern (INSPIRE, 2018), but for many people, this means supporting Go-Green Week. Go-Green Week is the People & Planet's annual national week of action on Climate Change in schools, colleges and universities in the UK. People & Planet are a student-led movement that empowers young people with the skills, confidence and knowledge they need to make change happen, at home and globally (People and Planet, 2018). Go-Green Week brings together a range of activities to UWTSD campus life for one week in February and includes public debates, film screenings, promotion of environmental campaigns, beach clean-ups and much more.

Finally, although the certificate described above is non-credit bearing, in other words, its completion does not provide credits towards formal education, academic staff are free to use its content to support delivery of teaching and learning around Sustainable Development and the SDGs within the University's degree programs. If Academic staff choose to do this, they must develop their assessment methods; but can do so with the support of INSPIRE if requested.

Discussion of Certificate Outcomes

The certificate on Sustainable Development and the Well-being of Future Generations first ran from October 2017, culminating in Go-Green Week in February 2018, with each of the eight online sessions delivered via Moodle fortnightly (with a longer break at Christmas).

One hundred and fifty participants signed up for this first run of the certificate. There was a cross-section of participants representing the entire institution and accessing the certificate through both the mediums of the Welsh and English languages. Undergraduate and postgraduate students including MA/MSc, PhD and MBA students and staff from both academic and non-academic parts of the institution (from facilities staff including cleaners, through to faculty staff including professors) were involved within the cohort. The current cohort of INSPIRE interns was asked to participate as part of their training (INSPIRE, 2018). 50% of the University's Green Impact teams were required to take part at some point in this academic year (the certificate will run again from March–June 2018) in order to obtain the highest (gold) award. Green Impact is a National Union of Students (NUS) scheme that brings together students and staff to green campuses, curriculums and communities (NUS, 2018). Universities can customize some of the requirements and set their targets within the framework.

Participants' levels of online engagement varied, as would be expected. Some participants were happy to 'receive' the pre-recorded online sessions, but reluctant to engage in the online discussions, preferring 'action' to demonstrate their engagement with the learning material (e.g. Go-Green Week). Others readily participated in the online discussions with a small faction proactively creating new discussions. These students appear to have benefited the most from the collaborative learning environment created through these online forums, with new learning creation where participants have actively interacted by sharing experiences and taking on asymmetric roles (Chiu, 2000).

Indeed, online contributions to discussions via Moodle have been enjoyable and engaging. Participants have been happy to explore the issues proposed, as well as posing and discussing other topics as they arose. For examples of the breadth of topics covered in the discussion forums, see Table 21.3.

Previous research has demonstrated the advantages and added benefits achieved from an online learning environment, as well as some of the disadvantages experienced (e.g. see Allen & Seaman, 2011, 2013). As an institution with no single 'main' or 'home' campus, it seemed logical to provide a course that everyone who associated with the institution could access equally and leave no participant feeling disadvantaged by geography and work/study schedule. To encourage inclusivity, it was important that the course was delivered via INSPIRE as the University's sustainability institute and not associated with a specific school or faculty. The flexibility and convenience of online delivery in this instance offset any arguments for face-to-face delivery. Indeed, the benefits of delivering the certificate online include:

1. Schedule Flexibility: Participants can access the certificate at any time, from anywhere, provided they can log on;
2. Ease of accessibility: Participants can readily review the sessions, their associated quizzes, resources and discussions. Individuals can also share their thoughts

with each other via the on-line discussion forums to facilitate collaborative and inclusive community learning; and
3. Participants control study time: Participants do not have to sit for an extended period to complete the sessions. Pre-recorded sessions are short (10–15 minutes maximum) and can be paused when needed; with the additional resources, discussion etc. read/written as convenient.

Benefits, in addition to the enhanced flexibility and convenience this form of delivery create, include a few participant enrichment opportunities that resonate with theories of inclusive and collaborative learning:

1. Chance for interaction: Online courses can be less intimidating than the traditional 'brick-and-mortar' classroom setting, and can help to increase participant interaction. By allowing everyone to have an equal voice, shared ideas grow diverse as well. Participants can also think longer about what they want to say and add their comments when ready. In a traditional classroom, the conversation could have moved past the point where the participant may be willing to comment;
2. Online communications: Academics can be more approachable in an on-line setting. Participants may feel more comfortable debating and discussion issues openly with the session academic (and their fellow participants) through online discussions, rather than face-to-face. Email and on-line correspondence also cuts out having to wait for office hours that may not be convenient for either party; and
3. Time to absorb material: Participants have the 'space' to absorb the material being presented and discussed, supporting their learning.

In addition to the benefits to participants as outlined above, there are cost benefits that include:

1. Little or no financial cost: The certificate is free at the point of use. In addition the on-line learning environment eliminates any costs associated with transportation, childminding, and other expense incurred when attending classes in a more traditional setting; and
2. No requirement to buy (expensive) textbooks: the certificate does not require physical textbooks, as all reading materials are available online or are downloadable free of charge.

Again, these financial benefits ensure the certificate is inclusive and accessible to all.

Informal Feedback

As might be expected, the students that contributed the most in the discussions forums have been more active in feeding back their experiences informally:

- "… really interesting to see how much is involved in Sustainable Development. Everyone can take on board and run with at least one topic".

Table 21.3. Example on-line discussion topics from certificate

Sustainable development/ well-being goal	Example discussion topics
A Globally Responsible Wales	Do you think the current system of using the international economy to measure "impact" is a good one? Do you think we should incorporate additional measures, such as looking at inequality or quantifying environmental protection, when accounting for "impact"?
A Prosperous Wales	Definitions of a 'prosperous' country relate to fiscal wealth or 'economic well-being'. Does a nation lack economic well-being when food banks seem to be required? If there was willingness from banks and perhaps Government to invest in small start-up companies, with initiatives and not necessarily money, would that encourage people to take that first step from unemployment to Employer?
A Resilient Wales	How do you think nature and the natural environment can be better used in an urban setting to promote environmental resilience within our built environments? Discuss what you think is the one big environmental issue that needs to be tackled before any other, and why?
A Healthier Wales	Are there any areas of health, which should be prioritised in Wales that you feel are not currently? Adverse Childhood Experiences impact upon both mental and physical health. How can this be prevented?
A more Equal Wales	Where would you place yourself on the continuum of sustainability theories? Does diversity lead to greater well-being?
A Wales of Cohesive Communities	How can we build our social capital in Wales and support our communities to develop? When you think about the communities you live/work in, how do you know that you belong to that community? Are there any that you feel more part of than others? Why do you think that is? What are the bonds that hold that community together for you?
A Wales of vibrant Culture and thriving Welsh Language	Discuss ways to promote the arts, sports and recreation for future generations? By 2050 the Welsh Government aim to increase the number of Welsh speakers to 1 milion. What steps can you think of that would support Wales to achieve this aim?

- "… I have really enjoyed the on-line discussions with people from all over the University".
- "… this has challenged my thinking on so many topics!"
- "I'm really enjoying this [certificate]. I've been grateful of the additional focus from INSPIRE during my MBA".

At this stage in the development of the certificate, no formal feedback loops are in place. Students regularly express 'survey fatigue', so it was felt that making feedback a requirement of a voluntary, non-credit bearing certificate was not a priority. INSPIRE will seek informal feedback during Go-Green Week and use it to shape the certificate for the next academic year.

It was also important for INSPIRE to 'check-in' with the team of academic staff involved in developing the certificate, all of whom have done so voluntarily and on top of their regular workload. Here is what they had to say:

- "It's been a good opportunity …".
- "I have enjoyed and learnt a huge amount!"
- "It's been a load of fun working through this with you all, I've really enjoyed it! And I'm so pleased the Certificate saw such strong uptake".
- "What a great opportunity … to work with a bunch of academics who are passionate about sustainability and prepared to stick their necks out and do something different".

Going forward, the certificate will run unchanged for a second time this academic year (between March and June 2018). Heads of School and Module leaders are now requesting that their entire student cohort sign up, so numbers are likely to increase in the short term.

CONCLUSIONS

Sustainable Development is about making better decisions using long-term values. It is about thinking about the impacts of today's actions on future generations and learning to live within environmental limits. It is about balancing social, cultural, environmental and economic needs in a way that does not compromise future generations. It is about building capacity now for a more resilient future (Hayles, 2015). The Well-being of Future Generations (Wales) Act 2015 is the first of its kind , where the well-being of future generations is central to (Welsh) government decision making. The Act ensures Wales will make a positive contribution to the achievement of the UN SDGs, which aim to end extreme poverty, fight inequality and tackle Climate Change through the introduction of its seven Sustainable Development or Well-being Goals. It is important that Welsh University's embed teaching and learning around Sustainable Development to support the aims of the Well-Being of Future Generations (Wales) Act 2015.

As detailed above, UWTSD as a University in transition pledged to embed sustainability within its core operations and culture. Previous research has shown that unless there is a culture of 'value' or 'priority' given to sustainability, and organizational and resource support for staff, as well as training for academic staff, instigating such a change during organizational renewal, fails (Cowell, Hogson, & Clift, 1998). By creating a Sustainability Directorate, serving the whole UWTSD group, INSPIRE has been able to work across academic and support structures to deliver on the University's strategic priorities and embed Sustainable Development through its learning, teaching, curricula, campus, community and culture.

The Well-being of Future Generations (Wales) Act 2015 has acted as a catalyst within the institution to support the development of new ways of working. In addition to providing learning and teaching around Sustainable Development and the Well-being of Future Generations, it has resulted in the advancement of academics' knowledge, skills and attributes in ESDGC pedagogy. In looking creatively at how to engage both staff and students in the spirit of the Well-being of Future Generations (Wales) Act 2015, INSPIRE at UWTSD has developed an inclusive and collaborative online certificate on Sustainable Development, centred around the seven Sustainable Development or Well-being Goals of the Act, with a group of self-selecting academics, passionate about ESDGC. This certificate, accessible to all staff and students associated with the University, has created a platform for discussion and debate around the principles of Sustainable Development. It also promotes practical action through INSPIRE internships and Go-Green Week activities.

By sharing UWTSD's whole-institution approach, and in particular the work of INSPIRE, it is hoped that other colleagues and institutions will feel empowered to design and deliver similar courses in support of the UN SDGs and broader Sustainable Development agenda. INSPIRE at UWTSD actively welcomes the development of collaborations and partnership with other institutions that promote and support sustainability embedding initiatives and willingly shares its embedding experiences, including the challenges it has faced.

REFERENCES

Allen, I. E., & Seaman, J. (2011). *Going the distance online education in the United States, 2011.* Retrieved January 29, 2018, from http://www.onlinelearningsurvey.com/reports/goingthedistance.pdf

Allen, I. E., & Seaman, J. (2013). *Changing course: Ten years of tracking online education in the United States.* Retrieved January 29, 2018, from http://www.onlinelearningsurvey.com/reports/changingcourse.pdf

Chiu, M. M. (2000). Group problem solving processes: Social interactions and individual actions. *Theory of Social Behavior, 30*(1), 27–50, 600–631.

Cowell, S. J., Hogson, S. B., & Clift, R. (1998). Teamwork for environmental excellence in a university context. In J. Moxen & P. A. Strachan (Eds.), *Managing green teams* (pp. 131–144). Broom Hall: Greenleaf Publishing.

Davidson, J. (2014). *Sustainability strategy 2014.* Retrieved January 29, 2018, from www.uwtsd.ac.uk/.../strategies.../Sustainability--Strategy--Approved-by-Council-10-7-14.pdf

Davis, P. (2015a). *The wales we want report: A report on behalf of future generations.* Retrieved from January 29, 2018, http://www.thewaleswewant.co.uk/sites/default/files/The%20Wales%20We%20Want%20Report%20ENG.pdf

Davis, P. (2015b). *The wales we want Report: Recommendations for local service boards*. Retrieved January 29, 2018, from http://www.thewaleswewant.co.uk/sites/default/files/Report%20-%20 Recommendation%20for%20local%20service%20boards.pdf

Fellows, R., & Lui, A. (2003). *Research methods for construction*. Oxford: Blackwell.

Fullan, M. (1999). *Change forces: The sequel*. London: Falmer Press.

Future Generations Commissioner for Wales. (2018). *Acting today for a better tomorrow*. Retrieved January 29, 2018, from https://futuregenerations.wales/

Hayles, C. S. (2015, July). *A case study of capacity building: Embedding sustainable development principles and practices at the University of Wales, Trinity Saint David*. Proceedings of the 5th International Conference on Building Resilience, Newcastle, New South Wales.

Hayles, C. S. (2017). An INSPIREd education, The University of Wales Trinity Saint David. In W. Leal Filho (Ed.), *Sustainable development research at universities in the United Kingdom* (Chapter 1, pp. 1–12). Springer International Publishing.

INSPIRE. (2018). *About INSPIRE*. Retrieved January 29, 2018, from http://www.uwtsd.ac.uk/inspire/about-inspire/

Moodle. (2017). *About Moodle*. Retrieved January 29, 2018, from https://docs.moodle.org/34/en/About_Moodle

Naoum, S. G. (2013). *Dissertation research and writing for construction students*. Abingdon: Routledge.

National Union of Students. (2018). *Green impact*. Retrieved January 29, 2018, from https://sustainability.nus.org.uk/green-impact/about

People and Planet. (2018). *Go-green week*. Retrieved January 29, 2018, from https://peopleandplanet.org/events

Quality Assurance Agency for Higher Education. (2014). *Education for sustainable development: Guidance for UK higher education providers*. Retrieved January 29, 2018, from http://www.qaa.ac.uk/en/Publications/Documents/Education-sustainable-development-Guidance-June-14.pdf

Senge, P. (1990). *The fifth discipline: The art and practice of the learning organization*. New York, NY: Random House.

Shore, S., Black, A., Simpson, A., & Coombe, M. (1993). *Positively different: Guidance for developing inclusive adult literacy, language, and numeracy curricula*. Canberra: Department of Employment, Education, and Training. (ED 371 112)

Sterling, S. (2012). *The future fit framework: An introductory guide to teaching and learning for sustainability in Higher Education*. The Higher Education Academy. Retrieved January 29, 2018, from https://www.heacademy.ac.uk/node/3573

Sulitest. (2016). *Building a sustainable future together*. Retrieved January 29, 2018, from Sulitest.org

Tisdell, E. (1995). *Creating inclusive adult learning environments: Insights from multicultural education and feminist pedagogy* (Information Series No. 361). Columbus: ERIC Clearinghouse on Adult, Career, and Vocational Education, Center on Education and Training for Employment, The Ohio State University.

UNESCO. (2002). *Teaching and learning for a sustainable future*. Retrieved January 29, 2018, from http://www.unesco.org/education/tlsf

United Nations. (2018). *Sustainable development goals*. Retrieved January 29, 2018, from http://www.un.org/sustainabledevelopment/sustainable-development-goals/

University of Wales. (2011). *University of wales merger*. Retrieved January 29, 2018, from http://www.wales.ac.uk/en/NewsandEvents/News/General/UniversityofWalesMerger.aspx

UWTSD. (2012). *Living within environmental limits*. Retrieved January 29, 2018, from http://www.uwtsd.ac.uk/inspire/inspire-activity/living-within-our-environmental-limits/

UWTSD. (2013). *University of wales: Trinity saint David strategic plan: 2013 to 2017*. Retrieved January 29, 2018, from http://www.uwtsd.ac.uk/media/uwtsd-website/content-assets/documents/inspire/Strategic-Plan---FINAL-AGREED-version-7-Nov-13.pdf

UWTSD. (2014). *Carbon management plan*. Retrieved January 29, 2018, from http://www.uwtsd.ac.uk/about/strategies-and-policies/

UWTSD. (2015). *About University of Wales: Trinity Saint David*. Retrieved January 29, 2018, from http://www.uwtsd.ac.uk/about/

Welsh Government. (2015). *Future generations bill.* Retrieved January 29, 2018, from http://gov.wales/topics/people-and-communities/people/future-generations-bill/?lang=en

Welsh Government. (2015). *Video – Well-being of future generations (Wales) Act 2015.* Retrieved January 29, 2018, from http://gov.wales/topics/people-and-communities/people/future-generations-act/future-generations-act-video/?lang=en

Welsh Government. (2016a). *Well-being of future generations (Wales) act 2015.* Retrieved January 29, 2018, from http://gov.wales/topics/people-and-communities/people/future-generations-act/?lang=en

Welsh Government. (2016b). *How to measure a nation's progress? National indicators for Wales.* Retrieved January 29, 2018, from http://gov.wales/docs/desh/publications/160316-national-indicators-to-be-laid-before-nafw-en.pdf

Welsh Government. (2018). *About wales.* Retrieved January 29, 2018, from http://www.wales.com/about-wales

World Commission on Environment and Development. (1987). *Our common future.* New York, NY: Oxford University Press.

Carolyn S. Hayles
Institute of Sustainable Practice, Innovation and Resource Effectiveness (INSPIRE)
University of Wales, Trinity Saint David, UK

DIRK FRANCO, ALAIN DE VOCHT, TOM KUPPENS,
HILDA MARTENS, THEO THEWYS, BERNARD VANHEUSDEN,
MARLEEN SCHEPERS AND JEAN PIERRE SEGERS

22. SUSTAINABLE EDUCATION

*Essential Contributions to a 'Quadruple Helix' Interaction
and Sustainable Paradigm Shift*

INTRODUCTION

For many of us, these phenomena are defined as a risk, for example, climate change, loss of biodiversity, the amount of clean water available and the diminishing variety of life in our oceans. On the other hand, many perceive the following trends as catastrophic phenomena: sea level rise, ice melt at the poles, increasing numbers of tornadoes combined with floods and forest fires, national security and the potential of 192 million climate migrants in 2060. C. Graciela (communication at the I-Sup meeting, Antwerp 2014) reported these findings.

Recently, environmental and social development has been newly integrated with the adoption of the Sustainable Development Goals (SDGs) (UN, 2015), the Millennium Goals (UN, 2000), more social emphasis and the definition of sustainable development in the environment (Brundtland Report, 1987).

Going forward, all stakeholders must play a crucial role in achieving the SDGs. Governments can set frameworks and stimulate innovation, NGOs can pay more attention to important issues, and educational institutions can develop their knowledge and educational programs. However, business communities and the private sector, also have an innovative strength and the potential to also take concrete steps. In such an interaction, Full Regional Innovation Systems (FRIS) (Cooke, 2001) or the Quadruple Helix model (see further) interact with the SDGs providing guidance in realizing a transition towards a truly sustainable society.

Through the years, there has been an increasing involvement from a wide range of actors to incorporate sustainability in their policies. This trend shows clear convergence with the shift from "end of pipe" technologies towards "clean technologies" including new concepts with new business models.

It is clear that we are moving from a *problem focused* (understanding systemic challenges and the need for transitions) towards *solution oriented applications* (identifying knowledge, skills and governance approaches for transition) (EEA, 2014).

Embarking on a path of sustainable development will require a profound transformation on how we both think and act. To create a more sustainable world and to engage with sustainability-related issues as described in the SDGs, individuals must become sustainability 'change-makers.' They will require the knowledge, skills, values and attitudes that can empower them to contribute to sustainable development. Education, therefore, is a crucial component for the achievement of our sustainable development goals. Education for Sustainable Development (ESD) should be understood as an integral part of a quality education and is itself crucial for the achievement of sustainable development. However, not all kinds of education support this. Education that promotes economic growth may also lead to an increase in unsustainable consumption patterns. The now well-established approach of Education for Sustainable Development (ESD) is seen as empowering learners to make informed decisions and responsible actions for environmental integrity, economic viability and society for all present and future generations (UN, 2017).

In Flanders, there is also a lot of attention for ESD (i"Duurzaam Hoger Onderwijs"). Recently, several working groups have been set up using the following themes: SDGs as a compass; Transition in knowledge; HRM; Interdisciplinary strategies in education and research; Research and innovation (LNE, 2018).

The shift towards solution-oriented approaches is not easy as many of the problems are defined as 'wicked' problems. In 1973, Rittel and Weber composed an article about planning dilemmas (Rittel, 1973). They distinguished between 'tame' and 'wicked' problems. The tame problems are relatively easy to solve because there is a clear solution for them. Whereas, 'wicked problems' do not have a clear solution because it is unclear what is the problem for which a solution must be sought.

Other characteristics of wicked problems include: (A) it is unclear when the problem is solved; (B) there are countless possible solutions, but it is unclear which combination is the most effective; (C) it is difficult to test the solution of the problem beforehand; (D) the problem is so intertwined in the society that a solution possibly translates into a new problem; (E) the problem can be explained in several ways, so that multiple solutions are possible.

In this chapter, we will focus our descriptions on the initiatives of two Higher Education Institutes (HEI) dealing with Education for Sustainable Development. Starting from three concrete "sustainable" courses, we will illustrate how these topics are closely linked to sustainability in other internal activities such as campus greening and research. As these issues are developed in collaboration with a variety of stakeholders (government, industry and society) there is also a clear link to the society as a whole. One specific case is the organization of a new postgraduate course in Energy Efficiency Services (EES) at the University College PXL.

The reduction of energy consumption together with the use of more renewable energies (decreasing greenhouse gas emissions) remains a priority on the climate agenda. As it became clear, even building professionals often lack the specific knowledge and insights to enable a transition towards a more energy efficient and low carbon society. The PXL has taken the initiative to organize a customized postgraduate course on EES (Franco, 2016). In addition, in the case of "school buildings," it is clear that the link in Non Energy Benefits (NEB) with combination

SUSTAINABLE EDUCATION

with other societal benefits are very significant. These examples have had the most substantial influence on individual behaviours (Freed, 2017).

BACKGROUND

Both HEIs Want to Play a Role in Education for Sustainable Development

The University College PXL is a centre of expertise for innovation, creativity and entrepreneurship. The PXL organizes its activities by starting from the quadruple helix model (an interaction between government, knowledge institutes, industry and society). Moreover, this university strives to work in an interdisciplinary manner in both its teaching and research domains. Consequently, in education its attention is directed towards authenticity for cases, teachers and students.

Hasselt University, the 15th Best Small University in the world, is a new and dynamic centre of expertise for teaching, research and service provision. It has as its social responsibility to contribute actively to a sustainable and innovative region. It aspires to be a hub in the innovation web. Therefore, Hasselt University pays more attention to the importance of cooperation with other centres of expertise, companies, government agencies and organizations in Limburg and beyond.

Paradigm Shift

Increasingly here is a drift from the linear way of thinking "take, make, dispose" towards an integration of the 3P's (People, Planet and Profit). This linear model is moving towards an innovated circular economy model. Before introducing new technologies and new business models, let us have a look at how many things are developing. Many phenomena in life follow the S-curve (Figure 22.1). This figure

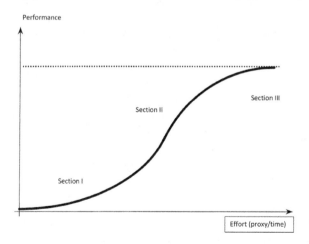

Figure 22.1. Profile of S curve

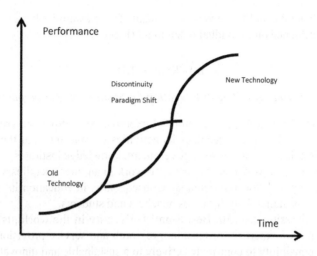

Figure 22.2. Position of S curves in transition

shows that after a more extended period of almost no benefit (section I), there is a (quasi) linear effect in which the performance or benefit strongly increase during a short period (section II). After this section, there is saturation and the economic costs strongly increase the performance, and the benefits are slightly improved (section III) (adapted from Christensen, 1992). We may have reached the limits of our current technologies. How can we improve these and reduce actual emissions? We need a transition towards new theories and new paradigms (Figure 22.2). These new technologies may cause a discontinuity, but they may also need to show a time overlap.

Creativity is inevitable in the reassessment or invention of new technologies. Transition experiments are different from innovative experiments as the underlying assumptions of innovation, integrated chain problems, impacts, methods, actors, and management are different. Therefore, a "Kairos time" may be necessary. The ancient Greeks had two words or ideas in dealing with time: Chronos and Kairos. The Chronos time is a quantitative time in our daily life. However, the Kairos time is the quality time dedicated to the Greek God for 'the right moment' and 'due measure'. Indeed, it refers to the right and opportune moment. These moments enable us to reconsider and to develop new mindsets. In this manner, a new sustainable and well-balanced paradigm can be discovered and developed (Hermsen, 2014).

Paradigm shifts (Figure 22.2), can also be explained by means of the Kuhnian Paradigm Shift (Figure 22.3) (Kuhn, 1962).

Innovation arises in two ways: quantitative because of the exploitation of an existing technological framework; and qualitative because of the exploration of a new technological framework. Quantitative innovation results in the re-articulation of an existing framework, wheras qualitative innovation is the shift to a *new* framework. Both kinds of progress cannot be pursued simultaneously, because the

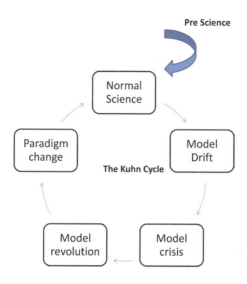

Figure 22.3. Kuhn Paradigm shift

same factors that promote their exploitation inhibit exploration of one or the other (and vice versa). Quantitative innovation results from sustained specialization and therefore requires an elaborate scheme for dividing labour, clear goals and strict rules to ensure mutual compatibility. Qualitative innovation results from a search process to find and develop new goals, a new standard for dividing labour and new rules. Such innovation is characterized by an essential tension between exploration and exploitation (Christensen, 2011; De Langhe, 2015).

Every agent must choose between exploiting and exploring but cannot do both at once. Changes in technological frameworks are typically accompanied by discontinuous shifts in adoption (De Langhe, 2014).

This is a consequence of the fact that the value of technological frameworks varies with the number of adopters. As more agents join a technological framework, their output will rise more than proportionally because of scale advantages, learning effects and other network externalities (Arthur, 1994).

Technology adoption is therefore typically caught in this 'chicken-and-egg' dilemma. New technologies are not articulated because there are no adopters, but the reason they have no adopters is because they have not been articulated. This explains why new technological frameworks can be adopted faster than expected after a tipping point of adoption is achieved. However, it also entails that old saturated technological frameworks are adopted longer than they should be. This is because declines in production are offset by the benefits of large adoption. Sometimes agents adopt inferior frameworks not because they are better: but simply because everyone else adopts them. Famous examples of this phenomenon are the adoption of the VHS video standard and the QUERTY keyboard (Paul, 1985).

Therefore, shifts in technology adoption can be promoted by reducing incentives for agents to exploit rather than explore, for instance, rewarding academics based on their number of citations is a strong incentive for exploitation and reducing the value of network externalities for instance, through anti-trust regulation or otherwise promoting competition. This is a political challenge, because of the essential tension between exploration and exploitation, promoting exploration will go at the cost of exploitation. The promotion of exploration will involve dismantling some of the very factors that were responsible for the successful exploitation of the existing technological framework, while the success of potential new frameworks has not yet realized. "We must bear in mind, that there is nothing more difficult and dangerous, or more doubtful of success than an attempt to introduce a new order of things in any state. For the innovator has for enemies all those who derived advantage from the old order of things, while those who expect to be benefited by the new institutions will be but lukewarm defenders" (Nicolo, 1971).

In order to address the wicked problems (see above) we need a threefold transformation (Rotmans, 2017) this includes: how we think; how we organize ourselves; and how we manage things.

Pedagogical Approaches

Three stages in a student's learning process (Boyatzis, 1995). We identify three different stages in a student's learning process: (1) the exploratory stage, (2) the elaboration stage and (3) the integration stage

(1) *Exploratory stage*
This first stage is often referred to as 'the problem stage' where students are not aware of their own behaviours. They now start to observe their own and others' behaviour and form their own opinions. Thus, the behaviour is no longer self-evident.

The student explores their own behaviours and asks what aspects of their behaviour are worthwhile. They also wonder whether there are alternatives to certain aspects of the behaviour that they would like to improve. If so, they may want to know whether you can learn how to apply these alternatives and whether they are interested enough to acquire these alternative forms of behaviour. A student has passed through this first exploratory stage when he or she consciously states that they want to change behaviour X and is willing to try alternative Y. Some students will be stuck at this stage and will not move on to stages two and three. In this case, students only gain theoretical knowledge from the social skills course. They study what is in their books, but do not intend to practice or apply these insights to their own behaviour. Their social skills usually do not improve.

(2) *Elaboration stage*
Students who have successfully passed stage one will now move from 'wanting to change' to 'knowing how to change'. They ask themselves "*What* is it that I need to do and *how* do I do it?" New alternative behaviours are analyzed, elaborated, taught

and practised. This process appears to be easy for some, but very hard for others: on the one hand, we have students who have successfully passed stage one and do not find it difficult to put a new insight into practice. However, others are very set in their ways and find it hard to change good old habits. At this stage, it is essential to give students the opportunity to practice and to give feedback on their performances.

(3) *Integration stage*
At this stage, students integrate or incorporate their new social skills so that they can start using them in appropriate real-life situations without having to think about it. Using the newly acquired skill should become automatic.. Integrating new social skills and thereby changing ingrained habits tends to be a long and challenging process that is to be continued outside the classroom.

Teaching Social Skills

(1) *Exploratory stage*
The exploratory stage is critical when teaching social skills. Getting students motivated to work on their social skills is a precondition for change.

Students have opinions and expectations of what they can and cannot learn or change their behaviour and in interaction with others. These ideas can be considered mental models or metacognition. A mental model represents a presupposition or mentality or way of thinking about a particular phenomenon. It is an aid to look at a more complex reality in a particular way. Although specific models can help us discover certain aspects of a phenomenon, they can also blind us to some aspects. Metacognitive knowledge is knowledge about cognitive functioning (Masui, 1999). It can be known about personal traits, tasks, strategies, procedures or condition and is partly objective (or general), and partly subjective (or personal).

Openness to personal mental models or metacognition is important during the social skills classes. Attitudes, metacognitions or mental models act as learning conditions. Let us illustrate this with an example. A student may be confronted with fellow students' positive reactions. He or she may conclude that this assertiveness is better than his or her sub-assertive behaviour. Now, if this student believes that they will never be able to react as assertively as fellow students because they are shy, then no change in behaviour will be brought about. By performing activities in which others confront them with the idea that assertiveness can be learned indeed, they may want to find out how to learn this. This is the first step in the direction of becoming more assertive. If one is convinced that changing or improving one's own behaviour is impossible, there is no motivation and willingness to learn.

To overcome this unwillingness, staff members can try to bring about changes in a student's mental model by having deep conversations. This method may not be successful though, because it is difficult to get through to people with very fixed ideas. One can also try to change attitudes or mental models by involving students in simulation games and role-plays. When acting themselves, students have to react to the given situation, and by observing their peers students may discover alternative behaviours. These personal performances and observations can then be questioned and discussed in-group. This method often works well. A final way of building attitudes is to touch people emotionally, but this method is tough to use and guide in a university course.

(2) *Elaboration stage*

At the elaboration stage, instructors need to think about how students can acquire certain social skills. It is indispensable to know what a person should do when he or she wants to change him or herself. Reflecting on your own and other people's behaviour can be enlightening: it is elucidating to see what one does and what the consequences of these actions are. When discussing this in-group, students are invited to think about behavioural alternatives. If there are any, they can try them out and practice them. Showing model behaviours or video cases may be helpful as well.

(3) *Integration stage*

The integration stage should be realized outside the classroom. We try to support and encourage students to go through this stage by creating open-task-tension and by focusing on long-term perspectives. Students should keep working on their own skills because they want to improve these skills and not because they have to pass an exam. At the end of each session, we ask students to write down one skill they would like to practice in the upcoming period. In order to get some feedback and support on their own performance, we ask students to pair up, so that they can continually monitor each other's behaviour and coach each other as necessary. At the end of the period students write down both positive and negative experiences and formulate ways to improve them. These will then be discussed later. The social skills course is wound up with a paper. Students write a paper in which they mention a few skills that they would like to keep working on and then formulate a plan of action. Two months later, they look back to their plans and their results and share this with their teacher.

KEY COMPETENCIES IN ESD

A list of key competencies people have to acquire early and update throughout their lives dealing with sustainability are given in Table 22.1 (LNE, 2017).

The above competencies also have common ground with research competencies, competencies of entrepreneurship as well as international and intercultural competencies.

RESEARCH IN ESD

As we must move from *problem focused* (understanding systemic challenges and the need for transitions) towards *solution oriented applications* (identifying knowledge, skills and governance approaches for transition) then also our research topics and approaches must undergo a transition.

Table 22.1. Key competencies in ESD (Ploum, 2017)

Name of key competence	Definition
System thinking competence	The ability to collectively analyse complex systems across different domains and across different scales, thereby considering cascading effects, inertia, feedback loops and other systemic features related to sustainability issues and sustainability problem-solving frameworks
Anticipatory competence	The ability to collectively analyse, evaluate, and craft rich "pictures" of the future related to sustainability issues and sustainability problem-solving frameworks."
Normative competence	The ability to collectively map, specify, apply, reconcile, and negotiate sustainability values, principles, goals and targets
Strategic competence	The ability to collectively design and imple-ment interventions, transitions, and transformative governance strategies toward sustainability
Interpersonal competence	The ability to motivate, enable, and facilitate collaborative and participatory sustainability research and problem solving

ENERGY (OF BUILDINGS) AND GHG

Since the industrial revolution in the 18th century, energy management has moved from short CO_2 cycles towards a longer CO_2 cycle as local biomass and local sustainable energy resources and no longer sufficient so we began to use fossil fuels. The rapidly increasing use of fossil fuels has led to a concentration of more than 400 ppm of CO_2 in the atmosphere (WMO, 2014). In 2007, the European heads of state and government stressed the need to increase energy efficiency and also lower the degree of reliance on fossil fuels.

Recently the EU also articulated a long-term goal for 2050 and the European commission decided within the 2030 Framework for Climate and Energy to increase these goals in comparison to the 2020 targets, in between brackets namely: a reduction in at least 40% GHG emissions (20%), at least 27% share of renewable energy (20%), and at least 27% improvement in Energy Efficiency (20%) and, 15% interconnection (10%) (EC, 2014).

As the conditioning of buildings is responsible for 40% of energy consumption and 36% of CO_2 emissions in the EU, there is a also a strong focus to reduce the energy consumption of buildings (EC, 2016).

The 2010 Energy Performance of Buildings Directive and the 2012 Energy Efficiency Directives are the EU's main forms of legislation. On the 30 November 2016 the Commission proposed an update to the Energy Performance of Buildings

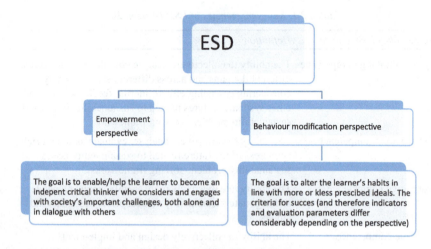

Figure 22.4. ESD from the empowerment and the behaviour modification perspective (based on Læssøe, 2009)

Table 22.2. Research transition in ESD

Research that is disciplined focussed =>	Research that is inter-and multidisciplinary
Research that has academic impact =>	Research that has social impact
Research that informs =>	Research that transforms
Research on technological and behaviour change =>	Research that focuses on social and structural change
Research as expert =>	Research as a partner
Research on people =>	Research with people

Directive to help promote the use of smart technology in buildings and to streamline the existing rule (EC, 2016).

CLEAN TECHNOLOGIES

Environmental technologies have been strongly modified since their first development in the early 1960's. The first environmental technologies, were designed as "end of pipe" technologies, and moved towards cleaner technologies with a focus on reducing their environmental impacts during the whole life cycle (Yarime, 2003). Clean technology is often defined as "any product, service or process that delivers value using limited or zero non-renewable resources and/or creates significantly less waste than conventional offerings" (Pernick, 2007).

At this time, clean technologies are divided into six subcategories: environmentally friendly energy and energy storage; the circular economy; sustainable water

SUSTAINABLE EDUCATION

Environmentally-friendly Energy & Energy Storage	Circular Economy	Sustainable Water Management	Sustainable Mobility	Resource & Material Efficiency	Energy Efficiency
Power Generation with Renewable Energy	Waste Collection & Transport	Water Procurement & Treatment	Alternative Fuels	Cross-sectional Technology	Industry-specific Energy-efficient Production Processes
Photovoltaic Energy Solarthermal Energy Geothermal Energy Wind Energy Bioenergy Sewage gas	Infrastructure Waste Separation & Sorting Technology	Groundwater Monitoring Water Purification	Biofuels Natural Gas Hybrid Drive Electrical Drive Fuel Cell Drive	Biotechnology Nanotechnology Mechanical Engineering/ Process Technology	Automation & Control Technology Efficient Engines Heat Recovery
Environmentally-Friendly Use of Fossil Fuels	Waste Utilisation	Water Utilisation	Alternative Drive Technology	New Materials	Efficient Appliances
Combined Cycle Power Plant Cogeneration Plants High-Performance Power Stations CO_2-reduced Power Generation	Recycling Thermal Waste Treatment	Components of the Water Distribution System Water Distribution Grid	Efficient Combustion Engines Environmentally-friendly Vehicle Design	Compound Materials Bioplastiscs	Electric Appliances Information & Communication Technology Illumination
Storage Technologies	Waste Disposal	Efficiency Increases In Water Utilisation	Infrastructure & Traffic Control	Material-efficient Processes	Energy Efficient Buildings
Mechanical Storage Electrochemical Storage Electrical Storage Thermal Storage	Safeguarding & Removal of Contaminants & Hazardous Waste Reduction/ Utilisation of Landfill Gas	Water-efficient Technology in the Residential Sector Water-efficient Technology in the Commercial Sector	Intelligent Traffic Control Integrated Traffic Infrastructure Electric Charging Stations Natura Gas Fuelling Stations	Optimisation of Existing Processes Utilisation of New Materials Reduction of Operating Supplies	Technical Building Equipment Building Shell (Insulation & Windows)
Efficient Grids	Environmental Remediation		Sustainable Mobility Management	Sustainable Design	
Smart Grid Local and District Heat grid	Land Rehabilitation Ecological Restoration		Carsharing Vehicle Fleet Management	Ecodesign Life Cycle Assessment	

Legend — Sector — Application — Technology

Figure 22.5. CleanTech categories (Berger, 2012)

management; sustainable mobility; resource and material efficiency; and energy efficiency (Berger, 2012). The most recent evolution in environmental technologies are directed towards the interaction between different industrial processes namely an industrial symbiosis; the waste from one industrial plant might be the input for another process (Braungart, 2002). In order to be successful new business models must be developed simultaneously (Bocken, 2012).

REGIONAL ENTREPENEURSHIP ECOSYSTEMS

Entrepreneurial ecosystems have also emerged as one of the most dynamic forces shaping the economic performance of individuals, companies and regions (Audretsch, 2017). They have become important for academic research, regional policy objectives as well as regional economic performance. This approach is related to the entrepreneurial university concept and its role in stimulating economic growth but also sustainability and adapted business models through cooperative relationships between higher education, business and government (Gibb, 2014).

Entrepreneurial Higher Education Institutions (HEIs) can act as 'anchor institutions,' embedded within and committed to a region and regional development. The entrepreneurial university as a regional anchor institution, therefore, has an important presence in the local community and makes a strategic contribution to the local economy (Culkin, 2016). These activities go beyond the business school, extend across the institution and embrace a more extensive network. This involves alternative forms of entrepreneurship education via pedagogical innovations and practice-based learning outside the classroom.

Regional entrepreneurship ecosystems are emerging with highly motivated student and academic entrepreneurs who are not just becoming future employees but alternatively are then setting up their own businesses during their study program or after graduation. The HEI's can provide support directly themselves or refer potential entrepreneurs to specialized start-up support services within the regional entrepreneurship ecosystem.

The proposed strategic model is that of the networked incubator (Hansen, 2000; Roseira, 2014). This is a type of business incubator that is well suited to grow businesses. It has features in common with other incubators such as fostering and promoting a spirit of entrepreneurship and offers economies of scale. A networked incubator can provide tremendous value to a start-up team through connections that help forge crucial strategic partnerships, recruit highly talented people, the forging of marketing and technology relationships between them and assistance in obtain advice from outside experts. Networked incubators also provide value through preferential network access, preferential access to potential partners and advisers. With the help of such an incubator, start-ups can network to obtain resources and forge partnerships with others quickly, allowing them to establish themselves in the marketplace ahead of their competitors. According to Segers, a country study for Belgium, the entrepreneurial spirit of educational institutions can enhance student's start-up intentions (1989). Student's participating in entrepreneurship education are more likely to start their own business and their companies tend to be more innovative and more successful than those led by persons without entrepreneurship education backgrounds (European Union, 2015).

RESULTS

Both HEI (PXL and UHasselt) are active in all domains of sustainable development (research, education, campus greening…).

THE STUDENT STARTUP PROGRAM (BOTH HEI)

An important feature of the emerging entrepreneurial ecosystem in the Limburg region is StudentStartUP, a joint venture of PXL University College and Hasselt University. The PXL Center for Entrepreneurship (the next StudentStartUP) project was set up in 2013 and motivated by the belief that graduates are not just becoming future employees but alternatively are setting up their own businesses as highly motivated student and academic entrepreneurs. Entrepreneurial thinking is a part of the PXL mission statement; "education and research are aligned with the development of the region and the regional entrepreneurship ecosystem."

StudentStartUP follows a 'quadruple helix' approach where the regional government, business partners, PXL University College, Hasselt University and the community (cities, civilians, and other regional stakeholders) are working towards a common goal of changing the regional mindset of risk adversity and nurturing a more entrepreneurial mindset.

The timeline concerning the StudentStartUP project is presented in Figure 22.6.

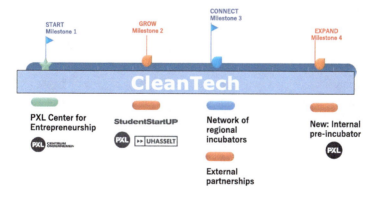

Figure 22.6. Timeline StudentStartUp PXL-UHasselt

StudentStartUP provides start-up support to foster undergraduate/graduate entrepreneurship. This is done by triggering and coaching student/academic entrepreneurs and helping them to connect with a growing network of incubators. Backed by a vast network of like-minded entrepreneurs and partners, StudentStartUP helps student entrepreneurs with their entrepreneurial endeavours. Aspiring student-entrepreneurs can also be granted a special status that provides them with a flexible study and exam schedule to make the best of their entrepreneurial venture.

Some strategic partnerships have also been formed. StudentStartUP is closely linked to a private-public partnership network with employers' organizations (strategy and support), law (IP) and tax advisory firms, banks (start-up incubation via Startit@KBC), human resources specialists, government organizations (Enterprise Agency; IMEC), local role models, business angels and the Blue Health Innovation Center (IT, health, media). StudentStartUP is also a founding member of Limburg StartUP, a regional startup association. Our student-entrepreneurs have access and are part of the new incubators that emerged in the Limburg region in recent years.

In Limburg, each incubator has its own focus. In the context of sustainability, we intend to emphasize the incubators GreenVille (the hotspot for Cleantech) and IncubaTHOR (focus on Energy). The activities of the other incubators include: Agropolis focusing on new agriculture; BikeVille aimed at the bicycle industry; BioVille focusing on health & care; C-mine Crib is for the creative economy; and Corda INCubator serves ICT. Student entrepreneurs can build partnerships with other start-ups and existing new tech companies and their (international) networks. They can also use various facilities such as dedicated workspaces.

In Table 22.3, the results for the PXL University College are represented.

Table 22.3. Start-up initiatives in PXL University College

Department	Numbers 2015–2016	%	Numbers 2016–2017	%
PXL Business	24	27	22	25
PXL Tech	14	16	15	17
PXL IT	14	16	27	31
PXL Social Work	10	11	4	5
PXL Healthcare	8	9	5	6
PXLMedia and tourism	7	8	9	10
PXL Art	4	5	1	1
PXL	4	5	2	2
PXL Education	3	3	2	2

These activities are very important: The results show that the incentives have a large recruitment so far. In addition, all departments of the PXL University College are active. About 350 student-entrepreneurs were coached by StudentStartUP in the period 2013–2017.

In 2016, At UHasselt, 35 students from all faculties signed up for the Entrepreneurship course to get them acquainted with the DNA of entrepreneurship. Through this course and from our many contacts with students, it appears that there is a need for training in the knowledge and skills of business planning. In 2016, the Faculty of Business Economics prepared two new courses as 'building blocks for a business plan, the theory' and 'drawing up a business plan, the practice' to include extracurricular or optional courses in the curriculum of the next academic year. Both UHasselt and PXL grant the student entrepreneur status that provides teaching and examination facilities at the request of the student.

UHasselt and PXL are also partners in the ERDF project PITCH PLEASE together with the city of Hasselt. This project aims to develop entrepreneurial ecosystems in student cities for youth and students (18 to 25 years of age). All relevant local stakeholders (the quadruple helix) (the city, higher education institutions, student associations, youth associations, intermediaries, profit and non-profit organizations) are connected in a collaborative endeavour to support youth in their entrepreneurial dreams and mindset.

By means of

(1) informational, inspirational and activating activities,
(2) community building practices and
(3) several support services (mentoring, (peer) coaching, learning sessions) young people get the chance to tap into this resourceful ecosystem to realize their entrepreneurial dream. Lecturers and youth workers are encouraged and supported in rendering entrepreneurial education.

In further work, we also report on the sustainability aspects and introduction of new business models. Although, it is clear that as the ESD concept is more and more introduced in both HEI (see further) and as there is a growing network of all stakeholders (quadruple helix), the behaviour of future generations, 'decision-makers,' is more and more directed towards sustainable transition. In addition, the UHasselt realize spin-offs activities. Spin-offs are companies whose primary business activity is based on university research results. Several spin-offs (11) have arisen within different domains (*ICT, linguistic, mobility, cleantech and life science*).

UHASSELT

General

Renewing an entire economy is not the work of one player. The FRIS model bundles all the players in the quadruple helix model. The Full Regional Innovation System (FRIS), is an innovative concept based on the idea that innovation is not a linear process from research on development to a marketable new product or service, but rather a web-like process with complex interactions between companies and knowledge institutions. These are at all stages of the research, development and commercialization process. The FRIS optimally anticipates this new reality that all actors are brought together and can interact at every stage of the innovation process. In this sense, the FRIS is a concrete design of a domain-specific and regional innovation web.

Cleantech Management

Cleantech is one of the foci of the Strategic Action Plan for the province of Limburg, where Hasselt University is located, after the closure of the Ford factory in Genk. One of the conditions for realizing a Full Regional Innovation System (FRIS) in such a policy focus is that a lifelong learning program is installed. CleanTechPunt, a non-profit organization for cleantech education, launched some elementary educational programs on cleantech in 2011. However, some participants indicated that they needed more elaboration on the academic program. During the academic year 2014–2015, a research group on Environmental Economics prepared a postgraduate program on Cleantech Management.

Curriculum development process. First, a *steering committee* was installed consisting of representatives of all relevant sectoral and educational partners in the province, (i.e. Hasselt University, university colleges PXL and UCLL, CleanTechPunt, the cleantech incubator Greenville and the umbrella organization i-Cleantech Flanders). The steering committee identified themes around which academic cleantech education should be provided: (i) energy, (ii) materials, (iii) building and mobility, (iii) ecosystem services and (iv) natural resources. Subsequently, *thematic working groups* consisting of cleantech experts at the educational partners were established in order to determine the required learning content and potential lecturers. Finally, a program was proposed to a *sounding board of cleantech companies*, which suggested slight changes. Hence, all relevant stakeholders in a FRIS were consulted in shaping the postgraduate program.

Goal and content of the program. The target audience of the program consists of the employees of firms who have a responsibility to make their organization more sustainable, and employees of government agencies that are responsible for designing policies for the transition towards a more sustainable and circular economy.

The goal of the new curriculum was to teach participants how to introduce clean technologies to the market. For this purpose, three categories of competencies were identified:

- *technological competences:* participants should understand the working principles of state-of-the-art clean technologies;
- *management competencies:* participants should be able to make a scientifically underpinned investment and policy decisions based on techno-economic and sustainability assessment;

- *communication competences:* participants should be able to communicate with and convince stakeholders for cleantech such as financial institutions, government agencies and the local community.

To be able to achieve these competencies, a modular program of 26 sessions were developed consisting of four technological modules (Energy and materials; Space, building & mobility; Ecosystem services and Natural resources). one overarching module related to management competencies (CleanTech Analysis) and a closing module on cleantech communication (CleanTech Impact). Evaluation consisted of an assigned portfolio for each of the four technological modules, in which participants had to show they had mastered technological knowledge by selecting from assignments tailored to their own professional needs. The CleanTech Analysis and Impact modules were evaluated using a postgraduate thesis, in which participants had to show they could develop a business case for a clean technology of their choice.

Awards achieved. The first edition of the course ran from January 2016 until August 2017, when the last of the participants defended their thesis. One of the participants, Pieter Grauls, won the award for best thesis in the category 'environmental professional' of VMx – the Flemish association for environmental professionals. The student wrote a thesis about 3D printing as an alternative production process for sealing rings at Saint-Gobain Performance Plastics Kontich in Belgium. He analyzed 3D printing both from an environmental and economic perspective. He performed a *techno-economic analysis* (TEA) for a first screening of the profitability of 3D printing, including uncertainty analysis in order to give direction to investment opportunities at Saint-Gobin. This combination convinced the jury to grant him the award.

Conclusion and future changes. A satisfaction survey among the participants also showed that they were delighted with the program: especially the module on techno-economic analysis (CleanTech Analysis). Moreover, participants indicated they would like to learn more about sustainability analysis (such as LCA) and valuation of environmental benefits. On the other hand, an enquiry amongst companies in the bio-based economy showed that companies expected future employees to possess of a broad range of competencies, including business-modelling techniques. Therefore, the postgraduate program is being revised in two directions: (i) technologically to include the domain of the bio-based economy and (ii) economically to include a broader range of business competencies. The revision has been made possible by the financial support of the European Fund for Regional Development Interreg Vlaanderen-Nederland and the province of Limburg.

Postgraduate Environmental Coordinator

The tasks, responsibilities and liabilities of the environmental coordinator are summarized in the Decree of 5 April 1995, Decree on General Provisions relating to Environmental Policy and VLAREM II, Part 4.

The program of Environmental Coordinator Level A at the UHasselt is made up of 3 courses, with an integration piece (final work) and company visits. In total, the education takes 1.5 years to complete.

This course has existed for more than 20 years but has always evolved with actual needs.

The target audience of the program consists of

- Managers and experts in profit and non-non-profit organizations responsible for making their organization more sustainable
- Consultants assisting organizations in designing and implementing sustainability measures
- Policy-makers responsible for the transition towards a more sustainable and circular economy
- Environmental coordinators as determined in Vlarem who wish to update their knowledge in cleantech

Many environmental issues are linked (ecotoxicology, environmental law and policy, environmental management systems) with quality, safety, sustainability and environmental technology. However, the interdisciplinary character of the association is a major challenge in these courses (technology in relation with economy, environment, people etc.).

This is reflected in the composition of our steering committee with external specialists from different disciplines (science, law, economist, society, industry, NGO, ….)

The training given by our own experts, connected to an interdisciplinary research Centre for Environmental Sciences, in combination with external specialists coming from all stakeholders (knowledge centres, governments, society) is not only focused on becoming familiar with legal requirements, but also with regard to *solution oriented applications* (identifying knowledge, skills and governance approaches for transition). We did not only want to inform them about trends like Green, Blue, Circular, Resource Efficient, Low Carbon, Bio, Smart and Digital Economies, we wanted them to understand the impact of these trends on existing and new activities in a proactive way. In this way they learn how they could create new and sustainable business opportunities.

In this context, it is useful to look at the evaluation of participants in the course

- Students have to write a paper dealing with the previous mentioned topics
- Students need to set up a portfolio in view of their communication skills.
- Students have a lot of open book/real cases to be solved during the exams and thes are tailored to the professional needs of the participant

SDG in Faculties in UHasselt

Very recently, an organization of working groups and workshops that facilitate the introduction of the SDGs in all faculties at UHasselt was launched. The well-defined goals of the SDGs, and their implementation into sustainable management policy and education is its task. In addition, special attention will be given on the SDGs and the importance of community engagement.

It is clear that at UHasselt the topics of sustainability have been introduced in many faculties and in different programs, some for an extended period. While it is evident that the content of the topics has been realized howver, the learning process has also shifted.

In some courses, there is now a co-creation between economics students and technical professors. They now interpret together academic papers dealing with technology and new (sustainable) business models.

As one example, we highlight a course in the Faculty of Business Economics: in the program "Masters of business engineering." Here a specialization of 'Technology, Innovation and Environmental Management' was introduced in 2008. This specialization covers courses like Technological innovations, Sustainability analysis, Business development for technology, Economic policies for technological development and Energy and environment: a multidisciplinary analysis.

This type of multi- and interdisciplinarity is also happening in our own research: with multidisciplinary cooperation within the Center for Environment of faculty from the sciences, medicine and economics. For example in the cleanup of heavy metal contaminated soils:

- Benefits: avoided medical costs (osteoporosis) of habitants involved.
- Cost: least costly through phytoremediation (remediation with plants) of heavy metal contaminated soils.
- Recuperation of the biomass as a valuable feedstock to produce renewable energy.

PXL

The University College

PXL is a centre of expertise for innovation, creativity and entrepreneurship. PXL organizes its activities starting from the 'quadruple helix model' (interaction between government, knowledge institutes, industry and society). Moreover, the university strives to work in an interdisciplinary way in both its teaching and research domains. Consequently, in education, its attention is directed towards authenticity for cases, teachers as well as for students.

Now, the PXL-Tech campus of the University College PXL is organized as a living lab for all occupants in the building and sustainability and this is a policy in the department because

1. Innovative answers are needed for many complex societal challenges
2. Social themes such as spatial planning, energy, agriculture, nutrition, social inequality and health care require a new approach.

3. Technology plays an important role here, sustainable action is, in a technological department, an important core value.
4. Sustainability is included as a policy theme in the institutional review.
5. Graduates are more broadly formed and thus have more opportunities on the labour market (Sustainable and circular economy, ...).
6. A growing group of students also expects the University College to incorporate sustainability into its policy.
7. Advantages to the outside world (making an annual sustainability report,).

PG EES (Steering Committee, Course Content, Dissemination of New Knowledge)

The reduction of energy consumption with the use of more renewable energies (decreasing greenhouse gas emissions) is a priority on the climate agenda. It is apparent that even building professionals lacked specific knowledge and insights in order to enable the transition towards more energy efficiency and a low carbon society. In addition, energy projects will not be a top priority if they are not linked to new business models. Therefore, the PXL has taken the initiative to organize a customized postgraduate Energy Efficiency Services (PG EES) course including new insights for the conditioning of buildings together with new business models. It was developed with the interaction of several dedicated stakeholders: BELESCO (association Belgium), Infrax (a public ESCo), Encon (a private ESCo), Dubolim (sustainable building) and the (local) government of the province of Limburg (Franco, 2016) (an example of a quadruple helix).

There are three core modules in this course:

1. Energy efficiency services dealing with buildings (with special attention towards iterative project cycles including the topics of audits, measurements and verification and the role for facilitators). In addition, the link between building and mobility is a subject, as well as attention to monuments.
2. In the second module, life cycle costing is the main subject. In addition aspects of the circular economy and green value/added value are explained. Special attention is also given to the new trend (and EC obligations) to incorporate sustainability into public procurement processes.
3. Communication.
   Special attention towards internal and external communication in combination with a change management strategy. Sustainability and sustainable business models are chosen to run through the whole course.

The course addresses (policy, technical and financial) interests from government, SMEs, energy agencies and energy experts, architects, consultants, schools, real estate companies, financial institutions, ESCOs and ESCO facilitators, and facility managers, The course is very hands on and therefore the evaluation consists of:

- Students have a lot of open book/real cases to be solved during the exams tailored to the professional needs of the participant

- Students have on-going evaluation for the communication module
- Students make calculations on real (public, private) EE projects with a special attention towards sustainability in procurement.

The PG EES was successfully launched, and other initiatives which are likely to affect the dissemination of this knowledge, have been taken. These include lectures, seminars, practical exercises, interaction with stakeholders, partners in the steering committee, matchmaking events, speed dating, master thesis, etc. with special attention towards the impacts of these EE projects in the public as well as in the private sector.

In addition, the students have started new businesses dealing with Energy efficiency. Sometimes these are subcontracts to assist the public sector in achieving its climate goals, working with innovative tools like an Energy Performance Contract (EPC) or by using an ESCO (Energy Service Company). Other graduates from the PG EES partnered with an established engineering company and an established installer to set up an integrated service covering the full ESCO process starting from screening improvement opportunities in prospective enterprises to advising on optimal energy solutions, to full engineering and project management including maintenance, surveillance and warranties for energy utilities. These solutions also include a full range of financing options.

EPC in PXL

The PXL also organizes a customized postgraduate Energy Efficiency Services (PG EES) including new technical insights and new business models. Based on a philosophy of applying the good practices taught in the PG EES to their own buildings. The the PXL also initiated an Energy Quick Scans (EQS) project in order

Table 22.4. Different Scopes for an EPC contracting

Scope of the EPC project	Actions
EPC maintained	Recommissioning Quick wins
EPC techniques	Measures in the fields of production, distribution and emission of heating and sanitary hot water with a payback time (PBT) of max. 12 years Renovation / optimization of stoves and fireplaces Renovation of Sanitary hot water installations Place insulating reflectors behind the radiators Relamping and relighting
EPC Building envelop	Improvement of the building shell (PBT max 20 y) Replacing old windows and doors, overhauling roofs Isolation walls

Table 22.5. Base and enhanced case PXL buildings

Topic	Base case	Enhanced case
Consumption Total (kWh/y)	9.891.356	9.891.356
Consumption Total (kWh/m2/y)	136.9	136.9
Consumption Total (€/y)	778.044	778.044
Consumption Total (€/m2/y)	10.8	10.8
Total investment (€)	2.610903	4.145.854
Total investment (€/m2)	36.1	57.4
Annual savings (kWh/y)	3.329.616	4.156.002
Annual savings (kWh/m2/y)	46.1	57.5
Annual savings (kWh/y)	3.065465	3.869.488
Annual savings incl rel (kWh/m2/y)	42.4	53.6
Annual savings (€/y)	242.569	296.581
Annual savings (€/m2/y)	3.4	4.1
Annual savings (€/y)	226.720	271.940
Annual savings (€/m2/y)	3.1	3.8
Annual Savings total (%)	33.66	42.02
Annual Savings total incl effect rel (%)	30.99	39.12
Payback Time (y)	11.5	15.2
Reduction CO2 (ton/y)	606	762

to assess the potential for energy savings. As at the PXL-tech campus, the concept of a living lab for all occupants is being applied and sustainability is now integrated into policy. The campus can function as a pilot project in the roll out of this approach.

The results of these EQS cases highlight the potential for heating, ventilation, cooling, lighting and insulation on the outer shell. The recommendations are described based on a base case (33,66% energy savings) and an enhanced case (42,02% energy savings).

Living Lab

The PXL-Tech department is a trendsetter in view of the living lab campus approach for all occupants as well as the introduction of sustainability in their policy and educational activities. Reecently researchers in a collaboration with students and the the campus manager set up some.an applied project financed by PXL and carried out in lectures eventually making recommendations regarding water consumption, electricity and gas consumption at the inuversity. With this experience and the interest of the building users, it seems evident that this PXL Tech campus can function as

SUSTAINABLE EDUCATION

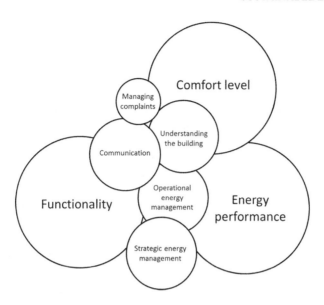

Figure 22.7. Different types of interaction in order to obtain good energy performance

a pilot project in the rollout of many new ideas. As this project facilitates further knowledge exchange, the PXL-Tech campus as living lab environment makes this the ideal pilot which can then be rolled out in other high-energy buildings in the PXL.

Figure 22.7 shows the interaction needed to come to a good energy performance of building (Franco, 2017).

Interactions between the physical environment and students' knowledge, attitudes and behaviours are crucial for EE projects in HEI. The link between sustainability and well-being offers the opportunity to shift the attention of students to corporate social responsibility (CSR) in combination with the UN's SDGs. The PXL will next undertake an energy literacy survey in the context of this living lab initiative and in strong collaboration with Plymouth University (UK) and University of Beira Interior (UBI) in Portugal to compare their results. Data on students' energy-related attitudes and the effects of EE projects on their health and wellbeing will be collected through a survey of students. This will take the form of a self-administered online questionnaire, based on that used in the UK and Portugal (Cotton, Miller, Winter, Bailey, & Sterling, 2015; Cotton, Shiel, & Do Paco, 2016). Future data from PXL University College will be situated within the context of a rollout of this approach to other locations.

In the next step, there is now a need to communicate clearly about future intentions. The PXL Tech department published a sustainability report (PXL, 2017). While the Global Reporting Initiative (GRI) is often used in industrial concerns it is also relevant in HEI. S ustainability reporting guidelines were used in this reporting while also providing background on what the organization communicates about its economic, environmental and social performance and impact.

CONCLUSIONS

Today's college and university students might be the first generation to face such intense economic, political and ecological instability simultaneously while also realizing humanity's growing inability to sustain living systems on the earth (Muligan, 2017). Therefore, it is important to involve students in possible solutions as these examples are among the first and strongest influences on an individual's behaviour. In addition, we have transformed our educational practices towards Education 3.0; teacher and student centre-stage, personalized development, room for professionals, a balance between knowledge and competencies, stimulating and motivating with minimal bureaucracy (Rotmans, 2017).

We are convinced that the given case studies in two HEI are an essential contribution in a 'quadruple helix' interaction towards a sustainable paradigm shift.

This offers in it an opportunity to shift the attention of all stakeholders (and student in particular) towards a corporate social responsibility in combination with the SDGs.

ACKNOWLEDGEMENTS

The revision of the cleantech program is financed within the Interreg V program Flanders-Netherlands, through a cross-border cooperation program with financial support from the European Fund for Regional Development. The views expressed in this chapter are solely the responsibility of the authors. The authors are very grateful to Christine Schoeters, Laura Franco and Viviane Mebis in assisting to finalize an earlier version of this chapter.

REFERENCES

Audretsch, D. B., & Link, A. N. (2017). *Universities and the entrepreneurial ecosystem.* London: Edward Elgar.
Azeiteiro, U. M., Caeiro, S., Disterhelft, A., & Filho, W. L. (2013). Sustainability science and education for sustainable development in universities: A way for transition. In S. Caeiro, W. Leal Filho, C. Jabbour, & U. M. Azeiteiro (Eds.), *Sustainability assessment tools in higher education institutions* (pp. 3–27). Springer International Publishing.
Breiting, S., Læssøe, J., Schnack, K., & Rolls, S. (2009). *Climate change and sustainable development: The response from education, Cross-national reports.* Aarhus: Danish School of Education, University of Aarhus.
Braungart, M., & McDonough, W. (2002). *Cradle to cradle: Remaking the way we make things.* New York, NY: North Point Press.
Brian, A. (1994). *Increasing returns and path dependence in the economy.* Ann Arbor, MI: University of Michigan Press.
Bocken, N. (2014). Sustainable business: The new business as usual? *Journal of Industrial Ecology, Special Feature on Industrial Ecology as a Source of Competitive Advantage, 1,* 684–686.

Boyatzis, R. E., & Kolb, D. A. (1995). From learning styles to learning skills: The executive skills profile. *Journal of Managerial Psychology, 10*(5), 3–17. doi:10.1108/02683949510085938

Brundtland, G. H. (1987). *Report of the world commission on environment and development: Our common future*. United Nations.

Bruyninckx, H. (2014). European Environment Agency 'Signals 2014', Well-being and the environment. Retrieved January 10, 2018, from http://www.eea.europa.eu/publications/signals-2014/download

Christensen, C. M. (1992). Exploring the limits of the technology curve. Part I: Component technologies. *Production and Operations Management, 1*(4), 334–357.

Christensen, C. M. (2011). *The innovator's Dilemma*. Harper Business.

Chichilnisky, G. (2014, September 1–3). *Closing the carbon cycle/avoiding extinction*. Paper presented at the I-Sup Meeting, Antwerpen.

Cooke, P. (2001). Regional innovation systems, clusters, and the knowledge economy. *Industrial and Corporate Change, 10*(4), 945–974.

Cotton, D., Miller, W., Winter, J., Bailey, I., & Sterling, S. (2015). Developing students' energy literacy in higher education. *International Journal of Sustainability in Higher Education, 16*(4), 456–473.

Cotton, D. R. E., Shiel, C., & Do Paco, A. (2016). Energy saving on campus: A comparison of students' attitudes and behaviours in the UK and Portugal. *Journal of Cleaner Production, 129*, 586–595.

Crabbé, A., & Meneve J. (2013). *Innoveren met materialen: economisch potentieel, economische noodzaak*. Tielt: Lannoo.

Culkin, N. (2016). Entrepreneurial universities in the region: The force awakens ? *International Journal of Entrepreneurial Behavior & Research, 22*(1), 4–16.

David, A. D. (1985). Clio and the economics of QWERTY. *The American Economic Review, 75*(2), 332–337.

De Bruyn, G., Lemain, S., & Vander Velpen, B. (2014). Publieke eindrapportage TaBaChem MIP3 haalbaarheidsstudie (projectnr. 3211) TAke BAck CHEMicals: Upgraden van een traditioneel verkoopsmodel van chemieproducten naar een lease-sale model RHDHV 820732. Report.

De Langhe, R. (2014). A unified model of the division of cognitive labor. *Philosophy of Science, 81*(3), 444–459.

De Langhe R. (2015). The essential tension between exploration and exploitation in science. In W. Devlin & A. Bokulich (Eds.), *Kuhn's structure of scientific revolutions – 50 years on* (pp. 105–114). Springer.

Eaton, M., Hughes, H. J., & MacGregor, J. (2017). *Contemplative approaches to sustainability in higher education, theory and practice*. New York, NY & London: Routledge.

Ecocampus, duurzaam hoger onderwijs [website]. (n.d.). Retrieved January 10, 2018, from https://www.lne.be/ecocampus

European Council 2016 [website]. (n.d.). Retrieved January 10, 2018, from https://ec.europa.eu/energy/en/topics/energy-efficiency/buildings

European Council 2016 [website]. (n.d.). Retrieved January 10, 2018, from https://ec.europa.eu/energy/en/topics/energy-efficiency/energy-efficiency-directive

European Council 2014 (23 and 24 October 2014). (2014). *Conclusions on 2030 climate and energy policy framework* [website]. (n.d.). Retrieved January 10, 2018, from http://www.consilium.europa.eu/uedocs/cms_data/docs/pressdata/en/ec/145356.pdf

European Union 2015 [website]. (n.d.). *Entrepreneurship education: A road to success: Final Report & case studies*. Retrieved January 10, 2018, from http://ec.europa.eu/growth/tools-databases/newsroom/cf/itemdetail.cfm?item_id=8056&lang=nl

Experpanel [website]. (n.d.). *De SDG's zijn voor bedrijven het nieuwe winnen*. Retrieved January 10, 2018, from https://www.duurzaambedrijfsleven.nl/future-leadership/24021/expertpanel-de-sdgs-zijn-voor-bedrijven-het-nieuwe-winnen

Freed, M., & Felder, F. A. (2017). Non-energy benefits: Workhorse or unicorn of energy efficiency programs? *The Electricity Journal, 30*(1), 43–46.

Franco, D., De Langhe, R., & Venken, J. (2016). *Energy efficiency services in buildings: A tool for energy transition Central Europe towards Sustainable Building* (p. 215).

Franco, D., Verhulst, E., Dubois, E., & Cruyplandt, E. (2017). *Energy efficiency services in buildings: The importance of social component between the quadruple helix partners*. 1st International Conference on Energy Research and Social Science.

Gibb, A. A. (2014). *The entrepreneurial higher education institution: A review of the concept and its relevance today*. Retrieved January 10, 2018, from https://heinnovate.eu/intranet/tef/downloads/HEInnovate_Analytical%20paper.pdf

Hansen, M. T., Chesbrough, H. W., Nohria, N., & Sull, D. N. (2000). Networked incubators: Hothouses of the new economy. *Harvard Business Review, 78*(5), 74–84.

Hermsen J. J. (2014). *Kairos, Een nieuwe bevlogenheid*. Utrecht, Amsterdam, Antwerpen: Uitgeverij de Arbeiderspers.

Huber, S., & Bassen, A. (2018). Towards a sustainability reporting guideline in higher education. *International Journal of Sustainability in Higher Education, 19*(2), 218–232.

Kuhn, T. S. (1962). *The structure of scientific revolutions*. Chicago, IL: University of Chicago Press.

Masui, C., & De Corte, E. (1999). Enhancing learning and problem solving skills: orienting and self-judging, two powerful and trainable learning tools. *Learning and Instruction, 9*(6), 517–542.

Mulligan, M. (2017). *An introduction to sustainability environmental, social and personal perspectives*. Taylor & Francis Ltd.

Pernick, R., & Wilder, C. (2007). *The clean tech revolution: The next big growth and investment opportunity*. New York, NY: Collins.

Ploum, L., Blok, V., Lans, T., & Omta, O. (2017). *Toward a validated competence framework for sustainable entrepreneurship*. Organization & Environment.

PXL. (2017). *PXL Duurzaamheidsrapport PXL-Tech*. Retrieved from https://www.pxl.be/Assets/website/media/pxl_in_de_kijker/documenten/Duurzaamheidsrapport_PXL-Tech_2016.pdf

Roland Berger, strategy consultants [website]. (n.d.). Retrieved January 10, 2018, from http://www.rolandberger.com/press_releases/512press_archive2012_sc_content/Green_tech_atlas_3_0.html

Rotmans, J. (2017). *Change of era: Our world in transition*. Amsterdam: Boom Publishers.

Rosiera, C., Ramos, C., Maia, F., & Henneberg, S. (2014). *Understanding incubator value: a network approach to university incubators* (FEP Working Paper, 532).

Rittel, H. W. J., & Webber, M. M. (1973). Dilemmas in a general theory of planning. *Policy Sciences, 4*(2), 155–169.

Segers, J. P. (1989). The spirit of enterprise in Belgium: current trends. *Journal of Small Business & Entrepreneurship, 7*(1), 54–57.

Stringer, C. (2012). *The origin of our species*. London: Allen Lane.

UN. (2017). *Communication materials* [website]. (n.d.). Retrieved January 10, 2018, from http://www.un.org/sustainabledevelopment/news/communications-material

World Meteorological Organization. (2014). *Assessment for decision-makers: Scientific assessment of ozone depletion: Global ozone research and monitoring project, 56*. Geneva: Switzerland.

Yarime, M. (2003). *From end-of-pipe technology to clean technology* (PhD dissertation). Retrieved from https://www.merit.unu.edu/training/theses/MYarime.pdf

Dirk Franco
Centre for Environmental Sciences (CMK)
UHasselt – Hasselt University, Belgium
and
PXL, Central Administration
Hasselt, Belgium

Alain De Vocht
Centre for Environmental Sciences (CMK)
UHasselt – Hasselt University
Diepenbeek, Belgium
and

PXL, Tech Universitaire Campus
Diepenbeek, Belgium

Tom Kuppens
Centre for Environmental Sciences (CMK)
UHasselt – Hasselt University, Belgium

Hilda Martens
UHasselt – Hasselt University
Diepenbeek, Belgium

Theo Thewys
Centre for Environmental Sciences (CMK)
UHasselt – Hasselt University, Belgium

Bernard Vanheusden
Centre for Environmental Sciences (CMK)
UHasselt – Hasselt University, Belgium

Marleen Schepers
PXL, Tech Universitaire Campus
Diepenbeek, Belgium

Jean Pierre Segers
PXL, Business
Hasselt, Belgium

THOMAS R. HUDSPETH

23. COMMUNICATING ABOUT GREATER BURLINGTON REGIONAL CENTRE OF EXPERTISE ON EDUCATION FOR SUSTAINABLE DEVELOPMENT (GBRCE) WITH SUSTAINABILITY STORIES

CONTEXT: THE NINTH WORLD ENVIRONMENTAL EDUCATION CONGRESS (WEEC-9)

Four decades after the Tbilisi Intergovernmental Conference on Environmental Education; three decades after the publication of *Our Common Future* or the Brundtland Report, in which the United Nations World Commission on Environment and Development (1987) placed the concept of sustainable development on the international agenda; and two decades after the 1997 NAAEE Conference in Vancouver, British Columbia, entitled "Weaving Connections: Cultures and Environments", established non-traditional inclusive sharing communities ranging from aboriginal and indigenous peoples, youth, world cultures to academic communities; the ninth World Environmental Education Congress (WEEC-9), entitled "Culture/Environment: Weaving New Connections", was held in Vancouver, Canada, 9–15 September 2017.

The highlights of WEEC-9 were: the nexus or close link – even inseparability – of Culture and Environment and the multidisciplinarity of EE/SE; a reminder that the dichotomy between environment and economy is a false one, and that sustainability involves addressing the three Es: Ecological integrity, Economic feasibility, Equity or social justice, or the three Ps: People, Planet, and Profit; recognition of the need to go beyond knowledge to action and empowerment, extending beyond mere tinkering to transformative change in the field of EE/SE and profound cultural shift or paradigm shift in our larger society; the necessity for active citizenship, using all the tools available to us; extending beyond individual change to also include structural change; emphasis on systems thinking and the importance of developing leverage points; acknowledgment of differences in the way we all see the world, in our ways of knowing, and the importance of the words we use, our language, in sending strong messages to each other, especially in this era of "fake news"; recognition of generational shift and emphasis on youth voice and youth action; welcoming any and all who can assist in working toward a more sustainable future – scientists, activists, organizers, artists, politicians, those who speak truth to power, etc.; the U.N.

Sustainability Development Goals (SDGs) remind us that we need to learn from each other, work together, and become a unified "we"; challenging, even disrupting, the status quo or business as usual, especially our addiction to overconsumption, greed, acquisition, and unsustainable lifestyles in the West, often using compelling stories to share alternatives to mainstream ways of thinking and acting; getting serious about addressing climate change head-on; recognition that community-building, social cohesion, solidarity, feeling of responsibility for each other (as we witnessed with forest fires in California and the Pacific Northwest, floods in the South, and Hurricanes Katrina, Irene, Harvey, Irma, and – in the case of Vermont–Hurricane Irene in 2011), and that having a shared purpose versus self-absorption and hyper-individualisim are key for resilience and for getting through uncertainty, and for countering the disintegration of social fabric and alienation that Putnam emphasizes in *Bowling Alone* (2000); we are exceeding our carrying capacity; capitalism is part of the problem, yet people are so invested in the current paradigm that they are not willing to acknowledge that or the necessity to rein in corporations driven to short term profits, rapid expansion at the expense of the natural world and our own well-being, and continued growth in a finite world with fixed amounts of resources.

However, undoubtedly the most notable and outstanding highlight, as passionately and articulately expressed by indigenous speakers Guujaaw and Jeannette Armstrong and emphasized by the other plenary speakers Wade Davis, Elizabeth May, Tara Cullis, and David Suzuki, was that indigenous peoples – by their proven track record and accumulated knowledge through experience that scientific insights will never duplicate – offer an alternative and fundamentally different worldview to the mainstream one, a different relationship with the earth that emphasizes connection to place and recognizes that the land inhabits us, we do not inhabit the land, and cherishes the importance of ancestors. Thus, their culture springs from a sense of place. Indigenous people are connected to the land and to all parts of the environment in a circular, inclusive way; they have a seamless spiritual connection to the land via spirit and recognize that the world is full of sentient life and does not just offer props for us to carry on our lives. The plenary speakers reminded us that we have to learn from indigenous peoples how to live a life in balance with nature – or, as poet and bioregionalist Gary Snyder (1999) asserts – our real work to do is to re-indigenize ourselves: "The most radical thing you can do is *stay home*". Indigenous people and their lifestyles provide an example or role model of sustainability. As David Suzuki reminds us in The Sacred Balance (1998), the traditional ecological knowledge (TEK) of indigenous peoples offers concepts, models, philosophies, and practices which can inform the design of new sustainability solutions. "Our elders tell us of the immense changes that have occurred in the span of a single human life; all you have to do is to project the rate of change they have experienced into the future to get an idea of what might be left in the coming decades. Is this progress? Is this way of life sustainable?" Four of these highlights of WEEC-9 are key elements of the Greater Burlington Regional Centre of Expertise on Education for Sustainable Development (GBRCE).

FOUR KEY ELEMENTS OF THE GREATER BURLINGTON REGIONAL CENTRE OF EXPERTISE ON EDUCATION FOR SUSTAINABLE DEVELOPMENT (GBRCE)

Need for "All Hands On Deck!": The U.N. Sustainability Development Goals (SDGs) Remind Us that We Need to Learn from Each Other, Work Together, and Become a Unified "We"

The Greater Burlington Regional Centre of Expertise on Education for Sustainable Development (GBRCE, also known as Greater Burlington Sustainability Education Network GBSEN) is one of 157 centres or networks recognized by United Nations University to promote multi-stakeholder cooperation at the local level and a global community of practice through the network of regional centres of expertise for education for sustainable development. The centres are networks of existing formal and non-formal organizations that facilitate learning about sustainable development in local communities.

The planet faces a number of sustainability challenges, from climate change and the rapid extinction of species to the necessary modification of our consumption patterns. International platforms exist to tackle each of these issues. Each of these global platforms needs to be implemented at a local level. With their official links to UN agencies, formal education institutions, and informal educators worldwide, RCEs are in an ideal position to do just that. The RCE network brings together multisectoral and interdisciplinary members who might not usually work together. As such, they are uniquely placed to help create solutions to sustainability challenges through dialogue, education, and learning. They are highly influential policy advocates, able to test policies individually and work collectively to bring policy to scale and advice on future actions.

Through these efforts, RCEs help prepare local leaders of tomorrow with the tools and information they need to make smart and sustainable choices for the future. RCE efforts encourage innovation and new approaches to sustainable development. They translate existing knowledge into concrete actions and empower individuals to make sustainable choices for themselves and their communities.

The success each RCE achieves on the local level is brought to scale through the global RCE Network worldwide. Local knowledge, expertise, and best practices are shared globally through the network and can be adapted and applied successfully in other regions. RCEs also play a central role in the transfer of global technologies, knowledge, and experiences at the local level through their programs and activities.

RCEs aspire to translate global objectives into the context of the local communities in which they operate. Upon the completion of the Decade of Education for Sustainable

Development (DESD) in 2014, RCEs are committed to further generating, accelerating, and mainstreaming ESD by implementing the Global Action Program (GAP) on ESD and contributing to the realization of the 17 Sustainable Development Goals (SDGs; see Figure 23.1). GAP has five priority areas of action: advancing policy by mainstreaming ESD, transforming learning and training environments using the whole-institution approach, building capacities of educators and trainers, empowering and mobilizing youth, and finally accelerating sustainable solutions at the local level. At all levels of society, RCEs play a crucial role in implementing these goals using their local knowledge and global network (http://www.rcenetwork.org/portal/rce-vision-and-mission).

Figure 23.1. Sustainable Development Goals (2015)

GBRCE is part of a network of 157 RCEs across the world. It promotes education, training, and public awareness to create a sustainable future for the greater Burlington region. Its goal is to promote the work of sustainability practitioners in this area and encourage collaboration to strengthen existing and new sustainability initiatives. GBRCE is a network of stakeholders from multiple sectors (see below) mobilized to both integrate education into sustainable development and integrate sustainable development into education in their local and regional communities.

Acknowledging that it will take all of us working together – involving discussion, dialogue, debate engaging *all* cultures and sectors and drawing on *all* academic disciplines – to address complex, "wicked", (large in scope and scale) planetary-scale problems and challenges of the Anthropocene such as climate change and poverty alleviation, the network recognizes the importance of working in transdisciplinary teams and of collaboration, teamwork, cooperation, coordination, partnerships, working together, linking, and networking. Further, it promotes diversity, inclusion, and equity in all aspects of its work and honours the beliefs, attitudes, language, interpersonal styles, and values of all individuals. Recognizing that a wide array of perspectives allows all organizations to be more effective, the network draws from:

1. culture and environment, closely linked and inseparable. The discipline of ecology should have recognized humans as part of the system early in the development of the science, but it has been a slow process. Urban ecology arose as a sub-discipline to begin to acknowledge that connection, but it took many years before coupled human-natural systems, and then social-ecological systems, began to take hold in our consciousness.
2. the three Es of sustainability: Ecological integrity or Environment, Economic feasibility, and Equity or social justice; or the three Ps of sustainability: People, Planet, and Profits.
3. various sectors: individuals, NGOs, higher education, K-12 schools, businesses, government, the faith community, media. It uses education as a tool to create a sustainable future for the greater Burlington region (the Vermont portion of the Lake Champlain basin) through promoting the work of sustainability practitioners there and encouraging collaboration to strengthen existing sustainability initiatives and stitching together on-going activities (versus creating new ones from scratch). To improve effectiveness and create tangible improvements in its communities, it uses *collective impact* (Hanleybrown, Kania, & Kramer, 2012) – a framework for cross-sector coordination/collaboration to initiate large-scale social change – to connect research and practice, to promote the work of sustainability practitioners, and to be *inclusive*, where all participants help "consciously create the future they want"(Wilson 1980), "tell the world of the future into being" (Flowers 2013), and devise a *shared* vision of change through effective envisioning approaches.
4. all five of the capitals recognized by ecological economists (natural, built/manufactured/produced, human, economic/financial/fiscal, and social; with emphasis on social capital given the size and scale of RCEGB and the importance of community in resilience).
5. individuals and groups working on all 17 of the United Nations Sustainable Development Goals.
6. examples from all WEEC-9 themes as well as many other related topics.

Effective Environmental Communication

As revelations increase almost daily about the severity of climate change and other sustainability issues, many people report an increased sense of urgency and a feeling of being overwhelmed with "doom and gloom", despair, paralysis, and inaction for lack of knowing where to intervene and how to make a difference. That is more reason for environmental communication to not succumb to focusing on fear, but rather on hope and inspiration. This is especially important in our present era where information from scientific sources is no longer being trusted, but in competition with other information which is not solid or backed by evidence; and where readers and viewers are exposed to "fake news" regularly.

Journalism, and the democratic functions it needs to perform, is in crisis. The state of the mainstream media has been degraded, along with the decline of its business models. Tens of thousands of layoffs, cutbacks, and closures have hollowed out reporting jobs and news coverage, especially away from the coastal large cities (the shift from print to digital has concentrated the news business more than ever in New York City, Washington, and a few other coastal cities), in rural areas, and at the local level. (Unlike most of the country, Vermont is fortunate to have a vibrant ecosystem of media – radio, TV, dailies, weeklies, monthlies – many of which are bucking the national trends of decline and attracting national attention for doing so). Meanwhile, remaining journalistic outlets are under assault from many directions, including the White House, the rise of "fake news" and misinformation and lies on Facebook and other social media, the continued rise of personalized social feeds and the content that spreads easily within them, filter bubbles (Websites we visit collect personal data about us and tailor themselves to us. Our past interests determine what we are exposed to in the future. Mostly we receive news that is pleasant, familiar, and confirms our beliefs. As a result, we increasingly each live in our own, unique information universe or "filter bubble"), social media outlets that exploit online news without contributing to it financially or otherwise, the collapse of trust in news, and more. Our current crisis of democracy and our political institutions must consider the many problems facing journalism.

Rosen (2016) reminds us that there are striking polarization and low trust all around. An emboldened and nationalist right-wing treats the press as a natural enemy. Reality itself seems to have become a weaker force in politics, and it is difficult to apply standard methods of journalism to a figure in power who is not trying to represent reality but to substitute himself for it as a show of strength. Prior routine is unsuitable as professionals in journalism try to confront these confusing conditions; a damaged economic base, weak institutional structure, and newsroom monoculture hinder any creative response; and there is a dawning recognition that freedom of the press is a fragile state, not a constitutional certainty.

Accurate information and quality journalism for a democratic society are as relevant as always; however, the contemporary environment makes it more difficult for readers and listeners to evaluate the quality of the information they encounter and recognize false information. It is essential that environmental communicators discuss the importance of journalism in a democracy, biases, the way news is constructed and newsroom norms, and the need to support quality journalism. The media landscape has changed, and we need to change as well. How do we help our students determine the accuracy of information they receive (to them, Breitbart News and National Enquirer might look just as reputable as the New York Times), decide which articles to believe, and challenge the Merchants of Doubt? Certainly there is a definite need for critical thinking and other higher-order thinking skills for them to be able to analyze news. Skills taught to K-12 as well as higher education students in media literacy programs, such as by Ithaca College's Project Look Sharp with its *Media Constructions of Sustainability: Food, Water and Agriculture* (www.projectlooksharp.org/?action=sustainability) are also extremely valuable. Also, including real, compelling stories of sustainability (Sustainability Stories, as discussed below) about many of the members of RCEGB can combat fake news.

Sustainability Stories: Using Compelling Stories to Share Alternatives to the Status Quo, Business as Usual, Mainstream Ways of Thinking and Acting

RCEGB is currently updating its website: http://www.uvm.edu/~rcegb. When completed, it will provide basic information about the RCE and the Global RCE Network; FAQs with answers; events; a blog with links to news about current partners, sustainability issues in the region, Vermont, and the U.S.; contact information; and a list of all the partners with hot-links to their websites and, importantly, in many cases, Sustainability Stories about those partners.

The author has carried out the Sustainability Stories: A Field Guide to Sustainability in the Greater Burlington Area project over the past quarter century (Hudspeth, 2016). He has written sustainability stories about individuals and groups in the area who serve as sustainability exemplars or role models for others to follow or emulate in bringing about the transition to more environmentally-sustainable communities; people who inspire, encourage, and empower others; "practical visionaries" who have a positive vision of a sustainable future environment – an alternative to the dominant social paradigm, the status quo – and take action to achieve that vision, to turn that vision into reality. He has also compiled stories written and videotaped by students in his senior capstone service-learning Sustainable Communities classes in Environmental Studies at the University of Vermont (UVM). The students serve as "credible biographers" for these pioneers or visionaries, these unsung local sustainability heroines and heroes, by profiling and celebrating such individuals and groups – utilizing such qualitative research methodologies as semi-structured interviews and analysis of documents and materials – and by spreading the word to others about these examples or role models in the community, so that these others can respond by giving them encouragement and helping them to get their jobs done or by starting their own initiatives for finding solutions to global sustainability problems and for healing the earth and for living more sustainably.

Not only are the stories of indigenous/traditional societies living sustainably (similar to those from the Pacific Northwest featured at WEEC-9), but also success stories of individuals and groups working at various levels to ensure a sustainable future. These demonstrate practical solutions to today's sustainability problems, thereby providing an antidote to "doom and gloom" accounts and also helping cultivate a sense of place and building community – both are key aspects of sustainability. In seeking to operationalize sustainability, make it more concrete, make it come alive, humanize it, and put a face on it, the Sustainability Stories offer hopeful, inspirational, local, place-based solutions with global implications. Further, they let people know what a sustainable future could look like – demonstrate that an ecologically-resilient and socially-equitable world *is* possible, *can* be achieved locally – and that there *are* alternatives to business-as-usual, overconsumption, "growth at all costs" model that we are addicted to. Sustainability Stories recognize that a much better future, an ecologically resilient and socially equitable world, *is* possible and that we already have working demonstrations and examples of aspects of it that need to be taken to scale and replicated. Experiments are under way *now*, all over the world, exploring how sustainability can, in fact, be achieved locally as people explore and test and share new and better ways to survive together; there are numerous promising developments.

Storytelling is an amazingly effective form of communication that helps us recognize new and better solutions to sustainability problems, to envision and work toward more sustainable futures. Because we are storytelling social primates who understand things better if they are told to us in a story, compelling narratives capture peoples' imaginations and connect them to their place and others. Sustainability Stories provide a change in thinking, a valuable means of shifting mental models and bringing about behaviour change and even paradigm shifts.

Fien et al. (2010) remind us that stories were the primary way our ancestors transmitted knowledge and values.

> Since earliest times most of our stories have related to our earth, how it was created, the relationship between it and its human inhabitants, and problems that arise when we fail to remember the importance of living in harmony with it and each other….We all love good stories, because they not only entertain but also hold our attention while we learn important concepts, skills, values, and attitudes.

Further, stories – especially with characters with whom readers or listeners can identify – can put a face on sustainability challenges and allow people to care on an emotional level far more than any facts and figures, statistics, reports, graphs, charts, diagrams, or "50 simple ways" types of books about how to live more sustainably. The powerful emotional responses evoked by stories help us to clarify the way we feel and can fuel the desire for change.

Frances Moore Lappe (2010) believes we can create the world we want by aligning our mental maps with conditions that bring out the best in people and for which we evolved: cooperation, empathy, compassion, efficacy, being courageous and doing rather than being fearful and feeling powerless, being active citizens instead of just consumers, and recognizing possibilities rather than decrying scarcity or lack. An enduring understanding of SE is that it all begins with a change in thinking, and storytelling is a valuable means of shifting mental models.

When she talked about leverage points, or places to intervene in a system to transform it for the better, Donella Meadows (1999) claimed that the most effective is to change the mindset or paradigm out of which the system – its goals, power structure, rules, and its culture – arises. This is similar to what Joanna Macy, David Korten, and others term "The Great Turning" and yet others term "The Great Transition", a paradigm shift, telling a new story or myth: a story of sustainability.

In *Dream of the Earth* (2010) Thomas Berry claims:

> For people, generally, their story of the universe and the human role in the universe is their primary source of intelligibility and value. ... The deepest crises experienced by any society are those moments of change when the story becomes inadequate for meeting the survival demands of a present situation.

Korten (2013) builds on that notion, asserting:

> We are a self-reflective, storytelling, choice-making species gone astray for want of a sacred story adequate to the needs of our time….a shared story reflecting our responsibility to….bring ourselves into balance with the generative systems of a living Earth ... before the economic, social, environmental, and political system failure wrought by inadequate stories becomes irreversible.

In short, we need to deconstruct outdated and inappropriate notions, narratives, and worldviews. Instead, we need to reconstruct the old model, revise our myth, and reimagine or generate a new story that better describes what is going on in the world and that reflects our creation of positive and empowering possibilities and opportunities from our envisioning. Wilson (1980) asserts: "The future is up for grabs. It belongs to any and all who will take the risk and accept the responsibility of consciously creating the future they want". Envisioning, creating alternative futures, and being "practical visionaries" are essential in SE, since to create a positive and sustainable future, we must first envision it (Milbrath 1989). Mindful of Meadows's (2014) Principles of Effective Envisioning, stakeholders engage in creating and communicating *shared* visions of a more sustainable future – what Elise Boulding (1988) called "public daydreaming" – and in identifying strategies, policies, and values for transitioning toward the kind of world we really want (not what we will settle for) – a more sustainable, just, ethical, secure, peaceful future that is based on systems thinking and learner-centred engagement and that focuses on solutions and psychological well-being, happiness, and quality of life; that is both ecologically sustainable and desirable to most people and sufficiently compelling to motivate positive change; that offers an alternative future to business as usual and that recognizes that our economic institutions and governance can be redesigned to address the ecological degradation and economic inequality produced by capitalism; and that breaks our addiction to overconsumption, fossil fuels, and an economic paradigm predicated on continual growth.

Giving a name to the world we want – sustainability – helps us create it, to "tell the world of the future into being" (Flowers, 2013), and sustainability stories are a powerful means of doing so.

The Sustainability Stories model developed over more than two decades has been presented to other classes at UVM, other colleges and universities, schools, and conferences in the U.S. and abroad. It has been shown to have transferability and it has been used effectively in urban and rural settings, in a variety of cultures and bioregions, and by K-12 youth and their teachers and non-governmental organizations as well as by university and college students. As far back as the 1997 "Weaving Connections: Cultures and Environments" NAAEE conference in Vancouver, the author organized a symposium on "Working Models and Success Stories of Sustainability". John Baldwin featured sustainability initiatives in the Willamette Valley in Oregon, Delia Clark presented initiatives in the Upper Valley of the Connecticut River in Vermont and New Hampshire, and he presented initiatives in the Lake Champlain Basin. His presentation included several Sustainability Stories about UVM, Shelburne Farms, Intervale Center, and more. Also, the Sustainability Studies project was one of the major features cited when, in 2015, the United Nations University Institute for Advanced Studies of Sustainability recognized the Greater Burlington Regional Centre of Expertise on ESD because of its collaborative and groundbreaking SE and sustainability programs.

Community-building and Emphasizing Social Capital for Resilience and Getting through Uncertainty

Most of the Sustainability Stories deal with social capital, which involves the norms of behaviour that bring us together as a community and help us be more productive and function better. Vermont is justifiably recognized as a leader in the transition to sustainable futures. Its high levels of social capital and sense of community, strong town meeting tradition, and manageable size and scale allow for interaction and cross-fertilization that do not seem to happen as well in larger places. The positive role models featured in Sustainability Stories are *not* presented as being exceptional or outstanding. Undoubtedly such examples exist in every community; however, one just might have to scratch a little deeper to uncover them in other places.

Former UVM President Daniel Mark Fogel http://www.uvm.edu/president/formerpresidentfogel/?Page=signatures_essay.html reminds us that UVM, as Vermont's university, is rooted in values long associated with the State of Vermont: "fairness, social justice, environmental stewardship, openness, independence, lack of pretense, and the achievement of practical results". Of course, many of these attributes are key characteristics of sustainability. In addition, they are linked with notable Vermonters and UVM alumni – George Perkins Marsh, Justin Morrill, John Dewey, Jody Williams (political activist from Putney, Vermont, who received the Nobel Peace Prize in 1997 for helping to found the International Campaign to Ban Landmines and working to eradicate antipersonnel landmines), and John McGill (doctor formerly with UVM College of Medicine and president of Doctors Without Borders, the U.S. branch of Médecins Sans Frontières, who received the Nobel Peace Prize in 1999 for providing medical care in out-of-the-way places to victims of famines, wars, epidemics, and other catastrophes) – who make UVM the distinctive university it is today.

CONCLUSION

Transitioning toward the kind of world we *really* want – a more sustainable, just, ethical, secure, peaceful future; that challenges the dominant social paradigm and offers an alternative future to business-as-usual; that recognizes our economic institutions and governance can be redesigned to address the ecological degradation and economic inequality produced by capitalism; that breaks our addiction to overconsumption, fossil fuels, an economic paradigm predicated on continual growth in a finite world, and a cultural presumption that bigger and faster is always better; and that has the potential to satisfy a wide range of human needs not being effectively met by the present consumerism-based society – has no charted course.

Managing such a transition toward a sustainable society that mimics the natural systems all around us, in which we accept limits, live gently and responsibly, and treat our fragile planet with dignity and reverence, will necessarily involve discussion, dialogue, and debate involving all cultures and sectors and drawing on all academic disciplines. Reimagined SE utilizing storytelling has the potential to play a significant role in addressing, confronting, and seeking solutions to profoundly serious planetary-scale Anthropocene challenges and working toward the transition to a more sustainable society at the local level, imagining the type of world we *really* want to create and identifying strategies for transitioning to such a vision of a sustainable, equitable, healthy society and future by offering positive, inspirational, hopeful, community-building, place-based approaches.

These stories are a powerful means of social transformation and behaviour change. Hopefully, they will help work toward a paradigm shift and a change in mental models to sustainability that will help society achieve a smooth landing instead of overshoot and collapse, and – along with an inclusive, collaborative, multisectoral approach and effective communications and emphasis on social capital – offer hope and optimism and provide inspiration and empowerment rather than despair and doom-and-gloom.

REFERENCES

Berry, T. (1990). *The dream of the earth*. San Francisco, CA: Sierra Club.

Boulding, E. (1988). *Building a global civic culture: Education for an interdependent world*. New York, NY: Teachers College Press, Teachers College, Columbia University.

Fien, J., Cox, B., & Calder, M. (2010). *Storytelling*. UNESCO. Retrieved from http://www.unesco.org/education/tlsf/mods/theme_d/mod21.html

Flowers, B. S. (2013, July 10). The American dream and the economic myth. *The Huffington Post*.

Hanleybrown, F., Kania, J., & Kramer, M. (2016, January 26). Channeling change: Making collective impact work. *Stanford Social Innovation Review, 1*.

Hudspeth, T. R. (2016). Hopeful, local, visionary, solutions-oriented, transformative, place-based sustainability stories and service learning as tools for university level education for sustainable development: Experiences from University of Vermont. In W. Leal Filho & P. Pace (Eds.), *Teaching education for sustainable development at university level* (pp. 191–203). New York, NY: Springer International Publishing.

Hudspeth, T. R., Baldwin, J. H., & Clark, D. (1997). Working models and success stories of sustainability. In R. Abrams (Ed.), *Weaving connections: Cultures and environments: environmental education and the peoples of the world: Selected papers from the 26th Annual Conference of the North American Association for Environmental Education* (pp. 344–347). Washington, DC: NAAEE.

Korten, D. (2013, July 13). It's a story problem: What's behind our messed-up economy. *YES Magazine*.

Lappe, F. M. (2010). *Why are we creating a world that no one wants?* TEDx Talks. Retrieved from https://www.youtube.com/watch?v=w_Lw5lt3J6c

Meadows, D. (1999). *Leverage points: Places to intervene in a system*. Hartland, VT: The Sustainability Institute.

Meadows, D. (2014). Envisioning a sustainable world. In R. Costanza & I. Kubiszewski (Eds.), *Creating a sustainable and desirable future: Insights from 45 global thought leaders*. Singapore: World Scientific.

Milbrath, L. (1989). *Envisioning a sustainable society: Learning our way out*. Albany, NY: State University of New York Press.

Putnam, R. D. (2000). *Bowling alone: The collapse and revival of American community*. New York, NY: Simon & Schuster.

Rosen, J. (2016). *Winter is coming: Prospects for the American Press under Trump*. New York: Arthur L. Carter Journalism Institute at New York University. Retrieved from http://pressthink.org/2016/12/winter-coming-prospectsamerican-press-trump/

Snyder, G. (1999). *The Gary Snyder reader: Prose, poetry, and translations, 1952–1998*. Washington, DC: Counterpoint.

Suzuki, D. (1998). *the sacred balance: Rediscovering our place in nature*. Amherst, NY: Prometheus Books.

Wilson, R. A. (1980, November). Interview by Neil Wilgus from Science Fiction Review, 37(9), 4. Retrieved from http://rawilsonfans.org/1980/11/

World Commission on Environment and Development. (1987). *Our common future*. Oxford: Oxford.

Thomas R. Hudspeth
Environmental Studies and Natural Resources
Gund Institute for Environment
University of Vermont
Burlington, VT, USA

ADELA TESAREK KINCAID, GLENN C. SUTTER
AND ANNA M. H. HALL

24. ECOMUSEUMS IN SASKATCHEWAN

Viewing Networks and Partnerships through a Regional and Project-Specific Lens

INTRODUCTION

Ecomuseums are community-driven organizations that encourage in situ heritage conservation and community engagement in ways that respond to local needs and foster sustainable forms of development (Saskatchewan Ecomuseums Initaitive, 2016). They have been described as "museums without walls" and are closely related to the concept of a "living laboratory" (Kakkarainen & Hyysalo, 2013; Westerlund & Leminen, 2014) in that both strive to create community-based partnerships. The idea of a living lab is pluralistic and post-disciplinary, in the sense that various actors from many backgrounds and from public and private sectors can be involved collaboratively and can "test" practical community-based ideas in real-life contexts (Westerlund & Leminen, 2011). As this chapter will describe, much like living labs, ecomuseums are heavily dependent on networks and systems. The living lab concept can add a research component to an ecomuseum by focusing on research opportunities linked to social or economic systems, ecosystems (Schaffers & Kulkki, 2007) or networks (Leminen, Westerlund, & Nystrom, 2012, 2014). We can view the ecomuseum as practical and functional, while the living lab provides a platform to directly engage with research. According to Borrelli and Davis (2012), 98% of the world's 400+ ecomuseums are situated in rural areas, where they focus on connections to local cultures and history, local natural and physiographic features, and agricultural practices. Given this breadth and flexibility, combining the ecomuseum with the living laboratory concept is likely to give rise to exciting research opportunities.

The ecomuseums concept has been applied at many locations in Europe, South America, Africa, and southeast Asia, but only sporadically in North America. While only one ecomuseum has been documented in the United States, the idea has a long history in parts of Canada, especially Quebec, where a number took root in the 1970s (Sutter et al., 2016). Ecomuseums did not exist in Saskatchewan until 2012 but since then there has been a growing interest in the model (Sutter, 2017). There are currently 4 functioning ecomuseums in Saskatchewan and 7 other communities are interested in applying the model.

Recent studies have identified ecomuseums as democratic, community-based endeavours where individuals and groups can work together to foster social, economic, and environmental sustainability (Simeoni & De Crescenzo, 2018; Borelli & Davis, 2012; Nash, Colwell-Chanthaphonh, & Holen, 2011) but these approaches provide only a limited understanding about practically engaging various community organizations with complex socio-environmental issues. This project, which describes the creation of a network and an educational program, was undertaken to fill this gap and advance the development of the ecomuseum concept by observing and documenting the evolution of local community partnerships. The results have far-reaching and longitudinal implications for rural Saskatchewan, as they contribute to debates about the role of ecomuseums and their potential as sites for citizen science and living labs. The focus is on a partnership between provincial heritage organizations and an outdoor education program designed to create bridges between three community organizations, with a common focus on sustainability.

In this chapter we describe two scales of networks related to the United Nations 2030 Agenda for Sustainable Development and specifically to several Sustainable Development Goals (SDGs). In the first section we focus on the process of building the ecomuseum network and the partnerships associated with it, as they help guide and develop democratic community development projects that focus on connections to local cultural and natural heritage (SDG 11). The second section provides an explicit example of an ecomuseum project addressing SDG 4.7.[1] Our case study concentrates on the White Butte Ecomuseum, which is situated in a rural part of southern Saskatchewan with increasing urban development.

BUILDING A PROVINCIAL ECOMUSEUM NETWORK AND PARTNERSHIP

Background

With roots dating back to 2011, the Saskatchewan Ecomuseum Partnership (SEP) has gone through several phases. As of April 2012, it was the Steering Committee for an exploratory project led by the Royal Saskatchewan Museum (RSM), which generated interest in the ecomuseum model across Saskatchewan and fostered several demonstration sites. The group continued to facilitate and track the use of the model as the Steering Committee of an informal ecomuseum network until November 2016, when it decided to rebrand as the SEP, and the Saskatchewan Ecomuseum Network (SEN) was launched as a member group of the Museums Association of Saskatchewan (MAS).

The possibility of ecomuseums in Saskatchewan was discussed in the 1970s, when the model was first being developed and applied in other parts of the world. None would take root here, except for Redberry Lake Biosphere Reserve (est. 2000), which follows ecomuseum principles but does not use the term. That changed in 2011, when the RSM rekindled interest in the concept. After key organizations and over a dozen communities responded favorably to a call for interest, the RSM, MAS, Heritage Saskatchewan (HS), and SaskCulture agreed to collaborate on an exploratory project which soon expanded to include all of the organizations in the current SEP. This group has been meeting to discuss the development of Saskatchewan ecomuseums every 6–8 weeks for the last 5 years.

At the same time, ecomuseums have taken root at four locations in the province (Val Marie, the White Butte and Calling Lakes areas, and the Regina Civic Museum) and seven other communities (Saltcoats, Nipawin, Wolseley, Moose Jaw, Humboldt, Middle Lake, and North Central Regina) have been working with the concept. All of these locations have been invited to join the SEN, which was formally launched by the MAS in April 2017.

The relationship between the SEP and the SEN is depicted in Figure 24.1, along with key connections to organizations that are not part of the SEP.

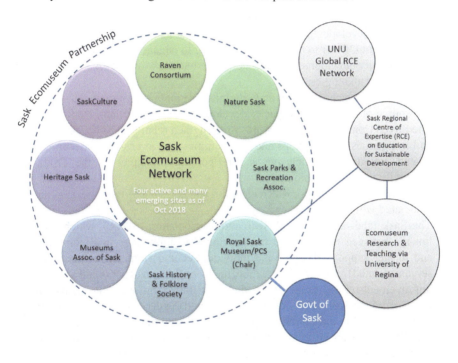

Figure 24.1. The Saskatchewan Ecomuseum Partnership (SEP) currently consists of 7 provincial heritage organizations, a group of Indigenous consultants (Raven Consortium), and a representative of the Saskatchewan Ecomuseum Network (SEN). The SEP is currently chaired by the Royal Saskatchewan Museum (RSM), which is also connected to other organizations involved in ecomuseum or heritage-related research and programs. The SEN is overseen by the Museums Association of Saskatchewan (MAS), with input from the RSM

Structure and Operations

The vision, purpose, and other guiding statements that have been developed for the SEP are provided in Appendix 1.

Members of the current SEP include:

- The RSM, which organizes and currently chairs SEP events, provides consultative services about ecomuseum development and the role of heritage in sustainability, and conducts and disseminates the results of ecomuseum-based research;
- MAS, which organizes and chairs SEN events and provides network services that include confirming membership, administering the Saskatchewan Ecomuseums Facebook group, maintaining a website about ecomuseums in Saskatchewan, producing documentation, and offering training workshops;
- HS, which hosts meetings of the SEP steering committee, publishes resource documents, advocates for the ecomuseum approach as a strategy for sustainable community development, provides the services of its Intangible Cultural Heritage Development Officer to communities looking to engage further with ICH as part of community development, and conducts research on living heritage, wellbeing, and other related topics; and
- SaskCulture, which develops and administers granting programs that provide a key source of funding and capacity development for ecomuseum work.
- The Raven Consortium, which works to strengthen relationships between the SEP and Indigenous organizations and communities and to ensure that ecomuseum-related activities are inclusive and reflect the principles of the Truth and Reconciliation Commission;
- Nature Saskatchewan (NS), which identifies and helps the SEP pursue opportunities associated with natural heritage;
- The Saskatchewan Parks and Recreation Association (SPRA), which provides linkage between the SEP and the provincial Communities in Bloom program and further supports the SEP and individual ecomuseums through consultative services related to parks and recreation, the identification of parks and community-improvement-related grant funds, the provision of information related to the *Framework for Recreation in Canada 2015*, and the dissemination of information to its membership through SPRA programs and communication tools;
- The Saskatchewan History and Folklore Society (SHFS), which identifies and helps the SEP pursue opportunities associated with local history, Intangible Cultural Heritage (in partnership with HS), and Intercultural Competence training (in partnership with the Multicultural Council of Saskatchewan); and
- The SEN, which is represented by a delegate selected by active ecomuseums as part of their Network meetings.

Being part of the SEP means committing to attend meetings, agreeing to the above mission, vision and values, and not making statements or undertaking activities on behalf of the Partnership that are contrary to its mission, vision, and values. Partner organizations are represented by positions that are able to make decisions about associated operations and programs without prolonged consultations, and all SEP decisions are made by consensus. When issues or concerns come up that cannot be addressed by one of the partner organizations, the SEP can bring in individuals or organizations for specific discussions or projects without increasing the size of the formal partnership.

The SEP conducts an annual evaluation of provincial ecomuseum-related activities and reports the results to the Minister of PCS. Key performance measures include: website and/or Facebook activity, as reflected by the number of posts and visits from within and beyond Saskatchewan; the level of media interest, based on number of press releases and associated coverage; and the nature and outcomes of site-specific projects carried out by individual ecomuseums.

Insights

One of us (GCS) has been deeply involved in the development of the SEP, shedding light on some of its ramifications. For example, as provincial interest in ecomuseums continues to grow, a body like the SEP has two important roles to play. First, heritage exists in many forms, from the tangible manifestations of human activities and natural processes, to the historic and current suites of values, attitudes, actions and customs associated with living cultures. Many organizations are working to safeguard and draw attention to the different aspects of heritage, recognizing them both for their potential or current economic value and as an irreplaceable source of skills, knowledge, and inspiration. These organizations often work in isolation, despite social, economic, and environmental realities that link different types of heritage together. The SEP gives like-minded organizations a place and opportunity to share ideas, discuss challenges and create strategies for ecomuseum development at the provincial scale, reducing the institutional isolation that might hamper this sort of work.

Second, all types of heritage have a role to play as people grapple with sustainability issues that range from global climate change and the loss of biodiversity to local concerns about air or water quality, food security, income gaps, urbanization, and other matters. Being familiar with the past and knowing about the current living heritage of a region is critical, but the scope of this work is beyond the reach of any one organization. One way to get a full sense of sustainability challenges and address emergent opportunities is through a broad organizational framework like an ecomuseum, an interlinked group of like-minded projects like the emerging SEN, and a multi-agency coordinating body like the SEP.

EXAMPLE OF AN ECOMUSEUM-SPECIFIC COMMUNITY PROJECT

Background

Researchers in many disciplines have addressed important aspects of community involvement (Flachs, 2013), community volunteerism (Gallo & Duffy, 2016), and local level governance (Gooch, 2004), but none have used ecomuseums to study cross-community partnership involvement and extended that vision to include a community-driven research component. Scholars thus have an incomplete understanding of the ecomuseum concept, including how interactions between organizations might be initiated while documenting concerns, observing partnership results, and incorporating elements of a living laboratory concept into the ecomuseum model. At the same time, scientific knowledge has come under scrutiny for being undemocratic, increasingly fragmented and specialized with a lack of unity (Nicolescu, 1999). In theory, encouraging the participatory citizen approach through ecomuseums will not only elucidate more fully the need for a more democratic science but also make room for community-based research and partnerships that will result in opportunities for community-engaged scholarship (see Chase & Levine, 2016; Kullenberg & Kasperowski, 2016, for citizen science examples).

Conservation Easement 'On-the-Land' Programming

Located about 20 kilometres (km) east of Regina, the capital of Saskatchewan, the rapidly growing Town of White City directly intersects with a rural landscape. White City has been spearheading the development of the White Butte Ecomuseum, which includes a section (1.6 x 1.6 km) of pasture land that is protected by a conservation easement and overseen by a partnership between the Town and the Rural Municipality (RM) of Edenwold. By offering educational programming on the easement land, this project aims to engage elementary school students in the ecomuseum concept (i.e. local natural and cultural heritage), resulting in wider community engagement to help build local identity (SDG 11). One of us (ATK) has been involved as a participant-researcher (i.e., embedded researcher), contributing to ecomuseum activities by drawing on community engagement theory and using elements of ethnography and participatory action research combined with situational analysis to map the interactions and projects that are created and executed by the White Butte Ecomuseum Committee. One such project it the creation of experiential outdoor lessons that engage local school children on the conservation land (SDG 4).

Conservations easements are legal documents that are agreed upon by the landowner and an outside organization, such as a land trust, a government agency, a municipality, or a non-government organization. The agreement is registered on title and protects the property for the number of years specified, usually for long periods of time. Under this agreement, the landowner manages the property based on jointly agreed-upon parameters that are beneficial for the environment and monitored by the specific organization (SDG 15).

In this case, the agreement is between a cattle rancher family and the Saskatchewan Wildlife Federation (SWF), which describes the easement process as follows:

> Currently there are over 9000 acres (3642 hectares) protected under the conservation easement program. Landowners identify to the SWF a portion

of their property that is good wildlife habitat that they would like to place a conservation easement on. The SWF will then get an assessment done on the property and based on the number of acres that qualify as wildlife habitat the SWF will pay the landowner 25% of the appraised value to place the conservation easement on the property. This is a registered interest in the property that ensures that the portion of wildlife habitat placed under the easement remain in its natural state for perpetuity. The landowner controls the access to the property but cannot remove any of the wildlife habitat. This is a great way to protect wildlife habitat and have the landowner retain ownership of his [or her] property. (2018, para. 1)

Partners in this project include (1) researchers at the University of Regina and the RSM; (2) a White City local elementary school; and, (3) the White Butte Ecomuseum, which is partially funded by the Town of White City. The project also hinges on consultation with the landowners and SWF. Interest in ecomuseums from the student body has been robust. Students from the University of Regina and beyond, across disciplines and in undergraduate to graduate studies have expressed an interest in participating in various roles related to this project (as volunteers, as part of their studies, enrolling in an ecomuseum class). Engaging community members and students is part of the research design which involves Participatory Action Research (PAR). PAR is typically community-based and involves collaboration between researchers and participant-partners in all phases of the project (Van Den Hoonaard, 2012, p. 37).

The goal of the partnership is to create local ecologically-based programming for local elementary school children in White City, which will be partially created and delivered by University of Regina students on the ecomuseum conservation easement land (SDG 4).

The results will illustrate how community partnerships between places of higher learning, local schools, museums, and community initiatives can be used to promote community development projects (SDG 11). Participatory science approaches can act as viable research tools that help identify and measure environmental and social issues and aid community engagement aimed at social and environmental sustainability. The novel concept of combining participatory science with the above partnership will result in opportunities for enhanced local awareness and actions for sustainability, and greater community-engaged scholarship.

Key learning components will include programming development that can be used to implement SDG-based curriculum and result in a curriculum toolkit. The project is currently funded through a combination of sources and is being executed locally by ATK, while the United Nations University-acknowledged Regional Centre of Expertise on Education and Sustainability (RCE) Saskatchewan is providing national and international networking opportunities. RCEs are a useful network that share effective practices and policies related to sustainable development, provide training workshops, and give more insight on sustainable related initiatives. RCEs provide connections to perspectives from various UN/International frameworks and connect them to community actions with the hope of leading to more unity and cohesion between the different RCE networks. Education for Sustainable Development (ESD) addresses and contributes to the implementation of the 2030 Agenda and the Sustainable Development Goals (SDGs).

Core Objectives and Methodology

This particular project resulted from research supported and encourage by the Royal Saskatchewan Museum and by the University of Regina. The objectives of the project are:

1. To create SDG-based lessons that (1) engage students with local heritage and ecology, (2) meet Saskatchewan curriculum requirements and (3) meet the needs of the Ecomuseum,
2. To strengthen connections between the three community partners,
3. To advance and connect theoretical and methodological approaches associated with objectives a and b, and.
4. To determine future opportunities for community-based science and research.

The methodology involves collaboration between the three participating partners: the ecomuseum, the University of Regina and a local elementary school. The University of Regina Faculty and students will create locally based lessons that engage elementary students with local heritage and ecology. Undergraduate or graduate students volunteered (as part of course work or of their own accord) to help develop the easement land program, with a focus on courses related to the environment, outdoor education/environment, policy, and community. The local elementary school and University of Regina education students helped to ensure that the lessons are meeting Saskatchewan curriculum needs and other educational needs. The third partner, the White Butte Ecomuseum, ensured that the program is meeting the needs of the community ecomuseum. As an embedded researcher, ATK observed, documented and participated in the process and made efforts to connect with and include various additional organizations such as the RM of Edenwold, the Town of White City, various university experts, other local schools and the Prairie Valley School Division.

Potential benefits of the project include: lessons for future public programming in the White Butte Ecomuseum; giving university students an opportunity to engage with a community project and gain practical experience in curriculum/ program design and delivery; and outdoor environmental/sustainability education opportunities for elementary students. The theoretical focus (Figure 24.2) is to map the organizational interactions and their positions using situational analysis and to advance and connect theoretical approaches such as PAR and citizen science, all practiced within an ecomuseum model. The final objective is to determine future opportunities for community-based science/research and disseminate results to

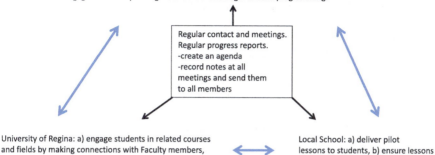

Figure 24.2. Theoretical project analysis: to advance and connect theoretical approaches to determine future opportunities for community-based science/research

the community and to the ecomuseum committee through presentations, e-letters, websites, and social media.

Program Details

The program has been designed as a set of lessons delivered as small groups of students circulate through a route, where each lesson is connected to the next. Each lesson (see details in Appendix 2) will be delivered by University of Regina students on the easement land, and is approximately 20–30 minutes in length. Currently, students in grades 4 and 6 will be participating and the content has been matched to the Saskatchewan curriculum and to the SDGs. The cumulating day will be facilitated by Nature Saskatchewan and will consist of a NatureBlitz that links the program to citizen science and includes a game about bird migration.

DEVELOPING PARTNERSHIPS AROUND ECOMUSEUMS: KEY INSIGHTS

Outcomes

Through its various stages of development, the SEP has produced a number of products and outcomes, including:

- A working definition of an ecomuseum as "a locally-driven, place-based organization that encourages sustainable community development, based on in situ heritage conservation and interpretation".

- Guiding documents, including a communications plan, a detailed concept paper, a feasibility study, and a development framework for newly-forming ecomuseums.
- Two published research papers and two ongoing research projects,
- An undergraduate course offered through Luther College at the University of Regina.
- Three provincial workshops that featured updates from demonstration sites, and
- A website and Facebook group for liaison with provincial, national, and international stakeholders.

Other outcomes have been achieved by ecomuseums that have taken root in the province, from community art installations in Val Marie and festivals to draw attention to water concerns in Calling Lakes areas, to the collection of digital stories and the development of plans for interpretive trails associated with the White Butte ecomuseum.

Recommendations

- Foster comparative research on the activities and strategies of ecomuseums in other countries, with emphasis on how their outcomes are, or could be, addressing local sustainability issues and related cultural needs.
- Make use of existing international portals, such as the Ecomuseum DROPS site (https://sites.google.com/view/drops-platform/home), to encourage interaction and knowledge exchange between regional and national ecomuseum networks, emphasizing the potential of ecomuseums as "living laboratories" for sustainability research.
- Encourage discussion about the connections between ecomuseums and sustainability amongst museum associations, heritage organizations, and community development groups at provincial, national, and international levels.
- Stimulate interest in ecomuseums and build capacity for research and development in this area by including discussions about living heritage (culture) as a basis for community engagement at regional and global RCE events.
- Make connections between the global RCE network and the global ecomuseum network. With some 600 ecomuseums in operation around the world and a shared interest in sustainability education, there would seem to be some untapped potential here for collaborative and mutually supporting initiatives.

Conclusion

The ecomuseum approach to community development is not biased towards any one aspect of sustainability (social, economic, environmental, or cultural). Instead, it offers a holistic, integrated framework that recognizes the value of all types of heritage (natural and cultural, tangible and intangible, fixed and movable). Where the different aspects of sustainability are useful is in categorizing and assessing issues that are encouraging ecomuseum development, since these can range from environmental or economic concerns to a desire for social cohesion and the preservation of local traditions.

Challenges. At the provincial scale we have gone from having no ecomuseums to having the start of a network, and a larger support system, mostly because we have spent time raising awareness about the ecomuseum model and responding to expressions of interest, both at the community level and with provincial heritage organizations. The change process here has mostly involved listening to concerns when they come up and giving communities and organizations the time and support they need to experiment with and talk about the idea. There have also been barriers, of course. There has been and continues to be scepticism about the concept, since it is difficult to define and can be perceived as either too "green" or not "green" enough. There have been concerns about adding another heritage-related activity to a provincial landscape that already includes many parks, a Main Street program, interpretive centres, and hundreds of small, community museums. And there are few examples of successful ecomuseums that are pertinent to Saskatchewan cultures or local sustainability issues. Now that some local ecomuseums and a strong provincial partnership are in place, there is greater understanding of the model, we are gaining insight about things that help and hinder ecomuseum development, and a base of support is developing within the university research community.

There appear to be clear connections between ecomuseums and living labs. The potential for ecomuseums to provide research opportunities has been realized through the University of Regina, where the model is currently the focus of a SSHRC-funded project on community engagement and graduate-level research will be concentrating on the links between ecomuseum development and knowledge mobilization. Ecomuseums are well-positioned to act as living labs by extending research into communities and providing democratic community research opportunities, including citizen science initiatives. In Saskatchewan, the potential for ecomuseums to act as living labs has been enhanced by the social networks and organizational partnerships that are currently playing an active and important role in ecomuseum development. From the production and promotion of information documents to networking opportunities through events and social media, steps that have been taken at this higher, systems level have helped individual ecomuseums attract resources, build capacity, and garner visibility for their work. As a result of networks like the SEN and support provided by groups like the SEP and RCE Saskatchewan, living labs can lead to knowledge mobilization which has been identified as one approach to finding resolutions to environmental issues (Cash et al., 2003; Reid et al., 2006; Fabricius et al., 2006; Olsson & Folke, 2001).

Partnership roles and sustainable actions. The SEP is a clear example of a larger regional network of partnerships, whereas at the community scale, the project taking place on the conservation easement includes partnerships that are more locally situated. For example, the partnership between the local school(s), the University of

Regina and town/municipality will provide opportunities for lessons taking place on the land that directly relate to the SDGs through education on sustainable actions.

Replication and scaling-up. Formalizing the SEP has been an important step, partly because it represents commitment to the idea, and also because it has clarified how various partners have been involved and the roles they will be playing as the movement continues. Development of guiding documents and a Facebook group has been important for scaling up and replication. Being able to spread the word through RCE Saskatchewan and the larger RCE networks has also been helpful.

NOTE

[1] SDG 4.7: By 2030, ensure that all learners acquire the knowledge and skills needed to promote sustainable development, including, among others, through education for sustainable development and sustainable lifestyles, human rights, gender equality, promotion of a culture of peace and non-violence, global citizenship and appreciation of cultural diversity and of culture's contribution to sustainable development (https://sustainabledevelopment.un.org/sdg4).

REFERENCES

Borrelli, N., & Davis, P. (2012). How culture shapes nature: Reflections on ecomuseum practices. *Nature and Culture, 7*(1), 31–47.
Chase, S. K., & Levine, A. (2016). A framework for evaluating and designing citizen science programs for natural resources monitoring. *Conservation Biology, 30*(3), 456–466 doi:10.1111/cobi.12697
Fabricius, C., Sholes, R., & Cundill, G. (2006). Mobilizing knowledge for integrated ecosystem assessments. In W. V. Reid, F. Berkes, T. Wilbanks, & D. Capistrano (Eds.), *Bridging scales and knowledge systems: Concepts and applications in ecosystem assessment* (pp. 165–182). Washington, DC: Island Press.
Flachs, A. (2013). Gardening as ethnographic researching: Volunteering as a means for community access. *Journal of Ecological Anthropology, 16*(1), 97–103.
Gallo, M. L., & Duffy, L. (2016). The rural giving difference? Volunteering as philantrophy in an Irish community organization. *Journal of Rural and Community Development, 11*(1), 1–15.
Gooch, M. (2004). Volunteering in catchment management groups: Empowering the volunteer. *Australian Geographer, 35*(2), 193–208.
Hakkarainen, L., & Hyysalo, S. (2013, December). How do we keep the living laboratory alive? Learning and conflicts in living lab collaboration. *Technology Innovation Management Review, 3*(12), 16–22.
Kullenberg, C., & Kasperowski, D. (2016). What is citizen science? – A scientometric meta-analysis. *PLoS ONE, 11*(1), e0147152. doi:10.1371/journal.pone.0147152
Leminen, S., Westerlund, M., & Nyström, A. G. (2012, September). Living labs as open innovation networks. *Technology Innovation Management Review, 2*(9), 6–11.
Leminen, S., Westerlund, M., & Nyström, A. G. (2014). On becoming creative consumers – User roles in living labs networks. *International Journal of Technology Marketing, 9*(1), 33–52.
Nash, S. E., Colwell-Chanthaphonh, C., & Holen, S. (2011). Civic engagements in museum anthropology: A prolegomenon for the Denver museum of nature and science. *Historical Archaeology, 45*(1), 135–151.
Nicolescu, B. (1999). *The transdisciplinary evolution of learning*. Retrieved from http://www.learndev.org/dl/nicolescu_f.pdf
Olsson, P., & Folke, C. (2001). Local ecological knowledge and institutional dynamics for ecosystem management: A study of Lake Racken watershed, Sweden. *Ecosystems, 4*, 85–104.
Reid, W. V., Berkes, F., Wilbanks, T. J., & Capistrano, D. (2006). Introduction. In W. V. Reid, F. Berkes, T. Wilbanks, & D. Capistrano (Eds.), *Bridging scales and knowledge systems: Concepts and applications in ecosystem assessment* (pp. 1–20). Washington, DC: Island Press.

Saskatchewan Ecomuseum Initiative. (2016). *Newly-forming ecomuseums: Development framework.* Regina: Heritage Saskatchewan and Museums Association of Saskatchewan.

Saskatchewan Wildlife Federation. (2018). *Conservation easements.* Retrieved from https://swf.sk.ca/programs/conservation-easements/

Schaffers, H., & Kulkki, S. (2007, September–October). Living labs: An open innovation concept fostering rural development. *Tech Monitor*, 30–38.

Simeoni, F., & De Crescenzo, V. (2018). Ecomuseums (on clean energy), cycle tourism and civic crowdfunding: A new match for sustainability? *Sustainability, 10*(3), 817.

Sutter, G. (2017). Growing Ecomuseums on the Canadian Prairies: Prospects for intangible cultural heritage. In M. L. Stefano & P. Davis (Eds.), *The Routledge companion to intangible cultural heritage* (pp. 453–464). Abingdon: Routledge.

Sutter, G. C., Sperlich, T., Worts, D., Rivard, R., & Teather, L. (2016). Fostering cultures of sustainability through community-engaged museums: The history and re-emergence of ecomuseums in Canada and the USA. *Sustainability, 8*(12), 1310.

Van Den Hoonaard, D. (2012). *Qualitative research in action: A Canadian primer.* Ontario: Oxford.

Westerlund, M., & Leminen, S. (2011, October). Managing the challenges of becoming an open innovation company: Experiences from living labs. *Technology Innovation Management Review, 1*(1), 19–25.

Westerlund, M., & Leminen, S. (2014, June 8–11). *The multiplicity of research on innovation through living labs.* Paper presented at The XXV ISPIM Conference – Innovation for Sustainable Economy & Society, Dublin, Ireland.

Adela Tesarek Kincaid
Department of Sociology and Social Studies
University of Regina
Canada

Glenn C. Sutter
Curator of Human Ecology
Royal Saskatchewan Museum
Canada

Anna M. H. Hall
University of Western Ontario
Canada

APPENDIX 1: SASKATCHEWAN ECOMUSEUM PARTNERSHIP – GUIDING STATEMENTS

Vision and Mission

To focus and motivate their work, the SEP crafted an overarching vision, where Saskatchewan is known for ecomuseums that help local residents and visitors understand, appreciate, and engage with heritage in ways that foster sustainable community development. The SEP also set out a formal mission, as a group that works to enhance the profile of Saskatchewan ecomuseums and offers guidance and services to encourage their development and viability.

Purpose and Goals

The SEP provides guidance to communities and organizations that are implementing the ecomuseum model across the province. The central aim is to enable interested groups and communities to be successful by providing leadership, a frame of reference, and by acting as a clearinghouse. To this end, the SEP works towards the following goals, in order of priority:

- Addressing the needs and increasing the number of ecomuseums Saskatchewan,
- Encouraging outcomes that are examples of sustainable community development,
- Raising the profile of existing ecomuseums and their outcomes,
- Drawing attention to funding opportunities that ecomuseums can tap into, and
- Fostering interaction and knowledge exchange with similar groups in other countries.

These goals are addressed collaboratively, with different partners taking the lead on different activities and depending on available resources and within their existing plans and programs.

Values and Principles

All members of the SEP have agreed to foster the development Saskatchewan ecomuseums based on the following values and principles:

- *Local Engagement: Striving for sustainability* – With the world moving into a new geological era (the Anthropocene) because of human activity, all sectors, organizations and communities have a stake in SDGs. Ecomuseums can help people and organizations address these goals by focusing on the environmental, economic, and social aspects of local sustainability issues and their cultural underpinnings. Instead of aiming to preserve heritage for its own sake, they can strive for outcomes that address real cultural needs and enhance the quality of life of their communities.
- *Living Heritage is Key: Sustainability requires cultural change* – Saskatchewan communities face a range of challenges, and in order to find lasting solutions, their residents need to reflect on past cultures, their current living heritage, and how they want future generations to live. The links between culture and sustainability are echoed in the HS definition of living heritage as "those values, beliefs and ways of living we inherit from past generations that we still use to understand the present and make choices for the future".
- *Relevance: Museums as catalysts* – As places that can stimulate reflection, discussion and ideas for action, museums of all types can play a key role in sustainability work. In keeping with MAS philosophies, ecomuseums can be catalytic, community-driven organizations that increase social cohesion and undertake activities "contribute to the understanding of the world and our place in it – our past, our present, and our future".

- *Holism: All aspects of heritage are valuable* – Just as sustainability can be viewed through environmental, economic, social, and cultural lenses, heritage can be separated into different types, e.g., tangible vs. intangible, moveable vs. immovable, natural vs. cultural. While these separations can useful at times, they can also be problematic, since they tend to create silos and obscure important relationships, including the fact that different types of heritage affect and depend on each other. The SEP agrees with the broad and integrated perspective offered by HS, where heritage is defined as "a valued and dynamic legacy that contributes to our sense of identity, creates an understanding of our past, is used to build communities in the present, and informs our choices for the future".
- *Appreciating Indigenous Perspectives* – People have been an integral part of Saskatchewan landscapes for thousands of years, creating a rich archeological record and vibrant cultures that continue to thrive and have much to offer where sustainability is concerned. The broad and holistic framework provided by an ecomuseum can be an effective way to recognize, strengthen, and celebrate Indigenous cultures and the insights they provide about land, water, and wildlife issues, equity and justice, respect for Nature, and other important considerations.

APPENDIX 2: OVERVIEW OF LESSONS

1. Mindfulness in the environment (SDG 11)
Anastasia

Area: Flat field
Material: Bring blankets to work on and a camera to document the projects made
Lesson Summary: Teach the concept of mindfulnesss by creating circular patterns (i.e. mandalas) out of natural material. The active understanding of oneself and place within society as it pertains to other individuals, groups, and objects; how we relate to them, and our understanding of our own actions, thoughts, and feelings. Using art this to explore the concept of mindfulness, students will gather natural materials to create and explore the philosophy behind mandalas.

2. Cow Management on Pastures
Brittany

Area: Trail walk to water body
Material: One bucket of soil and one bucket of water
Lesson Summary: Students will learn about good land management practices. Beef cattle farming, is a large industry in Saskatchewan and our goal is to teach children about a healthy ranching environment while connecting students to the food production process. The main objective is to teach students how to properly manage cattle and pastures. Students will be taught about cattle behaviour by walking through cattle trails. Students will learn about cattle behaviour and terminology, stewardship (the careful and responsible management of our environmental and natural resources), the benefits of cows in the environment and the detriments of overgrazing. Activities include a trail walk and cattle impacts observation, overgrazing activity and a soil compaction activity.

3. Climate Change (SDG 13)
Anna

Area: Anywhere that is comfortable to gather
Material: Game guide and related materials
Lesson Summary: In this lesson, students will learn about the factors that are causing the climate to change. Students will be able to differentiate between natural and human causes. Students will play a experiential game that illustrates the natural greenhouse effect, the human enhanced greenhouse effect and will be taught how to slow down the greenhouse effect.

4. Water Pollution and Water Scarcity (SDG 6)
Nadeeka

Area: Close to water body
Material: Water samples, pictures of water, pencils and note paper
Lesson Summary: Students will come to understand the importance of water and express the ways and means of water pollution. There are more than 326 million trillion gallons of water on Earth. Less than 3 % of all this water is fresh water and of that amount, more than two-thirds is locked up in ice caps and glaciers. Canada has one fifth of the world's fresh water in lakes, rivers, streams and wet lands. Students will compare and contrast pure and polluted water samples and learn about ways to protect water.

5. Perspectives of the Environment and Mind (SDG 15)
Roman

Area: Rock to water
Lesson Summary: Various perspectives will be discussed in relation to the earth and the environment. Students will be challenged to perceive the land from different angles. Using rocks as a metaphor for the earth, students will be challenged to find stones and to examine life sustaining elements that rocks uphold (moss, insects, etc). Getting the students to look down to try and track footprints of small animals in the dirt will enable them to focus on a new perspective. This perspective will be combined with the open land.

6. How to Use A Compass
Max & Derek

Area: Rock to dugout back to rock (we will need to narrow this area and keep them away from the water and dugout)
Material: Compasses, additional instructions set up at each location point
Lesson Summary: During our exercise students will be introduced to orienteering and the skills involved. Students will learn how to use a compass and map to navigate to specific locations. The ability to operate a compass and understand how to use a map is an important aspect of environmental studies and sustainability and has further applications to life such as survival skills and general navigating. The purpose of the activity is to become aware of your surroundings in the natural environment and use essential environmental tools such as a map and compass to navigate.

7. Human Impacts on the Land and Invasive plants (SDG 12, 15)
Allen & Jessica

Area: Tree forest area

Lesson Summary: The lesson focuses on how humans impact the earth. Examples of human impacts that will be discussed include: human pollution in freshwater that exceeds sustainability, species extinction or extirpation (i.e. buffalo on the Canadian plains), invasive plant species, environmental damage caused by human waste. Activities will include a search or interpretive group walk to look for and discuss industrial damage as well as identification and search for invasive plants

8. Saskatchewan Grassland Birds (SDG 15)
Michaela

Area: Rock loop

Material: Bird's nests, artificial eggs and pictures of each bird species

Lesson Summary: Students will gain a deepened knowledge of the different types of grassland birds. They will experience identifying different types of birds by their appearances, songs, and habits. Students will gain an appreciation for bird diversity. One outcome will be raised awareness of threatened and endangered birds. Students will discover six stations of (planted) nests and bird eggs by going on a hike with the facilitator and stopping at the bird stations to learn more about each species.

9. Aboriginal Storytelling (SDG 4)
Lara & Brenda

Area: Anywhere (around a treed area)

Material: Story to read

Lesson Summary: The goal of this lesson is to learn about different Indigenous viewpoints and contemporary society. The lesson will incorporate story telling that will include the history of Indigenous people, understanding different uses of bison, how food was obtained and how Indigenous people moved with the herds. The goal is to invite an elder to guide a culturally appropriate delivery of the lesson.

10. Journaling and Wellbeing
Melissa

Area: Tree forest

Material: Pencils and writing supplies

Lesson Summary: This lesson will incorporate journal writing to reflect on students' favourite place in Saskatchewan, their favourite activity to do outside and to think about a place they would like to visit in Saskatchewan. Students will be prompted to reflect and will be asked to write in a mini-forest (directly on the land). Discussion will include how students can incorporate nature in their daily lives and to identify and think about the physical and mental benefits of being outdoors.

11. Nature Saskatchewan
Lacey Weekes

A. Natureblitz (SDG 4): is like a bioblitz with a strong educational focus. It's a time-bound event in which citizen scientists and experts try to identify and inventory as many different living things as possible in a given area. It can be all encompassing or can just focus on a few groups of organisms.

B. Bird Migration obstacle course (SDG 15): Birds undertake incredible seasonal journeys of various lengths, a phenomenon called bird migration. Discuss that a bird's life can be full of dangers, many of which are presented in the obstacle course. Not all birds will encounter all of these obstacles every day, but many will encounter most of these along their migration route. Also, did you know that birds have to do this trip twice a year? One way is flying south for the winter, and the other is flying north for the spring and summer. The biggest threat is human disturbance of habitat.

KUANG-CHUNG LEE

25. WEAVING TRADITIONAL ECOLOGICAL KNOWLEDGE INTO INDIGENOUS YOUTH EDUCATION

A Case Study in an Indigenous Rice Paddy Cultural Landscape, Taiwan

BACKGROUND

In 2005, the idea of landscape/seascape conservation was introduced into the amended Cultural Heritage Preservation Act (CHPA) as a new legal subject entitled a "cultural landscape" in Taiwan. Unlike traditional strictly protected areas, namely the IUCN protected area category I–IV, the cultural landscape is a new concept to Taiwan that emphasises the interaction of local people and the land (IUCN, 1994, 2010; Phillips, 1995, 2002).

From 2005 until early 2012, 34 sites were legally designated as cultural landscapes. However, most of the designated sites concerned historical architecture preservation. Few of the sites employed an integrated landscape (or community-based approach) to benefit both local people and their living landscapes. In order to help the stakeholders of governmental authorities and local communities to apply this new instrument, the National Dong-Hwa University (as the research team) worked with the Hualien County Cultural Affairs Bureau (HCCAB) and conducted a two-year action research project from May 2011 to June 2013 (Lee, 2012, 2013).

The Cihalaay Cultural Landscape, the case study area, covers a land area of 1,040 hectares and is located in the indigenous Cihalaay settlement of the Fengnan village, Fuli Township, Hualien County of Taiwan. The boundary of the Cihalaay Cultural Landscape is a complete watershed of the Stonehouse Ravine Stream that is situated in the northernmost area of the Turtle Stream watershed. Right next to the landscape is the 1682-meter high peak, Ma-lao-lou, of the Coastal Range. The area is covered with rice terraces and irrigation channels and is home to the indigenous Cihalaay community. Downstream of the Stonehouse Ravine Stream is the core area of the entire cultural landscape, with 20 hectares of rice terraces and six irrigation channels constructed by local people during the 1920–1950s totalling 4,100 meters in length (Figures 25.1 and 25.2) (Lee, 2012).

Based on Lee (2013), the cultural landscape has 26 households with a registered population of 150, of which 99% are indigenous Amis. Due to the lack of job opportunities, only 70 people are living in the local area (with 28% from 0–14, 57%

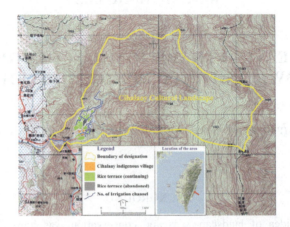

Figure 25.1. Location and boundary of the Cihalaay Cultural Landscape

Figure 25.2. The Cihalaay Cultural Landscape covers about 1,040 hectares and comprises mosaic landscapes of an indigenous village, rice terraces and irrigation channels, orchards, secondary forest, natural forests and streams

15–64, and 15% above 65 years of age). Most of the residents under the age of 30 have attained a high school education, whereas those above 50 for the most part have a primary school education.

Various formal and informal forums and workshops were conducted in the local area with the help of the research team to achieve stakeholder consensus on the designation of the Cultural Landscape and the formulation of its management plan. As a result of the above consensus, local people voluntarily set up a Local Management Committee in July 2011 and drew up a local Code of Conduct in November 2011 for the future management of the Cultural Landscape. With the help of the research team, the local authority (HCCAB) officially designated the site as a legal Cultural Landscape in May 2012, approved the Management Principles in November 2012, and completed the mid-term Management Plan for Cihalaay Cultural Landscape in June 2013 (Lee et al., 2016).

The Management Plan for Cihalaay Cultural Landscape was drew up in line with the Satoyama Initiative that aimed to revitalise agricultural production landscapes with environmentally friendly farming in rural areas as a way to help human societies to achieve the 2020 Aichi Biodiversity Targets concerning 'living in harmony with nature' (UNU-IAS, 2010a, 2010b). Five key perspectives of tasks were arranged in the Management Plan, including: enhancement of landscape diversity and resilience, cyclic use of nature resources, respect of traditional knowledge and value, multi-stakeholder collaboration, as well as socio-economic benefits. Consequently, one of the important follow-up activities after the designation of the Cihalaay Cultural Landscape was to develop a place-based or community-based environmental education (EE) programme for local indigenous youth.

In order to explore a feasible way of incorporating indigenous and local knowledge into the local school' formal EE courses, the research team went to visit the principal of the local school in mid-2012. However, the principal replied that those school children from surrounding indigenous communities had already known everything about their parents' local knowledge and practices from their childhood. The priority, he said, for school children was to 'see the outside world.'

In fact, most indigenous youth in Taiwan don't know their parents' local language and knowledge. Their parents and schools teach little of this because it is considered to be of 'no value' for their future. Paradoxically, many indigenous parents and elders interviewed by the research team actually valued their traditional ecological knowledge and worried about the dissappearance of their culture. This kind of worry and expectation gave the research team the opportunity to start working with the indigenous community in Fengnan village on developing and operating an informal community-based environmental education (EE) programme from late 2012 without help of the local school. The goal of the study is to provide relevant government authorities, rural communities and other stakeholders with reference so that they can work collaboratively on development of a more informal EE programme to help indigenous communities transfer their traditional ecological knowledge to the youth in rural areas.

RESEARCH QUESTIONS AND METHODOLOGY

This study explores the following research questions:

- What are the cultural landscape conservation issues involved in delivering community-based EE programme?
- What is the framework and teaching content of the community-based EE programme?
- Who are the stakeholders involved in the development process?
- What are the processes and outcomes of community-based EE programmes?

Concerning the theoretical basis, the study employs Healey's theory of collaborative planning (Healey, 1997, 1998) that seeks to enhance partnership and achieve consensus among stakeholders through a collaborative planning process. Social capital (relational resources), intellectual capital (knowledge resources) and political capital (mobilisation capacity) are terms used by Healey (1998) to describe "institutional capacity-building" which is a key concept in collaborative planning (Figure 25.3). The importance and influence of different stakeholders are explored through stakeholder analysis (Bryson & Crosby, 1992; DFID, 2002; Grimble & Wellard, 1997).

This study adopts a qualitative research methodology based on the belief that qualitative methods can provide a more in-depth understanding of "inner experiences," "language," "cultural meanings" or "forms of social interaction" than purely quantitative data can do (Silverman, 2000). The study also utilizes a range of different source materials to help maximise understanding of the questions (Flowerdew & Martin, 1997). Data collecting methods include document analysis, participant observation, individual interviews and group discussions. Each method provides a particular perspective that illuminates certain aspects of reality (Morse, 1994). The multiple-method approach also allows findings to be validated or questioned by comparing the data collected by different methods through a process of triangulation (Denscombe, 1998).

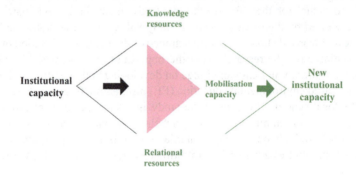

Figure 25.3. Theory of collaborative planning (Healey, 1998, p. 1542)

The method of transcript analysis of taped group meetings and interviews is based on Huberman and Miles' (1994) interactive model that comprises three sub-processes: data reduction, data display, and conclusion drawing/verification. First, with data reduction, the transcript is reduced in light of Healey's conceptual framework of the "institutional capacity" that consists of three dimensions, i.e. knowledge resources, relational resources, and mobilisation capacity (Figure 25.3). The process of reduction includes data summaries, coding, emergent themes and clustering of key issues. Second, the reduced set of data helps to construct an analytical diagram of the discussions. Third, conclusion drawing and verification involves interpretation and drawing meanings from the displayed data. Methods used include comparison/contrast, noting of themes, and triangulation.

TRADITIONAL ECOLOGICAL KNOWLEDGE IN INDIGENOUS YOUTH EDUCATION

RESEARCH PROCESSES AND OUTCOMES

Conceptual Framework of the EE Courses

After several meetings with local people in the Cihalaay rice paddy Cultural Landscape of the Fengnan village, Hualien, Taiwan in May 2012, they agreed on the fact that not only should they develop rural tourism to increase income, they should also educate the young about their own culture. Consequently, at the start of September 2012, the research team worked together with local people to launch a series of EE courses named *Pakalongay Interpreters Training Courses* for the youth of the village.

The courses were characterized in a way that local indigenous elders developed the courses mainly by themselves and acted as teachers to teach local young people. The students were all local Amis indigenous youth. The aim of the courses was to help them to learn about traditional ecological knowledge for edible plant collection, hunting and fishing, protection of forests and stream water resources, patrolling and maintenance of irrigation ditches, Amis traditional norms of age hierarchy, and for new technology on eco-agriculture, and interpretation skills for local green tourism.

In September 2012, the research team worked together with local indigenous people to launch a series of EE courses. Villagers gathered high elementary graders and junior high school students (considered *Pakalongay* in Amis age hierarchy) for class on weekends. Class content was discussed beforehand, and two of the community residents who were interested and capable were chosen to be teachers (Community Teacher A and B). The programme was called *Pakalongay Interpreters Training Courses* in Fengnan Village (Chen, 2013).

At the outset, the research team and the community teachers had expected to have the courses divided into *Basic, Intermediate and Advanced* Levels, but based on the concept of a community-based approach, there was no rush to settle at the content and teaching materials for each level of the courses. It was hoped that the curriculum for each level could be summed up gradually from experiences learned in the actual development process. Below are the development processes of each level of the Courses (Figure 25.4).

Basic Pakalongay Interpreters Training Course, September–December 2012

The Basic level of the programme started from September to December 2012. During the preparation for this brand-new course, the community teachers felt very difficult to come up with clear and certain content and goals. The research team encouraged community teachers to take the attitude of 'learning by doing' and believed that some kind of framework and operating system during the actual course development processes would come up eventually.

After several preliminary curriculum discussions, community teachers and the research team did reach a consensus on the courses as follows:

- Why? (Curriculum goal): be able to realize, cherish and present (by interpretation) local resources;
- When? (Course time): take place every weekend
- Where? (Teaching venue): the whole community area (the Fengnan village) as the learning field;
- What? (Course content): local natural and cultural resources;
- Who will teach? (Teachers): teachers are invited by local community residents;
- Who will learn? (Students): local teenagers join courses of different levels according to age and learning qualifications.

To put it differently, Basic Level students should be able to 'follow others' (experience), Intermediate Level students 'know how to do' (knowledge and skills), and Advanced Level students can 'lead younger siblings and interpret community resources to tourists (service, leadership and interpretation).

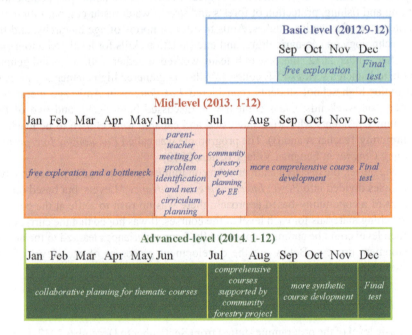

Figure 25.4. Development of basic, middle and advanced levels of the EE courses

The once abandoned Si-wei Branch School refurbished by the local community became the learning base for the Training Course, with the entire Fengnan village being an outdoor environmental education field. Students were mainly 10 to 15-year-old primary and junior high school students from Fengnan village. They came to class on the weekend. Community course teachers decided on the content after considerations of the week's routine farming activities, cultural activities, and related environmental topics. As for the research team, they played a facilitation role and took full participation in observation and recording, and in discussions with teachers both before and after classes (Chen, 2013).

Intermediate Pakalongay Interpreters Training Course, January–December 2013

The Intermediate level of the programme occurred from January to December 2013. Before the end of the Basic Training Course, community teachers and the research team held meetings to discuss follow-up curriculum connection issues and decided to advance Basic Level graduates to Intermediate Level from January 2013, and also invited high elementary graders in the village to join the second-year Basic Training Course.

There were not a fixed syllabus and a schedule at the beginning of the course, and the research team and community teachers still believed that the Intermediate Training Course could be developed in a flexible manner. Unfortunately, one of the teachers (Teacher B) who participated from the very start often failed to squeeze time out to come to scheduled classes, and thus was replaced by a female member of the Cihalaay Cultural Landscape Committee (Teacher C) who continued to work with Teacher A in collaborative teaching.

Likewise, the research team showed full collaboration by participation in observation and recording of the whole process and holding discussions with community teachers not only before but also after each class. In addition, since a number of students' parents reflected that Sunday was Church Day and so disagreed with having class on Sundays, the Intermediate Training Course was adjusted to take place every Saturday instead.

From January to June 2013, serious absences and participation declines caused the Intermediate Pakalongay Interpreters Training Course to enter a stage referred to as the *Free Curriculum Development Bottleneck Period*. One of the reasons behind this was that participating students were mostly on the track team and soccer teams, and two to three out of the six students usually could not make it to class due to frequent games which in turn caused the rest to lose interest. This led to serious absences in the second semester; in fact, only eight lessons were given from January to June 2013. Secondly, the themes of the Intermediate Training Course focused more on agricultural activities, which were similar to that of the Basic Training Course, this led to a gradual decline in interest and passion. Actually, it would be a good idea to have different themes interspersed throughout the course. For instance, in the camping and night observation class on 15–16 June 2013, it was apparent that students were eager to acquire knowledge and showed much liveliness. Thirdly, training courses were no longer on their trial stage; however, community teachers decided on the content shortly before class. This kind of flexible teaching that lacked theme variation and organized schedules came to a bottleneck.

Finally, it came to the point that the research team decided to discuss this dilemma with community residents for possible countermeasures. On June 20, 2013, the

Intermediate Pakalongay Interpreters Training Course Planning Workshop was held at Fengnan Community Centre. Of the eleven residents who took part in it, many of them were parents of participating students. The workshop started with event photos and briefings to review the origin and development processes of the Basic and Intermediate Pakalongay Interpreters Training Courses. It was then followed by discussions of possible themes for the next six months (from August 2013 to January 2014) with residents. At the end, all agreed on three main themes, namely, indigenous culture, agricultural experience, and natural experience, and the course titles and content.

In the seminar, many of the residents expressed that attending the meeting actually helped them to further understand the course content and implementation processes of the Pakalongay Interpreters Training Courses, especially on the recognition of learning traditional local culture and knowledge. What's more, children attending class on holidays meant that they had no time wandering outside hanging out with bad friends, therefore parents strongly hoped the course could become even richer and continue to run in the future.

Besides, the workshop was attended by residents, but also an officer that worked at Yu-li Station, Hualien Forest District Office of Forestry Bureau. He was responsible for promoting the Community Forestry Programme and he took the initiative to join the workshop after hearing about it. Having listened to the Pakalongay Interpreters Training Courses, he expressed that if the community applied the courses to run as a community forestry programme, the Forestry Bureau would be willing to show support.

With the assistance of the research team, Fengnan community held two local workshops on 6 and 13 July 2013 to discuss the possibility of bringing the Pakalongay Interpreters Training Courses to become part of the Community Forestry Programme. There were two main issues discussed. First, amendments were made to the decisions arrived at the aforementioned meeting on 20 June. Fengnan residents had agreed on the monthly themes for the Pakalongay Interpreters Training Courses for the period between August 2013 and January 2014. In the workshops, monthly themes, weekly content and titles, and teachers were again discussed, and also for a different period of time, that is, from August to November 2013 (duration of 2014 Annual Community Forestry Programme). The second was to confirm that the Fengnan Village Cihalaay Cultural Landscape Committee would take up the responsibility of implementation, funding control, and verification for the Community Forestry Training Courses. The person in charge in the community was also chosen in the workshop (Lin, 2013).

The period between August and December 2013 was the *Comprehensive Curriculum Development Period* subsidized by the Community Forestry Programme. Generally speaking, it took place in accordance with the themes come to in the three local workshops on 20 June, 6 July and 13 July 2013 respectively. Part of the course was put off until December owing to factors such as weddings, funerals, celebrations and holidays. A graduation test and an achievement exhibition activity marked the end of the Community Forestry Programme.

Advanced Pakalongay Interpreters Training Course, January–December 2014

The advanced level of the programme started from January to December 2014 and can be roughly split into three phases:

Collaborative planning for thematic courses, January–June 2014. This planning of the courses returned to the flexible arrangement of cultural activities depending on the season, time and agricultural activities. Community teachers worked on class content two weeks beforehand with the help of the research team. Early this period one of the teachers, Teacher D, who initiated to join the course, put great emphasis on students' expression skills, hence he required each student to share their afterthoughts with the whole class every single time. Not only did this succeed in training students' expression skills, but it also helped the research team understand students' thoughts. The teacher also recommended course Diary be produced weekly to make students aware of the content in advance. Moreover, team members suggested photos be added to the Diary to let parents understand students' learning situation.

Thanks to suggestions of the research team, the course was enriched with a few rice paddy field ecological observations in which students had the chance to observe the wildlife inhabited in the terraces of the Cihalaay Cultural Landscape. A number of experts with relevant professional backgrounds were also invited to come to support teaching, that is, to observe insects, plants and water quality. Furthermore, in order to highlight the importance of environmentally friendly farming, the research team proposed comparing the differences among organic farming, ecological farming, and conventional farming. To summarise, this period has shown growth on various aspects including teaching mode, curriculum planning, participants' expression skills and environmentally friendly farming education.

Comprehensive courses supported by the community forestry project, July–August 2014. During this period, community teachers, parents and the research team together finalized the course themes, and applied for the funding needed from the Community Forestry Project. Having previous implementation experience, both the community and the research team had so many thoughts about the course themes. In addition to the core agricultural course and traditional cultural course, the two parties came to realise how important the stream water quality was to the community. The local stream, which flows through the community, satisfies the needs for residents' drinking water and agriculture irrigation. To make students aware of the meanings of the water source to local livelihood, a series of classes about water resources was added in this period (Chen, 2015).

Integrated courses development, September–December 2014. During this period, most of the courses were taken place in the refurbished Si-wei Branch School. Due to the fact that Si-Wei Branch was regarded by local people as an Agricultural Experience Area located aside the Turtle River surrounded by mountains, it was relatively convenient to arrange traditional Amis collection activities like fishing and edible plant picking. Students got to experience from planting to picking, from cooking to eating. In the past, classes were almost always led by community teachers who jointly participated in picking, cooking and eating. However, in this period older teenagers were assigned the mission to lead the younger ones in activities which indeed promoted the goals of *Pakalongay* leadership and service learning and reached parents' expectations of Amis cultural heritage.

In this series of courses, growth in both teaching and learning can be seen. Community teachers who already accumulated one to two years of experience started to know what was worth to be taught. Traditional knowledge and skills of various kinds such as natural environment, cultural heritages and production skills and so on have been accumulated and passed on. In the past, reviews in the end of the class were done in a boring way in which teachers did all the talking and students just listened. After discussions between community teachers and the research team, content previously taught was reviewed in a lively, integrated way. This not only enhanced learning motivations, but also increased learning effectiveness.

DISCUSSION

An Analysis of Cultural Landscape Conservation Issues Related to Community-Based Environmental Education Programme

In the community-based EE programme in Fengnan Village, community residents who knew about Cihalaay Cultural Landscape resources were invited to be teachers to try to integrate into the curriculum related cultural landscape conservation issues. Details are given below:

Issues related to rice paddy field production and river conservation. Between January and June 2014, nature observation activities at the rice paddy field were included into the course many times. Community teachers, students and the research team discussed the advantages and disadvantages of various farming methods, such as: Were the insects observed in the rice paddy fields pests? Or were they beneficial insects? These questions were then explored in the community-based EE programme.

In 2014, the Cihalaay Cultural Landscape underwent two major storms which caused serious damage. The first storm caused some terrace ridges to collapse, and irrigation ditches to break. Rice paddy fields were dried out, so farmers were forced to let their land lie fallow. Terraces then completely dried out because of fallow land, and so they failed to survive the second storm and collapsed again. Local elders expressed that such disasters would never happen in their times because ancestral knowledge always warns them not to let farmland lie fallow. These issues had been involved in the class discussion.

Issues related to mountain and river conservation. The meaning of 'Cihalaay' in Amis refers to the Taitung river loach, which is ranked as a Rare and Valuable

Species in Taiwan by the Wildlife Conservation Law. However, the mountains and waters that Fengnan villagers feel proud of are faced with the threat of invasive fish species and illegal fishing. In 2013, The Fengnan village worked with the Hualien County to conduct a Stream Protection Programme and with HFDOFB to implement a Forest Patrol Programme. Issues of mountain patrolling and river protection were also integrated into the EE programme.

Issues related to local knowledge and traditional cultural heritage. Indigenous culture and mother language leaning have always been the concerns of parents. They repeatedly expressed the hope to teach the concept of the traditional Amis age class through the community-based EE programme. Amis shows great wisdom in the use of wild plants. Local knowledge and traditional cultures were usually the courses that interested the most students, and community teachers usually guided students to think about how to create a way of meanings to traditional cultures in today's modern life.

An Analysis of Stakeholders Related to Community-Based EE Programmes

This study categorized stakeholders into four different groups depending on their significance and influence on the development of the community-based EE programme (Figure 25.5). Interactions between the roles and functions of each stakeholder are shown in Figure 25.6 (Chen, 2015).

Community teacher ('Sinsi' in Amis language). In this study, community teachers refer to the community elders who give guidance to students in the community-based EE programme, who plays a role close to that of a school classroom teacher. They are the pillars of the entire course. The programme started with two male elder teachers (Teacher A and B); but Teacher B dropped out of the class in early 2013. Therefore, Teacher C was hired instead to teach Amis female knowledge to students. Later in the year of 2014, a community elder, Teacher D, joined voluntarily, so in each class two to three teachers led the students through the courses.

Community teachers were the core leaders in the course, and the three teachers each focused on something quite different from one another. Community teachers had decisive power affecting the programme's development, and they each were equipped with a strong motivation to participate; therefore, community teachers are regarded as highly significant and highly influential stakeholders.

Teacher A was good at taking advantage of the materials at the very venue to improvise in class; Teacher C concentrated more on physical and psychological development and teaching material preparation while Teacher D emphasized behaviour such as course rules and class management. At the start of cooperation, they were unfamiliar with one another's teaching style, and so they often either talked simultaneously or gave different instructions to students. Luckily, the three were willing to communicate in order to collaborate and find a way to work together gradually.

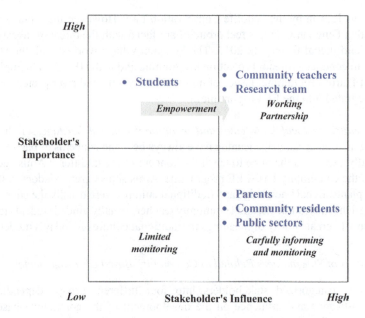

Figure 25.5. Stakeholder Matrix according to their importance and influence (based on DFID, 2002)

Students (Pakalongay in Amis language). Students who took part in this case study ranged from elementary to junior high school, which just corresponded to the Amis age group, *Pakalongay*. Youths of this age range are subject to the guidance of elders in Amis tradition; they also have to take up the responsibility of caring for their younger siblings; and at the same time, they need to attend to many matters at the Harvest Festival including tasks like pouring wine and fetching water. In 2012, there were only seven students at the age of 14 or 15. As time passed, more and more youths participated due to invitations from either friends or community teachers. Up until the end of 2014, the number of regular students reached up to 18, with 68% of males and 32% of females.

From interview data collected by the research team, what attracted youths to join the course lies not only in learning traditional indigenous knowledge and developing peer friendships, but also in killing time on the weekend. However, some students did not come to class on a weekly basis due to school activities or games, or family reasons. Students did not have much to say about the curriculum development because of the lack of opportunities, plus whether they came to class or not was usually affected by external forces; therefore, students are regarded as stakeholders with high level of significance but still low level of influence.

In August 2014, the four students who stayed with the course the longest finally graduated from junior high school, and in the same year they were promoted to a more advanced age group in the Harvest Festival. After graduating from Pakalongay,

Figure 25.6. Interactive framework of stakeholders' roles and functions in the development of Basic, Intermediate, and Advanced Levels of the Pakalongay Interpreters Training Course from September 2012 to December 2014

they continued to take part in Saturday classes. With permissions from community teachers, graduates led younger students in activities in part of the practical course. This was actually an act to try to get graduates more involved.

Parents. Parents' attitudes towards the programme have obviously changed. At the initial stage, there was a lack of communication between community teachers and parents. This led some parents to think that community teachers gathered students to make them work. Fortunately, community teachers actively communicated with parents to make them understand. Also, during the course chances were arranged to let students demonstrate their learning outcomes in front of the elders and their parents. What's more, parents got to see the weekly *Diary* produced. All these added up, and thus part of the parents softened their attitudes to become in favour of the course.

It is apparent that parental attitude played an important role in affecting students' participation. This study therefore categorized parents as stakeholders with low level of significance but high level of influence.

Community residents. Community residents have diverse knowledge and skills. If they can participate in the course, they can enrich the course content to make up for the areas community teachers are not good at, which is actually a very great resource for the community-based EE programme. However, it is easier said than done. Due to limited funding, the programme could only afford to pay two teachers the wage on a daily basis. Inviting other local residents to join teaching would mean that the community needed to apply for funding through other relevant programmes. In 2013 and 2014 respectively, fortunately, the Fengnan Community Association succeeded in getting grants from HFDOFB for the Community Forestry Programme, which enabled the courses to have community elders with diverse expertise to give lessons for about three to four months. This process, in turn, increased the visibility of the EE programme in the community.

Via interactions with community teachers and students, community residents further understood the content and operation of the course and at last showed recognition. Most of the residents invited expressed willingness in giving lessons again if opportunities arose. Residents participating in the course were relatively few in number; some had not joined still held doubts and therefore gave negative comments, which had formed pressure on community teachers indirectly. In this study, the other community residents were put under the category of stakeholders with a low level of significance but a high level of influence.

Research team. The duty of the research team is to get involved in curriculum development as a facilitator. At the end of each week's course, the team regularly met up with community teachers for reviews and discussions over matters like students' performance, the way teaching progressed, and course arrangements for the next week and so on. These after-class discussions were very much valued by community teachers as they thought this was the way through which they could get to clarify doubts, share thoughts, and brainstorm new ideas. They also felt that the way to collaborate with the team enabled the course to develop even more smoothly. In addition, the team assisted in arranging training course for community teachers and supplying a teacher candidate list from the community. To sum up, the research team offered help to community teachers in course planning, implementing and reviewing, and providing necessary resources through the programme. The Team also explored the feasibility of a community-based EE programme through the cooperation. This study has classified the research team as a highly significant and highly influential stakeholder.

The public sectors. This case study is related to the public sector through government institutions including the Hualien District Agricultural Research and Extension Station (HDARES) and the Hualien Branch of the Soil and Water Conservation Bureau (HBSWCB). The Community Forestry Project of HFDOFB provided funding for the training courses for local teachers for three to four months. As for the HDARES, it offered experts to support related agricultural and ecological courses according to community needs in 2014, such as basic knowledge of insects and plant management for landscape diversity of rice paddy fields. The HBSWCB provided funding to allow the community to restore water resources at the refurbished Si-wei Branch, which made it possible for the school to work as a fixed teaching venue for the community-based EE programme. In this study, the public sector is regarded as a stakeholder with a low level of importance but a high level of influence.

Primary Framework and Teaching Content of Community-Based EE Programme

Based on the themes, the course content for lessons given between September 2012 and December 2014 can be divided into four major categories, namely indigenous culture, production skills, natural environment and integrated activities, with each of them composing 29%, 21%, 19% and 31% of the total numbers of teaching hours respectively. Each major theme can be further divided into four to five sub-topics. When glancing over the percentage distribution, one might think that fewer teaching hours were assigned to natural environment compared to the others; however, the truth is that Amis local knowledge is imbedded in their daily lives and practices. It was difficult to extract pure 'natural' elements for teaching (Figure 25.6). Integrated activities such as outdoor games and interpretation practices were added into the course to make it livelier.

Figure 25.6. Local youngsters learnt to observe and record the agro-biodiversity data of the rice paddies

Indigenous culture courses refer to folk practices developed over different aspects, namely food (composing 41% of the total number of teaching hours), clothing (9%), housing (13%), education (19%) and entertainment (18%). Courses of different content were designed, for example traditional Amis food production, traditional headdress knitting, and building of traditional hut in an old-fashioned way and toy making.

Production skills are mainly about agricultural courses which were subdivided into rice growing (accounting for 44% of the total number of teaching hours), vegetable growing (34%), irrigation ditches construction and maintenance (17%) and livestock raising (5%). Agricultural courses can be extended from simply inviting students to particular agricultural activities to a series of courses of planting different kinds of crops depending on the season and timing.

Natural environment courses can be divided into edible plant resources (consisting of 17% of the total number of teaching hours), natural landscape and wildlife resources (47%), agro-biodiversity (25%) and water resources (11%).

Integrated courses were founded on the previous activities carried out. They were usually done through cross-theme training integrated with indigenous culture, production skills and natural environment to enhance learning capacity. For example, there were courses on interpretation demonstration and practice (accounting for 32% of the total number of teaching hours), graduation examinations (29%), integrated discussion (12%), nature games and creative arts (14%) and others (13%).

CONCLUSIONS AND SUGGESTIONS

Course Content Planned by Community Residents Covered the Entire Landscape Resources: Economic, Social and Environmental

It was discovered that the concept of landscape resources understood by community residents did not necessarily mean certain aspects of landscapes; instead, it covered a wide range of economic, social and environmental resources surrounding the community. The key concept of a living landscape focuses on interactions between people and the land (Sauer, 1925). Consequently, course topics and content suggested in related community workshops organized by the research team tended to widely cover the whole aspect of resources in the community. It is recommended that the diversity, integrity and daily life features of the landscape resources recognized by residents are carefully considered when it comes to promoting cultural landscape conservation and environmental education and interpretation.

Community Teachers, Parents and the Research Team Are the Key to Maintenance of Course Operation

Parents' attitudes have a huge amount of influence over students' participation. In spite of the fact that some parents refused to let their children join the programme due to misunderstandings or other personal reasons, and a few parents shirked their disciplining responsibilities to community teachers; most of the parents made a turnabout in their attitudes from banning to supporting their children to participate in the programme. Reasons summed up include the following: (1) Community teachers actively communicated and invited parents to participate in the course; (2) Changes in student were clearly witnessed; (3) Students were well taken care of by community teachers on weekends; and (4) The research team assisted in producing weekly Diary and facilitating curriculum planning meetings to help parents understand course content. In the planning and implementation of the course, the complementary relationship between community teachers and the research team is the key to maintaining the operation of the course.

At the outset of cooperation among Teacher A, C and D, they were unfamiliar with one another's teaching style, and there were often situations in which they either initiated talking at the same time or gave different commands to students, resulting in confusion. Fortunately, the three parties recognized the course as a medium to transfer traditional indigenous knowledge to the youth, and therefore were willing to communicate and coordinate their efforts to allow a better performance and a smooth class. Besides, the research team raised a suggestion to hold after-class discussions which community teachers thought were conducive for understanding each other's ideas, beneficial to cooperation and useful in finding a direction for the course in the future.

Sense of Belonging and Local Recognition Acquired through Community-Based EE Programmes

According to interviews, not only did students learn about traditional ecological knowledge, they also developed close peer friendships. To students, these were of far-reaching significance. Students in this case study belong to the Amis age group, *Pakalongay*, and community teachers kept reminding them of their age responsibilities and obligations throughout the lessons given such as duties at the Harvest Festival. The age group had even grown to be mature and responsible enough to care for their younger siblings. Students who gained promotion to a higher age level in August 2014 not only continued to participate in the course, but also led their younger siblings in learning under teachers' authorizations. It is obvious that age concept has already made an influence on students and started to show results. The community teachers hoped that local youths could understand and appreciate traditional ecological knowledge and livelihood skills from various angles; obtain sense of belonging; support the community and protect the environment, take up the responsibility for community development in the future.

Planning and Implementation of Community-Based EE Programmes Are Moving Towards Collaborative Planning of Multiple Stakeholders

Planners of the community-based EE programme changed from only community teachers into a cooperative between the research team and community teachers. There were several times in which parents, community residents, and the related governmental institutions were invited to contribute ideas at course planning meetings during implementation of the Fengnan Community Forestry Programme. A partnership platform involving participation of stakeholders such as the public sector, teachers, and students' parents was successfully established, and a complementary foundation was formed. What's more, the research team successively sent invitations to experts of related fields to give lessons for the programme and encouraged exchanges between experts and community teachers to share their knowledge. Through interactions community teachers grew more confident in teaching and students showed recognition for local knowledge.

Financial Resources from the Public Sector Can Enrich Course Content

Resources available and financial supports from the public sector are indispensable to the implementation of the community-based EE programme in Fengnan Village. They enabled the programme to be promoted in a continuous and steady way, provided the possibility of diverse teachers who contributed his or her own expertise (knowledge and skills), assisted the division of work and inter-communication, and established a new institutional capacity among stakeholders.

ACKNOWLEDGMENTS

I would like to show my gratitude to the Forestry Bureau and the Ministry of Science and Technology for their financial supports for the research. I would like to pay special thankfulness, warmth and appreciation to the local people of Fengnan village, Hualien, Taiwan who made my research successful.

REFERENCES

Bryson, J., & Crosby, B. (1992). *Leadership in the common good.* San Francisco, CA: Jossey-Bass.

Chen, Y. Y. (2013). *A study of the initial stage of indigenous Pakalongay young interpreter training course in Fengnan village, Hualien, Taiwan* (Unpublished master's thesis). National Dong-Hwa University, Taiwan. [in Chinese]

Chen, K. Y. (2015). *The development of the advanced level Pakalongay interpreters training courses in Fengnan Village, Hualien, Taiwan* (Unpublished master's thesis). National Dong-Hwa University, Taiwan. [in Chinese]

Denscombe, M. (1998). *The good research guide: For small-scale social research project.* Buckingham: Open University Press.

DFID. (2002). *Tools for development – A handbook for those engaged in development activities.* London: Department of International Development.

Flowerdew, R., & Martin, D. (Eds.). (1997). *Methods in human geography: A guide for students doing research project.* London: Longman.

Grimble, R., & Wellard, K. (1997). Stakeholder methodologies in natural resource management: A review of principles, contexts, experiences and opportunities. *Agricultural Systems, 55*(2), 173–193.

Healey, P. (1997). *Collaboration planning: Shaping places in fragmented societies.* London: Macmillan.

Healey, P. (1998). Building institutional capacity through collaboration approaches to urban planning. *Environment and Planning A, 30*, 1531–1546.

Huberman, A. M., & Miles, M. B. (1994). Data management and analysis methods. In N. K. Denzin & Y. S. Lincoln (Eds.), *Handbook of qualitative research.* London: Sage Publications.

IUCN. (1994). *Guidelines for protected area management categories.* Cambridge: IUCN.

IUCN. (2010). *Enhancing sustainable use of biodiversity through the Satoyama Initiative.* Information Paper on Satoyama Initiative.

Lee, K. C. (2012). *The preliminary project for designation of the Fengnan rice paddy culture landscape, Fuli Township, Hualien, Taiwan.* Research report for the Bureau of Cultural Affair, Hualien County. [in Chinese]

Lee, K. C. (2013). *The management plan for the designated Cihalaay Cultural Landscape, Fengnan village of Fuli Township, Hualien, Taiwan.* Research report for the Bureau of Cultural Affair, Hualien County. [in Chinese]

Lee, K. C., Kacaw, L., Chen, M. L., Shia, J. S., & Fan, M. L. (2016). Tailoring the Satoyama Initiative concepts to the national and local context: A case study of the collaborative planning process of a rice paddy cultural landscape in an indigenous community, Taiwan. In UNU-IAS & IGES (Eds.), *Mainstreaming concepts and approaches of socio-ecological production landscapes and seascapes into policy and decision-making* (Satoyama Initiative Thematic Review, Vol. 2, pp. 50–58). Tokyo: United Nations University Institute for the Advanced Study of Sustainability.

Lin, Y. Y. (2014). *The Analysis of institutional capacity of Pakalongay Interpreters Intermediate Training Process in Fengnan Village, Hualien, Taiwan* (Unpublished master's thesis). National Dong-Hwa University, Taiwan. [in Chinese]

Morse, J. M. (1994). Designing funded qualitative research. In N. K. Denzin & Y. S. Lincoln (Eds.), *Handbook of qualitative research.* London: Sage Publications.

Phillips, A. (1995). Cultural landscapes: An IUCN perspective. In von Droste et al., pp. 380–392.

Phillips, A. (2002). *Management guidelines for IUCN category V protected areas: Protected landscapes/ Seascapes.* Switzerland & Cambridge: IUCN Gland.

Sauer, C. O. (1925). The morphology of landscape. University of California Publications in Geography 2.2, 19–53. In J. Leighley (Ed.), *Land and life: A selection from the writings of Carl Ortwin Sauer*, 1963. Berkeley, CA: University of California Press.

Silverman, D. (2000). *Doing qualitative research – A practical handbook.* London: Sage Publications.

UNU-IAS. (2010a). *Biodiversity and livelihoods: The Satoyama Initiative concept in practice.* Tokyo: Institute of Advanced Studies of the United Nations University and Ministry of Environment of Japan.

UNU-IAS. (2010b). *Satoyama-Satoumi ecosystems and human well-being: Socio-ecological Production Landscapes of Japan– Summary for decision makers.* Tokyo: Institute of Advanced Studies of the United Nations University.

Kuang-Chung Lee
Department of Natural Resources and Environmental Studies
National Dong-Hwa University, Taiwan

DYLAN LEECH

26. DISCOVERING NATURE IN THE TECHNOLOGICAL AGE

INTRODUCTION

The medium, or process, of our time – electric technology – is reshaping and restructuring patterns of social interdependence and every aspect of our personal life. It is forcing us to reconsider and re-evaluate practically every thought, every action, and every institution formerly taken for granted. And they're changing dramatically. (McLuhan, 1969, p. 8)

There have always seemed to be two different types of experience that dominate my life.

First, there is the experience of electric "technology". This includes things like the experience of street lamps outside my window, but mostly I mean the active experience of the screens, speakers, and displays I, like most people, spend most of my day immersed in.

This experience, of electric "technology", seems to affect me in ways I have difficulty describing. I "feel" a certain way, I behave a certain way, and I am prone to seeing the world in a certain way when I am using these devices.

The second type of experience occurs when I am not using electric "technology", When I walk in the woods, camp, climb a mountain, or am otherwise distant from passive and active forms of electric "technology", I feel different. My mind and body seem to work differently. If I spend a long time in this non-electric environment, I seem to experience a cumulative effect; after a week-long camping trip I feel like I am a different person. For various reasons, I call this place "nature" and as with electric "technology" it seems to change "who I am".

It seems important to me to examine what these two experiences of the world mean, and what their difference is. Beyond just desire for knowledge, as a professional environmental educator it seems strange that I speak so often of "nature" while feeling so confused about what it actually is. Why are the woods different from the city? Why is a prairie vista different from a computer screen? Why do I think it is good and valuable to learn the different birdsong, but not as good to learn the language of modem tones?

To address this uncertainty within myself (and also to earn my M.A. degree!) I embarked on the project described within this chapter. By exploring relevant literature and my own experience during two 3-week experiments – one while embedded in "nature" and one while embedded in "technology" – I thought I might learn something that casual living could not reveal. I had hoped that from my own experience I could inductively build an understanding of the similarities, differences, effects, feelings, meanings, qualities and essences of "nature" and "technology". Thinking of "nature" as teacher, what would I learn if I looked deeply into it, or turn away completely?

To understand my experiences I used the methodologies of phenomenology (Van Manen, 2011) and autoethnography (Ellis & Bochner, 2000). Basically, I looked closely at how I felt in these different experimental conditions (phenomenology), and I have written my experience as a story (autoethnography). Also, I have tried to balance the tone of an academic work with a less formal tone. To express the phenomenon and experience of living in different ways I have attempted to "tell the story" of my experience, rather than report it like scientific fact.

This chapter is an adaptation of a much, much longer non-traditional Master's thesis. The original work was heavily descriptive, included significant interludes, deep theoretical explorations of important, but tangential topics. It was also written in a way that was meant to be "lean" and "of the times" using hyperlinks and crowd sourced definitions to say things in an efficient way. For brevity quite a lot has been removed or altered including much of the theoretical justification and tangential exploration. Gone are the pages of Wittgenstein's private language, along with Plato's cave, Prometheus' fire, and Campbell's monomyth. The focus of this work has been to express the key details, discoveries, and experiences while preserving some of the storytelling aspect. This undoubtedly makes this work seem "light" and of less consequence than I would like.

I also include many words in parentheses. I do this to remind myself, and the reader, that terms like "nature" and "technology" possess multiple meanings and contexts – we should be careful not to define them reflexively if we wish to understand them more completely.

RESEARCH QUESTIONS

In an open exploration of such an expansive topic it was difficult to keep myself focused within a specific boundary. I approached my research with an open mind and the belief that I should not anticipate what conclusions or feelings would emerge from my experiments. To organize myself I drafted the following list of research questions. These are the questions that emerged from my research, that I believe I made some meaningful self-discoveries about, and which I will report on in the conclusion.

Primary Question

1. What are the physical/psychological/emotional/spiritual/etc. effects of living embedded in electric "technology", and how do they compare to those of living in non-electric "nature?"

Secondary Questions

1. Does living embedded in electric "technology" and non-electric "nature" give insight into possible essential meanings and qualities of "technology" and "nature?"
2. What are some of the practical applications/outcomes of my experience living embedded in "technology" and "nature?"
3. Do "technology" and "nature" reveal themselves as being mutually exclusive, or are they able to co-exist in synthesis?

ON THE ASSUMPTION OF DIFFERENCE BETWEEN "NATURE" AND "TECHNOLOGY"

My research was based on many assumptions (some more widely accepted than others.)

First was the assumption that "nature" is a thing that exists.

As a "thing" I assumed "nature" had a physical/objective quality, as well as a cultural-linguistic quality; "nature" is both an object and a word. I also assumed that I could experience it and say something about it that might be meaningful to others.

I also assumed that to best experience "nature" I might also need to gain perspective on it by experiencing something that was "not-nature" This is consistent with philosophical ideas about meaning and language, specifically those of Ferdinand de Saussure, regarded as the founder of semiotics, who "emphasized in particular negative, oppositional differences between signs, and (that) the key relationships in structuralist analysis are binary oppositions (such as nature/culture, life/death)" (Chandler, 2014, para. 22).

I believe that the difference between "nature" and some form of "technology" is one most people would accept without much argument based just on how we use the word in conversation; it would be very strange to argue that while sitting watching streaming videos one is in "nature" as it is normally defined. But at the same time there is room for nuance here.

To justify the initial idea that "nature" and "technology" may have a relationship of difference I did the "natural" thing for someone my age; I Googled them.

According to Google, "nature" is "the phenomena of the physical world collectively, including plants, animals, the landscape, and other features and products of the earth, as opposed to humans or human creations" (Nature, n.d.). I took this to mean that, according to Google, "nature" consists of all things non-human. This would mean that its opposite would be a word that means "all things human".

To find a word that meant "all things human" I consulted Wikipedia. It informed me that "technology" is "the collection of tools, including machinery, modifications, arrangements and procedures used by humans" (Technology, n.d., para. 1). This, I thought, would be a good signifier to use when exploring a state of non-"nature", as its definition resembles the set of all things human, and human created including language, ideas and beliefs (which are all arrangements and procedures).

I chose to assume that "nature" and humans were not mutually exclusive things; a human can experience what we call "nature", at least on some level.

After a great amount of rationalization I chose to assume that not all "technology" was truly oppositional to "nature". Somewhere between the sticks and VR headsets some important thing happened to "technology" that differentiates it from "nature".

In the end, I chose electricity as being the fundamental characteristic of "technology" that was different from "nature". I chose it because it's ubiquitous connection with the most powerful and changing "technologies", because it created a useful physical characteristic for differentiation, because in thought experiments electricity and "nature" so rarely go together, and because it was the favorite term of Marshall McLuhan when speaking about new "technology".

ON TECHNOLOGY

This section answers the first half of my primary research question. It describes the different (physical/psychological/emotional/spiritual/etc.) effects of living embedded in electric "technology". From these effects I also begin to answer my secondary question about "what the essential meaning/quality of "technology" is as I experienced it?" I have written this section in a way that describes my experience, while drawing out meaning at the same time. I have done this because it is reflective of the processes of phenomenal lived experience.

Journal Entry Day 3 (Lightly Edited)

Last night, after 12 hours of playing the game I blinked.

It was 4am, and I had barely stirred since 4 in the afternoon. I shambled to bed and slept fitfully, my brain in a bit of a shocked state from the constantly moving images. For 12 hours the ultra-violence, and the anarchistic narrative overwhelmed me as the violence and sequence of events poured down nonsensically.

This morning, I awoke, headed downstairs and eyed the video game console's power button. Surely, I thought, I was too burned out from last night to engage with this sort of "monstrous" space again? I pressed the button, sat down, and suddenly it was 4:30 in the afternoon, and I had played, largely without sustenance, for another 8 hours.

By this point I have played the game beyond my interest in the narrative, until the game is a purely reflexive act. The game is just flashing lights in my brain.

Suddenly, the moment came this afternoon. Click. My body, almost without conscious deliberation, reached over and shut the game off.

I then started to manically march around the house, mildly hyperventilating. With no one to observe me I found myself absent-mindedly running up and down the stairs. I caught up on Facebook, made dinner, and began to learn what a Fractal is. By 9pm my finger was itching for the game world again. I began bargaining with myself to play more. In my head I thought "I can play because it is my research", or "I can play, but stop in half an hour to prove to myself I can", or "I'll play just one mission".

Experimental Design (FAQ)

Can you briefly describe your experiment? I wished to learn something about "technology" and how it differs from "nature" by spending three weeks (21 days) constantly connected to electric "technology". What this meant evolved as the experiment went on, but basically I surrounded myself with the electric "technology" I use most often (TV, computer, smartphone, microwave, etc.) and used it as much of the day as I could.

When did you begin your experiment? I managed to find a 21-day space August/September 2014. This involved juggling lots of work and personal obligations, as people did not necessarily understand the purpose of this electric "vacation".

What did you change about your life in this experiment? My goal was that when I could use electricity I would, and I would try to stay inside. I had thought about experimenting outside by using mobile devices, but I decided it was best to put strict limits on outside time. I wanted the purest "technological" experience I could achieve, and I was worried that if I spent time outside geocaching (Geocaching, n.d.) or playing with locative apps (Locative Media, n.d.), it might undermine my experiment.

I couldn't completely avoid the outside world, but I made sure my time there was sparing. In 21 days I spent about two hours of time outside in total. The time I did spend outside was composed of walking to and from my car and watering my parents' garden during the first week of the experiment.

While I was outside for these brief periods, I didn't feel non-electric, ensconced as I was in the electricity of the city, standing on pavement, cellphone in pocket, surrounded by electric human constructions.

Were you alone? During the first and third week of my experiment I was physically alone at my parent's house in Calgary, Alberta.

During the second week I was in a shared accommodation In Banff, Alberta. This meant I had many more face-to-face interactions. However, these interactions were strained and brief.

What did you eat? An aspect of living in "technology" was that food of all types was more or less instantly, and cheaply, available. I visited the supermarket to stock up before my experiment began.

I gave myself no specific dietary directive; I could eat as I pleased, and I did not think too critically about my food. I ate things that did not take much care or attention to prepare, and I followed desire rather than conscience. In the end I ate lots of sugary cereal, steak, candy, and freezer aisle pizza. I drank liters of Coca-Cola and coffee each day.

I also had medicine and brain-altering substances available to me; edible electric "technology". I limited myself to what I was legally entitled to have inside my body. This included ibuprofen when I had a headache, and an occasional beer.

What "technology" did you use? My "technology" was quite simple for our time. Lacking significant monetary backing for my experiments, I did not have access to anything exotic, like an Oculus Rift (Oculus Rift, n.d.), or experimental haptic gloves (Haptic Technology, n.d.). I had at my disposal a low quality laptop, an older model tablet and a smartphone, headphones, etc. At my parents' house I also had access to a 50 inch high-definition television and a PlayStation 3 video game console.

This meant I was living with "technologies" that had already seen mass adoption, rather than newer "technologies" that may never become popular, e.g. Google Glass (Curtis, 2015).

Are you a "technological" expert? I am a proficient user of "technology", but by no means an expert. I grew up with computers, so I have a good intuitive sense of how they work and how to make them do what I want them to. I consider my level of "technological" knowledge to be slightly above the average.

Were you physically active? Living embedded in "technology" meant I had little reason to move anything but my hands and eyes. I used my smartphone as a pedometer, and discovered I was walking between one thousand to three thousand steps a day on average, well below the recommended healthy minimum of *ten thousand* (Rettner, 2014). For exercise in Calgary, I would sometimes run up and down the stairs for a few minutes. However, as the experiment progressed I lost desire to do even that. When the experiment was over I found I had gained about 10 lbs.

Did you have a plan for how the experiment would go? Throughout the experiment I tried to do things by feeling, and to follow experiences where they led me.

Sometimes I used electric "technology" in a way that was new to me. For example, I tried to learn the finer points of Twitter, Facebook, and other social media; I tried to make friends in chat-rooms; I constructed a box to fit over my eyes and hold my iPhone; I talked to chatbots, and I created binaural sound pieces (NuMeditationMusic, 2015); I attempted online work filling out surveys, and even lurked on the Darknet using the Tor browser (Tor, n.d.). Some of this I had imagined doing before the experiment, but I would not say it was planned.

How did you document your experiment? I documented the experiment in a journal, but I found that writing about my experience often felt strange. Reflecting on my experience gave me the feeling I was changing my experience. In "technology" my impulse was to consume media, rather than create it. For this reason, the journal I kept consists of short entries spaced several days apart.

In addition to writing, I found other reflective ways of documentation. For example, I made sound art by recording household noises and running them through digital effects processors, photographed my food, and created 3D fractals. But these were difficult practices to keep up. The addictive, seductive experience of electric media precluded much reflection.

I also discovered passive ways of understanding my experience. I found a program that catalogued and offered statistics on my web usage, my computer logs, and my emails and text conversations.

Experimental Results

As I read what I have written, both above and below, I feel like it must sound to the reader like I was having an awful time in "technology". In reality, I might have been having the best time I have ever had in my life. As you continue reading keep this duality in mind; the things I describe sound like the worst, but my experience – in the moment – was also full of intense, deep, maybe perverse pleasure.

"Technological" heat. While in my youth I played video games quite enthusiastically, as an adult my engagement with the medium is better described as sporadic, occasional, or nostalgic. Upon beginning my experiment in "technology" I borrowed a new-ish video game console and purchased *Grand Theft Auto V*. I was obsessively consumed by the depth and vivid reality of this game for much of my experiment, and found myself playing for up to a dozen hours in a day.

My memories from these days belong half to me and half to the game, I remember mostly violence and criminal behaviour. While *GTA V* creates an open world where players are able to lead peaceful mundane lives if they wish, the purpose of the game is to allow and encourage characters to wreak insane havoc in this near-reality. The storylines in the game are thinly veiled reasons for high speed chases, assassinations, murders, and gang violence.

Sometimes, after hours at the screen, I would realize I could no longer remember why I was doing anything. The characters were unlikable, the story inane, and I was just performing rote actions for the ephemeral pleasure of the "Mission Successful" that signals an advancement in the game.

I think the English language ought to have a word for this type of media experience. Perhaps it already does. It might be a kind of temporary ego-death, or loss of self.

I was familiar with the words "magic circle" (Magic Circle, n.d.), "hyperreality" (Hyperreality, n.d.), and "simulacrum" (simulacrum, n.d.) before my experiment, and I had a feeling they might correspond with this feeling. But McLuhan's concept of "hot media" seems best to describe my experience; I was burning my brain, and I seemed to like it.

Flattening. While living with a "technologically" extended body, my actual physical body felt few typical sensations. I never felt the wind in my hair or the sun on my skin. I never got too hot or too cold. The feelings I did have tended to be diffuse, and difficult to pinpoint.

My diet, consisting of whatever I wanted that was easy to hand, ceased to be notable. Everything was the sweetest, or saltiest, or fattiest thing I could eat; a sort of uniform excess. I was never full, though I ate all day.

During the first days, I found myself subconsciously resisting this experience. My mind would become scattered. I couldn't seem to concentrate for long, and I would find myself pacing around the house in big circles. After the first week, my body ceased resisting and stayed in one place. I became accustomed to a flattened experience.

Emotionally, I began to feel disconnected. My physical life took on a sort of imaginary quality while my digital life began to feel more real. I began to have trouble dealing with the other people around me and felt better while alone than when people were around. This came to a head during the second week when my partner (now my wife) began to feel alienated and we had a long and emotional talk. We spoke of ending our relationship, and I didn't feel like I cared much at the time. I remember being frustrated that I was being pulled out of media. I remember thinking that the Internet would allow me to move on quickly if our relationship ended.

A part of my lack of concern for the real world might have come from the content of the media I watched. Looking over the media I viewed during my experiment, I find almost everything had a happy ending. I began to expect I would effortlessly attain a banal happy ending in my real life, because that was what I was seeing in media. Almost everyone lives happily ever after, right?

Hyperreallity/The essential meaning of "technology". It was in this strange, disconnected, flattened, over stimulated place that I found what I think was the essential meaning of "technology".

By "essential meaning", I do not intend to give a definition. Instead, I mean to give an impression of what I believe the submerged, hidden effect of "technology" is. McLuhan is famous for stating that "the medium is the message", and what I call the "essential meaning" is the closest I can come to articulating what my experiential experience was of the message of the medium, stripped from received cultural views, ideological assumptions, and explicit content and description.

It does however help to begin with a concept written of by others. Philosophers and semioticians might describe my condition during my experiments as a state of hyperreality: "a special kind of social reality in which a reality is created or simulated from models, or defined by reference to models – a reality generated from ideas" (Robinson, 2012, para. 1). To be in a hyperreal state means constructing your ideas of the world almost entirely from other ideas about the world.

During my experiment in "technology" I began to have difficulty seeing the physical world through "technology", and instead I began to see the physical world as "technology". While "technology" revealed the world to me, it also replaced the world; and this to me is its essential meaning.

To explain, any piece of "technology" can reveal the world. An axe can reveal aspects of a tree (like its use as firewood or building materials) in a similar, if less direct, manner as a television show about tree uses. As axe also replaces a person's ideas about the world; once you have an axe houses made of fallen branches might not seem so desirable (just as TV makes certain cars, clothes, or body types undesirable). After a while, the world without the axe becomes unimaginable; just as western people have a hard time imagining a world without roads, cars, antibiotics, clean water, or electricity. As "technology" becomes more portent, and more electric, the replacement becomes more and more complete.

Imagine being asked if you would like to visit the pyramids and replying that you had seen them on TV so didn't feel the desire. Imagine being asked if you would like to go on a date and turning it down because you were married to your computer. This was how I began to feel. Life became unreal and only the replacement was tangible, comprehensible, or important. I became content on artificial pleasure.

I am not sure how much I can expect you, the reader, to understand this. Without considerable explanation, or a shared experience, I am worried this seems like a wildly inappropriate rant (that has nothing to do with "nature".) As I write these words I feel myself passionate in a way that is inconsistent with what I think of as academic writing.

To conclude in a way that brings the conversation back around, my experience being embedded in electric "technology" was that "technology" replaces all other objects, including whatever kind of object "nature" is.

Summary. In attempting to answer my primary question "what are the different (physical/psychological/emotional/spiritual/etc.) effects of living embedded in electric "technology", I experienced a collection of effects.

I experienced the intense heat of the media, reduction in intake of what I think of as being important meaning, the flattening and loss of physical and emotional sensation, the shift in moral sensibilities, and finally my turning away from social bonds and non-"technological" experience to live almost completely in a state of hyperreality.

I believe the most interesting, and surprising discovery of my experiment in "technology" relates to the idea of hyperreality. I discovered a deep, felt, emotional connection to the idea that the essential meaning and quality of electric "technology" is that it reveals and replaces our world.

Aftermath

During the last week of the experiment, I had lost the desire to go outside, or be with people, or eat healthy foods. I was quite happy to live totally immersed in "technology".

In the following days I suffered several anxiety attacks – the first I have ever had. These might have had many causes, but I felt the most significant was the transition from my "technology" state to "reality". Somehow, my mind could no longer organize itself to deal with problems rationally, and my feelings could not be compartmentalized. Instead they overwhelmed me, and my heart would race and my body would be jittery until I found a piece of media to distract me again.

ON "NATURE"

Two weeks after completing my experiment in "technology", I drove from Banff, Alberta to Nelson, British Colombia to conduct my experiment in non-electric "nature". In this section I discuss the other side of my primary research question; what are the different (physical/psychological/emotional/ spiritual/etc.) effects of living embedded in non-electric "nature?" From these effects I have developed an essential meaning and quality of "nature", as I experienced it. I have tried to write in the same phenomenal manner as the previous section, though differences exist; the experience of "technology" and the experience of "nature" do not lend themselves to quite the same cadence and style.

Experimental Design and Overview

The location I chose for my experiment was on a friend's property in the Selkirk mountains. I headed out for my experiment on the last weekend of September hoping for pleasant weather.

The land I was on is part of a co-operative land-share that owns about one hundred acres of dense forest on steep mountain hillside. The northern property is a mix of second growth forest, full of birch, aspen, cedar, maple, and first growth moss covered gigantic cedars. The cedar forest areas had a very "magical" quality, you could almost expect to meet mystical forest creatures there.

During my experiment in "nature", I spent about the same amount of time near people as I did when I was in "technology".

I brought food that was in a relatively unprocessed state. This meant that almost everything required some cooking, or making, in order to become edible. I ate many potatoes and partially cooked dough. I estimate my average caloric intake was somewhere around 1000 calories. I also brought some treats, which I deemed "medicinal". These were one 750 ml bottle of whisky, and a four dollar chocolate bar. The medicine disappeared quite quickly …

I intentionally brought less food than I thought I needed. In "technology" I was able to "forage" from the store, and so I thought I should investigate how I might do the same thing in "nature".

For shelter, I lived in a canvas yurt my friend had built. It was a comfortable accommodation, and this gave me a guilty feeling; as if I was cheating.

My main experimental stipulation was that I would neither actively, nor passively, use any electricity. By this I mean I could not turn on a light, nor ask someone else to, nor linger in the presence of an electric light if one was near.

I also was mindful of how electric my non-electric items were. For example, I avoided items like lighters and chainsaws, in favour of firesteels and axes. However, I was pragmatic about how comfortable I wanted to be. I had a nice sleeping bag, metal pots and cutlery. If there was a greater lesson to be learned through being fully naked and destitute I did not learn it.

During my "natural" experiment I allowed myself to read by candlelight for a short time after dark, from books having little to do with electricity. Along with some collections of ancient Greek philosophy and drama, I had with me Cervantes' *Don Quixote* (2003), a book on edible plants (Kershaw, 2000) and another on bush-craft (Kochanski, 1998).

To document my experiment I brought several notebooks, some nice pens, and a children's painting set.

Experimental Results

During my experiment I felt and discovered many things. I was cold, hungry and afraid of the dark. I was lonely, bored, and filled with superstitious anxiety. I was also calm, joyous, contemplative, and even content. In my other descriptions of this experiment I tell long stories about how each condition came about. I wrote about weeping from hunger and frustration by the side of a dirt road after a farmer refused to sell me any milk, finding a dead bird and becoming convinced a family member had died, and spending a night sitting beneath a cedar tree in absolute darkness while monsters howled in my imagination (and in reality). Most of these stories re-inforce how I got to my conclusions about "nature", but few seem fit into the space provided here. The following is the bare essentials of what I discovered.

Perception of the relationship of objects. During my three weeks in "nature" I noticed a peculiar thing; my mind seemed so different.

While in "nature" I often found myself thinking about the relationships in the world around me. I spent my time thinking about things like how I was connected to the trees, and how the trees were connected to the birds, and how I could use the objects in the forest to satisfy my hunger. I thought a lot about how I was connected to my own "regular" life. What did all of these people, things, and cultural objects mean to me?

My thinking slowed. My writing became more thoughtful. The practice of putting pen to paper meant I had to consider the ending of a sentence more thoughtfully than with a keyboard (with which one can easily erase and revise).

I felt kinder. Less reflexive. I saw the world as it passed, rather than just the destination I was approaching.

Unlike in "technology" where I struggled to find the space to have and document thoughts about my experience as it occurred, I left "nature" with a full notebook detailing gesticulations of my "natural" mind; poetry, stories, dreams, ideas. Many fears and hopes as well.

The process of fire. Each morning I awoke, and the first thing I had to do was build a fire to cook breakfast. To start my fires I brought with me a tool called a Swedish firesteel, a small rod of magnesium alloy that creates a spark when a piece of steel is dragged across it.

It was more difficult to start a fire using a firesteel than I expected. It was revealed to myself, embarrassingly, that I really had no idea what I was doing. But as the days passed I began to notice something interesting was happening.

As the days went on I refined my technique. I learned that the brief flame I could spark in some hair lichen was enough to ignite the skin-like outer bark I peeled off a standing paper birch, and from that I could light the thicker bark I could strip off fallen birch which is rich in resin and burns well.

I learned which trees burned well, and which burned poorly. I learned which woods gave off a thick unpleasant oily smoke. I learned how to breathe a fire to life from embers, and how to do so without choking on too many cinders, or inhaling too much smoke. After a night of rain I discovered the importance of dry kindling.

I learned that I needed to have the fire going before the sun set, and that in October the length of daylight was more or less the same as the length of the night. I learned how to cook food I couldn't quite see. I needed the fire at night to light some candles, and from those candles I could give myself just enough illumination to read myself a bedtime story.

Every day, when I awoke, the embers from the previous night were extinguished, and I had to start my process all over again.

On community. In "nature" I often felt terribly alone. Being alone, hungry and starved of media resulted in a strong desire to bond with the people I was near. I wanted real friends. I wanted to get to know someone, I wanted to argue and fight, I wanted to resolve my differences. I wanted strong bonds. I wanted to be helpful, and to know that if I needed help I could count on someone. I thought often about what a real "community" was.

Francis Fukuyama, in his book *Trust* (1996), puts forth the notion that there exists a different level of trust in different cultures. He suggests that having high levels of trust means that you can make spontaneous connections, and this lubricates economies and helps a culture thrive. Two strangers can meet in the street and make a bargain, because they trust each other enough to begin negotiations. In low trust cultures, strangers cannot interact, they become tribally minded, othering and alienating those who do not belong to their tribal clique.

While in some ways "technology" increases our levels of trust, for instance when we hire a stranger for a job, in other ways "technology" seemed to reduce my trust in people; I preferred to interact from within the protection of my magic ring, or veil of hyperreality.

In "nature", I realized how false that was. Without trust, and without inspiring trust and affection in the people around me, life is more difficult, and can feel almost trivial. The words of Christopher McCandless rang in my head: "happiness is only real when it is shared" (Penn, 2008).

Process and Rhythm/Essential Meaning of "Nature"

The recurring theme as I think about my experiment in "nature" is that I found myself becoming more aware of the processes going on around and within me. For example, I became more aware of the progress of the sun across the sky, the warmth as the sun rose and the chill as the sun descended behind the mountain tops, and the quiet of the evening.

I became more aware of how it felt to be hungry, the pleasures of seeking out food, and the great relief that can come from a warm meal shared with kind people.

I learned and contemplated the complex relationship of objects in the world, including my own relationship to people, places, ecosystems, and all other things. I became aware of the anxiety of being exposed to the raw elements of "nature", while over time I became accustomed to "nature", and beauty emerged.

These were all experiences that repeated themselves with great regularity. I call them "processes" because the followed an order, and had a purpose.

Over time in "nature" I became more aware of these processes by their repetition or rhythm. Each night as the sun set I experienced the same elements of process and came to expect them, plan for them, and develop a relationship with them. The rhythm of a "natural" lifestyle was what allowed me to begin to form a relationship with the "natural" world.

In "nature" these processes and rhythms were at the forefront of my experience. I could not live a day without feeling them, and thinking about them. In "technology" a similar perception of process and rhythm seems to have been hidden.

Essential Meaning/Quality

In my section *On Technology*, I suggest there is an essential meaning/quality of "technology" that revealed itself through my experiment.

I would now like to suggest a complementary meaning to go along with my experiment in "nature". In comparison, the essential meaning/quality of "nature" is that it acts to reveal the processes and rhythms of the world to us in a way that gives texture and depth to our experience. This is a complex concept, but one that I felt deeply embodied by my experience in "nature", and perhaps one that might have a certain resonance with the reader. I feel it is something that when looked for, is strongly and clearly discovered.

CONCLUSION AND DISCUSSION

While I have described my primary research question "what are the physical/ psychological/emotional/spiritual/etc. effects of living embedded in electric "technology", and how do they compare to those of living in non-electric "nature?" in the preceding sections, in my conclusion I focus on my secondary research questions.

Question 1: Does Living Embedded in Electric "Technology" and Non-Electric "Nature" Give Insight into Possible Essential Meanings and Qualities of "Technology" and "Nature?"

Based on my experiences I arrived at the following summaries of how "nature" and "technology" revealed themselves.

"Technology:" It was my experience that electric "technology" had numerous effects including the intense heat of media, the trivialization of the information I took in, the flattening and loss of physical and emotional sensation, the shift in moral sensibilities, and also led me to turn away from social bonds and non- "technological" experiences to live almost completely in a state of hyperreality. The sum total of these effects has led to my theory/belief *that the essential meaning or quality of "technology" revealed in my experiment is that it acts to reveal and replace the world in my perception.* In particular, while expanding the amount of the world I was able to perceive, "technology" removed and replaced sensations of pain or displeasure creating a flat experience of the world. Finally, my experience was that "technology" did so in a way that felt coercive, or narcotizing.

"Nature:" While in "nature", I experienced changes in how I thought, how I wrote, and I experienced how much human influence permeates the physical world. Also, I confronted painful experiences, like hunger, darkness, and loneliness that seem absent from life in "technology". Textured experience of these phenomena over time gave me the impression of process and rhythm in the "natural" world, and something about the rhythm allowed me to develop a relationship with the "natural" world that was absent from my "technological" life. This led to my theory/belief that *the essential meaning or quality of "nature" revealed through my experiment is that it acts to make me aware of the processes and rhythms of the "natural" world, as well as become behaviourally and psychologically connected to them.*

An unoriginal conclusion. I do not claim that these are original discoveries. These essential meanings are not necessarily novel, new, or unique to my experience.

Soon after I "discovered" this essential aspect of "technology" I also discovered I was not the first person to discover it. Notably, Heidegger in his essay *The*

Question Concerning Technology (1977) characterizes "technology" as revealing the truth of the world, but also threatening to deny this truth by preventing people from experiencing "a more original revealing and hence to experience the call of a more primal truth" (Heidegger, 1977, p. 14). What I have termed' revealing and replacing", Heidegger called "revealing and concealing". It seems so obvious as to be near plagiarism.

Likewise with "nature", the idea that process and rhythm are important characteristics is common in academic and spiritual thought. This is explicit in panarchy (Gunderson & Holling, 2002) and process philosophy (Siebt, 2013), the god Kali (Kali, n.d.) and the worm Ouroboros (Ouroboros, n.d.). Implicitly, it is everywhere I look and see the word "nature".

What may be interesting is how hidden these meanings were from my understanding before, and how deeply I feel these things to be true now.

Question 2: What Are Some of the Practical Applications/Outcomes of My Experience Living Embedded in "Technology" and "Nature?"

To discuss the practical applications of my research in my own life I have drawn a somewhat arbitrary line between personal and professional impacts.

Personal. I left my final experiment in "nature" feeling that I had gained something valuable by moving away from "technology" and "technological" thought. So, after emerging from "nature", I came up with a variety of ways I could manage, monitor, and minimize the effects of "technology" in my regular life.

For instance, I vowed that the first thing I do every morning, or the last thing I do before bed, not be electric. I promised myself that I would eat better, be less dependent on coffee, and quit using social media. I also tried to spend some moments alone, still, and quiet outside each day. I can already attest to my failure in most of these tasks; each day once again the first and last thing I do is look at my tablet computer as I set, or respond to, my alarm clock. I also rarely find time to be still; I seem to always be on my way to some physical or digital destination.

This level of "technological" contact has come to feel inescapable. I live in a world that offers so much "technological" replacement, and at so little cost, that most of my desire to live in less contact with "technology" has been undone. This could be trivialized as weakness of will, but I feel that it is more than that. The power of "technology" is clear and overwhelming.

I suppose the best I can do is to be mindful about how much of my life is shaped or replaced by "technology". Exactly what this mindfulness entails is something I am still working on.

Professional. My research has already influenced my work life in many ways. Speaking from my experiences working for more than half a dozen environmental education organizations, I can see the ways "technology" and "technological" thought influence education about/in/for "nature", and in many ways I can see how "technology" replaces the "nature" educators present.

For example, "technology" is finding its way into educational programs as digital tools become more portable and affordable. The app replaces the guide and the process of human conversation, the "distance learning module" (Distance Education, n.d.) replaces the field trip and the process of phenomenal experience, and so on. As the national park I currently work for introduces free ubiquitous Wi-Fi (The Canadian Press, 2014) I sense the shift towards "technological" replacement increasing.

The most important replacement I find in the environmental education I deliver is the replacement of the informed anxiety that is a part of "natural" experience with misinformed hope. Most often the programs I am called upon to deliver have been designed in a way that presents "nature" as painless, accessible, and entertaining. In general, topics like politics or climate change are omitted from programs, or at least discouraged, because of the notion that they will negatively affect visitor experience, or even provoke anger from a visitor who disagrees. I have often been instructed that it is of paramount importance to leave visitors feeling positive and hopeful, and not trouble them to consider the often-dire state of the environment; that I ought not to spoil the innate enjoyment of "natural" experience by dwelling on aspects of it that draw away from its beauty by creating anxiety.

The balance between truth (or authenticity) and hope in environmental education continues to interest me deeply. My experience of the replacing power of "technology" has left me feeling suspicious of hope.

Question 3: Do "Technology" and "Nature" Reveal Themselves as Being Mutually Exclusive, or Are They Able to Co-Exist in Synthesis?

One of the secondary questions I had hoped to examine was whether or not "nature" and "technology" seem to be compatible with each other; can they co-exist? I feel that because of the seeming logical opposition of the essential meanings of "nature" and "technology, and the addictive character of "technology" that long-term compatibility is difficult to imagine.

Logical opposition. For me, "nature" has become not just process and rhythm, but also shorthand for a sort of pain. Living in "nature" means being in contact with simple pains like coldness and hunger, as well as with difficult emotions like anxiety, depression, and fear of death.

Electric "technology", on the other hand, has become the radical replacement of the perception of all pains. It removes our hunger and chill, as well as reduces our anxieties and fears through distraction and addiction. In "technology", even the smallest displeasure is removed before, or as soon as, it is felt. Most of the pain in my "technological" experiment came only if I ceased to consume "technology", and there was so much abundance and availability that it was difficult to see why I would cease my "technological" intake.

To me, logically, it seems as if our sense of "nature" cannot co-exist easily with our reliance on the radical replacements of electric "technology" if they stand for the oppositional values of pain, and not-pain respectively.

On addiction, pressure and dependence. My experience was that "technology" replaced physical and psychological pain in my life, in a way that reminded me of an opiate. My experiment reminded me of the addictive qualities of "technology" and the degree to which I myself am addicted.

My addiction comes both from within and without. I have an internal drive to escape hunger, and cold, and even boredom. There is also an external pressure to be addicted. Most jobs demand high amounts of computer use, and technological savvy; friendships and community are created and maintained through social networks and constant communication.

This addiction and dependence lead me to believe that my dependence on "technology" is existential. Inescapably, "technology" is who I am, and guides who I will become.

Use it or lose it. In the section *On Nature* I mention that experiencing the rhythm of "nature" seemed to play an important role in developing a connection to "nature". It seemed like after some time I developed the tools and strategies to understand and connect with "nature". I wonder if I would have been able to develop this connection with "nature" without my pre-existing experiences living in pseudo-"natural" ways.

The common adage is that you cannot teach an old dog new tricks, and I wonder if the opposite is true; can you teach a new dog old tricks? Can someone raised with all of the replacements of "technology" be enticed to the texture of "nature?" If you don't use it, do you lose it?

My suspicion is that the more I live in "technology" the harder it will be to connect with "nature".

FINAL NOTE

I had hoped to remove my terms "nature" and "technology" from parenthesis by the time I concluded, but I now believe this would be hubris. I still believe that I, and you, should be wary of these words. They still mean more than we think and are important in ways we cannot describe. They are wild organisms only partially contained within our linguistic, ideological, and perceptual realities, and like all wild creatures we can never be certain we understand them.

I also had imagined coming away with some kind of positive feeling about the future. I had imagined seeing beauty and promise in "technology", and a way for "technology" and "nature" to complement each other and make each other better. My experience was that there is too much opposition, that "technology" and "nature" are too disparate. Instead of mutualism between them, I can only see "technology" as being parasitic on "nature". I am still conflicted.

This being said, I still feel like I have learned some valuable things for a hopeful future. I have looked deeply at how "nature" and "technology" affect my life, and have come up with a speculative understanding of what they mean in our culture. I have felt and examined the phenomena of these different ways of living, and if anything I now have more curiosity about how the world is changing. I have also learned that an important part of a "natural" understanding is to lean into the pain and texture, rhythm and process, of my life.

I guess, as usual, there is no magic-bullet answer. "Nature", I think, is mostly unknowable. I will never be certain of the whole meaning, or the true power of "nature" and "technology" in my life, but I feel like, in a personal way, I have found a small part of their meaning that I can carry inside. The best thing I can hope is that readers can use this exploration to provide insight, and motivation, to explore the meaning and role of "nature" and "technology" in their own lives as well.

REFERENCES

Note: All digital references last retrieved on 08/01/2017.

Chandler, D. (2014). *Semiotics for beginners* [Online Book]. Retrieved from http://visual-memory.co.uk/daniel/Documents/S4B/sem02.html

Curtis, S. (2015, January 16). Has google glass failed? *The Telegraph*. Retrieved from http://www.telegraph.co.uk/technology/google/11350810/Has-Google-Glass-failed.html

Distance Education. (n.d.). *In Wikipedia*. Retrieved from https://en.wikipedia.org/wiki/Distance_education

Ellis, C., & Bochner, A. (2000). Autoethnography, personal narrative, reflexivity. In N. Denzin & Y. Lincoln (Eds.), *The handbook of qualitative research* (2nd ed.). Thousand Oaks, CA: Sage Publications.

Fukuyama, F. (1996). *Trust: Human nature and the reconstitution of social order*. New York, NY: Free Press.

Geocaching. (n.d.). *Wikipedia*. Retrieved from https://en.wikipedia.org/wiki/Geocaching

Gunderson, L. H., & Holling, C. S. (2002). *Panarchy: Understanding transformations in human and natural systems*. Washington, DC: Island Press.

Haptic Technology. (n.d.). *Wikipedia*. Retrieved from https://en.wikipedia.org/wiki/Haptic_technology

Heidegger, M. (1977). *The question concerning technology, and other essays*. New York, NY: Garland Pub.

Hyperreality. (n.d.). *Wikipedia*. Retrieved from https://en.wikipedia.org/wiki/Hyperreality

Kali. (n.d.). *Wikipedia*. Retrieved from https://en.wikipedia.org/wiki/Kali

Kershaw, L. (2000). *Edible and medicinal plants of the Rockies*. Edmonton, AB: Lone Pine Pub.

Kochanski, M. L. (1998). *Bushcraft: Outdoor skills and wilderness survival*. Edmonton, AB: Lone Pine Publishing.

Locative Media. (n.d.). *Wikipedia*. Retrieved from https://en.wikipedia.org/wiki/Locative_media

Magic Circle (virtual worlds). (n.d.). *Wikipedia*. Retrieved from https://en.wikipedia.org/wiki/Magic_Circle_(virtual_worlds)

McLuhan, M., Fiore, Q., & Agel, J. (1969). *The medium is the massage: An inventory of effects*. New York, NY: Penguin Books.

NuMeditationMusic. (2015, January 23). *Binaural sleep meditation music for positive energy: Sleep binaural beats, energy sleep meditation* [Video file]. Retrieved from https://www.youtube.com/watch?v=pKMEHgSJKkM

Oculus Rift. (n.d.). *Wikipedia*. Retrieved from https://en.wikipedia.org/wiki/Oculus_Rift
Ouroboros. (n.d.). *Wikipedia*. Retrieved from https://en.wikipedia.org/wiki/Ouroboros
Penn, S. (Producer/Director). (2008). *Into the wild* [Motion picture]. Paramount Pictures.
Rettner, R. (2014, March 7). The truth about 10,000 steps' a day [Online article]. *LiveScience*. Retrieved from http://www.livescience.com/43956-walking-10000-steps-healthy.html
Robinson, A. (2012, August 10). Jean Baudrillard: Hyperreality and implosion [Online article]. *Ceasefire Magazine*. Retrieved from http://ceasefiremagazine.co.uk/in-theory-baudrillard-9/
Seibt, J. (2013). Process philosophy. In E. N. Zalta (Ed.), *The Stanford encyclopedia of philosophy* (Spring 2013 ed.). Retrieved from http://plato.stanford.edu/archives/fall2013/entries/process-philosophy/
Simulacrum. (n.d.). *Wikipedia*. Retrieved from https://en.wikipedia.org/wiki/Simulacrum
Technology. (n.d.). *Wikipedia*. Retrieved from https://en.wikipedia.org/wiki/Technology
The Canadian Press. (2014, April 29). Wi-fi hotspots coming to Canadian parks [Online article]. *CBC*. Retrieved from http://www.cbc.ca/news/canada/wi-fi-hotspots-coming-to-canadian-parks-1.2625325
Tor. (n.d.). [Website] Retrieved from https://www.torproject.org/projects/torbrowser.html.en
Van Manen, M. (2011). *Phenomenology Online* [Website]. Retrieved from http://www.phenomenologyonline.com/

Dylan Leech
Royal Roads University
Victoria, British Columbia
Canada

Printed in the United States
By Bookmasters